Map of Life and Beauty

Fanny Barry

Blue Heron Book Works, LLC

Allentown, PA

Cover Photo: Megan Marie Greene

Cover design by Angie Zambrano

ISBN: 0-9968177-7-8
ISBN-13: 978-0-9968177-7-6

Blue Heron Book Works, LLC
Allentown, PA 18104
www.blueheronbookworks.com

TO LAKRA

Contents

ACKNOWLEDGMENTS

This memoir is dedicated to my dog Lakra. I doubt I would have stuck it out but for her. Then, of course, there is my mom who never doubted my sanity or my capacity to cope, my deceased father whose words of wisdom echoed in my mind daily, my good friends Sheba and Paul who encouraged me to finish, both the memoir and my abusive relationship, and my sisters and brothers who gave me an emotional safety net that allowed me to risk some things many cannot. I also thank my doctors and nurses and God and the universe for giving me the time to live and write it.

PROLOGUE

I was reading under the mosquito netting when I heard footsteps and turned to grab the flashlight I kept by my bed. The candle was still burning on the nightstand but I needed more light as I crawled from under the netting and stood in the oversized window. I lit the palm filled yard below and saw the moving shadow of a man. I felt a sudden chill despite the hot jungle night air. My dogs, sensing my fear, came to the window next to me and panted at my feet. Ama let out a nervous bark as the shadow, not caring he had been discovered, continued moving toward us. It was Amador. I froze. The dogs didn't move. Even the geckos stopped chirping as he moved closer.

I finally yelled, "Amador, go away," through what felt like a desert in my mouth.

"No. I no go. I want to talk to you," he finally responded, continuing to progress toward me.

I prayed he would leave. But strangely, a part of me loved that he wanted me, loved that he yearned to possess me. It was a sickness born of some sort of insecurity and low self-esteem, I knew. I had read the books, been to therapy, talked to myself in the mirror. I knew I was better than this. I was successful, I was together, I had hired and fired men with real credentials, real values. Amador didn't even wear shoes. God knew the last time he had brushed his teeth. I had more to offer than he would ever be able to handle or would ever care about knowing. Yet, I still loved him from somewhere deep in my soul.

His throaty, sweet, heavily accented English terrified me now and I finally understood everything. Where before, his voice had called to my heart and had seduced me into thinking he was the man I wanted; now I knew he was merely a selfish predator. The man I had believed in was my own creation. But he had become that man on occasion, long enough to get what he wanted from me, anyway. I finally saw that with me he had status, access, money to feed his addiction, comfort to quiet his pain. I had been his *mujer*, his rich *gringa*—smart, beautiful, capable of taking care of herself, a writer and an artist, an engineer who was an expert in her field. I scolded myself and reminded myself that I had provided testimony to Congress on environmental issues. That little voice on my shoulder told me it didn't matter. That was the past. Now, I was dealing with the drama of a drug addict who had taken most of my money, all my love and, worse, my sense of possibility. I had been clinging to the notion that he could love me, that he did love me, that I was capable of getting and keeping real love, that love could work. But now, we had crossed the line from love to hate. I was no longer rich and he was no longer loveable. I held Ama's mouth to keep her quiet. Her barking would only make it worse.

I told him, "I don't want to talk to you, Amador. Go away."

He advanced onto the porch and I strained to listen as he came up the wooden stairs. I jumped at the sound of breaking glass as he kicked a votive candle on the way. He was on the balcony outside the upstairs bedroom. I silently cursed myself. I had repeatedly vowed never again to live in these dramatic episodes, the victim of his tirades, an addict to the drama. Yet, here I was, like another fallen junkie. My hands were trembling in anticipation. I went to the double door and could see the outline of his body through the cracks in the oversized planks of dark tropical wood. I could hear his breathing as I tried to control my own. I put my back against the door, more to support myself than to keep him out and then, I exhaled heavily and leaned my head against the door, closed my eyes, and tried to gain the strength to refuse to engage him.

His voice suddenly snapped, "Open the door." I stood motionless.

He commanded in a tone I barely remembered, "*Oye, puta, abre la puerta,*" "Listen, cunt, open the door."

I put my back closer to it and tried to close my ears to his insults and told him no. I said firmly. "I don't want to talk to you." and then in a whisper, as if praying, "Please, go away."

"I not going anywhere *puta*. Open the door." he said forcefully but then, as if he really didn't mean the insult, he added in a voice filled with fatigue, "I want my dry clothes."

The tone was filled with pleading and reason as if I were over reacting. I hesitated, weighing my options and stayed silent, knowing it could not be so simple. Still, every nerve of my being was on fire with fear and anticipation of what could happen next. I unglued my body from the door and went to the bed, reached under the mosquito netting, and lifted my cell phone from the covers. I thought about calling the police but knew that he would hear me dial and it would infuriate him. Too, they were 30 to 45 minutes away and their concept of emergency did not include domestic disputes. The other times, they had left me feeling victimized and wasted by the people I hoped would protect me. Additionally, those encounters had cost me substantial cash that I no longer had. The police in Tulum did very little without payment.

I kept the phone in my hand and walked to the open closet to pull Amador's clean, dry clothes from the shelf where I had put them that morning with love. He had been working downstairs, I had washed his clothes, thinking we could at least be friends. I carried them toward the bolted double door but I was afraid to open it. Instead, I opened the big screen window and handed the orange shorts and white shirt to him around the wooden support column. My hands were shaking as he took his things from me gently, touching my hands as if to hold them. He touched me in an almost loving way. I was confused and wondered if I were overreacting. There was quiet for a moment. I exhaled and thought perhaps that was really all he wanted and he would quietly leave the way he had come.

Then, suddenly, he pounded his fist on the door. I screamed, a high-pitched, girlish sound and then inhaled and chastised myself for the cry's weakness, as if it really mattered. No one was listening. I pressed my body back into the door and he commanded, "Don't scream *puta.*" As I listened from the crack between the double doors, I could hear the spittle on the sides of his mouth and realized he was a rabid animal. I screamed again, fear overtaking my reflexes, and prayed for help. But I knew only the jungle heard me. My neighbors were close on either side but one set would ignore me, believing I deserved what I got from my ex-boyfriend for letting him back into my life. On the other side were Amador's buddies and they generally returned well after 3 am. Regardless, I knew their routine and abuse was part of it. It would take a lot for them to do anything to help me.

I jumped and screamed again when he yelled, "Don't scream or I gonna knock the door and kill you."

This time my instinctive scream was loud and forceful. I searched for the correct buttons on the phone to dial the police. Even in Mexico, they don't condone killing their women. I hit the send key as the door slammed against my back from outside and I fell to the floor, clutching the phone. The splintered deadbolt hit the floor next to me. Amador followed, an animal stalking its prey. When he saw me in the corner, he slowed and smiled cruelly as I pressed the phone to my ear. He reached me in the exact moment that the call was connecting and, with the same twisted smile, ripped the phone from my hand and threw it against the far wall. I screamed loudly in a rage of frustration but he grabbed my throat, forcing me to stop. I started to choke under his grip. His face turned to an old photo negative and then disappeared as I lost consciousness.

Part 1 - The Map

Chapter 1

I woke with the kind of snort that happens when you have your head resting back in the car or, more embarrassingly, at a meeting when you fall asleep at the conference table. I looked around, having forgotten where I was, dreaming I had been caught snoozing at one of those boring meetings I had come to Mexico to escape. I inhaled deeply as we passed a break in the seaside jungle and I saw the cobalt blue of the Caribbean Sea.

"Incredible," I said sleepily and then to my friend who was driving, "Lynn. Look." I pulled myself up in the seat and asked if we had arrived.

"I am pretty sure *La Vita e Bella* is around the corner," she answered.

We were on vacation in Mexico. I needed a break to do nothing. That was what people told me, "just stop." I had finished cancer treatments nearly 3 months before and although my doctors told me that physically I was doing well, emotionally I was a wreck. There were many days that I came home from work, laid on the floor and pounded my feet and fists against it, frustrated and angry that I could not change my life faster. But today, I was far from all that and driving a white VW beetle with a bimini roof that we rented at the airport in Cancun. We had been horribly lost in a maze of Cancun hotels and tourist bars, but now, after nearly 3 hours of clumsily driving this roller skate of a car, we saw the waves breaking over the reef as the jungle opened to expose Tulum beach once again.

"You made it," I whispered to myself, as we pulled into the sand parking lot of *La Vita e Bella*. I was south of the border with plans to relax and dream about starting over, perhaps here, perhaps somewhere else. I was determined to make a new life for myself somewhere. I told myself that this could be the beginning.

The hotel consisted of a group of brightly colored thatched roof cabanas called *palapas* that were tucked into the dune on the Mexican Caribbean. We checked in and the hotel manager took us to three different cabanas before he gave us one with two beds. People generally thought Lynn and I were lovers, but we were just very good friends. As we entered each cabana I would look up at the thatched roofs in awe, then toward the mosquito netting that covered the bed and the towel in the shape of a swan that sat on top of it. I almost didn't notice there was only one bed but Lynn made the manager understand that we wanted two. Finally, we pulled our suitcases along the sandy path one more time toward the *palapa* at the far edge of the hotel. Lynn went on ahead as I stopped to marvel at an iguana on the side of the path. I was engrossed with the dinosaur until Lynn called me to, "come on." Finally, there were two beds. We dropped our bags, peeled winter clothes from our sweaty bodies, pulled on bikinis and, before I could comment on the place, she led me down the stone steps to the beach and the beach bar. The sand was soft and pinky white and the gentle waves called us to enter.

"Fabulous," I exhaled.

"Let's have a margarita," Lynn said happily.

It was always a drink with her. I never objected. Actually, I loved the fact that I never felt I drank much around my Irish buddy. Like Lynn, I loved a cocktail. Unlike Lynn, tall, blond and very able to drink, I was a petite, mousey-haired athlete who could barely drink more than two glasses of wine without suffering for at least one day. After cancer treatments, I was even leaner, not so resilient and much less able to tolerate alcohol. We sat on the patio in the sand and looked over the undulating cobalt blue that gently caressed the shore in front of us. I wiggled my feet into the sand contentedly as we sipped our cocktails.

Before we could order guacamole, two tanned Mexican men in surfer shorts sat down with us. They didn't ask. They just occupied the 2 empty chairs at the table. They were slightly drunk and seemed harmless and amusing. Neither was particularly handsome. The one who sat next to me was charming and the yellow tipped dreadlocks that framed his face made him somehow exotic. It was after 3 pm and he still had sleep in his eyes. His smile was contagious but as he spoke, I couldn't help but stare at that speck of sleep still in his brown eyes. He spoke good English, certainly better than my nonexistent Spanish. I found myself not listening, staring at that speck and wondering if he ever looked in a mirror. Then I realized he probably did not. That made him irresistible. Without warning, he lifted the sunglasses off the bridge of my nose.

"Your eyes are beautiful," he said.

"I know." I put my glasses on the table as the sun had started to set. My eyes—green, sometimes a little yellow around the iris—are my favorite thing about myself.

I disregarded the compliment. Dying to get into the water, I took another sip of my cocktail and asked him if he wanted to swim.

"With you? Of course," he purred. Not hesitating, he took my chair from behind me, helped me to my feet and took my hand. Lynn raised an eyebrow.

"I need a swim," I told her as I left her with her 'friend' and walked down the few stairs to the beach with a confidence and flair I had only recently acquired. I was not sure if it was from surviving cancer, my surrender to taking a vacation and leaving it all behind, from the tequila after the long journey or from this indigenous man who was following me. But I felt like someone everyone wanted to know. I turned back to look at him as I walked into the warm water and smiled. He called to me to ask my name as I entered the sea. After I told him he volunteered his own, "Amador," with an accent on the third syllable and a roll on the "r."

"Hello Amador," I said successfully rolling my r as well.

I dove into the soft waves, and let the water embrace me. I immediately felt new, not necessarily happy, but clean. I started to cry, forgetting anyone was there I was so moved by the sea, the alcohol and the warm breeze that touched my face when I surfaced.

When Amador touched me, I was startled.

"I want to marry with you," he told me as I turned to face him and let the sun dry my tears. I laughed loudly, deeply, happily. I was flattered; even if his remark was meant to be amusing. I told him he didn't even know me.

"But I do," he said with a certainty that made me more interested in him, "and I want to marry with you."

I smiled and swam away from him, unsure how to respond. I wanted to enjoy the sea. I wanted a love affair with the Caribbean, not another man. From thirteen years with a sponge of a man to

7

months chasing a married man up and down the east coast, love hurt every time. Although I knew it was a fantasy, what he said made me feel good. I let myself be there for a moment as he followed me through the water. In combination with the warm air, the cool sea sparkling in the sun and this interesting dark man with blond tipped dreads following me, I was in heaven.

Amador swam up behind me and put his hand on my lower back. I turned quickly as electricity ran up my spine.

I treaded water and told him directly, "Listen, we can be friends, that's all. I am not sleeping with you, if that is what you are looking for."

I surprised myself with my frankness. I had never been so direct with a man before.

"Too bad," he said, as if we were both missing something. He smiled an incredibly infectious smile, which I returned.

I marveled at his self-confidence as, un-phased, he pointed to his side and asked me "See this scar?"

He put my hand above his waist and took my fingers to gently trace the outline of a 4-inch scar down his side. "Barracuda," he said.

I laughed and kicked my feet harder to stay afloat as he took my other hand and brought it to his thigh where I felt a 2-inch scar. I started sinking since he had both my hands but I did not pull back because, even though I feared it, I was enjoying the feel of a man. I smiled and replied, "shark?" as my head went under the water and I took back my hand to swim.

"How did you know?" he asked as I surfaced and he followed me toward the shore.

I walked out of the sea and onto the beach that stretched gloriously for miles. In my red bikini with orange accents, pale and marvelously thin with baby hair on my head barely half an inch long, I appeared different, alien to some. But I felt exceptional.

He walked me back to the table and asked, "May I kiss you?" I hesitated, and noticed the sleep was no longer in his brown eyes.

I made him wait a moment and then replied, "A little one," and kissed him on the lips with my eyes open. Lynn looked the other way. Her 'friend' had already started up the beach.

"Adios." he said, a little melody to his voice. Then he strolled down the stairs and along the beach, not looking back.

I finally looked at Lynn and we laughed. She shook her head.

"You should have seen how everyone looked at you. They didn't like that you swam with him," she reported.

"Why is that?"

"You know."

I did not and I asked her why again.

She said, "He's black" as if that should mean something to me.

Then I said with innuendo, "No, I know black and he is not." The last man I let butcher my heart had been African-American, Southern to boot. We both laughed. But the racist nature of the remark bothered me. Too, I could still feel the touch of his scars on my hand. I am still not sure which bothered me more: her reaction to his color or how good it felt to be close to him. Before I became confused, I finished the rest of my margarita and put my head on the back of the chair to feel the sun and be in the moment. I did not want to think about anything, so I forced myself to feel and not think at all.

Chapter 2

The next morning, I woke to the sun cresting over a magnificently calm blue Caribbean Sea with rolling waves gently breaking along the shore as a gentle breeze moved the palms in front of our cabana. It was as if I had entered one of those cliché Caribbean postcards. The sand on the beach in front of us glistened like snow. I had the illusion that we were in paradise until a file of soldiers with machine guns walked past. I shivered and then stretched my arms over my head, pushed the soldiers out of my mind, and relished the feeling of having nowhere to go for the first time in months. My life had been running in so many directions in the last year moving from my home town of Boston, to Washington D.C. for work, to Miami to be somewhere warm and try to start again and to Pennsylvania to visit my friends who were helping me create a non-profit foundation and finish books I was writing for cancer survivors. Every day I had somewhere to go, something to do because if I didn't I was afraid I might settle back into the life I believed had trapped me into a sadness and discomfort that gave me cancer.

Lynn was still asleep, sprawled out on the bed, under the mosquito netting. She had taken the larger bed and had put her own sheets on it. She said couldn't sleep in other people's sheets. When traveling, she brought queen sized 600-thread count Egyptian cotton sheets. I got the smaller bed with the hotel's crisp white sheets. Although I was happy in my little bed, it stung that she gladly took the better things, as if she appreciated them more, as if I didn't know better. But I was as much, if not more, of a princess than she. However, I was tougher and smarter, even though I was less engaging at a party. But I loved her for that. Everyone did.

I snuck out onto the patio. The sun sparkled brightly on the water and I closed my eyes to feel the breeze softly on my face. I inhaled deeply and started my yoga practice, the discipline that made me queen. Over the last 10 years, yoga had become the touchstone I believed would cure my internal melancholy, elevate me to happiness and cure the nagging pains I often had in my hips and lower back. I saluted the sun and thanked God for the moment.

As I dropped my feet behind my head into plow posture Lynn came to the door.

"Nice view," she joked and then sarcastically, "Hope you don't get stuck like that." I opened my eyes to see her standing in front of me, looking at the sea.

"Coffee?" I asked.

"Of course."

I put on my damp suit, a skirt over it, and sunscreen on my face, ready for the day. We walked the beach to the restaurant and sat down among the other guests, most of whom were couples. "Think they are all married or are some of them here with other men?" Lynn asked me motioning to the couples already eating. I laughed and asked her why she would think that. She responded that they were too lovey for married couples, as if marriage precluded romantic vacations. I wondered if after 20 years with my friend Fernando, Lynn was missing romance in her life. It had certainly been true for me and Harry.

I decided not to comment and looked around before motioning to a couple in their 70's and saying, "Well, the couple over there is definitely not fooling around," as we watched the woman cutting the man's eggs.

Lynn laughed. "You have a point," as she looked for a waiter saying, "Where the fuck is that guy?"

Pains of caffeine withdrawal were starting in the center of my forehead where my guru located my third eye when the waiter, a short brown man in black pants, a white shirt and bare feet finally walked over, introduced himself as Carlos and asked, "Café?"

"Si," we both said enthusiastically and then he left. He did not give us menus or tell us anything.

In 5 minutes he returned with two cups and a carafe of coffee.

Lynn asked for menus a little more loudly than necessary so he could understand. He said, "Si," smiled broadly and walked away again.

I chided her, "Your English won't become Spanish by yelling."

She told me to fuck off but I laughed. Lynn was always ready with a joke or an insult, trying to dominate, make people notice her. It usually worked but no one was noticing her now and she was getting annoyed. Not only was she strikingly beautiful, she was incredibly funny and incredibly mean at the same time. I knew that if I ignored the insults, we would both get over it.

Carlos returned with 2 menus and before he could turn to walk away, Lynn commanded, again a little too loudly, "Wait. I'll have the eggs, *the huevos*, scrambled, *revueltos*, with bacon." Then she added, "Hurry up and order something before he leaves!"

I asked for a plate of fruit. He nodded and left us once again. We waited 20 minutes for the breakfast. I had finished all the coffee and was happy to have more. Of course that took another few minutes after Carlos brought breakfast. He didn't seem phased by the constant return trips to the kitchen in the soft sand. We were learning that things here moved slowly.

We began to move slowly too. We filled the next 2 days waiting for service on the beach and making visits to Tulum *pueblo* when the sun became to hot, or the service for margaritas too slow.

Every so often, we would see Amador and Lynn would joke, "Look, your husband."

I would look and then turn away, not wanting him to see me yet enjoying the joke. Enjoying the fact that someone wanted to marry me. The last man I wanted to marry had dumped me. My relationship of 13 years had ended without marriage and with lots of pain. My other relationships had not worked out in a marriage sort of way and I was beginning to understand it was me. I was somehow afraid of men, afraid of their hold on me. From the very first man who put his hands down my shirt when I was 12 to the last man who made love to me as if I were a queen, helped me leave a my stale relationship, promised to visit me when I was sick with cancer and then stopped talking to me with no explanation, love hurt every time. It was unjust that I had no man's hand to hold when I was fighting for my life. Even though I was hardly alone through my cancer treatments and through my life, I felt that way.

So, later, as we walked down the Avenida Tulum and Lynn poked me and taunted, "Husband at 2 o'clock," I ducked. To her, he was a beach bum with whom I could play. But I was attracted to him and I had learned to fear my attractions. I asked "where," from behind a stack of Mexican blankets. She pointed to a small storefront where they had some sort of buffet. I saw his same blue T Shirt and the black surfer shorts from when we met. I knew the blond tips to his curly brown dreds. His back had a slight curve and he was further bent over the buffet, helping himself to food. I wondered if he had washed the sleep from his eyes.

"Duck," I cautioned as I moved deeper into the shop.

We joked about it and laughed a lot. Lynn and I rarely got serious. Everything could be a joke. Even when I was waiting to see if I needed a mastectomy, she would ask, "any news on the girls?" referring to my breasts.

With great pleasure, I finally announced, "The girls are staying" and we celebrated with cocktails at the 4 Seasons Hotel. We laughed like two sisters who had been through so much together that we didn't need to talk. In the pueblo, we walked and drank and made friends with the waiters who found us amusing and profitable. No one tips like Gringos. We wanted people to remember us and the surest way was to tip big.

Our third morning, as we worked on our tans in front of the crystal blue sea, Lynn saw Amador walking up the beach and said, "Husband at 9 o'clock."

I took the straw hat from my face, looked up, then put my head down again and replied, "yup," before putting my hat back.

"Would you give him a chance?" Lynn asked.

I left the hat on my face and asked her what she meant.

"Let's give the poor bastard some business," she said.

I peaked out from under my hat to look at her and asked incredulously, "You want to go fishing?"

She shrugged. "Why not?"

"I hate fishing."

Then she suggested a tour, something to get us out on the water.

I loved to be on the sea as well and I missed my sailing days so I agreed and said, "Why not, what's the worst thing that could happen? We get married?"

Lynn laughed and told me to try to get us a good deal.

Chapter 3

As if Amador heard our conversation, he changed course and casually moved towards us. He smiled and looked down humbly, as if thinking what to say.

Then he said, "Buenos Dias."

"Buenos Dias," we each replied as he bent to kiss us, Lynn on the cheek, me on the lips. I was a surprised.

Lynn seemed almost jealous and blurted, "We'd like a trip," as his mouth left mine. She gestured to the sea and said, "You know, one of those tours you do."

So much for the good deal, I thought as she asked how much it would be. She never stopped talking and never let him think he had to work for this one. I put my head back on the lounge chair knowing she was just getting started.

"For you two?" he asked.

"Who else?" I joked feeling that someone had to be disagreeable. We continued to discuss the date and the price until we settled on that afternoon and $60 per person. When we told him that seemed expensive, he offered us a price of 600 pesos, or about $60 US, but he would include beer and bait.

"I don't want either," I said.

But Lynn accepted saying, "I like to fish and I like beer."

We had a deal. Amador asked for a deposit and said he would be back by 1 pm. Lynn went to get some money and as she walked away, asked the time.

Amador looked up at the sun and responded, "almost 11."

I looked at my watch: 10:45.

"Pretty good," I said to him as I covered my eyes.

He smiled and let his eyes wander down my body slowly. I felt exposed. My green crochet bikini barely covered the scar on my left breast or the miniscule tattoos used to target radiation that I thought were so obvious or my pubic hair that was still growing back after chemotherapy.

He moved his gaze back to my eyes and explained, "That is life on the beach. I don't need a watch."

I reached for my sunscreen.

"That must be nice," I said wistfully.

Then he asked quietly, "Are you enjoying your vacation?"

"It's great."

"I could show you some things," he said. "If you want."

Lynn returned at that moment but he held my gaze. I did not look away. Lynn handed him the money and told him that we would be waiting at 1:00. He took the money, counted it and said he would see us then. He kissed each of us as he left. Again, he kissed me on the mouth and Lynn on the cheek. She noticed. I wondered if the permission of one kiss meant I had given him lifetime access to my lips. Regardless, I put my tongue over the place he had kissed me and told Lynn I hoped she did not lose 300 pesos. He walked down the beach; nodding to the people he passed.

"He'll be back," Lynn said and put her hat over her face to rest. I got up to swim, relishing the heat on my body as I walked to the sea. Amador was in the distance, walking away from us. I eased into the water, let myself float and let my mind drift away as the waves lifted me gently up and down.

Chapter 4

Amador returned promptly at 1:00 and asked us if we were ready. I actually was not. I threw on a black t-shirt over my bikini, deciding that was good enough, and Lynn grabbed her cowboy hat. She was already in shorts and a t-shirt. We walked together along the beach with the sun sparkling off the waves. A gentle breeze had picked up with the afternoon tide and Amador pointed to a white 18-foot whaler type of boat with a blue bimini.

"That is my boat. I go for the cooler. Wait me there," he commanded.

There was a tall Mexican man in the boat cleaning.

"Think he's the crew or the captain?" Lynn wondered.

I bet captain.

"Then what is our friend, what is his name again?"

I told her he was the owner but that I could not remember his name but I knew it began with an A.

"Better learn it if you are going to be his wife," she joked and continued, "I'm a door, remember?" she repeated and continued, "I'm a door, I'm a window. I'm a door. Got it?"

Amador returned with the cooler on his shoulder, introduced us to the captain as he handed the cooler to him and then helped us into the boat. It was not clean but seemed at least seaworthy. The engine sounded good. There was a heavy smell of diesel. But the 85 horsepower outboard started right away. Ten minutes later we were over the Great Meso-American reef. You could feel the surge of the waves moving over it. It was as if we were entering another world. The water turned less blue, more green and you could see the coral below the boat. The waves gently broke over the more shallow parts. I turned to show Lynn something and noticed she was slightly green. The captain slowed the boat to troll for fish as Amador made his way to the cooler to hand us each a cold beer. The boat was undulating up and down as he climbed around the boat gingerly, took a box of worms from the cooler and put a hook onto the pole for Lynn. She took it in her hands and cast the line gently toward the stern of the boat. I told him that I was not interested in fishing and then snuggled into the bow of the boat to sleep like I did when I fished with my brothers. Only now I slept even more, an after effect of radiation therapy three months before. Or maybe I just liked it and used sleep as an escape.

Regardless, I fell asleep before I could obsess on the fatigue. I dozed for what seemed like only a minute before Lynn touched my shoulder to waken me. Amador was putting the fishing equipment away. She told me she was sick. We were turning toward the shore. Amador was taking us back before she barfed. She sat down next to me and I put my hand on her back, giving her a soft back rub.

"Sorry," I said, my nature to apologize for things that were never my fault but I was still sorry they had happened. She was changing shades of green. I told her to put her face into the wind explaining that the air would make her feel better. I knew it was the diesel fuel because I had suffered the same symptoms many times motoring on the sea. She closed her eyes and let air fill her lungs. Breathing deeply, she regained some of her pink color.

Then I advised her to "Look toward horizon. Focus on

something steady, not the waves," as so many people had told me when I was sailing.

I had a long history of seasickness, carsickness and general malaise so I sympathized. I knew it would pass, often quickly.

Amador came up the starboard side of the boat to announce, "She asked to go back. Is she ok? We haven't been out for too long."

I tried to explain that it was OK and we only wanted to get out on the water. He offered Lynn another beer, obviously not understanding seasickness.

She motioned the beer away. He offered the can to me instead. I shook my head. He shrugged, handed it to the captain and dug into the cooler for another one for himself. In less than 10 minutes, they beached the boat so we could escape easily.

"Wait me here," Amador said.

Instead, we wandered up the beach toward a small bar with the name, "Paraiso" scrawled on a piece of driftwood over some swings that served as bar stools.

I took a swing until Lynn looked at me and asked, "Are you joking? Let's get a table. He can find us there."

Lynn put her head on the table, resting there until a young Mexican with a towel on his belt and a shirt that said, *Oregon*, came over and asked us what he could get for us in heavily accented English but with a broad smile.

Lynn lifted her head off the table long enough to say, "Margarita, en los rocks con salt."

I asked for a mineral water but Lynn interrupted with, "*Y* one for her."

"A water, too, please," I said.

At least I would have some water before the tequila. Just then Amador arrived and sat down, said hello to the waiter and touched knuckles with him, as if they were in some fraternal order of beach bums.

"*Y cerveza para* him," Lynn added.

The waiter brought our drinks and I licked the salt from the rim of my plastic cup but drank the mineral water and waited to enjoy the margarita. The view was spectacular. The afternoon sun colored the water differently, things were crisper, the blue more blue and the greens more green and the gentle caramel white of the sand more soft. The colorful fishing boats tipped in red and yellows and orange seemed more exotic.

Amador broke into my daydream to ask where we were from. Lynn told him that she was from Ireland but now lived in Boston. I explained that I was from Boston and told him we had met there years before.

She asked Amador if all her did was sell tours.

"*Si*. That is enough, no?" and he continued, "When I first came here there was nothing. I took coconuts from the trees in the morning to drink and then fished with a spear to eat. Some days, I still do that."

I imagined him fishing with a spear and climbing trees for coconuts. He looked a little soft for that sort of life, even with the scars. Lynn challenged him to get a coconut and pointed to one on a tree nearby. He said that of course but that the tree was not his. He told her to pick another one, farther down the beach.

Lynn smiled and said, "maybe another time. Here is what we owe you, right? Three hundred pesos."

Amador took the money and then told us that the food was good in case we were hungry.

On cue, the waiter brought menus. Lynn asked for guacamole with some French fries. I asked if we could share, something about eating someone else's portion was more fun and somehow less fattening. Most people hated it but Lynn indulged me. Amador distractedly looked for tourists and potential tours as we enjoyed our drinks. I examined Amador's milk chocolate skin and deep brown almond shaped eyes as I sipped my margarita. His eyebrows and eyelashes were long and pretty in contrast to his rugged face. His face was ugly and rough, so much so that he was attractive. He caught me looking and smiled his contagious smile. I smiled back and noticed his baby teeth: small, white and well formed. He had soft facial hair that was too long for stubble. It grew only around his upper lip and chin, a little up his cheekbones but that was it. His chest was clean, a few soft hairs in the center. He asked me if I liked the sea. I told him I liked it a lot.

He told me he did too and explained a tad dramatically, "Of course, for me it is my life. Without it I am lost."

His boat was moored a little way off. The captain was smoking a cigarette, waiting for Amador to find more customers.

He continued, "When I come here there was only that little *palapa* and a few places to camp. It was so different," he said wistfully. He had been here four years. In "Playa del Crimen" before that.

"You mean Playa del Carmen?" I asked.

But he explained that he called it Playa del Crimen because of all the criminals there. He and Lynn agreed that they did not like Playa much. I told them I obviously did not need to go. Amador asked what we did in the states with a mouth full of guacamole. I couldn't help noticing some of the green delicacy on the side of his mouth and I had to fight the urge to wipe it off. Lynn answered first telling him she had a store and sold furniture and things for houses.

"Cool," he said. "You?"

I told him I was an engineer and tried to explain the intricacies of a job I used to love, saying, "for environmental things. You know wetlands?"

He shook his head no.

"Places that have lots of water but some land."

"Oh! Like the manglers in Tulum out in the lagoons?"

"Basically," I said, tiring of the explanation, as I had tired of the job.

I always had a hard time describing what I did: middle manager in the government's wetlands program. I supervised very smart people and managed all sorts of studies, wrote papers and made schedules. I assessed recommendations to issue building permits to developers and I assessed my staff's proficiency at their job. At the end of the day it seemed I spun my wheels more than anything, trying to get some projects out the door and stop others. After nearly 15 years I felt I had accomplished one or two good things but mostly jumped a lot of bureaucratic hurdles created by men who wanted to justify their pay. I was burnt out. When I had breast cancer, I left my supervisory position and instead of returning afterwards, took a new job in Washington D. C.: 'headquarters'. I would start when I got back with hopes I could change my attitude and the world. I was still idealistic. But when people asked me what I did, it seemed complicated and nebulous, a reflection on how I felt about the work.

"Interesting," Amador said and I realized he barely understood what I had said.

Lynn chimed in saying that I was very smart and he should not think anything else.

"You look fit," Amador added looking at my body.

I admitted that I liked to work out.

"She could kick your ass," Lynn said

I kicked her under the table. Lynn always sold me, like one of her pieces in the store.

"Really?" Amador asked.

I told him "probably," and obviously moved my gaze over to his arms. They were not muscular, at least not well defined. They were long and his hands were smooth. Lynn asked to have us arm wrestle.

I rolled my eyes and became uncomfortable as Lynn told me, "Show him what you've got, Joanneo," playfully.

He was ready. I was embarrassed but always up for the challenge. I enjoyed giving men a run for their money. I loved beating them when I could. At 5'3" and at this moment 100 pounds of muscle and skin, I looked a lot smaller than I felt. I always thought I was big, if not fat then big. It was funny when I discovered how other people saw me: little and feisty. If I were a breed of dog, it would be pit bull terrier when I had some weight. But now I was more like a whippet: small yet agile and muscular. Cancer had worn my body thin and there were times when I felt like a piece of driftwood on the beach. But I knew I was strong, mentally and physically. Amador cleared the table. Lynn wiped it with a napkin.

We placed our right elbows on the wooden surface and grabbed each other's left hand underneath the joined hands. My arm was slightly lower than his and I had to adjust my seat to get my elbow totally on the table while still holding his hand. He waited. I felt the tequila running into my veins. With our hands together I felt a familiar electric attraction as well. I did not dislike it. I told him it wasn't fair since I was left-handed. He told me it was not a problem: he could beat me with either arm. I smiled, removed my hand from his and put my left arm up, waiting for his fingers to interlock with mine.

Lynn said, "Ready?"

I nodded.

"Of course," Amador sang.

When she commanded, "go," I immediately felt pressure in my hand and pushed back, holding my place and moving Amador's arm a fraction. I struggled to hold it there.

He smiled and asked, "You OK?"

I told him no problem and he added pressure. I felt unsure that I could hold on but pushed. The strain probably showed in my face. He allowed me to work and enjoyed my discomfort the same as I would have had I been winning. He locked eyes with me, pushed harder and moved my arm onto the table. I tried to make him work for it but suddenly my arm went down like a knife through butter. The contest was over.

"Winner buys the next round," Lynn said victoriously.

I stroked my left bicep with my right hand. It hurt.

"Nice try," Amador said with a smile as he put his hand on the back of my neck and kissed me on the lips as if I were his trophy.

"You are very strong," he said almost as a consolation and then added, "for a woman."

"Not strong enough," I replied, annoyed but wondering who the hell I thought I was.

It had always bothered me that men were generally stronger than women. But I needed to accept the fact or continue to embarrass myself. The days of me beating my brother's buddies in push-up contests were over. I was still reconciling myself to this: days of glory past. It was part of what had made cancer so hard for me. Another symbol that I was as vulnerable as everyone else. I was not Super Woman and I did not like it.

"No worries," Lynn said as she flagged the waiter for the check. Amador had gone to talk with one of his colleagues: a guy who rented snorkeling gear on a tricycle.

Lynn and I had an appointment to look at some land in the jungle. One of our ideas for starting over was to buy a place and do a business here or have a vacation home in Tulum. We stood and waved goodbye to Amador, who saw us push back our chairs to go. He ran up to us to ask if he could see us later. Lynn replied that we were going to see some land in the jungle but perhaps later we would be around.

He seemed very interested in knowing what we were looking for and then said, "But you just got here. You don't know much about the place do you?" as much to himself as to us.

Lynn told him we were looking, nothing concrete.

He nodded and said "*Hasta Luego*" as we made our way down the beach happily.

As we neared our cabana, I craved a nap. The margaritas, the sun and my inability to make it through many days without a rest caught up with me.

"While you shower, I am going to lie here for awhile, ok?" I said to Lynn.

She said we had time and went in ahead of me.

I put my pareo on the beach and fell on top of it, fatigued. I drifted away with the sun caressing the small of my back and the afternoon heat melting my bones. I let the gentle rhythm of the waves on the shore relax my body and mind. I dreamt of the time my little sister had brought me to the beach after the first surgery for breast cancer. I had felt so cared for in that moment. The sound of the sea made me feel that way again and I fell deeply asleep.

Chapter 5

I opened my eyes slowly and focused on the translucent limbs of a crab playing in front of my face. The crab's two black raised eyes were at the exact level of mine. I let my eyes wander past him and up the white sandy beach and slowly remembered where I was: sleeping soundly on the beach. Visually, I soared over the sand, the cushions on the lawn chairs and the bikini clad people until my eyes rested on Amador.

"I'm a door. I'm a window," I said jokingly to myself, remembering his name.

I shielded my eyes to verify the sighting. It was him. I rolled over and sat up on my elbows, looking in his direction.

He was not in a hurry but he was walking with purpose. He greeted the tourists as he passed them. He was smiling a self-conscious smile, appearing humble but confident at the same time. When he reached me he bent down and kissed me solidly and fully on the lips.

I withdrew, surprised and said, "Well, hello."

"Ola," he said, and then he kissed me again, this time placing his tongue in my mouth.

I kissed him back. It had been a while since someone had kissed me so I relished it. Since Anthony had stopped taking my calls and Harry and I had barely made love in the last 3 years of our relationship, I felt more than a little unattractive. I let Amador caress me with kisses and wash away some of my emotional trauma. His

21

kisses pulled on my lips with suction like a baby at its mamma's tit. It was unusual but I relaxed into it as if I were still dreaming. He put his arms around me and we kissed right there on the beach. After a few moments acting like high school kids, I remembered Lynn and our appointment.

I wrestled my lips from his vacuum grip and gasped, "I have got to go. We are supposed to meet someone and Lynn is waiting for me."

He asked me if I were sure I wanted to, smiling as if he were irresistible. I easily reassured him and took his hands from around my waist. I stood up self-consciously and looked up and down the beach. There were very few people and the blue water had a pink tint glimmering on the surface. I wondered out loud what time it was and Amador looked up at the sky again. Annoyed, I started to walk to my cabana.

He followed saying, "Around 4."

I didn't believe him since Lynn would have come for me if it were 4. Our appointment was for before 5. I turned to go to our cabana. Amador followed me. He caught up to me and made contact with his hand on my lower back as I climbed the stairs. It felt nice. He escorted me to the cabana and I tried the door: locked. Lynn left the key under the doormat. Amador stood in the doorway. I wondered why Lynn hadn't wakened me.

"I can't believe she left without me," I said, sitting on the edge of the balcony.

Amador said, "Good," and embraced me and we kissed again.

He pulled me close, overtaking me like a cloud overtakes the sun. I felt bliss and comfort and release all at once. I did not even think of asking him to stop. He pulled my little black t-shirt over my head and walked me backwards into the cabana.

"I have scars," I said self consciously as he undid my top.

"Like mine," he said and then kissed the scar on my left breast where the tumor had been. He touched it with his fingers, gently caressing the long dimpled scar that cut above my nipple. I remembered when I first took the bandage off after surgery. I cried for hours, not only because it hurt but I was sure no one would ever want to touch me there again. "It is beautiful," he whispered, kissing it again. I melted. He pushed me gently onto my bed and stood over me and took off his surfer shorts. Suddenly, I awakened fully to what

I was doing.

"I am not ready for this," I blurted and put my hands behind me to help myself up. He gently but firmly held me down on the single bed and bent down to kiss my belly button, moved his mouth down over my hips and over my pelvis with gentle kisses. He started to pull my green crochet bikini bottom off.

I stiffened and repeated more forcefully, "Really, I am not ready for this."

"Of course you are," he said as he pulled the bottoms around my ankles and pulled my legs around him.

"No, I am not. I really am not," I told him but he pulled me closer and I pushed my feet into his hips.

I pulled myself back away from him and he came forward, kissing me on the lips and said, "don't worry, *mi amor.*"

I think it was the "*mi amor*" that got to me. I softened and did not continue the fight with enthusiasm. He kissed me again and then he firmly grabbed my feet from his hips and pulled my calves and then my thighs toward his erect penis and entered me, gently at first and as he did so all my resistance softened. It felt so very good. I relaxed into it as he moved deeper inside me and then felt the weight of him pressing down on me, nearly suffocating me. Just before I couldn't breathe any longer, he lifted me up and balanced me on his lap, still moving us closer and closer together. I inhaled as he held my back and balanced me there. I felt the bliss of orgasm and we came at the same moment. He had overwhelmed me and I liked it. I adored it, in fact, and he knew it.

We lay together as night softly fell and the sea moved from its reflective pink haze into a deep, dark blue. I watched the colors change in the room. Amador's legs were on top of me and his arms were wrapped around me. I felt secure, safe and protected, as if I had entered a cocoon where I freed myself from my former life, from my illness, from any responsibility to anyone but this man and my need for more of him. I did not want the moment to end. The peace I felt had come without medication, alcohol, or therapy. I looked at Amador's sun tipped curls and the odd dreadlock and nestled my head into his shoulder. I believed I had found the one. Again.

Then I remembered Lynn. I did not want her to be the one to disturb us.

I gently moved myself to whisper in his ear, "Lynn will be back soon."

He said, "so?" not at all self-conscious about being found together in bed.

I pulled myself from under him and told him I was having a shower. He asked to shower with me and I said it was fine but that afterwards, I needed some space. He looked like an eager puppy that had been scolded. I did not feel badly and when he asked if we could have dinner together, I told him it was fine with me but I wanted to check with Lynn.

He said that the shower did not have much pressure. But when the hot water came, he was happy and he moaned softly as he let the hot water run down his back. He called me to join him. He scrubbed my back and kissed my breasts again and again under the hot water. We playfully fought for the single stream of water and then gave up, shut it off and toweled ourselves dry. He sat on the bed for a few moments and then, as if knowing what I wanted, told me he would be back around 8. It was only about six o'clock. Lynn still had not come home but I wanted to be on my own for a little.

"See you," he told me as he kissed me and walked into the darkness that had overtaken the beach.

How could you sleep with a beach bum? Was I a whore? Would he come back? Did I want him to? All my insecurities came to the surface. I sat down with my journal and wrote to take things off my mind. Since cancer, writing had been my release. If I got it on the page, generally it made sense or at least didn't torment me for a while. I coached myself to not let it get out of hand and reminded myself that, "It was a nice moment, nothing more or less."

Lynn finally sang through the door with a knowing look on her face. "How'd it go?" she asked me.

I blushed that she knew.

"What?" I said with a smile and then, "Why did you leave me here? Why didn't you waken me?"

She said I was awake when she left and she didn't want to bother me to look at land.

Then she said, "Will your beach bum husband be back later?" I sighed and explained that he did ask to have dinner with us.

Lynn agreed to let him come saying, "Yeah, let's take him with us," as if he were some funny pet. Then she dashed into the shower to get ready.

As the hour approached I started to feel that abandonment that had become so familiar: the slight preoccupation with the time, the sad feeling creeping over me, that slightly sick feeling in my stomach, the anticipation that the man would not want me.

"Let it go," I told myself again before reciting from my daily affirmation book, "It does not mean you are not loveable."

I sat in the hammock and waited for Lynn as I prepared for rejection. Then I heard singing as Amador came up the stairs. He had come back. I was desirable.

During the next week, he found me everywhere, both on the beach and in the town. I loved it. We camped out and made love and drank and laughed and danced. He introduced us to people. He showed me places: those pools of dark clear fresh water where the underground rivers come to the surface called *cenotes*, the *manglers*, the biosphere and the lagoon that wad on the other side of the peninsula. And we swam every day.

One morning, floating in the calm blue water, Amador asked me if I had children. I was pulled from heaven as I told him that I did not. Then he asked me if I wanted children, implying he was ready to give them to me.

"I cannot have children."

I left it at that. I was unsure how to explain to him that being pregnant raises your estrogen level and that was what fed my cancer. So, getting pregnant would encourage the cancer to come back. But he asked me why, seeming genuinely curious.

I inhaled and told him, "Getting pregnant might give me cancer again, it is a hormonal thing. And besides, I am a little old to have a first child."

He didn't seem bothered and said to me "Well, we could adopt a child. Maybe one from Africa."

A calm glass of sea separated us and I swam to him. I kissed him and told him I would like that. He said that we could adopt a nice black baby from Africa. And I fell more in love with him because I believed he would.

When our vacation came to an end, I extended the trip to stay with Amador for another 5 days.

"See you in a week," I assured Lynn hugging her at the airport security line.

"Take care, ok? Be careful," she cautioned and then followed with, "Have a good time."

I told her not to worry because he was a nice guy and then reminded her he was the nicest beach bum in Tulum. We had decided that one afternoon over lunch: an uninformed informal poll of two. We laughed and hugged again. I told her I wished she were staying. Then I tried to explain that I couldn't go back yet. Lynn told me she understood and to take care of myself, then walked through security handing them her passport and her boarding pass and then turned to wave us away. Amador was standing behind me, his hand on my waist. He made me feel loved and, ironically, safe. He had no shoes and was wearing surfer shorts and a peace sign T-shirt that Lynn had given him. They were all the things that made me love him.

He kissed me on the lips, slowly, gently and asked, "*Vamos?*" For some reason I was unable to speak and wanted to cry, not sure if it was sadness or happiness. We turned and walked toward the exit in one of those seemingly harmless moments where one choice you make reverberates through your life and changes it forever.

Chapter 6

I had taken a bite of pasta when the phone rang, number unavailable.

"Get it. It could be a date," Fernando said sarcastically, with a mouth full of food.

I had been back in the states for two weeks and was living with Lynn and Fernando. I couldn't face going back to the job I had left when I had cancer and I was waiting to begin the temporary job in Washington D.C. that had always been my dream. Now, after a year of special projects and sick leave, it had miraculously come true. I hoped it would make me feel less vulnerable in the world by relieving my financial troubles, softening my cancer memories and helping me escape my conflicted emotions around my breakup with Harry. I was excited to start but I still dreamt of those warm nights and the crystal blue waves crashing on the shore in front of my little love nest in Tulum, Mexico.

I had not heard from Amador and told myself to be realistic. We had wonderful moments and the 5 extra days I had with him were filled with laughter, love and an abandon I had never known. But, as

I wished on the first star each night, I asked myself if I could have anything more than a meaningless love affair with a beach bum on the Caribbean. Well, honestly, I actually thought I could have a life with this man. I knew I could pull it off but I told myself he would never call.

"Move on," I told myself in the mirror. I answered the phone and walked to the porch to talk.

"I miss you *amor*," Amador's scratchy voice was on the other end, sounding close and beautiful and then continued, "It is not so much fun here without you. Why not come back?"

I laughed and started to glow inside. He wanted me. I was still loveable. I was not a whore. I told him I would think about coming back.

Fernando raised an eyebrow as I returned to the table and sarcastically asked with his mouth full once again, "Did he ask you for money?"

I inhaled sharply, hurt, naively surprised and pretended not to know to whom he was referring.

He smiled evilly and continued to harass me saying, "It was your beach bum, wasn't it?"

I answered directly, yes it was Amador and no, he did not ask me for money.

But Fernando would not let it go and asked me "Why did he call then?"

Hurt, I told him Amador had called to tell me he loved me and to invite me back.

Then I asked him, "Is that so hard to believe, Fer?"

He apologetically told me no, always regretting his insensitivity after the fact. But he followed by telling me to be careful, then stuttered and searched for the polite thing to say. I told him to never mind since I knew he only said things to me because he cared. I wanted the conversation to stop.

Fernando did not. He asked me if I remembered the time he was in the Philippines for work, how they had a guide who they paid and through the week became sort of friends. I started to wash dishes and he came around to stand next to me to keep my attention. He told me that when they were leaving, the guide asked for more money. "He asked me for 300 dollars, just like that," he said obviously hoping this cautionary tale would resonate with me.

"Did you give him the money, Fer?" I asked.

He told me not to be ridiculous and that he didn't have that sort of money to give. He laughed and said, "I told him I was going to ask him for a loan."

I laughed with him and he reminded me that his point was that it was not too much unlike Mexico in the Philippines. It was third world. He told me sincerely that I was out of my element and that these cultures think people like us have money to blow. He finished by telling me that the people in places like Tulum and the Philippines were survivors.

And he added, "especially this beach bum guy." I resented his paternal attitude with me. "Aren't I a survivor, too?" I asked him. I had been through hell and back and had travelled all over the world and wanted some credit. He stuttered that I was a survivor but a different kind. "I just want you to be careful."

I hugged him. I appreciated where he was coming from. But I was tired of people looking out for me in ways that seemed to stifle my happiness. I wanted this and I was going to get it if I could, regardless of "third world." I knew I could handle it and I would not let him take it from me.

So I began hiding Amador's calls from the people who loved me. Not just Fernando and Lynn, everyone. I became afraid of what they would say, so I didn't tell them. I didn't want their opinion. Perhaps I knew they were right. Perhaps I knew it was an un-realizable dream. But I didn't want to analyze what felt very good. I didn't want to hear them analyze it either. I did not want to break the bubble of denial that at that moment was all I had to hold onto. My life had become unmanageable and Amador was my way out. Without him, I felt alone because I was alone. I felt tired and weak because I was tired and weak. My year of cancer treatment had left me that way. I was living on people's couches and moving from place to place, visiting people so I wouldn't feel alone and sick. I wanted to break free. I wanted a change. I wanted that something else that I believed was Tulum. I needed a break and a new start and I believed Amador was the only way I could get it.

So when he called a week later, and asked me for money, the words hit me like a train. He wanted $200 for a new motor on his boat and he asked me to "help" him with it.

"Two hundred dollars for a new motor. It's a good deal, no?"

Fortunately the connection dropped since I had no idea what to do. I finally confided in Lynn telling her that I didn't want things to be like that.

She advised me, "Then don't let it be. Don't send him anything."

It was that simple. But not sending him the money, to me, meant losing him. I was sure he would forget me. Too, I believed that if I loved him, I should help him. After all, I rationalized, $200 to me was not even half a credit card payment. It was a quarter of a visit to a doctor, if that. It was Amador's livelihood and if I saved his life, he would love me forever. I sent him the money by Western Union and told no one.

The calls from paradise continued, intermingled with the calls for cash and I lived for them.

Chapter 7

I cried as I left Fernando and Lynn's the following Friday to head to Cape Cod. My mom would drive to D.C. with me and help me settle into a temporary apartment I had rented in Foggy Bottom. It was on the metro line and finally, I had a job where I could commute to work by train. I was excited. We had packed all my belongings into the white Saab convertible 93 including a Tupperware full of cut watermelon from my sister, and headed south early Saturday morning. We had a telephone interview for the condo we hoped to buy in Florida on the way. The Condo Association called us south of New Jersey. I pulled over to take the call. After 15 minutes in the rest area, we were back on the road. The process left me feeling energized. It was as if I were taking my life back, moving, buying a place on the water, dreaming. I was healing myself. I knew I would be well again and powerful.

Eleven hours later, we arrived, exhausted. The next day we wandered around the neighborhood and found the Metro, a grocery store, the Potomac River and my office for Monday morning. We shared memories of the city where mom's brother, Uncle Bob, had lived for most of his adult life and my childhood. Our family often visited his amazing apartment on Connecticut Avenue close to the Zoo and Rock Creek Park. Bob was the first person I had travelled to visit alone and I felt glamorous when I did. He and my aunt Therese were glamorous people. My mom and I shared stories and laughs and the next day, after a night long discussion of our family history in DC, my mom decided to take a train home. The idea of spending the day in my apartment while waiting for me to come home from work was too much. I got her a first class ticket on the Amtrak and waved as the train left the station. It was Monday night before I knew it

I hustled to make it to the office before 9. I was the last one in. Most of the people there started at 6:30 or 7, my boss told me, "to beat the traffic."

I knew the rationale and disagreed with the concept.

I told him, "That is why I chose a place so close" refusing to cave to the concept that early was better. He continued my orientation without discussing hours any further.

I worked on Clean Water Act Policy Studies, writing reports and briefings. They were well-researched documents that I spent hours tuning in my obscure little cube on the 10th floor of the federal building on G Street. Sometimes, I spent afternoons in the Pentagon waiting to brief some assistant Secretary of the Army only to find that Mr. this or that would make the decision without my input.

The places were cool, filled with history and a sort of military drama. But, as they became more familiar, they lost their appeal and my work seemed less and less meaningful. I was spending my days in an air-conditioned, windowless cube, surrounded by men and women with whom I had very little in common. I was afraid to talk about my illness and year of treatment for fear I would be fired or treated as if I were contagious or not up for the job. But I was tired and often late in that environment of early birds. People were waiting for me as I looked for coffee at 9 a.m. I stayed until 7 to catch up. But that didn't seem to matter. They were rushing home to families by 2 pm and wanted more time with me. I loved the nearly empty office after 4. I could drink a tea, catch up on my edits, and listen for the phone to ring. But little by little, each late afternoon, I began looking for a way out of what I had thought had made me sick in the first place: working at something that did not feed my soul. Whatever that was, I realized I had to find it to stay well.

But for now, I had that subsidized apartment in Foggy Bottom just a 10 minute walk from the Metro. Taking the train to work had been a life goal of mine that somehow I had never realized. Now, I relished it. I loved the crowds in the morning and afternoon. It was almost as if I had a social life close to all those people. But after the train ride, I happily came home to my empty apartment and worked on my books and my art. My friends Sheba and Paul were a 3-hour drive away and I visited them when I had the energy. So that meant once a month. They encouraged me to start a non-profit.

"Don't kid yourself, Fanny. You can make a lot of money with a non-profit. And you can help some people too."

It sounded appealing as I searched for something to wrap my arms around and give my energy to.

In a few weeks my mom and I would close on a condo in North Miami Beach. I wanted something nice, in a warm climate. I did not want to die in the cold. Once you have to really think about dying, there are certain things you want. I believed I would die alone. Somehow, warm and alone seemed more appealing than cold and alone. My mom wanted something nice and to be with someone, especially me. I don't think she thought about dying. At least not the way I did. She had seven children so probably would not die alone. But she had almost lost her little girl to the same thing that took her husband 3 years before. I think she wanted me close. Too, we loved buying real estate, or at least dreaming about buying it. One of our favorite Sunday things was to look at the Real Estate pages and then go to open houses and dream of what we could buy. We were the curse of most real estate salesmen and we were both shocked when we qualified for the loan in Miami. My mom would be out of the cold winters. I would be warm and out of Boston, the scene of so many crimes against me.

Sometimes, Amador would call me during work. I would run out of the building, down the 10 floors in the elevator to talk to him outside. I knew all the phones inside were tapped. I had people surrounding me on all sides and I did not want them to hear my calls or my plans. Somehow I didn't want them to know that I had a friend in Mexico.

He always immediately asked, "Where were you?" and then question my answer.

Sometimes he would hang up when I said I was at work. It was so foreign to me, this sort of jealousy and distrust that I mistook it for love. But when he didn't hang up, he would generally end asking for cash. Needless to say, I knew all the places in D.C. that sent Western Union.

I didn't let any of it get me down. For these four months, I delighted in each detail of my life. I would say thank you for the coffee on a little balcony that overlooked a homeless shelter, the famous Watergate apartment complex and then the Potomac River. I said thank you for the ability to move, thank you for the work and the place and I would thank God for this life and ask him to pull me through my day. My *attitude of gratitude* was getting me through but I was struggling. I thanked God with every ounce of energy I had. I was alive wasn't I? I had been saved. And then I would run painfully along the Potomac with my slightly battered body and I would count every 8th woman. "One in Eight" was the statistic I had read. I wondered why I had been that 8th one and at the same time, I wondered if I was losing my mind. I had no idea where to go or what to do. When I didn't have work, I slept or wrote. No one was around to notice how tired I was. No one asked me to go places. No one knew me. I was hiding until I could go to the only place I felt good.

At the end of July, I told my employer I was going to the doctor and took a long weekend to visit Tulum. It would be enough. When I got off the plane, Amador was not waiting as he promised. He either forgot I was coming or he had a tour with his new engine. I waited for 2 hours before I got in a rental car, hurt at being forgotten. I was sad, not angry. But what could I do? I drove to Tulum in a red rental Jeep Cherokee. As I drove, the open sky lined with palms and flowering tropical trees and the odd deciduous pine that flourishes in the tropics reminded me how good I felt alone. The expedition to Tulum felt right.

I checked into *La Vita e Bella*, the hotel where Lynn and I had stayed, pulled on the same little red bathing suit, wrapped a pareo around my waist and walked down to the sea. I felt the warm sand on my bare feet and stood in the sun for a moment. Then, I dropped the *pareo* from my waist and continued to walk into the gentle waters of the Caribbean. It was a tonic. I swam and breathed and cried and thanked God with a fierceness that outdid every other thank-you. I came back to the beach and fell onto my pareo and slept, the warm sun soothing my body and bones. After awhile, I squinted toward where I remembered Amador's boat to be moored and wondered what he was doing, why he had forgotten me.

Lynn had given me a pair of binoculars, "So you can have a good look at things," she told me with a smile.

I put them up to my eyes and swerved the glasses north. To my surprise, there was Amador, with a cooler on his shoulders, waist deep in the water. I was surprised and then angry. I walked up the beach to confront him with an energy and confidence that was not at all in my repertoire. As I moved up the beach casually, I caught his eye. He smiled. I couldn't help but smile back. He walked toward me to give me a hug.

I pushed him away asking, "Where were you?"

When he told me he thought I was arriving the next day, I pushed him farther away, saying, "I really do not believe it."

He came back toward me, "*Amor,* I forgot. Ask Cain," he pointed to his captain and then continued, "I been talking about you. I even go to your hotel this morning to check but it was too late and I had this tour. Really, *amor,* I just forget the day," and he smiled gently and pulled me toward him in an embrace.

I allowed myself to smile and let him hold me. I kissed him self-consciously there on the beach and we walked back to my cabana.

And that was how it started: the trips, the mad love, the changed life. I had found who I wanted to be. I had this dream, actually this realization. Not all people worked themselves to death for "the man." People made it on their own. I wanted to be one of those people; the one's who opted out of the 9 to 5. And I felt better each time I would go to Tulum and worse each time I would be back in the states. So, I made a plan to save myself fully, to live the life God had given back to me. I would leave D.C. in October and go back to Mexico to organize a life there. I would return to Boston to work with Lynn for Christmas while working on my books and a foundation for cancer survivors. In January I would go to Miami to settle at my condo while I created a life in Tulum somehow. Amador would help me. I would be his woman. Together, we would manage building a house for myself and cancer survivors and move back and forth between Tulum and the U.S. I would publish my books, sell one million, give a million dollars to women with cancer, keep a few million for myself and change my world. And if it was backwards, saving the world to save myself, I didn't see it.

Chapter 8

I left DC on a cloudy Friday morning the beginning of October.

"I need a break," I told my boss sincerely.

I needed some time away from the job, from Amador, from my family, from my friends. I needed to meditate, to find myself, to just be. My therapist wrote me a note citing posttraumatic stress disorder. I felt ashamed, weak. I mean, I hadn't been through that much, had I? It wasn't as if I had been to war like my brother. But when I thought about it, maybe I had been to war. It was a war with myself when I had cancer. I had been my own enemy and many times I felt my body had betrayed me. So, perhaps I did have posttraumatic stress. Or perhaps I had chemo brain like my sister Calzi said jokingly. Or perhaps I was an entitled middle-aged woman who wanted a free ride. All I knew was I needed to stop.

I was granted a year leave of absence. Thursday night, my nephew Brendan came to help me pack and get back up north. I was still slow and, although I knew I should be happy to be alive, some days it was a challenge: both life and being happy about it. I had packed my life into a couple of small suitcases to move to D.C. I could barely fit what I had now in the car.

"Where did it all come from?" I asked Brendan as he held up one more pair of shoes saying, "Do you need these?"

Of course I needed them. They were shoes, for God's sake. He smiled and pushed them into the back seat. I loved that boy. I had since the day, at 2 years old, he ran up to me on the beach in Onset Bay with his arms open as if to give me a hug. I stopped and turned to him, flattered by his attention. I opened my arms to him and leaned forward for his embrace. Before I could close my arms around him, he took my right arm, wiped his nose on it and ran away, laughing.

When I lived in DC, Brendan lived in Baltimore, close even by eastern standards. Both of us were chasing dreams: he in real estate, me with my books, non-profit and Mexico.

If we complained of a bad day or not enough money or time, we would finish saying, "But, it beats working for the man."

We meant it. Brendan became my touchstone. Each time I felt I had made a mistake to leave my job, each time I felt I was wrong to be in love with a dream of a life in Mexico, each time I felt afraid, I would reach out to Brendan and he would wipe a snot on my arm so to speak and make me laugh.

There was barely enough room in the car for the two of us. I was leaving my dream. I had made it to Headquarters, Washington D.C. I had been to the Pentagon, to all the monuments, given testimony to Congress, pushed my agenda. I had been able to walk to work and ride the train and be in a conservatively hip urban environment. The things I had put on my 5-year list I had achieved in 3, despite the lost year to cancer. Now, I was quitting. I still did not fully understand it. But I knew I had to go.

"I'll take this last suitcase down?" he asked me, seeming to know how I felt.

I nodded and took another sip of coffee and said, "I guess we are ready, aye?"

I took a deep breath, closed the door behind me and got into the elevator. Walking out the back entrance of my Foggy Bottom apartment, I noticed the yellow and red leaves on the ground as I got into the passenger seat. It was autumn, what better time to let a dream die.

We drove past the monuments to leave the city. I felt drawn to them and proud of my capital city. We moved onto I-95 later than planned but still in time to make it north that day. We easily passed through Baltimore, then headed onto the New Jersey turnpike to get through New York and finally into Connecticut where I had worked for years with the Army Corps. Each road had a project, a memory, an experience, and many a crime against nature. I turned my attention to something else. I asked Brendan about his girlfriend Lexi. I liked her and casually asked him if he thought they would get married. Brendan almost drove off the road. I laughed that I had shocked him and told him I was just asking. He told me they were still far from that point.

I liked teasing him and continued telling him, "I don't know, I thought maybe you guys would want to have a baby some day?"
Then he tried to turn the tables saying, "What about you? Want a baby?"

It was a fair question but somehow it hurt, now that I could never have a child.

Instead, I said, "Brendo, look around. Where would I put a baby? On the roof?"

We laughed and he turned up the music.

Around 10 pm, we were passing through the familiar city of

Providence Rhode Island. At 11, tired, hungry and happy, we drove into my sister Calzi's driveway. She had a beautiful home on a cranberry bog in East Falmouth and was waiting at the door when we arrived. We opened a bottle of wine in front of the fireplace before my sister Susan called wondering where her son was. Brendo left after the first glass saying welcome home as he gave me a hug and headed off.

Calzi and I finished the bottle without him and then she showed me to the guest room. It was painted a beautiful white with cream curtains and a queen-sized bed with a coffee colored duvet. It was on the first floor of her 2-story ranch house. The closet was full of her two girls stuff but I had enough room to put the things I needed. The bathroom was right across the hallway by the back door. I could still smell the fire in the living room off the kitchen.

"Stay as long as you want, Fans. I love seeing you. Although when the weather gets cold I think we should go to Miami," she said with a smile.

Before I fell asleep, I said a prayer, hoping it would be ok. I was afraid to spoil my relationship with my sister by asking her to take care of me once again.

Chapter 9

Fernando turned on the lights at 4 am. and cooed, "Wakey Wakey."

"You're a child," I told him and stretched my feet out from under the down comforter. He laughed and closed the door. I lay there for a moment and checked my cell phone. No missed calls. I wondered if Amador would be there when we arrived.

Fernando, Lynn and I were going to Tulum that morning. We had things to do, land to buy, people to meet. We would be one big happy family and Fernando would love Amador. They would go fishing and hang out like guys do. Lynn and I would tan and shop, like women do. I would finally have what many considered a "real" life. It may not have been a real normal life but it was about as close as I believed I would get this lifetime.

As we were renting a Jeep at the airport, Amador called to tell me, "I be at San Francisco, baybe."

We met him there: barefoot with a slightly stained t-shirt over his surfer shorts waiting in the parking lot. He looked more than a little stoned because he was. He was dirty too.. Fernando didn't like him the moment he saw him Of course, Fernando suspected Amador's motives.

"He has been sick." I said trying to justify his appearance.

I knew because I sent him money to pay the doctor when he moaned into the phone, "I no can walk. No can walk, baby. You got to help me. Three hundred dollars to pay the doctor. My knee is swollen like a football. Can you help me?"

The direct questions were always the hardest to answer. I have a hard time with "no." I still practice every day. I even have books on the subject, "The Art of Saying No." I have that one in Spanish as well. I sent him the money in record time. My man would not be a cripple.

Amador squeezed into the jeep and I sat on his lap in the front. Lynn took my place in the back with the luggage as he directed us toward the apartment he had rented for us, with my money of course. He was thinner than I remembered and a weak cappuccino color rather than the deep chocolate milk I had left in July. His knee was swollen and still cut. I sensed disapproval from Fernando and sudden discomfort in Lynn. She had liked Amador before.

"Joanneo is with a beach bum," she said to Fernando on one phone call, "But the nicest one on the beach."

Now it seemed she was unsure.

We drove down the central avenue, Avenida Tulum, a quick right and then left turn into the pueblo on dirt and pot-hole filled roads to a building painted white with salmon and yellow trim.

"This is ours baby. I get another for them but first we go to ours."

"I think we will stay on the beach," Lynn said, suddenly changing her mind.

It had been her idea to stay in town and save some money. Fernando confirmed their decision as if they had some telepathic communication that I was not allowed to access. I couldn't fight with that. But we had planned on staying in town and I had asked Amador to get us places there, not at the beach. Amador looked at me, questioning. I shrugged and told him that they wanted to stay on the beach, as if I were some English interpreter. Fernando's body language said he didn't want to be around us. He was tense. I was too tired to care and too annoyed to do anything about it. I let them go and said nothing.

To me, the barrio wasn't so bad. After all, that was what I had signed up for, the native Mexico, a place where we could learn the language and the culture. I wanted a culture change. But Fernando and Lynn were experiencing culture shock.

"You are on your own now," Fernando told me as he dropped me at the apartment building.

They didn't even come up to see if it was ok. I was surprised and hurt and asked them if they wanted to hook up later, not believing they would ditch me so quickly and not even give Amador a chance. Lynn replied that they would find a place and come back for dinner. I let it go, as I had been practicing. After all, I had Amador. He was wonderful, even if he did seem less marvelous than I had remembered. He brought my luggage up to the small apartment where there were no towels and where the ants were busy making a caravan across one of the beds. After all the moving I had managed in the last few days, I was just happy to have running water and to see my lover. I fell into his arms and let him lick me dry after a cold shower.

I gave him the gifts I brought: a bottle of Jack Daniels whiskey was Lynn's idea, some shorts, sandals, and a couple of T Shirts. I had always loved buying things for a man and I poured myself into buying things for Amador in the times I was away from him. He poured himself over me in that moment pulled off my sweaty clothes and made love to me on top of the ant colony on the bed. I could have cared less. The bliss was worth a few dead ants. We lay on the bed for awhile, listening to the fan move and the sounds of the town: beeping carts, Mexican music and dogs barking. Eventually, I pulled myself out from under Amador and moved into the shower. There was only cold water and before I finished, Amador handed me a towel he had hung outside earlier. Then we dressed and went into town. I was high on exhaustion and love and I felt beautiful. Amador wanted to hold me all the time, wanting to touch me in some way, holding hands, putting his arm around me. He had this delicious habit of putting his leg over mine when we sat, almost as if to hold me down in case I would run away. I didn't understand it but I loved the way it felt.

Fernando and Lynn drove by as we sat at a little restaurant

called, *La Nave*, next to *Cocodrillos*, the little bar where I first danced with Amador. Either they did not see us or they had changed their mind about meeting us because they kept driving. I ran to cut them off on one of the side streets and managed to catch them two blocks down as we both navigated the dirt and pothole filled back roads, them in their jeep and me in my stylish sandals and a red and black leopard print top Lynn had given me.

"You look like a local whore," Fernando told me when I caught up with them.

I winced but said thank you anyway.

"How's the apartment?" he asked, sarcastically.

I told him it was a cheap Mexican apartment and then jumped into the car to show them where we were. Amador had not chased the car. In fact, he seemed disappointed when I returned with Fernando and Lynn. But we all sat down and ordered drinks. They had found a room at *La Vita e Bella* and were happy. As we sat, Amador put his leg over mine and kissed my shoulder.

Fernando mumbled, "Get a room."

It was going to be a long week, perhaps a very long next few months. I was planning on living with them and working with Lynn in her furniture store when we got back. I started to rethink that plan. They had a beautiful house on the water north of Boston and I had been looking forward to staying with them. I had actually bought the house for them with my good credit, a major benefit of suffering through years of the 9 to 5 grind. It was their money but they couldn't get a mortgage: the down side of years of artistic freedom and self-employment. They were always over-extended. Lynn liked to buy 500 dollar boots and Versace dresses and then, all of a sudden, houses.

"You have to do this for me," I remembered the call from Fernando one morning at my office. "If I don't get her this house," he paused, "I don't know what she will do."

They were my best friends and it felt good to help them, even though everyone said not to. In about a year they had taken over the mortgage so I hadn't lost anything but the opportunity to own a great house if they didn't pay. But owning a house hadn't changed them. I bought their tickets to Mexico on my miles as their cards were maxed out. And we were thinking of buying property in Mexico together. But I couldn't imagine it happening unless I subsidized the project. The parallels to Amador hit me in the face.

After dinner we made plans to meet in the morning. I went back to the barrio. They went to the beach. Amador wanted to party more. I was exhausted. He wanted to drink. I wanted to sleep. He wanted to fuck like an animal. I needed to make love more tenderly. We fought. He took the bottle of Jack Daniels I had brought and left me. I was too tired to care. As I listened to him talk and drink in the next apartment, I fell into blissful oblivion.

I woke early the next morning to dogs barking and cocks crowing. The air was clear. The fan overhead made its grating noise. Amador was next to me. The sheets were spotted with blood from the cuts on his perpetually bare feet. The door was open and I suddenly felt very vulnerable. I got up to close it and immediately felt ill. I told myself it was a hangover and moved toward the bathroom at the foot of the bed. As I sat on the toilet my head started spinning and I began to sweat. Sweat dripped off my nose in one of my usual bouts of angst and distress: my body's defense mechanism to stress has historically been to black out: "vaso vegal" or something like that, according to my nurse sisters: body temperature increases dramatically and then drops the same way along with your blood pressure. I sweat an amazing amount and then black out and drop to the ground if I don't find it gently beforehand. It had happened to me many times: with my dad in the hospital, on the bus in high school, at my first day of work, coming out of the hospital after my second surgery, times when I would stress my body with too much exercise or partying or worrying. It was happening now. I was always too sick to be afraid. I just let it happen, generally getting to a safe spot beforehand. This time, I dragged myself to the bed and let the fainting take me in. I cared about nothing. That is the beauty of being sick: nothing else matters but finding escape from the illness.

I am not sure how much time I spent unconscious but as my wet body cooled, I reached for something to cover me. I pulled the bed spread over me, forgetting the ants that had been there the day before. But I was still cold. Amador called to me. I told him I was ill and needed his body to keep me warm. But I couldn't move. Then a horn blared on the road below: Fernando and Lynn, I knew. I tried to call to them but couldn't make a sound. Amador went to the window.

"Tell them I am sick," I whispered. He didn't answer.

"Ask Lynn to come and help me."

I only heard some conversation and then the car leaving. They had left me. I slipped back into unconsciousness as Amador's leg covered my body and the weight of it held me there.

I woke hours later suddenly anxious to get to the beach. I needed to swim, to feel the sand in my toes, to see the blue and to remember why I loved the place. I was shakey. Amador was hungry. We went for breakfast and then took a taxi to find Fernando and Lynn at the beach by la *Vita e Bella.* I took a lounge chair and lay there, oblivious to the silent conflict all around me. I decided I didn't care if they didn't like Amador. I needed to rest. Eventually, Amador asked Fernando if he wanted to get high.

"That would be great," Fernando said.

I thought I sensed Fernando warming to Amador. I was thrilled when Amador said he would go for some pot. Fernando said he had his money in the room and I told him I could pay since I had my wallet there. Why I felt I should pay for Fernando's pot was beyond me. And then, even more ridiculous, when I went to give Amador cash for Fernando's pot, I gave him the purse holding my cash instead for some bizarre reason, perhaps to show them how I trusted him. But I did not go with him. I was still recovering and Amador would come back shortly. I kissed him goodbye and laid back in the lounge chair. If I believed in omens or signs, the clouds that came after he left and drenched us in a tropical downpour would have told me something was up. But I was not looking for signs. The rain was warm and I needed to rest. I let it wash the salt from my skin as tourists ran past me for cover.

Eventually, I had a beer with Fernando and Lynn. Lynn and I decided to take the car and go for ice and groceries and look for Amador and give him a lift back. But we didn't find him and the apartment was locked. I couldn't get in. We asked around but no one had seen him so we went back to the beach. After awhile we figured we would go for dinner. Still, no Amador. I was beginning to worry. Fernando and Lynn were beginning to wonder.

People from the U.S. seem to always think people are trying to rip us off. Perhaps it is because of the stereotypes we have of foreigners or maybe because we have so much. Or, maybe, because they are. Lynn and Fernando believed that Amador had taken my money and was not coming back. They told me this at dinner. I couldn't argue. He had not come back. I felt abandoned, taken advantage of, and very sad. Amador was a loser and a con. Fernando told me he knew Amador's type as we had a margarita at Charlie's bar.

Then he continued, "He is not good for you. You are a beautiful and intelligent woman. Is it for the sex?"

I smiled self-consciously but had no idea really. I only knew I felt passion for him. I called it love. Others may call it sex but in that moment I had no idea what to think. We had another Margarita and talked some more. Then we went to *Cocodrillos* where I prayed Amador would find us. We ordered a round or two. People asked for Amador. I said I did not know. I started asking people where he might be, if they had seen him. No one could help us.

Then I remembered my drugs. I was on Tamoxafin, a daily drug to reduce the chance of recurrence of cancer. I was nervous about not having it. And I was using Atavan, a sort of mood stabilizing anti anxiety drug, to help me rest. I wanted the Atavan more than the Tamoxifin but both were in my suitcase in the locked apartment. Finding Amador became more than an issue of ego. I wanted my drugs. Gisela, the woman who managed the apartment, came into the bar and I asked her for an extra key. She did not have one and was much less friendly now that I was with Fernando and Lynn. Fernando and Lynn started to panic and began imagining some grand scheme to rob all my things, drugs included.

"What the fuck will you do?" Fernando asked me.

I felt abandoned until he invited me to stay with them. I was now nebulous about how they felt about me where two days ago I would not have questioned staying with them. I wanted to crawl into one of the potholes in the road. Fernando joked and told me what else could they do, really. I looked down at my feet, feeling stupid.

Then he reminded me that we were friends and told me, "Anyway, Lynn and I got it on last night so we can let you stay with us tonight."

Lynn scolded him and then asked for the check. She paid the tab and we jumped into the jeep and headed back to the beach. We enjoyed the night air on our faces and the brilliant stars overhead. They had the same room Lynn and I had stayed in when we first came to Tulum. It was funny and more than a little nostalgic but I entered and looked for my little single bed.

We were tired and drunk and as we stumbled in Fernando looked at both of us and said, "Let's go swimming. For God's sake, we are on vacation."

He stripped his clothes and ran out the door naked and down to the water. Lynn started to laugh and so did I. His ass was the only white thing visible on the horizon under the ¾ moon shining on the sea. I shrugged, looked at Lynn and then stripped and followed him. Lynn was right behind me. We jumped into the waves that crashed toward the shore, oblivious to the possibility of sharks or other attacks. I let the waves wash all the damage from the past few days and weeks and months. In fact, it felt like all the damage from the past year, my break up, my cancer, my job, washed away for the moment. We laughed, played, and crawled into bed feeling renewed. I was ready to start over. If Amador had abandoned me, I would abandon him. After all, I was a beautiful, intelligent woman. Fernando had told me so.

Chapter 10

A shrill voice entered my dreams, screaming "Joanna, Joanna."

I slowly opened my eyes in the haze of new consciousness not quite sure where I was but feeling safe. I heard my name again and as if dreaming, quietly went to the door slowly, toward a blurry vision of a short, thin, blond woman on the other side of the glass. I motioned for her to be quiet, putting my index finger to my mouth. She had blotchy skin with big pimples and thin pointed features. Her eyes were frantic, open wide and pleading as she reduced her shouts to whispers.

"Amador 'ees in jail wit my boyfriend," she whispered a heavily Italian accented English as I opened the door.

I looked at her blankly trying to understand what she was saying. She continued as I stared at the pimples on her face, pulling myself out of the deep sleep. She explained to me that when they went to buy the pot, the police found them and took them both to jail. I was not sure if she were real or still a part of my dream. Then she asked me to help her pay and told me that if we didn't pay tonight, they would take both of them to Playa del Carmen where they could keep them indefinitely. When she asked me if I understood I nodded and then she asked for 2000 pesos. I let the number settle into my mind: 200 dollars U.S. I still had not said a word. It must have made her nervous because she continued to tell me that she had 2000 but that the police wanted 4000. She was probably wondering if I were mute or totally deaf and told me that if we paid, the police would let them out. Then she asked if I could help and if I had a car.

"Who are you?" I asked calmly.

She told me her name was Barbara and sounded annoyed with the question but continued to explain that Sergio was her boyfriend and he was in jail with Amador. She asked me again if I had a car explaining that she had a taxi waiting that she wanted to send home since he was charging her to wait. She was confident that if I had a car, I would help her. I was still in my dream state and told her flatly that I did have a car. But I made no other commitments. She asked me then if I would drive her to the jail and give her the money, directly and simply as if it were the most normal question in the world.

I nodded. "What a drag."

The driver appeared behind her and said something to her in Spanish. She waved him away. Amador had told me stories like this one about the police. I had no reason to doubt him. After all, he was "the one." I looked for the cash and for the keys to the car and as I found them Fernando awakened.

When he saw Barbara, he was startled and he asked me "Who the hell is this?"

I calmly said, Barbara, and felt like I was on some sort of drug as I shrugged. Then Fernando asked what she was doing in our room and I told him that Amador had been arrested buying his pot and that Barbara and I were going to bail him out of jail. I said it as if I had done it before. But I had no idea where the jail even was.

"What the fuck are you thinking?" he said, annoyed and incredulous. Then Lynn woke up. And we went through the same litany of questions. She was surprised and somehow frightened. When I explained the situation, I thought Lynn would understand. I thought she would be on my side since she had met Amador with me. The joke, "I'm a door. I'm a window," echoed in my mind. Instead she asked me if I were out of my mind and then said I could not go alone.

"Let me get dressed," she mumbled as she pulled herself out of the fine sheets she brought for herself.

She continued, rambling, as she pulled on her jeans, "I don't like this, not one bit. How do we know this woman?" and she asked Barbara how she knew Amador was in jail.

Barbara explained that she saw them and again talked about her boyfriend and then told her about the money. She pleaded when she said it. Lynn asked me what I thought. I told her I knew that the police were pretty corrupt and I thought that since we asked him to get the pot we might like to get him out of jail.

I told her I didn't mind going alone and she said, "Oh no. We will all go. Why didn't you come sooner?"

Barbara didn't answer and Fernando grabbed the keys. I wore the only clothes I had as pajamas so I took my money and credit card and we all walked out into the night. The moon was starting to set and the breeze was cool but not cold. Our feet fell softly on the moist sand and we walked single file to the jeep. There were no cars on the road and we pulled easily into the night. I looked up at the stars, admiring them, loving to be awake so early in the morning, remembering times bareboating in the Caribbean when we would night sail navigating by the stars.

As we drove down the deserted main street toward the only bank in town, HSBC, Fernando broke the silence asking where the jail was. Suddenly Barbara asked to be dropped off telling Fernando that the jail was behind the bank. Fernando wanted to go with her. She explained that if the police saw us, they would want more money. She said, matter of factly, "You look rich," and then asked for the money.

We all got skeptical. I told her I would pay them myself.

She repeated herself saying that if the police saw us, we would pay more.

"You look like wealthy tourists," she said and looked down at the money in my hand.

I didn't like it but it made sense to me. Fernando and Lynn said nothing. I handed her the cash, 2000 pesos. She took the money and walked into the night, immediately absorbed by the darkness.

"Kiss that money goodbye," Fernando said. I didn't respond.

But Lynn said that she hoped our stuff was still in our room when we get back, explaining that "they" often lure you out to rob you when you are gone. I asked her if she thought it was a scam. She shook her head, as if I were naïve somehow. Fernando pitched in to say that regardless, I lost 200 dollars.

I felt sick and confused and victimized as we drove back to *la Vita e Bella*. When we got back, Lynn opened the door and everything was as we left it. I was relieved. I didn't want to be responsible for a total robbery, "*robo total*," as they said in the rental car place. I apologized, crawled into my little bed and slept like the dead. I did not pray for resurrection but later that morning, I woke with the clear air and felt the same: renewed and clean. It was as if the fog had lifted. I went to the beach for a swim. Amador had not returned to the hotel. I wondered if I would ever see him again. So much for my fairytale love, I thought. I felt empty, but not bad, just cleaned out. We went to town and I hoped to get into the apartment even if Amador was not around.

"Drop me here, will you? I don't need any more witnesses," I asked Fernando and Lynn as we pulled in front of the apartment building.

If he were there, I would talk to him and I thought better alone. I was embarrassed. Fernando and Lynn wanted me to move out, get a place at the beach and relax with them. I felt the same but I wanted to talk to Amador first. I told them I would get my things and go back to the beach. I told myself to go back to the tourists, back to who I was, back to the same old thing. I walked up the open stairway that overlooked a wreckage of a building next door and some clothes hanging on a roof nearby. The apartment door was open. I walked in to find Amador on the bed. He looked pale and thin, dejected.

He asked why I had not come to the jail to find him. He looked like a little boy as he showed me where they had hit him and pulled his hair. He told me that the police had taken his shirt and new shoes. I was shocked and felt badly.

Then he started to cry and said, "Maybe I am not the man for you, Joanne. You need a different guy."

His chin trembled as he tried to hold back tears. I hugged him, apologized and told him it was all OK. And I explained that Barbara told us we would only make things worse, that they would want more money if they saw us. I explained to him that I didn't know what else to do.

Strangely, I started to feel better. I had not been abandoned. It had been a misunderstanding. Fernando and Lynn came up the stairs. Lynn peeked into the apartment asked if I needed help with my bags. Somehow, now, moving to the beach felt so disloyal. I told her we would take the bags down and then invited Amador to come to the beach with me.

I felt Fernando groan inwardly before he started talking to Amador, "Man, I hope you don't take this wrong, but really what could we do?" He continued, "I mean, we are only tourists and well, really, don't want to get involved. I mean what if they had taken the car? You live here, you are from here, you know how to handle it. We are just on vacation."

I glared at him during his little tirade. The whole thing was about him. It was his pot and all Amador's risk. I wanted to vomit but instead added that we would go to the beach with them since it would be safer for us all there. They didn't know what to say and there was a long pause until Lynn asked what they should bring to the car. We loaded the car and then went to *La Vita e Bella* to get a room. They were full. So was *Diamante K*, there was no place.
When I came back to tell Fernando and Lynn, Lynn said, "Don't you get it? It's him. No one wants him, don't you see?"

I told her I didn't believe it because it was too horrible to believe. Just then Amador walked in and said he knew a place and asked me if I wanted to go there.

We took the car and drove to the other end of the beach road. On the southern side, the road turned to dirt and there were long stretches of nothing. The pot holes were huge, larger than any in town. After about 4 kilometers driving, we pulled into a new little hotel called *Amansala*, "Bikini Boot Camp, Eco Chic Hotel," read the sign. Amador talked to the receptionist. They were happy to see him there. He knew the manager and the owner and they gave us a deal on the room. They had bicycles and a yoga studio. This was great. I brought my luggage to the room, changed and went for a swim. I floated and sighed "*perfecto*," one of the few words I knew in Spanish. I was finally feeling good. Amador didn't swim with me. He was smoking a joint with the manager, brother of the owner. After my swim I walked over to them. Amador introduced me to Matt explaining that he took care of things at the hotel. Matt confirmed his job description in perfect English and told me that if I needed anything to ask. Amador told me later he was from Arizona.

Regardless, he seemed genuine and nice, even if he was stoned.

That night I met Fernando and Lynn on the beach for a reggae party. Amador's cut feet were infected and he told me he was taking some powerful antibiotics that made him very sleepy. Matt, apparently now Dr. Feel Good, had given them to him but told him not to drink or dance so I went alone. Fernando and Lynn were at the bar. The band sucked but it was fun to be at the beach. The stars were beautiful, so close you felt you could touch them. The waves broke softly on the shore, glimmering with traces of phosphorous. We were in paradise.

I took a taxi home leaving them with the car.

Amador was stoned and in the hammock on our balcony when I arrived. We laid there together for awhile and laughed about nothing, enjoyed the night and went to bed. All the lights went out shortly thereafter. The distant generator stopped. There was only the breaking of the waves on the shore and then the squeak of the door opening. I tapped Amador on the shoulder but he wouldn't waken. I sat up in bed, my heart beating rapidly. In front of the door, outlined in the gentle moonlight was the shadow of two tails wagging. The dogs from the hotel had pushed open the door to sleep with us. I told them it was ok, softly and laid back down. In that little room, with no locks on the doors and next to Amador, I felt safe and comfortable, loved and happy.

The next day, Lynn and I met for a cocktail at *la Vita e Bella*. I sat with her on one of the too high stools at the bar, praying that mine would sink a little deeper into the sand so I could reach my drink. I was nearly falling off the seat to reach the margarita when she told me people had been talking to her about Amador.

"So, tell me about it," I said licking salt off the rim.

"They say he is a drug dealer."

I had known that and I told her how he had mentioned he dealt some drugs, mostly pot.

And then, trying to lighten things up, I told her, "He doesn't seem to be too good at it."

I didn't want to get into it, to be honest. I was finally having a good time.

But she continued and told me, "They say crack."

I stopped drinking my margarita and and asked her who actually does crack cocaine.

Lynn shrugged. "Apparently your husband."

I couldn't believe it and I told her so. For me, crack was out of my realm of consciousness. It was a drug for the ghetto, for people who had no hope, no life, no laughter. That couldn't be for my happy man from paradise. Why would anyone living here need crack. Why would they need to escape? I couldn't fathom it. And Lynn wouldn't give me the time to do so. She continued saying that he smoked crack, sold it and that "they said" he stole to support his habit. I had come to see her to have a drink and enjoy and now she was annoying me. I asked her who "they" were. She said that they were people who lived here, at the hotel, at the beach bar last night. She told me that they were people who would know and have nothing to gain by telling us. I told her that I didn't believe it and had another sip from my glass. Lynn was unsure too but she told me to look at things, remarking that Amador was not too popular on the beach anyway. She asked me to think why no one had a room for me and why I had to go all the way down the beach to find a place.

She touched my shoulder and said, "Joanneo open your eyes. You are way too good for this."

I closed my mind to her. I would not hear it. Gossip. What "they" said.

My father's voice echoed in my ears, "Who are they? You cannot believe it just because 'they' said it."

He taught me to learn for myself. But that was as it related to the New York Times and Scientific Journals. That was to encourage me to think for myself. I was not prepared to research small town gossip where I had no relative database. How could I know who was right? How could I give up something that felt so good just because "they" said so? Fernando walked in from the beach.

"Looks grim." he said as he kissed me hello on the cheek and asked Lynn if she had told me.

She shook her head.

"Seriously, Joanneo, it never should have gotten this far. I mean, what does he bring to the table? Nothing. Lose the guy now before you get in deeper."

I went numb and told him that life was not a balance sheet. Fernando found something interesting in the sand and told me that perhaps life was not a balance sheet but a partnership meant that each person would bring something.

He looked back up at me and asked, "What has he given you? Sex aside."

I smiled an embarrassed smile and reached again for the drink. Sucking at ice cubes. We were all uncomfortable until Fernando started to apologize but he stopped and told me he only cared about me, or he would never had said anything.

"I am not your father but he would want me to do something."

I was buzzed.

Seriously, I told myself, where could it go. I smiled and said I would go talk to Amador as I reached for my wallet. Fernando said he would get the drink.

"Don't worry. People break up every day."

I told them both thank you and before I turned to go told them I was sorry for all the shit and drama. And I meant it. It was the last thing I had wanted.

I left the bar and took a taxi to town. How I would find Amador was beyond me but I needed to get out of the bar and away from them fast. The hypocrisy of the whole thing gnawed at my inside. I mean, how could I break up, if that was even the word, with Amador for drugs when most of the people I knew did drugs. Wasn't Fernando getting stoned every morning? Didn't they make magic mushroom tea every time we would vacation together on Martha's Vineyard? Hadn't Amador been arrested because he was buying dope for them? Hadn't I had friends who nearly lost everything to cocaine? The whole thing seemed fundamentally wrong and if, in fact, I loved this man the way I told myself I did, I should stand with him, not abandon him when he needed my help. I started humming "Stand by Your Man" and then stopped myself.

And then, as I looked out the taxi window and saw the sun burnt tips of Amador's dreadlocks, I asked myself, "What would my dad tell me to do for a friend?"

The answer came to me quickly. "Help him," he would say.

"Leave the world a little better place when you leave than it was when you came into it," was what he always told us.

After you stripped all the religion and dogma we had been fed, it was what we basically believed was the purpose of our lives.

He caught my eye in the taxi and flagged me down. I got out and he jogged over to hug me. I asked him if we could have a drink, saying I needed to talk to him. He said yes as he kissed me on the lips and held me there. We walked across the street to la Nave and sat at a table in front. I decided to confront him and get it over with.

We had barely ordered when I asked him, "Amador, do you smoke crack?"

His face went pale and he asked who told me that. When I told him it didn't matter, he disagreed and told me that in the little town of Tulum, it mattered a lot who said what. I confided to him that I really didn't know but told him people had been talking to Fernando and Lynn. He shook his head and his face got red and he said people were jealous of us.

When I asked him what they would be jealous of us for, he told me dramatically, "Of our love."

I wanted to believe it with my heart and soul. But somehow I didn't. I told him I didn't know what to do and stared into the glass of wine Amador had ordered for me.

He wanted to know if I believed them. I didn't really know who to believe.

"You believe them?" he said and took a drink of his beer. When he put his glass back on the table he told me he knew I was going to "Cut" him. I knew he meant break up but I liked the word cut. So I told him, I did not want to "cut" him but that I needed some time alone. I wanted to get away from everyone and think. He asked me again if I was going to leave him because of what Fernando and Lynn said. It hurt me to feel so shallow and I told him that I needed to think about things by myself. He didn't get it.

"Don't think too much." he countered. I knew I had hurt him.

That voice on my shoulder chastised me saying, "of course you hurt him, you just called him a drug addict" and I pushed it away and asked Amador to come over in the morning but to give me the night to think about things.

"What can I do?" he said meekly.

I thought he would cry but he didn't. He stood up and pulled my chair out for me, like a gentleman and walked me to the curb. Before we hailed a cab he asked me for money to pay for the drinks saying, "I got nothing. You know that."

I was somehow moved by his poverty and felt sorry for making him ask me for cash. Somehow his poverty made him more authentic, another throwback to my upbringing. Weren't all the Saints poor? Weren't poor people the backbone of the world? I handed him

200 pesos and he escorted me to a taxi, said something to the driver in Spanish and then came back to me in the back seat. He the driver would take me back to the hotel.

Then he followed with, "Don't think too much. Feel what you need to do," and he kissed me on the lips and tears started to roll down my cheeks. I sniffed "OK" like a little girl.

He stood up straight and hit the cab to go. As we pulled from the curb and went toward the beach I leaned back and wiped my eyes and felt immediately lighter and suddenly hungry. I closed my eyes and decided to go eat with Fernando and Lynn. There was a party there and I needed to see them. When I asked the cabbie to change direction to La Vita e Bella, I had no idea that it would probably get back to Amador.

When I arrived to La Vita e Bella, they were sitting with a table full of people drinking and eating pizzas. They saw me and immediately looked for someone behind me. No one was there and I could tell they were relieved. Fernando asked me if I was hungry and Lynn asked me sympathetically how it went. I told them that it wasn't pleasant to leave someone because of small town gossip but that I talked to him about it. Fernando rolled his eyes as he handed me a slice and I devoured it. He repeated his phrase about how people break up every day and finished by saying it was not such a big deal.

"It is for me Fer," I told him and looked for the waiter to get a drink. Then I waved at GiGi Fernando's Italian friend across the table from me. He waved back but his eyes were swimming in something. They didn't seem to focus and they were red and blurry. I settled in and felt comfortable as I ate, feeling almost like I belonged there. Fernando and Lynn were the center of attention and I let them have it. I had another slice and a drink with them. Then I got up and went to say good night. Lynn asked me suspiciously where I was going and I told her that I was tired and wanted to rest. She looked skeptical and I told her not to worry.

I walked out to the road on the sandy paths as geckos darted across the walkway and the leaves from the palm trees rustled in the wind. I looked up at the stars imagining they were mapping my course. They were fantastic. There were more stars than I had ever seen. There was no moon yet and somehow I didn't want to let go of it all. Sadness consumed me. I felt I had let the possibility of changing my life slip away from me because of other people's judgment. It seemed wrong. But at the same time it was too hard, too confusing. My brain ached and I stopped myself from thinking until a taxi pulled up and brought me home.

I went into my cabana and climbed into bed. I needed to be alone. No Fernando and Lynn, no Amador, nothing but a need for comfort. I pulled the sheet over me and slept fitfully, moving from deep sleep to anxious moments and then back to deep sleep. Sometime close to dawn, I felt a presence in the room. I thought the dogs had let themselves in again but when I turned it was Amador. He looked like Zeus rising up from the sea. He was wet as he touched me under the *mosquitero* telling me he had walked the beach to find me.

I wasn't too awake and told him, "That was a long walk" and then put my arms out to him and let him hold me and then move into my bed. He laid next to me, feeling warm and wet. My body ached to have him.

We made love and he said, "Let me enjoy you this one last time."

As he held me close and put his leg over my body. I slept soundly. I felt good and whole and I cursed myself for listening to other people. We awoke to a rainy morning. I needed to pack and get ready to go.

Amador begged me to stay, "*Solamente dos dias, por favor.*" He looked in my eyes and held my hands, "*Solamente dos dias, por favor.* Stay."

But I needed to get away from the whole thing. I felt sick and confused and hurt once again. But I was feeling. It was anything but the numbness I had developed to survive the last years after my father's death, my stale relationship with Harry, my rejection with Anthony and then cancer. I watched him walk away from my cabana and I cried like a baby. Then, as I turned to go out the door for a last swim, he was there again. We embraced and cried for each other and how wrong the week had been, how wrong we both had been. He left in the rain and I walked to the beach to swim in the calm blue rain dotted waters of the Caribbean. It was a tele-novella and I was the star. I left him that day but promised to return as soon as possible. I would not cut him from my life. I would pursue this dream, even if it was a drama.

Chapter 11

"I'll take 5 dozen of the roses – people love them," I told my almost-friend Steve.

I was in heaven at the flower market in Boston: a warehouse for flowers and plants and, at this time of year, every sort of evergreen. The fragrance alone was intoxicating and the people were, well, flower people: cool and generally happy and kind. And although it was a "closed shop" of sorts and I was a newcomer, I felt happy and almost accepted. Like everywhere in my life at that moment.

From the warehouse on Kneeland Street, I would drive my Saab convertible loaded with flowers to Lynn's shop on Clarendon Street, a few city blocks away. I was working downtown with Lynn: shop girl and flower girl. It was a far cry from the Chief of Policy and Technical Support but somehow it seemed more meaningful. Lynn paid me $10 an hour to sell furniture and flowers. The flowers had been my dream since I started working as an engineer. And I had learned that if you didn't chase your dreams, they could slip away in an instant. Like the instant when the radiologist told me I had cancer over the phone. In that instant all my dreams slipped away: that I could be an artist, or have a flower shop or a yoga studio, have a child or a husband. Everything was taken in one call. I was determined to get something back before I got the next call.

Too, I wanted some beauty in my life and things had been ugly for awhile. Why I thought I had to work with the flowers and not just buy a few every so often escapes me at the moment. But here I was, surrounded by beauty rather than engineers in a windowless cube. Meeting people all day and responsible for none of them seemed to be what I was lacking in my life. Being a flower girl was much more fun and romantic, like the French girl I had role-played in high school language class, as I called, '*mes flores! ils son bon mes flores, ils son frais.*' Preparing for class, I would practice in front of a mirror and dream about the French gentleman who would come buy "*mis flores*" and take me away. I still had that dream, I suppose.

So in my early forties, after nearly dying from cancer, I quit my stable, well paid, career engineering job to sell flowers. My dad was not there. Harry was not there. I had no one to worry about but me and I knew I would not last forever. I was free. I could do what ever I wanted, just like my father had said on his deathbed.

"Joanneo, you can do whatever you want," echoed in my ears as I went to the flower market early in the morning and bought roses and anemones and talked to the men there who thought I was marvelous, who probably thought I was French.

Each day I would bring the leftover flowers to my condo or to friends. I wasn't making money but I was making people happy. As important, I was making myself happy. And who cared about the French gentleman. I had my own Caribbean gentleman calling me, waiting for me.

I had rented my condo in Boston to pay the bills. This work certainly did not. After Christmas I would move to the condo I had purchased in Miami with my mom and then take a month in Tulum in January. I was leaving my hometown. Somehow, as the snow started to fall, it felt right. And, at Lynn's insistence, I lived with her and Fernando until I would go south.

"So I understand if you don't want me living with you guys," I said from the back seat when we arrived in Boston after that more than memorable trip, "I totally understand. Lots happened in the last week in Tulum."

Lynn asked me what I meant as I explained that I understood that they might be tired of dealing with my "shit" and that I didn't blame them if they didn't want me living at their house. I wanted them to have an out.

Lynn answered for them both and told me she needed me at the shop and that "what happens in Mexico stays in Mexico." Fernando surprised me and told me, "that is what friends are for so don't go getting all dramatic on us, ok?"

I was happy they still loved me. So there I was, living with them in Gloucester.

When it got to be too much, I would visit my mom or Calzi on Cape Cod or Sheba in Pennsylvania. I was working on my illustrated books about cancer, drawing alot, painting a little. And I had more plans than selling flowers. I was creating a foundation that would help women with breast cancer using these absolutely beautiful books I wrote. I planned on finishing them when I went to Mexico in January and then publishing them, just like that. The profit from the sale of the books would bring women to a place I would build in Mexico with Amador. It was a stellar plan. I was sure I would sell a million books. If I only made 1 dollar a book, that would be

1,000,000 dollars. The rest would go for women with breast cancer. To give them cash for whatever they wanted: a babysitter, a manicure, a good meal. Then I would bring survivors to Tulum to show them how good you could feel if you stepped away from your life and got some perspective. What I didn't understand then was that some people wanted to step back into their lives. Getting back was what they had been waiting for during all their cancer treatment. Not all cancer patients were like me: fighting to get a second chance, to start over.

But it was a perfect plan because I needed it to be. I would have a wonderful life. So I filled my mind and my days with making it happen. I practiced yoga, sold tulips, laughed with my customers, researched non-profits and publishers while managing 2 mortgages, living with friends and taking calls from Amador. I became all the things I wanted: a gypsy artist, writer and an entrepreneur in the non-profit world with a foreign lover. I was interesting.

Chapter 12

My mom and I pulled into Jacksonville Florida at about 7:30 p.m. It was our 3rd night on the road.

"How do people do this in one day?" I asked her as I honked the horn signaling passage into one more state. She laughed and told me my brother Dan had done it to drop his daughter off at college and then turned right around and came back.

I shook my head and told her, "Sorry, but I am not Dan. And I need something to eat. You?"

She never refused to stop for food. So I told her we could make it to Jacksonville and I knew a great restaurant downtown.

I had been to Jacksonville several times before for work and play and then again after my radiation therapy. My doctors said no but I needed to get away so two weeks after I finished treatment, I put 6 bottles of Moet Chandon in a cooler in the trunk and drove south. It took me a week to get this far last time. I had been so exhausted. I called Anthony at the border and told him I had made it.

"You are nuts," he told me in what seemed a joking tone.

But when I hung up I said, "fuck you," to no one in particular and drove to find my friend from college and work, Susan. I got out of the car in my favorite black skinny corduroy Levis, the best boots

I had ever owned and a very cool hot pink top covered in black mesh. There was a big heart on the front that was muted by the fine mesh cover.

"You look like a heroin addict," she commented.

"Love you too Susie," I replied.

She knew she had hurt me and tried to make it up to me by telling me she only meant that now was the time for me to join a band. We laughed but I was hurt and the hurt stuck. It has been a long time since I've seen her.

But, here I was in J'ville again. This time, I wanted a good meal. We drove off the highway and into the city and parked the car in front of a little Italian place that I remembered. It was hip, which I liked. The greens were very green, another thing I liked. And the wine was good and served in a real red wine glass. The waiter put fresh Parmesan on my spinach raviolis. And we finished with a good cappuccino and tiramisu. I knew I could drive for awhile longer after that but my mom wondered after 2 glasses of wine. I told her I hoped so since she could barely see after dark. We laughed but were both tired. I told her we could look for a place but we could make a little more ground. We were almost there, almost to Miami.

We had waved good-bye to my sister Kathy the day after Christmas with my Saab once again "packed to the gills," as we say in my family. It was grey and cold and we were heading south. The family Christmas was a treat after the Christmas season as "shop girl." I was tired. People bordered on abusive. And I had been used to being the boss so it was a real adjustment.

"Wrap those for me, would you?," one client asked as she handed a stack of purchases to me and continued to speak to the owner, Lynn.

I thought Lynn would wrap her gifts after the sale but no. Here I was, shop girl. But, OK. I liked wrapping presents. I used our beautiful red paper. It was that or regular brown paper so I took the red. I finished the packages with a striped red and white bow. They looked adorable.

As I stacked the last one on the top of the $1000+ pile, the woman looked over from talking with Lynn and said, "Oh those won't do. I am Jewish."

Lynn said nothing but I looked back at the customer and asked, "Jews don't like red?"

Lynn rushed over laughing nervously and told her we had some nice brown paper and re-wrapped all the gifts. I walked away as she continued kissing the woman's ass. When I finally left the shop on Christmas Eve, I was beginning to understand why my dad pushed me into engineering.

But, now mom and I were excited to be heading south for a new start. We had bought this condo together. And we would be in a warm place for the coldest months of the year. I was nearly one year cancer free. I felt I had not accomplished anything substantial.

In moments of frustration when I confided in my mom she would tell me, "Joanne, darling, you should be happy you are alive."

I knew she was right but it was not enough. Everything was working but nothing was concrete. Nothing was definite. I was clawing at life, desperate to have something done. My patience had not improved with cancer. If anything, I had lost that sense of "steady as she goes" that my father had tried so hard to instill in me. I was not steady and I needed to go somewhere that was for sure. So we were going to Miami Beach. And even as I was moving to Miami Beach, I was planning to go to Mexico. It was incredible how fast I was pushing things.

It felt great to be on the road. We had stopped to visit my friends Sheba and Paul in Pennsylvania. It was way off the fastest route but I had to see them. They loved my writing and art. And I loved them.

Before they went to bed and my mom and I got into our air mattress, Paul told me, "Those books are good."

Sheba added that they were not just good, they were great. I needed that. If they approved of my work, other people would too. And I needed to know that someone approved of what I was doing. Leaving Pennsylvania, the traffic through D.C. delayed us for hours. We were in the left lane and the sun had set. My mom was driving. I asked her if she were hungry but she only wanted a cup of coffee. There was a place at the next exit if she could pull into the right lane we could make it. She asked me to help her but I didn't understand and asked her what she meant. She confided in me then that she couldn't really see at night.

"I don't think I mentioned that to you before," she apologized.

I couldn't believe it and asked her if that were why she had been in the left lane since sunset. I started to laugh and then guided her to the right lane and then onto the exit. She started to apologize again but I stopped her saying in fact that I was sorry. I told her I had never imagined that was why she was in the left lane for more than an hour. And then I told her I could drive at night from now on. As we pulled into Virginia it started snowing and then turned to freezing rain and we had to stop. There was a Comfort Inn right off the highway and I slid into the parking lot. The receptionist told us they had only one room left. We forgot that we were with the snow birds migrating south en mass.

The receptionist led us down the hall and into a room that looked as if it were a conference room with a king sized bed in the middle. It was a huge room with only this big bed in the middle, two side tables and nothing else. And the bathroom had a huge hot tub but there was one wall that was all window facing the area where the bed was.

"I don't even want to imagine what has happens in this room," I said to my mom.

She smiled and told me to check to see if the sheets were clean. Then she asked me if I had pijamas. I laughed and told her I was going to wear my undies and p.j. pants. The place gave me the creeps but I was so tired I crawled under the covers after checking for stains or roaches. I told her it was clean enough as I rested my head on the pillow.

And so, I kept driving past each Holiday Inn and Siesta Inn as we left Jacksonville and headed south to Miami. My mom asked me if I was ok as she rested her head back and prepared to doze. I told her I would stop if I got too tired.

But as she closed her eyes, I told her honestly, "I would really like to get there tonight. I want to be home."

"Me too," she said and she held my hand.

My mom's hands are the softest and most wonderful in the world. I smiled, told her to rest and promised to stop when I found something good. I didn't waken her until we were nearly in Miami Beach. We drove across the causeway at Hollywood Beach heading to A1A and that was when I wakened her.

"Look Mom," little sailboats," I nearly shouted as I looked at the causeway lined with Christmas sailboats.

Miniature boats sparkled with tinsel and lights. It was nearly 3 a.m. and the stars were gently sparkling in front of us, nearly guiding our way. The boats looked like the little wooden 12' sailboat we had called a beetle cat. My Uncle Dick had bought it for the family. We all learned to sail on that little yellow wooden boat: The Golden Apple. That little boat was my independence before I could drive. It took me everywhere: first kiss, first joint, first cigarette and beer. When finally, about 25 years through its history with my family it became the "sail and bail," my mom and I decided to have it restored at a school Providence RI. They would restore it as their boat building school projects. It came back as good as new. But, I nostalgically remembered as I saw those little boats, I had abandoned it again. I hoped my sister Kathy and her boys would love it as we said goodbye to the sparkling little beetle cats on the Hollywood Boulevard in Ft Lauderdale and followed the stars to Miami Beach and our new condo on the Atlantic Ocean.

A1A was empty and we cruised the last half hour of our trip. But we noticed that the supermarket was open.

"Look! Pubics is open," my mother said.

I corrected her and told her it was Publix but it never registered. We stopped for some groceries at 3:30 am before we pulled into the big red building on the corner of Collins Avenue and 73rd Street: The Burliegh House. We took the packages into the elevator and rode happily to the 12th floor where we quietly opened the door and, entering, inhaled deeply. It was fabulously dark but you could see the waves and the stars and lights in the shipping lanes in front of us. We had made it. We slept until 11 the next day. The drive had sucked the life out of me. I finally opened my eyes to the sun shining into my window and sat up to look out at the Atlantic Ocean. It was calm and a radiant blue green that morning. A few mega ships floated on the horizon. When I gently slid off the high platform bed, I could see the beach, dotted with the signature lifeguard shacks of Miami Beach, each one a fairytale of a different style, color and ambiance.

"Maybe I should become a lifeguard here," I whispered to myself as I gently crawled out of bed, "fabulous office, anyway."

I tiptoed into the kitchen where my mom was sleeping on the pull out couch.

As we put sheets on it the night before, she told me, "Don't worry darling, I love this couch. And I have slept on it on many occasions. It is actually a very good mattress."

Her back, at nearly 80, was better than mine. I was too tired to say no and really never slept well when I slept with her so I went into my bedroom calling good night over my shoulder.

Now, I put water on to boil for coffee and sat on one of the many boxes that were still scattered around the room. I watched people walk up and down North Miami Beach and decided to join them as soon as possible.

"Procrastinate as long as you can," I told myself as I gently touched my mom on the shoulder and sang, *"Buenos dias senorita."*

I brought her coffee in bed and we sat and ate toast and talked. I marveled at how we still had things to talk about, after nearly 36 hours of driving.

Lazy was the theme for the day. We swam and went to an early dinner/late lunch close by as we strolled Collins Avenue looking for whatever they had: food, clothing, art, drugstores, beauty salons. I started to sort out the neighborhood. In 2005, North Miami Beach was up and coming but had not quite up and come. It was almost as if I had left the U.S., there were so many people speaking so many different languages. And the culture was certainly not the North East U.S. Still, across the street from our condo I could buy a *Cuban Cafe con Leche* and walk up the street for Jewish *Rugallah* and dark black bread from a Kosher Bakery. And there was still an edge to the neighborhood. Homeless people lined the causeway that led to the beach. They were often using the outdoor public showers there. I told my mom, if I had to be homeless, I would certainly come south and Miami, well, had a lot to offer. Free fresh showers, a climate that 75% of the year was hospitable to living outside and tourists who, if you cleaned up a bit, might mistake you for a local artist or even celebrity.

In the afternoon, you could hear people yelling insults across the street as one drunk called to another. The park north of my apartment was a little bit frightening when the sun went down. The beach entrance to the condo building was closed at night so you didn't have to stumble over a sleeping drunk as you came down the last stair. And the building's cleaning staff was never able to eliminate the odor of urine from the area. But you could ignore it easily if you lifted your nose to catch the sea breeze and sent your gaze past the sprawling sea grape tree to the marvelous Atlantic Ocean directly in front. I had always been good at looking past undesirable realities to notice the desirable ones. Once you passed that gauntlet of marginal income and addiction, the beach was long and fabulous. The sea was a dusty green color near the shore moving into an emerald blue green once the water deepened. On the weekends and after 5 on weekdays, it was packed with people of every background and color. But as I looked out from the balcony by the second floor pool in our building, bums to the left and right or not, I saw only the tips of sun umbrellas and the vast blue Atlantic. I was south and I was on the beach.

And in a short month I would go to Mexico. That was the plan and so, I had lots of work while in Miami: my non-profit, my books, I was drawing and painting and now I had to become a life guard. My days were full with making it happen, research, contacts, appointments. I was sure I could do it all. I had contact with Amador through email and the odd telephone call.

And the calls were odd: "Baybe I so happy you answer me. It is always so hard to find you."

I told him I agreed and that he always seemed to call when I was busy. He asked me where I was and I told him I was on the beach and that I had found a great yoga studio close to my apartment. He sang "cool" into the receiver and I asked him where he was in that moment.

He told me, "I am in the San Francisco. I took a big shit in the toilet here."

I was shocked and told him that was really too much information and he told me, "Si but baybe it feel so good. It is a pleasure really."

I laughed and thought about it and decided he was right. Taking a shit is a pleasure that I often took for granted. I loved him more for appreciating it. After calls like this I was sure the simple life he could give me would be bring me closer to happiness with an appreciation of the little things that make life worthwhile. Like taking a shit.

I finished that call telling him I loved him and that I would be there soon. I hung up anticipating the next time I would be in his arms. I walked up the back entry, around the pool and into my building to take the elevator up to our 12th floor apartment. My mom was on the couch reading and I fixed us some lunch. Later I went to find an internet cafe and grab a few groceries. That was my routine and I loved it. If I didn't practice yoga, I ran or went to the gym. And then I was researching non-profits, contacting doctors, checking emails, writing and drawing and dreaming of going back to Tulum, Mexico. I had my tickets. My sister Susan and Tom her husband would come to visit my mom and keep her company and then I would come back before her birthday. While I was in Tulum, I would finish editing my books and finish the drawings that I was putting carefully on the pages. Fernando and Lynn would visit and we would organize ourselves with the land we had bought in the jungle. They would go and I would start to build. Things would be fabulous. I knew it. And until they were, I was manically trying to create a life other than the one I had known. Each day I would enter my routine searching for something more while holding onto the dream that I could have a simple life in both Mexico and the U.S.

Chapter 13

My mom brought me to the airport in Ft. Lauderdale. I would abandon the mother of 7 who had, in five short years, lost her husband of 48 years, her home of 47, nearly lost her daughter, lived happily but unfulfilled with 2 daughters, then moved with a third outside her home state to finally be alone. I told myself she could handle it: it was a gorgeous place and on the beach. Then, I told myself she would have to. I needed this.

Amador was waiting as I exited customs: dirty, bare foot and wearing a silver grey Puma soccer shirt. He smiled when he saw me. I jumped for joy and we hugged and kissed publicly. People stared. I liked it. He did too. We were the same in that way: wanting to prove something to the world but not quite knowing what it was. Extracting myself from his kiss, I told him I was happy he remembered me. Twice I had waited hours for him to come only to finally rent a car and drive to Tulum alone. But outside the hurt of being stood up, I discovered I loved being on my own in this oh-so-foreign place. He assured me he would never forget me. I melted with his words, but told him perhaps never *again*, to remind him of the other times. He took my bags and we walked to the rental car agency. Leaving, he suggested we go to Puerto Morelos for the night saying that Tulum was packed and that he wanted to rest with me now, kissing me on the neck. I loved that he wanted me and agreed.

Less than half an hour's drive from the airport, we took a left off the highway down a two-lane road that ran adjacent to a vibrant marsh. Behind the palms that lined the road, calm water shimmered in the sun, white egrets were feeding in the shallows and an osprey hunted from a dead tree that was jutting into the blue sky. Abruptly, the marsh disappeared and we were in Puerto Morelos' town square. They had filled a good portion of the marsh to build that town and my work of 15 years poured back into my mind. With it came a sadness. It was the same old thing. Everyone wanted their place by the sea regardless of what it did to nature. I pushed the energy from my mind and reminded myself that at least I had not permitted this destruction. I looked at Amador for directions.

We took a room on the beach which was adequate: clean enough, toilet in the room and shower with hot water. It was not as nice as I would have liked, but it was just for the night and we could explore the village. The sea air moved easily into the room once we opened the sliding door to the tiny balcony that nearly faced the sea. There were, of course, the universal plastic chairs and I cursed whoever had created these uncomfortable sticky excuses for garden furniture. I knew they were made in China, but I believed the guy who patented them was a Republican out of Illinois who used cedar patio furniture from the rainforest, purchased with the profits from these plastic atrocities.

I pulled my new computer from the bag to show Amador and to keep my mind from spiraling out of control toward other environmental atrocities. I opened my Apple OSX laptop and told him I would finish my books on this computer. He grabbed my waist and kissed my neck and back as he looked at the machine, only slightly impressed. He reached under my shirt and started to undo my bra.

"You are sweating." He said with concern.

I told him it was really hot and then kissed him and wiggled out of my tight and now sticky jeans. I had put on 2 annoying pounds and blamed it on the tamoxifin I was taking. My doctor told me it was preventative for breast cancer but he hadn't told me that it would make me feel bloated and anxious. I was sweating like never before and I slept fitfully. It had forced me into early menopause even though I thought chemotherapy had done that already. Even before cancer I only had periods every other month at most. Now they had stopped altogether. In my running days I had gone years without them. I thought I would have it easy where "the change" was concerned. But this drug sent my body out of control, robbing me of an illusion I held fiercely: that my body was mine. Lately, I had no idea what to expect. I would sweat at the slightest anxiety. I rarely got a good night's sleep and without the rest I often slipped into depression. To fight the blues, I would run. But I had so much pain in my hip that I was limping through the first mile. Yoga calmed me but it wasn't enough and the classes were expensive. It seemed that my body was betraying me and Cancer was only the beginning. Age would catch me regardless. But, Amador loved the gentle new curves telling me I looked good and helping out of my shirt. There was no tension, no self-consciousness and I relished that he found me attractive.

We made love with U2 singing on my compute above the sound of the waves.

Afterwards, he asked, "Swimming?" with a smile.

We dressed, walked to the beach and into the cool blue water. It was calmer than Tulum, a bay rather than the miles of endless beach. The reef was closer. There were more fishing and snorkeling boats and there was a soft, short seaweed that I did not recognize as anything that would ever grow up north. I told him I liked Tulum better. He said it was different in Puerto Morelos and suggested we rest in the sun. My pale thin body welcomed the warmth and his hand on my lower back.

We dined at a little Italian restaurant in the town square later. Amador wore clothes I had brought for him. He cleaned up well, although the shoes I brought for him gave him blisters and he quickly kicked them off unapologetically like so much trash. I wasn't sure how to feel as he kicked my gift into the street, cursing. But a part of me liked that he would toss away so easily what many would hold onto regardless of the blisters. We finished a bottle of wine with dinner and he ordered tequila afterward. I tried to talk to him about my plans and desire to find a place to settle and work but he was distracted and escaped into the alcohol.

In the morning we loaded my things into the rental car and headed south toward where I hoped to find a home.

About 30 minutes into the drive, Amador asked, "You been to Akumal?"

I told him no and he suggested I take the next left and we could have some lunch in Akumal Bay. There was a restaurant on the calm bay with tables at the water. As we ate, Amador mentioned again that it would be difficult to find something in Tulum and asked me if I wanted to stay in Akumal. I hesitated. I wanted Tulum. I wanted to settle. But I wanted him to be happy and it was nice to see new places so I agreed to stay for awhile.

I told him Lynn and Fernando were coming later in the month and that they wanted to stay with me. I commented on how it would be great to find a house in Tulum and all be together. He did not answer. I continued to talk about finding a place, not able to tolerate the silence.

Finally, he said, "You don't think I understand how it feels not to have a place?"

I never thought how he never really had a home. His stories of growing up with an abusive father and being kicked out of the house at 9 years old were hard to listen to and must have been harder to live through. But he chose to live in a tent or on the beach. I thought it was what he liked or he would have changed it.

He wanted to say something but stopped himself and told me we would look for a place soon, touching me on the thigh as he said it. We found a wonderful place for a good price and booked 5 days, settling into a gentle life of love-making, swimming, me writing, and him sleeping a lot. Our third night there, after dinner, Amador asked me if I was still interested in the land he had offered me. It was a lot inside the biosphere, right on the beach. We had driven there in July when I had visited from DC. It was where I had told him I could die.

He wanted $150,000 US for the lot and was under the illusion that I had that kind of money. But I did not and doubted I could get it. But I wanted it. At least until I researched it back in the states. A Texas Title Attorney told me that the title was not clear and that Amador's name was nowhere on the deed or in any of the paperwork. Too, they said his piece was not legally subdivided and inferred that he was trying to sell me something he did not own.

I had never told him. It had cost me $5000 U.S. but my attorney told me as I signed an equity loan on the condo I had in Boston, "If you cannot afford to research the title, you cannot afford to purchase the piece." I trusted his advice. The title attorney told me that when he inquired about this land, the notary didn't want to tell him anything. He told me, frankly, that he had worked with these people for years and when he mentioned Amador's name and the lot, their whole demeanor changed and they would not tell him anything. He finished saying, "My advice to you, Ms. Barry, is to leave it and look for land with a clear title." He told me he would send a written report the following week. I hated what the attorney had to say, so I put it into the "can't handle that now" part of my brain. I knew Amador had an explanation and would let him give it to me.

This was the moment. I told Amador I had wanted to discuss that with him and that I had researched the lot and basically told him that he didn't own it, at least not officially. I mentioned to him that whoever sold it to him did not put his name on the title or the deed. Then, probably sounding like his mother, I told him he needed to take care of that before anyone could purchase it and I offered to help him do that that while I was in Mexico. I congratulated myself for having said what I knew without accusation.

But he was looking at me in an uncomfortable way and asked me, "You got that paper?"

I pulled the folder from my portfolio. He took the folder from me and started to go through it. I got uncomfortable. I had other pieces in there I did not want him to see. He noticed my discomfort and asked me if I were hiding something from him. I was, in fact, but told him that I was not but that was my private stuff. I asked for the folder and told him I would find the paper for him. I reached for the paperwork.

He pulled the folder back, looking at me with betrayal in his eyes and said, "You keeping secrets from me, *amor*?" as he held my papers close to him.

I told him not to be ridiculous but they were my private papers. "Stuff," I told him I wanted to talk to him about before he went through it alone.

I was explaining rationally and smiled at him with my hand extended waiting for the folder. He did not smile back and I didn't feel comfortable at all. After all, I could have my stuff. I could do what I wanted.

He asked, "Like what things?" as he looked at the papers more closely.

I didn't answer him and he continued looking until he got to the paperwork on the jungle land, rudimentary sketches, bank transfer receipts, notes on how to get the land in my name legally.

I finally told him, "That stuff," bluntly and confessed that I bought the piece of land in the jungle with Lynn. In one of my weaker moments while staying with them, I had fronted the money for two lots.

"That piece you told me was shit?" he said to me.

His eyes were piercing and his face had turned to something I did not recognize. He frightened me. I looked away as he said sarcastically that I had bought land with my best friends. He asked if I had researched that piece as well and I lied that I had. Then I got angry believing he had no right to make me feel badly about this. I explained to him that the land in the jungle was a whole different situation in both price and the fact that there was a title. He asked me why I didn't tell him about it, looking hurt. I felt like shit and told him I didn't know why but that it was weird the way he and Fernando and Lynn all felt about each other. Then I reminded him about the last time I was in Tulum. He dropped the papers on the floor and walked out the door in silence. I followed him to the landing and called after him. He did not answer. I let him go and sat on the couch and stared at the papers on the floor. Finally I picked them up and started to put them away. I looked at the letter from the title researcher and started to cry as I shoved it back into the portfolio.

"Fuck," I said to myself and to that voice on my shoulder before she could say, "I told you so."

Not even 5 minutes later, he walked back in the door. He stood there. I apologized, not sure for what but I knew I was sorry: sorry his land was not in his name, sorry I had not taken the time to talk to him, sorry that it was all shit. I stood there, with the portfolio in my hand looking at him and then at the floor. He told me he had wanted to leave me but that he couldn't because he loved me too much. I dropped the portfolio and went to hold him.

He opened his arms and embraced me and then pulled back and looked me in the eyes, put his hand on my chin to hold my gaze and said, "But no more secrets, ok?"

I nodded through tears as he told me I needed to tell him everything I was doing. He was nearly scolding me. I nodded yes again, loving that he cared to know everything. He took my hand and led me to the bedroom, kissed away the tears on my eyes, then moved down to my mouth and throat and then to my breasts. He gently took my clothes off and we made love to. The next few days were heavenly.

But I still wanted Tulum and somewhere more permanent, more Caribbean, less touristy and I wanted to report to Lynn that I had a place where they could come and join me not only to pay them back for living with them but also to help me with the rent. I was living on a fairly tight budget and money was only going out. Nothing was coming in and I could not survive that way for too long. Lynn and Fernando did not know I would be with Amador but I didn't care. I emailed Lynn about Akumal. She, like me, wanted Tulum and told me that Fernando's sister and his friend Rob and his girlfriend were all coming so we needed a big place. She told me to try to find a place for everyone the last time I had called her. I said okay and hung up. Each time I called I planned on telling her about Amador but each time I failed. The sin of omission had always been my biggest fault.

I had learned from the master, my mom, as she worked around my father's desires and demands. Every so often she hid new pieces of furniture in our attic room because she never told my dad she had purchased them. There were the stacks of collectible plates in the closet that would take years to reach the walls for the same reason. I could still see the surprise on my fathers face when I told him I was indeed going around the world with "Semester at Sea" even though he had denied me months before. My mom and I had worked it out. When I asked about what my father would say she answered, "Lets cross that bridge when we get to it, darling."

We didn't get to it until the month before I left.

He was furious but my mom told me, "He will get over it, darling. You have a big adventure."

I cried at having deceived him but I was happy I would get my way. My mom was my co-conspirator in life. From her, I learned to be quiet about things I really wanted.

"Wait until things are ready, sweetheart. Who knows what will happen with your plans," she would caution me.

And so I became a quietly determined young woman who did not share plans. I moved quietly forward with them. And if people did not like it, well, as my mother would say, "that was really their problem."

But that strategy lost me a lot in weighing my options until sometimes it was too late. My mom forgot to mention, or perhaps I neglected to hear, that although it is great to move ahead to get what you want, it is sometimes good to consider other people's opinions, especially people who love you. I didn't want to hear bad things, I didn't want to face reality sometimes, didn't want to lose my dreams, so I rarely brought them up. Accordingly, I figured that Fernando and Lynn would have to face their prejudices when they arrived.

Finally, Amador and I left Akumal and drove to Tulum and up the beach road under the blue sky and the emerald border of palms heading south toward the biosphere. We stopped at hotel after hotel asking for a place for a month. No one had anything.

"With a kitchen," Amador would add. "And electric," he would say as they shook their heads no.

We were relentless and even as the sun started to set, we continued to drive and stop.

"*Oye*," he would stop a friend in the road and ask for advice.

Finally, we bumped into three youngish Mexicans at a small hotel called, "*Hamaca Loca*," crazy hammock. They started to talk with Amador and check me out. One, named was Gerry, started to pick at his face in the rearview mirror.

Grossed out, I poked Amador to ask quietly, "what is he doing that there for?"

Amador spoke to him in Spanish and he stopped but looked at me resentfully.

Finally, Amador said, "Gracias," and we backed down the drive.

"They know a place" he said, "We gonna go there now," we and headed up the road and drove under the stone arch that marked the entrance to one of the largest nature preserves in Mexico, the Sian Kaan Biopshere.

We bumped our way along the unpaved road past nothing but palms and potholes until after about 30 minutes we saw the sign for Cesiak, an Eco hotel with army tents perched on platforms. We parked and went into reception. They looked at us suspiciously, sort of from under their eyebrows. I wondered why but let Amador talk. He introduced me to the manager, Pepe.

They talked in Spanish and finally, in English, Pepe told us, "Please, follow me."

We walked towards the sea, past the remnants of a concrete building and along a small path at the top of a bluff. There were mosaic tiles scattered everywhere from what must have been a house wrecked by a hurricane. I looked from the bluff to the sea. The waves were big and crashed against a trash littered beach. But if you looked above the trash, toward the horizon, it was mesmerizing: miles of blue ocean in three directions: east, north and south and a fabulous sandy beach extending along its border.

I could hardly keep up with the guys who were more used to the view. We jumped over small brush and I glimpsed the odd salamander scurrying out of our way. There was a large iguana sunning himself on the concrete remnants of another wrecked building. Birds flushed from low-lying bushes chirped loudly as we passed. Black and white frigate birds floated above us. We came to a small, round unpainted concrete house with a glass door and a large triangular window overhead. All the glass still had tape from a recent hurricane and there was a thin film of sand across the floor. There was a small fridge, a gas stove and a sink.

"*Hay dos banos,*" Pepe mentioned referring to the two bathrooms and he walked up some stairs to show me the balcony.

I followed him up a winding stairway where there was a dining table and a grill. As I got to the upper level and looked out, I inhaled deeply. An incredibly large lagoon stretched before me. Where the Caribbean water was crystal blue and rough, the lagoon to the west was a milky green and calmer than you could believe possible given the state of the sea in front. I stopped and looked. Pepe ran back downstairs and spoke to Amador, who had not followed.

"Two bathrooms, honey bonny."

Amador called in a sing song. I went back downstairs and Amador came close enough to me to touch my ass and make a funny smile. Almost dancing with joy, I poked my head into the two bedrooms, one with 2 single beds and one with a queen and a single. Pepe continued to talk and told me they had solar power. I was high. The house was exactly what I wanted. It was as if I had found home. I asked him how much and he told me "24 hours a day."

I laughed but he didn't understand so I explained that I was asking about the rent. He told me $1500 US for the month. It seemed expensive but I wanted it. And I figured Fernando and Lynn would love it and would want to stay here. I looked at Amador but he was looking at the stove. Pepe was in a hurry and told me to think about it and let him know. I wandered around the house, sat on each of the 4 beds and looked over at Amador who was pulling some dishes out of the sink.

"You got a fridge," he said happily. I looked over at him, smiled and then ran to hug him fiercely.

"I love it. It is perfect," I told him.

He commented how I had everything: electricity, hot water, and a fridge. Then I asked him about the price. He said it was okay but a little expensive. Thinking out loud, I commented that if Fernando and Lynn came they could help me pay.

He looked at me and said, "If they come I not gonna be here."

I told him we would talk about that later and put it back into the 'can't go there now' part of my brain. We strolled back along the bluff to talk to Pepe and I took the house for a month.

I was ecstatic. We moved my things in and I went upstairs and into the hammock to rest. Amador stayed at reception for awhile and then wanted to use the car to go to town.

"I'll go with you," I said automatically. I didn't want to but since he had been arrested I was nervous about him using the rental car. After all, he had no license and the car was in my name. If the police pulled him over they would probably arrest him for stealing the car even though he had my permission. That arrest and the drama that followed had traumatized me. After all, my dad was a cop. No one I knew had been arrested. Well, at least not put in jail. So we drove together to town.

On the way, Amador looked over at me and said, "When you gonna live here. When we gonna marry."

I was surprised but I loved the concept. I smiled at the thought but asked him what I could possibly do in Tulum.

He thought for a moment and then said I could open a hospital, finishing with, "You could help lots of people with that."

I looked at him as he continued to tell me that my sisters could come here to help. He said it matter of factly, as if it were the most normal thing in the world. I would save the world and have my family close by. It was a recurring dream I had: all my family in one super huge dream house. All seven of us had a house within the house and my parents were there too. I told him it was a great idea but I was not sure they would come. I took his hand in mine and kissed it believing I had finally met a kindred spirit.

Chapter 14

The next morning was cool but the sun warmed the living room and front landing as it came through the window and into the house. Amador slept as I made coffee in an Italian coffee press that he had shown me how to use the night before. When I asked him what it was, he opened it for me. It was full of old grinds and mold from the last person who had been there. Apparently the cleaning lady had not known what it was either. But after a thorough cleaning, the coffee was delicious. I brought a cup to the front landing to sip as I wrote in my journal.

The morning reminded me of the crisp September mornings I had spent with my mom on Cape Cod. We ate French toast on the back stairs to stay warm in the sun, having skipped school to enjoy the beach for a few extra days.

"You can learn about enjoying life and you won't miss anything really," she would say as we put extra syrup on the cinnamon French toast and laughed the mornings away, postponing the inevitable.

For me, it would be the dirty streets of Dorchester, the rigors of Girls' Latin School and the nausea of daily bus trips. For my mom, the kids all back to school meant a certain loneliness that having raised a family of 7 ultimately engenders. I was as happy to help her as she was to justify to my father why she could allow me this indulgence. My teachers never forgave me but my dad eventually forgave us both.

The sea that January morning was wild but there was a scraggy bush growing atop the bluff that protected me. I sat in the sun, wrote and drew the gentle beach birds that were sheltering in the shrubs in front of me. Putting my pen inside the seam of my journal, I felt a kiss on the neck, turned to see Amador's smile and meet his lips.

"Breakfast?" he asked me, "Or first a swim."

I loved swimming with him. Until I met him, I had always been afraid of big waves. Now, I developed the courage to face them. Amador would hold my hand and guide me under them, ducking as they broke over our heads. It was exhilarating and I thought it was a sign that he would help me overcome other obstacles. I chose swimming first.

He closed the door and we slid down the bluff together next to the remnants of a set of stairs that had been washed away by the last big storm. I enjoyed the free fall and followed him to the water's edge. Amador took my hand and we dove into the crashing waves.

After the swim, we struggled back up the hill balancing on pieces of the old stairway. Shivering, I wrapped myself in a pareo before retreating to the sun-drenched balcony. Amador eventually brought me breakfast. We dined overlooking the lagoon, the murky blue green water glistening in the sun. I was as happy as I had ever been. We ate, laughed, made love in the hammock and lay there blissfully. When I went to shower, Amador went to reception to talk to people. Apparently, I was never enough.

He returned to tell me he was going to town with some of the guys from the Hotel mentioning that way he would not need my car. I detected a note of resentment but let it go and asked casually when he would be back.

"Later," he said, as he closed the door to the bathroom.

I continued talking and asked him how I could get in touch with him if I needed him.

"You can't," he said with a grunt that told me he was taking a shit.

I smiled, stopped talking but started thinking. Neither of us had a cell phone and although I was enjoying the disconnectedness, I suddenly felt very alone. Then I told myself to relax since, after all, I had everything I needed.

I heard the toilet flush and he came out smiling, and told me not to worry saying, "I never gonna leave you, honey bonney."

He wrapped his arms around my waste in a big bear hug, kissed me hard on the lips and then asked for 200 pesos.

I didn't hesitate. After living with Harry who never had money and then my cultural coaching that said if you didn't put out some money and even fight about paying, you were labeled a cheapskate, I was always there with the cash. Too, there was an element of control that I enjoyed in paying and in enabling. I handed Amador a 200 peso note, got another kiss and he was out the door. I called after him saying I loved him.

He blew me a kiss and said, "me too."

I knew his English was bad but the cynical part of my brain told me, "he said he loved himself, not you."

I asked that voice to leave and sat down at the computer to work. It was noon.

At 2, I went for a long walk down the beach, ignoring the stories of wandering the beaches of Mexico alone: robberies, rape, muggings, and walked for more than an hour in one direction, meeting no one. I felt someone behind me and when I turned around, noticed a dog following me. I called to him and he shied away. When I moved toward him, he ran in the opposite direction. He turned to look at me once he got far enough away to be comfortable. I continued walking and he followed me from a distance. It was nice knowing he was there. He was grey, skinny and his ears stood up on his head. Each time I would stop, so would he. We played a little, me stopping, him stopping, and he helped me generally enjoy myself despite a certain loneliness and displacement: seeing no one in all that time felt good and bad at once.

Close to 4 p.m. I arrived back. Rather than climbing the bluff in front of the house, I opted to go up the stairs by reception, the same way I had gone down. I wanted someone to know I was around, to miss me if indeed I never came back. I saw Pepe and waved. He nodded hello. I hoped to see Amador at the house but he wasn't there. The note I left him was still in the door. After I rested a while on the couch. I decided to practice yoga on the balcony as the sun set into the lagoon.

I prayed into the rich orangey reds that sank quickly into the blue green water as it became dark: dark like you read about. There was no moon and when you looked to the sea or the lagoon, it was like a dark hole had opened up in the sky. The only light was from reception: one lonely bulb. No light on the pathway to guide me if I needed to run. No light to guide me to the car if I needed it.

"What would you need to run from?" I asked myself, "The boogey man?"

I answered the rhetorical question, "yes," and smiled because I firmly believed in ghosts and boogey men and had never been this alone ever in my life. Sure it was beautiful but in the dark it was scarey to be there on my own. I wished Amador would come home and then noticed two bright spots behind the porch: eyes. I inhaled and looked more closely, then laughed, recognizing my dog friend.

"Hey you," I cooed standing still, "nice to see you. Are you hungry? I bet you are."

I wanted that little dog to stay and I was afraid to go back in the house for fear he would go away. But food would coax him more than my presence so I left the door open and went to the fridge. Wondering what he would like, I pulled a piece of cheese out, went back to the door and offered it to him. I waited for what seemed a long time as he tiptoed to me, took the cheese from my hand gently and then slid back a safe distance to eat it. I smiled and waited to see what he would do next. He lay down and looked back at me.

"It's okay, you can stay if you would like." Then I said, "I would like it," talking as much to myself as to the dog.

I looked up past that dark hole of a horizon and saw the stars. They were fantastic. As dark as the sky was, the stars were equally brilliant. I smiled and slowly went back inside to cook.

I went to bed at 11, locking the door. Amador had not returned. The dog did not leave and I was less afraid. I slept fully until I heard a knock on the window at what must have been 3 a.m.

"*Mi amor,*" the throaty voice I had been longing for, "Let me in honey. It is me."

I was not that happy to see him and only asked him where he had been. He shrugged and told me we were a long way from town and he asked me for another 200 for the taxi. I told him I had already given him money to get back. I was hurt that I was spending the night alone while he was obviously out partying. He kissed me and told me he needed some food and a beer. I tasted the beer and knew there had been more than one. He put his arms around me and kissed my neck as I continued to complain that I was alone. He continued to kiss me and then asked if I had any food. I told him I had just awakened but yes, I had cooked and could heat something up for him. And just as I would have done for one of my brothers when they came home late from a party, I heated the leftovers for him.

He pulled me close and kissed me hard sucking on my lower lip and nearly inhaling it. He liked doing that. I almost enjoyed it. Then he walked toward the bathroom and said, "That would be great. I have a lot of hunger." I smiled at his English. But I told him I would have liked to go out with him.

And when I asked if he enjoyed himself without me he told me, "Honey don start."

I was quiet. I did not want to be a nag and he was right to a point. I suppose I could have gone looking for him. But that was not my style. I hated going out alone. So I started the stove and heated up the stir-fry I had made earlier.

He inhaled the food and I worked on a helping myself. He told me he was happy I could cook. I laughed. He leaned over for a kiss, puckering his lips in a funny expression that made me smile. I gave him the kiss and cleared the plates. He took my hand and led me to bed. We wrapped ourselves around each other and slept deeply until the sun came up and shot into the room. In that little bedroom you could watch the rays of the sun move up the horizon, over the sea and then into your life. It was marvelous. I let the rays surround me and wrapped my fingers around his sun tipped dreadlocks and fell back to sleep.

That day and for several following, I would waken and write. Then Amador would make us breakfast and we would talk. Generally, he would look for a ride to town or I would drive him so that he could sell a tour or do one. He would come home late and a little drunk. I would walk the beach and practice yoga and wait for him. One evening he suggested we go to Belize and buy a cheap car so that he could always come home and have dinner with me. I was not even a fraction as excited as he was and I told him so. I mentioned maintenance and responsibility and he talked about how much I was paying to rent the one I had. I told him I would rather get a bike. He told me we needed a car and that he needed one for his tours. We started to argue. Finally, I asked him how much we could get a car for. He was unsure but wanted to go look. When I asked him when, he told me he wanted to go the next day. I had never been good at geography and had not recently seen a map of Mexico and how it related to Belize but I asked him how far it was. He said it was only 3 hours and we could go and come right back.

Then he got me saying, "They have cheap bikes there too."

I thought for a moment and then decided to try to be spontaneous, open and look forward to having a day with him.

We left early the next morning and headed south through town. It was somehow liberating leaving. The road was 1 lane in each direction and there was forest overhanging on either side. Cars passed recklessly. Every so often we passed a small town or a small *palapa* or someone selling oranges, coconut water or roast chicken in the road. But generally, it was fields and woods. After about 2 hours, the road expanded to 2 lanes in each direction and we started to see more houses, farms and traffic and a rotary with a sculpture of a

Spaniard and a Mayan woman. It was a sculpture of the first "*mestizo*" couple. The Spanish soldier who had married a Mayan united the village and turned back the Spanish invasion.

The rotary also marked the turn for Belize. As we approached the border, there were various used car dealers with their multicolored plastic flags rustling in the breeze. We stopped at a couple but since I didn't know much about cars and Amador knew less and I didn't really want a car, it was a hard sell. We left each one empty handed. Even if we had wanted to buy, they wanted cash and I was not prepared with 30,000 pesos in my pockets. We stopped at the Free Trade Zone that was at the border but couldn't go farther because Amador had no passport. I wondered what that must be like: to be always limited. But then I told myself it was his choice. He just didn't want to do the paperwork.

The free trade zone was a huge open flea market full of people buying stuff, not very nice stuff either. It was like a New York's China Town but without anything of quality. We looked for bikes, settled on two, loaded them in the car in their boxes and started the drive back. I was tired and not too satisfied with the day. But I had two bikes and had seen some of the country, enough to last a while. We dropped the bikes in town at a bike shop Amador knew so they could put them together and headed home.

Just before we reached the traffic light Amador commanded me to stop. He told me he wanted to see someone about a tour and that he would see me at the house later.

"No fucking way," I said, angry that he would drop me like some used piece of clothing and I told him so.

He countered that he had been with me all day and then moved to kiss me but I moved my face away and asked him if that were such a bad thing. Tired and angry, I reminded him that it was his idea in the first place. He didn't listen and told me he had to do some things. I would not listen and told him he could do them the next day or do them with me.

He looked at me then and said, "No *amor*, really. I need to go."

I pulled the car over and told him to go. When he got out, I told him not to come back and drove to the house, angry at him and at myself and then even more so as I remembered I had no idea how to get back to the bikes.

"Shit" I said and then, "Fuck the bikes. I can rent one."

Then I started to cry. I pulled through the arch and into the biosphere feeling very alone. But as I entered the driveway, I looked up at the stars and they took my breath away. I pulled the headlamp from the dash board and made my way up the sandy path to the house. The front light was on. The maid must have put it on and I found the key in my bag. I noticed my little dog friend there waiting. I said hello to him and he looked at me. I went to the fridge and got some cheese but he wouldn't come near me to take it. I left it on the ground telling him it was there if he wanted it. I let myself in, closed the door, washed up and crawled into bed, too tired to cry anymore.

At nearly sunrise, I heard a knock at the window and a raspy "*Amor*," in my dreams. I couldn't waken. I heard "*Amor*," louder and then "Joanne."

I heard it again.

"Joanne, it is me, *amor*, Amador," and I pulled myself from sleep.

"I told you not to come home," I said and rolled over trying to ignore him.

But he didn't stop. He kept calling. But then, I put my feet on the floor and walked to the door to let him in. He told me to relax and that he had things to do, as he came in and wrapped his arms around me.

Then he said, "But baby, I always coming back to you. Always."

I let him kiss my neck and hold me tightly. He walked me backwards toward the bed and kept kissing me and then he took my nightgown off and made love to me. I did not stop him. I embraced him back and let him make me feel good. I loved that he had come back. I was happy to have him there with me and too tired to make a stand.

"Don't do that again," I told him as he lay next to me.

He asked me if I didn't like the sex. I smiled and told him I meant not to leave me like that. I wanted him to come home with me or go out with me. I wanted to fall asleep with a man and I wanted it to be Amador.

He held me tightly and told me that sometimes he had to do things alone but then, he got up on one elbow and told me, "I gonna try."

Then he said that the next day we could go get our bikes and ride some places together. I relaxed and my mind drifted back to the times we took bikes from the hotels to ride for drinks or to the beach. I would be behind him and see his dreadlocks and his rounded shoulders in front of me. I wanted that again. I wanted to have some fun with him again. I fell asleep with the voice in my mind telling me that tomorrow everything would be great.

We went to town for the bikes in the afternoon. I never would have found the place. It had no sign, one bicycle out front and a few screaming kids around it. I thanked God he had come back so we could collect them. He went into the shop and I opened the back door to put them in. He came out with one bike and heaved it in the back and told me we had a problem. I looked at him with curiosity as he told me the other bike we had bought didn't come with pedals. I couldn't believe it but he told me the other bike would be ready tomorrow.

I was annoyed and Amador said, "The world is full of assholes baby."

Then he apologized saying the he should have checked and he asked me for money to pay for them both. He explained that they needed to buy the pedals. I wondered what kind of bike shop it was that had no pedals and told him why not just pay for one and then come back for the others. He got frustrated and told me to tell them and walked away from me. My Spanish was so bad I hardly knew how I to say anything. A fat Mayan woman in a tight skirt and blouse with fat hanging over every edge of the two pieces of clothing, was staring at me. I looked at her and smiled.

I called to his back that he knew I couldn't tell them and he told me, "Well then, you need to do what I say," he told me, looking back with a smile.

I was frustrated and paused for a moment, knowing he had me and hating it. I looked at the fat woman. She glared at me and I returned her glare saying the universal "bitch" with my eyes. Then I looked at Amador and asked him how much I needed to pay. I wanted that bike. He told me flatly that it was about 125 pesos. I gave him the money to pay her and got back in the car.

"You go ahead," he told me when he came back saying he had to do some things at his boat. I started to ask him to come with me but he interrupted me and asked if I would drop him at the boat. I happily agreed. His boat was on the part of the beach that was close to the ruins, close to the hippies and the campers and *Don Hernando's* where you could dance all night. People seemed cool and free. There was a beach bar with swings where you could get a margarita and sit and watch the day go by. The sea was calmer than by Cesiak and the snorkeling boats would wait on the beach until they had a tour. The crews would push the boats into the waves, load on a cooler and gear and head off with their tourists. It was where my Tulum experience had started, full of good memories and happiness.

We pulled up the potholed road that took a dip as you entered and then made a slight hill filled with potholes. As you crested the bluff, the base of the road turned to sand. Just as you thought you would be stuck, the road hardened and leveled allowing you a view of the blue water and the bows of at least 10 fishing boats. Each was 3 to 4 meters long with outboard motors and painted different colors with their names on the sides accompanied by drawings of fish and Mayan gods. They were marvelous, reminiscent of the boats we drove as kids on Cape Cod minus the Mayan gods. The beach was freckled with sun bathers, some hiding in the shade offered by the fishing boats. There were a few people playing volleyball. The beach bar with swinging seats and great margaritas was empty. Amador asked me if I wanted a drink before I went.

I wanted to feel that place again and told him yes. We sat at swings and he ordered a beer for him and a margarita for me. He quaffed that beer and said, "agua fresca," as he wiped his mouth with the back of his hand and smiled.

"Fresh water," I understood. After all, I had Irish roots and had worked construction in Germany where the motto was, 'beer is for drinking, water is for washing'. I was not unaccustomed to beer in the vending machines. And when I bicycled across Ireland in what seemed like my past life, Lynn would always want a beer by lunch and the pubs were packed with like-minded individuals. So I did not think anything of him ordering another before I finished my drink.

He spotted someone down the beach and quickly told me he had to go. He finished the beer, kissed me on the lips fully and repeated himself.

"I see you later."

"The check?" I asked as he walked away.

He turned toward me with a slight scowl and turned his pockets inside out and backed away leaving me. I was annoyed but finished my drink slowly there on the swing, looking out toward the ocean, enjoying the view if not the sensation of being left with the bill.

Then the margarita spoke and told me, "It is only money, for god's sake. Pay the bill." I did and left for home.

It was early morning when I heard the now too familiar knock on the window and opened the door for him to come in. Although I loved that he had returned, I was tired of the routine. I would write and play music and cook and talk to my dog friend and wait. I watched the sun settle into the lagoon and the moon come up and I would count the stars and wish on the first one I saw and any shooting stars. I mostly wished for Amador to come home. Then, I would lock the doors, check the rooms for "boogey men" and go to bed.

The next morning I wrote in my journal, "This isn't working. It isn't what I want."

And when Amador got up to join me I told him that I loved him but this wasn't the life I wanted.

I finished telling him, "I feel like a bird in a cage."

He cooed into my ear, "But you are my bird in a cage," then smiled and kissed me and explained that he had things to do and that he could not be with me all the time.

He finished reminding me that he had a life here before I came. Then I remembered that I had just dropped myself into his life and told myself that of course he had other things to do.

Then he started almost nagging, telling me how hard it was to get to Cesiak especially since I would not let him use the car. I got slightly defensive then and reminded him that he didn't even have a license and then joked, "It is not that I don't want you using my car. I don't want you losing my car."

We both laughed. But he finished telling me to let him do things his way. But I wouldn't accept that and told him to please see my side remembering that I was there alone and that I didn't like to go out by myself. He told me I didn't need to go out and that I had everything here. Then he asked me to be patient.

We were both quiet until he said, "I always coming back to you. I promise."

I questioned what I wanted then. I mean, what did I expect? I took a deep breath.

He knew he had won and followed with, "Now I gonna make

you a real Mexican breakfast. But first, swimming?"

Reluctantly, I agreed. As my mind raced over my limited options, he took my hand, helped me up and we walked together into the waves.

Chapter 15

As we ate *huevos rancheros* on the balcony upstairs overlooking the lagoon, I asked Amador if he wanted to go get his bike. He told me that tomorrow would be a better day and then smiled and reminded me I was in Mexico. I laughed and took the plates from the table. He asked me if I wanted to take a walk. I told him no and that I would bike later. My hips were sore from walking and driving and making love. I needed a break. He said okay as I washed dishes and he went to see the guys at the reception area. I took out my paints and sat at the table. I had barely wet my brush when he returned to tell me he had a ride to town and then asked if I wanted to meet him later. I told him of course and he told me Mar Caribe at 3 pm. When I told him I would ride the bike he told me that it was a long ride but I told him I could take it slowly and enjoy it. Then I reminded him that if he had his bike we could ride home together. He smiled, kissed me and left without a word.

Later that afternoon, I got onto my new silver grey bike and started down the dirt road toward Mar Caribe and what I hoped would be a fun afternoon. It was a beautiful road even if it was filled with pot holes. No one was on it. There was the occasional truck or van transporting people to Punta Allen at the tip of the peninsula. But mostly it was me and a few yellow birds flying in front of me playfully. I road past the bikini boot camp where Amador and I had stayed after he had been arrested, past Casa Banana where I felt pretty comfortable eating alone, through the new construction for Anna y Jose where we met Amador's friend from Spain. I continued across the intersection where the police kiosk stood, generally empty or with one sleeping officer inside and the cardboard and metal shacks on the beach across from it. Then I rode past the little beach cabanas with no windows at *Playa Condesa* and past Gringo Dave's where there was always the same "Fresh *Langosta* Today." I wondered how that could be but kept pedaling past the construction for the new Mezzanine and over past *La Vita e Bella*, where my

Tulum experience had begun.

I inhaled the smell of the *La Vite e Bella*: pizza and happiness with a dash of lime for the margaritas before I continued toward the fisherman's cooperative pulling around the potholes. As I got into the deep white sand, I dismounted and walked the bike for the few meters before I saw the blue of the sea, smiled and looked for Amador. It was past 3 and I knew he wouldn't be early. After all, he used his nose as a sundial to tell time. I put my bike against a palm tree, drank some water from my backpack and sat to read. I was tired. I watched the tourists and the fishermen hanging around, classifying them: hippies, yuppies, those on their first day and those who had been there for awhile. I waited half an hour. Then I waited 45 minutes.

I started gauging when the road would get too dark for me to ride home. I told myself to go at 4. That was long enough, I said as I started to get angry and then worried and then I wanted to cry. At 4:30, with still no sign of him, I got on the bike to head back up the road to my home in the jungle. I lost the urge to cry as I looked to the left and saw the break in the palms that exposed the sea. That view took me back to the first day I had arrived with Lynn: hot, pale and exhausted. The place had breathed new life in me then and it did so now. "Fuck him." I said to myself. "Fuck him Fuck him Fuck him," I repeated and vowed to tell him to go to hell the next time I saw him.

The shadows were lengthening as I passed under the Arch marking the entrance to the biosphere and I pedaled faster around the potholes to make it back. The sun was setting into the lagoon and I did not want to be on this road in the dark. Not just for banditos that tourists seemed to believe were everywhere in Mexico, but also for the snakes and scorpions that I had yet to see. As I was riding, bats started to come out and buzz in front of me.

"They eat 5000 mosquitoes a day. They are good," I told myself but they still gave me the creeps. I was recounting the childhood stories of how they would catch in your hair and you would need to shave your head to get them out. I tried to encourage calmness but failed. I was frightened, even though I noticed the beauty and appreciated the sound of the surf and told myself the bats were my friends. I felt betrayed and annoyed and foolish as I came to the landmark sign, "*se vende terenno*" that told me I was close. Soon, in the settling darkness, I came to the big fence that marked my house. I cruised up the driveway as far as I could go and got off the bike to walk the rest of the way.

My mind, a powerhouse of imagery, went wild. The adrenalin fed my feet and I ignored the pain in my ass from this first long bike ride in at least 8 months. I was tired and dirty and hurt inside and out. I pulled the key from my bag and noticed my little dog friend and went to pat him. He let me touch him and I started to cry. Long full sobs escaped my lungs from ages. I cried for my cancer, I cried for all the people who had hurt me and then I cried for myself. I was angry and tired of all this shit and people who were rude, ignorant and disrespectful and who I had to let go of because they would not change. And that, for me, sucked because truthfully, I liked them when they were good, but I hated them when they were bad. And I was so good to them. I gave my new friend one last pat and went into the house, turned on the hot salt water shower to let it run over me and mix with all my salty tears.

There was a big bug on the floor of the shower that I tried to avoid as I stepped in. It made it more difficult to relax but it was one of those beetle type things, too big to kill because that would be disgusting, but also too big to like having in the house. So I kept one eye on it all the time to make sure it didn't climb up my leg or something. I started to talk softly to it, trying to develop a rapport, like with a pet. It was that big. I told it to stay there and that I would be finished shortly so he could crawl away to a better place. I thought smugly that I needed to say those same words to Amador, because I knew he would come back. Maybe not soon, but he would come.

And, exactly as I knew it would happen, the next day as I was eating lunch, Amador came around the corner meekly, like a dog that knew it had done something wrong. I held back a smile. I was happy to see him. I couldn't believe it, but I was. He noticed and came forward with more certainty then. He bent to kiss me and I turned my cheek away.

"You mad at me?" he asked.

I let it all loose then and asked him how he would feel if he had been stood up. He told me I was right. I told him then that the situation was not working and that I didn't want to be a bitch or cramp his style but that I thought we were wrong for each other.

I told him, "I don't know if I make you happy. But you make me crazy."

Then I told him that we should forget it and stop before we hated each other. I started to cry. He stood there for awhile but then he came over and hugged me. I let myself go in his arms and I wiped my nose on his dirty t shirt. I enjoyed that. I looked horrible I am sure but it felt good to let go of all of it.

He held me close and patted my head and said, "*mi amor*, don cry, don cry."

"But," I sobbed and continued in staccato phrases, "this. was . supposed. to be. so great. You know?" I sniffled. "And. I. would. make. you. so. happy. and cook. for you and be your best woman ever. And I would write and paint and you would fish and bring it home to me and we would dance once in awhile. But this." I got my voice back and told him, "This Amador, is crazy." I paused and looked at him and said, "No. This is not what I want."

He looked at me and asked me if I wanted him to go. I told him that I thought it was what we should do and told him he didn't know what to do for me and I certainly didn't know what to do for him. I pulled away from him and looked down at my sandwich as it collected flies. I might still try to eat it I thought, surprising myself that I could think of food after all that but I was tremendously hungry all of a sudden. He looked at his feet and told me it was ok if that was what I wanted. He said he thought I was wrong but he would go.

Then he said, "I no disrespect you. Things are harder here than you think."

And then he said I was right. I didn't know what to do for him. It hurt to think that I wasn't good enough to be his woman. When I told him he could tell me what he needed, he told me I should know, as if I were not woman enough, as if I were not intuitive enough to understand his needs as a man. He paused after saying it and then turned away and walked down the path.

In that moment he put it all on me and I took it all on. It wasn't his fault that he didn't come home or that he wasn't there for me or that he was an asshole. It was my fault. I wasn't the perfect fisherman's woman. I started to cry again. This time, I not only felt hurt and abused and weary of life, but I felt I had failed. I was not enough: not understanding enough, not there enough, not Mexican enough, not free enough. Whatever it was, I felt not enough.

I sat down on the stoop again and started to eat my sandwich but quickly lost my appetite and started to cry. Little by little I threw the tuna sandwich to the birds and then to my dog friend who came around the corner to see what was happening. He liked the tuna. I sniffed my tears away and stood up, looked out to sea and then started walking around the house checking the bottle garden that I was creating from the glass bottles I would collect on the beach. I enjoyed the milky color that being in the sea long enough produced in them. Once I got them home I arranged them with pieces of coral around the dry garden that circled my house. I created what perhaps looked like the garden of a lunatic. But I liked it. When I would recite my favorite passage in Shakespeare's Hamlet, "Oh that this too too solid flesh would melt thaw and resolve itself unto a dew," I imagined myself the lovely crazed Ophelia, drowned with flowers in her hair. But then too, I knew my lunacy would not be so dramatic or beautiful as Ophelia in the movies. It would be an ugly craziness that would get me in the end. I clung to my sanity as I arranged some of my latest additions and then walked back toward the road.

He was still there, pacing back and forth across the road, kicking one thing or another, looking dejected and sad, the golden tips of his dreadlocks calling to me like the snakes on Medusa's head must have called to her victims. He looked up to see me. Our eyes locked. He called me by sweeping one hand in a downward motion from shoulder height. It was unlike how I called people by bending my elbow and wrist and pulling my hand up. I understood it but I stood still. He motioned for me to come to him again. I didn't move. I was afraid of what I would do. He started walking toward me and as he reached me I went to turn away but he caught my elbow.

"*Perdoname*," was all he said. I looked back at him and started to cry again.

"Oh Amador." I said with resignation.

Then he asked me to give him a chance. I told him I had given him chances, probably too many. And then I reminded him that he not only stood me up, he didn't come home at all. He told me he had forgotten the time and that by the time he arrived, I had gone. Then he asked me to forgive him and told me it would not happen again.

"You are right about that," I said not sure if I meant I was not letting him back in or if I had just conceded that we would try again.

He accepted it as the latter and pulled me toward him. It felt good to be hugged and he led me up the path, hand in hand, and took me to bed. We made love. I was no longer alone. Images of Ophelia left my mind and when we finished our short love induced nap, I put on the Dire Straights' song *Romeo and Juliet* and imagined myself on the balcony with Amador below calling to me with Mariachis. If my father had been there, and I thanked God he wasn't, he would have told me I was living in "fantasy land." But I pushed his voice from my head and I reminded myself that all life was a fantasy of some sort.

Chapter 16

Things improved for a while. Amador would be late but not so late as before. I would 'wait dinner' for him and often we would read Spanish together under the mosquito netting on the bed. He would correct my pronunciation. We would laugh. He would bring wine to bed. We would inevitably spill some and laugh more. Then we would make love and fall asleep in each other's arms. Some nights we went out together. If he slept in, I practiced yoga on the balcony overlooking the lagoon and then we ate together. We were making things work. For me, it was bliss.

One morning as I handed him coffee and eggs, he looked at my arms and said, "*Amor,* what happened? Someone hurts you? Someone grab you? What is that?" as he pointed to black and blue spots under my biceps.

I looked down and said, "What?" not understanding what he was talking about.

I looked in the bathroom mirror and noticed 3 or 4 small bruises under each arm and wondered where they had come from until I remembered I was learning the crow posture in yoga. In my daily yoga practice, I consistently attempted to put my knees above my elbows and close to my armpits from a deep squat and my lift feet to balance. Each morning I got a little closer. But, I guessed it was taking its toll. I explained to Amador and laughed as I looked at the marks. He didn't believe me and told me I could tell him if someone had grabbed me or hurt me. He finished saying he would take care of it for me. I smiled and loved his gallant try at protecting me. The suspicion surprised me, however, and I told him that no one was bothering me, it was really yoga and I modeled the posture for him.

He tried it as well and we both fell down laughing.

Then he kissed me and kissed the bruises, and commanded, "Stop hurting yourself."

I wanted badly to obey him but wasn't sure how.

Then Fernando and Lynn came.

"You are not with him," Lynn said to me the day I met them from the airport.

They were staying at *La Vita e Bella* for a few nights, checking out my situation before they committed to stay with me. Lynn told me she didn't know what to say. So I told her to tell me she was happy for me and come stay.

She told me Fernando, "would rather poke his eye than see Amador again."

I loved her Irish. Fernando was in the shower and we were sitting in low wooden chairs on the balcony sipping wine.

After a moment of silence, I told her it was good to see them.

She told me, "It is good to be here. It is cold as a nanny's tit back home."

Her language always made me laugh. Then she paused and asked me how things were going. I confided in her that it was more difficult than I had imagined. As Fernando came out of the shower I told her I was lonely.

Fernando barely said hello before Lynn blurted, "Amador is at that house with her."

I froze, gulped my wine and reached for the bottle to pour another.

"What the fuck is wrong with you?" Fernando asked me and then said, "What is it? Sex?"

I told him I wasn't really sure but then defended Amador telling Fernando how he helped me find the house, show me around and how he kept me company and made me laugh.

I finished saying that, "when he is around, I am not so alone," resenting that I had to search for an explanation when I never asked him what he got from Lynn. Then he told me I would be alone if I stayed with Amador since no one wanted to be around him. I didn't believe him. In the silence that followed, Lynn went to get another bottle of wine.

I looked at Fernando and told him, "Good to see you too Fer."

We paused and then he talked about his family a little bit. He told me his mother was in the hospital and that his sister, Jacqui, may not come for that reason. Then he told me his brother finally called him after 2 years and gave him a hard time for going away while his mother was ill.

He finished telling me, "I get tired just thinking about it."

I was already weary of the melodrama. When Lynn emerged from the cabana, she asked if he were talking about his family again. I shook my head and she asked him to please leave it all behind as she handed me another glass of wine and poured Fernando a bourbon. We sat and talked about nothing. But we all were thinking about how the next few days would go with me still with Amador.

My house on the bluff in front of the ocean would not work solely for Amador being there so Fernando and Lynn found a little house in town behind the main avenue. I was unsure how to feel other than to let them make their decisions even though to me they seemed racist and unforgiving. But they were my friends and I loved them and their company, most of the time.

I met them at the house when Fernando's sister Jacqui and his friend Rob came.

The next morning, I drove Amador to the Mar Caribe beach and told him I would be at *la Vita e Bella* with Fernando and Lynn, in case he wanted to come by. As I walked toward them on the beach in front of the hotel, I felt uncomfortable, as if I didn't fit anymore. Then, I realized I never had. They had always considered me the more stable one in the group of artists and entrepreneurs. And in a way, they looked down on me for it as if there were some disgrace in working for someone else. The ironic thing was that in my establishment job I never fit because of my artistic and independent ways. To my co-workers, I was anything but stable. It seemed I was stuck somewhere in the middle for most of my life.

But they were happy on the beach, having pulled 5 or 6 lounge chairs together. Fernando was playing music and making drinks. As I arrived, he was bent over the cooler mixing tequila and pineapple juice for the group and I touched his back.

He straightened up, somewhat surprised, kissed me hello and then looked behind me and asked, "Alone?" before he offered me a drink.

I took it with a smile telling him, yes.

He told me "good girl" as I sat down.

Suddenly, I was very homesick. I sipped my cocktail, looked out at the sea and then up and down the magnificent beach and asked myself homesick for where? I could hardly place home anymore. I had been running since I had been diagnosed with breast cancer, perhaps before but definitely that day as I ran to the waterfront to cry after receiving the diagnosis on the phone. Then running to doctors, running to stay with people, running to friends, running to Miami, running to Mexico, running to DC, running to my sisters', just running. I kept telling myself that I could carry my home in my heart. But it was becoming heavier every day.

The cocktail massaged my feelings and I walked to the waters edge for a swim. Just steps away from them, I found heaven in the alcohol, the sea and the sun. As I left the water, I noticed Amador walking along the shore, his trademark rastas shining in the afternoon sun. He was with a friend, strolling casually down the beach. He saw me and jogged over to meet the group, politely shaking everyone's hands. He kissed Lynn, nodded to Fernando and finally kissed me on the lips with a long soft wet kiss. I felt them all looking for a moment and then I felt them all look away. I loved Amador more after that kiss and that gentle act of saying hello, of standing in front of them, standing up to them. They all knew after that handshake and that kiss that they were in his territory, in his country, on his beach.

As he left he said, "See you later, right?"

He walked away, holding my hand until the last minute. But he had a sarcastic smile on his face. He knew it was Fernando's birthday and he didn't want me to go to the party Lynn was throwing. I didn't even think about letting him tell me what to do. But I suddenly wondered if he had a plan to punish me for my disobedience. It was strange but I felt something.

I let the thought leave my mind as Jacqui commented, "That your main squeeze when you are here?"

I told her he was and started putting my things together. Lynn asked me where I was going and reminded me and Jacqui about the party she was throwing at Mezzanine, the new bar down the beach. She reminded me to come at around 8. I nodded yes although I dreaded going. And I dreaded bringing or not bringing Amador. As I got into the jeep and started the engine, I realized that despite the cocktails and the swim, I was more tense than I had been for a long, long time.

I moved slowly to the main road, looked for Amador but found only hitch-hikers. I loved picking them up. Perhaps it was the thrill of doing something so forbidden back in the States. But too, even a few words with someone on certain days was priceless. I picked up the first couple I passed and after I heard their story and practiced my rudimentary Spanish, I continued up the road toward home. Amador wasn't there so I left him a note and took a bike ride. I needed to move to lose or sort the thoughts in my mind.

The golden afternoon sun sparkled on the mica in the nearly empty dirt road. There were not many cars anywhere and less shade. Sweat poured into my eyes as I pushed the pedals down until I reached the bridge across the entrance of the lagoon to the sea. I stopped there. Workers were rebuilding the flimsy wooden bridge that Amador and I had crossed our first time to the biosphere. It had been reminiscent of something from the mummy movies and had been a thrill to ride over with Amador that day. Every inch I was unsure if the car would fall through the old wooden planks that moaned as they bore the weight of our rental car. I walked my bike onto the bridge, remembering that day fondly and then noticed workers sleeping under the semi-trailers that lined the dirt road: siesta time. I became self-confident and turned back down the road toward home.

Amador was still not there when I returned so I went for a swim. I missed him and hated that I had no way to contact him. No way to talk, to know I had a friend, to explain what was up, to see if he understood or was angry, and also to know he was not in jail. I was anxious and lonely and a little miserable and knew the beach and the sea would help.

As it started to get dark, I realized Amador would not come home any time soon. I dressed and went to the party alone, putting on a black dress with a beautiful scarf that my sister had bought me from Lynn's boutique. When I arrived, Lynn was ordering appetizers and drinks for everyone. I couldn't help but find her generosity pretentious when she couldn't pay me the money she owed for the land we bought in the jungle. My father's voice echoed in my mind with, "neither a borrower nor a lender be," his favorite quote from Shakespeare. I chastised myself for not heeding his advice as Lynn came over and asked what I was drinking. I paused and told her it was a margarita as Fernando sent over a shot of tequila. The room started to fill with an entourage of young professionals that Fernando and Lynn had met in town and in Playa del Carmen. I did not feel less alone in their presence. In fact, they stayed together and drank and ate a lot at Lynn's expense. I couldn't help but realize that I would have had a better time if Amador had been there, regardless of the fallout. After watching a few games of pool, attempting some lame conversation and having too many drinks, I tired of the scene, wished Fernando a happy 40th and promised to take him out on the lagoon tomorrow. That was my gift to him: a day at the beach and a boat ride. I had made reservations for us all, paid for Fernando and Lynn and hoped they would enjoy it. In that moment, I regretted ever suggesting it.

Chapter 17

Flaco, my "skinny" little dog friend was waiting for me. He walked in front of me up the starlit pathway to the house. I rewarded him with some chicken I had brought from the party. I made a mint tea and sat on the balcony relishing my aloneness and marveling at my ability to do so. The stars spoke volumes and were good company. I had always considered myself a scaredy-cat, seeing and feeling ghosts and spirits around me. In this place I wasn't so very much afraid, even if I did sleep with a knife under the pillow. That was for humans, not for the spirits with whom I was trying to make peace. I was accepting what was around me, the place, the environment. I was trying it with Amador too. I was accepting if he came home later or not. I crawled into bed setting my intention to be ok.

I woke early and alone in the coolness of the morning. I looked out toward the beach through the sand blasted windows and pulled the blanket up. I missed Amador but I knew I had hurt his feelings going to the party and by hanging onto this friendship that did not accept him or the idea of him and me together. Yet, I found it hard let go of these friends, although, at the moment they were torturing me.

"Your best friends. Go with your best friends," Amador said when I would confide in him about them.

I told him what was in my heart and he mocked me. To a certain extent he was right but it was unkind.

I told him on many occasions, "They have been very good to me."

I would continue, as if justifying myself, to explain to him how kind they had been.

He would accept my weakness, kiss me and say, "I know *amor*, but you got to live in the now."

If I weighed it out, Amador had been good to me too. He had brought me to this little house. He helped me with simple things. Although he never sent me a plane ticket or anything, he was a big part of the reason I kept coming to Tulum. But, when I thought about it, Amador gave me mixed messages: not coming home, standing me up, making me wait hours and hours, taking money so easily. Not too unlike Lynn, I had to remind myself. Between all of it, I was confused about what a real friend was anymore. I asked myself how much loyalty was correct and when did it cross the line to self abuse. I really didn't know who could I count on anymore.

"Just yourself," I heard the voice in my head say, "Just count on yourself" as I went to the balcony to practice yoga.

I then made a solitary coffee and wrote in my journal both happy and sad to be alone in the sun with the quiet and the birds and geckos. Often this solitary existence felt like heaven and hell rolled into one.

"I guess that's life," I told myself, settling into the wonderful moment.

But then I wondered if it had to be so extreme before I closed my eyes and tried to be present.

In that moment, I heard whistling from the pathway. It was Amador but I did not know how to react. After all, he had not come home the night before. Now he was strolling in as if it were fine. *Flaco*, curled up in the shade next to me lifted his head to say hello. Amador came around the corner and smiled. I couldn't help but smile back. Seeing him made me happy. I couldn't deny it. He moved toward me and bent to kiss me on the lips. I pulled away, then changed my mind and kissed him back. He lifted me up to embrace me and as I felt my body against his, I cared less that he had not come home the night before.

He kissed me hard and pushed me into the living room, opening door in front of us and murmuring, "How are you baby," as he kissed my neck.

I asked him where he had been, mocking him by repeating the baby part, as he put his hand on my ass. I got aroused but reminded myself that I needed to be angry with him. Then I asked myself why before he answered that he had been at a party on the beach reminding me that I didn't want him to come to Lynn's party. He bit me on neck and the act sent a sensation to my toes. Then he told me he had gone to Mezzanine. I was surprised but did not say anything even when he reported that I was not there and he asked jealously where I was. I didn't answer and he reached into my pants playfully. I touched him on reflex and felt how hard he was.

I melted into him as if a different person had entered my body. I couldn't resist him as he took off my top and he kissed my breasts, taking time to kiss my scar softly. He appreciated every part of me. I stroked his back and he put me over his shoulder and carried me to bed as I laughed loudly. He dropped me on a stack of pillows and pulled off my pants. He easily stepped out of his shorts and moved into me immediately, hard and forceful. I let myself go completely, not caring if it was wrong or right. I took the moment, accepting that was all I had and I relished it. He made me climax first and then he came and fell on top of me, resting his weight on my slim body and pushing the air from my lungs. I had to move out from under him before I could inhale again. We lay there for a moment and then I asked him why he had not come home.

He told me, "I was angry, mi *amor*, and the road," he let the noun dangle for a few seconds and then continued, "it is too bad."

I put my hand on his back and made gentle circles with my fingers in his sweat. I felt sensuous, like a cat in the sunshine, and beautiful, like a woman adored. I lay there with him for a little while, wanting to stop time, to freeze the frame of this existence.

He moved first, putting his nose in his armpit, smelling himself and then smiling and saying, "I stink."

I laughed, nodded agreement but told him I loved it.

"Me too," he laughed, "But I think I will shower."

I told him it was a good idea and went to shower with him. I loved showering with Amador. He would wash my back and my front and kiss me under the water as he washed my hair for me.

I held myself close to him and told him, "My friends are coming here today, remember?"

He told me he had forgotten and his voice became softer and

sad. I reminded him that we were going on the lagoon in the boat and invited him again. He told me he had been in the lagoon a thousand times and told me he didn't want to be with my friends or pay the $50.

He was right. And I was buying Fernando and Lynn's for a gift and letting them sleep at my house. I scolded myself for being so kind and asked him to be here for me.

He told me, "Baby I always gonna be here for you. Don't worry," and then he kissed me gently, sincerely under the water.

He kissed my breasts and moved me directly under the stream to rinse my hair as he asked me what time they would arrive. I told him too soon and that I needed to put a pareo out front to mark the gate. I stepped out of the shower and dried myself off. He joked that I should forget to mark the gate and see if they could find us.

"Don't be mean", I told him smiling.

They found the red pareo and I heard them coming up the path carrying coolers and beers and bags of food and beach chairs. I inhaled deeply, fought the urge to run and hide and walked out to meet my countrymen. I had invited them and had prepared. But they brought more of everything: chicken to barbeque, avocadoes, steaks, fruit for some salsa recipe that Jacqui "had to make," tequila, beer, juices and of course chips. They were a swarming horde of ants and they took over the kitchen. Then we set up camp on the beach: lawn chairs, boogey boards, big towels, coolers full of ice and alcohol After lunch and playing in the waves, we moved toward the big house for our tour of the Sian Kaan Biosphere. The three story building had a restaurant, reception and class room area. It had been built on top of a bluff, that was now more of a cliff from several years of erosion. It had a magnificent view of the sea and the lagoon. Fernando and Rob finished beers they had brought and went back for more. I watched them walk the path back to our little house. They met Amador and I knew from their body language that they were asking him for a joint.

"Hypocrites," I thought.

Later, a small man with a smile full of gold covered teeth finally came upstairs and called us down. He was the *capitan* and we followed him under the palm trees along the sandy path and across the dirt road. His legs were so bowed it was as if they framed the path. We wound down another path through some brushy wetlands into the mangrove swamp and then to a narrow elevated walkway supported by thin pilings out to the dock, which was supported by the same marginal pieces of wood. Tied to the dock were 2 large skiffs each with four benches. We waited there as the captain went back for supplies. As we waited, the mosquitoes took notice of the buffet that had arrived. Out came the spray and the earthy smell of the lagoon was replaced with citronella and Off. The young Mexican who cleaned the beach came by with a wheelbarrow full of supplies: life jackets, cooler, and a canvas bag. The captain was behind him and motioned to us all to get into the boat and put on life jackets. When we complained about the life vests, he accepted, and let us go without. His job was to tell us to put them on, not to make sure we did. He jumped into the boat like a brown leprechaun, pumped the ball on the gas tank to get fuel into the outboard and then pulled the cord to start the 85 horsepower. He reminded me of a crocodile, his skin was so taut over the sinewy muscles. He pulled away from the dock, throwing the lines to his assistant who would wait there for our return.

I felt the spray of the water against my face, and watched the rainbow it made away from the boat as we drove along the shore, toward islands of mangroves where the water was a murky brown. You couldn't tell where the land started and the water ended, if in fact it did. The arms of the mangroves stretched into the water, creating the illusion of land where there were meters of water. We cruised the shoreline until the captain turned sharply, throwing the group off balance. Then he slowed moving toward the center of the lagoon. The water was deep blue and the brackishness of the shore had disappeared. He told us it was a *cenote* or natural spring. I explained the *cenotes* to the group having seen them with Amador: underground springs with clear fresh water. When they are in the sea they attract marvelous colorful fish. The water is cool, nearly cold compared to the lagoon water. In this one circle, diameter perhaps 6 feet, within the lagoon, the water was crystal clear and deep. You could see edges of the earth break away deep below the surface and small fish darting back and forth, clearly visible from the boat. We were incredulous and the captain was happy to have impressed us. He gave the engine some gas and moved the boat back toward the shore, through a break in the sand bar that was forming from the peninsula to one of the larger islands in the lagoon and then gunning the engine into the relatively open area.

He turned abruptly once again and slowed the engine.

"Crocodile," he said pointing.

Rob put his binoculars to his eyes and whistled and said, "That is a big one" before he encouraged Fernando to take a swim.

We laughed and parked there for awhile, gently rocking, the breeze gently cooling the heat of the sun. The peace of the moment was only interrupted by the snap of a beer can as Fernando and Rob cracked a couple of Heineken cans. They offered one to the captain who accepted it readily, happy to have a cold beer rather than the orange drink and Oreo cookies that they had packed for passengers.

I smiled thinking of this crew stranded in the mangroves for a day or two with only orange drink and Oreo cookies. I pictured Lynn and Jacqui in the trees with Rob and Fernando trying to catch some fish using the Oreos for bait. I was somehow absent from the fantasy. Most likely off trying to find a rescue or I had swum ashore and was having margaritas with Amador having forgotten my "best" friends.

I returned mentally when the leather faced Mayan captain with the overly bowed legs started the engine and we headed toward one of the green mangrove islands in the middle of the lagoon, I watched the sun start to lower and create a crystalline light on the water and the green islands. The colors were bolder somehow, crisper against the azure sky. The captain' orange life vest was nearly day glow and his dark skin a richer cocoa color than before, every wrinkle more clear, drawn into his skin by the sun and the weather and his incessant smoking. He lit one cigarette from the other as he stood over the gas tank and maneuvered a channel only he knew, his eyes creased more deeply as he looked for the shallows. No ray bans for this fisherman. His eyes were used to the sun and the weather and he needed the depth perception only the naked eye could offer. He pulled up to a green island and stalled the engine once again.

"This is the bird island. The birds come here from all over the lagoon to sleep. We will wait. You will see."

Fernando and Rob and the captain opened another beer as the birds started coming. First a pair of snowy egrets, the captain named them. Then a pair of roseate spoon bills landed, the captain named them again. They were huge birds and the trees seemed barely able to support them. Five or six frigate birds, long black bodies with a white tee drawn in their feathers, circled overhead, ready to land in the same boughs. I wondered if the island would sink. A rose colored bird in the heron family flew in with a couple of other friends. More egrets landed on other boughs and pelicans shared spaces with them. The captain knew them all and recited them for us. We watched as the sun turned the sky to a marvelous rose color, the shadows lengthened, more birds perched in the trees and Lynn started to yawn. The captain started the engine. I was happy to be going back: I had to pee badly and it was getting cold.

Chapter 18

Amador was waiting with Pepe when we returned. I loved that he waited but knew it would have been easier if he had gone away and not returned until tomorrow, like he had a few other nights I easily remembered. Funny how when you get things you wish for there is always a down side. I had run to the bathroom while the group had gone to the house. Amador waited for me and then we walked together toward the madness in the house. The small kitchen counter was full of food. Jacqui was cutting something for her salsa and trying to mix it in pans since there were no bowls. Fernando was using his leatherman to cut steaks and make burgers. Rob was drinking tequila from red plastic cups on the balcony while his girlfriend was in the shower.

"Been in there for days," Lynn remarked looking salty and tired. There was an empty bottle of wine on top of the fridge and she was opening another.

"Any ice trays around here?" Fernando whispered into my ear.

I jumped at the sound of his voice, I was so overwhelmed by their activity. I looked at him blankly and he repeated that we needed ice for cocktails and the beer. A weariness took hold of me until Amador told them he knew where we could get some. He told Fernando he would take him there. Fernando looked at him, not sure what to say. I laughed as I told him it was right down the street and suggested that the three of them go.

Fernando, who hadn't even spoken to Amador since months before, shrugged okay, and they walked out the door together. In two minutes Amador returned to ask for cash. Without thinking, I handed him 100 pesos. I would have given anything for him and Fernando to be friends. But I had learned that most times you don't find anything by trying too hard. I closed the door behind Amador and shook off the sadness that had overcome me in that 2-minute exchange. Then I laughed at how uncomfortable Fernando would be and went to shower. By the time I finished, everything was nearly ready and we were waiting for the guys to come back with ice and their appetite. I sat for a moment until Lynn asked me if I would walk to the big house with her to buy some wine. I agreed and we walked in the cool clear night with the stars lighting our way. When we asked for a bottle of wine, the waiter had no idea what to do. I believe that he had never sold one before. He checked the price and if they had enough. We ordered two glasses while we waited. Finally, he brought over two bottles that he felt he could spare, Lynn asked him how much. He told me he would add the wine to the tab Amador had started earlier, making a point with the last phrase. My eyes narrowed as I grasped what had happened while we were on the tour. Lynn just grabbed the bottles and we started back.

As we walked under the balcony, Fernando called happily that the steaks were on the grill. Apparently they had found ice and probably *ganga,* pot. Regardless, the house smelled wonderfully. Amador was unusually quiet, not even sitting close to me or touching me like I loved. I missed his leg over mine, his constant closeness. I missed him even though he was right there. But he was stoned out of his gourd. I wasn't sure what he and Fernando had smoked but Amador was definitely not present as we ate on the balcony, watching the stars over the lagoon. There was too much food, not enough light and everyone had consumed too much alcohol and perhaps other substances.

When Lynn was very drunk she would find someone to pick on. Tonight it was Amador. Fernando rolled his eyes as she started to hit Amador with little girly slaps. I was washing dishes and Amador was fixing the futon couch to be a bed when Lynn came at him asking him if he knew what he had.

I knew the routine as she told him, "You don't get it do you?"

He smiled, not knowing what to do. Lynn became more and more belligerent. She told him I was a treasure and that if he ever hurt me, she would kill him. Then she asked him if he wanted to fight. Amador was laughing by this time. We all were, a little.

"Here she goes," Jacqui said as we washed the pans and piled trash from dinner.

Lynn had him on the back of the couch and he was holding her hands, trying to pacify her.

"I'll kick your ass," she challenged.

Fernando told her to leave him alone as he walked into the bedroom.

Rob called "Good Luck," to Amador with a smile as he took his girlfriend to one of the tents they had rented for the night. Amador still seemed stoned but smiled and said, "What did I do?"

I got annoyed with Lynn and told her to stop but she kept thrashing at him. Amador finally pulled Lynn onto the floor, held her there, and asked again what he should do. I started to laugh and told him I had no idea but pleaded with her to stop and then called for Fernando. She told me she was doing it for me.

"Then stop for me", I said with a smile.

Hearing myself, I felt 10 years old emotionally but fatigue made me feel at the same time 100. Amador let Lynn get up and then ran over to me for cover, asking what her problem was. I explained wearily that she was just too drunk as she pulled herself up off the floor.

She looked disheveled, her blond hair matted down, her pants low on her hips and a little lip of fat hanging over the top of them, her skinny legs leaving plenty of room in the pant legs and her shirt pulled up just under her breasts. She pulled it down, brushed back her hair and went for another drink.

"Did you ever get a shower?" I asked her, hoping one would calm her down.

She didn't respond, too busy trying to get the last drops of wine from the bottle before she gave up and asked if there was another one. I responded hopefully that there was none and added that there was plenty of hot water if she wanted. I told her a shower would make her feel better.

"How about a swim?" she said devilishly as she stuck her head into the fridge and pulled out another bottle of white wine.

I grimaced, knowing where this was going and before I could stop myself, asked, "Don't you think that you have had enough?"

Jacquie told me to watch out and Lynn spat back at me, "Who are you, my mom? I can have one more. Just one more."

Her voice was high like a child. She was mocking me and then she asked me to go to the beach saying that Amador could come with us. It was ludicrous. Amador looked over at me and I told him he could do what he wanted but that I would not go, commenting that she was out of control.

He said calmly that he would go and, added, "You need someone to take care of your best friends."

I let the insult slide and told him not to even try. Lynn ignored me, got her drink and walked out the door and over the bluff. Jacqui followed with Amador. I reveled in the quiet. Fernando was sleeping. Rob had gone with his girlfriend and I sat down on the bed, dish towel in hand. I wanted to cry but instead inhaled and enjoyed the howling of the wind and the sound of Fernando snoring. My little dog friend *Flaco* came to the door with the yellow lab from the big house. The two dogs smelled the food but must have known to wait until everyone was gone.

"In tune with their preservation instincts," I told myself.

I fixed them each a plate and watched them eat, enjoying the peace while I had it.

The group returned in 20 minutes. No one had swum, not even Amador. It was too cold they reported. Once they all settled into bed, I went into my room and screamed loudly enough to waken them all. On the wall was a scorpion about 2 inches long. I had never seen one. Amador came in. Lynn came behind him and I pointed to the insect on the wall and asked what I should do.

"It is nothing." Amador replied. "Nothing," he repeated as he got a plastic cup, scooped the bug off the wall and put it outside.

I loved that he saved it. I kissed him and thanked him.

Then I tucked the gang back into bed and went to join Amador in mine. He put his arms around me and held me closely.

Then he moved away and looked at me and said, "Your best friend tried to fuck with me."

I was incredulous.

"Si. Your best friend want to fuck me."

I got the words but not the concept. Was she messing or did she want to really fuck him, just like that. I told him I didn't understand.

He just said, "Si. She a bitch," matter of flactly.

He pulled me toward him again and gave me a big bear embrace. I asked him what had happened, relaxing into his chest. He told me between his kisses that I didn't need to worry, she was not his type.

He finished saying, "I no like that bitch."

I smiled weakly and worried for a moment, but then he moved his body closer to me and was all over me, like an animal, as if his desire should communicate that he didn't want her. I pushed thoughts of my best friend hitting on my man out of my head as he brought me to orgasm in the full house. The fact that she had hit on him was just one more thing I pushed into the "cannot deal with that now" part of my brain.

Everyone was hung over the next day. The energy in the house was heavy and I was happy when they all left the next morning after coffee. I didn't see them for two days. Amador was around and I was more or less happy. But the night before Jacqui and Rob left Mexico, I went to visit them in town and we had dinner. Amador didn't want to go. I was secretly happy about it. I didn't want Lynn near him.

We ate at *La Vita e Bella* under the big *palapa* or thatched roof over the sand floor. Tropical wood bar, dining tables and chairs sat glistening in the sand. But the chairs were too high for the tables, or they didn't quite sink into the sand as much as the tables did. Regardless, it felt as if you took the wrong pill in Alice in Wonderland when you sat there. You were either too big or too small, depending on the reference, table or chair. Too, in the sand you could not pull the chair into the table without great difficulty. There were eight of us at the table, all a little tilted in the too high chairs. Someone would always be trying to move his or her chair to get it right. It made a nearly choreographed motion within the group. As I had my second margarita, I found it more and more amusing. Finally, I stopped trying to make conversation and just sat back and enjoyed the dance, engaging in it myself every so often when it was my turn to fidget.

Halfway through dinner, Lynn and Fernando started to speak to the owners about the land they had purchased and their plans to build. It annoyed me that they didn't even mention me. I had paid for everything. I gave up then, if I hadn't already. Lynn was smashed and she looked tired. Walking in the sand with the owner's one year old hanging on her arms didn't help her stability. Her tight jeans were hugging her hips. She had put on a few pounds so there was a slight overhang just where the child hit her. Her blond hair was back in a pony-tail and her face looked drawn. I thought about her trying to sleep with Amador. She needed attention constantly. Like right now, using the child to get at least his attention, if not the group's. I had seen it before but it always surprised me since she generally received so much.

As we left the dining room and said goodbyes, Lynn called out to me, "What is up now?"

I turned and told her I was meeting Amador at his friend's house in the village. I asked her what she felt like doing, knowing she wanted to make the night last longer. She looked at the group, they were all getting into the car. Then she asked if she could have a ride with me. I looked at her: glassy eyes, happy smile, and cocky attitude and decided I really did love her. In so many ways, she was a great friend. I just wished she hadn't made it all so complicated. She and Fernando had been wrong about Amador, or at least about giving him a chance. Lynn knew it and I knew it. And we both knew that we still loved each other. I took her with me to meet the gang for one more drink, some not so teary goodbye's and then went to see Amador.

I picked him up at his Italian friend Claudia's. They had a funny group of *palapas* just two blocks back from the bus station in town. They were finishing a lasagna and I had brought a bottle of red wine that they happily opened and poured into coffee mugs, nearly forgetting to offer me one. With a mouthful, he asked how dinner was and then washed the lasagna down his throat with a gulp of wine and suggested we go dancing at the beach. It was a clear night with a new moon shining as we headed back toward the beach club, *Don Hernando's* on the north end of the beach road. It was full of hippies and tourists swaying side to side to the music. Candles lit the dance floor and there were a few single light bulbs that lit the bar. Amador took my hand and led me in. A salsa band played some dance music to the diverse crowd. I recognized a few of the locals and nodded hello. The music was too loud to talk. I was happy for it.

"Drink?" Amador called into my ear.

I moved closer to him just to feel his warmth. The evening had left me cold and confused and I really did not know why. I told him I only wanted water and he took my hand and we danced a few steps before he asked me to buy him a drink. I handed him some money without thinking about it. I was distracted. I hung around the edge of the dance floor and then wandered out to the beach. It was a beautiful night. The crescent moon was over the water, sparkling on the waves. I suddenly wished I had asked for tequila. My brain was moving too fast and I wanted to stop it. I felt alone and looked for Amador but he was nowhere to be seen. I strolled to the waters edge, put my feet in and made little cicles of phosphorous in the moonlight before walking back to the bar. Amador met me as I was walking in, water in one hand and some concoction in a plastic cup in the other.

"Let's dance baby," he said handing me the water and we headed to the dance floor.

We danced well together. The coldness left my spirit as I swayed with him to some reggae music. After the band stopped, we had a tequila on the beach and then Amador drove us home. You could almost see the sun rising in the sky. The gate across the road was down and the guard came sleepily to the door and asked where we were going. "*Cesiak, vivimos alli,*" Amador told him. "We live there," I said out loud in English and then closed my eyes and imagined that we really did.

Chapter 19

The next morning I was a hung-over. I wanted to sleep, surround myself with Amador and the certain unconsciousness he often lent me. I snuggled closer and breathed in his soft skin, struggling to return to the same sleepy bliss he was enjoying. He put his leg over mine. The weight settled me down, calmed me for a moment. I so loved being with this man. He healed me emotionally, when he was around anyway.

"When he is good," I said to myself, "he is oh so good," and then the voice in the back of my mind finished the rhyme, "and when he is bad, he is oh so bad."

I wondered why I had thought of that and then told myself that if I could only be in the moment with him, somehow escape from all my past and all my neediness, I could be truly happy.

I rested for a moment more until my hip started to ache. Amador's leg was in the wrong spot. I withdrew myself from under him and limped into the bathroom. Jacqui was leaving today and Fernando and Lynn were moving to the jungle town where we had bought the land. They would stay at Tony's house, the guy who had sold us the land. I was unsure if I would see them again and felt an urgency to talk to them. I woke Amador to tell him. He pulled me closer to him and told me to stay and forget about them. I tried but couldn't let go of the need to talk to them. I moved away from him and told him I would be back soon. He rolled over and went back to sleep, saying he understood.

"He should," I told myself as I pulled on my clothes and drove to town, "he is always moving from his emotions."

As I reached the break in the tree line at Zama's, I breathed in the sea air and looked out on the water. It was calm that morning and there were only few people on the beach. I continued over the speed bumps or topes and turned toward town. It was quiet but not deserted, after all, it wasn't dawn, it was nearly 10:00 a.m. But that was early in this town, like in Miami. Part of the reason why I loved the *latino* culture was that they put no value on getting up early. I never felt inadequate when I slept late.

No one was home when I arrived to Lynn's house. The owner told me that they had just left. I drove slowly back through town, half looking for them. Then I grabbed a coffee at the Stop and Go and went to the Internet café to call my mom. Talking with her always helped. I dialed the number in the little booth and listened to the ring, picturing my mom shuffling across the tiled floor in Miami to answer it. I looked down at my dirty feet and suddenly longed for the civilization of condo living. When she picked up, happiness and comfort filled me. She was my touchstone to goodness and the knowledge that someone in the world cared about me. I said hello and nearly started to cry.

"Darling, it is so good to hear from you," she sang back to me, her voice a melody.

I told her everything, how horrible it was to have Fernando and Lynn there, how mean they were to me and to Amador. She sympathized but she couldn't quite understand because I had never mentioned to her the arrest and drug issues, committing the sin of omission she had taught me so well.

She finally said her famous, "I would just give them a wide berth if I were you."

I agreed and continued to tell her how I was so looking forward to having them and how lonely I was. I asked her if she would come visit. She sang into the receiver once again that she didn't even have a passport. I couldn't argue with that and was silent before I told her she would love it at Cesiak. She told me that perhaps when I had my own place. I reminded her that this was a place but she told me that perhaps a place with hot fresh water. I smiled and told her I understood, reminded her to apply for her passport and thanked her for talking.

She told me not to let Fernando and Lynn get to me and reminded me that if I was lonely, I could come home, saying, "Maybe this is all too much for you."

She sounded concerned and I was happy to know she cared, that she was there for me. I had been feeling very much alone in the world.

I thanked her for being there and before I could cry, she told me, "You never have to thank me. That is what I am here for."

"I love you Mom," I said before I put down the phone and cried in that little booth until I became self- conscious, wiped my eyes and left the booth to pay the obese Mexican dude behind the counter. He was always pleasant and he had a smile nearly as big as his waist. I liked him and he recognized me these days when I would see him on the street in town because I was in his shop about every day. But it felt good to have someone know me. I drove to Lynn's house once more but they were still out so I left a note and headed home. On the way through town I saw them seated at Don Cafeto's for breakfast. My mom's voice reminded me, "enjoy your day without them" and I drove past.

When I returned to the house Amador was still sleeping, I crawled in next to him and kissed his back. He woke, turned to kiss me on the lips and we made love. I had found the peace in letting go.

"What do you think I want from you?" Amador asked me as we were laying in bed in that moment when you feel nothing but peace, before you remember that there must be something you should do, before you return to the world of man.

I told him I didn't know and then asked him, "What do you want?"

Strangely he told me he wanted me to love him. He said it like a little kid.

I told him I did love him and then asked him, "Don't you see that?"

I turned around in the bed and I told him I wanted him to love me too. He got strangely philosophical and asked me what love meant. I decided he was stoned.

But I answered him saying, "Everything."

Then I paused and told him, "and nothing."

He smiled and said, "exactly."

We had decided that one night in a bar, the two of us chatting about love. It was everything and it was nothing. But for me, just talking about it was the best.

After a few more moments, I decided to go to a yoga class at Maya Tulum. I mentioned it to Amador.

"I think I have time, no?" I told my sundial of a man.

He said I did, looking out on the water, and then said he would go with me. Before I got my hopes up he corrected himself and told me he wanted a ride to Mar Caribe. I wasn't sure what I would have done with him at a yoga class, so I didn't make a big deal of it. We drove together and Amador said he would find his way home. I tried not to focus on it, working on letting go. As I was walking into the yoga hall, I saw Fernando and Lynn coming around the corner. I was surprised but not afraid or worried and that was absolutely liberating. I didn't care what they thought. I just knew that I liked them as people. They were my friends no matter how messed up they were and I was happy they were looking for me.

I asked if Jacqui and the gang had left and Lynn nodded, saying they were on the plane by now. She asked me what I was doing and I invited her to come with me to yoga. She declined but asked to meet up with me later. I told her I wanted to hang out now and needed friends more than yoga. I explained how I had gone to find them in the morning but that it had not worked out and then I asked them if they were going to Tony's.

They were moving up the road in the jungle near the land that we had bought. Well, I had paid for it but was sure Lynn would pay me soon. Our friend and realtor, Tony, had a house out there where they would stay for a few days.

Lynn said they were leaving in a while and Fernando followed with, "A night in the jungle."

I suggested we have a drink now so that they could get there before sunset. We walked out to the beach chairs and ordered Margaritas from the barman who came running up the beach. It was a different kind of yoga but it healed my heart to talk to them, to have had them look for me.

"Never again," Lynn said stirring the ice in her margarita, "We need to make a pact to not bring family and friends here again."

"Don't worry about me. You guys are my only friends who don't think I am crazy and my family is not coming to Mexico until I have a house with plumbing and they haven't seen me for a year or two."

We laughed but I did want my family to come. We would have a good time. I was sure of it. As the sun started to sink, we agreed to have dinner the following night at Tony's. I drove back up the road toward home, buzzed. The two margaritas had hit my petite frame like a truck. I hoped Amador would be home but stopped myself. I didn't want to get my hopes up or be disappointed. But I tried to stay positive. I got to the house and only *Flaco* was waiting for me. I patted him happily and let him into the house, fed him some cheese that he just sort of licked but didn't eat. He had become used to chicken and beef. I went upstairs to lay in the hammock. It felt good to just relax on my own, and watch the stars as they emerged from the darkening sky.

"More brilliant than fireworks and slow enough to follow, even the shooting stars," I said as I saw one and made a wish for Amador to come home.

The palm trees rustled, the gecko's chirped in the *palapa* roof and *Flaco* laid down next to me as I fell soundly asleep.

I woke to singing on the pathway. It was Amador. My wish had come true. I called to him and stayed where I was, too comfortable to move. He came up the stairs and kissed me on the lips, asking me about yoga as he settled into the hammock with me. I told him how Fernando and Lynn had met me there and how we had a drink on the beach.

"You are drunk?" he asked, almost accusingly, as if I had done something wrong.

I told him that I was not drunk any longer and that I had been home for awhile. I laid back and he swung the hammock and hugged me close.

"I have hunger," he said and then asked if I were hungry too.

I told him I could cook something and he said that would be great. He helped me out of the hammock and then into his arms. We searched the fridge for something to cook and came up with a stir fry option. He asked for wine and I told him happily that we were out. Then he suggested to take the car to Amansala and he could buy a bottle. I told him I didn't need it and started to chop an onion. He told me he wanted it. I told him it was too much trouble and it might be a good idea not to drink for one night. When he said it was only 10 minutes to Amansala, I felt a fight coming.

I did the math telling him it was 10 minutes there and 10 back, talking to him as if I were reasoning with a teenager. I continued to tell him he should just stay with me and then asked him why he needed a bottle of wine. He told me it would be nice for me and reminded me that I liked wine with dinner.

He put his hand out and asked, "You have pesos and the keys?"

I got furious about the entire exchange and said, "Why the fuck do I have to pay for everything?"

And when he responded matter of factly that it was because he didn't make money that day I told him, "Well then that means no wine," I said feeling like his mother but totally serious.

He stopped, looked at me and asked, "Why are you like this? What is wrong with you?"

I stopped to think about it and asked myself the same thing. Then I told him that I just didn't want him to leave. I told him I wanted him to stay and cook dinner with me.

He paid no attention and said, "I be right back" as if that were the end of the argument and asked me for the keys.

He was relentless when he wanted something. I looked at him standing there in front of me with his hand out waiting for the keys. I thought about it. It would be nice to have some wine and, really, why was I being so weird about the whole thing. Why shouldn't I let him go get some wine. I apologized and told him I hated when he left me home alone. Then I handed him the keys and 200 pesos. He told me he would be right back with the smile I loved and then he whistled his way out the door, having won.

After nearly an hour, he had not returned. I pushed thoughts of car crashes and abductions from my head, asking myself who would kidnap him anyway.

The paranoid voice on my shoulder told me, "Only someone to get to you."

I told myself that was from hanging out with Fernando and Lynn. After waiting 1½ hours, I ate alone with peppermint tea. It was good. I got undressed, laid in the hammock with *Flaco* on the floor beside me and made a plan. In the morning, I would bike to the police and report the car stolen.

"Asshole," I said to myself, "Fucking abusive asshole."

I told myself and then I asked myself how I could be so stupid and how he could be such a jerk.

I fed *Flaco* Amador's portion, realizing he was better than that man.

"Dog is really woman's best friend," I told the dog.

I wrote to try to stop anticipating Amador's return. With each car that came up the road, I hoped he would pull into the drive. But he didn't and I grew tired of looking for headlights. I called softly to *Flaco*, asleep in a ball underneath the hammock, to come downstairs, closed the upstairs door and got ready for bed suddenly feeling a fatigue that was more than I could bear.

"It is so much more than over," I said to the dog as I pulled the mosquito netting around the bed, surrounded myself with pillows and put the knife under the one supporting my head. *Flaco* laid on the circular rug next to the bed, my guardian. I was happy to have him there and reached from the *mosquitero* to say good night to him. When I looked into his eyes, I imagined I saw my father's eyes there filled with a certain confusion, as if he were asking me why. I looked away not wanting, not able to answer. I put out the light, tossed and turned for minutes that seemed like hours as my mind traveled light years, past tonight and into tomorrow and then into the next year.

None of it was good. I imagined the police station tomorrow and then filing a claim with the rental car people. The voice in my head asked about insurance and how I would even get to the police station. I answered the voice with a number of options as I threw my covers off and told myself to stop. I told myself it would all work out. I chanted Buddhist mantras. But they were not enough. I turned the light on to read. Shadows filled the room and the crash of the surf filled my ears, the wind pulled at the front door and my anger gave way to fear. I touched the knife under my pillow to make sure it was there, to comfort myself as I thanked God for the dog there and the lights up at the big house. I didn't feel so all alone. I read some Spanish and tried to sleep again. Still no Amador. Now, I didn't want him to return. I had my plan. The romance was over. I did not want this life. It was too much drama for me.

I allowed myself to take an Atavan, checked the lock on the door, kissed the dog once again and put out the light. I laid in the now dark room desperately trying not to feel betrayed and alone.

I told myself, "Get mad. Do not get depressed or sad. Get mad."

I took deep breaths until finally the Atavan pulled a cozy blanket of sleep over me. It was bliss.

It seemed only moments later that I heard him at the window, "Honey Bunny."

I fought consciousness. I would let the drugs and exhaustion keep me sleeping until, "Mi *amor*?" intruded.

I opened my eyes and didn't recognize where I was. I reached for the brown and green down comforter from home but instead felt the cotton Mexican blanket I had on the bed. The texture startled me. "Mi *amor*?" he called at the window again. I remembered where I was and got out of bed, stepping over *Flaco* carefully. I stumbled like some mummy raised from the dead to go to the door. I wasn't thinking, just reacting. He was at the door. I looked through the glass as if not really seeing him, imagining he was a dream.

Then I opened the door and rage enveloped me as I spat, "Fuck you, Amador. Where the fuck did you go and who the fuck do you think you are?"

"*Mi amor*, we just stop at a party."

"Fuck you and your parties," I said as I closed the door on him.

He came in behind me, like a dog with his tail between his legs. I turned and continued with a vitriolic stream that came from my soul as I confronted him about going to a party while he left me waiting for him for dinner. I called him an asshole and reminded him he was only supposed to go and get us wine. He just stood there. Possessed by hurt and anger, I asked him about the wine. I reminded him that he took my money and brought back nothing. I asked for the money and grabbed at his pockets pulling on them. He stepped away from me, not recognizing me, almost afraid of me.

I didn't recognize myself and I turned my back on him and said, "Just leave the car keys on the table and go back to your fucking party."

He realized I meant it but somehow I got the feeling he thought it was a game.

He moved closer to me and cooed, "*Amor*," and then reached out to touch me on the arm.

I nearly hit him and he backed off. He continued from a distance telling me he bought wine but then met Gigi and saw they were having a party there at Amansala. Then he told me they just forgot to come back.

"Sweet," I told him, "That is just what I wanted to hear."

Then I spat at him, "Fuck you Amador," and walked away from him.

The hurt started to settle. The anger was subsiding, I couldn't sustain it and the hurt at being left behind moved in.

Just like the time my family had forgotten me in the car for church. Then, it was understandable, after all, we were late, I was slow and there were 7 of us, 9 with my parents. But to me, that little child of 8, to be left behind was trauma. I watched them leave from the upstairs window incredulously and then waited on the curb for minutes until they came back. My dad had forgotten me. I wouldn't look at my dad or at any of my family for awhile after that. Well, at least 5 minutes, maybe a little more. But, I felt so betrayed. My father had brushed the tears from my eyes and I put the anger away but the hurt went deep into my soul as I realized then I was not everything to him. I was not so special. I vowed to try harder, to be so good that I would be special to him finally. But at the end I was neither more nor less special than any of my siblings. He loved us all pretty much the same. And now Amador had forgotten me. I was not so special to him either.

Amador was quiet for awhile.

The sadness kept coming and I told him, calmly now, "Just leave the keys on the table. Go wherever you want," I started to cry.

"But now I need to drive Gigi home," he said softly.

I snapped back to anger through the tears and asked him to repeat what he said.

He told me sarcastically that, "Gigi. Your best friends' friend," was in the car waiting for a ride home.

Amador explained he had no money for a taxi and Amador volunteered to drive him home.

I raised my voice again and asked him if that were my problem finishing with, "Since when am I responsible for the whole fucking village and their travel needs?"

Amador tried to calm me down saying he was just being nice.

I only got more angry and told him to be nice with his own stuff. And then I poked him in the chest and told him, "And get this. You don't leave me here for 5 hours while you go for wine with my money and then come back, no wine, drunk and with a friend you need to drive back to town in my car. Fuck you, being nice. No!"

He started toward the door saying he would tell Gigi he had to walk. He knew exactly what he was doing. I thought of Gigi, the happy little Italian man, small framed with beautiful greenish brown eyes and a beautiful face. He was a stoner and he drank a lot. But he had a beautiful family.

I shook my head and said, "Fucking A, man. Why do you do this to me?"

I looked at him with the tears still running down my face and then commanded, "Give me the keys."

He put his hand out with them and I grabbed the car keys from him, purposely tearing at his skin when I took them.

I threw a jacket over my sexy black cotton Calvin Klein nightgown and I walked to the door shaking my head and mumbling, "I don't believe you guys."

My hair was tousled from sleep and salt water, nearly matching Amador's when he asked me, "You going like that?"

I took my flip flops, a flashlight and said, "Shut the fuck up," as I walked out the door and headed for the car. He followed closely behind.

"Hola Joanna," I heard Gigi's adorable Italian accent from the car but said nothing. Another asshole.

"Everything is alright, no?" he said in his broken English.

I told him everything was not alright but he let his head fall back onto the seat. He was smashed. As I stepped into the car, I noticed an empty bottle of wine on the floor. I picked up the bottle and held it in Amador's face and asked him it that were my wine. He did not answer. I wanted to break it and smash it in his face.

Instead I just said, "You guys suck," and backed quickly out from the driveway and down the road. I drove fast to bounce the shit out of my two passengers, but it took its toll on me as well. I was furious and said nothing. My fingers gripped the steering wheel. We passed Amansala where the lights were still on. I would have enjoyed a party, I thought to myself. I would have liked to meet some people, some new people. Amador would have had to convince me to go, I knew. I had become somewhat reclusive, but I would have relented and had a good time.

"Jerk," I said under my breath and he looked at me meekly.

No one spoke and in the silence I could not help but notice the beauty of the stars and the fantastic blue of the sky. Even furious, I could not ignore the magnificent beauty of the place.

I was softening. Amador knew it. He put his hand on my leg. I removed it and continued driving past the opening where the sea was visible and the ocean breeze gently came across and stroked my cheek, comforting me. I took a deep breath of the clean air and slowed down over the speed bumps. Amador and Gigi were silently thankful, I could tell. At the main road we went left toward town, past the police who knew the car by now. How many times had we been by here? And how many times tonight had Amador driven by? I checked the gas gauge. Unless he put gas in the car, and that was unlikely, he had only gone to Amansala. We waited at the traffic light, the roads deserted and I resisted the temptation to run the light. Amador directed me past the San Francisco Supermarket and down a dirt road that looked as if it had never been traveled.

I wondered out loud if it were the right way and Gigi told me, "Si, Si, Graci, Joanne, graci."

Then in English he said, "don't be too mad ok?" and he touched my shoulder as he got out of the car and slid through a fence and into Lotte Numero 5, the housing development where he lived with his lovely wife and beautiful son.

I wondered if Suzanna had been cooking and waiting for Gigi. Amador asked if I wanted him to stay in town as I turned the car around.

I looked at him and thought about it. My anger had subsided but I hadn't forgotten how worried and sick at heart I had been just a few hours ago.

"I go if you want me to. Just let me out here," he said calmly. I tried to explain calmly and make him understand, "You know? I like a party. I would have loved to go to a party with you, with new people, people who like us both."

I let it hang there, wondering if he cared. Then I asked him if he wanted to come back with me.

I let the question rest for a moment and then continued, "Or should I go alone. You act as if you don't want to be with me." He told me that he wanted to be with me but said he was just an asshole sometimes.

Then he convinced me saying, "I never have someone as good as you, really. I don't know what to do. *Mi amor*, I want to be with you," he said.

I knew in that moment he meant it. He kissed me. I kissed him back.

But then I said as much to myself as to him, "Just don't pull this shit anymore," as I shifted into gear and took the left onto the beach road.

We drove home in silence. Amador put his hand on my leg and I left it there. It felt good. I wouldn't deny it.

Chapter 20

Tony's house sat on a gentle rise in the landscape at the end of a bumpy dirt road. It was an unfinished block of orange concrete with a deck that got a beautiful breeze from the jungle. The gaping hole next to the back door would someday be a swimming pool. Water entered the house from a garden hose tapped into the public water supply down at the street. The front door had no stairs. The neighbors had dirt floors and cooked on a wood stove. This was where Fernando and Lynn and I thought we could live.

I arrived at about 3 p.m. and Fernando told me we had an appointment at 7 in Playa to discuss the land with our attorney. I had no idea we were going, or that we even had an attorney. Tony's partner, Juan Carlos, had set it up for us. He and Lynn thought we should go since they would only be in the country for a few more days. We all knew that things here took time. We ate early, sitting on the deck, listening to the sounds of the village of Hu May: roosters crowing, the occasional truck down shifting as they approached the speed bumps and laughter and screams from kids playing in the street. All superimposed on the sound of the trees blowing in the gentle breeze. It was tranquil and cool, in its own way.

We drove together to Playa del Carmen, or Playa del Crimen as Amador liked to call it. But it turned out we did not have an attorney, we had an accountant who we met at a bar next to Tony's real estate office on 12th Avenue. He walked with us a few blocks through this teeming, dusty, ugly Mexican town to the Notary. In Mexico, everything happens at the Notary. We did not realize it then but I know now that Notary's are some of the most powerful people in the country, next to the *Narco-trafficantes* and politicians of course. The office was packed at 6:30 in the evening and we waited outside. Our accountant went in and spoke with the receptionist.

He came out and reminded us, "You have the 6000 pesos for the incorporation?"

I looked in my bag and shook my head. "I don't have that much," I told Lynn, "and I cannot get more out from the bank today."

There was a limit to daily withdrawals and I had approached that limit most of my days in Mexico. Between paying the rent for the house and my general living expenses and Amador's, I managed to run through the 3000 peso daily limit rather quickly. Lynn asked me how much I had and I pulled 3000 pesos in bills from my wallet. But told her I couldn't spare all of it. I was tired of paying for everything. So far, no one else had paid for the land, they had not shared the bill for the house I had rented and it appeared they wanted me to pay this most current bill.

"I can cover the 6000," Lynn said as if she read my mind.
She stood up, pulled up her jeans and walked out the door to find the closest ATM. Fernando and I waited in silence, both a little nervous she would not get the money. Nothing would happen until we paid. That much we had learned. But, she came back smiling, with cash and we breathed a sigh of relief.

We waited nearly an hour until a small and officially dressed Mayan woman came out from behind a closed door with a black ledger like the ones they used to use to catalogue library books before computers took over. She opened it to a page and directed us to sign. I tried to read it but everything was in Spanish.

"Who is the administrator?" she asked in Spanish.

The accountant translated for us and told us we needed two, an *administrador uno* and *administrador dos*. The *administrador uno* had rights to sign for the corporation. Fernando looked at me and told me since I would be here it should be me. Lynn wasn't happy. I could sense it. But I knew he was right and since they had not paid anything for the land, I agreed that I should be the *administrador uno* and as Lynn nodded consent, I told the accountant it was me. He directed me to put my name on the line and then to sign. Lynn signed after me. Then the woman asked for the money and told us the documents would be ready in 5 days. I would pick up the papers.

The Notary got us a receipt and when she returned she handed it to the accountant. He would meet me at the same restaurant in 5 days and we could pick up our Corporation documents. I got his number, which really wasn't helpful since I had no phone but I knew

I could call from the internet, and we pledged to meet in 5 days at 4 in the afternoon. We drove back, feeling as if we had accomplished one important thing to establish ourselves in Mexico although Fernando worried that he had just lost 6000 pesos.

They dropped me at the car in San Francisco parking lot and I decided to drive to town and see if I would bump into Amador. Sure enough, as I passed the glorieta he was crossing the street. I beeped, pulled over and he got in the car.

"I so glad to see you baby. How did things go?" he asked and he gave me a kiss.

I told him I was the *administrado uno*.

He was happy about it but corrected my Spanish, "*Administradora Una.*".

I turned the car around and headed back the way I had come, feeling somehow more legitimate in this little tourist town. I would see Fernando and Lynn in the next days and we would go over what I needed to do when they left. Then I would have the place all to myself again. When I started to worry about being lonely, I chastised myself to be happy about it. I would have only a week and a half without them to finish my books and to finish things with the Corporation. I was certain I could do both.

The day they left to go home, we had breakfast at Don Cafeto's on the Avenida Tulum. Part of me wanted to go with them, then part of me wanted to hurry them out of my life in Mexico. It had been so confusing, so tormented, so dramatic. I cried saying goodbye but then went back to the beach and took a long walk. Amador was not around. I would go to yoga at Maya Tulum and settle into a more regular routine, alone most of the time. But I was ready to walk the beach alone each day keenly aware that it would not last forever. There, I could be myself: that half happy half sad princess, excited about life, confident about who I was, happy to be alone but always waiting for my prince to come riding down the beach and sweep me away. I wondered what I would have done if he really appeared. If I would be confident enough to take off with him or be that frightened and insecure little girl who fought to send depression and insecurity back to the corners of her psyche. But that beach cleansed me with those long lonely walks and that blue unpredictable sea. I would bath in the shallows, noticing the fish and watching pelicans dive close to catch them. Sometimes a ray or barracuda would surface and I would run out of the water only to run back in to try and see them a little closer. On those walks and timid swims, I was home. I thanked God for my life and the experience and, yes, sometimes, the courage to be there.

The nights Amador came home, we settled into a sort of dysfunctional normalcy. I tried to enjoy our time together, even if that meant me ignoring his erratic appearances and near abuse. I would leave on the 21st of February, two days after his birthday. The days were closing in fast. Some mornings he was out and about before me. Other mornings he was just coming home as I was ready to head out. I accepted that he had a life away from me. I tried to accept that he needed to party. The thought he was with another woman never crossed my mind. Why would he need someone else? On the mornings he had breakfast with me or did yoga with me and then took off for work, it was my dream life: by the sea with my fisherman. He would work on the sea while I worked on my books and my art. My fantasy came true on those days. The nights he didn't come home until dawn, I lived my nightmares, hurt and insecure, pretending it was okay.

Far down the beach you could see a palm that grew nearly sideways from the dune towards the ocean. Most days that was my destination. I walked toward it, processing my thoughts, marveling at the beauty of the beach and the sea, at the huge pieces of driftwood placed in juxtaposition to the trash strewn along the wrack line from everywhere: shoes, bottles of every sort, toys, plastic, needles, a baby doll's arm and 50 meters further the same doll's leg. I knew because I had the arm in my hand. Later that week I would find her head. There was more trash than you could imagine. I wondered how it traveled to what I now considered my beach. I thought about the currents that brought the driftwood and the trash this far and knew I was right to stick to the shallows when I swam. The driftwood was generally barkless, polished smooth, speaking to me of long days at sea, powerful waves massaging each piece to reveal in their bark the colors of camel hair and dark mahogany. I would stand on the wood, balance there and feel its energy under my feet as I looked out to sea and prayed to channel the energy of these pieces and the forces that brought them this far. I prayed for my health and I prayed for Amador and I prayed for the man who I knew deep down he could never be. I prayed for a real partner and I prayed for help. I knew I needed the energy these trees once had to accomplish things. Like them, I felt somewhat stripped, but I prayed I could send out roots here and start again.

One morning, I noticed a heron, tall and white with pink hues, standing close to the shore. As I got closer, I slowed to try not to frighten it. He didn't seem to see me. He was walking along the shore, back and forth toward the waves. I was excited to get so close until I noticed blood on its neck. I wanted to help but knew he would never let me. He continued to walk just ahead of me, aware that I was there, just too weak to fly away. I backed off and watched. The stunning bird stopped, looked at me directly for a long minute and then continued to move slowly up the beach. I watched it move away, standing still, saddened by its condition and wanting just to stroke it and comfort it. But I realized that would only hurt it more.

"No more stress for you," I told him as I walked away, at first backwards, trying to maintain some contact and then I turned back up the beach.

I reminded myself, "Everything dies. Leave it alone, let it die in peace."

Then I said another prayer, "Let him die here on the beach, without too much hassle, from people or animals."

And as I walked away, I wished that for myself too: to die on that beach without too much hassle.

Chapter 21

We were hardly ready to catch my plane. Amador was moving to a campsite at *La Zebra*, a little beachfront campground. I left him what I wouldn't need in Miami: cooler, flashlight, headlamp, the cool hammock with the mosquito netting, the bike, my favorite little coffee cups from Belize, all that I had was his. I hoped he would still have it when I came back in a month but, too, I wanted to leave him parts of me. I wanted him to think of me and be comfortable. That was love, wasn't it? Wanting the best for someone. Amador did the heavy lifting, I did all the crying. When the car was jammed full, the bicycle was still on the side of the road. Amador volunteered to ride it to La Zebra where we would store it until I came back. I looked over the house one last time: the futon couch, the little stove and fridge. I felt the cold tile floor on my feet, the grains of sand that always collected there and the warmth of sun streaming through the big window over the door on my body. I walked up the stairs to the balcony and looked out over the lagoon, peaceful and glistening. I looked down at my glass bottle garden, all collected from the beach and surrounded by hundreds of white shells. Exhaling, I prayed to come back.

Flaco was in the drive. I knelt to pat him and give him a big hug. He had been my pal, my best friend here, really, and I was not sure if I would see him again.

"*Te amo, amigo,*" I told the dog and went to meet Amador at the car.

He was waiting with the bike and asked if I were ready to go, being cheery about the whole thing. As tears rolled down my cheek, I got behind the wheel and backed out of the drive. Amador came to the window next to me and told me not to be sad. He reminded me I would be back and kissed my tears saying he would ride on the side of the car and cautioned me to drive slowly. I nodded, shifted into first gear and moved over a few potholes.

"Easy, easy," he cautioned me.

He wasn't pedaling, just riding along next to me. His hair was blowing in the breeze and he was smiling. He was the happy man once again. I laughed out loud and so did he. A car passed and he had to let go. He fell behind until the car passed and then he pedaled back up to the passenger side as I slowed to let him grab the rear view mirror and then lock his elbow over the door. He was riding again and looking so beautiful that I forgave him all the hurts and oversights and stupid things he had done. All the misfit maladventures were gone from our history and it was just this wonderfully spontaneous and happy man that I loved there on the car, smiling and making me smile too.

As we pulled out from the arch and continued down the road, he called to me to stop. He dismounted the bike and told me that the piece of land in front of us was for sale. He asked me if I wanted it. It was a small piece of land on the jungle side of the road, overgrown and so full of palm trees that I really couldn't get an idea of it. I told him it looked nice but that I really didn't have time to look at it now. He said he knew but that it was only 25,000 US and it was 15 meters by 60 meters.

"Wow," was all I could say as I heard the surf pounding across the street.

He told me to think about it and to talk to some people back in the US. He reminded me that I could bring survivors here.

He told me, "We could have a little business, *amor*," as he got back onto the bike and reminded me it was a good opportunity.

He finished his pitch telling me, "And then you wouldn't ever have to leave."

I fell in love with the idea as he put his hand around my waist and kissed me on the neck before he clung to the side of the car again. I was more in love with him than ever as we pulled into the parking for *La Zebra*. He mentioned to the caretaker that he would need to store some things there and they sat for a moment. I wandered through the site and looked out at the water and felt the breeze, saw the communal toilets and showers and the little tents under palm trees. It would be good here for Amador. He could have people around and he would be at the beach. That was important to both of us. I wished it were a week ago, or a month ago and wanted in the worst way to turn back time. But at least I was only going as far as Miami. It would be ok. And I would come back to buy that land, if I could get the money. It was a good plan. I remembered his proposal of marriage that first day I met him and considered the idea. I watched him unloading stuff from the car and wondered who had more to lose, him or me. If I were rational, I knew it was me. But Amador gave me a way out and a future apart from my old life. I had destroyed myself with rational decisions and in this moment it seemed Amador was my only hope yet I wondered if living with me might actually destroy him.

I wandered back to the car, looking at my watch as Amador called to me with that underhand gesture that I loved, the one that was just the opposite of how Americans gesture to someone to move close. We needed to leave. I went to meet the owner and then we walked to the car. Amador drove. We were quiet. He put his hand on my knee. I put my hand over his and he asked me if everything was okay. Tears started rolling down my cheeks and I nodded yes.

"*Amor*" he said sympathetically, "it will all be okay. I gonna be fine."

I looked at him through teary eyes, pressed his hand tightly and told him, "I know, Amador. It is me I am worried about."

Part 2 - Life

Chapter 1

I resumed a distracted life in Miami, appreciating the luxury of constant electricity, refrigeration, fresh green groceries, sometimes even organic and the salt-free, high pressure, hot showers. But I was always thinking of Mexico and next steps. I tried to be present, to be there with my mom and appreciate the moments. She would be with me for only another month, until it got too hot. It was our plan when we had invested in the condo together, our second purchase since my dad died. He would never have allowed our real estate adventures. But we had found this wonderful place on a whim the one weekend we came to Miami. The purchase had gone smoothly. Investing was a thrill for us and though we hadn't been super successful, the banks were still giving us money.

My nephew Brendan and his girlfriend visited us for Valentine's day, the day after I returned. I was happy to see him but distracted and hurt because Amador didn't call. I told myself that I was cooler than all that Valentine's hype anyway. I had learned to deal with hurt by being cooler than it. Anyway, I had people around me I loved and who loved me. That should have been more than enough, but I wanted him to call. For once I wanted a Valentine.

He eventually did. I inevitably answered since I now carried my cell everywhere, obsessed with hearing from Amador, with knowing he had not forgotten me, knowing I had a future outside going back to a day job. I had to know my dream was alive. When he called, I calmed down. When he didn't, I was anxious and moody. And although he called to talk to me, he would inevitably ask about the land and if had I found someone to help me buy.

"Try harder, baby," he would say, "Try harder for us."

Although I didn't have many friends in the position to hand over

$25,000, I talked to them anyway. My mom and I discussed the whole idea. Compared to land in the US, it was not that much money. But my mom reminded me that a bank would not give me money for a project outside the US and one without title. Too, the project was philanthropic. I needed a donor, not a bank. My mom suggested I do the project on the land I bought with Lynn. It made sense but Fernando's voice echoed in my brain saying, "it is all about the beach really." I tried to explain but I left out the part about Lynn and Fernando never wanting to work with Amador, hating him, believing he was a drug addict. After all, I couldn't tell my mother that. She would be horrified. She had learned enough about me in the last few years. I had divulged a little about my sex life with Anthony while she helped me get over him.

She was in the room when, in response to a comment on how healthy I was to get cancer, I said, "those days of pot smoking in High School, the fags in Europe and those endless drinking parties sort of catch up with you."

My mom was only slightly shocked and I was actually glad she heard it from me. I didn't want her to think my cancer was her fault. My parents internalized everything. And in the end, it was really no one's fault. It just was and it didn't matter anyway. It was in the past.

I kept dreaming about the project on the beach and trying to manifest a way to make it happen and then I finally let it go and moved on with my small life in Miami. I was writing in my loft bed that looked out over the little guard shacks on Miami beach, when the phone rang. I jumped on the "unavailable" number thinking it was Amador. But Helen, my friend for what seemed like forever, answered. Helen and I had worked at the highway department together. Both of us hated the job: Helen because it was not enough of a challenge, me because it was just not enough. We met at the Christmas party our first year. She had come to work in Boston with a group of Irishmen and I immediately fell in with them. We became a gang of five: Pat and Jerry and Helen from Ireland, then me and a black guy whose name I forget, both of us from Boston. We generally gathered to meet for coffee in the late morning, cigarettes in the early afternoon and beers after work. We gossiped, talked shop and planned our next parties.

They were great parties. It was where I smoked in those days. I would swim like an athlete in the morning and then drink and smoke a few "fags" as the Brits call their cigarettes, in the evening. Once again, I was living a double, even a triple life: athlete, engineer and party animal. I remember lining up at a phone booth on Cape Cod one Monday morning as we passed the phone around us and asked for our respective bosses so that each of us could call in sick. We were at the beach swimming within minutes of hanging up, any guilt lost to the gentle brush of the cool water against our hangovers. We would cash in cans from the party the night before and buy breakfast at a local diner after the swim. The gang of five fell apart almost as quickly it had begun. I went to Germany to follow a man under the pretext of a job, Helen went home to Ireland and I never quite found out what happened with the other guys. I met the black guy from Boston once on Tremont Street in a store he had opened. He pretended not to know me. The two Irish lads could be anywhere. But Helen and I stayed in touch and visited each other regularly over the years. I was still searching for my life but she had found hers solidly in Ireland with a marvelous husband and now three children. She was also a major force in a start up engineering firm. I was proud to be her friend.

"Joanne," she chimed into the phone with her gorgeous Irish accent, "we have been talking, Georgie and me, and we'd like to invest with you in that land in Mexico."

Just like that. I asked her if she was sure. I got butterflies but I wasn't certain if it was from happiness or fear of losing my friend and her money. I told her I could not guarantee anything but that it was beautiful. She told me she thought it would be exciting and all they wanted in return was for me to hire their sons when they were in college. They could work for me and learn Spanish and a little bit about the world outside of Ireland, she told me. I told her I couldn't agree more and that although I loved Ireland, it was good to see the world. I told her I would talk to Amador about it and get back to her, mentioning the number of 25,000. She told me that was what they had and that George could wire the money to me when I needed it. I started to get nervous and asked her to think about it.

She told me she and George had and said, "Lets do it."

And with that, I had investors. I had the money to build in Mexico. Now I just had to get it there.

Chapter 2

"He doesn't has a bank account. You need to bring cash," Amador explained about Davide, the land owner.

I sighed. Twenty-five thousand dollars was a lot of money to carry. I had no idea how I would do it. But there had to be a way.

My nephew Charlie's voice echoed in my mind, "you never know until you try."

He had been talking about reaching oreo cookies on the top kitchen shelf. I reminded myself that this was a slightly different situation.

Legally, I could carry 9,999 U.S., "less than $10,000." If I declared more, I would be thoroughly questioned and taxed. More worrisome, the authorities might talk and send people to rob me on the way to Tulum from the airport. I decided not to declare it. My lawyer friend shook his head in disbelief when I told him I had investors and asked him about carrying the money.

"Just don't carry more than 10,000. Wire some before hand," was his legal opinion.

But to whom? Amador didn't have a bank account. Davide didn't have a bank account. Who could I trust in Tulum with that kind of money? I decided to make a trip with some, find someone to accept some more into their account and then bring the 9999 USD. This trip I could bring 5000 extended on my credit cards, see the land again and check the papers and then get the investment from Helen. Tickets were cheap from Ft. Lauderdale. I decided to camp with Amador at *La Zebra*, so we could save some money. If things seemed ok, I would give Davide a deposit.

This time Amador met me at the airport and stayed even closer than usual. He held my hand even after we arrived in Tulum and found the campsite. I loved the attention and closeness. Our tent faced the beach and the view was spectacular. Just in front was a bush with little purple-blue flowers that hid the tent slightly and offered some protection from the constant wind. There were palm trees extending onto the beach. Amador's campsite was simple and clean. He had clothes hanging to dry on a line that ran from the tent to the closest palm. My cups from Belize were in a stack of clean dishes in the hammock. He had the blanket from when we lived in

Cesiak and his shampoo and toilet paper were tucked into a corner of the tent.

"It is nice, no?" he asked as I looked around, trying to find a good place to put my stuff.

I told him I thought it was lovely, although I wasn't sure I could live that way for long.

We walked hand in hand to the big open deck with a *palapa* roof where people hung out and sometimes you could get a meal. We sat at a picnic table that had oversized chairs with cushions in a zebra motif. No one came to see if we wanted anything so Amador went to ask for drinks: a beer for him and water for me. He came back and sat next to me. We looked out on the water, our legs touching slightly. He put his hand on mine, looked into my eyes and told me it was good that I was back. I agreed and told him honestly that it was exciting. He told me that in the evening we would meet with Davide, the land owner.

I could tell he hadn't been speaking much English. I loved it. If he had been from the U.S. and spoke that way, I never would talk to him again. But as a foreigner, his accent and bad English courted me. The voice on my shoulder said, "Imagine if his Spanish is the same!" Horrified at the thought I put it out of my mind and held his hand. Then I asked if Davide would want money tonight. Amador sang, "Of course" but then told me we would not give him anything. He explained that we needed to have him sign a contract first and finished by saying, "Amor, we not gonna just give him cash with nothing, come on?"

He was acting like the all knowing macho man I generally scorned but for some reason appreciated in this moment. I defended myself and mentioned that Davide would want some sort of down payment. I wanted to secure the land and put the cash somewhere more secure than a tent or my handbag. Amador told me that the next day we would have a meeting with an attorney. Then I would be able to pay Davide and be certain that I had the land.

Amador pressed on my hand when he finished talking and told me, "One thing, *amor*. The contract gonna be with Davide and me. You are a foreigner and you cannot own land here in Mexico."

I would have a contract with Amador where he transferred the land to me. Amador told me that it happened all the time. He was my *preste nombre*, literally the "name loaner". It is one way that foreigners, like the owners of *La Zebra,* could own land. I nodded that I understood but asked him how it was that I could own the jungle land without a Mexican. The mention of the land in the jungle bothered him. He had never gotten over the fact that I could still be friends with Fernando and Lynn when they had been so difficult with him. But he explained to me that the beach was different because it was *ejido* land, he said. The government had not given titles yet.

And then he looked at me and told me, "That is why it is so cheap."

The government would give titles in a few years, he explained and then the land would be worth a lot more. I didn't really care about two or three years from now. I just wanted to do this correctly and just Amador and Davide on the ownership papers seemed weird.

"Won't we have anything like a title?" I asked him.

"When we finish we get a *constancia de posesion.*"

"Like a long term lease?" I asked him.

"*Exactamente,*" he said, pronouncing each syllable clearly and then assured me that, "the lawyer gonna 'splain it all to you *mami.*"

I hoped so since I needed to 'splain things to Helen before I used her money. Something like a lease for 99 years or more would be fine with me, but I needed to be able to explain it to her.

He kissed me and said, "Hungry?"

I was and he suggested we go to the pueblo for some dinner. We had a pizza and wine at a newish Italian restaurant called *Basilico* and then went to find Davide on his *rancho* by the beach. We parked on the side of the road and Amador took my hand and led me into the jungle. I was skeptical but I could see the light of a fire and hear voices. A barking dog came toward us and I moved closer to Amador who ignored the dog and kept walking, enjoying that I was afraid. I clung to his arm and saw some people at a picnic table on the other side of the fire. They didn't move to help us even though the dog was barking at our heels, running toward us and then running away. We moved close to the fire as the guy at the head of the table threw something at the dog and shouted, "*caiate,*" or "Shut up." The dog ran away crying.

"*Buenas noches,*" Amador said loudly and everyone at the table finally looked up. There were 3 men and one woman.

"Amador!" the guy at the head of the table called pronouncing a clear accent on the last syllable and rolling the final r and then he smiled broadly.

My jaw dropped. His teeth were all gold capped. And when he stood up you saw that he was shorter than my 5 foot 3 inches. He had a handsome face and an impish smile but the tooth thing mesmerized me. He was wearing a grayish button down short sleeved shirt and khaki pants. He wore flip flops and his feet were extra wide. I was still behind Amador and wondered if the guy saw me.

Then I scolded myself, "Of course he sees you. You are not invisible."

He extended his hand to Amador and put the other one around Amador's back to look at me. Amador introduced me.

"Joanna?" Davide asked as he took my hand, shook it firmly and then kissed me on the cheek.

"*Mucho gusto*, Davide." I said.

I had been practicing Spanish and wanted to talk and say, "I have heard so much about you. Where did you get those teeth done?" but, thank God, I didn't have the vocabulary.

So Amador did the talking. Davide introduced us to the others. They were not so pleasant. They nodded and looked up at us, uninterested. I noticed a chicken pecking the dirt close to my foot and then saw a rooster just a few feet behind her. Davide gave her a slight kick and she ran into the darkness clucking. The rooster ran close behind. Then Davide motioned for me to sit. He smiled broadly and cocked his head to either side. I wasn't quite sure if he was an idiot or just trying to be charming. He and Amador talked in hushed tones. I smiled at the other people at the table.

The woman extended her hand and reminded me her name was Maria before saying, "I speak English."

I don't know what came over me but I joked, "Me too."

She laughed and then shared the joke with the other two.

"Don't get too crazy," the voice on my shoulder told me. I looked over my shoulder to see Amador walking away with Davide. "Great," I said to myself and clutched my bag full of money tighter. I had brought it with me because, what could I do, leave it in the tent? Leave it in the car when Amador had the keys? I was surprised that I didn't fully trust him.

"Everything changes with money," the voice on my shoulder said.

Then Maria introduced her husband and told me that they lived in a placed called *Pino Suarez*. She was short and chubby and her English had a little twang that was almost endearing combined with the Mexican accent. She was barefoot and wore a shift dress. Her hair and eyes were dark, definitely Mexican. She told me to make Amador take me to their lagoon, saying it was beautiful. Then she lowered her voice and told me that if I wanted to buy land, it was a good place. She knew why we were there. The other man was looking at me so I extended my hand and introduced myself. "Mauricio," he said and shook my hand with a smile that revealed a missing tooth in front. He looked goofy all of a sudden rather than tough and I had to fight a bout of nervous laughter. Taking a deep breath, I looked behind me for Amador but he was nowhere to be seen.

A mosquito buzzed my ear as Maria continued expounding on the beauty of *Pino Suarez* Lagoon. The mosquitoes began gnawing on my feet and I rubbed them together to scratch. No one else seemed bothered. I didn't want to be rude but I was being eaten alive.

Maria lit a cigarette and blew the smoke away from me and then said, "You'll get used to the mosquitoes after awhile."

She went on to explain to me that there were lots of bats who ate the mosquitoes and flew everywhere. I heard a little swishing sound passing my ear. I did not mind bats, in case she was trying to frighten me. I had studied them in my wetland days, encouraging people to build bat houses and studying their cute yet ugly faces in bat books. Their faces reminded me of the characters in the Star Wars movies. I told her, "cool," happy she had failed to scare me.

I looked for Amador again and saw the branch of a palm tree moving as he and Davide strolled toward us, still talking. Amador stopped and motioned for me to come toward him, drawing his arm from shoulder height down in the uniquely Mexican gesture that meant "come here". I excused myself and walked over to where he was. As I passed Davide, he gave me his golden smile and touched my shoulder gently as he continued toward the table. I kissed Amador and told him I had been worried. He walked me back toward the road, told me I didn't need to worry and then said Davide promised to sign everything tomorrow with the lawyer.

I was ready to celebrate until Amador told me, "but he needs 500 dollars deposit now."

My spirit dropped and I became uncomfortable. Amador continued saying that Davide needed the money and that he would deduct it from the total but he wanted it now. I nervously calculated some things in my mind. I had wanted to talk to Helen and make sure she understood what we were getting into and see what the attorney said tomorrow.

As I hesitated and tried to think, Amador touched my arm and told me seriously, "You gotta give it to me and I give it to him."
I hesitated again and he commanded in a tone I had not heard before, "Now."

I felt a fear and adrenalin rush and asked if Davide shouldn't sign something for receiving the money. Then I asked why I couldn't give him the money. I raised my voice, trying to stand up for myself.

Amador got stern and asked me, "You want do this alone?"

I looked him in the eyes and shook my head no. He repeated that Davide would sign the next day and asked again for the money in a not very nice voice. I nervously reached into my bag and counted out 500 dollars, feeling eyes all around me. "Are you mad?" that voice inside me said as I handed the money to Amador and he shoved it into his pants, escorted me back to the table, put his hand on my shoulder to help me sit down as he and Davide walked back towards the road. I sat, weighing my options and then smiling at no one in particular. The next 5 minutes seemed like an hour until Amador came back for me and Davide walked us out to the car.

When we got inside I asked Amador if Davide signed something to acknowledge he received the money. Amador just told me he would sign tomorrow. I was nervous and sure I had made a mistake. I told Amador that no one saw him give Davide the money.

I reminded him that everyone was at the table and nearly started to sob saying, "No one witnessed it."

I was afraid I had just lost 500 dollars.

Amador laughed and said, "You mean the *squadron del muerte*? (Squadron of death)."

He looked at me and told me that I didn't want that group to witness anything. Then he put his hand on my leg and told me not to worry, that everything would be alright. Then he started to hum the "Don't Worry Be Happy" song, as he started the engine and moved away from the curb. He felt good. I was still nervous and unsure of what had really happened. As we drove down the dark, palm lined road I asked him why Davide's gang was called a *squadron del muerte*? The term gave me the creeps. He said that was exactly what they were. I shivered at the thought.

He looked over at me, smiled and said, "Don't worry baby, you got me."

I asked him if they were mafia and warned him it could be dangerous. He told me that it was in fact dangerous and so were they. Then he was silent for awhile. We both were until he told me "but they not mafia."

He repeated not to worry and said, "They happy now. They got some cash and someone to buy the land. You not gonna have problems."

I wondered what sort of problems he was referring to but before I could ask, he put his hand on my knee and suggested we could go for a beer. I told him it was a good idea and then looked out the car window in silence. I didn't want to think what I had just gotten into but told myself not to be so Hollywood about it. After all, that crazy Mafioso stuff only happened in the movies.

The next day we waited nearly an hour for the Attorney Rizzo: Amador, Davide, me and of course, his *squadron del muerte* just outside the door of the attorney's tiny office on the main Avenida Tulum. Davide would go out to talk to them every 10 or 15 minutes. Amador visually followed his every move. Finally, the secretary motioned us in.

Amador whispered in my ear, "He speaks English. Ask him any questions you got."

We sat down and Amador explained to him why we were there. I trusted him to tell the attorney what we wanted. When the attorney asked me if I understood everything, I told him "*Sí*" because Amador had explained it to me the night before, not because I understood Spanish.

Then the attorney said it again in English, "You understand that this land has no title. Titles may come in time but there is no guarantee. But you will have the right to live there and to do a business there."

I nodded my head and asked him how long that right was for asking if I or my heirs could live there forever. He said there was no limit on the *constancia de posesion* and that when I died I could transfer it to someone else. I felt better then and thought Helen would be happy with that. But then he continued to tell me that I could not be on the paperwork. I had to have a Mexican on paper and then have a contract with him or her. That person, he explained, is called a *preste nombre*, meaning they have loaned you their name.

He looked at me a little skeptically and asked, "Do you understand all this?"

It was more or less what Amador told me so I nodded my head yes. Amador put his hand on my knee. The attorney then spoke to Davide in Spanish. I tried to follow. It seemed he was basically telling him he had explained everything to me.

I looked at Amador and said, "He knows we don't have all the money today, right?"

Amador told me the attorney would talk about that now.

And sure enough, once the attorney finished talking to Davide he turned to me and asked, "So how much can you give Davide to hold the land."

I used this opportunity to mention the 500 from the night before and told him I could give him 4000 as a deposit and pay him the rest in a month or less. He raised an eyebrow when I told him about the 500 and then said that we would do a contract that said I was giving him $4000 dollars deposit today. Attorney Rizzo told me to give him the remaining $3500 and he started the paperwork, turning to his file cabinet. He pulled out some forms and started to fill them in by hand. I felt as if I had been beamed back to the '70's before computers when people still used white out. The fan above me rattled noisily as the attorney put the papers on the table in front of me and looked at me for the money.

I reached into my bag and pulled out a stack of bills and started counting. Everyone noticed that I counted $3500 and put $1000 back into my bag. I scolded myself for not preparing it before hand. The attorney counted the money, handed it to Davide and then put the paper in front of Davide to sign. He signed, then I did and then Amador did. He asked us all for ID. I looked at the paper and noticed my name was nowhere other than as a witness.

As I reached for my passport, I asked about it. Attorney Rizzo reminded me that I could not appear anywhere on paper. I didn't like that and told him that at least they could say I paid the deposit. He took Davide's ID and then looked at Amador while he told me that we would do a contract between Amador and me that would give me the rights to the land. I told him I thought something that said Amador was doing the deal on my behalf would be appropriate. I hated that I sounded so business-like but it was not even my money. I had to take care, for me and for my friends. The attorney told me he could do the contract and asked Amador again for his ID. Amador looked blankly at him and then admitted he didn't have anything.

He looked at me and said, "It was all stolen," as he shrugged his shoulders.

The attorney sighed and told Amador he would need an ID before he could sign. Then he went out the door to talk with the secretary. The three of us just sat there. Davide appeared happy but he was fidgeting. One leg was always moving. Today he had on dark pants and a clean white shirt. His hair was combed to one side. It was slicked down with gel or grease, like a little boy. Every so often he would pat it down, look at me and smile, showing his gold teeth. I still couldn't take my eyes off them.

The attorney returned with the papers and he handed one to me. It was a paragraph that said Amador gave 90% of the property to me and kept 10%. That seemed fair. I wanted him to have something.
Amador read the paper over my shoulder and said, "You don't need to give me anything, baby. I do this all for you," and he touched my knee as he said it.

I melted and told him I wanted him to have something. I signed, then Amador signed, the attorney signed and the secretary signed. The attorney made copies for all of us, shook our hands and told us to come back with ID when we were ready to finish buying. We all filed into the bright, dusty, hot Avenida Tulum.

Somehow it felt cooler than being inside even though the *squadron del muerte* was waiting. Davide said a shakey goodbye and walked with them down the street. I had no idea where they were going but couldn't help imagining it was horrible. I looked at the four little men walking away from us. They seemed so harmless and I reminded myself that looks could be deceiving. Amador touched me on the back. I looked slightly up at him. He kissed me and asked if I wanted to go to la Nave for lunch. We could celebrate our first step.

Chapter 4

"I only gonna be two minutes," Amador told me, "Wait me here."

I didn't mind waiting. I enjoyed being on my own for even a few minutes, actually. I took out my journal to write under a tree in the parking lot. We were trying to get Amador a replacement ID in Playa del Carmen. And so far this trip, I felt as if I were never alone. I wasn't quite sure why but I always felt someone watching me, someone close: the staff at la Zebra where I was camping, the other campers, the locals who stared at my blond hair and green eyes.

Too, camping was getting to me. This particular morning there had been no water for the toilet or for the shower. I had swum in the sea for my bath and we both stopped at San Francisco to use the toilet. It was fun being such a vagabond but I had never been good at not having my creature comforts. I had waterless cleaners, but I yearned for a shower, even a short cold salty one would do. But for now I was happy to have a little solitude, the shade and a gentle breeze.

I was barely settled when Amador walked out of the building. I put my journal away and went to meet him. He told me they would give him something next week and then shrugged, accustomed to the bureaucracy. Neither one of us was too crazy about the dirty little tourist town of Playa del Carmen. The beachfront was exclusive with little public access. Too, I mostly associated it with attorneys and notaries. Once I had a drink on the water with Amador and we walked the beach. It was crowded and reminded me of Miami Beach. The sea was gorgeous, crystal blue and almost prettier than Tulum, if possible, but overbuilt. Tulum beach was empty and stretched for what seemed like forever. In Playa you had to dodge lounge chairs, vendors and the odd rope marking the entrance of a new section of hotel beach. I preferred the remoteness of Tulum and with only two nights left on this trip, I wanted the Tulum beach as much as possible. We headed right back and Amador drove fast. He loved to tell me how good a driver he was as he passed cars on the two-lane highway. It was common to pass but it gave me the creeps. There were huge trucks and there was enough traffic to make it dangerous. Needless to say, I was very happy when we were back and I asked him to stop at San Francisco Supermarket to use the toilet, "just in case."

"Good idea," agreed the man that appreciated a good shit.

When we arrived at *la Zebra*, Amador went directly to the beach and came back with a joint after about 15 minutes. He was smoking it as I was organizing my things and cleaning out our little sleeping space, playing house. He handed me the joint and I took a drag only because I loved the smell and the taste. The effect for me was normally a slight paranoia so I took one hit and handed it back to him. Paranoid was a drag. Amador inhaled deeply and holding his breath, asked me if he could take the car to town. I was surprised since we had just come from town. I asked him why he wanted to go back. On his exhale he told me he would be back soon, avoiding the question. I did not relent and asked him again why he needed to go. He just reached into my bag and took the keys. I protested and reached for the keys but he pulled them away with a mischievous smile as I asked him again why he wanted to go to town. He told me he had a couple of things to take care of and that he would be back.

I asked to go with him, understanding that he was going whether I liked it or not. He told me to enjoy the beach and that he had to do some "business." I did not want to fight and decided to enjoy the time alone. Although having him use my car made me nervous, I told myself to let it go and to be happy he had not asked for money. I zipped the tent and walked to the beach with my bag. I still had nearly $1500 US in cash and I knew better than to leave it in the tent.

As the sun went down, I decided to wait for him on the porch. I didn't like how I felt: worried and uncomfortable. I sat on the deck and wrote but looked up each time I heard a car coming. I noticed that the couple working looked away each time I looked up. I told myself it was the pot. I ordered water and was getting hungry but there was no menu and I didn't trust their ability to make something great just off the top of their heads. So, I waited, apparently still learning to do so. I remembered something I had forgotten at the tent and went back, ducked inside to find it and then decided to organize Amador's shower stuff. I cleaned around the tent before it got too dark to do so, pulling at some weeds to pass the time. I gently pushed my hand across the sand and felt something plastic and soft.

I pulled my hand back and looked at what I had exposed there in the soft sand next to the tent. It was a condom. Disgusted, I wondered if Amador had been sleeping with someone there in the tent I had bought for him. I couldn't believe it. I kicked sand over the condom, not wanting to touch it. Just then Amador whistled to me.

I looked at him, kicked the condom with my foot and asked him, "What is this?"

He came closer and gave me a kiss before he looked at it. There was a guy behind him, keeping his distance but waiting and paying attention to me. I asked him again and pushed the condom in the sand to give him a better view.

He told me, with a slight smile on his face, "It is a *condon.*"

I asked him what it was doing there by our tent and he asked me, incredulously, if I thought he had used that with someone.

He looked at me skeptically and said, "Baybe, you no trust me?"

I told him that there was not much else to think. I waited for an answer or an excuse or something.

He shook his head, repeated, "You no trust me," and started to walk away past the guy who was waiting. I realized he had the car keys and went after him. But it was more than that. I wanted to go after him. I didn't want this to be happening so I tried to change it and when I called him he stopped and turned. I couldn't believe I did but I apologized. I wasn't really sure how I felt. I just knew I did not want to be abandoned here and knew that was the only way to keep him with me.

He turned, opened his arms to me and told me exactly what I wanted to hear, "Don't be jealous. I only want you."

I melted into his arms and felt foolishly happy. He kissed me and asked me if everything was ok. Then he told me not to worry and he introduced me to the guy who was waiting, Miguel: a young, handsome, hippyish Mexican. He explained that he was going to live on the property and watch it for us. I shook Miguel's hand and asked if we needed to pay him. Amador told me he would take care of the property in exchange for a place to live.

"He works for me now," Amador said proudly but I worried that Miguel would need a house or toilet or something but Amador said, "He be ok," and went to talk to him.

They both looked back at me. I smiled.

They walked toward me and Amador said, "We go to town now to dinner and then we bring him back. He gonna sleep there."

As I grabbed my bag, Amador put his hand on my waist, pulled me close to kiss my neck and whisper in my ear, "Don't be thinking crazy things, *amor.*" I nuzzled his head and blamed it on the pot. I would not let that condom ruin my plans. He took my hand and we walked to the car together.

We went to la Nave and ordered pizza. Miguel kept coming and going. But he ate his share. They both had a few beers and Amador paid the tab. Normally, I would have waited until he asked me to pay and then I would take the check. I always wanted him to acknowledge when I was paying. But this time, he didn't even look at me about the check. He just took it and paid. I liked that and didn't let myself think where he was getting the money. It wasn't my business. If he could pay, I would let him pay.

When I got back to the car, there was stuff in the back: a machete, a few candles, some bottles of water and some beers. I asked Amador about it and he told me that Miguel would need some things. "Right," I said. I had learned that Mexicans all needed machetes, and of course water for washing and beer for drinking, just like in Germany. We stopped at *La Zebra* on the way back to check on some things. I waited in the car with Miguel, enjoying being part of a tribe. Miguel and I didn't have much to say to each other. But he seemed like a nice guy.

Suddenly Amador pulled open the car door and took the machete. He looked furious and yelled in Spanish to Miguel who opened his door and got out. Javier, the manager of the campground was walking towards us. But he suddenly started back with his eyes bulging as Amador and Miguel ran toward him. Amador was waving the machete and yelling, "*pinche perro*" or something like that. I knew they were not kind words. I got out and walked too calmly to where Amador and Miguel now had the guy against a palm tree and Amador was waving the machete over his head threatening to kill him or at best just cut him up. I screamed over his cursing to ask what was going on. Amador yelled that the manager had said we had not paid and was holding Amador's papers until we did.

I told him, "Well, lets pay him," trying to be rational and then scolded, "You don't need to cut him up."

I removed myself from the drama but was intrigued and felt a slight adrenalin rush that reminded me of my racing days, that tingling in your stomach and lower intestine just before a race. Amador looked over at me and explained that Javier said we owed about $500 US. I laughed, told him that was ridiculous and asked if Amador was paying for a year. Amador got angrier and started to swing the machete again as Javier's short, fat wife came running toward us with her son in her arms. She put her son between Amador and her husband. Nice woman, I thought, wondering if

Amador might grab the baby and threaten to cut him up too. She was yelling some things, some I understood, like *cuenta* and *paga* and *policia*. I at least understood that the shit was hitting the fan.

I suggested we call the police. Amador looked over at me in disbelief. I shrugged and told him that his violence would not solve anything. Feeling the peace maker, I touched the arm in which he held the machete and told him I didn't want him to go to jail so we should just go get the police right down the road. He didn't want to let it go and for a moment I thought he would pull the machete away, cut me up and then go back to Javier and his family but he finally softened. He lowered the machete and said okay. Miguel backed off as well and we walked to the car as Amador spat more venomous Spanish words at them behind his back.

"I'll drive," I commanded.

Amador tossed me the keys and we drove down the road to the little shack of a police station that marked the entrance to the south side of the beach. Amador and I talked to the police while Miguel waited in the car. Actually, I just looked at them while Amador explained. We both understood they would do more with a tourist there than they would with just a couple of Mexican guys. Finally when Amador stopped talking, one of the cops said he would follow in a police pick up truck.

We headed back toward *la Zebra* guided by the lights of the police truck. I reassured Amador that it would be much better if the police sorted things out for us. I told him he shouldn't get so crazy and rubbed his neck.

"You right, *amor*, you right," was all he said as he sat and stared ahead of us.

As we pulled into *La Zebra*, Javier and his wife and a couple of other people moved into the drive to meet us. We were now out numbered. I checked the rear view mirror to make sure the police were behind us. The lights pulled into the drive and I exhaled. The group stopped moving toward us but did not disperse or back up. I got out to meet them and the police. Amador took a while but finally got out too. I looked at him for support. He just stood there. I walked with the police to Javier and tried my Spanish.

"*Tienes los papeles de Amador?*"

I was impressed that he understood me. But deflated when he started to speak rapidly to the cop. I couldn't follow and then his wife started in. The crowd stayed behind them, backing them up. Finally, Amador came to the discussion and started to speak. I was relieved until it turned into a shouting match. I looked to the cop for guidance. He finally put up his hands and yelled for them to be quiet. Then he let Javier speak first. I tried to follow and caught most of what he was saying. He told the police man that Amador owed him money and that was why he was holding his papers. Then the wife chimed in about all the meals he had eaten and how he had not paid and then she said something about women, "*muchas mujeres*," that hit me like a rock in the head. I wished then that she had just taken the machete and cut me badly enough to render me unconscious.

Things moved in slow motion for me then and all the other voices went into echoland. After a little while, things settled down. Javier came out with Amador's papers and I am pretty sure we had to pay something but I really don't remember. I do remember going to get my things and leaving, dropping Miguel off at the land with all of the stuff and looking over at Amador.

"What was that she said about lots of women in your tent?" I said finally.

He looked at me blankly and just said, "What?"

I told him I knew what I had heard and that it was lots of women associated with him.

I asked him again, "What was she talking about?"

I waited for an answer in the car, homeless at about 11 pm after a confrontation that involved the police and my man and I wanted to know what was up. If 'timing was everything', as my dad had always said, I had chosen a bad time to confront things.

"You no understand nothing," he said in bad English.

"No, it is 'I don't understand anything' and you are wrong. I understood what she said," I was not moving without an explanation.

"*Amor*," Amador said tiredly, "you know I know lots of people. Sure I got some girls who are friends. But that is all. She just ugly and fat and jealous."

I looked into his eyes and he stared back at me. He leaned over, kissed me and asked me where we would stay now. Suddenly exhausted, I decided to let it go. I told him I didn't know where we could stay and rather than cry, I looked at his smiling face as he said he knew a place. I smiled back and we drove up the road toward the arch and just before it, pulled into a long sandy drive, finally stopping at a *cabana*. Two barking dogs met us as Amador got out of the car. He told me to wait. I looked out the window at the stars thinking it had been a pretty wild few days. I knew I would sleep well, if we got a place. I closed my eyes to rest just in case.

I am not sure how long I rested, but Amador came back with Yuri, a tall, handsome Mexican with a big smile and very white teeth. I got out of the car to greet him and he welcomed us to *Saphiro* and then politely told me he had a *cabana* for us. He pulled my bag from the car and we walked toward the beach and a small *cabana* with a *palapa* roof. He opened the door and lit a candle, explaining that electricity was coming. "So is Christmas," I thought to myself but Yuri was kind and I was just happy to see a mattress. I didn't care about lights.

He put my bag down, told me to have a good night, and then asked, "You want some ganga or a beer?"

Amador answered for me, saying I didn't drink beer but asked if I could have some wine. Yuri shook his head no and said he had Mezcal if I wanted. I said yes and in a moment he came back with two shots and excused himself. I sat on the banister to the small balcony and drank with Amador, looking at the stars, listening to the surf. Then we crawled under the mosquito netting, made love and fell soundly asleep.

Chapter 5

I woke, stretched my arms out over my head and unsuccessfully tried to move my leg from under Amador's. I gave up and looked up through the mosquito netting to see a huge palmetto bug dead on top of the net.

My eyes opened wider and I thought, "Good thing we had a mosquito net."

I noticed the door was wide open and I looked over to make sure all my bags were there. I saw them and relaxed into the space between sleeping and actually waking up. It lasted only a few seconds before I had to pee. I forced my way out from under Amador and went to the bathroom. There was no door but it wasn't planned to have any. You walked around a circular tiled wall and there was the toilet and on the other side was the shower. I turned on the faucet and happily found water. I peed, flushed, said, "Not bad," to myself and grabbed a *pareo*. I wrapped it around me and walked out to the balcony where the sand was softly caressing the stairs with the breeze from the sea. The beach was savage, lightly cleaned of plastic but not totally of seaweed and driftwood. I looked out onto the sea and exhaled.

There was no one around and I noticed there were 3 *cabanas*. The one to my left as I faced the water, seemed larger than the others and there was one to my right that was identical to mine. Further up the beach to the right or south was a two-story house, open at the bottom with a *palapa* roof that was open in front. I did not want to presume I could go inside, so I just sat on my balcony. There was no chair so I sat on the bannister and leaned against one of the wood posts that supported the roof. I wrote in my journal and took out out my sketchpad.

Finally the dog who had come to attack us last night passed by and said hello with a bark, waking Amador. He called to me from the bed, just coming out of his deep sleep. I went in, touched him on the back and said, "*Si.*"

He rolled toward me and grabbed my waist asking me where I was scolding, "You know I hate when I don' wake up with you next to me."

He pulled me back into the bed. I loved that he liked me close. I felt loved that he wanted to always know where I was. I told him I had been waiting for him.

"Wait here, next to me," he said in a voice more serious than I recognized.

I laughed and told him I would waken him next time and then asked him if he wanted to go swimming. He told me he did but he pulled me into bed and we made love before we swam. I was in heaven. The beach was deserted and the hotel was slightly derelict but cleaned and cared for, just the way I liked it.

Yuri met us as we walked back from swimming and said hello in English. I thanked him for taking care of us the night before. He dismissed the gratitude politely and invited us to see the house. I would only have been happier to be invited for coffee. I had a headache brewing that could only be cured with caffeine. But I politely waited to be asked as we walked to the house and then up a set of stairs on the side into an large open dining area with one small table and a couple of plastic chairs. There was a stove and sink at the back and a bunch of coolers under the sink. Off the kitchen was another set of stairs that led up to a *cabana*. It was open in front but there was a roof over the entire space. I looked over the sea and was transported far away until Amador came behind me and commented on how nice the view was.

I turned, looked at him and impulsively kissed him fully on the mouth and then told him, "Magnificent."

He had rescued me from *La Zebra* and brought me to heaven once again. We walked back downstairs to meet Yuri there. He asked if we were hungry mentioning he had cereal and milk. I took the opportunity to ask him for a coffee and accepted the cereal. Yuri smiled and took out the cereal and some powdered milk and then made coffee in one of the Italian coffee makers I had grown so fond of at Cesiak.

We had breakfast together and he asked, "So, for how long are you here?"

I couldn't help noticing that he even put his preposition where it belonged, rather than ending his sentence with it. I liked him more. Amador had told him that we were buying land down the road and Yuri offered to help with whatever he could. He told us he had done some research on the *ejido* issue and he would be happy to share what he had learned.

He finished saying to me, "It can be a little tricky sometimes so let me know, Joanne, if you need anything."

Amador ate silently so I asked Yuri if he had the *cabana* for another night. He said yes and told me the price was $65 per night. I just agreed to the price. I knew I would hear about it from Amador later but I didn't feel like bargaining, especially since he didn't seem to want to help me. We finished breakfast and went back to the *cabana*. Before I took a shower, Amador told me I could have gotten a better deal if I had negotiated. I told him perhaps and then asked him why he didn't help me. He answered me with an attitude and told me I needed to learn.

I became annoyed and told him, "No Amador, you have got to help me, ok?"

I didn't want to learn. I wanted help and he was my guide, my teacher in this culture. He didn't answer but as I jumped into the shower, I asked if he wanted to go to town for second breakfast.

I asked, "*Chiliquilis?*" knowing they were his favorite breakfast.

I would be munching on yogurt and granola and he would eat those two eggs on top of tortilla chips with a cream sauce smothered in spicey green salsa. I got heartburn just thinking of it but knew I could use a little more to eat.

After breakfast we stopped by Davide's house in town to say hello. It was on the far southern end of town, where the main avenue turned into a highway heading toward Belize. Just past a shop for tires we took a left and drove up two blocks. There was a palm tree painted the colors of the rainbow on the corner and we pulled in just past it. Davide's front yard was littered with construction debris and trash and children's toys. There were two hammocks in front. The house was a concrete slab with a big window in front. Several men were standing and sitting idly in the yard and two skinny dogs lay in the driveway. The guys and the dogs all looked at us as we pulled in. The dogs relaxed when we opened the car doors but the men continued staring.

"Wait me here." Amador commanded and he left the car running as I closed the door to preserve the air conditioning.

Then, I turned the engine off, opened the windows and congratulated myself on having the car keys again. I heard a rooster crowing and waited and enjoyed the fresh air until Amador stuck his head in the window and told me Davide wanted money.

"What?" I asked him, not understanding.

He repeated that Davide said he needed money and wanted to know if I could give him something. I told Amador that until I signed, I was not giving him any more money. Amador pressured me saying I had to give him something and suggested 500 dollars. I lied and told him I didn't have it. He asked for 300. Davide came out of the house and Amador got nervous. I wasn't sure why but I told him I could give Davide 200 US if he would sign for it. Davide came to the window.

I reached into my notebook, pulled out a page and asked Amador to help me write a receipt, saying, "How do I say, I received $200"

Amador grabbed the paper, started writing and told me to just get the money. I said hello to Davide and got out of the car to greet him.

He told me, *"Hola Mi Reina,"* "Hello Queen" and I smiled as I kissed him on the cheek.

He smiled back, blinding me with his gold teeth. Amador came over, stood in front of me, put his hand out and asked for the cash. I double checked that Amador had the receipt ready and I reached into my bag and handed him a pen, rather than the money. He took the pen, asked Davide to sign and then gave him the money.

I knew he didn't like it but I needed to take care of these things. I was wondering why we even came here if Davide was going to demand money from us. Amador went over, handed him the bills and they shook hands and he came back to the car. He motioned for me to get in and I waved goodbye to Davide. As we drove away from the curb and Amador said told me I didn't need to get out of the car and kiss Davide hello.

I laughed at him and said, "I was being polite, for God's sake. What would you have me do, just wait for you in the car?"

He told me that would be better and then he said, "Listen, *amor*, these guys," and he paused, "You don't want to get too close to them, ok? They not nice guys, ok?"

I understood what he was trying to say. I was always too nice. I apologized. We drove in silence for awhile until Amador broke the silence asking me if I wanted to "take some sun." I smiled at his use of the English language and agreed. We stopped at 'Stop and Go' for supplies and back at *Saphiro* put beers, ice and Perrier along with some other supplies in a cooler. We went to the beach, me with my green yuppie Perrier bottle and Amador with two beers.

It was heaven laying there next to him, the breeze from the sea cooled our bodies as the sun warmed them.

After an hour or so, Amador got up and said, "I gonna go see some people down the beach."

I told him that was fine until he asked for the car. I told him I might need the car but he said he would be right back and asked for the keys again, mentioning he could go get them in my bag, if I wanted. I didn't want him to know what I had in my bag, namely, more money, so I went for the keys myself. I scolded myself for not trusting him but then told myself it was ok to have my own things. I came back and handed him the keys and said, "Right back, ok?"

He kissed me as an answer and headed out the drive. I walked back to the *cabana*, got my things and took a long walk. The little dog, whose name I learned was LoLo, followed me. I came back after awhile, showered and then went to sit in the kitchen with Yuri. He was there with another guy who was playing guitar.

"Hola Joanna," he said to me, "This is Javier."

The guitarist just looked up and nodded. I offered them beers and they accepted. As I served them, I noticed Amador had taken one six pack. That bothered me but I let it pass. It was his style and I told myself it was ok.

I sat with my Perrier, shared the beers and listened to the music. It was beautiful. Javier was a short guy with a beautiful face. He wore a little cap on his head and looked more Turkish than Mexican. Each time he would finish a song he hugged his guitar, folding over it protectively. I clapped, he smiled and sang another as if the guitar were part of him and it took no energy to play. The sun went down and when Yuri asked if we were hungry, we all said yes to a stew he had been working on. I listened to the music, let the sun set and the stars come out like a map in the sky as we ate the stew Yuri served. I shared the wine I had and laughed with them. When thoughts of Amador came to mind, I pushed them from my consciousness asking myself what I could do?

At around 9:30 Amador came to the kitchen with a friend, Mauricio, and a big Tupperware container full of ceviche. He was stoned but I could care less. We all were a little, so I couldn't say anything. We happily listened to more music until Javier stopped playing. Amador and Mauricio wanted to have a a night cap in the town and I tagged along.

We came back late. The stars were incredible, drawing courses in the night sky and I imagined being on the sea and looking at them for guidance. The night was still, with no moon and no wind as we crawled under the mosquito netting to sleep. I was tired and tried to sleep but Amador kept waking me up for the heat and the mosquitoes that managed to come through the holes in the mosquito netting. "No see ums," we called them in my sailing days: tiny bugs that seemed to be all teeth. He kept swatting at them and of course, missing.

Finally he said, "*Ven amor*," "Come my love," as he pulled the sheets off the bed and walked outside.

I followed in my black nightgown as we went to the beach. He pulled two lounge chairs with cushions together and put a sheet on the bottom and then one on the top and put his arms out toward me. I went to his embrace and felt as safe as in my mother's womb there in the open on the beach. The breeze cooled us and kept the mosquitoes away.

"Better, no?" he whispered into my ear.

I agreed. It was cooler and you could breathe better and relax. He spooned his body with mine and pointed to the stars. A shooting star moved slowly across the night sky. He whispered to make a wish. I did, wishing the moment could last forever as I drifted off to sleep and the dog, Lolo, came to sleep underneath us. Before I fell asleep, I thanked God for bringing me this man.

Chapter 6

Over the next month back in Miami, I would dream of that night and prepare to go back and buy my piece of paradise. Amador would call and I would be homesick for our lounge chair under the stars. We talked of him coming here. I told my family and friends other than Fernando and Lynn, of course, about him. I lived in the dream of being with the man I made of Amador: wonderful, funny, smart, a fisherman but a Renaissance fisherman if there could be any such thing. He was anything but the drug dealing addict Fernando and Lynn would have me believe he was.

That month, my friend and partner in the Foundation, Bathsheba, came to Miami. We met to discuss our project and map out next steps. Finalizing my emotional support books was one of them. Going over artwork and finding a printer were others. Her husband Paul was my editor. I loved working with them. We talked about my books candidly and how we would help women with breast cancer. Mexico always came up.

"Was I sure I knew what I was doing?"

I had no idea. But I knew I could learn. After all, this was new territory. I had worked for someone else my entire life. Now I needed to navigate on my own. I knew I could do it. When they would ask if I would move to Mexico, I smiled. How long did everyone think I could continue living from place to place, searching for somewhere. Did they realize how lonely I was? Did they understand how good it felt to be in Tulum. How good it felt to be with that man? How good it felt to be free of my past? How I needed a new map for my life? When they wondered how I would run the Foundation from Mexico, I confronted them with the modern world: planes, cell phones and computer conferencing? And wasn't that why I had a Board of Directors?

I listened and justified myself for awhile. Then I put all their questions into an imaginary balloon and sent it to explore in space. I stayed on the ground and focused on each day, what I could accomplish and what I couldn't. I tried to keep a sense of purpose to my life, something that I was having a hard time regaining after leaving my 9 to 5 and finishing my cancer battle. All of a sudden, I was my own boss. It was exhilarating but it felt strange. I suddenly understood how my father felt after his retirement.

When your days are mapped out weeks and months in advance and then suddenly, you map your own days, it is difficult to adjust. I needed something to work toward every day. I didn't understand yet that each day is enough. I would remind myself how Amador would say, "Lets see what great things can happen today." And I would remind myself to love him madly as well. Because if I didn't, what was I doing?

My mom would return to Cape Cod just before I would go back to Mexico. Although I would miss her terribly, I knew that alone was bad for her in Miami even in the winter when she was rescuing herself from the cold. In those months, she could walk and go to the beach on her own at any time of the day. With the heat of summer coming, however, she would isolate herself, staying in the condo and reading under the air conditioning except for the early mornings. There was no reason for her to stay. She could be on Cape Cod with my sister for the summer and enjoy life and a family I was afraid thought I was crazy. But I would not let losing them allow me to lose myself. I needed my new life and I promised myself that they would understand one day.

I stayed in Miami alone and then planned to go back to Mexico. I needed to focus on finishing my books, getting them to cancer patients and figuring out how to get to Mexico with 25,000 undeclared dollars on my body to buy my place. I sent Amador an email about the latter asking if he couldn't find someone trustworthy to accept some of the money in a bank account.

"Why are you dealing with these scumbags who haven't even got a bank account?" Paul asked me one day.

I defended them and told him they were not scumbags and that I could not even get a bank account in Mexico. Paul chuckled and said that I was a foreigner.

He said with a smile, "There have to be Mexicans with bank accounts. Why don't you meet them?"

Paul was a realist from New York City. If he had a problem, he told you about it. Too, he understood the world better than I did. He knew the capability of the criminal element. He could see the hardship I was setting myself up for and was blunt about it. I defended my friends in Tulum saying how it was a third world sort of place and that the guys I was dealing with were basically just fisherman.

Paul continued, "I just don't get why you would want to deal with people like that. I mean, don't you know any rich people there? Or not even rich people," Paul knew my working class philosophy, "Just normal people like us. I don't get it, Fanny."

I thought for a moment and then admitted that I didn't get it either. But I told him that I knew it made me happy to be there. He wouldn't stop, even after that. He told me that basically there were cultural differences I could not overcome. He said I would always be the foreigner, the American and that the sooner I realized that the better I could take care of myself. He was preaching but I appreciated it and understood to a point but I knew my situation was different.

Then Sheba said with a chuckle, "Maybe you should move into a double wide and meet some people you like here in the States."

I laughed but the thought horrified me. Although, what was the difference? Perhaps I was just romanticizing trailer-trash from a foreign country.

We were shopping in a leather shop in South Beach, looking for a good bag to carry money to Mexico.

Sheba knew she had sort of freaked me out with the trailer concept so she continued and told me, "I don't know Fanny. It just seems so difficult, as if you don't have enough on your plate."

But I wanted more than enough on my plate. I needed to fill my life so full that the other shit I hated would fall out or be pushed out, never to return. Didn't they see that? Then she held up a brown leather bag. It was beautiful. The proprietor came over to show us the secure lock, the hand stitched detail and how easily it locked. I put it on and looked in the mirror. The Arabic man trying to sell it told me I could dress it up or down. I doubted I would dress it up but I felt the lock, liked the look of it and decided it was perfect. I wasn't sure if I meant it or if I just wanted to change the topic of our conversation to where we would have dinner. Over the next few days we completed the Foundation paperwork, organized our Board of Directors and finished most of the work on my books. We would print when I went to visit them in Pennsylvania in May with money I had saved and my credit.

In one week I would go buy the beach property in Mexico with Helen's money. I would see my mom over the summer. I had a map for my new life and people to work with on it. I pushed every day to get a little closer and told myself I would be happy if it killed me.

Chapter 7

Amador and I practically ran into our old cabana at Saphiro. "Swimming?" he said to me happily as he put down my bags. Then he came over and kissed me, reached under my shirt and undid my bra. As I pulled off my shirt and the bra fell to the floor, so did a wad of US dollars, $4,500 to be exact. The other wad of $500 dollar bills stuck to my breast since the pressure from my bra and the sweat had cemented it onto my body. We looked down and started to laugh. Amador reached to pick up the wad on the floor as I peeled the one off my breast. He opened the chunk of money in his hands, flipped through the bills and handed it back to me as he kissed both my breasts and moved his hands down toward open my pants. I stopped him and reached in to withdraw another bunch of money from my underwear, laughing as I did so. Then I wiggled out of the blue jeans and into his arms. He moved me toward the bed and I put the piles of money under the pillow. We made love on top of them. My pants with $2000 in each front pocket lay on the floor by the bed. The door was open to the sea breeze. I finally stopped worrying for a moment about where the money was and who might know I had it.

We ate later at Don Cafeto's on the Avenida, watching people go buy. I kept my bag close but was not so preoccupied about the money as before. I felt safe. Amador suggested that we visit Davide, finished his food and asked for the check saying that Davide needed to see me, to know I was in town, to know the deal was still on. I wondered if that was wise since I knew Davide would want more money.

"We just take it off the price and make him sign," Amador said matter of factly.

I reluctantly agreed. One block before Davide's house we stopped for beers, Amador's idea. I thought we had to bring something so I conceded. Something, that was, besides all that cash. Davide's house looked the same, 3 or 4 guys out front just standing around or lying in the hammock, a chicken pecking the dust and two dogs sleeping close by. This time, Amador told me to come in with him. He opened the car door for me and took my hand in his to walk past the *squadron del muerte*. They said subdued *hola's*. I held Amador's hand tightly as I stepped over the discarded broken concrete blocks and trash that were everywhere and asked myself if I were the only person who noticed all the trash.

I couldn't believe the *squadron del muerte* didn't at some point turn into a *squadron de limpio*, a cleaning crew. It was gross. The trash attracted flies. And these were not dirty people. They were well groomed and clean and not stupid. But the trash made them look dirty and ignorant. We stepped up two concrete blocks that made the stairs into Davide's house and we walked directly into his bedroom. He obviously had not read anything on Feng Shue. One of the squadron pulled up chairs for us, moving quietly from behind. I hadn't even seen him following and made a mental note of his stealth.

Davide was lying in bed, his wife sitting next to him. His hair was slicked back as usual and he still flaunted the gold smile. But his teeth were tight on his jaw. I had seen that sort of smile before but couldn't remember the context. Before we sat, each of us shook his hand. I kissed his cheek and then greeted his wife. Mayan women do not generally like white women. I felt his wife's distaste at having me in her house, not to mention her bedroom. Davide introduced her only as *mi esposa*, my wife. She was beautiful, petite with large brown eyes and long, curly, dark brown hair. When she politely extended her hand and smiled, she showed off the same gold filled mouth that Davide had. It was wild.

Then he pointed to a few family photos on the walls and said to me with that gold smile, '*mi familia*', again almost grinding his teeth. The photos were formal portrait style and the family was young, two girls and a boy. The boy I recognized as a younger version of one of the squadron out in front of the house. He was handsome, like his parents. He had not smiled at me but I knew that one of these days he would crack a smile and I would see gold. Amador handed Davide the beers. Davide took the six pack, took one and handed another to Amador, then offered one to me. I refused politely and he offered me some orange drink. I accepted trying not to be rude. His wife accepted a beer. He exchanged some words with Amador and they laughed. Then he put his attention to me. He was smiling that tight wide smile again and he said, "*mi casa*" and put his arm in a gentle arc around the room. I smiled and shook my head and said "*bonito*" and then I recognized the smile. It was a cocaine smile. People on coke had that tight, tooth grinding type of smile. Now I understood the constant need for cash.

Amador said, "You should see Davide's birds," and then looked at Davide and said, "*Tus pajaro's, verdad?*"

Davide shook his head emphatically and directed his *esposa* to show them to me. I hated to leave. I wanted to see, even if I couldn't fully understand, what was going on. But Amador was sending me out. I did not like it and wondered if it was on purpose. Then, "of course it was," said the voice of reason on my shoulder. Davide's wife opened the door and took me around back. There, in an aviary that couldn't have been more than 5 feet wide and 7 feet long were two large peacocks and several other small exotic birds that I did not recognize. I pretended to be impressed and I was by the birds but I was horrified at the small cage and the dirtiness of the place. It had not been cleaned for some time. I smiled at the *esposa*. She did not smile back but turned and led me back to the house. Amador was shaking Davide's hand as I entered.

They both looked at me so I commented, "*Bonito, muy bonito*".

He smiled, sort of nodded, and shook my hand.

Then Amador took my arm and led me past the squadron once again saying Davide needed some cash.

"I told you so," I chimed triumphantly but Amador ingnored me.

He suggested we give Davide a hundred. I joked if it were dollars or pesos but Amador was not amused. I handed him the money and told him Davide needed to sign for it, adding an emphatic "*por favor*" as I gave him a paper and pen.

Amador didn't want to take it but I told him it could go on for awhile and commented, "He is a coke head and is going to want cash every day until we sign."

I knew I was right but Amador seemed surprised that I realized

Davide had a drug habit.

"Am I wrong?" I asked.

Amador looked down at his feet, then took the pen and paper and the cash and told me to wait for him. I was suddenly tired and hot so I started the car and put on the air conditioning. As I rolled up the windows, I told myself that the whole thing was getting a little too interesting but, as long as he signed, everything would be fine.

"So long as that stealthy *'squadron del muerte'* doesn't come in the middle of the night to kill you," the voice on my shoulder said.

I brushed the voice away as Amador came out from the house and said, "Let's get the fuck out of here," in slang English that tourists had taught him.

I asked if things were ok and Amador said that Davide wanted more, 100 was not enough. I prayed we could sign the contract the following week.

We stopped to see the lawyer before we went back to the beach. But his secretary said he was out until Monday. I started to get depressed and to save myself, we decided to go back to the beach stopping for groceries and ice, some beers and wine. On the beach road we passed Amador's friend Mauricio in a loud red Toyota station wagon with Vermont license plates. Amador stopped to talk with him while we blocked the road.

Then he said, "I gonna go with him for a few minutes, OK?"
I told him he needed to at least come back with me to put things away. He apologized and told me I was right. He explained to Mauricio and we drove to *Saphiro*. Mauricio followed and helped unload the car before he and Amador grabbed a six pack of beer and got into the red car. I yelled for him to come back.

When he got to me I asked him, "You would leave without even saying goodbye?"

He apologized several times and then gave me a long kiss on the lips saying he would be back in an hour and asking if I would be there. I shrugged, wondered where else I would go and felt actually happy to have some time alone. I was happier that he was not taking my car.

I knew he would not be back in an hour, or probably even in two. When it started getting dark, I went to the kitchen to put things away, since there would be no light later. I had lost my appetite but did not want the rats to get into my food. Then, I went to the cabana, opening the door with a knife as Yuri had shown me since the key had been lost and never replaced. Once in, I lit candles and looked for the flashlight to prepare for the night. I walked back to the house and lit candles in the kitchen. As I finished, Javier from upstairs came down and remembered me from the last time I had stayed at Saphiro.

"Back again," he said with a smile and kissed me on the cheek.

I mentioned that I had seen him at the Weary Traveler the other night and told him I was glad he was still at Saphiro. He started to cook and I got some wine to share. I enjoyed his company and let watching him cook take my mind off the fact that Amador seemed to have forgotten me. We did not talk much. I poured wine and he made a concoction with tuna and rice. He fed me some to taste. It was delicious and simple. We shared the meal, drank more wine and talked. It was hours since Amador should have returned but I was more than ok.

As if he knew I had allowed myself to enjoy time with someone else, Amador finally walked in with Mauricio and a huge platter of ceviche. They were stoned or drunk or both and happy. They couldn't imagine or didn't care to think that I would be upset at all. It was this Mexican thing that ½ hour can mean anything, from one hour to three or even 24. I needed to get used to this if I were going to live here or I would become a sad, anxious, bitch. Determined not to become that, I opened another bottle of wine. Javier went upstairs as Amador, Mauricio and I drank, talked and laughed. The wind blew softly and created a coolness that smelled of the sea as the nearly full moon sparkled on the water.

Amador went upstairs and convinced Javier to come back to play for us. I couldn't help but notice how quickly things could change and made a mental note of that. One minute I was feeling lonely. The next I was surrounded by men and listening to Flamenco guitar under the light of the full moon and a couple of candles, feeling lightheaded and happy. Amador smiled at me. I couldn't decide if his erratic schedule was really a cultural thing or just Amador. At the moment I didn't care. But sooner or later, I needed to figure it out.

Javier went upstairs and found a third bottle of wine to share. I knew he was used to camping by the way he kept all of his things to himself: the olive oil that he brought out only after we fed him pasta without it, the raisin bread that he fed me the other morning once I made him a coffee and now the wine after we had finished 2 bottle of mine. He had been taken advantage of before, I was sure.

As he finished another song and we finished his wine, Amador said "lets go to *Acabar* for one."

I knew that it would never be just one. Mexicans are so Irish, I thought to myself. Javier said goodnight and headed upstairs. We thanked him before Mauricio, Amador and I jumped into the rental car and headed for town.

Acabar was the newest bar in Tulum at the time; hip and trendy with recessed lights and low cushions for sitting. I knew most everyone there: Yuri and Nanette, his girlfriend, Puff behind the bar. Alex from the internet shop and his brother were playing the music. Each acknowledged me with a kiss or a nod. It was nice to be recognized. Amador and I danced. He smiled that wonderful, boyish smile and made me feel as if I were the only woman with whom he would ever dance. When the bar closed Amador talked with someone while I waited by the car. The night was balmy with a soft breeze blowing through the sweat that had gathered at the back of my neck. I was wearing a black dress that made me feel cool and together, a rare occurrence in Tulum. Mauricio got into the car with us and Amador drove, but in the wrong direction. I asked him where he was going and he said, "Just a stop," nothing more, no laughter, no touch on the leg, just driving and looking for the "stop." I was tired but suddenly on edge and I wasn't sure why, yet.

It was about 3 am and we drove to where the streets got third world at the far western end of town. There were one-story cement block buildings side by side, like an early fifties housing project, only worse. The potholes were huge and we bounced along next to the houses. Small lights flickered and you could see hammocks and TV sets through open windows and doors. We came to a garage and Amador asked me for 100 pesos. I stared at him incredulously. I had already bought all the drinks now he wanted me to buy his pot. Mauricio looked on from the back. I did not want to make a scene so I handed Amador the money. Then he motioned to the biggest Mexican I had ever seen to come over to the car. They traded packages. But Amador received a small package containing white powder. I couldn't believe it. I didn't believe that anyone really did coke anymore.

"You are disgusting," I said to him.

He pretended not to hear and drove away. Mauricio waited in the back. I looked out the window, away from the two of them, silent and annoyed but not knowing what to do. I could get out, but not in that neighborhood. I could ask them both to leave, but I didn't want the hassle and I didn't want to find my way out of the 'hood alone. I decided to confront things when we got back to *Saphiro*.

Halfway up the beach road, Amador handed the packet to Mauricio who opened it, cut 4 lines and handed them to Amador who offered them to me. I looked at him and told him flatly that I didn't do cocaine.

"You mean any more," he said and then he repeated, "You don't do it anymore."

I let the insinuation slide and told him that was a long, long time ago when I had done coke a few times.

"I gonna do some," he said as if it were a challenge.

I looked out the window, heard him snort the two lines and then listened as Mauricio did the other two in the back seat. We dropped Mauricio at his campground and home, *Playa Selva*, and continued up the road to *Saphiro* in silence. I wondered how much fun that must have been: alone in his campground stoned on cocaine and no one around to talk to. That voice inside my head told me to chill and reminded me that it was not a big deal. But I hated it. And I hated that he did the lines in front of me and even more so, that he had asked me to pay. I hated that he had ruined the night for me. I hated that he disregarded my opinion. And I hated that I had absolutely no control over him and that, in this place that I was beginning to love, he had control over me.

When we returned he followed me to the cabana. I went directly to the bathroom to get ready for bed. As I finished putting on moisturizing cream, lost in my thoughts of what to do, I turned and saw him, waiting at the foot of the bed, his hair wild and his eyes burning a hole into me.

"*Mi amor*," he moaned.

I could literally see the desire in him. It made me feel high.

"Why you keep me waiting so long?"

I smiled, laughed at myself and him and decided to let it all go, let him do what he wanted and let it be. I walked toward him and kissed him long and passionately. I loved the way he wanted me. We were wonderful in bed and sleeping with him, entwined in his body after we made love, his body heavy against mine, made up for everything else, at least for that moment.

Chapter 8

I asked Amador about his ID over lunch the next day, wondering if he had gone to Playa while I was in the US.

"No," he said as he scooped ceviche with a tortilla chip and then dipped it into a spicey green salsa, "I forget."

I was annoyed but knew it didn't serve any purpose so I reminded him that he needed an ID to sign for the land. I only had so much time before I headed back to Miami and I wanted to get rid of the cash and put the paperwork in order. He flagged the waiter for another beer, but I told him we could have a drink after we got his identification.

We headed to the municipal offices in Playa del Carmen. I waited in the car again and he went in: surfer shorts, no shoes, dreadlocked hair. He smiled his way into places.

He emerged in 15 minutes and dashed my high hopes saying, "They no gonna give me nothing."

He opened the door and looked to me for the keys.

I stared back at him and asked, "What happened?"

He looked sullen and dark. He put out his hand out for the keys. I asked him again. He snapped and asked me harshly what I wanted from him. I looked at him, hurt and surprised by his tone of voice. I tried to explain that I only wanted to know what had happened and said, "Is that too much?"

His face turned to a scowl and he opened the door and told me it was all too much. I reached for his arm but he pulled it away telling me he didn't need all this shit.

He got out and yelled it again, "I don't need any of this shit," loudly enough to turn heads in the parking lot.

I didn't understand what he was so upset about or why he was taking it out on me and I asked him what was wrong.

He turned and looked at me and spat, "You know what is wrong with you?" in a loud voice so everyone could hear, "You don't understand nothing."

I wanted to correct the double negative but I was getting good at stopping myself. I got out of the car and went toward him. He kept walking away.

I followed until he said to me, "Leave me alone. I don't want to talk to you."

He put his right hand over his head and pushed it back behind him as if to shoo me away in a gesture that I knew was the Mexican version of giving someone the finger. I asked him what I had done and he started to run. I stopped, hurt and not understanding. He kept running for awhile and then continued walking away from me.

I could not believe this was happening. After a moment, I walked slowly back toward the car trying to comprehend what had just happened. He had disappeared. I got into the drivers seat and put the key in the ignition, wondering what to do, where to go. I felt abandoned and sick. I asked myself if that was the end. I don't remember how long I sat there but finally I turned the key and decided to go back. My mind went over what would happen with our project, if he was not willing to help anymore. I raced through options and thought about bringing all that money back to the States. Then I wondered about the cash I had given to Davide. I would lose it all. I surprised myself by feeling relieved, almost, if God had stepped in to clarify things. I put the car in reverse and turned to go.

As I stopped to leave the parking lot, I saw him on the corner, looking at me with a blank, sad look on his face. I smiled at him and he walked toward me. I put the car in park, left it in the middle of the exit and got out of the car to meet him.

"You would have left me?" he said.

I asked him what I could have done in disbelief.

He opened his arms and said, "Wait me, like I would wait you."

I was totally confused as we embraced and he said, "*Perdoname*," and buried his head in my shoulder. I held him tightly there on the street, still not really understanding what had happened but I told him that of course I would. A car beeped behind ours, trying to get out. We jogged back to the car and headed for the highway. I finally asked him what happened with the ID.

"You not gonna believe this," he said, "but welcome to Mexico. I get so frustrated sometimes. I need to get my original birth certificate. They only gonna give me the id with that."

I felt defeated. I didn't have my original birth certificate and I lived in a house with walls, not a tent on the beach. I wondered if my mother even had a copy. But Amador was optimistic and told me he knew his sister in Cancun would have a copy. We had found the house once. She lived in a modest but nice 2-story town house next to a park on *Avenida Paleque*. I was not sure I could find it again and I asked Amador if he knew her number. He did not but told me she had a friend in Playa del Carmen who would have it and directed me to take a left and head back toward the city.

He went to a small neighborhood and a three story house painted cobalt blue with a cast iron gate that made the shape of stars. He knocked on the door and when no one answered he yelled up to an open window. Finally, a young woman's head poked out the window and smiled broadly when she saw Amador. A minute later, she opened the door. They embraced. Amador pointed to me in the car. She waved. I smiled and waved back and the two of them talked for awhile. Finally she went upstairs and came back and handed him a slip of paper.

They hugged and he came back to the car, smiling, and said, "Got it."

We went to a pay phone and arranged to meet Hayyde's husband in two days with the birth certificate. I would probably need to change my flight if I wanted to accomplish something but we were getting there.

Driving back Amador told me we needed to explain to Davide why we weren't paying him and ask for more time. He reminded me that Davide wanted all the money soon. I knew that. But how were we going to make that happen with no ID for Amador? He suggested that we sign for the land the same day we pick up the birth certificate. I thought it was cutting it close but he was positive it would work. His attitude was contagious and I agreed.

We went back to Tulum and scheduled things for Monday. Then, we visited Davide, stopping to get beers first. We walked the gauntlet of the *squadron del muerte* and handed Davide the beers so that he could offer us each one. Amador accepted, I declined and we discussed the appointment Monday afternoon in Playa. He would be there. We shook hands leaving and planned on picking him up. I was in the car when Davide called Amador back. I waited in the car, knowing Amador would return for money.

"I told you so," I said with a smile as he came back to the car door.

I handed him 300 dollars in pesos and a piece of paper and asked him to have Davide sign for the money. When he came back in

10 minutes, I was dozing in the passenger seat.

He opened the door and said his customary, "Let's get the fuck out of here," with a smile.

Monday morning the sun peeked into the shady cabana and Amador's eyes opened with mine.

He looked at me and said, "Swimming?"

I smiled and nodded yes and stretched the full length of the bed.

"*Vamos*," he said to me happily and pinched my butt before he wrapped a *pareo* around his wasted and walked out the door. I rushed to pull on a suit and followed him. It was heaven in the sea and swimming was my favorite ritual. I practiced yoga on the beach before we showered and got into the car to go to breakfast and then get Davide. I was nervous that we needed to meet his brother in law before we could sign and pay. I was unsure we had time and worried that the papers wouldn't be there for us. So many things could go wrong in the short time we had to pull everything together. And we had to do it all while I had about $20,000 US in my bag.

We stopped for beers after breakfast and went to Davide's. He was neatly dressed in a grey-blue shirt and dark, pressed pants. His hair was neatly combed and he had that easy, golden smile as he met us. But his hands were shaking as Amador handed him the beer in the back seat. He immediately opened one and drank with gusto. I looked over at Amador as he pulled from the curb and reminded him that so far we had given him $900 US. I had brought all the papers to prove it. But Amador was somewhere else mentally. He didn't acknowledge me or what I said. I hoped he would return mentally soon.

After a few moments of silence in the car, he looked over at me and said, "we got to call," and pulled over at the next pay phone.

When he came out he seemed happy and told me his brother in law was in Playa with the papers and he would meet us at Playa Car, a gated community on the outskirts of the downtown area.

We were there in 40 minutes and when the security guard met us, Amador gave him my license and an address that he knew. We went into the neighborhood and followed some circuitous tree-lined roads with houses on either side. They were mostly concrete or stucco in a Spanish *hacienda* style. But the lots were small. It reminded me of the wealthier neighborhoods in Miami where I always believed the narco traffickers lived. Swimming pools, limousines and Mercedes waited behind the manicured hedgerows of bougainvillea. This was a different part of Playa than I had known. Until now I believed that Playa was water front hotels and dirty city streets that faded into dusty *barrios* filled with the poor workers from the hotels and restaurants. This neighborhood could have been anywhere. We passed golf carts and security cars. Suddenly I was aware of a motorcycle next to us beeping. He was on my side, passing from the inside. He kept pace with the car and kept beeping. I was afraid the police had decided we were undesireable and discovered the address Amador had given was false. Amador didn't stop but I rolled down the window and Amador looked over and called, "Jacobo!." His brother in law had found us.

We pulled over and Jacobo pulled up to Amador's window. He handed him a manilla envelope and they shared some words in Spanish. Jacobo had no time to chat, but Amador quickly introduced us and then Jacobo took off again. Amador looked through the package and pulled out a legal sized paper that was his birth certificate. Now we could get his id.

"Lets go," he said.

We drove out of the gated Playa Car and back to the Playa del Carmen I had known. The contrast was starker now, as we left the cool shaded avenues for the hot streets of the city itself. We drove to the municipal offices and Davide and I waited in the parking lot once again as Amador walked in to retrieve his ID.

He came out 20 minutes later smiling and he told me, "*Si, amor,* I got it," beaming as if it were a college degree.

I had been clutching my bag to my chest most of the drive, the remaining cash solidly pressed to my abdomen, where I felt a growing sense of that same uneasiness I would get before a race or a speech to a hostile audience.

We found the notary and confirmed the appointment with the secretary. Just as we parked and the three of us left the car, a white ford sedan pulled up with the *squadron del muerte*. Davide met them and talked with them for a moment and then Pancho, who I knew from the first night I met Davide in the jungle, got out of the car. He looked nervous and was wearing jeans and a clean but oversized shirt and what looked to be a pair of women's sneakers. They were pumas but definitely women's shoes. You could tell by the cut and the color. I smiled when I saw them. Davide was still shakey and he brushed his hair to the side in a nervous manner as Amador opened the door and we all went inside.

All contracts, land sales, business development, births and deaths are registered in the notary offices. As Lynn and I discovered when we formed our corporation, there were still no computers, just big ledgers where the notary entered names and dates and numbers. Rumor has it that some notaries leave blank pages so they can fill in false dates and back date transactions. I sat down between Pancho and Davide on a black *faux* leather couch as Amador paced the room. Finally the attorney entered and Davide and Amador handed him their ID's. *Abogado* Rizzo talked to me briefly about the contract, did I understand and did I have any questions. Then he went to talk with the Notary but he came back out looking concerned.

He spoke to Amador and I watched Amador's brow furrow as he looked up at the ceiling and cursed quietly. The secretary heard him and scowled at him. He apologized quickly before he pulled me up from the couch and took me outside to explain that the ID was no good. He told me the notary wanted a passport or a military ID or something federal. His was just from the state. He needed a federal one. I felt defeated and felt my shoulders slump as I relaxed my grip on the bag I had been holding so tightly. Amador said nothing and I asked him what we could do.

He looked me in the eyes and said, "We need to go to Mexico City or we forget the whole thing.

I knew Davide wouldn't give any of the deposit back and I didn't trust anyone else to sign. Actually, I didn't know anyone else who would sign. I was focused on the concrete ground when Attorney Rizzo came to speak with us. He said he had an idea. He looked at me rather than Amador and told me that we could sign now and when Amador got his ID the notary will file the papers. That way, Davide can get his money and we can move the process forward. He looked at me and told me I could go back to the states until Amador got his ID in Mexico City and could formally sign. He said he would write a contract to clarify everything. I asked for a contract with Davide as well. Amador started to walk away. I think he had decided again that it was too much trouble but the notary came to the door and called us in. She was ready to have Davide and Amador sign.

I whispered to Amador, "when do we need to pay?"

But he just put his hand on my knee in a signal for me to wait. The notary brought us inside her office and took out the large ledger. She explained something to Amador and Davide and I was pretty sure she was telling them she would reserve this page and the appropriate line on the register for them. Attorney Rizzo brought out two hastily written contracts and the two started to sign. I felt as if I would vomit. They initialed each page and signed at the last page. After, we all shook hands with the notary, and then walked outside. Davide was looking at me and Amador took my hand and told me we were going to pay Davide at that moment.

"Here in the street?" I asked incredulously.

He fired a "no" at me and signaled to Davide that we would be back. He took my hand and led me across the street to a stationary store or *papeleria* across the street. We bought a pen and paper, wrote out a receipt for the 24,100 dollars that I owed Davide and made a copy of the receipt for the other money we have given him. Then he asked me for the cash. I looked around and moved into a corner of the store to count it out for him. He took it all and told me to wait as he crossed the street and asked Davide to sign. Davide signed and Amador handed him money, there on the sidewalk in front of the notary. Davide took it and put the thick wad of dollars into his pocket. Amador came back across the street to make copies of the signed papers and told me that we would all go to lunch as we waited for the copies. I told him I didn't want to. I felt sick to my stomach. But he told me, "You have to," as he took the copies and left me to pay for them.

Chapter 9

I had heard stories about Mexico City: dirty, dangerous, poor, underground cities and smog that burnt your eyes. I was excited to go, get Amador's ID and finish buying the land this trip. It didn't make sense to return to the US with the sale pending. Too, Amador's erratic behavior worried me although the entire concept was thrilling. We left *Saphiro* the next day, ready to make it happen. We had no reservations, no idea where we would stay and really no idea of how to get his identification. But we knew we could not get anything accomplished in Tulum so we headed to the airport, dropped the rental car and went inside to buy tickets.

I flinched when the Mexicana representative told us the next flight left in 4 hours and it would be $4000 pesos each. I had expected cheaper flights. When I hesitated, Amador got angry and nearly yelled at me saying he knew I couldn't make it happen.

I tried to explain that it was a lot of money but he shouted over me, "I told you not to start this if you didn't have the money."

I mentioned that I had not counted on this sort of expense but he wouldn't listen. Instead he raised his voice and told me that we needed to get his identification. Then he told me that if I couldn't help him he would find someone who would and started to look around the room, checking out other women.

I lowered my voice to make him lower his and to calm him, but also to be serious and not dramatic. First I told him not to be ridiculous and then I told him to give me a moment to figure it out.

He commanded, "Then do it."

I did not want a scene and needed a moment to work the figures out in my head. I knew we needed to go, I just had to feel comfortable spending the money. I could tell that Amador enjoyed my discomfort and his power over the situation. It confused me but I needed to finish this, secure the paperwork and my friend's investment. Too, I wanted it to happen for me. I reached into my bag for my American Express and said to no one in particular, "Cost of doing business," as I handed the card to the sales agent. In less than 8 hours we would be in Mexico City.

We arrived late and rented a car. I recommended a taxi, thinking of rental car costs on my credit card. He asked me if I wanted to be kidnapped, in a tone you would use on an ignorant child. I noticed that since I had paid Davide his attitude had changed. It didn't feel like love anymore. It felt more like entrapment. I knew Mexico City was a place renowned for crime and kidnapping. Holding people for ransom was only one of the articles I had read. But I had Amador. I had traveled the world. And as we said in college, I had a deal with God. Those things would not happen to me.

"Just like cancer wouldn't happen to me," that annoying voice from inside reminded me.

My credit card felt hot as the rental agent returned it to me with my license and Amador drove out of the lot. He pulled onto an overpass, telling me the agent would not care if he drove and we headed into the city.

I was desperately tired but excited at the same time as I watched the passing streets of the mega city fly by. Amador drove fast. I watched the people, the lights, the places passing from the car window. Suddenly, the thought dawned on me: no one knew I was there. I smiled feeling so free. I hadn't checked in with the people who loved me. Suddenly I felt the emotional stress of the past few days and I closed my eyes. They already stung from the pollution and it felt good to just let go of my consciousness. It was as if I were on a treadmill and couldn't get off. Amador kept pushing even accelerating. I was on full force during all my waking hours. If I had been incapacitated for the year of cancer treatment, I was making up for it now.

I opened my eyes as we came off the highway and into the *Zona Rosa*. It reminded me of the upscale Back Bay neighborhood in Boston and I was surprised that this was the same Mexico City I had read about. There were trees, four story walk ups and hip people wandering to and from street bars and cafes. This was not what I had imagined. I asked Amador if we could stay in this neighborhood. He grunted and told me it would be about $300 US.

Surprised, I asked him, "Seriously?"

He pulled the car over abruptly in front of one hotel and told me to go in and see for myself. I looked at him, not feeling capable. After all, it was Mexico City and my Spanish was not too good and I was so tired. But he looked at me as if he thought I couldn't do it. My red burning eyes narrowed at the challenge. He was not taking care of me the way I wanted but I would be damned if I let him intimidate me. I asked him how I would say it in Spanish.

He told me to ask, *"Tienes habitaciones?"*

I repeated the phrase in my head as he derisively asked me if I knew how to say how much. I left the question unanswered, opened the door and walked the stairs to the reception. It was gorgeous: large lobby, chandeliers, polite, if aloof, help.

I called on my whiteness to help me and walked to the desk with attitude and asked, *"Tienes Habitaciones?"*

The receptionist told me yes and when I asked how much she told me $250 US. She asked me if I wanted to see it and I told her yes. I wanted Amador to think I was renting it. I wanted to punish him for being so mean. She got a key and I followed her to the elevator and to one of the rooms on the 5th floor. It was beautiful but very much like a Hilton in the US. Compared to the lobby it was nothing special. I thanked her and she escorted me to the reception where I walked back to the car.

Amador told me, "Satisfied?"

I got back in only because I had no other option. I told him it was beautiful but not that special. He shook his head like he didn't believe me and then drove down the street slowly, looking for something.

Finally, with a smile, he said, "There," as he pulled onto a small exit ramp onto an elevated highway.

We left the highway a few exits down and entered a different neighborhood: more offices, fewer trees and more people on the street, some just walking, some preparing to spend the night. He said we would try here and then pulled over to ask a man in a business suit if he knew of a hotel. He directed us down an alleyway saying, "*Filipo's*."

The lobby of *Filipo's* was a diner of sorts. Amador sent me in again, although I didn't want to. I asked the now familiar question, "*tienes habitaciones?*" The concierge gave me the creeps. He had greasy hair, a white shirt with a stain where it tucked into black pants. I was humbled by his toughness and indifference. He showed me a room that was acceptable: clean enough and cheap, $50 per night. As we came back to the lobby, I motioned to Amador through the glass double door to come in. I told the man we would take the room as Amador came in with the bags and asked about parking. A part of me loved proving that I could handle things alone.

The concierge gave us a key to a different room than I had seen, saying they were all the same. The big surprise was that the room had a Jacuzzi tub. Amador started to fill it with glee while I pulled the sheets down to check for cleanliness. I thought nostalgically of Lynn and how she brought her own sheets to a hotel. I touched the sheets thinking of her and decided they were clean enough. I jumped into the shower and let the hot water steam my cares away while Amador waited for a full tub. I went to bed to the sound of the jets of the Jacuzzi and later woke to Amador sleeping next to me, snoring. I kissed him and went back to sleep, spooning in his body. He did not waken. We did not make love.

A sliver of light came into the room through the blackout curtains the next morning. I stretched and checked my cell. I touched

Amador and kissed him gently on the lips but he did not waken. I took a towel from the bathroom and used it as a yoga mat. I knew my practice would help energize my body and quiet my mind.

He woke when I was in shoulder stand and asked me, "Baby, what you doing?" before he farted loudly and blamed it on me, saying, "Honey, not again."

It was our joke. Adolescent, I admit, but I loved it. I laughed as loudly as he had farted and moved out of the posture to give him a kiss. He wrapped his arms around me but the smell was foul and I pushed him away. He laughed and went to the bathroom. I finished my yoga while he was there. He told me from the toilet that we would go see his family that day. I asked if he knew where they lived, joking. But I did have my doubts. The joke my father would tell about his family moving when he went to the war and him knocking on the wrong door on his return echoed in my mind.

We left without coffee and headed into the early morning city. It was a rush of traffic and dead ends as we searched for his mother's apartment. At one point, a tractor-trailer nearly backed into us as he moved into reverse to manage a left hand turn and get out of the traffic. Amador slammed on the horn since we could not move back with the total gridlock. The truck came a hair short of hitting us and then shifted back into drive to make the left and escape. Amador ran the red light to follow and we drove along a large boulevard that reminded me of most current downtrodden U.S. Cities: old industrial warehouses intermingled with 3 story houses that now were selling cable television, tortillas or used clothing. I liked the feel of the unplanned neighborhoods. I didn't feel threatened or shocked.

Amador pulled into a maze of one way streets, double parked and looked at me seriously, "Stay in the car and only move if the police come. Then don't go far."

I laughed, wondering if he thought I had never been in a city. He had no idea that I loved this type of neighborhood, albeit because it had never been my only option. When I hung out in China town and the mill districts of Boston it was because I liked it, not because it was necessary. When I was in the worst sections of the city, it was because I enjoyed the ethnic food, the music and I wanted to be bohemian. But I was not authentic. I always had my day job and my checking account. I was somewhat street wise from taking the train to get to an inner city high school and running from kids who wanted to beat me up. But I was the white nerd in a tough black neighborhood. I was not tough but I was not country or suburban.

Regardless, I waited while he went to the corner and looked up. He yelled, waited a few minutes and yelled again. A head appeared in the window. I could see him smiling but could not tell if the other person was. Regardless, in about 2 minutes, someone opened the door and Amador entered. I waited, like he told me to do, constantly looking in the rearview mirror for the police. No one came. Less than 10 minutes later, he came back to the car. I asked if they were coming down to meet me and he told me tomorrow. He said we would meet for breakfast at a place he knew.

I sighed and asked him, "Now what?"

He told me we would go get his identification.

We went back out to the boulevard. Amador maneuvered the streets while I enjoyed a sort of tour of the city. He drove relatively well although aggressively and I was free to just observe. He did not guide me or talk about neighborhoods or history but I could see and smell and feel one of the great cities of the world. It was as eclectic as my china: patterns from every aspect of life. The nice neighborhoods were super chic. The bad ones were so bad you could feel it. And the hills and valleys were pockmarked with derelict buildings that housed more than half the city's population. You could feel humanity there. The struggle to move above the person on top of you was palpable, an invisible lightning storm of emotional energy. The people who made it in this town were survivors, more so than I and in a very different way.

We found the neighborhood for government offices on the outskirts of town after having stopped half a dozen taxis and people on the street. The buildings were impressive, if not elegant with a mix of architectural styles: some very old, some distinctly 50's, and then a few patchwork projects of modern buildings. Amador pulled over and instructed me to wait in the car again. I did as he asked and watched him speak to a soldier. The soldier pointed to a building and Amador disappeared into it. I wrote distractedly in my journal, looked for him and watched people. Finally, after about half an hour, he came back to the car appearing tired and slightly frustrated. He sat behind the wheel and said we had to be back the next day with photos but now he wanted to get back to the hotel. I asked to walk in the city.

He agreed but for later saying, "You cannot go alone."
I wondered if the city were really that dangerous or if he were trying to control me.

When we got to the hotel Amador needed to sleep. I used the internet in the lobby to tell my family where I was. In all this anonymity and mass of human beings, I wanted someone who cared to know where I was. When I returned to the room an hour later, Amador was still sleeping. I wrote, I read and then I laid down beside him and tried to sleep. But I needed to get out and walk. Here I was in Mexico City and all I had seen was from a car.

I touched Amador's back and called softly, "*Amor.*"

Nothing.

"*Amor,*" more solidly this time.

Again nothing.

Finally I said, "Amador, wake up," and shook him.

He mumbled something and then sat up in the bed, looked at me, gave me a kiss and rolled over to go back to sleep. I pushed him once or twice and told him I wanted to go out. He said he would but then rolled over and closed his eyes again.

I shook him awake, and wined, "Lets do something."

He reluctantly agreed but then farted loudly and once again blamed it on me. I laughed at the joke and he got up and went to the toilet. I waited for him to shower and change and then we walked. It was already 5 p.m. We could easily walk to the downtown, to the fabulous *Palacio de Bellas Artes*, along the boulevard called *Reforma*. I loved it. We held hands. I felt safe. He explained everything about the city to me and would pull me back from the curb each time I got close.

"You want to get taken? Stand back. They can grab you so fast," he cautioned snapping his fingers to demonstrate.

He told me he would never see them and I would be gone. I didn't believe him and did not realize that I appeared wealthy to anyone who was even middle class here. I had no sense of myself in relation to this world and thought I could belong anywhere.

The next day we dashed out of the hotel early to meet his family outside a supermarket, not in front of the house. His mother, Fatima, his sister, Hayde and her deaf son, Carlos, and a baby girl, Amanda were waiting for us. I liked them even if I didn't understand much of what they said. His mother seemed timid and was checking me out. I knew she was not more than 10 years older than I. It made me self conscious. His sister was beautiful, chubby but she had a nice shape. She had died her hair blond and it looked interesting with her brown eyes and darkish skin. Amador called her "*gorda*," fatty. I could never get over how people did that in Mexico. If you were fat, they called you on it. Same if you were skinny or even ugly. And no one got offended. They just sort of said, "ok, that is how I am, big deal." I thought it was healthy but didn't really want to hear what they called me. I knew they said, "*gringa*," but didn't want to hear the adjectives to support it.

The six of us had breakfast together at 'Sanbornes', a Mexican 'Friendly's'. I would have preferred a nice café but it was a treat for them. The process took hours and the restaurant was packed. At the end I paid for us all. I felt somehow obligated and Amador didn't offer to help. The family couldn't. We all went to take photos. I paid again. It didn't feel good somehow and when we said goodbye's I was happy and sad to have met them. I would have liked for it to be different but when I asked myself how, I had no answer. But I had no time to contemplate how to change things since we were rushing to submit Amador's papers before the 2 pm lunch break. We made it only to be told to come back the next day.

When I asked Amador how many days we would need to be in Mexico, he told me curtly, "*I don't know.*"

I tried to be patient. I sensed he was on edge between the traffic, the family and this sort of urban living and I didn't want to push him. I was almost afraid so I practiced not saying anything.

Before heading back to the hotel, we drove back to the neighborhood where his family lived and drove around in what seemed like circles through neighborhoods of 5 floor walkups, gated houses and small variety stores. Finally, Amador pulled onto the sidewalk in front of a house with a large, ornate metal gate in front.

"Wait me here," he recited the now all too familiar line.

I slouched in my seat and pouted. He said he would only be a few minutes and went and knocked on the door. When no one answered, he yelled. After a moment, a bald man opened the door and looked suspiciously at Amador. After just a moment more, however, he smiled broadly, opened the door and embraced him saying, "Rodrigo" his family name: Rodrigo Amador Rosales Mandujano. I loved every one of the names for no particular reason.

It was like the German man I fell in love with skiing 15 years before: Bertram Otto Rudolf Slovokovski. I could still recite his name even though he had broken my heart when, after I followed him to Germany, I discovered he had a wife. I was praying not to meet Amador's Mexico City girlfriend.

They talked for awhile and then walked toward the car. Against orders, I opened the door and got out to say hello. Amador told me the gentleman was his cousin. We shook hands and then they continued to talk, discussing family and friend issues. He never invited us in. Never talked to me. Then, we all three got into the car and drove a few blocks to a large industrial space. The cousin took several locks off the door and opened it to show a huge vacant warehouse of sorts. Amador told me that they were thinking of building a bar and restaurant. I waited as he talked to his cousin but grew impatient and wandered outside. I didn't tell Amador, I just strolled out and stood by the door. There was a small stone wall in front of the place and the day felt remarkably cool so I sat there and watched the traffic, the trees and the people.

Suddenly Amador came out from the building looking around and, when he saw me, he nearly ran to me asking me angrily what I was doing. I looked at him as if he had two heads.

He commanded me to stay with him saying, "Why you have to be so stupid?"

I got angry and told him I was not stupid but that he was if he thought I would have problems.

He took my wrist too tightly and told me, "They gonna take you so fast."

But I looked at him and told him that no one was going to "take me" and pulled my hand from his.

He said, "No?" and took my arm tightly and nearly pushed me back into the warehouse.

His cousin was talking to someone on the phone and Amador continued to hold me until I pulled myself free of his grasp. Then, he took my hand. I rubbed my shoulder and decided that, although I liked him taking care of me, this was just too much. It was suffocating.We returned to the car and talked about what to have for dinner as we drove back to the hotel. Amador wanted Chinese. I succumbed and we drove to a place he liked. We were on *Avendia Reforma* when we got caught in traffic once again. *La Reforma* is a boulevard that runs into the city. It cuts through some of the nicest and most historical parts of Mexico City, the *Distrito Federal*, not the worst place to be stuck in traffic.

But as we neared the monument, I saw women standing in the green tree lined median strip. They had placards on their chests, like the ones vendors used in the 20's to sell things: big cardboard pieces which covered them in front and in back with writiing on them. As we moved past them, I noticed that they were all naked. They were indigenous women, with dark hair, full figures and they were all looking down. I expected to see Diego Rivera painting them from somewhere. I couldn't stop staring until we neared the rotary around the Angel of Independence. There we saw men on the base of the sculpture of the angel facing inward with their pants down around their knees baring their asses. Amador laughed loudly and he told me it was a political protest.

The contrast struck me of the women stripped naked in one of the wealthiest neighborhoods in Mexico. I couldn't get the image out of my head and didn't eat much when we went for Chinese. Amador was not bothered and devoured everything we ordered before we went back to the hotel to watch a movie.

When we finished, Amador told me, "I going to see my cousin again."

I shrugged and said OK not really caring until he said, "I need the car."

I automatically said no: fast, concise, no room for argument. So he told me he was taking it. I held my ground and said no again. He told me to give him the keys in a tone I did not like and I told him no again, reminding him he didn't even have a driver's license. He got up off the bed and went for my purse.

I grabbed the bag from him and said, "Go if you want, but not in my car."

He looked at me with a meanness I had not seen before. But I stared back at him, refusing to be intimidated. He lunged at me, pushed me away and pulled the handbag from my hands.

He dumped everything out, took the car keys and walked toward the door, saying "I be back in 2 hours," with a grin, knowing he had won.

Then he opened the door and left.

I was stunned. I thought of going after him, running down the stairs and into the street screaming as if it were a crazy idea. Then I did it. I ran down to the garage and looked for the car. He was driving out and I stood in front of him. He looked at me with a grin and stepped on the accelerator as if to hit me. I stood there.

He stopped, put his head out the window and said, "*Amor*, I got to do some things. Don be crazy."

I was angry and I felt crazy and I told him I didn't want him in my car. Suddenly, he pulled the emergency brake and jumped out saying that everything was mine. He threw the keys into the street and ran away. I stood still for a moment, digesting what had happened. People passing pretended not to notice. I came out of my trance and walked slowly to the keys in the street, picked them up and motioned to the attendant that I would go back in. I was calm, too calm. I got into the car, pulled into the street and turned it around to go back into the garage. Just as I did, Amador came to the window.

I jumped and he apologized as I asked, "What was that?"

He was kind again, my happy, nice man. He apologized and told me that he was not used to asking for things.

I told him, "So you just take?"

He said yes. I felt as if I were speaking to a child and I told him that was not the way things worked. Then he told me he wanted to do some things with his family. When I offered to come, he told me I couldn't. I told him to go in a taxi then, thinking of my German lover's wife. He got angry again telling me that would cost me a lot. I told him I had no intention of giving him money for a cab and he started to boil, I could see it in his eyes but he couldn't get the car from me now. I was in the driver seat. I had possession.

He started to explain things to me, that he would be right back and then he swore on his mother that everything would be ok.

I told him, "Don't swear on your mom" and he asked me what he should swear on.

He was begging when I told him not to swear on anything, just don't go.

Then he said to me, genuinely pleading, "Help me with this one thing. Look at all I am doing for you."

I could not answer and said nothing.

"*Por favor?*" he pleaded and I looked into his eyes and succumbed.

He promised to be back in two hours. I doubted it. But I got out of the car anyway and handed him the keys. I regretted it the minute I did it. He kissed me fully and dramatically on the lips and jumped in.

As he left he told me through the open window, "Go back to the hotel and stay there," saying he would not leave until I was inside.

I smiled. I liked that at least he cared I was ok and wanted to protect me. But I felt freer in the street, the air was better, I felt I belonged somewhere. I didn't want to go back inside.

I wanted him to take me with him and I stood there until he commanded, "Go."

Finally, I turned and walked back to the hotel imagining what the garage attendant thought. After I pushed on the glass doors and entered, I turned back to see he was gone.

I couldn't focus once inside. My mind went to all these terrible places, as I channel surfed through Mexican television. Amador was dead or arrested or with another woman. I tried to force the images from my mind. He left me. I would need to find my way through the city alone to the airport and get home. I was frightened to even go out.

I told myself out loud, "You have traveled all over the world without a man. You can handle this."

But he had the rental car.

"Report it stolen" that voice on my shoulder told me.

I picked up my cell phone to dial the police but abruptly called my mom instead. Surprisingly, I connected. I felt like I had all those times I had called her to come and get me out of some uncomfortable situation. But that was before when she had my dad. She was easier back then. Somehow against the background of a strong man, she didn't have to be the heavy.

I had interrupted dinner at my sister's house. I could hear the happy voices around the dinner table and I pinched myself for being such a child. They would all know. I knew they all thought I was being irresponsible just by being free and experimenting with my life. Regardless, I was happy to hear my mother's voice. We talked for awhile and I finally conceded, "I am so over my head in all this," hoping to have her save me somehow.

"Well, you have always been a good swimmer," my mother replied.

I smiled, then I laughed. We both did. She was setting me free too. Here I was in the most densely populated city in the world, where they routinely kidnapped people and where I didn't know a soul and my mom had all the confidence in the world that I could handle myself and manage the situation. It felt good, actually, in a difficult way it reminded me that I was responsible for myself, that I needed to take care of things and that I could. I hung up with "I love you's" and told myself that at that moment, all I could do was sleep. I filled the hot tub, took an atavan and went to bed.

At 2:00 am, I woke sleepily to Amador knocking on the door. I did not go to open it, not remembering where I was. He knocked again and I walked like a mummy to the door and asked who it was.

"*Mami*, it's me," Amador said.

I opened the door but went right back to bed, without saying hello.

He crawled into the bed next to me and said, "I always coming back to you. Don' worry."

I was asleep before he could finish but I felt my body soften and he slept there, spooning with me.

We took the next three days to get Amador his ID. Each day was a new tour of the city and another test of our perseverance. Amador was incredible, and I was incredible next to him. Each time one of us would lose heart, the other found it. When we had to wait, we did some sightseeing. We took a tour of the *Palacio de Bellas Artes*, the gold district, Mexico's City's Chinatown. The last day we picked up his ID we celebrated with lunch at *"La Polar"* a *cantina* Amador told me was famous. It was in the heart of the city in a *barrio* called *San Rafael*. We celebrated like tourists with soup, beer in huge steins, *mariachis* singing for us, and finally, photos of the happy couple. It was fun but I was missing the beach and Tulum and I was tired from the city and its pollution, traffic and drama. From *La Polar* we went directly to the airport to return the rental car and jump back on the plane. Amador drank while I watched from the window as we ascended from the megalopolis called Mexico City. Eventually, he fell soundly asleep and I looked at the clouds. It felt good to leave and to be floating in that relative space between two worlds: that of the air and that of the earth.

We landed with a jolt in Cancun. Amador woke and we started to move again. We walked down the stairs onto the tarmac like rock stars: Amador dressed in black, carrying my lime green designer bag. His curly hair was smooth and shiny around his shoulders with those sun-touched ends. He walked with purpose, sunglasses covering his otherwise bloodshot eyes. I followed, with my overly hip sunglasses, my ripped jeans, white t-shirt and red silk Puma sneakers. I didn't even look at the credit card bill when I rented another car to head to Tulum. It was more frightening than the city had been. But we would finally sign all the papers in earnest. It was a victory I relished because, deep in my heart, I knew it would be short lived.

Chapter 10

This time, there was no lunch or celebration. We signed the papers with the attorney in Tulum. No money changed hands, so no one else thought much of it. But I knew now was the time for real work. I needed to stop moving and focus. There was a lot to do to create my dream. Being a gypsy had been liberating for awhile, freeing me from my thoughts. Now it was exhausting and I couldn't think. My edge was giving way. I was tired of sleeping in hotels and other people's beds, alone except for when Amador was there and he was not there enough. Weary and sad, I wanted to go home. But I had to find it first. The Miami condo life and the anonymity of that city wasn't coming together. Tulum opened its arms to me but it held a whirlwind of distractions and obstacles. Boston held so many sad memories. "Find home in yourself and you will be at home anywhere," I heard that voice inside me say. I told it to, "Fuck off" and decided to spend some time at my sister's.

Calzi had always done things well, even when she lived with her family in nurse's housing she had guest rooms, champagne, good champagne glasses, and down comforters for the beach. Even if it was from the Christmas Tree Shop, she presented things well. Now, she had a big house on Cape Cod and had invited me to stay. I decided to go north and stay awhile.

I flew to Miami with papers in hand and took a solitary month to pack before I would head "home" to Cape Cod. I would come back to Miami in September and planned on going to Mexico in October to check the construction. Amador would take care of things there, making sure Jeraldo Bustamente our General Contractor was working. I had decided Gerry was good enough. Amador had introduced me to him and had shown me other projects he had completed. His quote for my project: a yoga salon, bathrooms and showers for after classes, two suites for cancer survivors and a penthouse suite for me was $40,000 US.

"Everything?" I asked, incredulous.

He assured me it was everything except for some permits. It seemed low, considering what I wanted. He saw me hesitate and told me again that he could do it for that price, winking at me and explaining he had good connections. I looked for help from Amador but he was smoking a joint with Mauricio on the other side of the room. Stalling, I asked Gerry for a formal proposal. I figured if he were serious and professional, he would get back to me. If not, nothing lost. We shook hands and he went to smoke with Mauricio and Amador.

The next afternoon he came to find me with a detailed 5-page proposal. That was it. I had a contractor. Amador would be my man on the ground. I just had to get Geraldo $10,000 US to start the project. As I packed to go north from Miami, I wondered how I would pay for the construction. Because I couldn't see the answer, I pushed it from my mind and focused on what would I need for the month up north. I would write alot, work on my business, be close to the bank and figure out how to make some money. The whole starting over thing was becoming more of a project than I had imagined. But I thanked God for the chance. Regardless, it wasn't a choice. I couldn't go back to whom or what I had been. And I didn't need to pay the government back for all my sick leave until November. I still had some cash to get me through and I would figure out how to get more money to build.

In the meantime, I ran, swam, wrote and practiced yoga at a studio called Nirvana in the basement of a Holiday Inn on north Miami Beach. The yoga classes and workouts at the gym or visits to a coffee shop were my only social situations. The rest of my days, I wrote, drew and dreamed away. It wasn't what I had expected. Without work outside myself, without friends, I had misplaced my sense of purpose. Each day I struggled to regain it. Little by little, it was coming. Sundays were the hardest days. I would sit in my window writing and drawing the life guard shacks that lined the beach: small huts, each designed with a different Dr. Suess-like motif.

They were colorful, linear and uniquely north Miami Beach.

After watching the beach fill with families preparing for a Sunday cook out, I put on yoga clothes, packed a bathing suit and walked the half mile to the studio where I would practice and search for my own Nirvana. Sometimes I would find it either there on the mat or on the beach walking home as I people watched and listened to the various languages they spoke. There was more Portuguese, Spanish and Russian than English. The body types were larger and more robust, the attitude more dramatic. I was less than a voyeur in their lives. I was invisible. It gave my existence a surreal nature that, after cancer, had become nearly normal. Yet I longed to be recognized.

After the second Sunday ritual of that month, I came home to check my phone. Three missed calls within minutes of the other: Amador. My heart did not bounce like it usually did. I felt sick in my stomach as the phone rang again and I answered.

"Where have you been?" his throaty voice demanded.

Before I could answer he told me he had an accident and that he was hurt badly and finished saying, "Baby you got to come today."

I sank down to the floor and sat against the wall, putting my hand to my head. When I asked him where he was, he told me he was at the police station and that they would not help him until I came for him. He was bleeding and needed me to come take care of him. I tried to reason with him and explained that there were no flights, but he cried into the phone that he would die there without me. I told him to get a grip and assured him he would not die. But when I said it he moaned that they were going to put him in jail and let him bleed to death.

He sobbed into the phone, sniffed loudly and then angrily told me, "If you don't come now I never want to see you again."

There was no sound for a moment and I almost thought he had hung up on me until a calmer voice came on and said he was a doctor in Playa del Carmen. He asked for me by name and I acknowledged who I was. Then he explained that Amador had been in a bad car accident and had broken his collar-bone. He had some other cuts, he told me and then continued to explain that he may need some blood, surgery and pain medicine.

He asked me very matter of factly, "Can you come to take care of him?"

I had to think quickly. I mean, why couldn't I? The man I loved was nearly dying as far as I could tell and couldn't I come for him? I committed to going the next day. The doctor told me that he would trust me to come and so would give Amador pain medicine. I was surprised that he needed me to be there before he would do that and then it dawned on me: he needed me to pay. I nearly vomited but then asked him where I should go. The doctor explained where he was and how to get there. I hung up the phone and booked a flight for the next morning. I would save my lover.

I contacted Amador's friend Gisela who had been managing the apartment where Amador and I stayed in town the time Fernando and Lynn had vacationed with us. She never answered my email. I let Alvaro my neighbor know what was happening in hopes he would meet my flight. No answer either. I was afraid I would get lost in the maze of one-way streets, slums and luxury hotels that made up my version of Playa del Carmen. Amador had always insinuated that even for him it was a dangerous and difficult place. I knew the police couldn't be trusted so decided to use a taxi if no one met my flight. I packed for 5 days and reserved a taxi to go to the airport the next morning.

When I came off the airplane in Cancun the next morning, Gisela was there. She had a beautifully crooked smile, bad but white teeth and happy eyes. She was a joy to be around: rotund with long brown hair and always up for a party or a chat. I was relieved and happy to see her. She was with a handsome man who had a car, "*mi ex marido*," she explained, her ex husband. Neither spoke English but knew where the hospital was. It was a clear Monday afternoon by the time we got there. The streets had that harshness that the afternoon sun imparts to tropical urban areas. The streets seemed empty and I attributed it to the low season, the heat and siesta hour.

We drove into the back streets of Playa looking for the hospital called *Hospiten*. Gisela had lived in the neighborhood before so we found it easily. We walked into the lobby and found the doctor who led me to a small door on the other side of his office. There was a police officer in front of the door. Gisela waited. The doctor passed him, opened the door and allowed me to go in. I inhaled sharply when I saw Amador on a small metal bed, handcuffed to the side covered in blood.

His hair was matted to his scalp and his face was dirty but the smile that came across it made me cry.

"*Amor*," he called to me and I made my way over to him with tears in my eyes asking him what had happened.

I knelt beside the bed and kissed him lightly on his cheek. I was afraid to touch him for fear of hurting him. He held me with his free hand as I asked him what they had done to him. He told me he knew I would come and moved his hand from my back to stroke my hair. I felt like a heroine. Gisela had come to the doorway and behind her was another police officer. I asked him then what he had done. He told me he had ruined some public property in the crash and the police wanted him to pay. I didn't understand and asked him if he was in pain. He told me he was better now that I was there. I felt whole. It was as if my lover, my child, and my soul were all together laying in that bed, hurting, needing me. It gave me purpose to save him.

I kissed him again. Gisela said something in Spanish to Amador. As they spoke I looked at the bed. It was dirty. His shirt was covered in blood at the shoulder and his feet were bare and covered in cuts. His knees were bruised and his shorts were filthy and torn. Amador saw me looking at him and he squeezed my hand and told me he had fallen asleep and crashed. I was speechless. I looked around the room. It was not cold but not hot. There was a noisy air conditioner in the only window. The walls were off white with nothing on them. The police officer was in the only chair. I stayed on the bed and Gisela stood. There was quiet for a moment.

Then the doctor entered and asked to speak to me outside.
I brushed the tears from my eyes and got up, squeezed Amador's hand and said, "Thank God you are alive."

I kissed him on the cheek, let go of his hand slowly and followed the doctor to the door. Once outside, he turned to me and said that Amador would need x-rays and surgery for his shoulder. We continued down the hall and into his office where he put some preliminary x-rays on a light screen and pointed to a break in his collar bone saying that if they did not repair it, Amador would lose the use of that arm. I wondered what he meant by, "not repaired." In my mind, we had to repair it. The doctor continued and told me that he needed to go to Cancun for the operation. He explained that he could arrange for an ambulance and a good surgeon in Cancun. He finished with, "But it is expensive."

When I asked how much he told me it would be around $5000 US, including the ambulance. I looked down and breathed deeply.

The doctor didn't wait for me to weigh my options, he asked me if I had 1500 pesos to pay for the x-rays, just like that. I realized with clarity now that the doctor wouldn't treat him unless I paid. But in that moment, I was numb to the numbers. I would have paid anything to get him out of there. I wouldn't leave a dog chained to the bed like that let alone the man I loved. Absent-mindedly, I asked him if he took credit cards.

The police removed Amador's handcuffs before the doctors moved him onto a stretcher to wheel him out of the room and into the ambulance. They got in with him and I went to join them but they stopped me. Gisela was behind me and I asked her to tell them that I needed to go with Amador. The attendants looked at us blankly until the doctor told me I could go with the driver. I nodded and moved to the front as Amador screamed for me not to leave him. I told him I would be in front but he didn't seem convinced. But I had no option so I let them close the door and tapped on the glass between us once I got in the front seat. It was the best I could do.

We entered the highway 307 to Cancun with the siren blaring. But no one pulled over so the driver really couldn't speed. He just drove very badly in and out of the traffic, trying to go fast without success. I was happy that Amador was not in worse shape. In under an hour we pulled into the emergency entrance of Hospitan and the attendants wheeled Amador through double doors into what looked like a meat locker. There were two other people on stretchers already waiting for a doctor. No one spoke to us for some time and a new police officer waited outside. Amador screamed with pain. The people on the other stretchers were also moaning and looking for help. It seemed to be an inferno. I held Amador's hand.

For some reason, the nurses refused to acknowledge me until finally a doctor came in. He nodded at Amador and took his hand, lifting it to check his range of motion. Amador screamed as the doctor calmly asked me if I spoke Spanish.

"*Pocito*," I said honestly.

He asked if I spoke French and I told him English.

"He will need xrays," he said to me as he touched Amador's shoulder and Amador moaned deeply.

I handed him the ones from Playa del Carmen but he told me

they were not enough without even looking at them. He sent me to an office behind the emergency room where I could pay. He candidly asked me if I had cash. When I told him I could pay he told me they would not take a credit card. His eyes were on the diamond cross around my neck. I felt him judging who I was and where I was from. His gaze moved to my eyes and I held him there. I believe he saw something there, perhaps love, perhaps *naivete*, perhaps just hurt and he softened. He told me in a softer tone to talk to them in the x-rays and he could start things.

He said, "In the mean time I will get him, Rodrigo?"

Amador shook his head and said, "Rodrigo Amador," with his famous roll on the final "r."

The doctor finished his sentence saying, "some pain medicine."

I kissed Amador, squeezed his hand and went to find the xray office. There was only an access from outside the hospital. I walked outside in the waning hours of light and pushed on the glass door. I finally made them understand that I needed xrays for someone in the hospital and they told me how much. I nodded agreement and the gentleman looked at me, waiting. I asked him if he needed something more. He said I needed to pay. I was surprised that they wouldn't wait for payment until after the xrays but I shrugged and asked him how much. He told me 3000 pesos but when I took out my credit card, forgetting what the doctor had told me, the man shook his head and told me "cash": the universal concept. I only had 2500 and asked if he would accept that to start and I would pay the rest later. He refused and told me I had to pay it all. I couldn't believe it but I walked out the door to find an atm. After a short tour of Cancun City Center, I came back with the full payment. After I handed it to him and he laboriously gave me a receipt, we walked together to the emergency room.

At the end of the day we moved upstairs to a nearly empty but large room with a private bath and one big window overlooking the roof of the hospital. The bed was a single stretcher and they moved Amador onto it. He moaned a lot, not one to suffer in silence. It was embarrassing. I mean, I knew he was in pain but couldn't he "suck it up," as my brother the marine always told me. T-Bird had endured much worse in the 3 wars where he had served and, to be honest, probably so had I.

Finally they gave him intravenous pain medicine and he quieted.

I sat in the one chair and wrote for awhile, drawing him, drawing the room and writing in between the poor sketches. I wondered what I would do, what I was doing. Then I would look at him and not doubt anything. I wanted to save him, now more than ever. I had no idea how he had been driving and fallen asleep. But the idea that he had been smoking crack cocaine for days on end and was driving to get more before his body collapsed was nowhere in my mind. The idea that he had been doing it with all of his friends, Gisela included was even farther from my reality.

After a few hours, I went into the hall to move around and was surprised to find a police office waiting at the door. I nodded at him and then went back inside. Amador was still sleeping. I waited and finally the doctor came in. He told me that the fracture was bad but clean and that he could fix it. He said he could perform the operation the next day and that he would give me a time in the morning after he could see what was available. He told me the nurse would keep Amador comfortable with pain medicine and he checked the IV on Amador's arm. I took the opportunity to ask him what the police officer was doing outside the door.

"They have some business with your husband," he told me.

I allowed him to use the word and said it was just an accident but my tone implied a question so that he could correct me if I were mistaken. He didn't say anything other than that he would talk with them for me. We passed a moment or two in silence before I asked him what the police might want. He told me he was not sure but that he thought he might need to pay the state for some damaged property.

He finished telling me, "Be patient," and then he extended his hand,said, "Until tomorrow," and walked out the door.

As he shut the door I started to cry. I let myself sob at the injustice of it all and then pulled myself together and, since Amador was still sleeping, walked out the door, past the policeman, down the beige hallway, to the open stairway, through the lobby and into the street. The heat wrapped itself around me like a soft blanket. I had been in closed and air conditioned spaces since the day began just about 12 hours before. Suddenly, I was very hungry and followed my instinct to a café on the *Avenida Tulum*. I ordered a sandwich and a cappuccino and felt that certain bliss that comes with exhaustion. I didn't care that I was a woman sitting alone. I focused on the food and wondered what the hell I was doing.

Suddenly someone touched me and pulled me from my stupor. It was Gisela. She was with two other friends who I absentmindedly greeted. I didn't really want company but she introduced me to her friends: one a very thin woman with long brown hair, Akim and one a thin Mexican man named Moises. The Italian spoke English and told me that it was Moises' car. I didn't say anything more than, "oh," when she told me. We made small talk for awhile and they ordered a coffee.

At one point, Moises looked at me and said, "You know, I can make trouble for Amador if he doesn't pay me for the car."

The women became quiet all of a sudden. I just asked him what he meant. Moises told me he could "demand" Amador. I was cool, too tired to get angry and I asked him to explain what, "demand," meant. He said it was a process whereby he might put Amador in jail. Suddenly the police presence made more sense. I was quiet and looked out at the street to think. I couldn't handle any more so I put it into the file cabinet in my brain labeled "can't handle that now".

"What do you think?" Moises asked me after awhile.

I turned my head toward him and inhaled. Then I exhaled and still said nothing.

I locked my gaze with his and wearily said, "If you think I will pay for your car, you are mistaken."

I took another breath and he looked down as I said, "That is between you and Amador. Talk to him."

I shocked myself with the forcefulness of the statement but I did not show it. I turned and asked the waiter for the check.
"Together or separate?" the waiter asked in Spanish.

I looked into Moises eyes, reached for my walled and said, "Separate."

Chapter 11

Gisela and I walked behind Moises and his girlfriend. We barely talked. Not that I had nothing to say, it was just too difficult to say it in Spanish and too tiresome to make Gisela understand my English. Once we reached the hospital, we all went into Amador's room. Amador took my hand immediately and kissed it, wincing dramatically from the pain as he did so. I touched his face and whispered in his ear that he needed to talk to Moises. I wanted them to discuss things alone and looked at Gisela and Akim to leave, but they did not move. I shook my head and closed the door but waited outside for awhile to hear voices. There was nothing. I imagined getting a glass to eavesdrop against the door but noticed the police officer still there. I changed my mind and decided to get some fresh air.

I sat in front of the hospital for what seemed like only a few moments imagining what they were saying upstairs. I watched people come and go, wondering what they were doing, wondering what happened to bring them here. Finally, Moises, Gisela and Akim came out the door. Moises looked sullen and dark. The two women were quiet. Akim seemed ready for something, quick to smile but the smile faded just as quickly. She was playing with her long brown hair, pulling split ends. I had nothing to say to any of them. But I did not want to be rude and asked how things went. Moises told me Amador would try to fix things. He said it sort of sideways, not looking in my eyes. He was thin and pale and his dark long hair made him look more sinister than sympathetic. I told him I hoped it would all work out and I meant it. After all, he had lost his car. He told me he might see me the next day, Akim said "*adios.*" Gisela gave me a hug and they left together.

I watched them walk away feeling weary. Finally, I stood with great effort and walked up the stairs to Amador's room. As I crested the last landing, I saw an empty chair where the police officer had been. For a moment, I was elated: one less thing to worry about. But when I came around the corner, I saw the officer standing, talking with the nurses. Disappointed, I nodded to them before pushing open the door to Amador's room. He immediately asked me where I had been. I told him I was outside giving him some space. He reached his uninjured arm out to me and told me he didn't need space. He needed me.

My gaze moved from the needles in his arm to the cuts on his face and then to his smile. I started to sob. He asked me what was wrong and invited me to come over to him. I went to hold him gently and tried to pull myself together but couldn't.

He told me, "Oh *Amor*, I gonna be alright, don worry."

I told him I knew he would be fine but that I was so tired and weary and sad.

I stopped to sniff and then finished saying, "it seems our dream is turning to a nightmare."

He patted my back softly and told me it was all going to be ok. But I was not ok. I told him how Moises wanted me to pay for the car and how he said he would put Amador in jail. I sobbed more. Amador touched my hair and kissed my neck softly to calm me down, telling me it would all be fine. I suddenly lost the energy to cry or talk or even think. Amador invited me to lie down with him. I crawled into the bed and got as close as I dared. I felt the warmth of his body and inhaled his smell of hospital and iodine and fell asleep. Later on, the nurses woke us but I didn't move. I was not going to let anyone take that comfort from me.

Early the next morning, I had a cold shower, took a blanket from the shelf and practiced yoga on the floor. Amador slept until the doctor knocked to come in. He sat with me a moment while the nurse helped Amador to the bathroom. He told us that they would operate on Amador in a few hours. I was happy. Amador was afraid. The doctor left and Amador and I talked before he drifted off to sleep. Then two male nurses came to bring him to the operating room. There was a police officer behind them. I could not believe they would stay with him through the operation and wondered what he had done to bother them so. Amador cried like a baby as he left the room and begged me not to leave him. The nurse had to take his hand from mine. He would not let me go. I told him that everything would be ok and waved as the swinging doors blocked him from my sight. I wanted to cry but inhaled to fight the urge and went to the café on the *Avenida*.

I stayed with him the next three nights in the hospital. We shared hospital food and hospital sheets. I cleaned him and got him extra medicine when he couldn't stand the pain, which was often. I made him laugh and practiced yoga on the floor in front of him. He made me smile and we played cards and watched television. He always wanted to touch me so I stayed close. I wrote and drew while he slept, drawing hospital scenes on some pages, drawing his face on others and then filling between the lines with my words and thoughts. I couldn't think of anything nicer. I still cannot.

Chapter 12

The police left just before us, handing me a paper Amador needed to take to the police in Playa del Carmen, where he had the accident. We moved to Amador's sister's house the same day. Gisela had found Hayyde and brought her to the hospital. Here, she had more substance, more color, more life than when I met her in Mexico City. It was as if city living in her mom's high rise apartment sucked the life out of her. She and Amador hugged and laughed more than in Mexico City. After she left, Amador told me we could stay with her saying he wasn't ready for Tulum.

I laughed and said with a smile, "I am not sure Tulum is ready for you."

We took a taxi to Hayyde's modest town house on the fringe of downtown Cancun. The doors had security bars and were padlocked even when they were inside during the day. The living room was small and dark with wall-to-wall carpeting and soft, oversized furniture. It smelled moldy. The big windows also had bars and plants growing over them from the outside that kept the light out. The 2 children slept together in bunk-beds just off the living room. Carlos, the deaf son, was jumping up and down to show us when we entered. He took Amador's hand and made noise without words and used sign language. When he calmed down, Hayyde showed us the small kitchen packed full of stuff and organized around a dining table and chairs. It was hard to maneuver but opened up to a small overgrown, unkempt back yard enclosed with a wall and barbed wire. Bugambilias sprawled over the barbed wire, their red and pink flowers turning brown on the tall grass. Two canaries sang from a small cage just outside the back door. I could not help but wonder if they were fed regularly. The family lived downstairs. Hayyde told me that the second floor was unfinished and their two Sharpee dogs lived on the roof. They never took the dogs outside and I am not sure if they ever cleaned upstairs. I didn't let myself go there: not my place, not my culture.

Hayyde and her husband Jacobo had moved from their bedroom to the living room to give Amador and me their room. We did not sleep well. Amador was in pain. He tossed and turned and groaned loudly. The room was packed with stuff: toys, clothes, accessories, furniture. I could barely get in the door, let alone make space to practice yoga. But I managed a short practice on a sliver of moldy, hairy carpet. The bathroom was the same: packed with stuff. There was no space to put even a toothbrush, let alone my face cream. I tried to appreciate their hospitality, and enjoy the little things. But it was difficult. I needed to get out but Amador hated it when I left him. He would actually cry and almost demand that I stay. I attributed it to the drugs.

The next day, Hayyde and I rented a car and drove to Playa to talk to the police. We had the paper they had given me. Hayyde wanted to avoid future problems and we both knew Amador would never do it. We found the building easily, stopping only twice to ask someone. It was an ugly city office building with an open space crammed with metal desks that were stacked with papers so high they almost hid the police officials sitting behind them. We waited and watched the police officers come and go until they called us to one of the desks in the corner of the room. Hayyde demurely explained the situation, omitting the fact that her brother was probably drunk or worse. Finally, after more than an hour of waiting and explaining, they stamped the paper without fining us, put it into a file and gave us a copy. After saying thank you several times, we walked out the door quickly and congratulated ourselves in the car as we rushed home.

Amador got better and more demanding each day. He wanted to come everywhere with me but he was slow and loud, sharing his situation acoustically, groaning and moaning as if he were dying. Too, everything became a dramatic family affair. The entire family came to the grocery store the next day. Amador limped over to one of their automated wheel chair cars, with his arm in a sling and bruises still on his face. He could barely drive but he was determined to do so and he took his nephew with him to help. Screaming with laughter, they moved in staccato bursts alternating pressure on the gas and the break until Amador got the rhythm down.

His face was still black and blue and it contrasted weirdly with the bright orange cart. His nephew sat next to him signing words to give him directions under the high Mexican flag extending from the back of the vehicle to identify them in the aisles. We sent them for items that were far away to see if they could find them and then us when they returned. It was absurd but childishly fun. I bought the groceries, cooked for them all at that night and wondered how long I could manage it.

The next morning I woke early, practiced cramped yoga in the dusty space between the bed and the door and then snuck out for a coffee and to find an internet cafe. The morning air was clear and I enjoyed being by myself, walking in the city. I people watched with a cup of coffee before I found an internet cafe at the end of the road. There was not much news, no new emails, no new work so I walked up the road to sit in the park before going back. As I nearly turned the corner to the park, I faintly heard my name called from behind me. It was Amador's half cry, half command to stop. I turned to see his big hair framed in the morning sun and his silhouette with his arm in a sling and the button down shirt I had bought for him to leave the hospital. He impatiently yelled for me to stop and wait. I loved that he was so attached to me and waited for a moment, absorbing the blue sky and his aura of smokey orange as the sun rose behind him. He nearly had a halo. I walked slowly back to him and kissed him gently on his black and blue lips.

He pulled away and demanded to know where I had been. I laughed and told him I had been working. He looked at me suspiciously and I laughed again. His jealousy was beyond my comprehension and I mistook it for a demonstration of love when he scolded me not to leave him. I held him gently there in the road and surprised myself by starting to cry. He held me tighter to make me stop but the closer I got to him, the harder I cried. All the tension from the last 6 days came out of me. I sobbed everything into his arms.

He patted me on the back and tried to make me stop saying, "*Amor*, don' cry. Don' cry. I gonna be fine."

I pulled away from him, looked into his eyes, sniffed, and finally told him, "I know Amador, it is me I am worried about."

He smiled, kissed me softly and walked me to the park where we sat for awhile, silent, just holding each other. We seemed so together in that moment. In hindsight, I know we were very far apart.

Chapter 13

"Let's go to Tulum and check on the proyect," Amador asked the following day.

I jumped on the idea, tired of being in other people's spaces. I looked forward to a trip with him. I needed time to talk candidly about things, about what his responsibilities and where he would stay after I left. I wanted to make sure he would be ok and thought I could organize things enough to continue to take care of him. But when we mentioned to Hayyde that we were going, she immediately included herself and the kids in the plan. I took a deep breath. It would be another long family day. I vowed to enjoy it.

We loaded into a rental car and headed south, Amador and I in the front and Hayyde and the two children in back. No radio so we could only talk. At one point in the drive Amador turned to me and asked about Gisela saying that perhaps she could help with Gerry who was not advancing in the construction. I told him that was his job. He laughed and told me to take a better look. I reminded him he would be better soon and that he needed to contribute something to the project. He hesitated a minute or two and then told me she could help with the paperwork at least.

I smiled. Gisela: his *comadre*, godmother. He was so wonderfully amusing to me. It was as if he were in the land of lost boys and Gisela was Wendy, there to take care of them all. But I wanted that job. Or did I?

Amador said, "Well, *amor*, you always going back to the states and leaving me here. I need some help."

I laughed and asked him what he thought I had been doing this last week. He touched me and said he understood but that Gisela needed a job. I wondered out loud how much I would have to pay her and mentioned to him that I had been spending too much. He didn't register the comment and only suggested we go to her house and ask her.

I agreed and took the right turn off the highway into Villas Tulum, a subdivision with masses of identical concrete boxes they called houses. The streets were numbers and Amador maneuvered us around them until we came to Gisela's house. I knew it by the pareo with a gecko hanging over a broken screen that she used for a window curtain. It was still early by Tulum standards and Gisela was just waking up. She let us all in and made coffee.

I strained to understand as she and Amador talked in rapid Spanish. But I got enough to know that she was unsure of the work and what she could do to help. Amador said he would help her.

I wondered who would help whom before she looked at me and said in her beautifully broken English, "I try to help as best I can."

I smiled and gave her a hug. Then I looked at her and asked her how much in what I hoped was beautifully broken Spanish. Amador threw out 200. I looked over at him and told him I could not. He got annoyed, stood up and walked out the door. I calculated quickly and told her 100 dollars a week. I knew I could manage that, nothing more. I waited. If she agreed I was committed. If not, I was off the hook in one sense but on it in the other: who would take care of the property if not Amador. I was confused since our deal was for him to work the project, not just to sit around while I paid someone else. He was turning it all around now. If Gisela was taking care of everything, what would he do? His remedial concept of "boss" was amusing at times but becoming annoying.

I came back to the moment when Gisela said, "*sí*" with a smile.

The voice on my shoulder said, "fuck" but I extended my hand to her and invited her with us to go to the land. We walked into the trash strewn street where dogs ran wild and children ran far from their parents to find Amador just standing by the car. He was leaning on the side smoking a cigarette. I gave him a dirty look as we all got into the rental car, now with 4 in the back, and drove out to the beach. I asked Amador if he had the key to the gate.
"Gisela have," he said absent mindedly.

It was as if he had suddenly shut off, gone somewhere far away. Gisela reached into her bag and happily pulled out a set of jingling keys. It made me wonder. Had Amador been doing anything all along? I pushed the thought from my mind since I could do nothing about the past. I could only work on the present and perhaps the future.

We crossed the break by Zama's and my heart and spirit lifted. The view from that point out into the Caribbean always made me happy. After the police check point, the road turned from bad to worse and we bumped along for what seemed like miles of palm trees, past Amansala and then several hundred more meters to my place on the jungle side of the road. My neighbors were building too. But I had paid for the fence that ran along the common side of the property. I wondered about that but then forgot it when we opened the door. The land had been cleared and there were large pieces of wood of about 6 meters in length on the ground just as you entered. Empty plastic coke bottles were all over the place. There was a small concrete structure for a bathroom and the beginning of two structures, one that would be a yoga and meditation palapa and another that would be a three story palapa with two suites for cancer survivors and one suite for me and Amador to live on the third floor. Some of the supports were there, most were definitely missing. I noticed more wood out back as I walked further into the property alone. The kids started to play, Amador walked back to the road and Gisela and Hayyde stood around and waited. I needed to think.

I climbed to the first level that reminded me of old half finished industrial buildings by Boston Harbor: it was a mess. I looked at the cement floor and asked myself what I had done as I looked into the palms and then into the sky and prayed to God to help me.

"What was I thinking?" I asked myself. Then I sat down and tried to clear my mind.

I didn't hear Gisela when she came up behind me until touched my shoulder and said, "We can make it happen. I will help you."

I smiled and nodded ok before I noticed the tears running down my cheeks.

Before I left Cancun, I booked a hotel for Amador so that he could recuperate close to his sister. It was just a block from the Hospital.

"I cannot be here longer," I told him when I brought him to the hotel.

The hotel had a pool and his sister could come and stay with the kids. The doctor wanted to see him again in a two days but my 5-day visit had already turned into 7 expensive days. I was devastated leaving and he was angry that I would go. He begged me to stay but I needed to figure out how to pay for the hospital, our project and for myself. I wanted to bring Amador with me to the states but it was impossible. Even if I married him it would take months and somehow that didn't seem feasible or wise. Slowly, I was learning what a marriage to him would mean. And although I loved losing myself to him, something held me back from taking that final step. Without marriage, there was no chance that he would ever get a visa. We talked about it. I wanted it to happen and I told him what he needed to do. Then I did something uncommon and difficult for me. I let it go. I held him responsible for that at least. If he started things, I would help him finish. But he had to start. I kissed him from the taxi window and headed back to Miami, certain that he was ok.

Just a week after I returned, my mom flew down to Miami and we drove north together. We loaded the car and got two Cuban coffees from across the street to start the trip up A1A, the old coastal highway that went from Florida to Maine. I was moving again. I wasn't exactly excited about the trip but I wasn't sure what else to do. I was confused and needed to be around people who loved me, who I could trust and who would take care of me. My grip on life was slipping and Amador was sucking me dry.

I was afraid of going back to my old job and at the same time of not having it. I was trying to do art and write and publish my books and rent my place and build in Mexico and keep it all together while I felt very, very alone. The tamoxifin I was taking made me feel weird, teary, bloated and nauseous and I was sweating uncontrollably. I went everywhere with a towel. Calzi and her girls had always been my touch-stone. I decided to take help from them once again. I had plenty of work so I would be away often. I needed to go to Pennsylvania to work the foundation and my books and to New York to talk to publishers. I had other family and friends to visit as well. Too, Calzi worked long hours so we would not be on top of each other.

But the truth was, I wanted to be around her. Somehow my little sister, the one I was supposed to take care of, had been taking care of me, physically and emotionally for awhile now. I felt a comfort with her that was uncommon. She had raised her two girls alone, survived a horrible marriage and financial distress and had risen to come out shining. I was in awe of her and happy to have the opportunity to be living close.

She met us with champagne at the doorway and told me to stay as long as I wanted.

Then she smiled and said that, "when the weather gets cold I think we should go to Miami," and put her champagne glass out for me to touch.

I felt loved. She gave me the guest room with my own bath and room in the driveway for my Saab convertible. I was close to the kitchen but far enough away from everything. I could plug into her internet and use her desk. I had a certain paranoia about intruding into her family space and maintaining my privacy so I quickly fell into a routine of making myself slightly invisible. Too, I didn't want them to know everything I was doing in Mexico. I didn't share the fact that I was sending money to someone to build my place. I couldn't maintain my strong denial that something was wrong if they confronted me, so I held my cards close.

I got up after everyone left in the morning and went out several nights a week. But there were wonderful nights when we were all there. I forgot my feelings of failure and stopped wondering if the girls thought it was weird that I lived there and allowed myself to enjoy being around my family. I tried not to let my insecurities ruin our time together. One night after dinner and a bottle of wine, Calzi asked me how it was going and I started to tell her about Amador and his accident.

"My God Fans, how could you go there and pay for everything?" she asked me.

I tried to explain but wasn't sure she understood. When I told her about the police and that he was chained to the bed, she didn't seem shocked. When I told her how he screamed in pain for so long she mentioned that drug addicts feel pain a lot more severely, especially when they are not getting their drugs. I asked her why she was telling me this and she said he seemed to be having more pain than normal for that injury. Then she reminded me he smoked a lot and told me she was just putting two and two together.

"You might give it a thought," she told me as she gave me a kiss and went to bed.

I vowed not to confide in her again but couldn't sleep for a while.

That weekend, I went to Pennsylvania, paying attention to the fact that it always felt good to drive out of Boston. It was a message. I would work with Sheba and Paul, my muses. With them, I was creating art and finishing my emotional support books. We were self publishing my emotional support books and creating a non-profit foundation for women with breast cancer. It was a fantastic project. But, when I would talk with them about Amador or when he would call, they would smile and shake their heads. Paul would tell me to get real. Sheba told me I would find someone more suitable. And although it sounded so class conscious, deep down I knew he was not suitable. But I didn't want it to be true. Somehow I had taken on this man as a project. I would make the world see it that our love could work. It had to. I believed I had nothing else. So, even there, after a few days I would feel the familiar urge to leave.

"Houseguests and fish start to stink after 3 days," I would quote, and pack my bags.

After my experiences at Fernando and Lynn's, it felt wise to keep going and sharing myself with people sporadically. Even though everyone said, "Stay with us," I knew very few people who really meant it. I hoped Calzi was one. Sheba and Paul were my gamble for the others. But I needed to learn to live a gypsy life, just in case.

One night driving north from Pensylvania on I-95, I stopped at the rest area. As I nearly ran toward the entrance, a kitten came running out toward me, as if it knew me. It ran right under my feet and I stopped quickly to pat it. It would not let me move forward until I finally picked it up and put it into the bushes. I loved that it loved me. On the way out, I stopped to get some chicken McNuggets in case the kitten was still there. Knowingly, the kitten was waiting and followed me to a picnic table where I helped it devour the nuggets. When we finished, I couldn't leave or rather, I didn't want to leave it. I asked a person sitting close who looked local if they knew of a shelter close by. They said it was horrible and quickly added, "we have 2 dogs at home," before I could ask them to take the kitten. I called Calzi. She didn't pick up. I called 3 times more and then called Megan, and told her about the kitten.

"Bring it home. Mom won't mind," she told me confidently.

That was all I needed. I put it into the car. At first it clung to the inside roof, hanging upside down. It stayed there as I went to get gas and I wondered how I would make the 3 hour drive home with a frightened cat on the ceiling.

But as I pulled out into the traffic, it settled in on the floor and slept the whole way. I loved having it there, having the company. I loved rescuing it. When I got home, Megan found a box and we put the soft ball of fur in there and into my bedroom. Megam asked me what we should call it.

I told her, "Lucky, because he is lucky he found me."

Megan told me she liked it but said, "Lets see how lucky he is after mom finds out," with a smirk before she kissed me and went to bed.

The next morning, she stayed in her room while I listened to the lecture.

"I will not be the crazy cat woman of Falmouth."

My sister was on a roll and asked me how I could possibly bring the cat to her house. She wouldn't even see it and told me to find a place for it. I brought Lucky to the vet and called Lynn as I waited for him to have his shots.

Lynn told me to bring him up here to the city and she would find someone for him, saying, "Poor little guy."

That night after bringing the cat to Lynn, I knew Calzi would not want to see me so I went to visit my mom at my sister Kathy's. Kathy had a beautiful house on the beach with a nice apartment for my mom. Both my older sisters were together. They had good marriages, nice children, stable jobs and homes. I felt inadequate around them but Kathy was away so I was happy to see just my mom. We made dinner and sat on the back porch to watch the nearly full moon rise. It was a beautiful mass of yellowish orange against a dark blue sky, lines of clouds stretched across the horizon in front of it. I had a split of champagne that we shared as I thought how everyone would be watching this moon, Tulum, Afganistan, California, Hawaii. It was a miracle that we were so far away but still could experience common things in nature. I thought of Amador, full moons were his downfall. There were always too many parties and too much energy in Tulum.

My mom and I sat in silence for awhile watching the moon and sipping champagne. Finally we talked about how my brother in law would help me work my foundation and how I wanted to invite them for dinner but it was weird in other people's houses.

I added, "especially now with this cat thing."

My mother agreed and then asked about the cat. I told her that Lynn would take care of him. My mom smiled and said that the cat would be spoiled sooner than we could imagine.

Then she put her hand on my leg and told me, "It was a good thing you did. Calzi is frantic right now. Two teenage girls are not easy."

I thanked her for saying it, and assured her I was not sorry for taking the cat, only sorry I upset my sister when she was being so good to me. "She certainly got to vent. I had no idea she was so concerned with her image," referring to the crazy cat woman remark. "I think that is why I am so attached to Mexico. I have no image there," I said naively not realizing that I did in fact have a big image. I really wanted to have my own place and to help cancer survivors. I told her she needed to see the place.

I was almost talking to myself. "Maybe it keeps me hanging on too tightly."

My mother let silence answer me.

I wondered out loud if I could take care of everything.

"I mean look at me. I am trying to do all this stuff to take care of other people. For God's sake, I can't even rescue a cat and I am going out with a homeless guy."

My mother, I'm sure, was wondering the same thing.

I chuckled. "I should be going out with the president, well not *this* president but you know what I mean."

She smiled knowingly. "You could, but you wouldn't like that kind of man."

It was true. I was getting pretty comfortable on my own.

She sighed that men could be difficult. Her eyes reflected the light of the moon.. Her blond hair fell softly around her face and I marveled that even this woman who had been with my father for 48 years and slept beside him on the day he died, knew that it wasn't easy being with a man, even if he was a great man.

"Thank God for chemistry," I said.

We both laughed and took a drink of champagne. I silently thanked God for the moment and for my mom. Amador called the next day, the first call in nearly two weeks. He asked for money.

Chapter 14

Shortly after that, I went back to Miami. It was enough time living in other people's lives and having them live in mine. In Miami, I was free. If I wanted to pick up a cat from the highway, I could. If I wanted to send money to a man, I didn't have to hide it. I decided I liked the anonymity of the place, my Cuban coffee and pastry across the way and the great yoga studio up the street. There I answered only to myself. I was lonely but getting used to it.

I worked most of the day on That Barry Girl Foundation issues at the oversized kitchen counter, right next to the best painting Harry had ever done.

It was a 5 by 6 foot canvas he had hauled home from the trash saying "Fanny darling, I cannot believe someone would throw this away."

I told him I could. The painting was horrible, a mess of dark colors with no form or cohesiveness. He scolded me saying that he didn't want the painting, he would use the canvas and paint over the other artist's work. From the original mess, he created a beautiful landscape, colorful and textured. It was during a time when I loved him so much. He labored over it for weeks after I thought it was finished.

"Laquer the shit out of it and it will get more depth," I remembered telling him.

He looked at me as if I had no right to say anything about painting. I told him meekly, that was what Sheba told me. He respected her as an artist.

"Fanny Darling," was all he said, dismissing me.

But the next day he started laquering the shit out of it, so I was vindicated. I never got smug about it. I knew I was right, again.
But there I was, next to this piece of art and very far from him. Actually, I was surrounded by his art. When Harry moved out, he never came back for a lot of his things. I had to go through all of them, throwing a lot away, giving a lot away with seemingly endless trips to Goodwill. But I couldn't throw the paintings away. When he never came for them, I moved them to Miami with me. In the oversized living room with the view of the ocean, surrounded by all that art from someone I used to love, I would write and call people and look out at the ocean and notice how fast the days went until I would go up the road for yoga.

One afternoon, I was finishing work when the phone rang. It was Charlie, my nephew. I told him about the storm that I could see moving down the coast as I watched a wall of darkness come down from Ft Lauderdale, north of me. It was charcoal colored, moving fast and full of lightening.

He told me impatiently, "Joanneo, I think that is the hurricane I was calling to tell you about."

I had no idea and he asked me if I even had a radio. I told him no but I was sure I would be ok as the windows started to rattle. I told him I would go downstairs to check but commented that it was certainly impressive. He chuckled and told me to get some water and some canned food or at least a flashlight. I told him I had one with a smile and I told him I had candles and food and water. I hadn't thought of the possibility that it would be any more than a big storm, that I could be without electricity. Hurricane Wilma was going to be more than that. But I told him not to worry. When he asked if I wanted to talk to my mom, I told him I would call later. I was suddenly nervous to get more water and some more food. I wanted to get out before the rain. I panicked as I watched the dark cloud descend on north Miami Beach.

The wall of water I had been watching enveloped the building before I could hang up the phone. You could hear the wind howling in the elevator and the lobby floor was wet and slippery as the rain hammered the building. I went across the street to get water, letting the impulse to stock up take over. People were running to escape the rain on the street but they had to fight the strong winds to do so, leaning into them and moving with effort. The wind was so powerful that my umbrella was nothing. I didn't bother opening it. The energy around the city was suddenly natural, incredibly strong and frightening. A1A was full of water. It felt good to be around people and I hesitated in the lobby before hauling my gallons of water back up to the apartment to watch the hurricane that would hammer the coast from Florida to Mexico and then into the Gulf. Windows shook. Lights flickered. People called to caution me about various things. I was unsure if I should sleep in my bed so close to the window. I was afraid, had no one and had no idea what to do. I finally decided to put in my ear plugs and go to sleep.

I dreamed that my mother was with me on the couch. In the dream, the storm broke all the windows and my mom and I fell out into the sea, which had come around the building and moved in to flood the neighborhood. But we floated on our mattresses, she on the couch, I on the whole bed, base and all. We were getting soaked and moved by the winds but we didn't fall against any buildings or into the sea. We floated above it. And we could always see each other. I was calling to her, telling her to look at a car crushed by a tree when I awoke. It was dark, still raining and 7 a.m. The worst of the hurricane had passed and there were people on the beach. I made coffee and went to join them.

I pushed my way out to the beach and walked into the wind. The beach was lined with seaweed and trash and many big pieces of wood and, sadly, fish. Lots of them had been caught in the storm and washed up. I walked for a while and tossed ones that were still alive back into the sea only to have a lifeguard caution me to stay out of the water. What did he think, I would go swimming? Apparently, yes. There had been 2 surfers lost in the storm. The best waves come with a hurricane, the guard explained to me. I could see the helicopters north of us still searching and decided to walk back and get the paper. I looked at the paper and the photos of, yes, cars crushed with trees. I read about damage, areas without electricity, flooded neighborhoods. I looked at the satellite imagery of the storm and noticed the trajectory of the storm had been through Cancun, Mexico and it was still there, battering the coast with high winds and heavy rains. I wondered how things were in Tulum.

In less than a week, Helen and George and their family would visit Tulum. Amador was organizing a house for us all and I was going to show them the project. I was so excited to see my friend and then to show them our work. The Cancun airport was closed but I didn't think much of it. I still had 4 days before I would go.

Chapter 15

Two days later, Helen called to say their flight had been cancelled. Cancun airport was still closed. Hurricane Wilma had hovered over Cancun for 3 days straight and the damage would keep the airport closed for at least another week. Aer Lingus would reschedule her flight but with each day's delay they were losing part of their vacation. She thought it might be better if they came another time and we talked about March or April. I was disappointed but accepted that they could not come.

Amador had rented a house for us all. Well, he found it and I paid. Hopefully, we could reschedule, but I doubted it. I had not heard from him in a few days. After 3 days, the airport opened and there were some flights from Ft. Lauderdale. I was desperate to see what had happened in Tulum. The stories of destruction and the poor response of the Mexican government to the situation had been all over the news. Thousands of tourists stranded, evacuated from the beach with nowhere to go inland, no power, looting. I was once again excited. I felt like an adventurous executive as I boarded the nearly empty plane. Landing, I understood why. Cancun had been hardest hit by Wilma and where normally you saw the colors blue for the sea and green for the forest, now you had the same blue, perhaps even deeper, but the forest was brown. The leaves had been ripped off the trees and square miles were flooded.

The airport had been destroyed. Even the concrete roof had been torn off by the constant and high winds. The terminal and immigration had been relocated to a hastily built structure that resembled an army bunker. I quickly passed customs since there was no line. Amador told with an email he would meet me and I waited in front of the dilapidated building. A white truck pulled up to the curb and my neighbor Bali got out and came toward me.

"Amador asked me to come get you," he said with a smile and a kiss on the cheek. He took my bags, looked around and said, "come, we go to Tulum now. It is not so bad there."

I had hired Bali one night while having dinner with my great friend Susan Lee. She and I had worked together for years and now that I was on an informal leave of absence, I tried to see her when I was in the city. We were having dinner when the phone rang. I knew it was Amador and I asked to be excused. I went outside and he told me that Gisela quit and we needed a new person. He said that Bali could manage the project and put him on the phone. I was unsure but finally told Bali to contact me with email as I watched my friend start to eat her dinner alone. He sent me a long email that night with a proposal that we discussed the next afternoon. I decided it could work. Amador told me he was a good guy with construction experience. We started to work together. He seemed to be working and at least had a bank account so I could send him money. He sent me photos and things seemed on track. I was unsure how things would be after the hurricane but Bali told me it had not been too bad. We drove to Tulum against the backdrop of a brown jungle and obvious destruction. I humbly passed billboards that the hurricane had bent and overturned as if they were made of aluminum wire rather than steel beams. Wilma had doubled over streetlights like play-dough. Where I remembered palapas, there was nothing. It was as if I were driving in a desert rather than a tropical paradise. But as we passed through Playa del Carmen, the forest became more green. Palm trees were standing and, although bent, they at least had leaves. The palapa roofs had holes but structurally, they were there. I was tired and shocked by how bad things were in Cancun.

I barely knew Bali. He owned the lot next to mine with my neighbors, Alvaro, who owned a hotel in town, and Filip, a guy from Poland. Amador told me they were friends and we had shared a beer once or twice in town. Bali was a young, handsome Hungarian. He told me how he lived in Playa del Carmen for years before coming to Tulum.

After a few minutes of silence, he looked at me and told me, "Amador got a problem." He told me that he used a lot of drugs. I told him I knew in an embarrassed sort of way. At least I thought I knew he used drugs like marijuana and cocaine. I didn't want to seem like a stupid or naïve girlfriend so I pretended I was at least aware of his drug use. I thanked him for telling me and asked how bad the problem was.

Bali answered me, "Pretty bad."

But then told me that Amador was better now, or at least trying to get better. I am not sure if he only said that so he would have a job or so Amador wouldn't kill him. But it was what I wanted to hear and I believed him. I had known people with drug habits. All of them seemed to be able to give it up finally. I knew people who had blown a nostril from snorting so much cocaine. They had eventually quit and taken their lives back. What I didn't understand was that they had wanted to. What I didn't know then was that Amador loved his drugs and had no real reason to quit. I mean, besides me and our project, what did he have besides the party?

Bali interrupted my thoughts saying, "We gonna find him."

I asked him if he had not seen Amador and he said no but that he was "around." I knew that Amador was always around. Then, I recognized we were coming into Tulum. The road gently curved and you could see the traffic light in front of San Francisco Supermarket. I felt a nervous anxiety in my stomach, an adrenalin rush that felt good and bad in the same moment. I had no idea what to expect and then Bali asked me where I would stay. I didn't have a reservation since I thought Amador would help me. I asked Bali if he could suggest a place. He told me he would think about it but first he wanted to find Amador. I had the distinct impression that he wanted to get rid of me. He was tired. I felt badly for a second and then reminded myself that I had been paying his way for awhile. It was ok for him to help me out.

The town looked sad. It was grey. There was no sun that late afternoon. Bali repeated that we would find Amador, as if he were hiding or something. I wondered why but didn't say anything, so lost in my thoughts: thoughts of rescuing Amador from drugs and thoughts of how to rescue myself. I was in deep financially with this guy for whom it was now official: "he got a problem." I wanted to save him, sure, but I also wanted to save myself. Too, I had invested other people's money to do this project. And I was planning on bringing cancer survivors and doctors here and being famous with Oprah. How could I do that if I were running it with a drug addict. My mind was going in 10 different directions as we drove the Avenida Tulum to la Nave, our favorite bar and restaurant. Amador was there, having a beer. I didn't see him right away. Bali pulled the car over and I got out.

"He is there," Bali told me.

I looked over and knew why I had not recognized him. All the wonderful dredlocks he had and the golden tips of his black hair had been shaved off.

Amador walked toward me. I opened my arms.

"*Amor*," was all he said.

My mind stopped racing, I smiled and hugged and kissed him there in the street and then ran my hands over the stubble of new hair growth that he had.

"What happened to your hair?" I asked.

He told me he had lice and then asked if I didn't like him without hair, if I would still love him. I assured him it was not for his hair that I liked him and kissed him again. I decided it would all work out and pushed the drug and money issues to the back of my mind. Years later, when his friend went to jail, I learned that they shave your head there to prevent you from getting lice. But for now I would believe his half-truth. Amador asked me where I was staying as if I had been here awhile. I told him I had just arrived and needed a place, thinking his questions were weird. I told him I thought he would have come to the airport to meet me. I noticed he looked over at Bali and said nothing. Then I changed the topic and asked him where he was staying.

He told me it was a "scarey place" and then repeated himself, "I staying in the scarey house."

I invited him to find a place with me.

He purred, "Of course. I always gonna help you."

I wrapped my arms around him again and hugged him like a young girl would hug her father. He hugged me back and I believed that was all I needed. We would be ok.

Amador said something to Bali in Spanish and then said to me, "Get in. He gonna take us to a place. You want to stay on the beach, right?"

I thought it would be nicer and closer to the land. I mentioned that I was excited to see what had happened. Bali said we could do that tomorrow and I relaxed as they spoke in Spanish again. I sat between them in the front seat and we drove out to the beach to a place on the south side of the beach called "Luxury Cabanas." I found the bad English amusing and interesting and especially liked the way people put things together. To me, Luxury Cabanas, was one more instance of something that wasn't actually wrong but didn't sound quite right. Anyway, we pulled in and Amador got out to talk with the owner. Bali waited with me and after Amador was far enough away not to hear us, Bali told me that he would be OK I shook my head in agreement and told him I was confident that things would work out. Then I confirmed that we could see the project the next day. Bali said he would pick us up as Amador came back to the truck and put his hand out to help me down saying he had a nice cabana on the water.

A positive energy entered the air that had been heavy around me. It seemed like more than tension between Bali and Amador and I couldn't shake the feeling. Amador went for my bag and pulled it up the sandy walkway. I followed behind after saying goodbye to Bali. The hotel had been saved much of the damage from the hurricane because it was only half built. The view was spectacular, however. Entering from the deck in front was a king size bed and then a bath with a beautiful shower.

The *cabana* had a high palapa roof and a small closet. The headboard was the wall for the bathroom. The construction was white concrete. The lights were low but good enough to see and the white reflected the light. The deck had a beautiful white hammock with fringe down the sides. I started to unpack as Amador lay on the bed. I gave him a polar fleece blanket and some shorts and a pair of sandals. I picked up things like that for him since he always needed things. He was good at losing things or wearing them out or God knows what, but he never had anything.

He told me, "Thanks baybe," with his crazy accent as he wrapped himself in the blanket and got into the bed.

I went to the bathroom to wash up. I wanted a hot shower and ran the water for awhile but nothing even warm came out. I told Amador there was no hot water and, rather than going to ask about it, he said, "probably not." I forced myself under the cold water. It was exhilarating to say the least. I walked back to the bed in my towel to find Amador already sleeping, wrapped up in his new blanket, like a child.

I kissed him on the forehead and he wakened, saying "*Amor?*" in a surprised tone.

I told him that of course it was me and asked him who else might be here.

Then he told me, "They coming for me. They gonna be here any minute."

I asked him who "they" were and started to feel strange and afraid as he continued to tell me some guys were coming to bring him "some."

I asked, "Some what," not really wanting to hear the answer.

I knew it wouldn't be champagne and strawberries for his girlfriend and was not surprised when he told me they would bring him some cocaine. A chill ran up my spine and I wanted to vomit but instead I told him no one was coming, more to deny it or try to will it not to happen. But he only asked me if I didn't hear them coming. I told him no and became very afraid. After I said no one was coming, he told me he needed to go but he didn't move. I told him he couldn't go anywhere because I needed him. He was still laying on the bed, not moving but talking, almost in his sleep. He told me he needed a little.

I found his need for drugs and his hallucinating frightening and told him to go back to sleep. But he continued to say they were coming and asked me if I didn't hear them. I told him to go to sleep and lay next to him in my towel with my hair still wet. Then the lights went out and the fan stopped. I wrapped my body around him and the polar fleece blanket he had become attached to and told myself, "only the end of the generator." Here on the beach, if there was light, it was only until about 10 p.m. when people turned their generators off. It would be earlier if they ran out of gas. I thought it was earlier but was unsure. Regardless, I pulled part of the blanket off him and over me and wrapped my arms around Amador for comfort and to make sure he didn't slip away to get drugs. I began to understand the "problem" that Bali had mentioned.

Chapter 16

Bali picked us up at about 11 to go to my project. Amador was slow and difficult to move. He wanted to sleep all the time. When not sleeping, he was throwing up or with diarrhea. He didn't want to eat but I was always hungry. He was pale, almost grey, hardly the chocolate colored beach bum I had fallen in love with. He hardly had energy for sex and it felt like sex, not like love. I became more confused with every passing minute. I was happy for the diversion to go to the land.

When we entered, I noticed that Bali had all the keys. He pushed the swinging doors open as if they were his. The piles of wood that had been there before were gone. But the trash was not. There were beautiful coco palm trees and some smaller chit palm trees rising out of a lot of trash, mostly coke bottles and cans of beans and tuna and a few Styrofoam Nissan soup cups. There were materials and then three shells of structures rising from the landscape. They reminded me of naked mannequins waiting for clothing. I was embarrassed to look at them. Entering to the right was the concrete structure that Gerry had built. One day it should be a bathroom. Then, there was a 2-story building with no walls or ceiling. One day it should be my meditation and massage center. At the back of the land was a 3-story skeleton. I looked at the wood and didn't recognize it from the long sturdy trees I had seen on my land before. These were shorter and thinner and had to be joined in the middle to reach the height and support the building. To do that they cut a piece of the end off and put a huge bolt into the place where they joined the two trees. The building moved when you walked into it.

Each structure was full of construction materials: a bag of pvc elbows for plumbing and bags of flexible orange tubing. A porceline sink lay on the floor and next to it the base of a toilet on top of bags of hardened cement that had apparently gotten wet during the rain. It was total chaos, and although I wanted to attribute it to the hurricane, my spa reeked of neglect. I became more depressed with each step. Amador was totally absent mentally and most likely focusing on how he could get to town to score some drugs. Bali was preoccupied and probably nervous about how I would react since the lot was a mess, over the top disorganized and looked as if vandals had been rummaging through things to take what they needed.

Then I realized that was probably the truth. I understood the same about the wood. I wanted to scream not only at Amador and

Bali, but also at my neighbors and at the universe. I felt betrayed. Then I noticed a nice palapa, nearly complete next door. The wooden supports were smooth and strong, without any junctures or bolts. I couldn't say they were mine since I had never really known the posts, but they looked similar in quality. There was a new well beside the house that was half on my property and half on my neighbor's.

I asked Bali who's house it was. He told me it was his. I said nothing but then I asked about the well. He told me it was mine but was hoping we could share it. I looked at him suspiciously and asked him if we had shared the cost. He looked at his feet, kicked the earth and told me that it didn't work very well. I shook my head and told him I didn't remember the house being there the last time I visited, before the hurricane.

Amador finally said, while looking at Bali, "He finish his house with your money."

He was agitated but I couldn't tell if he was angry or needed a fix. I couldn't understand why Amador hadn't done anything to make Bali work on our place. Bali defended himself and said he had only used his money to finish his house.

I didn't want this to be happening but there was no way for me to deny that Bali had been ripping me off. I told them that I had seen enough. I turned to walk off the property. Bali followed me saying it wasn't what I thought. I told him I really didn't know what to think but that it looked like he had been robbing me. He got defensive and told me he had been doing good things with the money.

Amador chimed in to say, "good things for himself," but Bali gave Amador a look that seemed to say, "be quiet or I will tell some other stories."

I saw it but I had checked out mentally. I couldn't focus and kept walking toward the gate. I stopped halfway in front of two beautiful coconut palms that were growing together to form a place where you could sit. I touched them and looked around at the mess I had made on this pretty lot of land. There was debris everywhere and three half built structures that I didn't know how I would finish. I felt guilty for damaging the earth and I wanted to get away from it as soon as possible. I moved toward the gate more quickly. Amador followed me and Bali was right behind. They had been talking. I hadn't cared, nor did I imagine they would have a plan to keep me in this project.

But when I reached to door, Bali called me to wait and blamed things on the hurricane saying he would make progress the week I was there.

I said, "I expected a lot more, to be honest."

He told me it was not what I thought and I asked him what he expected me to think. When he didn't answer, I asked him what he would have thought if he were me. I waited for the silence to get stale and then told him I was happy my friends were not here to witness this mess.

I waved my arm toward the back part of the lot and said, "And your house is done."

He whined and said his was simpler and it only looked finished but then he changed his tune, grabbed my arm before I walked away and told me, "Listen, ok. Of course I gonna build my house. I need to live here. But yours is coming. We working on it."

My jaw dropped open and I looked at him, my thoughts racing over how I could start over again. I looked over at Amador and knew that I was sinking. Bali was the only one throwing me a line.

Amador walked past me to the truck and said softly, "He been ripping you off."

I looked at him angrily, almost not believing what he had said and asked him to repeat himself. He did, insisting that I heard him. Bali complained that it was not that at all. I stood there in shock for longer than a moment and then reminded Amador that he had been working with Bali. Second, I reminded him that he had recommended Bali.

He came close to my face and asked me loudly, "You think I let him do this?" with his features contorted in anger.

There was spittle on the side of his mouth and some of it touched my face when he finished the sentence. I wiped my face and started to say yes but he cut me off saying he knew I would side with Bali.

Then he said to me, "You been fucking him, right?"

Where that came from I would take forever to understand and I almost laughed. But he was still in my face and I was frightened. He continued to say he knew he could never trust me. Then he called me a whore, or "*puta*." He became so angry he started to speak only Spanish and, although I could tell it was cursing, I had never heard the words before. Finally he turned around abruptly and walked away, throwing his arm over his head as if to keep me from following.

I called after him. Bali stood close by but didn't get involved. I called Amador again and then jogged after him and grabbed his arm. He turned like an animal but I didn't let go. I spoke softly and asked him what he was thinking. He started to calm down but was still very much on edge and he asked me if I thought he was ripping me off with Bali. I told him honestly that I had hoped he would help keep Bali from robbing me, yes. I reminded him that I had trusted him to manage that sort of thing.

He calmed down, looked at the ground and let his defense fall and said, apologetically, "I let you down."

"Yes, in fact, you let me down," I told him and continued, "but I hoped that we can fix things."

He looked at his feet. So did I. They were dirty and cut, as always. He never wanted to wear shoes. He caught me looking at them and smiled. I smiled back. Then he asked if we would still work with Bali and looked over toward where Bali was still standing, waiting. I thought for a moment and told him we could try. I thought that at least we knew Bali and we knew we needed to watch him and manage him. I took Amador's arm and told him that would be his job. I looked in his eyes and seriously, asked him if he could do it.

He looked at me and said, "You been fucking him, right?"

I let go of his arm, shocked and disgusted and told him not to ever say that again. I reminded him that I loved him and that there was no one else, not in Tulum or in the US. Too, I told him it wasn't even about that. I asked him again, could he do the job. He calmed down, apologized and told me yes, he could do it. We walked back to talk with Bali and made a plan to talk about the work over dinner later. Bali assured me he could finish the project well.

That night I had dinner with Bali at Las Ranitas to discuss next steps. Amador was sick and stayed at the Luxury Cabanas that were not so luxury after all. Bali acknowledged that he had been working for Amador and, although he didn't say it directly, he hinted that Amador had been taking money for drugs and even selling materials when the cash ran out. I didn't know what to think. We talked about how to move forward, control the money and how to find Gerry who had run out of town with $10,000 of my money. I got depressed and couldn't listen any longer after that. I asked him if we could talk the next day explaining that I was suddenly very tired. I paid for our dinner and walked back alone on the beach. Amador was asleep on the bed. I sat outside for a while thinking. Later, as I got under the orange blanket we shared, Amador woke and asked me if "they" were here yet.

I felt afraid and bored at the same time as I asked him, "Who, Amador?"

He told me in a semi sleep state, "They coming. I just need a little. They gonna bring it to me."

I knew he was referring to drugs and I told him that no one was coming. He repeated in a dream state that they were coming. I wanted to cry but held him instead, listening to see if "they" in fact were coming. Then I wondered who it would be while it took me hours to fall asleep.

Over the next few days, Bali, Amador and I met each evening to go over the construction, how we would move forward and how I would pay. That was my job: get the money. I trusted Amador and Bali to do the rest. For the time I was there, I was Amador's nurse, sponsor and caretaker. He mostly slept and when he woke it was with diarrhea or dry heaves. I waited for him to feel better while I wrote, drew or hung out at the beach. Some days I wondered if he could ever get better. But, slowly, he did.

The morning before I left to go back to Miami, I swam and relaxed over breakfast with Amador. Then he helped me find a taxi to the airport and, for the first time, he didn't come with me. He bargained with a taxista for a decent fare and then kissed me fully on the mouth, opened the door and grabbed my ass before I got in. I laughed, opened the window and kissed him again. He was feeling better. I told him I loved him and asked him to call me later as the driver pulled from the curb. Amador told me he loved me back and said he would try, but wisely made no promises. As we drove through the traffic light and headed toward the airport, I started to cry but then put my head on the head rest, closed my eyes and slept.

Chapter 17

I was sitting in front of the oversized windows looking over Miami Beach with the computer open, feeling lonely when the phone rang. It was Bob Brumbaugh, a colleague and high level executive from the Corps of Engineers. He offered me a job in Alexandria, Virginia, writing policy papers for a group called the Institute for Water Resources. They held courses and did research on water related issues. The work would be on a national and more academic level than my previous field-work with the Engineers in Boston. It was something new, something different and something far away from everyone who knew me. For some reason, that was what I wanted: some sort of security but on my own. I kept trying to get away from everyone. I wanted to redefine myself and I couldn't do it around all these people who knew me so well. Too, alone I could do what I wanted with Amador. I could give him my soul. I could trust or pretend, actually, that he was good without anyone telling me that he was not. Away from the people who cared about me, I could deny reality yet still not fully live in the craziness I was creating.

Too, I needed income. Any savings I had were almost gone. My credit cards were high and I had nothing coming in, although I knew it would. This job could help me get over this interim period. I accepted the job and would go to Alexandria, do research, think and be around smart people while cultivating my other life in Mexico. I could finance my dream from there. Amador would be the man I wanted. I would show everyone when it all worked out and God would help me since, after all, he was on my side.

I moved my things and drove myself south from Boston stopping for one night in Allentown, PA. I stayed with Sheba and Paul. They always gave me hope. I was a star with them. I had potential. A visit with them was like an injection of vitamin B-12 for my ego. I left the next day, full of energy and ideas and found a temporary apartment in the fringes of Alexandria. My mother would fly down in two weeks to help me find something more permanent. It would all be ok.

Amador called me on the drive.

I had missed several of his calls and when I couldn't answer, he would get nervous and demanding leaving messages like, "Honey I try to call you but where are you or who you been wit? I call you later."

Then he might call right away but he might not. I hated missing his calls but sometimes thought it made him take me less for granted. I knew it made me more attractive to him in some weird game playing way, and often, I let it happen. I picked up his call close to DC on I-

211

95 and the first thing he did was reprimand me for not answering the day before. I loved the concern and the jealousy although I knew it was unhealthy. I told myself it was somehow only unhealthy in other people's relationships. Then I explained that either I didn't hear it or had turned it off for yoga. He asked me where I was.

I told him I was in my car and joked, "I am living in the car."

He told me he had retrieved a Ford Bronco that he had sold to pay the rent. I assumed he had actually sold it for drugs. Apparently he had gotten it back. He told me he was living in the car but he was enthusiastic and happy.

My shoulders slumped and I said to him, "So we are both living in our cars."

I did not want to believe it: both of us living in cars, both of us homeless.

That voice on my shoulder told me, "This is where he will bring you, living in his car."

I ignored that voice and said, dreaming, "I wish we were at least in the same car."

But then I remembered our trip to Chiapas in July. We had met Jerry the contractor and he was giving us an estimate for our project. Amador wanted to get out of Tulum. I thought it would be fun to travel. We were on the tree lined two-lane highway heading toward Palenque when I said something he didn't like. I had been in a pissy mood that day and I said something to him about the music. I thought it might make him angry but didn't care and never imagined the response. Without saying a word, he pulled the emergency break up and skidded the car into the middle of the two-lane road sideways. We were blocking the road when I noticed a bus in the distance coming in the opposite direction. He jumped out of the car, swearing at me and telling me to get out of his life. Then he ran away, leaving me there. I looked the bus barreling down the road towards me, jumped into the driver's seat, straddling the stick shift and managing to start the car and begin a three point turn as the horn from the bus blared into my ears.

I stalled once and cursed over and over, "fuck fuck fuck how the fuck could he do this fuck fuck fuck," adrenalin flowed through my body. "fuck fuck fuck…."

I moved the car over and onto the shoulder seconds before the bus swerved around me, I could see the driver cursing back and people in the rear of the bus looked out the window at me, wondering what sort of lunatic I was. My hands were shaking and I couldn't breathe. I looked around for Amador. He was nowhere. I waited to regain some composure. Cars passed and beeped their horns. I stopped shaking, slowly shifted into gear and moved to the first intersection where I could turn. As I did so, I saw Amador. I moved the car toward him and he started running. I called from the car window and asked him what his problem was. He spat back at me that I was the problem.

I was surprised and hurt. I thought I was his love. He kept moving and I followed him in the car and asked him if he were going to leave me. I had no idea where I was. I wanted to hit rewind on the last hour and play it over differently. He yelled that he never wanted to see me again and jogged to get away from me. I was incredulous and angry and stopped the car and let him keep walking. I told myself I would be fine. But then I looked around. I was in the middle of nowhere and I did not want to be by myself. There was nowhere to stay, nothing. I did not even know how to get back to Tulum. Everything had turned around for me. I shifted the car and pulled in front of him to block his progress. He shouted at me to leave him alone but I commanded that he would not leave me here alone. Then I started to cry. I didn't want to but I did.

He walked around me and said, "go away."

I told him no, sniffed to stop crying and told him, "Alright. I am sorry, whatever I said, I am sorry. Please don't leave me here. Get back in the car. Please? It is ok. Really. I will be good."

I couldn't believe I was actually saying that. I was shaking and was unsure why I was apologizing but I was. I didn't want him to leave. He could hitch back to Tulum, I knew. I was unsure I could drive and sure I didn't want to. And without him I had no reason to go back. I reached out to him and said the magic word, "please?" He looked at me for a few moments that seemed like an eternity and then took my hand and asked me why I did that to him. He pulled me close and hugged me. He had thrown his shirt in the bushes and was sweating and smelly. But I liked it. I felt whole again. I felt possessed and taken care of. I started to cry and he held me closer.

We got back in the car, he curled up in the seat beside me and went to sleep telling me not to talk to him for awhile. I obeyed, steadied my hands on the steering wheel and turned the car back to the main road. The voice in my head wondered what the fuck that was all about and why I was with this mad man.

"What are you doing?" it asked me.

I knew what I was doing to a point. I was going to leave him but not until I got somewhere I knew I could handle. It was bizarre. I had been around the world. I didn't understand what was so different now that I couldn't handle it. But at that moment I could not. I needed him, at least for now. But at the same time, part of me was making a plan to get him out of my life. As I drove along fields that seemed to extend forever, I reminded myself that each time I had problems in the many places I had travelled, someone had saved me. Each time I looked at Amador, I knew I wanted him to be the one. But I also knew he could never be. I let him sleep and focused on the fields dotted with cows, the hills off in the distance and the green grass alongside ditches and flowing rivers as I pushed any thought of him being "the one" from my mind.

Since that day, being in a car with him put me slightly on edge. There were more outbursts but, so far, none that drastic. However, the possibility was always in the back of my mind. He had started to condition me. I did not realize it then but I behaved differently with him after that. I became afraid of upsetting him. Harry had done that too. But he had exploded only once and he only yelled at me in public. He had never tried to intentionally kill me in a car, although his driving skills said otherwise.

But that time as well, I had no idea what to do or what I had done. But I knew I didn't want a scene. I didn't like them. I didn't need them. I did not know how to handle them. So as I drove to Alexandria and waited for him to speak, I knew I did not really want to be in a car with him. I was happy to be alone. Then I started to cry. I wasn't supposed to be alone after all this and I hated that I found myself there.

Amador told me, "Honey don cry. When you come back, September?"

I told him I didn't know and asked him when he thought would be good. He told me, "tomorrow." I melted emotionally, felt better and told him I loved him. Although I meant it from my heart, I was beginning to realize that it was dangerous. There was a pause and before I lost the connection, I asked him if he had received the money I had sent.

He said, "Yes, thank you." I loved it when he said thank you. We talked for a short while longer and finished with him telling me that he would take care of things and that I should not worry. I hung up the phone and trusted him to do just that because isn't that what you do with people you love?

Chapter 18

I let Amador take care of things in Tulum and I settled into my temporary house in Alexandria, Virginia to fund our dream. I worked with a small group of scientists, mostly PhD's, in a windowless office with a door, a computer, one file cabinet filled with other people's old files and 5 telephone lines. The work would have been meaningful if I thought anyone ever looked at it. But I soon discovered that my reports to Congress and Assistant Secretaries of this and that were piled up on desks of people who responded only to connections. The supervision was sparse, like the coaching and encouragement. My secretary knew more about where I was and my work schedule than my boss. The people were kind but were all in a very different place than I was. Gradually, I developed a routine of workouts and denial to fight the depression I knew could kill me. After work each day, I would run, then work on my foundation and my art in a studio I set up in my apartment living room. I lived in an apartment complex where, each time I came home, I needed to check the apartment number to make sure I was in the right place. After working the day in my office, I came home to an empty apartment to work again until exhaustion overtook me. I was anonymous. I was invisible. Only my dream in Mexico and my foundation kept me from slipping over the edge and into some limbo between the rote numbness of the workaday world and the frustrated desperation of an artist who wouldn't let herself be good enough.

I waited for Amador's calls and any drama he gave me reminded me I was alive. When I would lose contact with him, I became numb and slipped into a place where I would try to control everything by working hard and not allowing myself to feel. When he re-established contact, even if it was just for money, I was alive again, my dream was alive again and I knew that this life was not the end. I was like a patient that exhales what seems like the last breath and keeps her lungs empty for a moment too long. Amador's calls reminded me to inhale.

I still had so many doctors it was sometimes unnerving to think about them all. But they were in Boston so I didn't have to think about them all that much. My appointments were important although after cancer treatment I was happy not to have to see someone every day. But it was interesting how I missed the medical staff's advice, their consoling smiles, the laughs we would have. They had been a major part of my social life for nearly a year. Some days, especially during radiation, they had been the only people I would talk with. During those treatments, I managed a routine that was more than tight. I woke exhausted and stayed that way most of the day. At 7 am. I would feed the birds, make coffee and start the computer to begin my work. At 12, I went to the gym and was back by 1:15. By 1:30 I would have showered, eaten an apple and cheddar cheese, put a wig on, penciled in my eyebrows and would be out the door for my 2:15 appointment. I was at the Shapiro Radiation Center in the basement on time since punctuality was important. There were always other people waiting. If you were late, you messed everyone up. So, I was not late.

Thank God they gave me parking and from there I nearly ran onto the table when Sam, the technician, would call me. He always gave me a hug and a smile and then I would prepare myself. The other technicians would chat with me. I am ashamed now that I don't remember their names but they were always encouraging for the 3 minutes I was there. I would dress afterward trying not to look at the growing burn on my left breast. It got worse each day as did my ability to handle it. I would rush back before the traffic generally crying. Home by 4, I would start the computer again, return phone calls and try to stay awake to finish my work. I was beyond any exhaustion I had ever known. It was in my bones and I pushed my body as if I were finishing a marathon just to get through each day.

At 5:45, I would turn the computer off and heat up soup or whatever someone had brought me to eat. Everyone who visited brought me something cooked so I would not have to do it for myself. They knew I could not. I would turn the television on and watch first Seinfeld and then The Simpsons with my dinner. They were my friends and, no matter how pathetic it was to have television friends, I treasured and laughed with them. Finally, I would wash the dishes, put cream on the growing burn and my face, take an atavan, put a cap on my bald head and fall asleep. In those months, next to my TV friends and my family on the weekends, my doctors and the medical people were my life. I still looked forward to seeing them and flew to my appointments every 3 months.

So after my first two months in Alexandria and before I moved in with my first room-mate ever, I flew to Boston to see my doctors for breast exams, pap smears, bloods and then family, not necessarily in that order. It was early November, still beautiful in Boston. The trees and the air were crisp. I loved it and I combined seeing all my loved ones into one trip.

On my return to Alexandria, I moved into a new subdivision where I learned to identify my apartment by where I could park the car. I didn't have much and I moved myself. I had a found a roommate at 43 years old. I couldn't afford to live alone but I was embarrassed that I had to share rent with someone. But then I discovered that I actually liked it. Sona was fabulous. Her mother had breast cancer and we talked about it every so often. She was a dentist and we worked very different hours so it worked well for both of us. I wasn't on the lease, I didn't pay utilities and I could leave at any minute with a few days notice or a month's rent. We had a fireplace that turned on with a switch and a gym with a treadmill where no one would talk to each other. I knew I would not get attached and could remind myself that I was moving to a tropical adventure soon. I still had my car. I still had Amador calling me. I still had a dream.

One morning, before I went to work, the phone rang and I jumped for it. I always jumped for the phone in those days since I was afraid that if I missed a call from Amador, he might not call back or he may get angry and act out. I wanted to talk to him but he had been acting weird, needing money more than before. Sometimes he would call and sound stoned and then drift off in the middle of our conversation.

I would call, "Amador? Are you there?" before he would come back to the line.

Some days, he would say, "I got to go Babe," and hang up.

But this time it was not Amador. It was my doctor, the woman who had saved my life by finding the tumor on my breast.

I was happy to hear her voice but immediately got nervous about why she called. She was a busy woman who normally, mailed me a post card that said everything was alright. I didn't like that she was calling me, no matter how much I liked her personally. I liked her less when she told me that the results from my pap were slightly abnormal and showed signs of a potential pre cancer. I sat on the floor as energy left my body. She said I shouldn't be alarmed, but that I should be checked by a specialist. The C word echoed in my mind and I asked her what sort of cancer it could be. She sensed fear and told me it was nothing to worry about but that the readings showed something that might progress to cervical cancer. She told me not to worry and gave me the name and number of a specialist in Brookline for the next time I was in the north. I thanked her before she asked me to follow-up with her.

I hung up the phone and looked at the number on the paper for a few moments and then dialed it. It went to voice mail. I left my name and number. I didn't know what to think. I didn't know who to call. My lover? How ironic that I didn't even have a number for him. I put the phone down and got ready for work. I would process it all later. Now I needed to move and pretend everything was normal although "abnormal" was becoming normal for me. I couldn't get the words, "cervical cancer" out of my head. I kept hearing the echoes of her voice in my mind, the "don't worry" mixed with the word, "cancer" in a bizarre sort of contradiction. Did she remember who she was talking to? Did she understand how much that word frightened me? I spent my day in a distracted sense of suspension as I researched the habits of piping plovers on barrier beach islands and wondered with whom I could talk about my situation.

I ran the trails behind the office after work, before sunset, to process my feelings. There was one hill I sprinted to a pine grove at the crest. I stopped there, my breath making smoke as I listened to the silence. I walked for a few moments and looked up at the sky. It was crystal grey and the green of the pines was more brilliant against the grey background. I started to cry and then, to stop the tears, started to run back down the hill, across the beaver dam and past the migrating Canadian Geese. I finished my tears and my run in the parking lot behind the brick laboratories at work, took a long hot shower and called my sister as soon as I got in the car. The seat heater warmed my back and my aching hip as I relaxed into the heat, explained the situation and asked her what I should do.

She was wonderfully calm and told me to take things one step at a time: make the appointment and try not to worry. She reminded me that it might not even be Cervical Cancer. If it was, Calzi said, it was slow and could be a simple thing. Then she said it could even be a mistake. I decided to believe the latter but then confided that I was frightened. I looked out the car window and waved to some colleagues leaving the office late. I felt so different. For that second, I was jealous of their organized lives, going home to a family and the TV news. Abruptly, I told myself to stop and reminded myself how lucky I was to have a different life. I vaguely heard my sister tell me to make the appointment.

She finished saying, "I wish all this shit would stop for you."

I agreed, decided to wait until the next day for the doctor and drove home the back road. It was a curvy road that cut through some orchards on the fringes of booming subdivisions to my empty apartment that I decided had probably been the same rolling orchard until yuppies like me moved in. I shrugged off the guilt as I climbed the stairs, pushed my way into the door with my workout bag and some books from work. I put things away, cooked some pasta, poured myself a glass of red wine and sat by the fake fireplace until I fell asleep there dreaming of escaping to Mexico.

I woke when Sona entered the apartment. She asked if I had fallen asleep and when I nodded yes, she told me she did that all the time. I smiled and almost drunkenly picked up my plates and the glass and turned off the fireplace. Blaming the wine, I said good night. She told me to get some rest as she made a cup of tea. I walked to my room, turned on the computer and looked for a flight. If I were going to face this again, I would need a trip to Mexico first. I would have to see Amador and take care of things there. I booked a trip for Dec 8 for 6 days. It was the best I could do and I knew I could get the time once I told them I was sick again. Like a manipulative child, I would work their sympathy. The dream of doing something in Mexico had become my touchstone. I couldn't let go of it. Not yet.

Chapter 19

The wall of heat that hit me as I exited customs felt good. No snow and a green Christmas but no lack of Christmas spirit: images of Santa and the Virgin Mary were everywhere. The holy family was on every corner. People ran or biked with torches leading trucks filled with people and decorated with oversized images of the Virgin Mary. Similar parades ran all the way from Cancun to Tulum: people making pilgrimages to honor the Virgin. Some would go as far as Mexico City, I learned later. Some would run with a statue of the Virgin on their backs. It was tradition.

Our new tradition was to meet at the San Francisco Supermarket rather than having Amador fail to pick me up at the airport. I hated waiting for him, losing the time to be let down because he had forgotten me. It was depressing so I told him not to come. Too, this trip, I had a sense of urgency that I never had before. We had suspended work with Bali, stopping construction altogether. Things had not worked out between him and Amador like I wanted. I had no idea who to believe but I was losing money and not getting much accomplished. Either one blamed the other. I couldn't get my arms around the project and felt beaten by it. Too, I wanted to focus on other things and I wanted to get my finances in order before the next rip off. Or better, I wanted to figure out how to avoid another ripoff. But mostly, I couldn't get there fast enough because I was unsure when I could come back. The doctor's voice in the back of my mind saying, "just have it looked at," sounded too familiar.

As I drove toward the only traffic light in Tulum, I saw him. He was waiting there, nearly in the street looking for me. First, I saw his hair, that mass of dreadlocked curls that you could only touch, never get your fingers through. It had all grown back. I started to smile. Then I saw his long legs and his bare feet and I started to laugh. Seeing him and knowing he was waiting for me made me happy. I think still, if I were to see him, I would have to smile. Who knows? But that day and for a long time, he made me smile from the inside out.

I honked the horn lightly and waved. He waved back and I pulled into the parking lot. He half walked, half jogged to see me and put his head in the window to kiss me before I could open the door.

"*Amor*," he said.

I repeated the phrase, kissed him and then got out of the car to give him a hug. He pushed me against the car and kissed me again asking me where we could go, implying sex. I smiled, enjoying that he wanted me. I whispered that I had no idea. He pushed himself into me and told me there was a new place in town that I would like.

Then he kissed me on the neck and sent shivers down to my toes. I inhaled but then told him I needed to eat something first. He grabbed my ass, said OK and drove us once again to *La Nave*.

When we finished we drove through town past the last of Tulum's holiday lit stores and onto the dark highway that led to Belize. There was nothing but forest on both sides of the road, a few tire repair places and mechanic shops. Amador turned at a small sign that said, *Don Diego de la Selva*, and continued down a bumpy road about 500 meters until we came to a hotel with a huge concrete entryway and arched wooden doors. To the left was another concrete building of two floors for what looked like an artist studio. From the entryway you could see one bare bulb in what appeared to be an open empty space. There were plants everywhere but the garden was young. They were still finding their way, you could tell.

There was no one to greet us and we walked in and found the pool. I put my foot in and commented that the hotel was nice. Amador seemed to be annoyed either at my response to the hotel or to the fact that no one was there. But he had definitely changed his attitude. He insinuated that nothing was good enough for me. I told myself that I was being insecure but then caught myself and realized that actually, it wasn't good enough. It was nice but it was in the middle of nowhere, actually worse. It was in the middle of the wrong side of town and I was not entirely comfortable.

But I told myself to get over it because I didn't want to annoy him. I wanted to be happy. I wanted him to be happy. So I tried to like what he wanted me to like. The proprietor finally came down from his studio. He had a French accent and was handsome and reserved. I liked him immediately but he was cool toward us. At the time I couldn't understand it. He showed us to a room that was nice enough and we settled on a price I considered fair. Amador jumped on the bed and called to me. I went happily towards him, looking for comfort. I had not told him about my health issues. After all, I had no idea what would happen, so I preferred to keep it to myself for the moment. He kissed me, started to undress me and I let myself forget everything else.

We laid there after making love, resting in the dark, relaxing, enjoying the moment and suddenly I blurted out that I might be sick. His arm was under my neck and I had my hand on his stomach but he got up on an elbow and asked me about it. I explained that my doctor thought I would need another operation. He wondered if it was on my breast and I told him no, that it was my cervix. He asked me where that was and I touched my groin.

He put his hand over mine and asked, "What you got there?" with concern.

When I told him I might have cancer there, he asked me what I needed to do. I explained that I was not sure yet and needed more tests. I lied and told him that was why I could not stay for Christmas.

I paused before I added, "I am afraid."

He held me tightly for awhile and I let him console me with kisses. He told me not to be afraid and that everything would be ok. I drifted to sleep, loving him more for having accepted my issues. He knew and was not repulsed by me. I could relax.

Until a voice entered my dream, saying, "I got to go out. I gonna take the car."

In my mind I said, "here we go again" and sleepily recited my "no" mantra, telling him he was not taking the car. He told me he was only going to town. I asked him why he needed to go. He got angry and got up off the bed saying that he was going to shower and go. I told him that he was not going in my rental car. I stayed in bed, exhaled fully and then lifted my body and followed him to shower.

He said I could come with him to town. I complained about him leaving me in the hotel after I had come all this way to see him. He grunted and said he had things to do and that I had to understand. He said it matter of factly, as if I should know.

Without thinking, I told him that he needed to understand and then asked him, "Who is more important to you than me?"

He did not answer and let the hot water wash him as he moaned, "wonderful," and then motioned for me to join him. I did and let it wash the day's dirt off my body. It did feel marvelous. We washed each other's backs and once we were dry we put cream on each other and then we dressed and went to town.

"You can drop me here," Amador said to me when we got to a bar at the end of town.

I looked at him incredulously and asked him, "What? You don't want me to come with you?"

He stuttered and told me how he knew I was tired and that I needed rest.

I finished his sentence and said, "so you are sending me back to the hotel."

I couldn't believe it.

He opened the car door to get out and told me, "Look at it how you like, but I got people to talk to and you cannot come."

I grabbed his arm and told him to wait. He looked at me angrily and told me to go back to the hotel and rest saying his famous, "I be back," as he pulled his arm from my hand and got out.

He walked over to the driver side window to kiss me and then he asked me for money for a taxi back, reminding me that I was a long way out of town. I got angry, told him no and reminded him that he put me a long way from town.

His eyes narrowed to slits and he said, "Then maybe I stay in town."

I told him that was fine and drove away. Immediately, I regretted that I did knowing I would probably not see him tonight, perhaps not even tomorrow and I only had a few days in Tulum. But I had shown him that I had limits, that I would not be discarded. I thought about going for a drink but felt weary and went back to "Don Diego de la Selva."

I barely spotted the small yellow sign for the hotel. I slowly turned the car and immediately sank into a deep pothole. It felt like where my heart was. I downshifted and pulled out of it only to enter another and then another as I moved up the bumpy road. The soft yellow lights of the hotel appeared like a mirage in the desert of potholes and I parked in front. I pulled myself out of the car and looked up to the stars to remind myself how happy I was to be back in the tropics, closer to my dream. Then I glanced into the tall building across the street as the yellow glow of the bare bulb shone into the dirt road below. The shadow of a man flickered on the wall and I heard low jazz music coming from somewhere inside. I wished for someone who could stay home at night, someone who liked to be in his own space, in his own creativity. I thought of Harry and decided perhaps not. I really wanted a blend. But it was the first time I thought that Sheba may have been right. Amador may not be at all suitable. I walked past the pool and around the garden to my room and then crawled into bed and fell soundly asleep.

Amador didn't come to see me that night, or the next. I got used to having breakfast alone and writing most of the day. The first day without him, I took the car to the beach at *Mar Caribe*, where we had met. The second day, I drove out past Cesiak, where we had lived before. On the way I stopped at the land. Nothing was happening but there was a fence with a padlock. I had paid for it but didn't even have a key. I got back in the car, pensively, and drove south to the bridge over the place where the lagoon met the sea: *la Boca*. I parked on the other side of the bridge and walked along the edge of the bay to the sea where I could put my feet in the water and swim in the shallows. On the lookout for crocodiles, I walked back around the marsh grass along the edge of the water and sat by the bridge to watched people fish.

Back in town, I bought a roast chicken at *Pollo Bronco* to eat at the hotel. Eating breakfast alone in the restaurant was enough. And I didn't want to bump into Amador. I was done but remembered that I was committed to him with land and other people's money. I cursed but knew that beating myself up over it wouldn't help. So I let it go and vowed to not let him rip off my friends or me. At least no more than he already had.

Just as I had given him up, he came into the lobby. I was eating breakfast that third morning. He looked exhausted and dirty. His hair was matted into a shape that was not at all the same as his head. It was comical, actually and his smile was contagious. No matter how hard I tried not to, I smiled back. He asked me if I were angry as he sat down and looked at my food and then took my spoon to sample it. Before I said anything, he practically spit it back out onto the plate, saying it was too sweet. He stopped talking for a moment, looked around and asked me if I wanted to go for a Mexican breakfast. A part of me wanted to. I had been lonely and wanted to see him, to be with him.

But, I realized I couldn't let him walk back in on me. I said no. I knew right from wrong and suddenly, he disgusted me, even if I were smiling. He was dirty in a different way than when he lived on the beach. I was lonely but I didn't want to be around him and told him I was already having breakfast. He got up without a word and left, puffing out his chest as if I were the one missing something. I let him go and finished my deliciously sweet breakfast with another cup of black coffee.

I drifted through the next few days, writing, calling attorneys, going to the beach, some people may say brooding but I didn't look at it that way. I was thinking, working things out as best I could. Amador came by the next day, cleaner, less obnoxious. I liked him better and we did some things. Sometimes he was charming. Sometimes he was an asshole. When he was the latter, I tried not to his behavior to affect me and I would ask him to leave. That was what the self-help books said, corroborated by the Buddhist philosophy of non-attachment. But deep down, I somehow believed that if I cleaned him up, if I touched the part of him that I knew loved me, I could fix him and he would love me the way he had before, the way I wanted him to. As I moved through each day, with him or alone, I did what I had learned to do best. I denied there was something I could not fix and I planned how I would fix it by trying to change myself.

The night before I left for the states, weary and lonely, ready to go to bed, I heard a knock on the door. It was Amador. I stopped and waited, not knowing exactly what to do. I argued with myself about him not deserving to see me, about how much more I deserved, about what a jerk he was. Then he knocked again and, like someone in a trance, I opened the door. He was standing there, smiling. Not a happy smile but that smile he must have learned as a child that makes people want to forgive you. A smile that says, "sorry but I know you love me anyway." I let him in and gave him a "hold" as he called a hug. I smelled his hair and brushed my face against his soft new growth of beard and let myself melt into him.

"*Perdon*" he said and then said it again, "*Perdon*."

I asked him why he did all those things and he told me, "I am an asshole."

I pulled away from him and told him, "But I don't want an asshole."

And I reminded him that he was not an asshole before and asked him what had changed. He didn't answer but asked to come in. I opened the door wider and asked him to sleep with me. I couldn't believe I was saying it and that voice on my shoulder asked if I was some sort of lunatic or glutton for punishment as I held him and led him into the room. But before I let him into my bed, I did one sane thing. I asked him to take a shower. He looked at me and asked if he smelled. I told him yes, he did. He looked at his dirty feet and told me that a shower would be good. We scrubbed each other's backs and fronts and made love there. It was beautiful and real and I still don't care what anyone says, it was more than the physical act. We went to bed after, our hair still wet, our bodies smelling of soap and each other. We slept intertwined with each other and I felt bliss in his embrace and in being around him. I had no cares for anything but this man. I still have no idea why but it was good to lose myself in him. I woke with the sun, refreshed and committed to him again.

Chapter 20

It was cold with a clear cobalt sky when I arrived at National Airport that night. I took a taxi to my apartment and struggled up the stairs with my suitcase thinking only of other places and things. I had barely seen Amador that morning. He and I had breakfast but then I dropped him at his new place not far from the hotel where he acted like some sort of outlaw, kissing me dramatically in the middle of the road and then walking away. I had time for more but he told me he had things to do, adding, "honey boney." I accepted it. After all, what could I do? I drove away and a few kilometers out of town, stopped at Gisela's to say goodbye and Merry Christmas. I wanted to give her a gift. Why, I am not sure. She had let me down with the work but in a way had helped me. I had never really had the money to pay her so her quitting was a gift. I had time and so I followed my instincts and stopped at her house. She was there with Moises' ex girlfriend, Akim. We had a coffee and when we embraced I slipped 500 pesos, about 50 dollars, into her hand and said, "Feliz Navidad." And then I asked her to tell Amador that I loved him. I wasn't sure he knew. She nodded and told me of course she would. They both hugged me and I went to the airport believing I had friends.

Now I was home. Amador had called when I was in the taxi and apologized again for being "bad" as he called it. Then he told me he would do the best for us. I told him it was alright. I reminded him that I was going to the doctor the next week and asked him to call. He told me that of course he would call and then reminded me not to think about sad things. It was as if he didn't want them to bring me down. I tried to explain that it was not sad but something I wanted to share with him.

He cooed, "Of course," into the phone and asked me to come back soon saying he would be missing me.

I added, "because you hardly saw me this time."

He reminded me again to not talk about sad things and then I told him a near lie.

I told him, "I believe in you, Amador" even though I did not believe we could work together any longer.

But I said it anyway, since, after all, I had to believe in someone.

When I entered the apartment, Sona and her boyfriend Steve were having dinner. They asked me how things went. I lied again and said, "progressing" when actually everything was stalled. They invited me to eat with them but I declined, afraid I would have to lie more. I couldn't admit how badly it was going and how I was getting totally ripped off and taken advantage of. I think the logic, if you can call it that, was that if I didn't tell anyone, it was less real. I was living in the land of make believe and telling the truth would make it all crash down around me. Suddenly exhausted, I excused myself and crawled into bed to sleep with the phone by my head in case Amador would call me. I wanted to talk to him more. I always wanted more. But when he called the words escaped me somehow. Bottom line, I did not want to ruin the moments by talking about "sad things."

From the window in my bedroom, I could see the train tower in Downtown Alexandria and, of course, hear the trains coming into the station. On that clear, cold night, I could also see some stars. Before I drifted off to sleep, I reminded myself that things were good. I was charting my course. In a week it would be Christmas. I would fly to Boston on Christmas morning. Lynn was sending a limo to take me to her store for champagne and then to my sister's house on Cape Cod. I was a celebrity in my own mind and I didn't care if I had a boring job that I didn't like. I was moving to Mexico. I would live by the beach. I had a beach bum boyfriend who would call me at dinnertime and who would love me forever. I had a non-profit and had fundraisers and sold my art. I was changing the world, and myself too. No one had to know that I might have cancer again, that I could not love my beach bum forever and that I was so broke I was financing food and the little medicine I still took. I would fake it until I could make it.

So I walked to the nearly empty metro station Christmas morning already dressed for dinner in silk pants, heeled boots and a furry leather jacket. The sun was warm on the platform even though the wind was cold. People were happy and on the train, you could feel the festive mood where normally no one allowed themselves to feel anything. The plane was not full and it was on time and people didn't care if they had to work or to travel, they were in a good mood. After all, it was Christmas.

The limo was waiting as I stepped off the plane and when we got to Clarendon Street, I tapped on Lynn's store window. She had already closed for the day and was wrapping some last minute gifts. Opening the door and ushering me in before any last minute shopper could see her, she told me, "I have something for you." I protested as we walked to the back of the store, reminding her we said no presents. She shrugged and handed me a small package wrapped tastefully before she went to the basement for champagne and glasses. The sun was shining through the large plate glass window in the storefront. "Fresh Eggs," the store name, was outlined backwards on the light wood floor. Lynn called to me to take the bottle of champagne she was passing from the basement. I took it and she came up the steep ladder with 2 glasses.

I opened the bottle with a pop and filled our glasses saying "Happy Christmas."

We both took a sip and I opened the package carefully. It was a small paperback book with a black cover. On the cover was a drawing of two white-gloved hands holding the same book. I opened it slowly and saw those hands holding a heart shaped paper cutout.

"You flip the pages," Lynn said, "Like this," and she demonstrated, flipping the pages to reveal the white gloved hands opening the heart cut out and, like an old moving picture, revealing the words "I love you" in hearts.

It was beautiful. I started to cry and told her thanks. She told me she meant it.

I brushed the tears from my eyes, gave her a hug and said, "I love you too."

I hadn't told Lynn that I might have cervical cancer. I didn't really want anyone to know but I needed to tell someone. It was this strange combination of a need for privacy but a need to share. I thought I could trust her.

So I told her, "I might be sick again."

She almost dropped her glass but instead put it down as I told her how the doctor had called me and explained that I would go for tests this week saying it was too early to tell. I wanted to cry again as I went over what the doctor had told me, the weird results, the possible cancer. She gave me a hug and we both were quiet and drank the champagne.

The limo honked gently and Lynn said, "That is for you," with a smile on her face.

I knew he probably wanted to get home for Christmas dinner too.

I thanked her again, reminding us both that, "its not like either one of us has any money really."

She asked me if I seriously thought she would let me take a bus on Christmas. I lied and told her there was nothing wrong with the bus. But I was still smarting from the fact that no one in my family would pick me up at the airport. I was, in fact, relieved that I didn't have to take the bus and promised to see her the week I was here and visit my birds since Lynn was taking care of them.

"Your babies are waiting for you," she sang as she went to open the locked door.

The limo driver greeted her and opened the door for me. Lynn came to the window and told me not to worry, that the driver gave her a great deal. She winked at him as she said it, told me I was a star and went inside to finish wrapping presents. I took the book out of my bag and flipped the pages to remind myself how much I was loved.

I relaxed and dozed nearly the entire trip knowing I would need some peace before I arrived at Kathy's house. We always had a full house on Christmas. With immediate family, there were twenty-one of us. And generally there were a few of what we liked to call "blow ins," the girlfriends or boyfriends who we figured may not last long. Ages ran from 2 to 76 and we were all loud. I could see from the front window that the table was set with my mother's china: white with burgundy and gold leaf. I knocked on the door as the limo driver brought my bags. Kathy was putting out the sterling silver and the crystal glasses. No one had even noticed that I had arrived in a limosine.

"So much for being famous," I said to myself.

Regardless, they were happy to see me and I looked at the table sentimentally. Those plates and sliver had graced every holiday I had ever known and I touched them and the embroidered linen table-cloth that was fragile and nearly translucent from so many bleachings for wine and gravy stains. When Kathy asked me to serve the potatoes and gravy, I obeyed, not only because I loved the food, but because I loved the tradition. I reminded myself that with this support, I could do anything.

I slept on Kathy's couch after dinner. We had toasted my dad with port and pecan pie. I had given my nieces and nephews each a photo of him I had found packing one day. They were proofs from his official portrait when he worked for the Governor of Massachusetts. He was about 50 in the photo. He was not smiling but not angry and his steel blue eyes were penetrating. Even from this old proof, you could feel his energy telling you to "do the right thing." It had been the quote that followed me out the door every night I was allowed out in my life. Even after I had moved out of the house, he would remind me to do the right thing. Everyone cried when they opened those photos, even me. Carolyn scolded me fondly saying, "leave it to you, Fans."

I smiled thinking of it as I crawled out from my blankets to look at the harbor. The house was quiet and warm but I could feel the chill from outside, almost pressing against the windows and the floor. I couldn't sleep, thinking too much and having eaten too much. The water and the sky were both dark midnight blue. The bright stars seemed far away but called me, twinkling. I reviewed everything in my mind: the feel of a good sterling knife on the Lamouge china plate, the sturdy red goblets from our childhood, my grandmother's silver candlesticks, the happiness in the 21 faces sitting around 3 round tables put together so we could all fit in the dining room, the conversations and the jokes, especially "the three chairs for the deceased," where we all saluted my dad, and how loud it was. I smiled as I remembered my brother in law Walter coming to the table with his earplugs and Kathy pulling them from his ears. Before I could cry, the coldness of the floor started to move up my feet and into my legs and I went back to the couch. My mom gave a loud snort in the bed just around the corner and I laughed, pulled the covers up and fell sound asleep.

Chapter 21

Calzi met me at the doctors. We checked in and waited a

moment before the secretary ushered me upstairs to the ultrasound. I hadn't peed for 2 hours and was dying with my, "full bladder." I tightened my butt muscles and wiggled my legs to control myself as the technician put jelly on my stomach and pressed the cold instrument against it to take the picture. I felt an incredibly profound sadness as I thought of all the belly's where there were babies and reminded myself that would never be my case. The emotion surprised me since I had never worried about having kids. I had so many children around me and in my life that I had never before felt a lack. And I never felt I had the right man for raising a family or for adopting. But in that moment, I wanted to cry. Instead I remembered the time I told Amador I might be pregnant and he said, "cool" like he wanted a child with me. It made me feel less alone, less hopeless even though I had not heard from him in days. Regardless, the sadness slowly lifted with that memory. The technician finished, wiped my stomach softly and told me I could pee. I pulled on my pants and ran to the toilet.

Shortly after, the doctor invited us into her office: nicely furnished, pictures of family, nice art, comfortable chairs, and a big window with the curtains drawn. I braced myself. She shook my hand and asked me if I understood this was not a big deal. I asked her if it was cancer. She smiled and said, "no". My shoulders relaxed. My face softened.

A weight lifted off my shoulders as I listened to the words, "pre-cancer abnormality but definitely not cancer."

Calzi touched my thigh and smiled. I started to cry. The doctor told me I was fine and reached over to touch my hand sympathetically. I kept crying while Calzi explained that with my history it was easy for me to get overwhelmed. The doctor explained to me that I really didn't need to worry. She could remove the "abnormal cells" right then, Calzi could stay, no anesthesia and 10 minutes later we were done.

We laughed about the whole thing over lunch and, although I felt embarrassed, I was elated it was not a big deal. Too, I was happy I had told only a few people. I apologized more than once to my sister for dragging her up for the appointment. She reminded me that if it had been something, I would have needed her. Then she asked me if I remembered what the doctor had told me. I admitted that I had no idea. I had been so lost in my relief and embarrassment that I had not really paid attention. Calzi explained that the doctor said it was something I needed to keep an eye on. She made me promise to do my regular physicals and checkups. I promised.

I sat in the car for a moment or two after I had waved goodbye to my sister. I thought about it all and thanked God that it was not cancer. I started the car and drove to Lynn's shop on Clarendon Street. She was behind the register with our friend Mario. When I entered he came to me with arms open saying he was sorry. As he hugged me I knew that Lynn had told him. I pulled myself from his embrace and told him that I was fine.

Then I looked over at Lynn with a smile and told him, "I am really well, actually."

Lynn smiled at me and although I smiled back, I was disappointed. I thought I could count on her not to tell everyone and here she had told Mario probably in bar conversation or worse, conversation over drinks in the store with other people. Lynn hung up the phone and before I could scold her or even be mad, she came over to me and gave me a hug and said, "So?" I told her I was fine and explained that it was a pre-cancer that the doctor removed. She hugged me again and then told me it was another reason to celebrate. Before she could go downstairs for some champagne, I asked her to wait until later and confided in her that I was pretty tired and it was a long drive. She agreed and told me she was ready to close up so we could get on the road.

We drove to Gloucester and Fernando greeted me saying, "Lynn says you are dying."

Then I did want to hit her but laughed instead and told him I was sorry to disappoint him but I was very healthy.

He said, "Then let's eat and not be depressed. Lynn told everyone you would die, so we were kind of depressed. Now I feel better."

I shook my head, looked at her with a "how could you" look and went to talk to the birds as Fernando opened a bottle of wine and started to cook. People were getting weirder by the minute. I was happier that I lived far away.

I spent the night and the next morning with them. We had coffee overlooking the salt pond that framed their backyard. It was a fabulous house. They had bought a mess and turned it into something magical. Even in winter the garden was beautiful, perhaps even more so as snow and ice hung off the dead flower petals that still clung onto the last year's plants. I drove Lynn to the shop and we stopped to pick up some things on the way. I loved shopping with her. She was fast and knew exactly what she wanted when she saw it. And if she liked something, she rarely hesitated to buy it, no matter what the price. For me, that was fun. For Fernando, it was an issue.

Before I went back to my mother's, I met my good friend Sue Lee in the city. I was catching up on old work gossip and we were laughing when the phone rang. I let it ring through and then waited. If it were Amador, he would call again. Sure enough, in less than two minutes, the phone rang again. I excused myself and left the room feeling slightly rude and hypocritical as I remembered walking out on my boss when she took a call as I was telling her I had breast cancer. But I couldn't call Amador back so after Sue told me it was okay, I walked outside to take the call.

Amador asked me how I was and I told him that things were good but I was at the doctor's days ago.

When I asked him why he didn't call he told me, "Bayby, it been hard here. There is nothing and I don't get to the phone."

I told him sarcastically not to worry, that I was fine.

He told me that I was always going to be fine finishing with, "You with me."

I laughed before he became serious and told me he wanted to hire Bali back to finish the work, saying, "He gonna help us more and he not gonna rip us off again. And really, it wasn't his fault before. It all was from that Gerry."

I couldn't help thinking we were blaming a lot on Gerry. Amador passed Bali off to me but at least told me he loved me first. I was still in mid sentence saying I loved him as well when Bali started to explain about the issues we had before and how he would correct them. But I was ambivalent, if anything, about the project. I told him to put things in a proposal and send it to my email.

I looked at the phone after hanging up and felt sad as I walked back to find Sue Lee waiting. I apologized and told her it was Mexico. I felt international and cool and much more than a drop out from Corporate America.

I told her I had another contractor and said, "So that is good, right?"

She said, "You tell me."

I thought about it for a long time later but really never could say either way.

Chapter 22

Once back in Virginia, I opened Bali's email. The numbers, the positive attitude and his interest in seeing the project through made me reconsider. I closed the email and decided to let him wait while I thought long and hard about my goal to build and bring women with breast cancer to Mexico. I thought about it as I drove to work and as I ran and as I looked at numbers in that windowless office and tried to make sense of them. I thought about the project as I wrote papers for the Pentagon and sat on the metro and as I waited for the work to be reviewed. I thought of helping woman with breast cancer as review meetings were cancelled and decisions were made without the input they had paid for. I thought about Mexico as I wanted to scream on my way back to the windowless office with a door and finally, I decided that it was my way out. Three days later, Bali asked to start work again and I said yes: to a new life and to an exciting project that might help some people, even me.

The next few months were full of calls and messages and, of course, wiring money. I was becoming an expert at sending wire transfers to Mexico. I liked progressing in something. But I heard more and more from Bali and less and less from Amador. And when I would ask for photos and nothing came, I asked again and waited.

I would eventually accept whatever excuse he would tell me: "I sent them but they didn't go through." Or, "They are all too big for sending on computer and it will cost a lot to mail them to you, but I will if you want." And then finally, "What, you didn't get them?"

I told him it was ok, preferring to believe he was doing what he should, helping me finish and creating a good project, than to believe that he was scamming me with Amador.

When I would ask Bali about Amador, he would tell me that he was around and that he visited the project. Eventually, Amador would call and tell me not to worry. I would feel better for awhile but would get anxious and preoccupied when he hadn't called in about a week. I didn't need much, really. I needed to know he was on my side. I needed to know we were still together, whatever that meant. And the angel on one shoulder would say to me, "How together can you be if you cannot even communicate?"

To answer that angelic voice, I started chanting a mantra of, "we are together in our hearts, we are working together, we will have a life together."

I worked in my office with no window but a door and every time I got afraid or lonely, I chanted that mantra. I believed it would all work out if I kept pushing. I would run and use the gym and pump endorphins to feel good and then go home, cook a sparse meal and paint or work on my computer. I gave myself no time for doubts. I had to get this right because I could not stay in this work or in this place or in this life. I would not be alone. I would not be normal. I would not fail. So, I did what I did best. I pretended that everything was okay. And for awhile that worked.

Then one night Amador called and I couldn't pretend any more. He cooed "baybe" into the phone when I answered. It was late on a cool September night and I pulled the blanket around me while we chatted, pulling myself from my dreams. Suddenly he told me I needed to fire Bali and it woke me like a slap in the face. After all this time and money, I asked him why, mentioning that Bali communicated with me better than he did. When I implied that he had been slacking, he got angry and asked me if I didn't believe him. Before I could answer, he said, "You want to fuck him or something?"

I asked him what he was talking about and reminded him that Bali had a wife and child. I tried to explain that I only wanted to know why he wanted to fire another contractor after it had been his idea to hire him again. He told me it was not my problem to know why. I angrily told him since I was the one paying the bills, I had a major part in the decisions. If he thought I would do exactly what he told me, he was mistaken. I wondered if he seriously thought he could use my money and then tell me what to do to be the heavy. I finally told him I had no time for this shit.

He told me, "You will see," and hung up.

I was shocked and afraid of what he would do. I wondered what I had gotten into and, no matter how I manipulated it, I couldn't pretend it was good. Like the time he nearly killed me on the highway, I couldn't deny that it was totally fucked up. Yet I looked for a way. I didn't sleep that night. The next day, I didn't let the phone out of my hand, and in meetings, I put the phone under my butt on vibrate in case he called. I would have run from a meeting with the president if I had a felt a thing. But I did not. I ran with the phone in my hand but nothing. After work I sent Bali an email asking how things were and waited for the response. For 3 days I couldn't function, couldn't focus, couldn't breathe.

I practiced yoga in the morning forcing the worry from my mind only to have it return the minute I finished praying for a positive mind, positive words, and a positive heart. But I was positively a wreck. He had done that to me so quickly. At the time I didn't see it, but he was conditioning me, like you train a dog, to think twice before I questioned him again. However, unlike a dog, I was thinking how I could cut him from my life. I became schizophrenic, trying to love him in my fantasy world while trying to protect myself from him in the other. Even after the car incident in Palenque, I had always carried love for him into both worlds: intellectual research engineer and entrepreneur in Mexico. I was in love with the beach bum in both places. After this, the dual nature of things reached my heart. I would allow myself to pretend to love him, knowing it would eventually all fall apart. My preservation instinct was talking to my heart and finally saying, "this is not at all okay."

He finally called on the third day as I was heading off to run after work. It was perfect. I was outside the office and on my own time. I told him immediately to never hang up on me again.

"Sorry, baybe, sorry," he said but then followed saying I needed to trust him.

He always turned it around. But I reasoned with him that he needed to consult me, not tell me what to do. He told me I needed to let him work things on his end. I told him it was still my project and he needed to include me. We went back and forth as he said that I needed to include him and then accused me of sending Bali money without telling him. He added the insult that I talked with Bali all the time and trusted him more. We continued fighting. I told him to get real and reminded him that I could not send him money since he had no bank account.

Then I said to him, "Bali calls me. You don't," and then I stopped myself, afraid he would hang up.

I didn't want to lose contact. There was a new vengeful tone in his voice and the possibility that he would hurt me or betray me entered my mind. I tried to keep him calm the same way I watched my mother placate my dad. The same way I had manipulated my bosses with kindness as much as intellect, I reminded myself that I could do it with Amador. But I had to control myself.

I took a deep breath and calmly asked Amador what had happened with Bali. Amador told me that he was not working well. That was it. I couldn't believe how stupid Amador sounded and told him he needed to work with Bali and show him how to do things better. I put the emphasis on him and tried to make him see that he could do something to make it all happen. Then I reminded him that was his job: to make Bali work well.

There was silence on his end of the line. I prayed he wouldn't hang up and I prayed he would think Bali could do the project again. I prayed for the comfort of my illusion. I wanted so badly to pretend that everything was fine.

Finally he spoke and said, "You right. You always right."

I exhaled and told him I knew he could do it, like a cheerleader. Before he hung up I asked him to stay in contact more, explaining that I needed to hear from him. He promised me he would and then thanked me.

Then I told him one more thing, "Never hang up on me again."

We said, "I love you's", and hung up the phone.

I sat for a moment and stared into space, wondering how it would go. I pushed the doubts away, looked at my watch and realized I had no time to run. I went anyway. I didn't care anymore. I ran through the woods, stretched and showered before going back to my windowless office where I had to tell myself that I was different from all these people in their predictable lives, in their cubes, happy until retirement. I knew that for me, that could not be my plan. That would not be my life.

I contacted Helen to see if they could go to Tulum in March. They had the credit from the cancelled flights and we planned around the kid's vacation. I would check on the condo in Miami and then meet them in Tulum to see the project. If I didn't look at how much money I was spending and how little I was making and how crazy I was feeling and how absurd my life actually was, I felt like a huge success. I was an international real estate developer. I had finished my books and they were beautiful and would be popular. I was an artist and would help lots of people. This was a rough spot and I reminded myself that it would all be ok. Then I prayed for a positive mind, positive words and a positive heart.

My father's words echoed in my head, "The power of positive thinking, Joanneo. Stay positive."

Chapter 23

I made it work with Bali. Amador didn't call me more often. Bali did. Bali sent updates but didn't really ask for money until one day he called to tell me the site had been shut down for not having permits. "But I paid for permits," I told him sincerely, not understanding. And then there was this litany of how yes, I paid but that really was for bribes and now they wanted more and if we didn't pay he couldn't work.

I found it so confusing that I just said, "Okay. Don't work anymore."

He was surprised. I was not. I may be way too nice most of the time but once I have had it, that is it. I don't budge. And I didn't with Bali. He was silent for a moment and then he started and I asked him to stop and wait for me. I told him I would be there in a month and we would figure things out then. He stuttered that people might rob the place. I told him he was still responsible for my property. When he told me Amador had the key I reminded him that he had one too. Hearing myself, I sounded like the boss I used to be. I liked it but knew that it was not so easy. I would pay for being so stubborn. However, I held my ground and in doing so probably lost some things from the site and what momentum I had but I gained some peace and respect. I needed that the most.

Amador called me a few times after that and I told him to wait too. Strangely enough, he accepted it. Perhaps he needed a break too. He was never as into the project as I had hoped he would be and it was taking longer than he thought. I felt the same but knew construction projects take patience and attention. I had both. He had neither.

In March, Helen and George and their three children and I went to Tulum. We rescheduled the trip from October. I was excited to see them and excited to see the project. But I was nervous to see Amador and Bali. Before I left, Amador called to say he had fixed the issue with the permits. I was happy but couldn't help think it was convenient that I would not need to investigate the issue now. That voice on my shoulder told me it had been a ploy to get more money. That thought made me tired and sad and nervous all at the same time. So I stopped thinking it.

I arrived a day before Helen to make sure things were OK. They were not. No one met me at the airport. I rented a car and drove down myself. I had not heard from Amador since he had called about the permits. When he asked for money to continue the project I told him we could talk about it when I arrived. So he was punishing me now with silence or I was no longer interesting for him if I was not sending money. I was at the point where I really didn't care. I almost didn't care if I saw Amador. Almost.

The drive south from Cancun always made me feel free. Since the first time Amador stood me up, driving along that road alone gave me joy. It still does. There is no other word for it. The road south is so flat that there is always lots of sky. You see all the cloud formations, especially in the afternoon when the cumulus clouds rise full of the moisture from the day. Somehow there is a very different energy in this sky compared road trips in the northeast. There are always those magnificent deciduous trees competing with the blue sky and when they lose their leaves, the sky is generally not so blue. Too, there is the warmth on the road in Mexico and by that time, I was renting the cheapest car I could find which normally meant no air conditioning. I was truly happy as I sang and let the wind blow through my hair in the non air-conditioned, no radio rental car.

Suddenly, I panicked as I entered the pueblo and realized I had nowhere to stay and needed to organize a place for Helen and her family. Usually Amador helped me. But this time I had no contact from him. I drove up and back the main street just in case I would have an, 'A sighting'. I didn't see him and if he saw me he chose not to come and find me. He was punishing me in some weird passive aggressive way, I knew. I also knew he would find me sooner or later and I went to the beach to look for a place for us. I found a nice hotel on the beach called *Luna Maya* where we could all stay.

It was at the part of the beach closer to town where there was a sandy cove before rocks and cliffs took over. For kids, it would be good and I thought that perhaps Amador wouldn't find us there for a few days. I wanted to chill before I got back into things with him. He was so exhausting. The one night before Helen arrived, I stayed at

Hotel Latino in town. For town, it was nice enough and cheap enough and I felt safe enough. Amador's friend Alvaro and my neighbor on the beach owned it but he was not around. I took a walk in town and had some dinner at *la Nave* but still, no Amador. I was tired and went back to the hotel to sleep.

About midnight I heard a tap on the door. I thought it was a mistake but then I heard it again, louder. I became afraid.

And then someone whispered softly, "Joanne."

It was Amador. I thought for a moment about not answering and considered what could happen. Then I heard that person moving the doorknob to get in. Then I heard him trying to pick the lock. I got angry and went to the door and when I opened it, Amador nearly fell to the floor.

"*Amor*," he said to me.

He was drunk but at least he was happy. He embraced me and started to kiss me, telling me he forgot I was coming. I told him I had heard that before.

He frowned, said, "You no love me anymore." He lowered his head, looked at his feet and shook his head saying, "no, no, you no love me."

I told him that I didn't like how he treated me if that was what he was talking about. And that I didn't like that he never called and that the few times he did he asked for money. "No," I agreed with him, "I don't love that."

He told me, "Baybe, you no understand."

He sat on the bed and reached his hand out to take mine. I gave it to him and sat next to him as he continued to tell me that it was not so easy here and that he couldn't call me when ever. He went on for a while but I was not sympathetic. Finally, he stopped talking and asked how I had been, finishing with, "You looks good,"

Then he reached over to kiss me. I kissed him back and tried to move but the room was so small that there was really nowhere to go. I asked him why he hadn't called me or met me or even looked for me that day reminding him that he could always find me whenever he wanted. I wanted to know why he chose not to find me. I asked him, "How is that missing me?"

I could be very honest. He never liked it and he told me it was the same sad old song but reached over for another kiss and pulled me closer to him. I resisted and then succumbed to his grasp and his charm. And as was becoming my habit when I saw him, I asked him if he wanted a nice hot shower. He smiled and acknowledged that he probably smelled. I nodded and turned on the hot water. We made love in the shower and then fell asleep together and woke when the light entered the room. Amador kissed me and asked the time. I wondered out loud what had happened to my guy who could tell time with the sun. He laughed and told me the sun was not in the room as he rolled out of bed and went to the bathroom. He came out and started dressing saying he had to go.

I found it strange and asked, "No breakfast? No swimming?"

He said, "Sorry Baybe, but I see you later."

I reminded him that Helen and George were coming in the afternoon but I didn't tell him where we were staying.

He was in a hurry and said, "I find you later."

That was all. No plan, no schedule, no time, just a promise or, perhaps, a threat. He came to the bed and kissed me, I asked him for a key to the land and he told me he didn't have it.

"But I bring it later" he said and then hurried out the door.

I felt betrayed and confused but decided to get up and do some yoga on the patio in front of my room. I had an uneventful day of reading, writing, and relaxing until I met Helen and George in front of San Francisco in the afternoon. We went to the hotel.

The rooms were perfect: one with a queen sized bed and 2 individuals and then a couch for Helen's baby. I had a big room with a king sized bed and one long side table in it, nothing more but a pole hanging from two lines where I could hang my clothes. I loved it. I had plenty of space to practice yoga and there was a small balcony where I could feel outside. Not that you ever feel too inside in a *palapa*, mind you. It is like you have brought the outdoors in. I was hoping that Amador would not find us until we had some time together. My prayer was answered. We settled in and had dinner at the hotel. The kids were tired. George took them to the room to sleep and Helen and I had another glass of wine and talked about nothing and everything: family, my life here in Mexico, her life there in Ireland. Then she asked the million-dollar question: how were things going on the land. I told her honestly that I wasn't sure, that I still had not been there since I had arrived and that Amador told me the site had been closed due to some permitting issues.

"I am prepared for a bit of a let down," I confided in her.

Helen touched my shoulder and told me to not be so negative. I tried to explain that it was not as easy as I had hoped and that there were many more issues that I couldn't really deal with too well from the U.S.

"It is an ambitious project, that is for sure," she told me.

I told her, "I'll drink to that," and we raised our glasses for a toast before Helen had to go tuck the kids into bed.

"I still cannot believe you have 3 kids," I told her as we said goodnight.

"Me neither," she told me with a laugh.

I climbed the stairs to my room and fell into bed, exhausted.

The sun shining through the spaces between the reeds in the *palapa* roof wakened me. I practiced yoga in that light and then went downstairs to have breakfast with the gang. I was surprised that Amador had not come to see me. Something was up for sure. But I pushed the thought to the back of my mind and focused on my friends. This was our time and I would not let him mess it up.

But I needed the keys to the land. I told Helen I would go to town for a few things and see them in awhile. I passed Bali's house: a trailer before the only traffic light in town. I climbed the stairs and knocked on the door. His wife was there but she did not want to talk to me. My Spanish was still so bad that it was easy for her to brush me off. As I was giving up, I looked around saw Bali's white Ford Bronco coming around the corner. "Yes!" I told myself and I waited for him to enter.

He didn't look unhappy but he didn't look happy to see me either. We said hello with the customary kisses on the cheek and I asked him what was happening with the project.

He looked at his feet and said, "Amador didn't talk to you? He said he would. Listen. He is not too easy to work and I have other opportunities."

He was quitting. I had stood up for him and now he was letting me go. Funny how things work.

He handed me the key and said, "Nothing against you. I wish you a lot of luck."

I found the family as they were leaving the beach. It was time to get the luminescently white kids out of the sun. There was no sunscreen available that would protect them. We went to Zama's where the kids could be in the shade and get spaghetti with butter.

George could get a beer and Helen and I could get a decent cocktail. I told Helen what had happened.

She said, "I cannot wait to see this Amador."

I cringed inside, hoping he would be on good behavior. Regardless, I explained how I at least had the key and we could go see the property.

"No worries, you will find someone wonderful to take his place," Helen told me.

I was not so sure.

We drove up the bumpy dirt beach road to the property and pulled into the drive. There was a tall fence of poles with a chain and a padlock, as I had remembered. The key fit. Relieved, I opened the gate and we all walked inside. My jaw dropped to my chest. The place was a mess.

"Typical construction," George said, "no concept of trash collection."

I laughed. If that were the case, all of Mexico was a construction site. The dirt was dark and dusty, almost like a powder. I remembered walking in it when we went to visit Davide before I bought the property and how black my feet had been. But there were those two stellar coco palms growing together as you entered. And then lots of smaller chit palms. I had the beginnings of common bathrooms on the right as you entered and then the beginnings of a house directly in front. But only the beginnings and they had been beginning for awhile now. The second floor still didn't exist, just some posts sticking up from the floor that was full of water. There were no walls and only supporting beams and the thin poles they placed side by side to make the ceiling. On top of the poles laid down next to each other, they put a tarp and then they would place the cement on the tarp. Every 50 poles or so, there was a thick, sturdy support beam. George, Helen, Sean and I couldn't stop looking at them.

"Bizarre," was all George could say.

"Hope it holds," Helen followed with a smile.

Her son Sean said, "Well, these indigenous cultures know how to build their structures. They have been building thatched roofs longer than the Irish. And they have some rudimentary techniques that are quite more than adequate."

We all looked at him and then started to laugh.

We walked through a mess of wood to the back structure. I

wanted to cry. It was 2 stories where there were supposed to be three, my "penthouse" being the 3rd. There were no walls, it was built pretty much the same way as the house with all these skinny poles covered in cement except the supporting beams there did not look so good. They had to be joined together to get to the height I wanted. The structure was lower to the ground but at least not on it. I could have impacted the earth more, I supposed. The back room was full of stuff: six of the back parts of toilets but none of the seat part, what seemed like thousands of meters of orange electric tubing, PVC tubing all over the place and in a maze of different sizes, cuplets and elbows in both copper and PVC. It looked as if a child had been let loose with a credit card at the hardware store: Amador.

My shoulders sank when I realized that, use it or not, I had paid for all of it. Then my eyes wandered to a nice looking palapa, almost finished, next door: Bali's house. He had in fact used my money to build his house. And he had continued after I left. I knew then that it was my wood: nice, thick, long, supporting beams. Now he had finished his house and had quit. I wanted to cry but not in front of Helen and George.

"It will take awhile to shape up, Joanne," Helen told me, "That is what construction is all about: making a mess and then pulling it back together."

I looked at her and sighed, "Then my life is a construction project."

She scolded me to not get negative and we talked about how beautiful the lot was and how certainly I could salvage the project. George and Sean were wiping sweat off their brow and suggested we should go back to the beach. And that was it. I couldn't really show much to my friends who had backed me in this project and who had believed in me so much. Helen and I went downstairs and the boys were playing among the debris. George was standing on the first floor looking at how they had built the roof and floor.

"Amazing," was all he could say.

"Let's go guys," I told them and we all headed off to the car.

As we were leaving, Amador came onto the property. I groaned inwardly to look at him. He was obviously stoned or drunk. His clothes looked as if he hadn't washed in a few days. As always, he was barefoot. But I loved that part and he had that little boy smile that I couldn't resist and a non-chalant attitude that made you believe everything was cool and nothing was his fault. I wanted to be angry with him but couldn't. And I didn't want a scene in front of Helen and George. So I said hello. He gave me a big kiss on the lips and then introduced himself to the family. He really could be charming. And he got all the answers to the questions he wanted. Where and how long they were staying, what they wanted to do, how they liked Tulum, even what they thought of the property. He found out everything that I wasn't so sure I wanted him to know. It was strange how I had this feeling that I should not expose people to him. I told myself not to be so paranoid and allowed myself to join in the conversation. The mosquitoes were killing the Irish people and then they started to bite Amador so we decided to go. When I asked Amador how he got here he pointed to a white van across the street. Now I remembered. He had wanted to buy a car for his "job" supervising the construction. We discussed it but since Bali had a car I saw no reason why I should buy another one. He could ride with Bali and he hitched everywhere and he seemed to always be successful so I didn't see why. Anyway, somehow he had gotten that car. I didn't really want to know how but I knew I needed to talk to him alone. I told Helen and George that I would drive with Amador and meet them back at the hotel.

When I got in the van he asked me how I liked it. I asked how he bought it.

"I got ways," he told me. Then he added, "You not the only one who can buy things."

I let the comment slide. He asked me what I thought of the site and I honestly told him I was disappointed.

He put it all on me saying, "What you think, it easy? I told you to fire Bali."

I told him that he quit and I started to cry. I am not sure why but I got so sad that I lost it. He softened then and I learned something about him for a change. He told me not to worry and that things would be alright and that he would help me.

"I gonna send you someone," he told me as we pulled up to the hotel and waited for me to say goodbye.

"You're not coming in to have dinner with us?" I asked him.

"Baybe I can't. I got things to do but I see you later."

I was suspicious but relieved in a way. It was either drugs or another woman or both. I couldn't handle any of it so I pretended it was okay and went to enjoy my friends.

He called his famous, "I coming back," as I closed the door after my kiss. I was weary and wanted to understand but realized it was too much work for me right now. So I did what I had been working on for the last 4 years. I let it go.

Helen and the family were not home.

"Must have stopped for dinner," I thought to myself and went to my room to rest and clean up.

With the heat and the dust from the property and the mosquitoes, I felt dirty. After a shower I fell onto the bed and looked up at the ceiling before I heard Helen calling my name. I went onto the balcony and we decided to have a glass of wine at the bar on the beach. I ate there with her and we talked and laughed and then walked to the sea and looked at the moon. I so wanted to be a tourist again all of a sudden. The thought surprised me since I never liked being a tourist. But I was beginning to understand why people went home. Helen and I started to feel the sand fleas and we decided to go to bed. I crawled into the oversized bed and imagined her family downstairs: all together, all pretty happy, all pretty responsible, even the kids. They were not necessarily boring but they fit a certain mold and it made their lives easier. Then I thought of my life and laughed out loud. Nothing fit and it was not making my life easier. I felt lonely but pushed the thought from my mind and fell sound asleep.

Hours later, I heard a knock on the door. I woke and the person knocked again. I imagined it was Amador and I stumbled to the door in my slip nightgown. I was right but when I opened the door he told me to come outside. He was really stoned or something. His eyes were pools of blood rolling around in his head. But he was super happy. I told him it was late and I was tired and in my nightgown but he took my hand and led me to the balcony.

"*Mira*," he said, "look."

Below me were 4 Mariachis, each one in his black tight suit with gold buttons down the outside of the pants and the front of the shirt. Two had guitars, one a trumpet and one sang. And he started to sing. It was fabulous. But it was loud. But it was Mariachi music and we were in Mexico. I let myself enjoy the music and the attention. I loved it and felt so much better for it. They sang a song called "*La Llorona*", that says "*canta no llores*" or sing don't cry.

It was confusing me as I mistook *llorona* for crier but really it is siren. Anyway, my heart melted. I thought that would be it but he came back up the stairs and handed me a paper rose. I imagined he would come to sleep with me but he kissed me as the mariachis left and he walked me back to the room and took my hand and brought me to the side of the bed and asked me for 250 pesos to pay the guys.

I was stunned, shocked, outraged whatever you can imagine. He didn't care. It was a cruel joke.

When I told him to get out and no, I would not pay he said to me, "then I gonna call the police and you gonna have trouble with those 4 guys."

I couldn't believe him. The way his mind worked was so perverse and mean. I knew I would never understand it. I never wanted to either. So I gave him the money and told him to get out saying I didn't want to see him again.

He told me, "No. I see you tomorrow," as if what I wanted didn't count.

I went back to bed and cried myself to sleep.

The next morning I woke with a "*mariachi*" hangover. I was sad but when the sun came into the window and I could hear the waves on the shore I decided that life was good and I went down to breakfast with my friends. "Fuck Amador," I told myself. I felt clean. I felt powerful. I felt happy. Then he showed up. As if nothing had happened the night before. He walked in, kissed me on the lips and shook hands with Helen and George and said hello to the kids. They were fascinated by him, his dreadlocks, the fact that he wore no shoes, probably too his dark skin. And he loved them. They talked awhile and then he asked us if we wanted to go to a *cenote*. Helen looked at me. She sensed something was not right. George had no clue and accepted the offer. I was not sure how I felt about it but we all decided to go. Amador would take us in the white van.

When we opened the door an adorable puppy came rolling out to meet us.

"Meet Tambor," Amador told us.

The kids went wild for him. He couldn't have been more than 2 months old and he wasa ball of brown and white fur. Super sweet but he had pooped in the back. The kids laughed when they saw it. I went for something to pick it up and cleaned it while the kids followed the puppy. Finally, we piled in with the dog as Helen started looking for seatbelts. Hardly any of the locals wore them and you would see families of 4 or sometimes even 5 riding a moped. But tourist parents couldn't let go of the need to get their kids into something safer. After practically tieing the kids into their seats, George rode shotgun and I sat behind Amador and next to Helen who had the baby, Rochean, on her lap since the car seat could not be fastened. The boys were in the way back with Tambor. There we were: me never wanting to see Amador again, Amador driving with no license in a car that I imagined had no papers, Helen and George wondering what the hell had happened to me. I smiled for no apparent reason.

We went to cenote *Escondido*. The first cenote I had visited with Amador. It was special for me, close to Tulum and exotically beautiful. As you walked in there were orchids and bromiliads hiding everywhere under the jungle canopy. The cenote had a platform close to the water from which you could easily enter and a cliff where you could jump in. The kids were in the water with snorkels and masks before you knew it. Sean, the older of the two, jumped from the platform with George while Donal the younger watched, afraid. He stayed with Helen and the baby entering from the dock.

Amador didn't go in and almost took care of the puppy but then went to smoke a joint behind some trees. I relaxed into the cool fresh water until Amador waved to me underhand to come to the dock and talk to him. When I swam over, he told me he wasn't feeling well. He wanted to go back. I decided to take him and come back later since the kids were having way too much fun. We took the puppy since he was Amador's, after all. Before we could get into the car, Amador vomited by the front passenger seat. I felt badly for him but was happy there were no witnesses. He climbed into the passenger seat as if he were 100 years old, put his head back and waited for me to drive.

"Where are you going, Amador?"

I had no idea where he was staying.

"Hotelito", he moaned.

It was the hotel his Italian friends owned on the Avenida. I had never been inside and didn't ever want to. So I dropped him at the curb. I reminded him about the dog but he asked me to please take care of him and he would come for him in the evening. Why not, I thought since the kids loved him and he was sweet. So Tambor and I went back to the cenote and Amador slept whatever he needed to sleep off in Hotelito.

It was all excitement when I got back. Donal had overcome his fear and jumped from the cliff into the cenote with George. It had been a stellar day. The kids were excited to see the puppy. Helen and George not so much and I wondered what I would do with him. But when we got back to the house, I snuck him up to my room. I hoped Amador would come for him soon but knew better. For the next three days, the last three days I would be in Tulum, I had that puppy with me everywhere. He was great but I didn't need a dog in that moment. The hotel people were cool, but it was a bit of a burden for everyone. I never saw Amador. We probably had a better time for it, but I was sad and hurt not to see him and angry that he left the dog with me. Despite it all, I enjoyed the visit with my friends who I probably would not see for a very long time after. And now that they knew all my problems, I wondered if I would ever see them again.

My last afternoon of the visit, I was sitting on the beach writing while the puppy ran when a tall thin young man came over to me. It was Moises, Amador's friend from the accident. He told me that Amador said I was looking for an architect and offered his services. He said it all before I could even get in a word about anything. His English was good and I forgot what an ass he had been when Amador was in the hospital. I saw in his eyes a kind person and he won me over with his humble smile. I shook his hand and said "thanks," and told him I needed help but wasn't quite sure where I would start or how. I needed some time. We exchanged emails and phone numbers and he told me he would get in touch in the next few weeks. He explained to me that he knew the land, had visited with Amador and had some ideas what we could do. He had seen the original plan for the spa and he loved the idea to bring survivors there. I smiled, said "me too", but I cried when he left.

The day I was to head out to the airport. I still had the puppy. Helen and George were going to Chichenitza and they would drop me at the airport. But I couldn't take a dog home. There was no way. So first thing I took the car to town and stopped at Don Cafetos and waited for Amador to pass. After about 20 minutes he did. But he didn't stop. I left money for my coffee on the table and ran to the car and followed him. He pulled around and made a stop in front of Hotelito. I double parked next to him and handed him the dog saying,

"I am leaving now."

He took the animal, looked confused and said, "OK I see you later."

I told him that he didn't understand and tried to clarify but it didn't sink in. He said he had things to do, calling me "baby". He got out of the car and gave me a kiss on the lips that I probably should have refused but I didn't and then he left. I went back to the hotel for Helen and George and packed the car. Finally, it was over between me and Amador. I wondered what I would do now. But I couldn't focus on it. I had to get back to work and my friends had to get on the road to Chchenitza.

As we closed the trunk, Amador parked behind us blocking our exit. I wasn't sure how to feel. But a part of me was definitely happy. He got out of the car and said, "You mean you are going back to the States?"

I had to laugh. He was such a clown sometimes. I told him yes, and he got angry and said that I couldn't go. I laughed harder until I realized he was serious. He was not going to move his car. Helen and George and the 3 kids were all waiting and I knew they were tired of his tele-novella bullshit. I took Amador aside and talked to him like a child wondering if that was the attraction for me. He was my child/lover. Sick, I admit, but there was something in his unrealistic childish approach that appealed to me. Ten minutes later he gave me a long kiss on the lips, told me to come home soon and moved the van so we could all leave. I breathed a huge sigh of relief as we made it to the highway.

Helen looked over at me and said, "He didn't slip the dog into the trunk did he?"

I laughed but made George stop the car so I could check anyway.

Chapter 24

I was not exactly miserable in Alexandria when I got back. I was flat lined although I looked for beauty everywhere and thanked God for each day. But there was a loneliness and disappointment inside of me that I couldn't shrug. I was a robot moving through my days; waking at 6, practicing yoga, out the door by 8 and into the my windowless office with a door by 8:30, 9 if I stopped for a coffee. I would mentally wander around my projects until 1:00 when I would go to the gym. By 2, I was back at my desk and eating out of a bag whatever I had brought for the day. By 7, I was home again and trying to market my non-profit or working on art projects, but always dreaming of Mexico. If my room-mate came home before I went to bed we talked, mostly about Mexico. Otherwise I would eat in front of the computer, check emails and write letters to potential sponsors, then crawl into bed with the phone under my pillow and fall asleep counting cancer booklets.

One afternoon, I was home before the sun went down. I had a meeting in downtown DC and rode the train to get there so I got home before dark. The day had been enjoyable and different. I did not have to drive and I was out and about on the streets of a city using public transportation. I had a love affair with trains. It came from my days on the subway in Boston and the fact that I totally believe in public transportation.

"If I were queen," I would tell my father coming home from the city in traffic, "I would stop all cars from entering the city and make the busses and trains free."

He would smile and tell me, "good idea Joanneo."

I sat in the sunny window by our balcony with a cup of tea and checked email. My heart skipped a beat when I saw an email from Moises. I hadn't heard from Amador for more than a month yet I still woke fitfully through the night to check the phone under my pillow for messages or missed calls. I had dreams about my neighbors taking all those bottom parts of toilets and the orange electrical tubing. I knew I couldn't leave the place and expect anything to be there when I returned but I did not know what else to do. So I was deciding to let it go by doing nothing. There was always a decision, even when you thought you weren't making one.

I clicked on his email and read his broken English saying how he would like to start to work on the property with me. He told me he had been there and was sure that we could use everything, clean up the area and move forward. He had attached photos and finished with one that said, "funny pet." It was a picture of a black and white dog in the middle of the building in the back, amid the debris and supplies. The dog looked at me with big eyes and a skinny, long, very young body. I started to sob. I wanted that dog and that project so badly. I did not want to give up. I asked Moises what he would need.

He wrote me back the next day with the answer: money. I was not surprised.

But he also sent a list of things he would work on and photos. We made a budget and little by little, I liked working with him. He was not totally responsive, sometimes answering my questions after 3 days but I was learning that in an underdeveloped Mexican town, that was how it had to work. There was no cell phone coverage in all of the beach and internet only in a few places in the town. Even those were not always reliable. So I learned to stress less when I didn't hear from him. I trusted him more than Gerry and more than Bali and, I had to admit, more than Amador. Regardless, it seemed things were progressing.

With Mexico more active, I could somehow focus more at work and accept the meaninglessness of it all. I was managing a conference in Baltimore, MD for our eastern coast offices. It was a big deal and there was more than one scientific big shot attending. None of it meant too much to me but I had a lot of responsibility, logistically anyway. And I enjoyed it since I was good at it and it was not at all mind numbing. I somehow felt powerful again with everything working.

At the close of the second session, my phone started to buzz with a number that was unidentifiable. I noticed but did not answer. It was not the time, if it was Amador or anyone else for that matter. I was busy. But when the 6th call came in during a break, I answered. Moises was on the other end and told me, "we got a problem."

I said nothing and he followed with, "Amador is in jail."

I am pretty sure my jaw dropped and the color left my face but I slowly walked to the terrace outside the conference area to talk. Moises continued to tell me that Amador was in jail for selling and using drugs. I sank onto the concrete floor of the outdoor space where no one was on this cool, rainy afternoon. I couldn't believe that just as things were going well, this. Moises continued to explain to me that they were going to take Amador to Playa del Carmen. From there he would go to a prison outside of Cancun unless, of course, I paid. And even then, they would only accept the payment for him to go to a rehab center. When I asked how much, he told me $1000 US. I asked to talk to Amador but Moises told me I could not. The police would not allow it. He told me I needed to decide now and send the money today. I was incredulous.

They had absolutely no idea of my life. But then I scolded myself "why should they? You always pull through."

I was quiet for awhile. Moises called my name into the phone but I had no idea what to do. I did not want Amador in jail. I did want him in rehab and I knew I had a $1000 overdraft on my bank account. I decided to do it. I told Moises he would have to wait but to please tell the police I would pay. So after my successful day at the East Coast Regulatory Conference when I should have been networking and celebrating with my colleagues, I excused myself to look for a Western Union pay station in the downtown area of Baltimore to pay for a beach bum to stay out of jail. Then I nearly jogged back to my hotel room to send Moises the pickup number by email. I called room service for dinner and I fell asleep with the tray on the floor outside the room.

The craziness started again. When Amador went to Rehab, Moises told me I needed to send him food and clothes. He offered to bring the things to him if I sent him money. I believed him when he told me he was visiting Amador each week. After all, why wouldn't I? Moises confided in me that he had done a similar treatment for drugs and it was the best thing he had ever done. It had turned him around. I wanted that for Amador.

I wanted to turn him around and I asked for an address to send Amador letters and gifts. I sent him the "little prince" in Spanish and love letters and letters that encouraged him to stay well and be well. After the initial shock, part of me felt very safe that Amador was under control. I was happy that he would get well, I would finish the construction and who knew, perhaps when I got back Amador would be well and we could start over. Things were looking up.

Chapter 25

It was springtime in the northeast and I decided to visit my family for Easter. I picked my nephew up in Baltimore and we drove to Manhattan together to have lunch and pick up Lexi, his girlfriend. We packed the three of us into the Saab and headed north with Brendan driving, Lexi sitting shotgun and me curled up in the back seat. Crossing the I-95 bridge by the industrial park that marks

Bridgeport, Connecticut, my phone rang. It was Moises. He told me things were going well but then, hesitated before he told me that he wanted to tell me something. His tone was mysterious all of a sudden and I assured him I was there.

He said, "OK. Did you know that Amador sold the piece of your land in front?"

I asked him to repeat what he had said. Moises asked me if Amador had told me that he had sold a piece of my property. When told him I had no idea what he was talking about, he explained that Amador had been in jail before this time, and again for more than a joint or two. It was a big deal and part of the reason why this time was a bigger deal. My head started to hurt as he told me that Amador had called my neighbor Alvaro to get him out of jail. Alvaro told Amador he would pay the police if Amador signed the front part of my lot to him.

I let silence convey my shock until Moises asked me if I was still on the line saying, "I know this must be bad for you."

Bad? The space behind my eyes was darkening and I thought I would pass out. Bad was not the word I would have used. I asked him why my neighbors didn't call me. I didn't understand. I thought they were my friends and they called me for everything else. Bali had my number I told Moises before I asked Moises why they would do that.

He took time to answer but finally answered simply, "They want your land."

I didn't know what to say but hung on the line before Moises told me he was sorry to be the one to tell me but he thought I should know. I pulled myself together enough to say thank you and that I could not believe Amador would do this to me. Then I asked him when it had happened. Moises told me it was months ago, before I came with Helen. I asked him what I should do. He told me to get a lawyer and protect myself and my land from Amador. I hesitated.
He could hear it in my voice and so he reminded me that Amador had problems. I told him I was aware of some of the things but obviously not everything. Then Moises said he had to hang up but that we could talk later by email. I said okay.

But then felt very much afraid and asked him to wait, saying, "Don't go yet."

But I could not think of anything to say. I knew I didn't want to get off the phone with him. My head was spinning and I felt the world closing in on me as I sat in the back of the convertible and listened to the highway zoom past. Everything slowed for a moment. I heard each guard-rail pass and the oncoming lights started to blur. I took a deep breath and told him thank-you again. He said, in his accented English, that it was nothing.

I told him, "No. It is everything," before he hung up the phone.

I let the phone fall away from my ear in disbelief. "Why? Why? Why?" I asked myself silently.

Brendan looked at me in the rearview mirror and said, "You okay, Fans?"

I told him I didn't know and that the call was a mind blower. Lexi turned in her seat to check on me and I took a deep breath and realized I needed to confide in someone. Brendan was a love and Lexi was more than cool. My mouth opened, suddenly not connected to my pride and I told them that the guy I was in love with, named Amador, and with whom I was working in Mexico had a drug problem. I explained that my Architect, Moises called to tell me that Amador had sold a piece of my land to get himself out of jail. I couldn't believe I had said it: that I loved a drug addict in Mexico and that my great project was not so great after all. I felt like a joke.

Brendan said, "Wow. That is a lot."

I told him that wasn't all of it. I couldn't stop my mouth. I told him that Amador, my love, had sold the land to my neighbors who took it from him when he was in jail. Brendan called them assholes. I continued. I told him that just last month, the last time Amador, my boyfriend, the love of my life, got in trouble, Moises called me and I paid to send Amador to rehab. I confided that it was costing me more than I could afford and now I had discovered this.

There was silence in the car until I almost cried and said, "Oh Brendo. What am I going to do?"

Lexi said, "Drugs suck, definitely," from the front seat and reached back to take my hand.

I leaned back in the seat and found the head rest and exhaled. I felt lighter for telling them. I still had no idea what to do.

Suddenly, I got nervous and pushed my head between the seats in front and said, "Don't' tell anyone, ok?"

I was not exactly proud of the whole thing. When I thought about it, I actually felt pretty foolish. But Brendan and Lexi told me

255

they could keep a secret. I said thanks and then closed my eyes. Brendan asked me if I were okay and I told him honestly that I was not and that I needed a bathroom. He asked me if I was going to throw up and I laughed and told him no. Even he knew my weak spot.

He finished telling me I shouldn't be embarrassed and said, "You are a really good person."

Then I started to cry. I didn't feel good at all.

We got to my sister Kathy's house late. My mom had been waiting for us with my sister and although I appreciated it, I would have preferred to crawl in unnoticed and lick my wounds the entire weekend. Brendan and Lexi went to stay with my sister Susan and my mom made me cocoa and we chatted into the early morning. Then I let it all go, climbed into bed and slept fitfully, dreaming of phone calls and lost opportunities.

The next days were filled with Easter eggs, food and laughter. But I was so preoccupied, I hardly enjoyed it. I told myself that on Easter, Christ rose from the dead after three days and so perhaps I could come out of this too. I drew the analogy that only a part of me died: that naïve part that trusted Amador to not damage me. I told myself that I may not be Christ but I had a relationship with him. When I was sick, I received every piece of good news with, "Thank you Jesus" like some bible belt person. It was half joke, half serious. That weekend, I reminded myself that I would be okay. It was not as if I had cancer again. Finally, on Easter Sunday morning I accepted what had happened but prayed to keep my dream alive and get back what my neighbors had stolen from me. I blamed them and prayed for Amador who I decided was a poor drug addict who needed help. I braced myself to fix him and decided not to let my dream go.

The drive home was long. We left at 5 am Monday morning to have Lexi to work in New York on time. We sat in traffic just past the city and it wasn't until 5 pm that I was home in my apartment in Alexandria. I was used to I-95, almost liking it, when it was moving anyway. When I walked into the apartment, the light was coming in the side window reflecting off the cherry tree in front that was in bloom. No one was home. It was beautiful. It was enough.

"Why do you need any more?" I asked myself, wishing I didn't.

At that moment all I wanted was a normal boyfriend and a normal life. I had a good normal job and a nice place and there were guys interested in me. I went to my room and saw the tower at the train station, put my bags down and felt the 400 thread Egyptian cotton sheets.

"It should be enough," I told myself. But it wasn't.

I made a cup of tea and went to the computer to talk to Moises by email but he was not on line. I called my mom and told her I was home safely. I called Brendan and said hello, told him the same, said thanks for being there for me. Then I sent out some inquiries for my books and went to bed. I had work early the next day and I was tired. No one called me that night. No one bothered me. I slept like the dead and dreamt that perhaps I would not rise again after all.

The next month was full of "chatting" emails with Moises asking about Amador, if he had food, couldn't I visit, what was happening in Tulum, in my project and was he sure I couldn't visit? We planned. He was my friend and I was grateful to have him. Yes I was sending him money but he was working for me so it was okay. And things were moving along. My dream was coming true. I planned a trip to Miami to see my mother for Mother's Day, the first weekend in May. We would spend the weekend hanging around. Things in Mexico were good, Amador was under control and I did not need to go visit the project for awhile. For now, I could take care of things like a normal person, and my mom was first on the list.

The night before I left, I was sitting on my carry on to force it closed when I got a call, number unknown. I missed a beat of my heart thinking it might be Amador, I was nearly afraid but not really. But it was my neighbor, Alvaro, the one who had robbed the front of my land and never told me about it.

"Alvaro?" I asked and then, "want to sell me my land back?"

I could hear the smile in his voice.

"No," he said and then continued to tell me he did not know what I was talking about.

But, he told me that Amador was out and that I had a big problem. My shoulders slumped and I almost hung up on him but listened as he told me that Amador was trying to sell the rest of my land to anyone who would buy.

"Fuck," I said into the phone.

Alvaro told me, "I told you to find another person to work this. Now you need to do something."

And he had. When I was working in Miami and Amador was in

Tulum, Alvaro had told me, "Find another friend," telling me that Amador was just not right. I did not see how I could do that. Tell my lover that I did not want to work with him and wanted someone else on the contract?

My head was swirling caught between the past and the present when Alvaro pulled me from my thoughts and told me, "Come here and fix this."

I didn't say anything.

Alvaro continued, "For God's sake he is in the street trying to sell your land."

I felt as if someone had punched me. I asked him distractedly for the name of an attorney and he gave me the name of Mario Vela telling me he had helped him a lot. I took the name, email and phone number and hung up without my customary, thank you. I didn't accuse. That night I wrote an email to Mario Vela, the attorney in Playa del Carmen, explaining the situation: "I loved this man and wanted to marry him but it seems he loves drugs more than me. I need some help."

Chapter 26

The next day I met my mom in Miami, our last weekend in the condo we bought together. She planned on spending the summer on Cape Cod and we were both unsure about what would happen the next year. The winter had been good for her weather wise. But she had been lonely. I was moving toward living in Mexico, at least part time and she wanted to be near family full time. But neither one of us discussed it openly, although we both knew what was in our hearts.

I arrived on time and walked out to the pick-up area. My mom was just arriving too we embraced.

"How are you darling," my mom nearly sang to me as I hailed a cab to take us home.

I told her I was great now that I was there with her. We are friends. We are confidants. But I still could not bear to tell her what was happening with my dream, with my life and with this man. I had defended myself so many times that now that it was clear they had been right all along, I could not stand it.

We chatted about normal silly things like my job, the foundation, my health. But in the back of my mind, I was thinking how I could tell her that I booked a trip to Mexico so that I could save my land from Amador. My new attorney, Mario Vela, told me he could have the paperwork ready Monday and he emphasized that the sooner we had Amador sign, the better. The plan was to have Amador sign his rights to the property over to Mario's associate Carmen, until I could find another Mexican to be on the papers. In the back of my mind, I hoped Carmen would stay on the paperwork forever, whatever that might be.

But I had 3 days from work to take care of things. My mom and I were supposed to leave together but I rescheduled everything to manage Amador's mess. We had planned a long weekend to talk about what we would do with our investment there and to spend some time together on Mother's Day. But I cut it short and felt like a shit. I hated Amador for it but I needed to do some damage control.

We walked into the condo and I rolled my suitcase over the big square white tiles and looked out over the Atlantic Ocean directly in front of me. The emerald green was breathtaking, my favorite painting of Harry's on the wall next to the 4 triple pane windows looked perfect. Below it were the curved stairs I had custom built for my old condo on D Street. I mentioned that I sometimes forgot how beautiful it was there. She told me she was thinking that too. We were both silent for a moment thinking that it was a beautiful place. But it was a lonely place.

I broke the silence and said, "But it is just a place. And we can move anytime we want to."

I wanted her to know that. She said we would talk about it over dinner and asked me if I had gone to the office. I told her I had but only for a few hours. I tried to remember exactly what I had done but couldn't. I had gone through the motions, saying hello, answering emails, checking documents, looking at the research paper I was putting together, compiling numbers and statistics. I wondered how it had come to that but then pushed any depressing thoughts from my mind and pulled my suitcase into the bedroom. The bed was up high, on top of my flat files full of art, a lifetime of trying. I started to cry but stopped myself and looked into the mirror and told myself it would all be ok. I took a deep breath, threw some water on my face, put on more mascara, colored my eyebrows and then called to my mom to go.

We headed down the elevator and across Collins Avenue,

"A1A," then down one block and up another to a café on the side street where we had been many times before. There were lovers in many of the seats and a family of five at one of the bigger tables. I looked at a quiet table for two and asked my mom if it would be okay. She was always agreeable and said it would be perfect.

We ordered an antipasto with more cheese and less meat and two glasses of red wine before we even thought about a main dish. Then we decided to share and as the wine arrived, my mom asked me about Mexico. She knew. I could hide nothing from her. I took a long savory drink of my wine and told her things were not going so well. I took a deep breath and told her that on Easter weekend I discovered that Amador had sold a piece of the property to my neighbors to get out of jail for using drugs. And I told her that I was paying to keep him in rehab but now he had finished and was trying to sell the entire piece without my permission. I looked at the cheese and drank some more wine.

She said she was sorry and asked how I could afford that.

I told her I couldn't but reminded her, "you know how good I am with credit cards."

My mom shook her head and actually called him a bastard. I started to defend him but then knew better. My mother didn't say a thing but her eyes told me not to be so naïve. I continued and told her that I knew it was my fault for trusting him. But I told her that I needed to go to Mexico to get his name off things and start over. I couldn't look at her. I was embarrassed. She asked how I found out and I told her that my architect told me Amador had sold the first piece and now my neighbor had called to tell me he was trying to sell the rest. I thought out loud that it was funny how they wanted to help me now. But how they acted as if it were all my fault.

My mom didn't say a thing. I agreed that I could have been smarter. Thankfully she stopped me and told me that I could not change how I felt about him.

But she took my hand and made me look into her eyes and told me, "now you need to take care of yourself."

Then she asked me when I would go. I told her I had a flight for Monday morning even though we had planned on leaving together on Tuesday. She told me not to worry about her, but there was a sadness in her voice that crushed me. I had not only let her down by not staying there with her, I had let her down by being so stupid. I had let everyone down by not paying attention to what was real and what was not. Amador was a jerk and a con and I should have seen it. But all I saw was this marvelous needy man and I thought I could be his all and we would be happy.

We finished the antipasto in silence and my mom finally said, "I am so sorry that this is all happening." The waiter brought the lobster ravioli and we both inhaled the aroma of the sauce. Then my wise mom told me to not let him spoil the time we had together and commanded me to, "Enjoy," as I served us both.

We relaxed and swam and talked about selling the condo and about all the great things we could do with whatever profit we made, if any. And on Monday morning she drove me back to the airport and I abandoned her once again. She told me not to worry and to be careful. I reminded her that the driver would be there and could help her with her luggage. I gave her a strong hug and fought back tears as she got into the driver's seat and I waved and watched as she drove away. I cursed Amador as I moved into the Spirit Air terminal and checked my bags. In under two hours I would be in Mexico. In less than 4, I would meet with the attorney. All I had to do was figure out how to get Amador to sign.

Chapter 27

Moises was supposed to pick me up. I looked for his white van as I waited outside the airport. The heat was more than in Miami and there was something about being so far away and on my own that felt good. Perhaps it was the challenge. I still don't know. But I felt better there, even with all the shit.

I leaned my suitcase against a wall and stood next to it remembering how many times I had waited there. I thought back to all the times Amador had left me waiting for hours and never showed up. Then I thought of the wonderful times he would show and I felt a tear forming in the corner of my eye as I remembered the time Bali had come for me and an anxious pit grew in my stomach before I saw the white van move into the access road. I took a deep breath, grabbed my bag and walked towards it as the driver pulled into a parking space close by. When the door opened, I stopped and inhaled sharply. It was Amador.

He looked at me, smiled and said, "*Amor*," as he walked toward me.

I opened my arms and we embraced. I couldn't help myself. I hugged him and then we kissed. It was absurd.

When he released me I asked him, "Amador. What is going on?"

He looked at me and told me I should know and then asked why I had sent him to a horrible place. He looked at the ground and shook his head. I asked him if he would he have preferred jail. He looked at me and asked who told me that. I told him honestly that Moises and Alvaro both. He said they knew nothing and started to get mad. I told him that none of it justified him selling my land. I watched as his jaw started to tighten and a line grew between his eyes. I backed off, said nothing more but I did not back down or apologize. He took my bag and we got into the car. I touched his hand as he pulled from the parking space.

He did not pull away but I waited a few minutes before asking, "Now what?"

He looked straight ahead and said to me, "We go to your attorney right? I need to sign some papers and get off your land. You want me out of your life."

"That is not true at all," I told him and continued to tell him how I wanted him in my life but not this way. I told him that I missed my happy man on the beach and finished telling him that this was not our dream.

He looked at me, sincerely, shook his head and said, "*No, verdad?*" No, for sure.

I looked at the scenery, the billboards and trees flying by. I rested my head and closed my eyes and imagined I were in a different time, riding down to the biosphere with him, ready for a swim and a picnic.

He called me from my dream, saying, "It is not so easy, you know."

I told him it wasn't so hard either, something he had once told me. He smiled and looked over at me and took my hand. Neither one of us had anything to say. I looked back out the window.

I thought of the email I had sent my attorney: "We were supposed to be married but it turns out he loves drugs more than me and now he is trying to sell the land I paid for."

It would be embarrassing to meet him. But I knew it was my only chance. Amador felt badly in this moment and I needed to use it to my advantage. I never knew when he would snap. I directed him to the office on Tenth Avenue and told him the attorney's name. He knew the location and found it easily in the organized maze of Playa del Carmen. We parked and walked hand in hand into the office, me in jeans and a white linen shirt with sandals from Kenneth Cole. Amador wore his beach shorts, his Puma soccer club T-shirt that he probably had slept in and no shoes. The secretary looked at us slightly sideways but was polite and escorted us to a conference room. I was grateful for her manners. We sat next to each other staring at the three stacks of papers on the table. We waited five long minutes staring at them silently with me nervous and ready to scream and Amador able to walk at any minute. But he stayed calm and was still more or less on my side.

Finally, Mario Vela came in and introduced himself. He was polite, with dark hair, taller than many Mexicans and light skin, probably Spanish ancestry. I liked him. He sat next to Amador and in a soft voice, directed him to sign the papers one by one. He explained each and every page, each and every clause. I caught myself holding my breath and coached myself to breathe and think positive thoughts. Then he gave me the contracts to sign, again, page by page, explaining every one.

And then it was over. I could exhale. Amador had no formal power over my land. I had a contract with Mario Vela's associate who had signed a contract to give all rights and responsibilities to the land to me. As we left the conference room, Mario, now my attorney, took me aside and asked if I would be okay.

When I shook my head yes, he told me, "You need to take control of this. You need to get on that land, physically."

I did not fully understanding what he meant. Didn't I have control now? I mean, we signed all the papers. Amador had given Carmen all the rights and she had given them back to me.

But Mario told me, "you need to make sure that he does not try to take this property away from you." I had no idea what he was talking about and asked him how that could happen if Amador had signed everything.

"People do strange things when land is involved, that is all," he told me seriously and then continued to tell me that if I wanted my project to happen on this piece of land, I should move there as soon as possible to make it happen.

I let the advice settle in, inhaled and asked him if I could call him if I had any problems. He handed me his card telling me I could call anytime. We shook hands and I left the office. Amador was waiting outside to take me to Tulum.

"That was easy," I thought as I settled into the front seat.

That voice inside my head said, "Way too easy."

And then it began. Amador told me I would have problems without him on the land documents. I chuckled and told him I certainly had enough with him on the land so I would not be surprised. We took the left turn onto the highway and I felt his attitude shift. He mumbled that I had sent him to that place. As if I were his mother, I told him he sent himself. But it was as if he didn't hear me. He continued to get agitated saying that I never came to see him. He was almost crying when he looked over at me and told me he had waited but I never came. I felt like a shit and tried to explain that they told me I could not visit. He asked me who told me that and when I told him Moises he said, "Fucking Moises."

I explained that I sent money to Moises to take care of him and that Moises said it would be better if I stayed away. I told him I thought that was the program. He said I should have demanded to see him, or at least talk to him. Then I asked him how I could have known. He didn't answer, and I told him I was trying to do the right thing. I felt frustrated, almost as if I were failure as his woman. He became quiet. I had reached a place in him somehow. I exhaled knowing he wouldn't kill us in the car just yet.

We arrived in Tulum as it was getting dark. I was hungry but didn't say anything. Amador told me he needed to see some people.

I said sarcastically, "Just like always."

He asked me what I knew about anything as we pulled into a back road and Akim, Gisela's friend, now Moises' ex, apparently, came out of a house and ran up to meet me and gave me a hug. I was distracted but happy enough to see her. Amador told me he would be right back and went into the house with her. I put my head back on the headrest and closed my eyes thinking to myself that the day had been a lot.

"There's a lot more," the voice inside my head responded as Amador came out and reached over to kiss me.

He told me we would go to get Moises and give him his car. He pulled away from the curb and as we headed deeper into the village, I asked Amador where I should stay.

He told me it was not his problem finishing with, "I don't want to send you to places."

I was weary of the entire thing and asked him if he didn't want to stay with me. He told me flatly that he would not stay with me anymore. I was sad but did not understand why. I caved into myself emotionally but then came out again. He was punishing me and it hurt. But I knew it was for the best. I had done nothing wrong. I didn't deserve this but here it was. He had taken a piece of my dream, what I thought was our dream, and thrown it away. He was lucky I still wanted him. But in a way, I was only pretending he was my man. It made no sense. Somehow, my reason was not translating into action. Regardless, I asked him why. He went back to the rehab issue telling me I had sent him to a bad place and that I trusted Moises more than him. He finished telling me to let Moises help me find a place.

We were back on the main avenue by this time. I was so weary of the whole thing I finally reconciled the two parts of my brain and told him to let me out of the car preferring to get a taxi to help me. My emotions for the last year spewed out without control.

I told him, "I did what I did out of love and if you cannot see that and forgive me, if all I am for you is a mistake then what is the use."

I went on to tell him I loved him, of which I was not entirely certain but I told him I was there for him. I told him he had to understand. I finished telling him that I had a life as well and things had not been so easy for me either. I reminded him that I had been working for us and that had been the plan. And then I got deeper into it and asked him where he was when I was in the hospital.

I said to him, "Did you fly to see me? No. Did you sleep beside me or even hold my hand when I was afraid? No. So, really, Amador, fuck you."

He smiled and then actually started laughing. I got angry and opened the door while the car was running, getting ready to jump. He reached over to stop me and told me not to get crazy. He told me it was okay and grabbed my arm. But I fought to get out until he told me I was right.

He said, "you always right" and then I closed the door when he agreed to help me find a place. "Don' worry," he said.

But first we had to find Moises to give him the car.

I started to calm down. I asked him if he understood where I was coming from and told him we all made mistakes. I reminded him that I forgave him and that he needed to forgive me. I was talking as much to myself as to him but in that moment, he stopped the car in the middle of the road and kissed me.

"I love you Joanne," he said.

And I believed he did. I still do.

We drove to the end of town then two or three blocks back and to the left and found Moises. The neighborhood was dark now. There were small houses close to each other and trash everywhere. Moises had been waiting for us and I thought he looked thinner than I had remembered. Perhaps it was the new beard he was wearing but his face was long and his eyes looked tired. He smiled when he saw the car and when he saw me in it. I knew that feeling.

He said, "Hello Fanny Barry."

I greeted him and gave him a hug. He asked me how things were and Amador answered for me, saying things were fine and telling him to get in that we were going to the beach.

Moises obeyed and got in the back asking where I would stay. When I told him I didn't know, he told me there was a new place called Jade. He said he had done some work for them and he was sure they would give me a good price.

"I know them too," Amador said, as if knowing them was a privilege, and then he said we would go there.

I relaxed for a moment. I felt my shoulders soften. I felt cared for and loved as we took the right turn toward the southern side of the beach. As we passed the break in the palm trees and the restaurant Zama's, I inhaled, smelling the Caribbean, and smiled at the first glimpse of it, with rocky outcroppings that sheltered the beach ahead. We passed several makeshift shacks that stood in the face of the hurricanes, wiped out every season and then re-built as the owners, who were fishermen and drug dealers, tried to hold onto that piece of land that was really being loaned them by the sea. The road turned to dirt after Maya Tulum and we bumped along. I held on and was suddenly very hungry. I told them but Amador told me he was not as he gripped the steering wheel and maneuvered around the big pot holes. I could see he was getting angry again. Moises suggested to check with the hotel first and then we could go to eat. I realized he was kind and polite, whatever else he was in addition.

After what seemed like a long time but what I would find on my bike to be about 3 km, Amador took a left up a narrow drive where the sign said, "Jade, Sueno Primitivo." The driveway was full of palm trees and we stopped in front of what seemed like a small concrete cottage next to a set of stairs that led to an elevated wooden walkway to cabanas and a huge palapa. The elevated cabanas were like tree houses. It was dark and I couldn't see much but you could hear and feel the ocean as we parked badly and got out of the car. There were only two other cars in the driveway but we managed to block them all. Amador didn't care. I said nothing, afraid to infuriate him. His angry mood was palpable. We walked into the concrete area which was a combination of a reception and kitchen.

Moises and Amador went in ahead of me. I stood outside and looked around. I felt very tired all of a sudden and looked up at the stars. They were incredible, sparkling, nearly calling me. Amador called me to come in and he introduced me to Juan and his wife Martha. Juan was tall and sturdy, not fat but not slim either. I couldn't tell if he was handsome since he had a big beard but his dark eyes were happy and welcoming. He extended his hand to me. Martha, his wife, did the same. She had dark long hair, beautiful dark eyes and was mysteriously cautious and melancholy. But they both smiled and offered me a room for $75.

I accepted but felt self-conscious somehow. Perhaps it was my bad Spanish but I could feel them checking me out. As if they were wondering who I was. Finally Juan spoke in good English and told me his worker, Fabio, would show me to my room. As if on cue, a beautifully tattooed man came into the room and smiled broadly, and theatrically said, "*buenas noches*".

Then in a heavily accented English, "Come with me, come with me" he said, almost as if he were pretending to be some sort of funny servant or quosimodo bringing us up the stairs.

He carried my bags to a room in the first row of tree houses. The walkway and all the cabanas were 2 meters above the beach, nestled into the trees. Everything was made of wood. Fabio opened the door to a small room with a queen-sized bed, windows on both sides, wood floors and a nice, simple bath. Amador was behind me but Moises was nowhere to be found. Fabio mentioned to me that the handle on the door worked backwards. I looked at him oddly as if to say I could handle it and he shrugged.

We went inside and he told me, "You got everything you need," as he pointed to towels and extra blankets and then started to open the windows for me.

The sea air moved in. There was no fan and it was stuffy inside but the breeze entered the room and quickly pushed the stuffiness away. I knew I would sleep well. Fabio asked me if I had any questions and, when I said no, told me that he would see me later and continued, "If you need anything I live here."

I thanked him and noticed that I felt less tired around him. Amador still said nothing. I put my bag in a corner, sat on the bed and told him it was nice. He said yes and then that we should go. I asked him to give me a second to use the toilet but I didn't dare to show him that I was annoyed. His mood was shifting and I knew I needed to be careful.

He walked outside and waited for me on the balcony to go back downstairs. Amador talked to Juan in Spanish and then Moises appeared from the beach. We said good night, I left a deposit for one night and we went up the road to a place on the jungle side called Casa Banana. It was a funny place, with sails for the roof and surf boards on the walls. The floors were wood and not level. There were too many tables for the space so the chairs were difficult to get into. But it was still open so we sat down, ordered and Amador started on Moises.

"She says she sent you money but you never give me nothing. Nothing."

I looked at Moises. He said nothing. Then Amador accused Moises of selling his wood to Alvaro. I was incredulous but Moises denied selling the wood and told me that he had used the money I sent to pay the police and some other things. I asked him about the packages I sent.

He told me he gave it to the people at the rehab center but finished saying, "But I don't think they ever gave it to Amador."

Amador said he never received anything. I got sad. I looked over at him and noticed that his face had changed. He did not look beautiful anymore. He looked mean.

I wanted to cry but instead I ordered food. I needed some energy. They didn't order anything and I ate while Amador kept accusing Moises of things and Moises defended himself. I listened and discovered what had been happening and how many mistakes I had made. Amador was only drinking. When the bill came, they looked at me to pay. I did and they drove me home. Amador walked me to the door and told me he did not want to stay with me. I was almost too tired to care. But it hurt because I wanted to talk to him, however useless it might be.

I asked him, "I would like some time with you. Please stay?"

He said no. I would not ask again. I opened the door and looked back at him, waiting for him to go.

He started to walk away and then turned and said, "I see you tomorrow."

I couldn't even speak. Tears were moving down my cheeks. He walked back and told me not to cry. I asked him how I could not cry, remembering the time he left me before at Amansala.
I looked at him and stated, "You are leaving me."

But he told me it was only for the night. I asked him to promise and he did and then he wiped the tears from my eyes and kissed them both and then kissed me on the lips telling me I would be okay. He then commanded me to sleep and gently pushed me inside, closed the door behind me and walked away.

Chapter 28

The next morning I woke with the sun. I felt it rising more than seeing the light. The ocean was calling me and I walked outside. What I could not see well in the night I could now notice. My room was almost inside a big sea grape tree, *uva del mar*. The limbs came over the balcony and we were tucked into one of the creases in its limbs. Nothing had been cut of this valuable shore-stabilizing tree. I liked Juan and Martha more. There were 2 small chairs to the right of the door so that you could sit in the shade. I walked to the left on the boardwalk above the earth toward where Juan and Martha had built a stairway down to the beach. I didn't go down, I sat on the stairs watching the sun rise. There was no one around. The morning was my own. I stayed for 10 minutes watching and then went back to my room, left the door open and practiced yoga in that space in front of the door, next to my bed. I wasn't really happy or sad. I was whole somehow. I accepted everything, all the bad and the goodness around me and knew I could still do my project. I still had my dream.

Martha and Juan served a continental breakfast: coffee, toast from a package and orange juice. Juan said he made the best coffee in Mexico. I watched him hand grind it in a big metal grinder attached to the counter near the stove with a handle on the side. He would fill the receptacle with the beans and then work the handle around with great effort about 15 or 20 times. He said it was good for his biceps, smiling. He didn't use any extra electric appliances because of the solar power. Everything had to be planned and budgeted, he told me. Down to every light bulb. I had not yet told him that I would build here, afraid that if I mentioned it to people, the whole thing would disappear. Too, Juan and Martha were polite and friendly but somehow standoffish. There was a barrier between us that was more than just client/owner. I was their only guest and I brushed it off to a cultural issue. I never dreamed it was the company I was keeping.

Fabio was brilliant; always moving, never too close but generally there when I needed something. He and Juan seemed more like great friends than owner/employee. They were like guys always working on something. You could feel that they were all there for love. It was in the planks on the floor. I was safe there. I knew it.

Amador did not visit me that entire first day. It made me more firm in my conviction to continue. I actually felt better. Life was nicer. Moises did come to see me. I was sitting in a low wooden folding chairs to the right of my door, in the shade of the sea grape around 11 when he came up the front stairs to see if things were ok and to talk. I was happy to see him, thanked him for his help and told him the place was wonderful. He was genuinely happy. We talked about my project and then we walked the beach together to my land. We entered the large wooden gate made of poles. Moises had the key to the padlock.

"It is a new one," he told me explaining that they had to cut the other one off. Amador had lost the key.

Entering, I could see there was not really that much. It was cleaner. Moises had done that. And I still had to pay him. The first time anyone had extended me credit in Tulum. Things were more organized and you could see that the strip of jungle land had been cleared with care. None of the palms had been cut, at least not that I could see. If Bali had cut some, the stumps were under the houses. There was that small concrete building, a box really, as you entered to the right; the bathroom for the spa. It was vacant but for a pipe for the shower and a drain in the floor. But the drain didn't drain. Moises told me he had checked it and we tried again together, just to make a mess I suppose. It was an ugly concrete box: no windows, no style. It could be a storage space, Moises told me.

There was still some wood running along the side of the property. I looked at the shells of my mediation and yoga salon and what would have been my house, a three-story structure rising above the chit palms and noticed that at least they were not resting on the land. They were not as well done as Jade but at least there was a crawl space below each building. I shook my head remembering all those years of environmentalism and here I had fallen into the development trap. We climbed two ladders to the top of the back structure, my house, where we could look out over the *manglers* and then up toward the lagoon. If God was anywhere, he was there. We were silent for awhile and then Moises cell phone rang. He politely went down to answer it. Without him there, I cried. I sobbingly told God and the *manglers* all my troubles and apologized for being such a fool.

For the next 3 days I made that trek my routine. After a continental breakfast with Juan and Martha, I would walk up to see my place. I started to take ownership mentally at least. I would climb to the future pent house, the tree house actually, and check in with God and the earth. I looked out on the great wetland system known as the *Sian Kaan* Biosphere, one of the largest nature preserves in Mexico. I felt small and powerful in the same moment. The advice from my attorney echoed in my head. Occupying the land was always running around in my mind. I knew I could do the project alone but it would be difficult. I had thought I could count on Amador but realized he was more of a liability than anything. Too, he had not come to stay with me the entire time I was here so I figured he had someone else. Unbelievably, I missed him. But I knew I missed the person I wanted him to be, not who he actually was.

Moises came to Jade the morning I left. Juan had organized a taxi for me and I was waiting, packing the few things I had brought. "What you gonna do?" he asked me.

I smiled and told him I really didn't know but that I wanted to continue. I felt I had to. He told me he could help me, reminding me he was an architect. Once again I heard how a guy could organize everything, send me pictures, get workers and help me have my dream.

Once again, a guy told me, "It is a good project. It is a good idea."

And once again, I committed to working with him. I wanted this so badly that I took the help I could get. Moises was more genuine and at least an architect. Too, he seemed to be speaking from his heart. He was respectful, understood I was the boss and we were not lovers so it would be easier. I felt better as I got into the taxi for the airport and committed to come back the next month: June.

As the taxi was backing down the drive of Jade laboriously, avoiding the palm trees, Amador came walking up. I was not happy or sad to see him. I was more afraid and not sure why. But he smiled when he saw me so I knew he was in a good mood and I smiled back.

He stopped the driver as if he had the authority, looked into the window and said, "Baybe, where you going?"

He seemed so innocent in a way. I got out to give him a hug, or a hold as he always said, and told him I was leaving.

I started to cry and he held me tighter and said, "I so sorry."

I pulled away to look at him and said, "me too."

We kissed and I got back into the cab and drove away.

Chapter 29

I had stayed in Mexico longer than I had planned. I could have stayed forever in that tree house hotel that floated over the dune. It felt so right there, so much in harmony with the natural environment and in such a comfortable way. But I had a million things going on back in the US. I was running my That Barry Girl non-profit with my friends Sheba and Paul while working full time as a policy writer for a national program. It didn't matter if it was water supply, birding programs or consistency with the law, the programs were important to someone and they paid. A couple of people wanted to put my art in shows. And there were my books. I needed to sell a million to finance my project. People loved them but the numbers were not adding up. I spent endless hours on the computer looking for a sponsor. But at the end of it all, the most inspiring notices I received were the emails from Moises about every 3rd day sending me plans of what he felt were good ideas for the project in Mexico.

I had dreams and doubts and long conversations with myself about it, especially regarding the money. But they were conversations with only myself. I didn't let anyone else in for fear they would tell me it was unrealistic. I knew I had resources and believed I could swing it. After all, I had paid for graduate school with credit cards. Why not pay for my dream? So I started to balance my credit against my dream. I would fund my project, if no one else would. Mexico would not slip from my "three pronged approach to fighting breast cancer: emotional, financial and recuperative support." I truly believed happiness was the cure.

The money that came into the foundation, we used for expenses and gave away as grants to patients in treatment for breast cancer. Money made a big difference when you were sick. And Mexico? People loved the idea. But I had tired of asking for help and then answering for it. So, I did it myself. That way I didn't have to tell my board of directors, or my sisters or brothers or my mom what was actually happening. And a part of me was more determined to finish it since Helen had financed the land and had faith in me, even after seeing the mess it was. But truly, I did it because I wanted it more than anything else and I knew it was a good idea. So, finally, it didn't matter that Amador didn't call and it didn't matter that he had someone else. I would not slip back into my old life. I would be spectacular and change my small world.

I cashed in some retirement stock since I believed I would die before I retired, especially if I stayed where I was. And I kept working until I could make a plan and since I didn't know what else to do. There was a part of me that could not let go of the 9 to 5, the prestige, the little power I sometimes had, the routine that had been my whole life and the constant paychecks. But a part of me knew this was not the road to my health or happiness. The two sides were fighting. I had one foot on the dock and one foot on the boat and I was stretching and stretching until I could stretch no more.

Practicing yoga every day was the thing besides running that kept me grounded. And one of the few things I was doing that didn't cause me pain. At 5:30 am I rolled out my mat next to my bed and stood in tadasana with a view of the train station tower and the last star of the night while the rustle of the early trains wakened the city. I would begin. My practice was routine, almost the same every day, constant. It was comfort in motion. I gently opened my body with the motion and quieted my mind.

One morning, as I lay in the final relaxation pose, *savasana*, with my mind clear and my body relaxed in this heavenly pose that focuses all your practice on the breath, a voice came inside my brain and said to me, "You are afraid."

It was so vivid it pulled me out of my meditation. It was that strong, as if there were a person beside me saying it.

My eyes opened and I said, "I am not," shocked and looking for who said that.

Then I thought, "Am I?"

I rested with that thought for a moment, but then finished with Om and my prayers and went to prepare for the day. But the seed had been planted and after awhile I finally had to agree. I was afraid to change, afraid to let go of the security I had known all my life. I was afraid to let go of what I thought was approval from my family and from my father, now 6 years out of the physical realm.

Suddenly, all the other obstacles cleared themselves away and I knew it was only fear holding me back. I needed to face it. I made an appointment to meet with my boss. I planned to give him notice and pursue my dream. I put on the Crystina Aquilera song, "The Voice Within" when I drove home in my turbo Saab convertible that night, still the mid level executive, still feeling powerful and in control under the spring canopy of fading cherry blossoms. Fear was something I could work with, something I could overcome, I knew. Suddenly, I felt free. I just didn't understand all that freedom meant.

I practiced what I would tell my boss as I drove to work the following morning: "I am going to leave in a month," "I have some other options I want to pursue," "This isn't working out for me," anything but the truth.

I was afraid of what he would say if I told him the truth. It was sunny and there was a chill in the air but I had put the top down regardless and breathed in those same fading cherry blossoms from the night before. I would enjoy my day. And since driving to work was a part of it, I would enjoy the drive. Too, now there was something impermanent about it: it would not last forever. I would quit today. I was elated yet so frightened I was shaking. My mind was racing. *Savasana* had held no revelations that morning, only that fear was real and it could be consuming.

I barely could think of my breath for focus on the question, "what the fuck was I doing?"

But there was that part of me that was secure and committed. I would go through with it. I would have a life.

I stopped at Starbucks and treated myself to a café latte.

Even there my mind played tricks on me, saying, "Enjoy it, you won't be drinking lattes too long without a job."

I chastised myself for that negative thinking and told myself I would always live large. I pushed the thoughts of poverty from my mind and cruised to work in that same executive style: convertible foreign car, Italian leather boots and a designer suit, bought on sale of course, but it was hip nonetheless. As I went through security, I wondered what they thought of me. After nearly a year of daily entries and exits, they hardly said hello. "Different worlds," I said to myself. Then I quoted my self-help books that what other people thought of me none was none of my business as I sipped the end of my latte and parked the car. The day was vividly clear, beautiful blue sky with crisp white clouds. Later it would be warm, nearly hot, but now it was cool.

I walked into my windowless office and somehow it felt not so stuffy. I would not be there more than one more month. My appointment with Bob, my boss, was for 11. I had two hours and tried to focus. I went through emails, checked to see if I had any money left to send to Mexico, checked for contact from Moises. Finally, I sat and watched the clock and rehearsed in my mind what I would say. And at 5 minutes before 11, I got up and walked down the hall to my boss' office, palms sweating, legs weak, stomach in an uproar. He was on the phone when I got there but he motioned me to enter. I sat in his oversized leather chair and waited, looking around at the clutter on his desk, the calendar on the wall was one from the Alexandria Rotary Club but from the month before. It seemed out of place. There was one very nice painting that his wife had done and some photos of his family. The place was over flowing with stuff: papers, books, magazines, every imaginable resource for water resources. Finally he hung up the phone.

"Thanks for waiting. That was Mark. He wanted to talk about those survey numbers again."

The fucking survey. I was working on some statistics for our headquarters and they were all messed up. They pointed toward us not making our goals. But the goals had already been reported and made a huge difference in our funding levels. No one wanted to accept them. So we were trying to justify them and it seemed almost modify them. I had new data to add every day and couldn't keep it straight. I couldn't get my arms around organizing it. But I also couldn't help but think they were scamming me with the data. Each time I found something that didn't look good, a new data set came in. I was not a conspiracy theory person and never felt as if I were in a position to worry about it. But something seemed odd.

He finished asking me if I could go over the numbers with him again. I told him certainly but then reminded him that there had been some problems with the reporting and that I was having a hard time reconciling everything. He understood that it was not the clearest data set but wanted to take a look at it. I told him I would get it but first wanted to tell him something. He raised his eyebrows and waited.

I inhaled and said, "I think I am going to stop working here."

How definitive. He asked me what had happened and I told him that I was not feeling particularly challenged with the work and that I didn't feel as if I were contributing and I that I was going broke living here, so I would move back to Miami and see what I could find there. It was a long sentence and I looked at the floor finishing it, knowing it was almost all lies. I couldn't tell him about Mexico. He would have me committed. Leaving a secure government job with benefits to go live in the jungle? Insane.

"I see," he said. "I know it has not been the most interesting work," he paused for a moment.

He was a good man. He really did care. He asked me when I would leave and I told him I would wait the month.

I told him, "I can finish some things for you with these numbers and the water survey and the bird study. That is really all I have."

I felt slightly embarrassed at how little I had contributed. "Well," he said. "A month. Well, lets talk. Perhaps we can work something out and you can still work with us. I think you do very good work and I hate to see you go."

I couldn't believe what I was hearing. Good work? I felt I sucked there. But here he was, telling me otherwise. I told him thank-you and I would love to hear what he had to say. I was honest. I needed the money so I would keep my doors open.

I told him I would get him the numbers. "Oh, right," he said, "Let's take a look at them."

I left his office smiling. I had conquered that fear. But as I collected the folders he wanted and went back to his office, a new fear of being broke crept in and I fought to keep it away. "It will all work out," became my new mantra. The month passed. I was not prepared to go but managed. I didn't have much. No one at work really knew I was even going. I was never good at good-bye's. My colleague and friend, Mike, Mr. Hawaii as I called him, helped me with my work things, promising to send them to me wherever I was, promising to come see me and help me build. I promised to visit my other friend Diane in Tajikistan. I knew it was all a lie, they didn't realize it yet.

I told my roommate Sona the same day I had given notice that I would be out of the apartment the next month. She gave me the news that she was now engaged. Her boyfriend would be moving in at the end of the month. It would work out well.

She made her now-fiance, also a dentist, clean my teeth before I left saying, "God knows what sort of treatment you will find in Mexico. And you don't need a toothache out there in the jungle."

She had been a gift to me. Having a room-mate at 43 was not so bad after all.

Chapter 30

Of my family, first I called my nephew Brendan, my touchstone to entrepreneurship and adventure and my best friend in the neighborhood. He lived in Baltimore, an hour up I 95. I would miss the proximity and our weekly visits. "Brendo my friendo" was excited for me. Then I called my mom who said coolly, "well, you have not been too happy there anyway." I relaxed knowing that at least I would not have any huge arguments with people I cared for the most. The rest of the family had to accept it. They all wanted me to be happy and if they were afraid for me, they didn't show it, except for my sister Kathy.

She sent me an email saying, "Listen Joanneo, I can help you get situated here and we can find you a job on the Cape. You will be close to us all and to your doctors. It would be nice to have you here and so much less dangerous than in Mexico. I mean, really, have you been watching the news?"

I cringed. At that moment the drug wars in the northern parts of Mexico were out of control. News casts of mass murders greeted you every time you turned on the news. I hardly ever watched TV believing it was a mechanism to control the population using fear and mental garbage. My father had always told us that and I took it to heart. That was except for a few great programs like Seinfeld and the Simpsons which absolutely saved me when I was home with cancer.
I tried to tell Kathy how that was not the part of Mexico where I was. I tried to tell her how safe it was in Tulum but then caught myself. I had no idea really how dangerous it would be. I was moving to the jungle without much of anything. There were some wild animals like boa constrictors and jaguars and the odd scorpion and tarantula for God's sake not to mention the crazy drug addict friends of Amador and Amador himself. I would be isolated and fairly vulnerable. But that somehow didn't bother me and I knew I had to go. I told her I wanted to try this and I hoped that if it didn't work out she would help me and that if it did perhaps she would come visit me. She said no, she would never go to Mexico. She hoped I would understand. My other brothers and sisters they felt the same way about Mexico. Selfishly, perhaps, I disregarded their concern.

My friends Sheba and Paul, partners in That Barry Girl Foundation, were happy for me. Understanding how much I was doing and how frenetic my life was, they encouraged me to leave the job. But they were ambivalent about me going to live in Mexico. It would make our work more complicated, sure. But we worked things out so we could stay in touch with internet and a skype calls. My books for cancer patients were getting some attention and I had a few fundraisers organized. And the thing was, Mexico was part of the foundation. People loved the idea of bringing people out of treatment to a tropical paradise to rest and relax. More importantly I loved the idea and needed to make it happen.

Sheba and Paul understood that I needed to be there or forget the whole thing but had witnessed Amador's abuse during a drive through the rolling fields of western Pennsylvania. We were on our way to a conference with a Public Relations and Publicity expert. We had put together a presentation for the That Barry Girl foundation and he was helping us fine-tune it. Amador called and immediately asked me to send him money. Shocked and embarrassed to talk about it in front of Sheba, I told him I couldn't do it. I didn't feel the need since I hardly considered him my boyfriend the way he had treated me my last few trips to Tulum. The thing was, at the time, he was still my *preste nombre* on the paperwork for the land. He got anxious and told me he needed the money and I needed to help him. I told him it was impossible and that I would get to it as soon as I could without elaborating. He started to yell at me over the phone. It was so strange to me his, "I never gonna see you again" and "you don' help me with nothing" and "people gonna take all your stuff" and he even added, "I gonna sell all your stuff." At that point I had no idea he had already started.

I didn't want to talk back in front of Sheba but also because he was not rational in that moment. I listened before explaining that I had no access to a place where I could send the money.

He told me, "you fucking better find one then."

At that I asked him if he were threatening me, not caring I had a witness and before he could answer, I hung up the phone and turned the ringer off.

I was shaking and wondering how I could get him out of my life and out of the project.

Sheba looked over at me and said, "You need to put a lid on that before he beats the shit out of you."

I was shocked she would say that and did not believe that he would ever touch me. But the call had unnerved me and I was preoccupied through our meetings with how to "put a lid on it". When we left I had 12 missed calls, "unknown number": Amador at a payphone. I imagined the scene as we drove through soft wheat fields and Menonite communities: Amador ranting, barefoot, surfer shorts probably no shirt, crazy hair and yelling in front the pay phone at San Francisco supermarket where the hippies hung out in those days. Everyone passing him realizing what a lunatic he was, just as I was starting to realize and now as Sheba understood. Perhaps the jungle was dangerous after all. But I was committed to at least give it a try.

Part 3 - Beauty

Chapter 1

The car was so full of stuff that I could barely see out the back window as I left.

"I should not let you drive this way." Mr Hawaii said to me.

"She'll be fine," my French friend, Diane, said to me as I pulled out the back gate and onto the access highway behind the apartment complex to I-95.

I would stop in Baltimore to see Brendan and then continue north. It was only 10 hours after all. I would have plenty of time to think and plan. But I needed to see my nephew Brendan who I would miss very much. He was one of the best things about my time in Alexandria. But we both wanted out. He would go to New York soon. Better for me if I left first.

My place in Boston was rented so I drove from Baltimore directly to Cape Cod. Calzi said she would store some things for me. She had forgiven me the cat episode and I would see her, my family and Fernando and Lynn. They knew nearly everything about the project in Tulum and were excited for me to the point that they would help me build a place to live on the land. I had spoken to the lawyer and to Moises and we would get something together so I could finish the project. Moises was coordinating workers and when I got there we could start. He said he would start without me and have something ready for me when I arrived. But I had at least learned that it would be better to pay for a hotel and build when I was there rather than send any more wire transfers to Mexico.

I wasn't frightened. I was more nervously excited, perhaps because I had no real concept of what it would take. I knew I had to:

"occupy my land." Fernando would help me and we would all stay at Jade together. I wondered what Amador would do and prayed the answer was to forget me. But I knew he still believed he was involved with me. It may have gone back to the contract he and I signed that gave him a 10% interest in my project. Perhaps he had forgotten he had signed his rights away or he felt that the contracts he had signed were a fraud. But I couldn't run my life around him even though I secretly hoped he would turn his life around, apologize for all the shit and be the man I had imagined when I met him: my happy beach bum. Regardless of my illusions, he had made his choices. I needed to make mine. I knew my happiness lay in Tulum and I would be happy if it killed me.

But, I had no intention of never coming back to the US. It was a modern world and I was about to become an international philanthropist and artist, flying between Boston, New York and Tulum, Mexico. Perhaps even LA. But some of my family and friends were not so sure. Calzi suggested I had "chemo-brain" and went on to explain that it was something medical people were researching. She said that it did seem logical since chemotherapy killed a lot of fast growing cells, among them brain cells.

She finished saying, "Perhaps it has inhibited your ability to make decisions."

That was not so subtle. I was trying to find my way and knew my ideas were great, even if she couldn't see it. I left her house the next day and went north to visit Lynn who I knew wouldn't tell me to stay unhappy. Better, she had no idea about new medical research.

But she did say to stop trying to do everything, counseling, "Don't work, don't look for anything, don't talk to Amador, nothing. Just clear yourself."

I told her I couldn't and started to cry. She hugged me and we went out in her dingy with her dog, Cash, to enjoy the afternoon. I vowed to get out of there before they made me change my plan.

I flew to Miami the next week to organize things at the condo before I went to Tulum. We had decided to sell. It was too much for my mom alone and I was not going to move there. Renting something so far away would be a nightmare. Before I went to Mexico I contacted a realtor, met him at the condo, set the price and gave him the keys after we signed the contract. I was hoping for a quick sale and flew to Mexico two days before Fernando and Lynn. I went directly to Jade. They had room for me and I rented a room for Fernando and Lynn who would come with their other dog, Murphy, a small terrier with a big attitude. Lynn couldn't imagine leaving him home. I groaned inwardly at the thought – another American tourist who cannot leave her dog and has the luxury of bringing it. It was so bourgeois. Juan was cool with the dog being there. I was happy they were coming at all.

I checked in and went for a swim. The water calmed me and made sense of what I was doing. The sea felt good on my body. I floated and went over my plans. I would pick Fernando and Lynn up in two days. We would relax a bit and then do some work at my place. The concept of "my place" floated over me as the water suspended me. It sounded wonderful and I let go of my other planning and decided to enjoy the beach instead. Lynn's instructions echoed in my head, "just do nothing." But I walked to my property the next day and met Moises. He had a design that I thought would work. I only needed a bathroom and some walls and I could live there and map out what to do. We began the septic system and plumbing for the toilet the next day, moving forward in a more organized way. I felt good about things for the first time in awhile and naively believed that Amador didn't even know I was in Tulum.

I was at the San Francisco supermarket when I saw him. He looked at me strangely, as if at first he didn't know who I was. Then he looked angry. I was nervous, unsure how I felt about him. Then I smiled, like always. When I did, his demeanor changed. He smiled back and walked toward me. I waited behind my shopping cart unable to move and not really sure why I wasn't running in the opposite direction.

"Baybe," he said as he approached and reached out to touch me, "you looks good."

He went to kiss me but I turned my face and offered him my cheek. He started to get angry but caught himself, as if he knew he would give himself away with a scene at this moment. He was calculating.

"Amador," was all I could say.

I looked down at my shopping cart and he said, "I so sorry about everything." He sounded sincere.

I told him, "Me too," sincerely.

I was sorry about the whole thing: not moving sooner, sending him to rehab, trusting other people, trusting him with more than he could handle, not seeing things clearly. But mostly I was sorry it hadn't worked out. I looked at him, bare feet, surfer shorts, dreadlocked hair with sun-bleached tips and I still saw my dream.

He asked if we could go for a coffee.

I told him no, explaining, "You'll get angry or accuse me of something else that I have done wrong. I am pretty tired of hearing how stupid I have been to be honest with you Amador."

He promised me he just wanted to talk and told me he missed me, touching my arm. I was skeptical. I felt as if I shouldn't even talk to him on the one hand but I so wanted to talk to him on the other. I wanted to talk to anyone actually. I was lonely. And here was my dream gone bad right in front of me. I wanted to reclaim it and not be so very let down. I told him I needed to finish shopping. He said he had nowhere to go and offered to help. I shrugged okay and we shopped for the few things I needed, him offering suggestions every so often, me making the decision on whether or not to put it into the cart. It felt like old times. I was calm, trying to be friends with this guy who had helped me change my world and who I still loved, regardless of how ill founded that love was. I had no idea that to the world of Tulum, we looked like a couple back together after a lovers' quarrel. And I had no idea that Amador felt the same.

We went to Don Cafeto's for a coffee and Amador told me he had stopped drinking.

"Really?" was all I could say.

I did not believe it but who knew? People could change.

As I thought it, I heard my grandfather's advice from when I was a child, "People can change, but it is not likely."

After awhile, we ran out of conversation. I was about ready to go when he asked me if I wanted to see something cool. I generally loved the places he showed me, so I agreed. He asked for the check.

I sat back and asked him, "Who's paying?" sorry I did as soon as I said it.

Not for insulting him, but afraid he would fly off the handle and walk away. But then I told myself not to care anymore. He had left me. I had money to pay the bill. If he had a fit, that would show me who he was.

But he smiled, and said, "I don' got ten pesos, baby. How am I gonna pay?"

I told him that if he didn't have the money, he shouldn't invite people. I heard myself and thought I sounded like his mother or a pompous ass. I wasn't sure which I preferred as I reached into my bag to pay the bill.

We walked west into the pueblo, past the apartment we had rented in what seemed another lifetime and he showed me the new sports complex, "*el campo deportivo*." The town had just finished it. We talked the whole way and then sat there and talked some more. I was happy he was so calm. I believed in him still, even after all the shit he had put me through.

Then he said to me, "I want to see you again."

I told him it was a small town and I was sure he would see me.

He chastised me and told me I knew what he meant. I told him I didn't know. He touched my arm and I got nervous. I told him I had lots to do and that Fernando and Lynn were coming to help me.

The minute I said their names, he changed. "Oh your friends," he nearly spat the word "friend."

I told him yes, my friends and I reminded him that Fernando was a builder. He became defensive and told me that I didn't need him then. I wasn't into this sort of bullshit so I asked him why he didn't like them. He told me they were racists. I laughed and told him I had to go but mentioned I was at Jade if he wanted to come for dinner. I still trusted him and didn't even know why. He looked at me as if searching for something.

Then he asked, "Can I kiss you?"

He didn't wait for an answer. He kissed me on the lips. And I kissed him back, right there on the street, not understanding what it all meant. Then I got in my car and drove to the beach.

He didn't come to see me at Jade. I was happier. But I could have used some company at Tita Tulum for dinner. I hated dining by myself. But I walked the beach from Jade under the countless stars and a new moon and thanked God for my existence. I drove to Cancun Airport the next day and smiled when I saw Fernando, Lynn and Mr. Murphy, the dog waiting at the curb: Lynn in her 500 dollar cowboy boots and terrier in her arms and Fernando in his jeans and standard white T, looking pale but happy. Murphy barked when I gave Lynn a hug. I told them we had rooms at Jade, even Mr. Murphy.

That is so funny," Lynn said, "That is where Normand told us to look."

She could never let me know more than she did about Tulum, even though I was coming back and forth, even though I knew people. She had been there first and had brought me. She would be the one in the know.

We talked our way down to Tulum happily but as we entered the pueblo, I got a queasy feeling in my stomach: nerves and the Amador dynamic. I knew, we would see him and I wasn't sure how it would go or how to handle it. I had told him everything: where I was, who was coming, what we were going to do.

"You talk too much" that voice inside my head said.

And at the same time I heard my dad talking to my mother, "Do you have to give them your whole life story?"

He hated how she told everything to everyone down to the milkman.

"I have no secrets, Charles," she would say. I smiled at the memory but realized I had not inherited my father's ability to keep things to myself.

Juan met us at the entrance and Fabio took Fernando and Lynn up to their room, #6. It was the nicest room in the hotel. Up high off the ground, in the "*uva del mar*," it had a private access and a small balcony with a hammock overlooking the beach and the sea. It was spectacular and as we climbed the stairs, Fernando could only say, "Sweet." I was happy they were happy. I was in the back, the cheaper room, #1. I still had access to the ocean and my own hammock and bath. I didn't need the ocean front suite or the pricetag that went with it. I would be there for awhile.

We played that afternoon and the next day. Fernando would go to town for supplies; beers, wine, grilled chicken, whatever he thought we needed or wanted. Lynn would hang on the beach, sun-tanning and swimming. I could only tan for so long and then would walk to the land and climb to the top of the back structure to look out over the marsh. Sometimes I would talk to God or my Dad but mostly I would marvel at how beautiful it was. I always invited Lynn and Fernando but they would say, "too hot" and "we'll go when we build that space for you."

The second afternoon, I came back from the land, Fernando was talking to Juan and having a beer and Lynn was on the beach. I walked down to meet her. I sat down and looked down the beach.

Amador was walking towards us. I knew his stride, the silhouette of his big hair. I took a deep breath. I didn't move. I didn't get up to greet him. I let him play his hand. Lynn sensed my anxiety and sat up in her lounge chair and said, matter-of-factly, "Here we go." It was as if she had been waiting for him, as if it had been a question of when. He arrived at our spot with a smile on his face. I smiled back. Lynn frowned. He kissed me on the lips, paying me back for my indiscretion the other day. Lynn noticed. Murphy started to bark from under the lounge chair.

Amador said, "Hello Lynn. Welcome back. Is that your dog?"

Lynn introduced Mr. Murphy and held him in her arms to keep him from attacking Amador. Amador asked about Fernando, about her shop. He remembered everything. I could only hear "blah blah blah" since my ears were ringing and I felt sick. Then he excused himself and told us he was visiting friends up the beach. Finally I found my voice and I invited him to come to dinner, regretting it the moment I did. But I wanted him to be a part of my life. It was unrealistic, I know now, but I thought he could fit in and be with anyone. I thought people would accept him the way I did. Nothing could be farther from the truth.

Lynn looked at me as if to say, "What the fuck," but then told him to bring his friends as well. He said thanks, politely.

Then he bent down toward me and said quietly, "See you later. *Te quiero mucho*," and kissed me again.

I wasn't sure what had happened but, as he walked away from us, I knew I was in for an interesting night.

When he got far enough away not to hear us, Lynn asked me "what the fuck was that all about."

I sighed and told her I was not sure. She asked me if I were still with him and I told her I didn't think so but explained how I had seen him two days ago and we had talked and had a coffee. I confided in her that it seemed harmless enough at the time but that now he had the wrong idea. Lynn told me that was an understatement and that he acted like he owned me. She told me I needed to straighten him out telling me that if I didn't, I was "fucked in this small town." Lynn knew small towns and the men in them.

She often said that Tulum was not so very different from her hometown of Dunleer, Ireland, "just a lot warmer and it doesn't rain all the time and the water was crystal blue and swimmable instead of a manacing green and freezing."

Other than that, she would remind me, the small town bullshit was still the same.

She put her cowboy hat over her face as Mr. Murphy crawled under her lounge chair. I went to see what was happening with the guys at the hotel. I walked into what constituted the dining area at Jade: a sand floor area below what they called their meeting *palapa*. The roof was low but not so low that you couldn't stand, it just made it feel tight and dark. You had a view of the sea but only through support pilings. It didn't really capture the beauty of the area. But we would eat there. Fernando and Juan were talking about tables. There were 3 square tables for 4 people each maximum. Fernando wanted a big table, for a big dinner and was trying to explain that to Juan who didn't quite understand the concept.

Suddenly, Fernando asked if Juan had tools. Juan replied, "*si*," and then Fernando asked about wood, long planks and nails. Juan systematically replied, "*si*," to each question and then smiled, finally understanding where Fernando was headed. Fernando said, "Well lets do it," with a big grin on his face as he followed Juan behind the house to look for tools and wood. Fifteen minutes later they were dragging out saw horses and planks and a sander and saw and drill. Twenty minutes after that, Juan was smiling in front of what appeared to be a very nice bench table.

"Just don't lean to hard on either side," Fernando said smiling and scratching his head, his tee shirt filthy and saw dust all around his neck.

He loved stuff like that. So did Juan. That night we would eat at the 30-minute-table, as Juan would tell the story for years later. Lynn came just as Fernando had finished and we started to cook and set the table. Before we finished cooking, Amador came to the kitchen door with two friends and two quarts of beer in oversized brown bottles. He greeted Lynn and me and then, extended his hand to Fer.

I held my breath but Fernando shook his hand and said, "Amador. Fancy meeting you here."

Amador introduced his friends, Sergio and Gisela, who I had known from before. We all stood awkwardly in the kitchen for a few moments until I brought them all outside to check out the table that Fernando made. It was crowded in the kitchen. Lynn was finishing her sauce and pasta and Fernando and Fabio were marinating beef and chicken. We looked at the table and Amador asked what was so great about it but Gisella said, "chido," or cool, as I explained it was from scrap and they made it in about 30 minutes. Amador was not impressed and opened a beer and asked if I wanted to get high.

"I thought you weren't drinking," I told him.

He blushed, caught in his lie from earlier. But then he smiled, and told me it was just one "to be social" with a mischievous smile. I let it go but told him Fernando and Fabio would love to share the joint. Amador went in and offered them the joint. They accepted happily. Gisela and Sergio joined them around the now glowing coals and glowing joint. I poured myself a glass of wine and finished setting the 30-minute-t able.

Serge, a mutual friend of Fernando and Juan's arrived saying, "small world" as he embraced them both. He was tall and lean with short grey hair and sharp, handsome features. He was impeccably polite and saluted everyone, including Amador and his friends. We sat down to eat after a few drinks. Fernando was red in the face and happy. Lynn was hovering over her sauce and the table, looking for serving plates and utensils. It was a feast and before we started, Juan raised his glass and toasted, "to the 30 minute-table." We joined him but afterwards, Amador left.

I almost didn't notice but Lynn hit me in the side with her elbow and asked, "what is up with him?"

I told her I had no idea and continued to eat expecting him to be right back. Gisela and Sergio were laughing and eating. After more than a few minutes I noticed Amador was on the beach alone so I excused myself and went to see what was up.

I called to him from behind and asked if he was okay. He told me no and asked me what he was doing there.

I told him, "Um, having a nice dinner. Enjoying some friends."

He said they were not friends and called them racists. I reminded him that they had invited him to eat with them and that they had been very nice the entire time. He didn't want to hear it, glared at me and said he was leaving.

I told him I didn't understand him and then added, "You are the one who wanted to be here. This is what it is to be with me."

I let him go. I walked back up the beach to the dinner and poured myself a glass of wine. Juan had started playing his guitar. Fabio was banging on his drum and Fernando was playing a washboard. Serge was in the house looking for spoons and Sergio and Gisela were dancing. Lynn was washing dishes, smiling and adding sarcastic, witty commentary. She looked at me when I came in and before she said a word, I assured her I was fine. Amador came into the space to talk to Gisela and Sergio before they excused themselves and said goodbye and thank-you to everyone. I asked Gisela what was up with Amador when they came to say goodbye.

She shrugged and said, "You know mens," before she gave me a hug and told me to take care, "*cuidate.*" They followed Amador.

"How rude," I said out loud.

Lynn told me to forget it and have some fun.

By now, Serge had broken out cigars and was smoking one while playing his spoons. He looked devilish with his impish smile, red cheeks and a halo of smoke around his head. Fernando had brought bourbon from his cabana and was glowing as he strummed the washboard. Juan was strumming the guitar while singing Mexican folk songs and at times grabbing his throat to make a warbling sort of sound with his voice. Fabio was in his own world on the conga. Lynn and I poured drinks and sang along. It was a Mexican hoot-a-nanny with all these "cosmopolitan" types, every one at the table from an urban background, even Fabio from Rome, here under the porch by the Caribbean, playing the most basic instruments and having the most basic very good time.

It seemed late when we all went to bed but it wasn't even midnight. I sat for a few moments in my hammock, looking at the stars, noticing how beautiful they were, waiting for a shooting star to wish for love and then chided myself for being pathetic. I felt comfortable there, we were the only ones in the hotel and no one would bother me. Chile, Juan's dog, came up to sit with me and I stroked his head. He had brought a coconut with him. The dog was addicted to coconuts, always carrying one, waiting for people to throw them for him so he could fetch. I didn't throw the coconut but he patiently waited.

Then I heard my name, "Joanne," deep and husky and familiar. Amador. The dog hadn't even barked.

He asked me, "What you doing here, baybe?" calmly.

He was relaxed and not so angry. I asked the same question back and he told me he had been thinking of me. I told him it was late. He said he wanted to talk. I asked him why he left and he told me he was an asshole sometimes. I told him not to be and that I knew he could be charming and polite and reminded him that it was rude how he left the party. He said nothing but he moved to sit with me in the hammock telling me softly that I still didn't know how to sit in a hammock. He pushed me over to get sideways so that there was room for him. I always sat in the hammock length wise but if you open them wide you can put two people in it perpendicular to the weave and it is super comfortable. He eased his body in next to mine. I loved sitting with him there but was unsure what was happening.

He held my hand and said, "baybe."

But I told him I was not his "baybe" anymore. He asked me why not, surprised.

"Oh Amador, there are about a million reasons."

He put his hand on my leg. It felt good but I was afraid of it. Afraid I would want to stay with him. I put my hand over his, not letting him move it. I wanted to forget everything but couldn't. I put my head on his shoulder and told him it was funny how he wanted to be around me now, after having left me alone for all that time. Then he told me I had been bad and had sent him to "places." I cut him off, lifted my head off his shoulder and asked him if he had been punishing me. He said nothing but put his hand back on my head to calm me down. I told him that everything I had done was to help him.

He told me rotely, as if he had said it to himself a million times, "But it was all wrong. You did nothing right. You got to learn."
I didn't grasp what he was saying but I was annoyed. I wanted to see the stars and relax and forget all my mistakes and now here I was resting in a hammock with what was probably my biggest mistake. I asked him where he would sleep that night.

"I got places," and he moved to get up. He puffed out his chest as if he were preparing for a speech or a fight. I was not going to tolerate either. I was weary and sad that it did not feel good having him around. But then he told me he wanted to check on me and make sure I was alright. Then he bent over and kissed me on the lips, pulling my lips towards him on an inhale, almost bruising them, stood up and said goodbye. I said goodnight as I watched him disappear down the elevated walkway and wondered where he would go. I lay there for a few moments longer and patted Chile's head.

"Some guard dog," I said looking down at him.

Chapter 2

The next day, Fernando, Lynn and I took a walk up the beach to my land. We climbed the steep, well-vegetated dune to half jog down the sandy rolling hill that meandered under several palm trees to the dirt road. We opened the dilapidated fence and wooden gate to cross to the jungle. This was their first time visiting my land and as we opened the fence to cross the road, I got nervous. Moises was going to meet us with the plans. I knew Fernando would be critical but hoped he thought I had done some things right. Mostly, I hoped he would help me. After all, he could make a table in 30 minutes.

"It's fucking hot here," Lynn said as I opened the gate to the property.

I agreed that it was hotter than on the beach for sure, my defenses rose.

Fernando defended me saying, "No hotter than the jungle," referring to the land Lynn and I had purchased in a jungle *pueblo* 20 kilometers inland.

I pushed the 2-meter high wooden gate open and we entered. The palms gently rose from soil that was dusty, not sandy, and dark grey, nearly black. Each time you put your foot down, a puff of dirt would rise up around it and then take its time to settle. It was quiet but you could hear the ocean and the wind in the palms. Then you saw my project. I sighed to look at what I had done. It was still a mess although it was cleaner. Moises had cleaned the construction materials from the front and stored it neatly in the house out back. But it made the back structure appear to be filled with trash. We stood in front of that building silently.

Finally, I said, "This was supposed to be for the cancer patients: two suites and then the penthouse for me."

I turned to walk back out front. Fernando took out a sketch pad and started to draw. Lynn climbed the stairs to the second floor. I sat on the stairs of the middle structure. They were outside the walls and they were sturdy.

After a few minutes Fernando came back and asked me, "And this one?"

I told him it would have been the yoga studio and meditation area as well as the reception.

"And over there?" he asked pointing to the concrete building surrounded by bags full of trash. It was supposed to have been bathrooms for the people who would come for yoga.

I let my head drop to my chest, wanting to cry and scream and stomp my feet on the floor. All the money I had spent and now, just another embarrassment.

Moises came to the door. He looked thinner than I remembered, his eyes more sunken and dark. But he smiled and was polite, his English was very good and he was happy to meet Fernando and discuss design. I hardly listened as if it were not even my business. I had no reason to trust myself any more.

I heard their voices like an echo in a tunnel as Moises said they could start the next day. He motioned to the stack of materials out back and told Fernando that we only needed a few more materials because really, everything was there. Fernando asked me what I thought. I looked at him with a blank stare.

He told me that the middle house, where I would have had a reception area, would be the easiest to finish saying, "Out back is a serious project."

I didn't say it but for me the whole thing was a serious project. Fernando told me he would do a plan for the entire thing but recommended that I work on the middle structure and get a place where I could live. I accepted it because I was overwhelmed. But I had never wanted to live in the middle house.

Fernando said we could put a bathroom in the far left corner and, in front of it, a kitchen area with a gas stove. Moises added that it would not take too long. And Fernando told me that we could make a screened in area toward the right side so that I could sleep away from the bugs. I looked around and pointed to the area inside the chain link saying, "here, right?" Fernando nodded and I suddenly felt very tired. Fernando put his hand on my shoulder and told me that I could figure out what I wanted to do with the rest afterwards. He said I should stay here for awhile and then "put a roof on or whatever," as he looked at me seriously. I sensed he thought this would get the whole idea out of my system and I would come to my senses eventually and move home.

I thought about the concept of home. I felt the wood stairs under me, looked at the palms around me, listened to the sea and wondered where home could be.

"Maybe here," I heard inside my head.

Lynn tapped me on the shoulder and said, "Hey, the view from out back is gorgeous but I am sweating like a pig."

She was ready to go. Fernando was still writing in his book but Moises answered her quickly saying to her and to me that all we needed was some money and we could start. He had people ready to work. I was the money person. I loved and hated it at the same time. Lynn wanted to go back to the beach and Fernando, Moises and I planned on going to the bank and then to buy materials. We were starting. I allowed myself to be optimistic and excited. And even if I was not designing or getting exactly what I wanted, I realized that without me nothing would happen. "The power of the purse," my father's favorite saying about how money controlled things, rang in my ears. I was the one in control and responsible, whether I wanted it or not.

We walked quietly back to Jade on the beach, all of us lost in our thoughts. I wasn't sure if they disagreed with what I was doing or they were just thinking. I didn't dare ask. At Jade, Lynn went to the beach and Fernando, Moises and I went directly to town.

"Let's get things started," Fernando said.

I asked Moises about his car as we drove and he told me he felt like taking a hitch. I wondered if Amador still had it, but decided not to pry. When I came out of the bank, I asked him what he needed and he told me about 2000 pesos, reminding me that we had a lot. I almost didn't want to be reminded as I gave him the money and asked him to bring me receipts.

He told me, "Of course Joanne. You don't need to worry with me. I not gonna rip you off like those other guys."

I inhaled and said, "Good. I hope we can work together for awhile," and gave him a hug, trying to forget the hurt of those other cons.

He had saved me, actually, with his call that Easter weekend, the almost consistent contact and the photo of the "funny pet". I owed him this chance.

The guys shook hands and Fernando asked Moises if he wanted a lift somewhere. Moises declined saying he wanted to look for a few things. He assured us he would see us Monday at the property. Fernando would not commit, but I told Moises I would be there around 9.

Fernando chuckled in that superior early bird tone and said, "That is almost lunchtime for me" as we left the parking lot and drove to Cocopesa, the construction supply store in town.

They were pulling down the metal grates and closing shop: Saturday after 2 p.m. Everything was shutting down. Sunday nothing would be open. We decided to try at least to find the wood store, the "*carpinteria.*" I remembered it was at the end of town and we headed in that direction, passing Moises along the way. Just past the very last speed bump, or tope, on the main Avenue, we found the *Carpinteria* and *Madereria*. We pulled into the driveway, walked into the yard and looked around. No one came to help us but Fernando wasn't bothered. He started picking out pieces here and there saying, "These should do." He was looking for a longer one when the owner came out wiping his mouth with his sleeve. It was time for the main meal in Mexican culture, between 2 and 4 p.m.

The men greeted each other, I said hello but the owner didn't respond. Then the fun began as we tried to communicate what we needed, showing him the materials we had, using our hands and arms and remedial Spanish to try to explain. After a hilarious 20 minutes, we had what we needed and put it on top of the car. I used my hands to hold it as we drove back, feeling the pioneer. We planned on getting the screen and some tools Monday. As we turned the road to the beach, Fernando asked me how my arm was. It was starting to ache and I asked him not to drive so fast and to please stay away from the palms on the side of the road. But I was laughing. I loved this sort of adventure. We dropped the wood on the land and went back to Jade to find Lynn lounging on the beach. I went for a swim and then relaxed with her.

I was falling asleep on the lounge chair when she asked me if I thought I would be okay living there. She finished telling me it wouldn't be that easy. I did not want to hear it and told her it would be a big adventure.

Then I opened my eyes and asked her, "what else do I have at this point, Lynn?"

I told her that we could do a nice business there. She promised to help me and took my hand in hers and said that after all, we were "sista's from another mother." That was our joke. We thought nothing could come between us. But then, Amador had. But I thought that if I built this place and if they helped me, when I didn't bring survivors we could rent it and make some money. I decided it would be great since, after all, I was going to be a famous author and philanthropist. Lynn had all the contacts for interior design and she had a style I believed I lacked. Together we could make something happen. I didn't want to do it alone. I put my head back on the pillow and dozed.

Monday morning I walked up the beach and waited until almost 10 a.m. before Moises came. I didn't mind waiting. I had lots to think about. He arrived in his van with a pickup truck behind him. Four Mayan guys climbed out from the pickup and stood behind him as he greeted me. I opened the gate so he could bring in the materials. The workers waited outside and did not follow until Moises invited them with a wave of his hand. Then they brought all the materials in without saying a word.

One spat on the ground close to me and I said to Moises, "Can you ask him not to do that?"

If I were paying these guys I would have a few things my way. Moises said he would but said nothing to the worker.

I waited and then said, "Well?"

Moises looked at me as if he did not know what I was talking about. I reminded him to tell the guy not to spit on my property. Moises looked at me as if I had a problem. But I waited until he walked over to the guy and spoke to him in a low voice. They both looked over at me. I was used to it from my days with the Corps of Engineers. Most contractors had looked at me that way when I told them they could not build where they wanted to, or when I asked them to re-plant things in a more random form rather than straight lines. So just like with those men, I stood tall and answered their stares with my own. They backed down. The workers went for more supplies without spitting and Moises and I headed for the house.

We planned to do the bathroom first, realizing that I needed that before anything. Moises showed me his plans and we went over what I needed just to get there and live. After what seemed like a short while, I felt weary of construction. I had been over plans and plans with so many people that I was numb to ideas. I wanted to be putting on Egyptian cotton sheets and down pillows. I had no idea how far away that was. So I asked him the million-dollar question: when would we be done. He looked at me strangely, seeming not to understand my question and I asked him again. He stumbled and told me it would take a few weeks, explaining that the toilet was the most difficult thing. He pointed to one super thin man who had darker skin than the rest and his eyes were deeply sunken into his skull and told me he would dig the *"fossa septica,"* the septic tank. We walked out to see the area as Moises told me the plumber was coming later and that the other workers would build the walls and do the sink and mix cement for the bathroom inside. Then he explained to me that the one who spat was the *albanile* or cement worker. He was the boss in the hierarchy of the workers. I was happy that at least I had started at the top to let them know I was the boss.

Moises looked around and said, "Right. I am going to talk to them now and we will get started with things. You know you need to bring them lunch, right?"

I shook my head no and Moises told me that either he or I had to bring something. He explained that they couldn't buy the street food they were used to here on the beach and that all construction projects fed their workers. I wondered what I would get them and he told me that a chicken from town or some tacos would be fine. He told me we could share that work if I wanted. I felt even more tired but knew that I would be going to town with Fernando shortly so I could get a chicken at least. Moises said he would be there for awhile to get things started correctly and, of course, wait for the plumber. As I was opening the gate, he called that they liked Coca Cola. I raised an eyebrow and he told me that if I wanted them to work well I would bring some Coke.

I walked back the beach and found Fernando and Lynn in the lounge chairs, Mr. Murphy under Lynn's. They looked happy. Lynn was reading. Fernando seemed figity but relaxed. He was always looking for something to do, something to create. I called him a renaissance man to his face but sometimes I wondered if he had ADD.

He smiled as I walked toward them but the first thing he asked was, "Want to go build something?"

I told him we needed to get materials and he jumped up, ready to go. I would have killed for 10 minutes in the lounge chair but needed to take advantage of his enthusiasm. Lynn came with us. She was used to being Fer's helper and was good at it. I still had to have him tell me everything he needed where Lynn had the intuition that 15 years of living together would bring. And each pair of hands could help.

We bought tools first. We had borrowed a drill from Moises but we still needed the basics: hammer, screwdriver, staple gun, hinges, nails for the concrete and screws for the wood and something to close the door with.

Fernando looked at the latch I had selected and told me it was not going to be too secure asking, "How are you going to lock it?"

I reminded him that I had the gate out front that I would lock and then asked him, "do you seriously think someone will try to come in and get me?"

I was making fun of Fernando for a moment but he got serious all of a sudden and told me that yes, someone might come for either me or my money or passport. I told him I could lock things in the bodega we were going to make from the concrete bathroom. I did not think I would have any problems telling him that the gate out front was like my front door.

We bought simple things that I knew I had paid for once, perhaps even twice, with other contractors. I told myself it was in the past and to let it go. Then we bought yards, meters actually, of screening, "mosquitero." Everything was in meters except nails and screws. They were in inches.

"How crazy is that?" I asked Fernando as we were trying to figure out how to order things.

He shrugged and accepted it all. Before we headed back to town I got food for the workers, chicken and coke, and some things for us. But Lynn whined that she did not want any more chicken. Fernando pleaded with her to have some. He loved it.

She told him that she had "had enough roast fuckin' chicken, alright?"

We had been eating it every other day but it was good. I got one chicken for the workers.

We drove directly to the land with all our materials and got started. Fernando talked to the workers first, joking with them and asking questions. Then he started. He was amazing. He moved quickly and ordered Lynn and me around like apprentices. He got Moises to help after awhile and it happened in front of my eyes. We replaced the chain link fence with Mosquito netting. After four hours, Lynn was in the air conditioned car having almost fainted from the heat. She wandered back and forth checking on us and looking for sympathy. Eventually, Fernando and I were sweating over the final details, checking that things were about right. Moises and the workers had gone before we were finished. Things were shaping up. I had a door, a screened in area and an area to hang a bed.

Fernando suggested hanging the mattress, like in some of the *cabanas* on the beach saying, "seriously Jo, there are God knows how many types of bugs and animals here. You should be off the floor."

It felt good to have someone care. And I had never thought of it really. I mean, I am not sure I understood what it would take to "occupy" my property. I let the concept sink in. Fernando continued and mentioned that perhaps Moises had a carpenter who could build it for me since we lacked some of the carpentry tools. We decided to tackle that one the next day and Fernando went back to drilling screws into the door frame. Then, it was finished. He opened and closed the door several times.

"This should work," he said to me, wiping sweat off his forehead and telling me to go inside for a minute.

I did and he closed the door, put the bolt across and started to walk away. I looked for a way to open the door but there was none.
He was laughing and he called over his back, "See you tomorrow." I laughed and yelled at him to let me out. He turned to help me and from a distance I saw the prankster I imagined Fernando to be at about 8 years old.

He opened the door grinning and said, "We put the lock on the wrong side."

Then he took the drill and fixed it. I was set. I had a screened in porch and I could sleep there, once I got a toilet.

I took my time shutting the gate and looked around a bit. It was a mess, I had to admit. And my more than disrespectful neighbors had had cut through my property and built right on the line leaving walls of unfinished concrete block as my view to the side. But the palms were beautiful and there were many more growing. You could hear the surf. There was a gentle slope to the land down toward the swamp in the back and there was a calmness that I wanted to pull into my soul, that I wanted to preserve. I would be okay here. I could feel it.

Chapter 3

Lynn was not so sure about the project. In the car on the way back she asked me how I would live out there. Surprised, I told her what she already knew: I would build my house and bring survivors each month and rent the place when survivors were not there to support the project. My books were going to sell and I would be fat and happy making a difference in the world.

She shook her head and told me I was getting in pretty deep questioning, "Living there by yourself?"

I was already in pretty deep and said it was my last chance asking her where else I would go. She told me once again that I could live with them and work with her. I wanted to scream that I was not her handicapped sister and remind her that I had survived cancer, not succumbed to it. Instead, I told her had a strength and capacity they were obviously not aware of. I didn't tell her that I liked visiting, not living, with them and I hated working retail.

I knew Fernando didn't want me and I told Lynn with confidence, "You will see. I will do this and then we can do our place in the jungle."

I reminded her to get ready since we would soon be running from New York to Boston to Tulum and my foundation will be giving away millions. She didn't answer. I massaged Fernando's shoulders from the back seat.

Lynn said, "I need a fuckin' drink and a swim. I am nasty from all that sweat."

Murphy barked agreement as he sat on her lap and we pulled up the narrow, tree-lined driveway to Jade.

I went to the land again the next afternoon. I walked out back to find the one dark, thin guy digging shirtless in the back part of my land. I noticed his eyes again and this time saw that they were nearly yellow on the outside. He was standing in water over his ankles and digging up a grey mucky clay. We said "Buenos dias" and I looked in the hole to see what the soil was. I had done that so many times in wet areas that it came naturally. He stopped digging to watch.

There was a layer of dark soil, the black dust we walked on, about 4 inches deep. But underneath it moved directly to clay, almost a white grey color, we would have classified it a gleyed soil back in my wetland delineation days. At about 3 feet maximum, there was standing water. I had denied permits to build in areas like this about one thousand times. Moises came up behind me in that moment and told me that here in the peninsula it was all that way: water at more than a meter of depth. I looked at the massive structure I had placed nearly on top of it and wondered about the stability of the thing. I felt stupid to the bone. First, because I knew better than to build without studies and soil tests and second because I had been so scammed in this project. I was happy Fernando wasn't there.

Moises explained that this would be the septic system. He explained how we would dig a big hole, create a container of cement with block and then put a huge plastic form into it to hold the black water, the shit. Eventually, we needed to create a treatment area, or humedal, but for now we would use this system that called for pump out. It was basically a holding tank. I understood and planned on doing something better soon. But now I wanted to get there. In a year, he told me, I would need to pump out. With just me on the land there would not be so much shit. I told myself it would be okay and then looked at the guy in his bare feet, his black skin glistening from sweat as he shoveled the sulpher filled muck that smelled like rotten eggs off to the side. I told Moises I would go get some lunch and coke for us and be right back.

In the next few days, Moises continued working on the bathroom. Fernando would pass by and talk to the workers and see that they were doing things correctly. Things were progressing. Moises was competent and kept the place looking moderately clean like I wanted. He managed to keep the guys working well. One afternoon he told me the plumber was also a carpenter and could make me a hanging bed. Fernando put in the supports to suspend it from the ceiling before he left, just in case they didn't get it.

"Moises, man, you have someone making that bed, right?" he asked as he finished screwing in the eye bolts.

Moises answered yes, that it would be ready the next day while he watched Fernando work. He was amazed at how fast Fernando moved.

That night we celebrated and went to town for dinner. We were all tired of cooking and eating on the beach. Town was more fun with more options and many more interesting people. We already knew a lot of them. I had not seen Amador since the night of the dinner party and was happy for it. It was over. I had finally realized that not having him around made my life much easier. We had dinner at la Nave and headed back to the beach around 11, happy and slightly drunk. As we turned right at the traffic light we saw Amador standing by the side of the road, in front of a dive shop called Acuatic Tulum, as if he were waiting for us. He ran out to stand in front of the car just as Fernando took the turn. Fernando stopped the car to avoid hitting him and Amador came to his window and started hurling insults at Fernando, including calling him a racist. Then he called Lynn a whore. At that, I got out of the car.

Lynn told me, "Don't go Joanneo. It is a trap."

I thought she was ridiculous and asked Amador what he thought he was doing.

He looked like a rabid dog and told me, "You. I wan talk to you. But not with them."

I told him whatever he wanted to say he could say it in front of them. He was crazy, his eyes pools of red and his hair wilder than usual. There was a crease between his eyebrows I never noticed before and he was pale. He had not been to the beach in awhile. He still had the same classic barefeet and surfer shorts but he could have been naked he looked like such a wild animal.

Then he said, as if he had authority, "You come with me. I take you to the beach."

I laughed out loud but Lynn screamed from the car that I would go nowhere with him. He moved to leave Fernando alone and came to talk to me.

I relaxed and asked him calmly, "Amador, what are you doing?" in a voice that was soft and clear.

I didn't yell, I wasn't angry. I did not understand and I let my voice communicate that.

He came over to me, softened and said, "Baybe, I just want to talk to you."

I started to tell him I was not his "baybe" but then let it slide, and said, "Sure, Amador, we can talk. What's up?"

I said it calmly like one of those police officers on TV trying to get a gun from a madman. Fortunately there was no gun. He told me that we would not talk in the street. He wanted to talk to me in the van. I looked over and saw Moises' white van parked further ahead. He must have seen us in town and driven here to cut us off and make a scene. Or perhaps to start a fight with Fernando and put him in jail. But maybe he was just stoned and wanted to talk to me. I was not sure. But I was sure I didn't want to get in the van with him at that moment.

I had to do something so I said, "Couldn't we talk another time? I am tired and it is late. Too, Amador, you are stoned. Let's talk tomorrow."

He stayed soft. It was strange.

Then he said, "Mami, you know I not so bad as people say."

I assured him people did not say he was bad. He continued to tell me that was all he wanted to say, that he was not a bad guy.

Then he said, "but your friends are assholes."

And instead of saying it in a bad way, he smiled like a little kid with a joke and added, whispering into my ear, "and that bitch is a whore."

I almost laughed with him. He was coming down from all the adrenalin or testosterone or whatever and he was the happy beach bum again, making jokes.

I took advantage and told him gently, "Well, I like them anyway. Let's talk tomorrow okay? You know where I am or I can find you if you tell me where you live these days."

For one very long minute he said nothing. Fernando and Lynn were waiting in the car and I was almost holding my breath.

He looked over at them and then back at me and said, "yeah. And you are just like them."

He told me he would find me in the next few days. Then he puffed his chest out, inhaling deeply, he took my head from behind with his hand and kissed me on the lips. He let me go and repeated that he would find me, as if it were a threat. He walked away, got in the van and tried to start it but it wouldn't start. I almost laughed at the comedy of the whole drama but controlled myself.

After the third attempt, the engine turned over and he skidded away, disappearing around a corner. I stood there on the side of the road, incredulous. Fernando called to me to get in. I went to the back seat and I suddenly felt exhausted.

Lynn asked, "What the fuck was that all about."

No one knew or understood and we were pretty quiet on the way back to the hotel. Until Lynn said, in a softly accusing tone, that Fernando had not defended her.

"No I didn't. And it was because that asshole wanted to fight and put me in jail. You have to understand, both of you. Here you have no rights against these locals. If you mess up, you will go to jail and they will be free."

He held my gaze in the rearview mirror and asked if I understood. I didn't really believe him but I nodded to say yes and avoid a discussion. I was weary of it all.

At breakfast the next day Fernando told me every time he heard a dog bark in the night he woke up and imagined Amador was coming in the night to kill us all with a machete.

I told him not to be ridiculous and then said, "He would just kill you."

Fernando didn't laugh but advised me to take Amador seriously. He told me he could hurt me. I drank my coffee in silence after that. I did not believe Amador would ever hurt me, but he had frightened me back there. I finished my coffee and took a swim to heal me and remind me why I was there.

Then their vacation was over. They were leaving me. I had my screened in room and the bathroom was nearly done. The carpenter had made a wonderful very rustic hanging bed. We had placed it beautifully in the center of the room. I just had to wait for the plumber to put in the toilet. And I had to get a good mattress, but I had an air mattress. It was all coming along. Moises reminded me every day.

I drove them to the airport and cried as they left. Fernando told me not to give the workers too much shit. He reminded me to think things through logically and take my time. He assured me Moises knew his stuff but told me not to give him any drugs. Apparently they had smoked some dope together and the outcome was not so great. I smiled and thanked him sincerely. He had been my angel. Lynn gave me a hug and told me she was not sure if it was good or bad but that she would help me where she could. She took my shoulders in her hands and told me to be careful.

"Lynn, it is not like I am in the middle of nowhere," and then remembered I was.

She reminded me in case I forgot. I shrugged and told her that God was on my side. But she stayed serious and reminded me that God didn't take sides. We hugged again and she made Mr. Murphy kiss me before they walked to the terminal. I watched for a moment and then got back into the car and started the drive back to Tulum. The radio didn't work. Fernando had taken the ipod. I was alone.

As I pulled back into Tulum, I got nervous. I checked for

Amador sightings at the San Francisco and in front of Acuatic, where he had stopped us before. He was nowhere and I thanked God. I took the left turn toward the beach and headed back to Jade. I went directly to my room, put on my swimsuit dove into the waves. As I lifted my head from the water, coming up like a dolphin, I believed Lynn was wrong. God was on my side.

Chapter 4

Over the next few weeks, I would check emails every day to see if my government contract had been signed or if they needed additional papers. I told them I was in Miami. It seemed easier. When I needed contact, I made an excursion to the *caseta telefonica* in town to call my mom or Fernando or Lynn. Cell phone reception was nearly non-existent on the beach. I loved it.

Sheba and I would chat on email about her meetings with hospital people and my internet inquiries and email contacts. My mom was sending out my books. I had put together over 100 sets for her to send out, ready with letters of introduction, addresses and postage. I asked her to mail 5 a day so she could have a walk to the post office. She was happy to help. Each day, I bought lunch for the workers: coke or sprite, a chicken for them and half one for myself. When I tired of chicken, I looked for places to eat where I didn't feel alone or weird or exposed. Eating was the hardest part of hotel living. But I was figuring it out, going through the paces. And every day I sorted my thoughts and cleared the confusion in my journal.

Mornings were precious. I practiced yoga on the balcony by my room and then swam and had coffee with Juan and Martha. They would introduce me to any other guests. Eventually they would ask what I was doing there for so long. Juan often joked that I was the resident of Jade. People were intrigued and asked me how I managed it. I loved saying, "my project is..." and telling them how I was building a place to bring cancer survivors. It seemed so noble and they were genuinely interested and it was mine. I finally had something great that was my own.

One day Martha told me over coffee that she had seen me practicing yoga on the balcony and asked me if I would teach her. I was flattered and thrilled and explained to her how I had been certified to teach yoga right before my first surgery for breast cancer.

My dream had been to have a yoga studio and gym in the city when I retired. I told her how it had been a dramatic final yoga exam for me and how I cried in savasana the last practice of the course knowing that in two days time I would be on the operating table.

I explained to her that I had lost the dream since life seemed to take it's own course with cancer treatment and work and trying to pay people back and to create my own human being again.

She smiled with her beautiful dark eyes, and said, "Joannis, this is your chance to start."

We began a morning practice in their beautiful palapa in front of the Caribbean sea. I had never built my studio but it seemed Juan had built it for me. We would move and breathe and laugh in the shade of his immense *palapa* sheltered in the palms, cooled by a breeze that held a hint of ocean. We used my mat, a gym exercise mat that Martha had and Juan practiced on a synthetic animal pattern rug. Without electricity in the *palapa*, the music was the sound of the waves crashing on the shore and the light was filtered sun. It was the most real yoga I can imagine, full of heart and the desire to breathe truth and energy into our bodies.

After our practices, I would walk the beach to my property and climb the dune that rose steeply from the beach after several harsh coastal storms. It was eroding so substantially that sometimes I had to pull myself up on the exposed roots that held the sand. I wondered how long this little barrier beach would support us and then let it go. The long term future was my last concern after I crested the dune and looked back at the magnificent coastline behind me. Then I would turn and jog the path that wound down the hill, open the gate that was hanging on one hinge and cross the road to my lot.

Generally, Moises and the workers were already there, having breakfast in my house and planning their day. But sometimes I arrived before them and had a little time to look around. I would wander around and check things out, look at how far, or how little, they had progressed on the bathroom, check what supplies I had, what I needed. Then I would walk out to the structure farthest back where I had planned to live and climb the two stories to the top. Once there I would sit and talk to God. Sometimes in a raging voice but most often looking at the wonder of His creation. I believed, actually, I knew, looking out over that vast stretch of wetland and grassy savannah, that He could do anything.

I wanted Him to do a few more things for me and each day I asked Him believing that when the time was right, He would give them to me. Then I would sit there until I heard the workers arrive. Feeling less comfortable, I would go down to see them. They tolerated me because I was the owner, *la duena*. I paid. I tried to communicate with them and have them show me what they were doing but they would act embarrassed and not understand my Spanish. We laughed at my frustration with the language and their inability to understand what I wanted. Generally, I gave up and put notes on the walls and floors for them. Fernando had marked counter heights and levels before he left but they either did not understand or they ignored them completely. If Moises were there, I would talk to him. But often he thought he knew better than I did and my ideas got lost in translation. They wore me down slowly to the point where I was happy to get anything at all completed.

But the place started to take shape. They built the bathroom. We dug a new well and ran the plumbing for the water and the toilet. There were two big tanks called *tenaco's* on the roof out back and we ran the pipes from the well to fill them with water. Gravity would bring the water to the toilet, kitchen and bath. Jose, the plumber and the carpenter, was also an electrician. He installed a water pump and put in a breaker and a switch so that I could plug the generator in to get water. The generator was my nemesis. I was afraid of it. It was loud and had way too many moving parts and flammable contents.

But I needed to master its operation if I were going to live there. Electricity was a thing I could manage without. Water was something I could not. And even though it was push button start and I did not have to pull a cord, each time I started the *planta* I would say a prayer, close my eyes and look away as I pushed the button. And each time it started without an explosion I would smile and feel competent. Then I would flip the switch for the pump, run to the back of the property and up the stairway and then the ladder to pull myself up to the top of the structure out back where the water tanks were to see if the water was pumping. If it was, I would touch it as it came out the spout and realize the miracle I had initiated. Then I would wipe the water on my face and say thank you to God and the universe as I looked out over the immense wetland system behind my property.

If water was not pumping, I would run back down to the

generator, lower the switch for the pump and then prime it by holding my hand over it to create a suction and get the water flowing. Once water sprayed out of it, I would try again. Generally it worked. It was such an important part of my life there that I was always preoccupied with the fact that it might not. I had never been good at mechanical engineering or mechanical things for that matter. I had no interest until now, alone on this little piece of land. I became fascinated with how they worked. The generator was my connection to a good life. Sure, there were people living on the beach with no water, using the sea as their bath-tub, the dune as their toilet. But I had not come to Tulum for that. I would live well and water was part of it. Candles at night were romantic, but a dry toilet and no way to wash your face or your body in this heat was not my idea of living. I learned to love my well, my pump and even my generator.

The plumber, electrician and carpenter, Jose, began to like me more than the other guys. I must have been paying him too much. But he showed me everything. How the pipe from the toilet had the exact right angle to bring the shit into the septic system. We discussed plants and soil to create a proper treatment system. He put cables into the house so that if I ran the generator, I had light. But I hated the noise and pollution from the generator, so I only used it for pumping water. Manuel, the *albanile* who I forbade to spit that first day, slowly started to appreciate that I was an intelligent person or at least generous with chicken lunches. He built the bathroom sink too high but it was absolutely beautiful. The group seemed to do things by how they felt rather than with measurement. And for a generally short population, they liked things high. The sink was too high, the countertop too. But over time, noticing I was there every day and noticing that I paid every week, they let me in a little and listened.

Manuel and I mixed the die to color the walls blue by filling one of the water tanks and adding bag after bag of deep cobalt blue die to the water. He would stir it and I would say yes or no to the color. It was fabulous. Then he used the water to make the cement. It wasn't enough die and the walls came out lighter than I had hoped. But it was fun regardless.

Mixing the die, working with them, I felt a part of something. I believed they were starting to know me and perhaps understand the project. Next to the bath, Manuel built me a concrete closet for my clothes and a space to put shelves in the bathroom for towels. Moises and I selected fixtures for the shower and sinks and bought a kitchen sink. Slowly, it was happening.

But each day was one more day that I had to pay a hotel room and one more day where I had to look for a place to eat where I didn't feel alone. I longed for my own space. I started cooking at Jade but felt I was invading on Fabio and Juan's space. Martha was back in Mexico City and although I wanted to be alone, really, I didn't want to feel alone in a place where you were supposed to be with someone. This was a place for couples and vacationers. I wasn't meeting any real people. I loved that the tourists were interested and I loved teaching yoga there but I was an anomaly and if I were going to be a weirdo, at least I wanted to be in my own space.

Too, each day was one more day where my focus was on construction when I needed to focus on writing and managing the non-profit and continuing my dream. It had been three weeks since Fernando and I had constructed my bedroom and I was still in the hotel. The new joke with Fabio was how much he needed to pay so that I didn't come back. We laughed but I was tired of Juan and Fabio as well. I was tired of them knowing how alone I was. I wanted to be far away in a place where no one would say, "How weird is she, so alone." The Doors' song always came to mind, "never saw a woman so alone, so alone." Well I didn't want anyone to see me so alone. I was getting all mixed up and lost.

And then I bumped into Amador in the supermarket on a not so good day. I was feeling weak and alone and anxious. Some days I feel that way and this was one of them.

I was in the check out line, paying for my things and he came by, touched me on the shoulder and asked, "Joanne, how are you?"

He caught me by surprise.

"Amador," I said flatly, wanting to cry, "How do you think?" as I tipped the woman who bagged my groceries and started to push the cart with the roasted chicken and 2 liters of coke for the workers in it to the door.

He told me I didn't look so good. I thanked him and told him that was nice to hear as I continued to move past him in hopes he would leave me alone. But he stayed with me. I stopped and asked him what he expected and what did he care anyway. I was getting mad just being close to him, being close to my dream gone bad. And he wouldn't let me escape. I turned and walked to the car. He continued to follow. As I loaded groceries into the car he offered to help. I told him I could handle it but he smiled politely, took the bags from me and put them into the car. I softened. It felt good to have him carry my things and I remembered the time at La Vita e Bella when Lynn was leaving our little hotel and I started to help Lynn with her things but he came and took them from my hands saying, "I can do that." It felt nice to have someone help me. I felt that way again for a moment: cared for, protected.

It was as if my world improved for a minute. When I closed the door he came close to me and kissed me on the cheek and told me he cared, "very much" about me. I told him he had a funny way of showing it and got into the car. He held the door open and put his body between it and the car frame so I couldn't close it. I wanted to run away. I was everywhere with my emotions and nowhere that felt good. His energy and my response to him were too confusing. He stood there and looked down on me and asked if he could come to see me and have breakfast together one day. I told him it was not a good idea and that I was busy. He reminded me I had to eat. I asked him defensively if I looked like I had not been eating.

He told me, "No. You look good."

I reminded him that he just told me I didn't look so good.

He explained, "I just say that because your energy seems low. You got to keep your energy positive, you know? People see your energy."

He said it as if he cared.

It always fascinated me how he could say things that were so intuitive and on a level so much greater than the drug addict I knew he was. I was so in conflict with who he really was. Still, I appreciated someone caring for me even that little bit. I had been so beaten up in the last years and months that even alittle attention meant so very much.

"So I gonna come by one day and we breakfast together, okay?" he said as he moved away and started to close the door.

I told him I didn't think it was such a great idea. He closed the door and I rolled down the window and started the car. As I turned to back up he was still standing there, smiling. I smiled back. I couldn't control it. And I had to admit, I felt happier somehow.

I started to back away and he called to me, "Joanne," I stopped and he said, "Good to see you."

I wanted to respond in kind, but somehow couldn't. I shifted the car into reverse and pulled out of San Francisco parking area and waited at the light. I looked into the rear view mirror and noticed that he was still there. It was like old times for a moment, how he used to wait for me there. I drifted mentally but then noticed the light had turned. I let my foot off the break and drove away, still looking at him in the rear view mirror.

After yoga class the next day when I was walking the beach to the property, Amador was waiting in front of Jade.

I walked past him but he called "Joanne," after I was about a meter in front of him. I stopped, turned, said hello and then kept going.

"You pretend to not know me?" he asked incredulously.

I stopped again, looked at him and told him, "No. I know you. I just don't know what to say to you anymore."

I started walking again. He caught me and walked with me asking where I was going. I told him I was going to the land. I had no reason to lie. He asked me if I was still at Jade and I told him it looked like it. I was tired of his questions. He smiled when I said it. I laughed as well, at my bitchiness. Then he asked if I wanted to have breakfast with him. I was hungry. I had coffee with Juan but wanted more. I was walking to the land to figure out what I would do that day. I stopped and looked at him and asked him who was buying.

He answered the usual, "I don' have a coin."

I shook my head and started walking again but he followed, like a lost little puppy that just won't give up. I turned on him then and I was taken over by an honesty and anger that surprised me.

I told him, "You know? Just once in this fucking country of yours I would like someone to buy me something: a fucking coffee or a fucking glass of wine. I am so fucking tired of paying for every fucking thing I and everyone else consumes. So don't fucking invite me to fucking breakfast if you cannot pay for me or at the very least for yourself."

I finished and started to walk faster. He stayed with me, telling me to calm down with a smile. It was as if he loved to piss me off, as if he enjoyed my anger. He wouldn't stop. He followed me telling me he was just a poor guy. He started to almost beg saying I was going to eat anyway and that we could share something. I turned to unleash another tirade, looked at him and saw myself. What was I, mad? He smiled. I inhaled, smiled back and told him, "Okay." He laughed. I laughed back and told him that sometime when he had some cash from a tour, he should invite me to a meal. He said of course. We walked back to Jade to get the car and go to Don Cafeto's on the beach. I loved it there and the workers could wait. Too, Don Cafeto's was at the end of the beach by the ruins that I always called, "Mar Caribe."

I got nostalgic as we pulled up the pothole filled road and asked him about his boat and Cain, his captain. He said the boat had been sunk in a storm. I didn't believe him but I didn't ask any more. I didn't want to know. I wanted to enjoy this place where I came first with Lynn. This was where Amador's boat had been and where we had margaritas and our arm wrestle. This was where Amador took me dancing on the full moon. Then I caught myself. This was also where people told Fernando and Lynn that Amador was a crack head. It was where people told me Amador was with another woman. It was where people thought I was crazy or doing drugs with him. I took a deep breath as we walked into the restaurant and pretended not to care what everyone thought.

I ordered a fruit plate and coffee and Amador ordered his usual *chile-kiles*: a plate full of tortillas with two fried eggs on top and a mixture of what looked like three different salsas: red green and a white creamy one. They created the Mexican flag in a messy sort of way. Then he ordered a beer.

I raised my eyebrows and he told me it would be just one. The food took awhile and we talked about nothing really. I had no idea what to say to him anymore. We used to laugh and flirt and make plans. I used to share my dreams with this guy but now, I didn't want to share much with him. I wondered, really wondered what I had seen in him. He smiled at me then and I hoped he wasn't reading my mind. Amador was incredibly intuitive. He touched my hand on the table and told me he missed me. Surprised, I asked him why. He changed then. I saw this dark cloud come over his face. The waiter brought the food and I started to pick at my fruit, letting the question hang in the air.

He challenged me saying, "You don't believe me?" and then finished his beer and raised it to ask the waiter for another.

I told him that perhaps he thought he missed me and I thought I missed him too, sometimes.

Then I candidly said, "But think about it. I just make you angry all the time."

He agreed with me but then told me he loved me. I believed he meant what he said, but he had put me though so much. I asked him what "loving me" meant to him. He didn't know what to say. His second beer of the morning came and he drank it fast. He wasn't really eating and his plate started to get soggy and the colors that had been clear and bright before started to melt together. The whole thing started to look grey.

I told him his eggs were getting cold, sounding like his mother. That made him snap, for whatever reason I will never know he got angry again. It came over him like the storms that moved in from the sea. He told me he wasn't hungry and that the eggs were shit. I didn't say anything and stopped myself from apologizing. It was his own fault that he didn't eat them when they were hot. A woman came in and sat at the table behind us. She was heavy set, pale, and loud, telling everyone that she had just arrived. I decided that the next day she would be red and, hopefully, look happier.

Amador looked over at her and said, "Not bad. Maybe I go to meet her now."

I was shocked. After all he had just said he loved me.

"Really?"

"Si" and told me that I had sent him to places. I was a bitch and a "*puta*," whore.

I said, "Okay," in a singsong way and looked for the waiter. I knew where this was heading and I didn't want to go there. But I couldn't stop him.

"Yes, okay. You are just a fucking bitch who sends me places and leaves me there."

He was back on the rehab issue. I braced myself and tried to stop him by saying that I refused to have the conversation again. He told me he was going to go with the woman who had just sat down saying she was better than I was. I stood up to get the bill but he grabbed my hand and told me I was not going to leave him there.

I tried to be calm as I told him I would not listen to his bullshit finishing with, "So, unless you calm down, I will leave you here."

He held my wrist tightly and it started to hurt so I sat down. He was ugly. I had never seen him like that. I picked at the fruit and the waiter finally came with the check but Amador said, "*Una mas*" to add one more beer onto the bill. I glared at him and he smiled back. The waiter went for his beer and Amador told me that he might go drink his beer with that woman.

"Suit yourself," I said and I got up and walked over to the register to pay, hoping that I could get out of there before he came after me.

The waiter looked at me, confused, and asked, "*Todo bien?*"

I would not acknowledge otherwise and said, "*Sí, gracias.*"

I paid, walked to the car and got in. As I backed out of the parking area, I saw him leaving the restaurant, looking for me. I shifted into drive, hesitated for a moment, made eye contact in the rear view mirror and drove away shaking. I couldn't believe or understand what had happened. It was as if I had been talking to a mad man.

"Never again," I told myself, "Never talk to him again," I repeated out loud.

I stopped at the break where the hotels ended and the sea came up to the road. I needed a moment. I got out of the car and inhaled the sea air deeply. Then I started to walk on the beach there. Just as I got in front of the car, a pickup truck drove by and I saw Amador in the back. He saw me. I looked away and kept walking.

There are two large outcroppings of rock at that point on the beach. People climb them to meditate or take photos. I began to climb and with each step felt a little better. I reached the top and sat down, looking out over the Caribbean. I calmed down and closed my eyes. Then I heard my name, opened them and turned to see Amador behind me. I was shocked and a little frightened. I asked him what he was doing and he told me he didn't know.

Then he said, "I sorry, *mami*. I don't know what happened," as if he were not in control of his behavior.

I told him it was ugly and I didn't want to be around it, feeling powerful and honest. The fear left. He apologized again but told me I made him crazy and then asked me why. I told him that was not my fault and that perhaps, if I made him crazy, he should not ask me to breakfast.

He reached for me and told me, "I love you," as if that made all the abuse okay.

I told him that behavior was not love and that it felt a lot like hate. I pulled myself free of his grasp and got up to leave. He asked to come with me, like a little street dog once again that wouldn't go away. I said nothing. He took my hand to help me walk back down the rocks and he followed me to the car and asked for a ride to town. When I didn't answer, he asked me to show him the project reminding me that it had been ours at the beginning. I looked at him, not believing how he could change and not believing how I felt sorry for him. I told him I would take him to town. He apologized again as he opened the door for me.

I was so confused. It was as if I had been in a bad dream for a few moments. But now, I was awake and here he was again, kind and loving. I let him into the car, started the engine and drove him to town. He kissed me as he left the car. It was a soft gentle kiss on the lips and I held onto it. I wanted things to be different so very much. I sent my wish into that kiss. A part of me said, "Are you nuts?" but another part looked into his eyes and told him "so-long."

"I love you Joanne," was his reply.

"You have a strange way of showing it," I said and I smiled at him.

He smiled back, shrugged his shoulders and started to walk away. I had no idea where he was going. I wondered and then pushed the thought from my mind. I started the engine and drove away. When I looked for him in the rear view mirror, he was gone. I decided then that I needed to get out of there. It was obvious that I was in some sort of never- never land and I needed to escape.

Chapter 6

Finally the kitchen and bathroom were ready. The bathroom was a pale shade of blue grey, even after all the bags of cobalt blue dye we added to the water. But it was beautiful and softly polished. The sink, in the same shade of blue grey, was a masterpiece, even if it was too high and too long according to Fernando's architectural standards. The kitchen was efficient and Moises loaned me a small camping gas tank so that I could cook on a two-burner stove we bought downtown. Before he left that last day, he helped me inflate the air mattress with the generator so that we could carefully place it on the hanging bed that the carpenter/plumber/electrician had installed the day before.

I hung an orange mosquito netting above the bed and put on sheets Lynn had given me for my birthday. They were brightly colored stripes of orange, red, yellow and white that met the Mexican aesthetic head on, especially under that orange netting. I had new pillows and pillowcases I had made for the foundation embroidered with my bird logo. We hung a silver tarp outside the wall by the bed to keep the rain out and put a piece of wood on two concrete blocks so I had a table. Moises helped me set up a spot in the kitchen for the huge drinking water jugs called "*garafones*" the same way and we tucked the cooler under the concrete counter top. The window in the kitchen looked out onto the brown wooden fence next door but I didn't care. It let light and air in and I hung some crystals from nails that were still in the beams.

When I returned to Jade, Fabio asked me again how much he would have to pay for me to stop staying there. I told him he didn't have to. I was leaving. He laughed and clapped his hands and told me congratulations. He helped me move my things to the car and promised to visit. I paid Juan with hugs and tears in my eyes and thanked them from the bottom of my heart. He had given me a safe place that had been my comfort on more than one starry night. But I was excited to move. And I would see them for yoga practice. We would keep our 3 days a week and the thought of it made me smile and made it easier to move. They had become friends, rather than hosts.

I had bought a set of frying pans from the little hardware store on the avenue and I couldn't wait to cook. I planned on cooking pasta or quesadillas with a big salad that first night. I did not want any more roast chicken from Pollo Bronco. I was eating one nearly every other day. They were cheap and easy to carry so I didn't have to sit in a restaurant alone or risk seeing Amador. But Juan and Fabio had started calling me the "chicken woman," while Martha smiled and after awhile, they wouldn't even share it with me any more. I hoped the workers didn't feel the same.

I drove up the road with anticipation. The rental car was far from full and I remembered driving from Alexandria a few months before with all my belongings in the convertible. Then I thought I had only a few things. Now I felt lighter than air. I had a few groceries in a cooler in the back of the car and about 6 large citronella candles so that I could have some light and keep the bugs down. I got to the house at about 5 pm. There was plenty of daylight. I pulled the rental car inside the gate and closed it securely behind me. Putting the chain through the posts twice. I dragged the cooler along the dark, powdery dirt, leaving a trail like an oversized snail between the palms. I pulled it up the concrete block stairs and pushed it under the sink next to the other one. Then I did the same with the big orange plaid suitcase but I put that into my bedroom on top of 2 more concrete blocks so that I could use it for a sort of dresser for my clothes.

I took a few things from the suitcase for the kitchen: my favorite wine cups that my niece Katelyn had brought me from Spain, my oil painting of a pig that Carolyn had given me ages ago on D Street, two plates from my Uncle Bob that I could at least serve myself a meal on china, an Elvis Presley tray from Graceland, 4 coffee mugs that Helen had brought me from Ireland and a few good spoons from my collection and a set of drinking water glasses I had found at a store in town. I set my kitchen up between bites from little orange flies called *"tabanoes"* and then cooked myself a quesadilla with tomatoe and a slice of avocado. I sat on the top of the outdoor stairs to eat it with a glass of red wine. It was by far the best quesadilla I had eaten in my life. I listened to the wind in the trees and the waves on the beach and several different birds whose names I had yet to learn and I smiled from the inside out. I was home.

I unpacked and stored some paperwork in the little bodega Fernando had helped me secure into the concrete structure at the beginning of the property. Then I decided to have a swim. I opened the gate and looked up and down the dirt road. There was no one. I crossed the street and pushed the gate open, climbed the dune and ran down to the beach, leaving my *pareo* by a little palm tree that was growing sideways there. I dove into the sea and floated. It was not calm but it was not rough and I enjoyed the up and down motion of the waves. I looked at the blue sky and smiled to myself and to God. I played in the waves and on the shore and then lay on the palm tree to dry off, letting the trunk run along my spine and my arms fall out to the side to open my heart. I was alone on the beach and I loved it. As the sun began to set, I walked back to the house and lit candles. Although there was light at the beach, it was getting dark on the jungle side of the street. I took a hot shower saying thank you for every warm drop and then went to the roof to watch the stars with a box of Teddy Grahams from the Stop and Go, the little store across from San Francisco. They had some of my favorite things at inflated prices but I paid regardless, happy to find these cookies from the "healthy cookie list." Bats flew by my head as the mosquitoes arrived and I pulled the citronella candle closer. I laid on the cement surface that eventually needed to be my second floor and watched the stars and the bats for about an hour. Then I crawled downstairs, put a candle next to the sink to wash, put the 6 citronella candles around the bed and climbed under my mosquito netting. The bed swayed side to side and the air mattress made a soft, squishy sound. I put three pillows under my head, a head lamp on my forehead and journaled about the day. But the light attracted more bugs so I quickly turned it off, abandoned writing and tried to sleep.

The noises were amazing. There were the *zacatas* and the tree frogs that I was not so sure were not monkeys. There was clicking from the blue crabs that roamed the land at night and the gentle chirping of the gekkos. That first night alone in the jungle, the noise was a cacophony and each new tone made me jump. Finally, I settled down and slept better than I had in a long time, even if every time I rolled over the bed moved a little and the light and heat from the 6 citronella candles was almost too much.

I woke the next morning with the sun, stretched and noticed huge bugs on the outside of the mosquito netting. They were large brown masses with wings nearly twice their size. They did not move until I did. Then they flew around looking for a way out. But were stuck inside my little screened in room. Finally, one stopped moving and sat on the door. I imagined he was frightened and, speaking to him softly, snuck up from behind to gently cup my hands over his body. I prayed that he didn't bite and I slowly moved him off the screen. He rested on my finger. I prepared for a bite and kicked the door open with my foot before opening my hands on the other side, imagining he would fly away. But he didn't. I imagined he was too afraid to move or he was getting ready to sink his teeth into my finger.

I took the opportunity to look at him closely. Apart from the amazing enormous translucent wings, his eyes were huge and his body was armor shaped, like an armadillo. As I bent closer to look at him, he flew away. I jumped back, chastised myself for being such a scaredy-cat and went in for the other 3 bugs. I took each one out with care, enjoying every second of it, especially the part where they flew to freedom from my finger. I watched the last one fly away, made a cup of coffee and drank it on the stairs before I put my yoga mat on the floor and began my practice. I didn't last long outside the screened room. The mosquitoes and biting flies were fierce, so I created just enough space inside and sweated, breathed and moved my energy into the little jungle hideaway.

Chapter 7

I went back to Boston ti visit my family and see bankers. I stayed a little more than a week. Returning, I stopped in Miami on a Sunday, not my favorite day to be alone in the Latino community with its focus on family. But my very favorite day to go to the yoga studio up the beach called Nirvana.

It was in the basement of a Holiday Inn. But it was my sanctuary, like Maya Tulum was for me in Mexico. I loved the smell of the incense that called me in from the park I walked through to get there. The teachers were good and the people were nice enough. In a place where I had no one, this was my community. The little space felt like home. And my practice developed there. After the weeks with my family and before I could deal with things in Mexico, a day to find my balance with some like-minded people was a gift.

Monday morning, I stood in the security line in Ft Lauderdale airport and noticed the overwhelming smell of feet. The new security measures seemed only to dirty the air since I did not feel safer as I took off my shoes and added my foot odor to the smell that permeated the area. I tiptoed through the ex-ray machine to keep as little surface area as possible in contact with what must have been a giant petri dish for foot fungus on the floor.

As I put my converse sneakers back on in the metal chair exiting security, I thought about Amador and couldn't help but think he was my personal terrorist. Homeland Security couldn't help. I had hoped my brothers would come to Tulum and get rid of any guys bugging me, help me pound a few nails, or paint a wall or hang out so that I was not always the woman alone. But that was not going to happen either. They were never going to come and help me build my dream in a place they thought was a "jungle hell hole."

Tom told me, "Put a 'For Sale' sign on there and get out."

He reminded me that it was okay to give up, especially when the battle was not worth fighting.

"Keep the big picture in mind, Fans, don't lose too much" he counseled, as we shared a bottle of good red wine.

It was always a war analogy with T Bird, the marine and he always ended with the recommendation to figure out what I wanted because he couldn't accept that I was actually doing what I wanted.

I finished tying my sneakers and as I walked down the ramp toward the gate, started thinking of all the things I would change if I could. I would have Amador pull himself together and grab onto something good, namely me. I wanted to hold on long enough to pull together a decent relationship. I would have him be my helper in the project and make him work well and honestly. What I didn't understand then was that my "picker" was broken, as a friend told me. I saw too much of the good in people and not enough of the bad, said another.

And instead of protecting myself from these men who would use me and looking for someone "more suitable," I kept pouring my energies into them. It was sad to think about how hard I tried. I felt like a kid who had not been selected for the team: the scrawny, strappy little kid who keeps trying but never quite succeeds. I hated the feeling. What I really needed was to learn the lesson of accepting and letting go. I had to accept that my family didn't like me in Mexico and Amador was not a good person and let go of the disappointment. Walking past the windows and looking at the planes still on the ground I decided to let it all go and pour myself into succeeding in the jungle in Mexico.

I came off the flight with that resolution in my head. I rented a car and started the drive south, stopping at Sam's Club to buy a mattress. It took awhile as I joined the "club," bought a very good mattress, organized transport and had them follow me to the property. I kept them in my rear view mirror as we drove down the 307, the main highway from Cancun to Tulum. We pulled into the parking area of San Francisco Supermarket and they asked for the address.

"*No hay un direccion verdad*," I tried to explain that there was no real address but told them the house was on the beach.

The two guys looked at each other and got back into the car slowly and followed me down the unpaved road to my house. Once we arrived, they asked for more money to help me carry the mattress inside and because they had driven to the beach. I was tired of people trying to rip me off because I was a white girl. We argued in Spanish but I knew they understood me. And when I would not pay extra, they left the mattress at the door and went on their way.

T-Bird's voice echoed in my head as I watched the truck drive down the bumpy road, "it is OK to lose some battles."

Winning was not so sweet as I opened the gate and clumsily walked the queen-sized mattress into my property. It was hot and humid and the mosquitoes arrived as it started to get dark. I was sweating rivers and swatting the biting insects as I finally reached the house 20 meters down the dusty path. I opened the chain link fence I had put around the house to keep things safe while I was gone and sort of lifted and sort of pushed the mattress inside. I pulled the deflated air mattress off the bed and then struggled to get the new one onto the hanging bed before dark. Each time I pushed, the bed went with me, until I moved over to the far side, put the wood against my hips and pulled the mattress into me. It was painful but sweet once I laid on the mattress that was fully on the hanging bed frame.

After a moment, I walked outside and leaned on the post in the corner enjoying the slight breeze and wiping sweat from my face. Then I heard my neighbors talking, laughing a little. They had been watching. I couldn't believe they had not offered to help. I looked over at them and they said hello. Bali, my old contractor, asked if I were moving in and I told him I was. He smiled and shook his head in disbelief. Filip, one of the other neighbors tried to soften the impact and told me I would be the first.

"No one else is living here yet," he called across the yard.

I told him that was better for me. Then he asked why I didn't ask them for help.

I told him I didn't see them and looked him in the eye and said, "Anyway, I don't need it."

Memories of the 'help' Bali had given me, the rumors about how Filip had stolen my materials and that they had both known when Alvaro had stolen my land came rolling into my mind like a tidal wave. I did not need their kind of help. No matter how desperate I was, I vowed not to ask them for anything.

We said goodbye and I looked at my place. There was a puddle of water on the floor. It was almost dark. With no light, I knew it would be too much for me to try to organize things tonight. I needed a bed and some food. I closed the fencing once again and walked slowly out to my car, weighing my options in my head. I needed a safe place, a calm place. I would go to Jade for one more night. I pulled into the drive and saw Juan in the kitchen on his computer. "Jo-anna," he sang to me like he had a million times when I was living there. I smiled and he asked me how I was. I confessed that I was tired. I told him about my day and asked if he had a room.

They were full. I was disappointed but said it was okay. He offered me a coffee and I told him it was too late for that, I was thinking of where I could go. I decided I had time and told him I had some wine in the car and asked if he wanted a glass. He nodded and said, "*claro que sí*." I went to the car and we had a glass of wine and chatted. Martha was in Mexico City making her jewelry and he was alone with his daughter for the night. I finished the glass and told him to save the bottle for me and I would come back to share it with him.

As I put my bag on my shoulder he said to me, "You could sleep here with Sophie and I will sleep in the hammock."

I asked him if it was for real and when he said yes, I hugged him around the neck.

He told me, "Only for you," smiling at me like a brother. I wanted to cry, but this time for joy. It was the first genuinely nice thing anyone in Tulum had done for me, the first time anyone had held out their hand with no hidden agenda, no desire for me to buy something or do something for them.

"Thanks Juan," I told him as I filled both glasses and we finished the wine and we shared quesadillas and avocado.

He led me up to his apartment in the sky, a tree-top penthouse that had a view of the ocean and the *mangler* swamp behind the road and the moon and the stars. His *palapa* penthouse moved nearly 20 meters up into the sky. It was "*chido*" as the Mexicans would say, "very cool" in my language. Sophie was already asleep in her single bed and he motioned me to his.

"*Que descansas*," he told me, "rest," as he headed back down the stairs.

I loved him for that. I washed in the sink briefly and then laid down. For a moment I looked out at the stars, feeling truly blessed, whole, loved and knowing my course was right with them guiding me. Finally, exhausted and slightly drunk, I fell quickly to sleep. I woke to see the sun rising over the sea and meditated on it for a few moments, calling my energy. I had a big day ahead of me.

Juan woke Sophie at 6:30 and I went down with them to have a coffee. Sylvia the cleaning lady wouldn't arrive until 7 so I started the coffee on my own. After having lived there for 6 weeks, I knew the routine: grind the coffee by hand, use the fresh water and then just wait. It wasn't difficult but Juan was particular about his coffee. The coffee at Jade reminded me of the coffee I had in Germany: strong and robust. It lacked the good bread and cheese that would go with it, or the great chocolate cookies that they would so very often serve in the bakeries in the square in Neurenberg. I got nostalgic about German food for a moment until I remembered the 18 additional pounds I had on my hips after a year there. I heard the gurgle of the coffee pot and went to pour myself some.

"Stir it first," Juan called to me as he descended the stairs.

Sylvia walked in as he was cautioning me and smiled. *"Hola Joanna, aqui otre vez?"* "Here again?" she asked me.

I looked down at the floor humbly and told her that Fabio had not paid me so yes, here I was. We laughed and she poured coffee. Juan took his with him to drive Sophie to school. I put my bag back into the car to head up the road to move into my house. But before I did, I stood in the driveway and looked back at what had been my home for more than awhile and where I knew I had at least one friend, maybe more if you counted Juan's wife, Martha, Fabio and Sylvia. Little by little, they were my family here and I was learning to love them.

Still, I was excited to be leaving, excited to be in a place where no one would see me every day, a place where I could make my own coffee, stir it or not and put my things wherever I liked. I would pull my special stuff from the bodega once again; the special cups from Ireland, the Spanish wine glasses from Madrid, the plates and the Elvis tray. I had the stuffed pig that Kate and Megan had given me ages ago in my suitcase. There was a zipper on her belly and when opened, there were 6 little baby pigs inside. The girls had given it to me one day.

Megan told me as she handed it to me, "Katey and I want you to have this. It is your favorite after all and you don't have kids so...," she let the sentence hang.

I always kept that little pig close. This time she also held a statue of the March Hare from Alice in Wonderland in her belly. My mom had given it to me one year for my birthday. It was one of the many *limoge* china statues she had been collecting. It was perfect, about the size of your thumb and even had a little stopwatch, since he was always chanting, "I'm late, I'm late."

Alice in Wonderland was my favorite book and that little rabbit was one of the nicest things I owned. He had lived with me in Germany and New York and Miami and had come with me all over New England. I could not leave him behind on this trip. I had cleaned the special sheets that Lynn had given me before I left and left them with the citronella candles, some regular candles and flashlights in the bodega. To add to all of that light, my colleague and friend, Mr. Hawaii had sent a new headlamp to replace the one Amador had taken when I was in Cesiak. I couldn't wait to unpack my things as I pulled the oversized bag up the dirt pathway and opened the chain link fence around my home. Anyone seeing me would have thought I was mad. I still am not sure I wasn't. But one thing for sure, I was happy.

I opened the screen door Fernando had built and started to sweep the water out from under it. We had only covered one side of the house and water came in easily through the other. "You need another tarp," I told myself.

Too the level of the floor was off and the water collected in the middle under the bed. It was a torturous game to try to sweep it out. I had to go all the way to the door opening to get it out. That was the only free space where Fernando and I had not put some wood to block its passage. We never thought of the rain coming in. I was learning.

When I finished, I took my things from the bodega and hauled them up to the house. Then I sat on the bed to look at what I had. Mosquitoes started to bite me and I lit a citronella candle and looked for the mosquito netting that I stored before I left. I stood shakily on the bed and put it up, sweating like never before. I stopped to look for a towel to clean my face. When I finally had the netting draping over the bed, I sat on the edge of my bed and looked around. There were palm trees on most all sides even in front of where my neighbors had built, exactly on my line. I noticed that my neighbor,

Alvaro, had extended a piece of his house onto my property while I was gone. I was surprised at how bad people could be. And the meter wide extension was ugly as well, as if it were an afterthought. The concrete blocks were not finished and looked unsupported as if they might tumble in at any moment.

I turned my head and looked out toward the front gate. There were new chit palms growing practically everywhere. And I had some gorgeous older coco palms as well. In the middle were those two which I imagined had been coconuts that had fallen together and then sprouted. They had grown together for all these years, gently touching at the roots while exploring in opposite directions. Those two gorgeous palm trees made a perfect place to sit and rest for me and for all my workers. They were like an old couple that didn't always need to be in the same place but were always connected. I was sure that it was the security they found with each other that allowed other people to feel secure around them. They were like an embrace for the property. As I thought of that, my loneliness left. I didn't notice all the work I had to do. I felt my dream and freedom coming true in a strange way. And it made everything okay.

I stood up and closed and zipped my suitcase to keep bugs out. I was intensely aware of them not only because everyone had told me about bugs in the jungle but mostly because they were everywhere. You could hear them: the cicadas, the termites, the mosquitoes and the biting flies, those pesky *tabanos*. If you looked, you could see them, waiting for an opportunity to get into my space. I opened the screen door and closed it quickly behind me to keep them from invading and went to the car where I had some other supplies.

I had purchased one of those linen closets that before I would have put in my basement to keep storage clothes. Now it was my furniture. I pulled the car far into the property and closed the gate behind me. I didn't lock it, I wanted it closed and I wanted a shorter distance to the house to unload the few things I had bought: more citronella candles, some torches and citronella oil to go in them, lighters, wine and some cheese, a new pan to cook on, tortillas for quesadillas. As I pulled my closet out of the box I remembered my calphalon pans and my bone china and pushed elitist thoughts of "how low could you go," from my head and started to set myself up. There wasn't much and it was actually fun, although putting the closet together was a bit of a nightmare. I had never been good at puzzles so these 'made in china', put together yourself deals were not at all my *forte*. But I persevered and by one in the afternoon, I was not only starving but I had a little closet where I could hang my clothes. I sat on my swinging bed and then, after two or three bug bites, crawled under the mosquito netting and checked the bed out. "Nice," I said to myself. I had moved into my first house, of sorts anyway.

After lunch and a swim that afternoon I hung a hammock from two of the support beams on my roof that were for an eventual second story. I brought a citronella candle up with me and lit it. Even though the sun had not set, the mosquitos were emerging. I lay in the hammock and looked up at the sky as it changed color with the sunset. It would soon be dark and I needed to get things ready. I took a final look at the sky, pulled myself out of the hammock and went down stairs to find some candles. I had a flashlight and I would get into bed and read after I ate something. I checked the car and the gate before I took a candle to the bathroom, washed up and then crawled under the mosquito netting. I left the citronella candles on, enjoying the light. Outside it was dark. The same black darkness from when I had lived in Cesiak out in the biosphere. I had a knife under my pillow, just like there, for whatever good it would do me. And I put a machete under the bed. And then, I fell soundly asleep until early morning. The calls from the birds woke me and when I opened my eyes, I saw my bug friends from before: the cicadas.

"Welcome home," I gently told myself with a smile.

I opened the door and the 'cicadas' flew away. I went to the bathroom and there was a big spider in the shower. I washed keeping one eye on him and then took my yoga mat and practiced inside my little screened-in bedroom. I breathed in the morning air, listened to the birds and the humming of the cicada and the buzz of the flies and the bees and I moved through my practice until I was finally in Savasana and all the noises blended into one. No voice told me I was afraid. There was only a voice that said, "you are home." And in that peace, I cried with tears of sadness and joy all combined. When I rose from corpse pose to sit and say "*om*" I felt sure I could make a life here even if I had to do it with only God to help.

Those days moved slowly. I was lonely and knew very few people. I didn't do much more work on the house. I was waiting for money and that gave me time to think. Something I couldn't do with people around all the time. So, quietly, each morning I would waken and look at the concrete wall in front of me that was my neighbor's house and then quickly turn my head to the right or left and look at the palm trees, look at the green. The earth was dusty on my land. On a couple of rainy days, I watched as the dusty soil repelled the first few drops of water, "viscous force," I reminded myself from Chemistry class. Once it reached saturation, the soil absorbed the water quickly. I wanted to be like that soil and once I had held things for long enough, things like love, hurt, hope, or anger, I wanted to let them go. I put that intention into my life and my yoga: to let feelings move through me quickly so I could get ready for the next emotion, finally to release them all.

I moved into each day with yoga, journaling and then a walk on the beach, walking across the street and up the sandy dune that was dotted with petite blue flowers and the yellow porchulacas that I remembered growing in my roof top garden in the summer. There were other coastal beach flowers I recognized and although easy to ignore in contrast with the vista of the sea and the beach that you took in as you crested the dune, I treasured them. Some mornings I said hello but then cautioned myself not to let them talk back to me. I was afraid I might be losing my mind talking to the plants and bugs and flowers. If they ever spoke back, it would confirm my fears. When I reached the top of the bluff, the beauty of the sea healed me. I didn't care anymore if I were crazy or alone. I was in paradise.

Moises stopped by every so often. He was kind, helping me with the stove that often didn't work, finding gas when the little tank he had given me was empty and he helped me with the generator. I told myself he was genuine but then reminded myself he wanted work. After all the cons, I suspected people had motives other than liking my company, other than wanting to help me. I had experienced how each person had his or her own agenda and it had changed how I felt about myself and how I felt about them. I didn't believe in many people any more.

Three days a week, I would teach yoga to Juan and Martha and their guests, when they had them. It was low season and there were not too many people around. I preferred it that way. Juan and Martha and I had a good time and they were progressing in their practice. It felt good to have students and, on more than one occasion, when they didn't want to practice, I forced them into it asking, "Why do you think we call it practice?" They would slowly come up the stairs and work through the poses breathing heavily and moaning sometimes but we completed a practice and then had coffee. It was my social network. Sometimes I would stay and talk to Fabio and Sylvia but more often than not, I would walk the beach home. Now that I didn't live there I felt redundant. I had my own things to do and they had theirs. And honestly, I preferred my own place, even though the view was better from Jade. When I got home, most days the little dog from next door, Goliath, would come to visit and I would share food with him. He was good company and our relationship was clear. If I had food or affection, he would come. He gave me back affection and company. I could practice my Spanish with him and he wouldn't make fun of me. I could bring chicken home every day and he wouldn't complain or tell me I was boring. He always understood or at least accepted.

I spent hours writing and working That Barry Girl Foundation going to town to use internet to contact my family and friends, trying desperately to establish contact with a person or business who would buy my books. I had my mom sending out orders and I called her from a pay phone every week to say hello and to see if someone wanted to buy a million books. Cell phones still didn't work well in Mexico.

I liked the isolation. I actually needed it, like an animal trying to heal, not only from cancer but from sadness and betrayal. It was good that I was far from everyone, licking my wounds, finding my way, trying to sort out what had happened in my life. I talked by internet with Sheba and Paul about the books and the foundation. We planned publicity and events. I didn't socialize for fear of seeing Amador and of being the topic of gossip in this small town. Too, I didn't trust myself around him. I was out of my element in Tulum social settings.

In the evenings, I listened to my neighbors to the south, Amalio, the drug dealer who was two lots away. He had pulmonary problems so bad that he would often waken me at night with coughs and groans. I knew him only by reputation. Amador and Moises had informed me on separate occasions that he was the Godfather of Tulum. Anything you needed, you could get from him. If you were his friend, you were safe. If you were his enemy, you had problems. I thought I was anonymous, invisible and therefor safe. It couldn't have been farther from the truth.

Chapter 8

One day, driving through the town, running errands, I passed a store selling motorcycles and bikes. They only had a few bicycles, as if they were an after thought. I slowed passing the store and looked inside from the passenger window. There was a pink one that caught my eye. I remembered the old one I had bought in Belize and Amador had probably sold for drugs. He claimed someone had stolen it but I was finally seeing a pattern. I parked further up the *Avenida* and then walked back to ask the price. I settled on 1000 pesos including a basket and a lock. The salesman helped me put it into the trunk and I drove back down the bumpy beach road with the handlebars sticking out and the trunk cover banging against the frame. But I was excited. Cycling always made me feel free.

Now I could ride my bike to the other parts of the beach when I needed to get away. Normally I went to Mar Caribe where I had come first with Lynn, then with Amador and finally with Lynn and Fernando. I was comfortable there and mostly on my own. I had one person who liked to talk to me named Reyes. He sold hammocks and on my first visit with Lynn we bought a few. I knew now that I had paid too much for them. But I didn't hold it against him. One day I was writing under a palm close to the beach and he came to talk to me, telling me he needed some help. I saw something coming and I dreaded it. But he continued to tell me that his father died and his family needed money to bury him. I listened waiting for the imminent question. He asked me to lend him 1000 pesos, about $100 US.

The words my dad recited from Shakespeare echoed in my head, "Neither a borrower nor a lender be." Lynn and Fernando said Reyes was a family man. His family made hammocks in the country and he would come to the booming metropolis of Tulum, live by the beach and sell his family's work. Then he would go home to be with his family and share the wealth. But I had seen him dining with various women in town and found that inconsistent with the "family man" model.

"I don't have that kind of money, Reyes," I told him honestly. He didn't accept it and told me it would help him so much if I could make that loan, as if he didn't hear a word I said. I didn't know what to do. But I did know that whatever money I gave him I would never see again. So, I opted for a purchase. I told him I could buy a hammock or two since I did not loan money. I also told him I needed a mosquito net for the hammock and would buy them both from him to help him. He smiled knowing he had made a deal and went to his cabana for the hammocks.

We looked at the bright and colorful hammocks together. He showed me each one and opened the ones I liked: fabulous, expansive weaves in colors across the spectrum. I chose a blue and brown pattern, not the most colorful but I liked the combination. It was subdued compared to the others, sort of the way I was feeling at the time. He looked at me afterwards,

"Another?" he asked.

I told him I needed a mosquito net more. He looked slightly perplexed for a moment and then told me he didn't have any but could get me one. He promised me that when he came back he would bring it.

I had no reason not to believe him. After all, he had been selling me hammocks since my first visit to Tulum. I had a picture of him and me at la *Vita e Bella*. He was holding a bunch of his hammocks in his dark hand with his dark hair in a pony tail and wearing jeans and a long sleeve shirt. I contrasted marvelously with nearly no hair, white skin showing all over in a bright red and orange bikini. Reyes often helped me with my Spanish in the months I had been living there. We sometimes talked about how bad Amador was. He seemed to be a nice guy, even if I doubted his family loyalty. I agreed to pay first and have later. I told him I would go to the bank and pay him tomorrow. He looked disappointed rather than happy.

He told me he needed to leave that evening. I got annoyed imagining he saw me like a walking bank or some sort of mobile ATM. Angry, I got up to leave, not wanting to make a scene but not trusting myself not to. I told him that I didn't carry money everywhere with me and told him that was the best I could do.

Reyes just stood there. Silence was his tool and no matter that I knew it, I did not have the practice he had. Too, I was not desperate. I didn't need the 100 dollars for my father's funeral. I looked at him, standing there with his eyes on the ground and lost all respect for him. But pity took its place.

"Listen Reyes," I told him, "I will see if I can get the money tonight and come back. Will you be here?"

He told me the bus to his pueblo left at 8 pm. I told him that I would be there before then. I walked back to my bicycle not feeling so great anymore.

He called after me saying, "Thanks," and then, "Gracias, Joanne."

I got on my bike and headed back to my house on the bumpy beach road. "At least you have a hammock," I told myself.

The bike ride made me feel better. Pumping endorphins was always my answer to sadness. That was really why I missed running so much, and why I loved a rigorous yoga practice. I could work my cares away. When I got to my house, I relaxed for a little on my bed under the mosquito netting and thought. I couldn't stop thinking about going to town for the money but I hated coming home after dark. It gave me the creeps to open the gate, always fumbling for the chain and knowing that my neighbors heard every move I made because I certainly heard them. Amalio's constant coughing, the vomiting when they had too much too drink, the subtle laughter, that rusty chain on their bucket as they would pull water from the well and then scream as they poured it over their heads in the morning. I heard it all. There was a gang of them and I knew each voice, although at the time I still had not met any of them formally. I knew the "leader's" voice and its intonations. I was accustomed to hearing his orders, his laughter and although I didn't understand each word, I got the meaning.

At night I would wait for the sound of his car starting and then breathe a sigh of relief, knowing that they had gone out for the night to party or whatever it was they did. Some nights I never heard them return. Other nights they would come back at 3 or 4 in the morning. I would hear women's voices and then music from the car. They would play it loudly until the car battery ran out. It never took that much time. But I was always half intrigued to hear the party and half mortally afraid that they would start to wonder who was this crazy woman living in the jungle and come to visit me. I had no idea that at the time, they knew exactly who I was and were as fascinated by me as I was by them.

I got up from my protected nest and went to go get Reyes his money. I stretched, closed the mosquito netting around the bed, opened my little screen door and walked to the car. It would be nice to be in town for a moment or two, so long as I didn't bump into Amador. I generally went to town in the morning to avoid him. I knew he was not a morning person, having waited hours for him to go to breakfast with me. He was a creature of the night. And why I ever believed he was an early rising fisherman was beyond me.

I drove to the one bank at the end of town without incident or "A-sighting." One part of me would play with his stalking tendencies while the other was trembling with fear. Together those two voices would caution me, "A-sighting at 45 degrees, north intersection," and I would panic and turn the car or walk in the other direction quickly if I could. But sometimes I wanted him to see me, I wanted him to recognize me as something in his life. Regardless, I was always too late, he had a sense for me. Always on the lookout, he had an eye for his sustenance, for his "sales" or whatever I was to him. That afternoon, he must have been out of town because, most strongly, he had a sense for me when I went to the bank.

I withdrew some cash, looked in the windows of some shops and then drove over to Reyes' beach around sunset. The water was calm, the sea a mirror of the clouds that reflected the sunset above. I parked and walked down to the water's edge and waited for a moment before I went to look for Reyes, thinking how bad it must feel to have to ask someone you hardly know for money. It seemed so desperate. I tried to put myself in his shoes and felt genuine sympathy.

I believed that by buying these hammocks, I somehow became his friend. I didn't understand that he would ask any white woman the same thing. I felt that I was somehow special, part of his inner circle of friends. I was lost in my thoughts, trying to put myself in his shoes, or actually sandals, as I walked back up the path where the *palapas* with sand floors and hammocks for sleeping were nestled into the dune. Reyes came out to greet me with hammocks in his hand. I kissed him on the cheek and told him,

"I got the money that you need."

He handed me my hammock and said, "And I will get the mosquito netting when I come back. My family will make it especially for you."

I handed him the money and he said thank you.

"*De nada*" I replied, took my hammock and went back to my car.

I arrived home before it got dark, happy that I would not need to open the gate without light. I brought my hammock in from the car and laid it next to the canvas closet that I used for my things. I stretched my arms over my head and looked in the cooler for a yogurt or something before I went to sleep. Another day in paradise.

The next day I put the new hammock under one of the palms, tying it with some of the hammock ties I had bought one day with Lynn and Fernando.

"These are great," Fer told me in the San Francisco supermarket.

He advised me to buy some for when I wanted to put up a hammock or two. They had that purchase mentality and it was somehow contagious. I put two sets in my cart. Now, I was happy I had. I put my body into the hammock under the palm gingerly, hoping the knots would hold. I had never been able to learn my knots in sailing. I still am not sure why. My mother told me it was probably something with being left handed. I accepted it and reminded myself of it that morning as I recited, "if you can't tie a knot, tie a lot." The several knots held and I relaxed there under the palms.

"Life is good," I reminded myself and I let my mind wander for awhile before I started my day with errands and the obligatory trip to the internet and town.

The next two weeks passed uneventfully. I was developing a routine. Sheba my friend and partner was still working with me. Most other people had lost interest. She was my muse, always encouraging, inspiring me to write and paint and live. We chatted by email. Somehow, not always being able to contact people was comforting. It made my life less crazy. I would schedule the time for that and then, somehow, the rest of my life was simpler. It was as if I had lost the capacity to focus on the world outside my dream, outside what I wanted my life to be like. Each day when I would go to the internet, I would mentally pull myself back to the planet and let go of Tulum for awhile, focus on bills, calls from creditors, letters of inquiry and hospitals that might want my books and then my own doctor appointments. Once again I would face the real world and my mortality with it. So when I shut the computer off and went back to building, I left those issues behind. I let them go and cleared my mind, free of worry and trouble and all the things I couldn't control anyway.

In those weeks, I started looking for Reyes and my mosquito

net. I would lie up on the roof at night and be eaten by mosquitos. They would literally chase me from my spot under the stars. I had become addicted to looking for shooting stars, wishing on them and on the first star at night. It calmed me down before I went to bed and I knew they were guiding me. I didn't know what else to do. I was tired of pushing and by nightfall, my last effort was wishing on a star. I was tired of people ripping me off and I wasn't going to let Reyes do it. So I made it part of my day to stop at Mar Caribe and look for him. I asked at the *palapa* where he hung out but they shrugged and shook their heads. I would go away and return to ask for him again in a few days. Then at night I would lie under the stars to focus and dream and wish on the stars only to be forced from my hammock into my screened in bedroom under the mosquito netting that protected me from further damage. I was accustomed to leaving a few citronella candles lit by my bed but little by little I was blowing them out when I fell asleep. I had to go to Playa del Carmen to find them, so I started conserving. Too, I enjoyed the darkness. I slept well without artificial light and started to embrace the pitch black.

Then one night, I didn't. I was sound asleep and as if someone had entered my dream, I heard a voice commanding me to wake up, telling me I was in trouble. I couldn't stop it but I didn't want to wake up. The voice pulled me from my dream. I rolled onto my side and moved to sit up and then looked behind me to see the figure of a man on the other side of the mosquito net. It was a dark moonless night and I almost didn't believe what I saw until a few seconds passed and it was clear: someone was there. When that realization hit me, I screamed loudly, with force and hoped that someone might hear me and come to my rescue. But once I started, I couldn't stop. I kept screaming. The person tried to quiet me. He didn't try to come in or hurt me, he just wanted me to be quiet. He was trying to make me hear him but I kept screaming, unable to stop myself. Finally, I heard him say something familiar, "Reyes" I thought I heard him say.

And then again, "Please, it is Reyes."

My screams got less forceful and then I took control of myself and repeated what he had said.

"Reyes?" I asked and took a deep breath in.

"*Si*, it is me?" he answered.

"Reyes?" I said again.

He told me yes, it was him and asked me to please stop

screaming.

I started to swear instead, asking him what he was doing here and how he got in.

I suddenly became furious rather than afraid. He explained that he thought I was looking for him. I asked if he had my mosquito net. He looked surprised, as if he had forgotten and said no. Then he told me he had come a long way to see me and he had jumped the fence. He was babbling about it being very far and that he had walked all the way.

I stopped him from talking and told him he could walk right back and said, "Get out and go the same way you came in, you asshole."

He must have thought I would invite him to sleep with me because then he asked me what I meant. I became even angrier, got out of bed, opened the screen door and started pushing him telling him he needed to leave.

When I got closer, I smelled the alcohol on his breathe, and said, "Oh yes, you definitely need to go."

He went on about how far he had come and telling me how hard his life was but I would not hear it. My eyes rolled back in my head. I knew he had a hard life. Why did he think I bought hammocks from him. I was weary of people thinking I was there to save them when I could barely save myself.

"For God's sake," I said to him, "Just stop will you and go."

I explained that I had only been looking for my mosquito net and reminded him that I had paid for it awhile ago. He looked at his feet, his shoulders slumped and he told me he was tired. I told him I was too and he should get out of my place.

Then he asked me, "Won't you drive me home?" I couldn't believe what I heard and asked him to repeat it. He did, this time adding he was so very tired.

Amazed, I asked him if that were my problem, reminding him that he was drunk, had jumped the fence to break into my house and waken me and "now you want me to drive you home?"

He wined that he had no money for a taxi. Again, I told him, not my problem. He had found his way to the house and now he could find his way back. Exhaustion overtook me. I wanted to go back to sleep. So I walked into my little screened in room, closed the door and let him sort things out. I got under the sheets and closed my eyes. But I could feel him standing there. I opened my eyes to confirm my suspicion. He was there looking down at his feet. I got incredibly annoyed, asked him what he thought he was doing and commanded him to leave. He said he was too tired to go. I put my head on the pillow and told him to sleep on the concrete if he couldn't walk. I closed my eyes to go back to sleep. But I couldn't imagine leaving him there or worse, waking up to him there in the morning.

I told him, "Reyes, just go," from under the covers.

He wined that I had a car and said, "please just take me home." That did it. It was the "please." My mother had been right all those years ago. It was the magic word.

I got out of bed, cursing, grabbed my bag that I kept under my pillow, slipped the knife I had under there in my bag and walked out to drive him home.

"Come on," I said. "You wanted a ride, no?"

We got in and I opened the gate and drove him to the other end of the beach in silence. I wanted to hit him the entire drive. Finally, when I let him out at the end of the road, I told him I wanted my mosquito netting that week. I added that I would come for it, not wanting him to misunderstand.

He confirmed and said, "*Gracias.*"

I drove home and as I pulled open the gate I couldn't help but smile.

I shook my head and said to myself, "That was fucked up."

I went back to bed, hardly believing it had happened at all.

I became more cautious after that, more aware of my actions. I stayed even more to myself. I felt as if everything I was trying to do was misunderstood. One night I had closed the gate and finished my ritual of lighting candles and reading with the headlamp when I heard a beep at the gate. I didn't take notice since generally no one came to see me. The word must have gotten out after the Reyes incident. But, then, there was another beep. I waited, listening intently to the silence until I heard another and then my name, "Joanne."

I wasn't sure what I felt but I knew that unmistakable, throaty, coarse voice: Amador. I told myself I was imagining it. But when I looked toward the door, I saw the headlights of a car. I got out from under my mosquito net and walked toward the entrance with my flashlight. It was Moises van. I smiled and started to open the gate.

335

But Amador got out of the passenger side. Shocked, I stood there with the gate half open. How could Moises do that? I asked myself. My heart was racing. Why would he be here? He walked toward me. I stood there under the *uva del mar* and the stars, in the cream colored slip that I used for a night-gown and waited.

"Joanne," he cooed to me. "I so sorry. What you doing living here?"

He looked around as if it were a ghetto or something and then looked back at me and told me he thought I was still in the hotel.

I told him dramatically, "I am making my dreams come true, Amador."

And then I told him I was building the house. I was surprised that he really believed I would or even could live at hotels for all this time. There was a part of me that wanted to show him all that I had done and to have him come back and finish it with me. I let that part lead me. I opened the door and let him in asking if it were Moises driving. Amador said yes but he told him to come back in a few moments. I wondered about their relationship for a minute but then let it go, confused enough with my own emotions.

We walked down the sandy pathway to the house, the candles flickering outside the entryway, a couple still lit in the bathroom. The sky was littered with stars. I commented on them as magnificent as we walked under them. "Like you," Amador replied and he touched me on the lower back. I jumped a little although the touch felt nice. I moved away from him and climbed the two concrete blocks that made the front stairs to the house. I pulled myself in with the chicken wire that still enclosed the space and began to show him around. He opened the door to the 'bedroom' and looked at the water entering on both sides. He shook his head. I proudly showed him the bathroom and how I had a little stove for a kitchen. But he asked me why I would put the kitchen next to the bathroom. I ignored his criticism and told him that there would be a door eventually.

He sat down on a concrete block .

"Joanne," he said and then he started to cry.

I was surprised. I couldn't understand why he was sad. It wasn't as if I had left him or done anything horribly wrong. I asked him what was wrong and told him not to cry mentioning that I was fine in my little house.

And for some reason I felt okay. I really hadn't thought about the material things but I was getting things together and sure I didn't have much but it didn't matter. I was living a life outside of the corporate scene. I was in paradise and drawn to it and happy. Sure I cried about every night. I prayed for God to help me. I prayed for a man in my life. Sometimes I even prayed for Amador.

But in some weird way, I was making a difference. And that meant the world to me. I had a purpose in my zen hideaway. Perhaps it was more like third world zen, but it was zen. I would bring survivors to recover. I would help change people's lives in a good way. I didn't get what he was crying about.

I walked over to the cooler and asked him if he wanted something to drink. He sniffed and asked me what I had. The selection was juice, wine or water. He asked for beer and I repeated the selection. He said wine. As I opened a bottle, he asked if I were angry that he had come. I laughed, and told him I thought it was strange and then asked him if he expected me to be waiting for him here with beer in the cooler.

Since I had the opportunity, I told him, "I have been here awhile and you never came to help me or to see if I was okay, right? So, now?" I let the question hang.

He mumbled, as if it were a justification for whatever he did to me, that I had sent him to places. I told him not to start and reminded him that I did what I thought was right. I spoke from my heart but I was frustrated to talk about that again. He stood up, walked over to put his arms around me and cried on my shoulder, saying he was sorry.

He stopped crying enough to tell me I was right and said, "You always right," still holding onto me.

I told him I hated being right and reminded him that he pretty much abandoned me. I finally took my hands from my side and hugged him back. It felt good. I started to really miss a man and when I realized it, I pushed him away and told him that I thought I had done a pretty good job of putting something together. I walked to the other side of the room, confused, and served him some wine while I tried to organize my thoughts, one side of me wanting to take him back and the other wanting to push him as far away as possible.

I held the Spanish wine glass that my niece Katelyn had brought me and tried to pull good energy from them. I needed some help. I needed to ground myself with this man. I pulled a citronella candle closer to us and sat on a concrete block next to Amador as I raised my glass and said, "*Salud.*"

He said to me, "Cheers, big ears," mimicking Lynn from when we first met.

I smiled and got nostalgic, of all things, and wanted to cry as well but stopped myself. How could I be sad? How could I want a guy back who would sell my land and take me for granted and take most of my money and leave me waiting. No, I told myself not to cry. I reminded myself that I should be celebrating that he was out of my life.

But I felt sad. I was disappointed that he wasn't who I had hoped and that he had not pulled himself up to be a better person. I was sad that I could not bring him up to his potential. I was disappointed that I couldn't control the way he loved me. Maybe all those people who said I was a control freak were right. But I saw so much good in him.

My sister Susan's voice echoed in my head, "You always see the good in people Fans and that is a good thing. But you have to accept the bad too and be careful for yourself."

I pushed the voice away and told him how I wanted to put a garden in next to the house to hide the neighbors' ugly concrete building. Amador told me it was a good idea since I had to look at it every day. He agreed with me that they were assholes.

I said, "They suck."

It was so easy to blame them. It made me feel better about Amador and I thought it made Amador feel better about himself. I often wondered how he could live with himself and knew it made things easier with him and me against them. They had taken advantage of us, him with his addictions, me with my trust. So I held onto that and I let myself to believe that it was them, not us.

I broke the silence asking him where he was living and then added, "With the Italian?" referring to Akim.

He looked at me and I raised my eyebrows and looked back, letting my question hang in mid air, not sure I really wanted to know but wanting him to know I knew. He said he stayed with her sometimes but that he was not living with her. It seemed an honest answer. It didn't hurt too much anymore. I had known it. He had been fucking Akim. I wondered for how long but there was a beep at the front door. It was Moises. Amador hesitated but finally stood up, telling me he would help me. I asked him how, bluntly, honestly, because I really didn't see it happening.

He said, "You will see," and told me he would come back. I told him I would not be waiting. I was not doing that anymore.

He said, "I know, I know."

Then he told me he was going to help make my dreams come true as he started to cry again and we walked to the gate together. He helped me open the chain and then he slipped out. Moises was waiting and I waved to him before Amador kissed me on the lips. I am not sure if it was a reflex or loneliness or that I did really want to but I kissed him back. He felt it and I realized it. He closed the gate then and told me to keep the door locked, saying it was dangerous for me to be there alone.

"I have been okay so far," I told him defensively. I hated how he tried to frighten me.

He said, "So far."

I said goodby and finished closing the gate. He got back into the van and Moises drove away. And just like that, Amador was back in my life.

Chapter 9

He didn't come back the next day. I almost expected him to, wanted him to and didn't want him to. I caught myself waiting, listening for a car door or a beep. But there was nothing. I scolded myself for being so naïve. I chastised myself for even caring. The next day, I waited for him less. But I was waiting and it amazed me. I let it go on the third day and didn't expect it, didn't even think of him. I had a quiet mind focused on my life again. It felt good. I relaxed but I still left the door open, just in case. At about 10:30 Amador walked in as if he owned the place. I inhaled when I saw him. His chest was puffed out as if he were pulling confidence from the air around him, creating his own oxygen. He smiled when he saw me writing at the little bar I had, doing some work, enjoying my morning coffee.

We exchanged hellos.

I didn't move and then he told me, "I came to see you, just like I said."

I told him I could see that, and I smiled. I always smiled when I saw him. Seeing him made me happy. I still cannot explain it, but it did. He walked over to me, kissed me on the lips and asked me what I was doing. I was surprised but pulled myself together and told him I was working. I sipped my coffee and waited for him to say something. He looked around and walked in a circle around the space. Then he asked me when I would build some more. I told him perhaps when I got some money. I didn't want to commit to anything with him and I was happy with no one else on the land. I needed a break from having people here each day and explained that I liked the peace and quiet.

Then he asked me if Moises was going to help me. He used a mean tone of voice, as if he were still angry that I had done anything with Moises. I reminded him that he had introduced me to him and I told him honestly that I wasn't sure. He was quiet for awhile, looking around as if assessing the place before he asked me if I still wanted the garden. He mentioned that he knew a guy who could do it for a good price.

I hesitated and he told me, "If you don't want, it is okay."

I didn't really have the money to do much. But I wanted to put something in to block my neighbors. So I told him we could talk about it. Suddenly, I wanted him to go. I was getting annoyed with his sensitive and childish nature and the fact that he wanted to use me to get work. I had been happy before he came but when he started to walk around the property, I immediately felt self-conscious. I finished what I had been working on quickly and went to find him. For some reason, I felt he was assessing my place and seeing what he might be able to get out of it.

I remembered my papers in the bodega, and all my credit cards as well. I hated that I even thought that he might take them but I couldn't deny the fear. So I closed my computer and went to see where he was. I walked the property but didn't see him anywhere. Then I knew where he was. In the less than 10 minutes I had asked him to wait he had climbed out back to the top of my third building. That was the building where we had planned to live: two suites for survivors on the second floor and then the penthouse on top for us, a communal kitchen and living area on the first floor, gardens all around and an aviary. That had been the plan. Now it was a shell of a building battered by the sun and the rain. I climbed the ladder to find him there, sitting on the edge smoking a joint. As I reached the top, he offered me a hit.

I declined but he told me it was good for me and said, "*toma*", "take it," pushing the joint closer to me as I sat down beside him. I obeyed against my better judgment and pushed the internal voice that started to scold me away. I inhaled deeply and looked out over the magnificent wetland system in front of us. We sat for awhile in silence, looking at nature, not touching but sitting close. I could feel his energy and I knew he felt mine. He broke the silence and asked me to have breakfast with him. I was stoned, just one hit and I was light headed and forgot all the things I had to do.

I loved it but I would beat myself up for it later as I told him, "Sure," and then suggested Mar Caribe.

He said it was a good place but I told him, "Don't go crazy on me again, okay?" referring to our last ordeal there.

He smiled and promised he wouldn't get crazy that day. He stood up and offered a hand to help me. I took it. It felt nice to have help.

I closed up the house, locked my computer in the bodega and went with him to the car. He opened the gate and closed the lock and we took off down the dirt road toward the other end of the beach. I felt as if we were on rewind and cautioned myself to not let him repeat his antics.

"Leave as soon as you need to," the voice inside my head told me.

I silently said yes, continued to drive and Amador asked me if I had any trouble living alone on my land. I wondered if he had heard something but said "no, not really". I regretted saying it as soon as I did. He asked me again if something happened. I reminded myself that it was a small town and that there were no secretes. I told him that someone had jumped the fence and come in but that nothing had happened. I finished telling him that I knew the guy anyway. His eyes widened. Stoned, I continued, wanting to share it with someone. I told him I was frightened and screamed but no one was there to help me. Then, as if he had not been listening before, he asked me seriously if someone had tried to get in. I smiled and told him that it was Reyes.

I explained that I wasn't sure what he wanted but I had awakened to find him in my house. I laughed and told him how I had screamed for awhile but then kicked him out. Amador couldn't believe that the hammock man had come to my property. I asked him not to say anything. I was not sure why but I was embarrassed for Reyes. He probably didn't even remember. But I continued telling Amador the story mentioning that he was drunk and that I thought he wanted to sleep with me but that nothing had happened. When I said it I wished I hadn't and I started to scold myself for so honest. I blamed it on being stoned.

Amador asked me what I did and I said I told Reyes to get out. I continued to say that Reyes begged me for a ride and there were no taxis so I drove him back to Mar Caribe. Amador smiled and told me I was crazy. Then he asked me if I liked him and if that was why I would drive him home. I got hurt and I defended myself explaining that I wanted him out of my space. I told Amador how Reyes had sat on the steps crying that he was tired and begging me for a ride telling me how his feet hurt and how far he had walked, selling his hammocks.

I finished, wishing I had never started and told him, "I wanted to go back to sleep."

Then Amador laughed, loudly, happily. And I laughed with him.

"You are too much," he told me giving me a hug as I drove.

I shrugged my shoulders and took the turn up the drive to Mar Caribe Beach. We went into the restaurant and sat as close to the sea as possible. It was windy and fresh, totally different from the jungle side. I wasn't stoned anymore and I actually could not believe I was there with Amador after our last experience. But I had to accept it so I ordered a fruit plate and Amador ordered his *chilekiles*, this time without beer. He ordered an *agua de papaya,* instead. As we waited for our orders, Reyes walked past with his hammocks. Amador got up to speak to him. I asked him not to and said the magic word, please, but it didn't work on Amador.

He told me he was definitely going to say something finished with, "He gonna know I know," as he walked over to where Reyes was.

I slouched in my chair not wanting to be seen, somehow feeling like a snitch, but not sure why. After all, I hadn't lied. I had told exactly the truth so why should I feel as if I had broken some confidence. Amador came back with a smile on his face.

When I asked him what he had said, looking satisfied, he told me, "I just called him 'fence jumper'."

I shook my head, amazed at the whole thing. But I knew it had not been a dream. Our breakfast came. Amador inhaled his. I played with my fruit thinking how weird it was to be in such a small place where people knew everyone. Then Amador asked me if I knew what could help me live in the jungle. I looked up at him and raised my eyebrows in a question.

He told me, "You need a dog to protect you."

I told him I felt pretty safe and reminded him that I might be leaving soon and that a dog was a responsibility. He got concerned when I said I was leaving and asked me where in a possessive way that I sort of enjoyed but resented at the same time.

I asked him, "What is it to you?"

And before he could answer I reminded him that I was here on my own and that I had things to do finishing saying, "Remember? I have to become rich and famous."

I was referring to the times we would daydream about the future and how I would sell one million of my books and be on Oprah. He got serious then and told me I meant a lot to him.

I laughed when he said it and he protested seriously, "Don' laugh."

I put my fork down and explained, very matter of factly, that he had abandoned me and that I didn't feel I had to tell him anything. He held my gaze for a moment but then stood up and walked away. I let him go hoping that finally it was over. Each time I was with him I walked on eggshells until something happened and he would explode. I wasn't going to do that anymore. I looked out to sea and enjoyed my coffee. The waiter came by and I asked for the check. I had known I would pay. As I walked out slowly to the car, I looked toward the sea and Amador jogged the path to catch me with a black and white dog next to him.

"You need a dog out there," he repeated and then offered the one beside him saying that she needed a home.

He told me that the people there and the police did not want her around.

He finished telling me, "They trying to get dogs off the beach."

I was not sure I believed him but the mid sized dog came up to me and rubbed her head against my leg. I patted her and thought it might be nice to have a dog. After all, it had always been what I wanted. I asked her name as I patted her.

He told me, "Lakra."

"Lakra," I repeated and as I opened the door to the car, she jumped in.

She sat on the back seat in a funny way with her belly hanging out from between her hind legs. As she did so, I saw a bunch of bloody sores on her stomach. I asked Amador what happened to her. He shrugged and said we should take her right to the vet. So we did. I had her cleaned and that day, I left her for an operation to remove what were small bloody tumors. Juan the vet told me it was skin cancer. I waited for her in town. Amador had "things to do," asked for money and then got angry and stormed away when I told him no. I was used to it but then thought, "Would 200 pesos kill you?"

I debated with myself over the concept of giving him money but then got bored of it and went to the internet to wait for my new dog.

I picked her up at 6:30 with a big bandage around her belly and guided her to the car to take her home.

She was still groggy from the anesthesia and as I bent down to lift her into the car, I heard, "I sorry Joanne."

I jumped back, startled, and let the dog almost fall to the ground but relaxed when I saw Amador. I asked him where he had come from.

"Around," was all he said and then he gently moved me away and lifted Lakra into the car.

She sleepily wagged her tail. I thanked him and told him, "Now I have a dog," with a smile, although I was unsure if that was what I needed.

He asked me where I would go now and I told him I would take Lakra home to rest.

I thanked him for helping me and he told me, "She famous, you know," as he patted her head.

"Really?" I said, surprised. Then I added, "Well at least one of us is," and Amador laughed.

If nothing else, we still had our joke. Little did I know then that in the *pueblo* of Tulum, I was almost more famous than my dog.

He told me he was going but he might see me later. "Don't make promises you won't keep," I told him calmly and reminded him that I was not going to be waiting for him anymore.

He smiled and told me if I was not there he would find me. He kissed me on the cheek this time and walked away. I was so alone that I enjoyed the thought of someone looking for me no matter what their motive.

Lakra and I went home. She was still wobbly and slow from the anesthesia and could hardly make the step to get into the house. I lifted her butt up to the first level and smiled wondering what I had gotten into. I made a comfortable bed for her to sleep on with some old blankets and reminded myself that I was responsible for one more thing. But then I told myself that dogs were easier in Tulum and could come everywhere. Too, it wasn't like I had to leave her to go to an office every day. I was happy to have her. She slept under my bed that night. I didn't feel any safer but it was nice to have company.

Chapter 10

My dog Lakra came everywhere with me. Even though I wanted her to stay on the land, she would tunnel under the gate or squeeze through the fence and chase me down the road whether I left on foot, on a bike or in the car. She sat under the table at restaurants and she walked the beach with me, staying a little behind but always with me. She chased other dogs and she chased cars. But she loved people and she was famous, just like Amador had said. More people knew her than knew me. They all loved her, asking, "is that Lakra?" and then telling me a story about how they had camped together or how she had been with them for some months until they left her and travelled more. It was a hippy life for them and for Lakra. But now she had a home. She slept under my bed, above where the puddle of water was. When it rained she moved to the driest corner of my little room and curled up. She rubbed her head against my leg in the morning to say hello and howled with glee when I fed her. We fell in love easily and she would sleep under the hammock with me while I watched the stars. I wasn't so lonely anymore. I had my dog.

Lakra hated any workers and would bark as soon as they arrived to let them know she was there. She did not like my neighbors either. It was fine with me. The first time my dog friend Goliath came to visit from next door, she chased him away too. But eventually, she let him in. Sometimes he would walk the beach with us and then I had two black and white dogs, one a little chubby, one pretty skinny; one that loved people, and the other who would bite anyone who came near us. Goliath always went back to his house and Lakra stayed with me. I would never even think about taking my neighbor Malio's dog regardless of how neglected I thought he was.

Lakra loved Amador. When he finally came to the house with a tall blond American guy who said he was a landscape architect, she howled, ran to meet him, jumped on his leg and started humping him. She wouldn't stop. I laughed as he introduced me to Christopher, while Lakra was on his leg. Shaking hands, Christopher said he was a landscape architect from the northwest US. I asked him what we could to cover the neighbor's construction that hovered over the property line. I explained that because I would be doing more work, it would be silly to plant more of the lot. But I told him I couldn't wait to block the ugly view and the bad memories.

He told me he understood and looked into my screened in bedroom. Without commenting, he illustrated his idea on a small pad of paper, suggesting ficus trees along the wall and then flowering plants and colorful tropical greens. He drew a curving border of rocks with the plants inside so that at points there was almost 2 meters of garden between me and my neighbors and at other points very little space. That would give the garden more depth. I had to agree with him on the plants. Although, I knew many plants from the North, here in the tropics I was out of my element. Christopher looked around told me I would need soil, mentioning he would give it to me for a good price, "since I was Amador's friend." The word stung like a hornet. "Amador's friend" was what I had become.

I looked over to see Amador quietly waiting by the gate and noticed he was smoking a joint. I shook my head realizing that, actually, "friend" was better. Chris estimated the cost at 15,000 pesos. I told him it was too much. He explained that at the end of the project, I would have a real garden, not small plants that needed a year to grow. I wanted something beautiful in my life and too, I wanted to do something I knew. I knew and loved plants and gardens. So I decided to wait to build more and plant with the little money I had. But I asked him to do something for about 1000 US. He told me he would see but that if I gave him a deposit he could start tomorrow. I started to feel sick. I was starting another money run. But instead of saying no and stopping, I told him we could go to the bank now. We would meet in town in front of HSBC, the only bank in town at that time. I committed to a project I was unsure of once again. He and Amador left and I loaded Lakra into the car and locked the gate behind us.

When I got to the bank, Christopher was waiting in a big black pick up with his wife and two children inside. The woman introduced herself as Lucretia. She couldn't introduce the kids because before she could finish saying hello the little boy started bashing on his sister's head and she had to stop him. I walked toward the back of the truck where Christopher was waiting to escape the mayhem and gave him his deposit. As he signed for it, he told me he would be back with soil the next day and then the plants later in the week.

Just like he said, the next day he brought about 50 bags of rich dark earth. But he also brought his wife and two children. His wife didn't stop talking and the two children didn't stop fighting and crying.

She kept asking, "You living there?"

Or would say, "You need to be careful here in the jungle alone," between reprimanding her little boy for hitting his sister or eating dirt.

Lakra hid. Finally Lucretia asked if her son could use my bathroom. I did not want that devil in my space but could hardly say no.

So, I helped him up the stairs as she held the infant and continued in her non-stop littany, "There was a murder up the road last year, you know."

I knew but did not pay attention since I was trying to count the bags of soil Christopher unloaded and keep track of the boy in my bathroom. I prayed they would hurry. Her son was crying for help so she went in, handing me the infant as she did so. I almost dropped the kid the diaper was so wet and the baby immediately started to cry. Lucreti kept talking from the bathroom, asking how I knew Amador.

Before I could answer, she continued, "He is a great guy. He will help you alot."

I had my doubts. When they came out of the bathroom, I handed her the infant without a word and walked toward her husband.

She followed me commenting, "You should put a screen in the bathroom window" explaining that a scorpion could fall on my head when I went in at night.

I had never thought of that. I shivered as I looked at this horrible little family. The boy was running down the steps to get to me and he hit me hard on the butt as he ran past to play in the dirt. Finally, Christopher said that was it and yelled to his wife to get in the car. When they were all loaded in, he told me he would come back toward the end of the week.

I surprised myself by asking if he would come alone. He smiled and asked if the kids were bothering me. My mother would have been ashamed.

But I told him, "Not so much the kids," and looked down at the dirt.

He laughed and told me he would see what he could do but there were no guarantees. His wife came up the walkway to get in the car but before she did she asked me if I had seen the black widow spiders yet. I shook my head and told her no, but that I was sure I would. She agreed and told me to watch out for them. Christopher told me he would be back in a few days with some beautiful plants. And they drove away taking Amador with them.

I went back to my house and sat for awhile in silence. But then I started to look around for insects. I caught myself and said to Lakra, "lets go to the beach." I was thrilled to be alone again, especially after that woman and those kids. Ever since I asked Harry to leave my condo 3 years earlier and I danced to be alone, I was learning to enjoy my solitude. It was no easy accomplishment considering I came from a family of seven kids but here I was, passing the test.

Christopher came by the next week with beautiful plants just like he said but he brought the family. Thankfully they went to the beach. Amador helped the first day but then didn't come back until it was time for me to pay. I noticed I was happier when he was not around. He always had some criticism of the house: the bathroom was too close to the kitchen, nothing was finished, the sink in the bathroom was bigger than the sink in the kitchen, always putting the place down. But at the end of it all, I had trees to look at rather than concrete. I smiled as I stretched on that little hanging bed of mine. Out of the blue one morning, Amador came back. I made coffee and we sat on the steps to drink it.

Before we could finish he asked me, "When you gonna finish the roof? When you gonna get into a real house?"

I shrugged. I had grown fond of my little screen house. I knew it was weird and that I needed to do more but for now, I didn't really want to deal with it. I had lots of other stuff to do. He reminded me that if I was ever going to bring anyone to recuperate or even visit, I needed to do more. Then Amador offered to help. And again, he told me he could do it for a good price. I told him I would consider it but, in Amador's mind at least, I was going to work with him.

The next afternoon he came by with a contractor named Felix: a short Mayan guy with a nice smile, no gold teeth. We went over what I needed using the design Moises modified slightly to add some curves and more windows. Amador never hesitated to give his opinion or to make fun of something I wanted if he thought it was wrong. I started not to like him. Felix would smile when he would correct or change something I wanted. I didn't like that at all and would change it back. Felix listened patiently to us both and said he would have a proposal in the next few days.

"*Tienes telefono?*" Felix said to me.

"He wants to know if you have a phone," Amador said.

I had understood and told Amador he didn't need to translate for me. I was tired of him bullying me.

"Well, then?" he asked.

I answered in Spanish, "*No. No tengo*".

I had bought several. But each time I left, I had given them to

Amador so he could keep in touch with me. He always lost them or smashed them when someone gave him bad news. He never had them for more than two weeks. So I never bought myself one, even when I moved. I used my US phone and let people find me. I enjoyed being inaccessible. I didn't wait for calls because no one could call me. So, it soothed my mind and I could imagine people trying to reach me, missing me, and wondering about me. Whether it was true or not, I was happier with the illusion than facing the reality that perhaps everyone had forgotten me. Amador told me I needed to get one and then said the same in Spanish to Felix.

"*Aqui es miyo,*" Felix said, "*Llamame cuando tienes tuyo.*"

I struggled to translate. I was pretty sure he was giving me his number and asking me to call with mine when I bought it.

I hesitated while I constructed a sentence in my head and then pushed the words out of my mouth, "*Te llamo cuando lo compro.*"

I prayed it conveyed that I would call him once I bought one. Amador smiled and Felix put out his hand to shake mine.

I was still unsure of what I had said and finally asked Amador, "Was it right?"

He smiled, nicely, warmly and told me, "*Si mami,* it was perfect."

I smiled back. At least I had learned something.

Felix left and Amador walked around my little place.

"You gonna stay here while they work?"

I asked him where else I could go. He told me it would be weird with me living here and all the workers around. I told him matter of factly that I needed to make sure they were working and check on their progress and the details. I looked at him and asked him if he had been planning on doing that.

"No," he said smiling, "You are right."

I continued, taking advantage of the opportunity to vent and told him I really didn't have the cash to stay at a hotel anymore and that I liked having my own place. I reminded him that had been the plan. He looked me in the eyes then and put his arm on my lower back. I felt a tingle that I loved and hated at the same time. Then he kissed me on the mouth and told me he remembered. It felt very nice. I asked him if he remembered telling me he would never leave me, pushed him away and turned to walk back to the house. He grabbed my hand and said he was here now.

"For how long?" I said seriously, knowing he would leave soon and I would never know when he would come back, or if he would.

He said, "long enough," with his eyes sparkling.

He really thought I would have sex with him just like that. He moved closer to me, grabbed my waist and kissed me hard on the lips and started pushing me back toward the house, step by step.

I pushed against him but almost fell backwards until I started walking step in step with him. He moved his hands up my back and pulled me closer to him. He was almost carrying me and I was surprised at how strong he was. I mean, I am not a big person but I am heavier than I look, dense, all muscle, I like to believe. And he was soft and I thought out of shape. But he had me off the ground and in his arms and took me up the stairs like it was nothing. I remembered our arm wrestle as he kicked the door to my room open and we fell onto the bed. He had already undone my bra. I was amazed at how fast he was moving and started to push him away but then I wanted it. I wanted to be close to someone and when I thought about it, sex was as close as I could get.

I couldn't deny that I had chemistry for this guy, this con artist, this small time crook. I wanted him and loved being overwhelmed physically. It seemed that was the only way a man could beat me and although I loved winning, sexually I enjoyed being dominated. I didn't understand why and didn't yet realize that coke heads/crack heads were hypersexed. I honestly thought it was me and loved believing that. When he pulled off his shorts, I wiggled out of my favorite green pants and he was all over my body, I was so happy to have someone actually see and touch me that I forgot for that moment what a shit he actually was. I saw him as the guy I wanted. We both had problems but we would overcome them and as he entered me I pulled him deeper into me. When I climaxed it was a release of months of misunderstanding and hurt and he came with me. We fell back onto the swinging bed and rested. I was unsure if the dizziness was from sex or from the bed constantly moving or a combination of both.

We laid there for about 20 minutes. I held his hand. We were both sweating. He was breathing heavily and then he fell asleep. I stayed awake. I looked over at him after a few moments. His face was peaceful, soft. His curly hair, some parts in dreadlocks with the tips bleached a blondish red from the sun, wound around his ears. One curl fell on his forehead. He had a scar that I noticed for the first time above his cheekbone, close to his left eye. It was new. He had been fighting. I looked away and thought about something else, like what the hell was I doing sleeping with this guy? I looked down at his feet and remembered the Pablo Nuruda love poem that I had read so many times when I lived in DC and was studying Spanish and working to keep the whole project together.

"I love your feet because they brought you to me," the poem said. I had sent that to Amador in emails. Now I wondered as I looked down at his dirty feet that were cracked and bloody and covered in dust from the street. He still never wore shoes. I looked up at the long thing poles in the ceiling, as he rolled over and covered me in his arms and his leg and kissed the back of my neck. I would have a hard time getting out of this one.

Chapter 11

Finally, I bought a phone. I could communicate with Felix as we built my little house. Amador came by most days. When he came, I would feel cared for, not so weird and alone. I wondered where he went when he was not with me but I told myself it was better this way. After all he had put me through, I preferred to not live with him. But, truthfully, I had no option. He did what he wanted. Showed up when he wanted, had dinner with me when he wanted, took me out when he wanted, stayed over when he wanted. I had no idea how to make him stay nor did I want to play the games necessary to make him do so. So when he showed up I was happy. When he came to the door at 2 a.m. I opened it, glad to see him. When he didn't come, I watched the stars and relaxed in the hammock, almost not waiting, about as happy as I had ever been.

Each morning, I woke early and practiced yoga next to the ever-present puddle under my bed, Lakra waiting in the corner. Then I would feed my dog friend, make coffee and wait for the workers. They generally came at 8. I often served them a coffee, using the Elvis Presley tray I had brought from Memphis, Tennessee. I loved placing the Italian coffee maker next to the Irish cups on the tray with Elvis, an American icon, on the concrete floor for the Mayan workers. It fed my soul somehow to have so many cultures around me, no matter how misrepresented.

The workers were a happy bunch of guys. I enjoyed them. They were all short and stalky and a berry colored brown. You couldn't really tell how old they were. Their skin was smooth and their hair generally dark, without a hint of grey. They were incredibly strong and they moved agilely, framing the roof in two days using no cranes, no machinery, not tied onto anything, just these 4 barefoot guys pulling 5 meter poles about 10 meters up to the peak to form my little *palapa*. The roof had to have a good incline, Felix would explain, so that the rain would not come in. It looked too high but I trusted him.

There was constant hammering to create the frame of poles that would support the thatch or *guano* roof. The only motorized equipment they had was a chainsaw and they used that or a machete to cut everything, from the thinnest pole to the planks they used to support themselves once they got to the top. The *guano* that would form the roof was palm-fronds from a palm native to the area called just that, a *guano palm*. Moises had explained to me that the *guano* roofs were a Mayan style more than the grass or *zacate* roofs. There had to be thousands of *guano* palm fronds stacked in my yard that the workers would first cut a little with a whack of their machete, then bunch about 15 together before hauling them with a rope and pulley to the guy who was weaving them together like a carpet from the top of the frame. It smelled sweet and was green when they wove it into the frame of the roof, frond by frond. It was gorgeous.

Finally, I was protected from the rain. The puddle under my bed gradually dried and now that we had the roof, we could create inside. We built walls and the guys fixed the floor that had cracked from exposure to the sun and rain. At Amador's suggestion, I added a balcony. Felix put waves into the walls and, although he didn't get it exactly right, I was happy enough with what he had done. Little by little, the house was shaping up. We put huge spaces for 2 oversized windows in front and in the back and two peaks at the top of the *palapa* to let the wind pass and air circulate and let light enter. It was a beautiful tropical house. In less than a month, I no longer had a puddle under my bed and I could only see the stars if I went out to the front yard. But I finally had real shelter. Felix was proud of his work and we talked about him finishing the other buildings. But I was running out of money and I still needed to find doors and windows. We decided to move the kitchen. But I would wait, since that was my living space. I was afraid I would have to move out. I also needed to figure out what to do about supporting myself and even though I was still consulting for the Corps of Engineers, I was spending more than I was making.

Too, it was nearly time for me to see my doctors back in Boston. Breast Cancer awareness month was coming and we had a few fundraisers planned. I had been neglecting myself and my foundation and I needed to leave for a few weeks. But now I had a fantastic dog. I loved her dearly and wondered if Amador could take care of her. He was always around in a weird sort of way, if not coming by, calling to check on me. But I was unsure if he would take care of my stuff and more importantly my baby Lakra.

One day as I was leaving for the beach to have a swim, Akim came by. She was waiting for me in a small blue car with a friend. I don't know for how long she had been there but I was surprised to see her. When I opened the door she got out. She was in a beautiful long knit cream colored dress. She had flowers in her long hair. She told me they were going to a wedding and then stood there for a few moments in an awkward silence. I did not help her break it.

She finally inhaled deeply and then started to speak in poor English. I understood that she was apologizing to me for something with Amador and she continued saying that it just happened and she never intended it to be that way. Like a fog lifting over the water, the meaning became clear to me. Amador was with her when he was not with me. He had been with her all the time that he was not coming by, not coming to the hotel and the days he was not sleeping with me, he had been sleeping with her. I let her finish but said nothing. She gave me a hug. I did not hug her back. I let her drive away without saying much at all. I was unsure what to say so I walked to the beach with Lakra and jumped into the ocean and started to scream and cry.

I had hoped he was only with me, living so in denial that I figured I could create this place where we could have our little island of existence on the land. And if he needed more social life, I let it slide but I never allowed myself to imagine he was still with another woman. I was so naïve I wanted to kick myself. I stayed in the ocean awhile, submerging to scream into the water and coming up to breath. I probably looked as if I were drowning and decided finally to come out and I sat for awhile with my Lakra. At least I had her. At least I had the beach. At least I had a new life.

After awhile, I stood up and we went back to the house. I had a long hot shower and counted my blessings. I had water and hot water at that. I had food for me and my dog, I reminded myself as I made some quesadillas and shared left over chicken with Lakra. I had a cooler and I had loads of small bottles of not so great wine but I was living large. I was alive. I had even found some baby bib lettuce in Playa del Carmen so I had a salad. I lit the candles and my new Coleman lantern and enjoyed my dinner alone. I would be happy with what I had.

As I was sitting there with Lakra, I heard a motor scooter pull into the drive. The driver touched the horn gently 3 times and I realized it was for me. I walked out to the gate to find Akim again, this time with her friend Gisela, who spoke better English. Gisela asked if they could come in. I told them yes, although I wasn't really up for it and not sure what they wanted. I would at least have a glass of wine with them. I found something to sit on and we sat around the lantern as I poured them wine in my Spanish wine glasses. Their faces were blurs of shadows and the scene was surreal as the light of the Coleman lantern and the candles was interrupted by the shadows of the bugs circling around them.

I notice Akim and Gisela looking around and I felt judged: my clothes in the linen closet, the cooler, the small kitchen sink and the disarray. I was not a house-keeper, I told myself and pushed feelings of inadequacy away. Gisela started talking first. I had always liked this chubby happy woman even when we were at the hospital in Cancun. I let her speak and she mentioned that that Akim thought I knew about Amador and her saying that Amador promised Akim that he had told me. I told her he had never said anything. They started to ask about his habits. I became defensive but I told them the truth: that he came to visit me but I never knew when or asked him where he was going afterward. Gisela asked me if I didn't care. My eyes narrowed and I told her that I knew I couldn't control him so I let him be who he was. She translated everything for Akim and I opened another of my small bottles of wine to share with them when there was a knock on the door.

I went to answer. It was Amador. The tele-novella was unfolding. He gave me a kiss on the lips as I opened the door and he asked if I had company, almost jealously. I told him yes and to please come in. Lakra was humping him as usual and he patted her and pushed her off his leg so we could walk to the house. I did not mention who was there. I wanted to see his face when he realized we were all there together. I watched him as he climbed the stairs and looked at the women. He smiled. He liked the drama, I could tell. I saw that little sparkle in his eye. He kissed them both on the cheek and asked for a beer. I told him I had none but he could have a glass of wine.

No one said a word until Amador broke the silence with "You been talking bout me?"

I wanted to hit him. Hit him and Akim and Gisella and kick them all out of my house and lock the door behind them. But I didn't. I smiled for some ridiculous reason and didn't say a word. Part of me liked the drama too. The shadows on the faces were flickering as a bug passed around the Coleman lantern. There was silence for awhile and you could hear the cicada bugs. Then Akim started and then Gisela and they spoke in Spanish and English and my head started spinning trying to follow the conversation. It all seemed so sophomoric and something that I was not able to follow linguistically or culturally. The whole my man, your man, you can't sleep with 2 woman, confrontation and bullshit blew my mind. It drew me in but more, it exhausted me.

Finally Akim stood up. I had said nothing. I had nothing to say. She told Amador he had to make a choice and then she walked away. Gisela followed, thanking me for the wine.

Amador looked at me and said, "Baybe she gonna be here for me when you go back. She take care of me and she know how." He kissed me fully on the lips and ran after her.

Shocked, I walked to the door. The air felt thick and I moved slowly, the light of the vespa illuminating the walkway. When I got to the gate, I saw Gisela getting into a taxi and Amador standing in front of the vespa while Akim sat ready to leave. Finally, she handed him a helmet and he jumped on behind her. I watched them drive off. Lakra rubbed her head against me as I stood there and watched the light of the vespa fade down the road. I patted her head, shook my head in disbelief and closed the gate. I did not cry.

We walked slowly back to the house, toward the light from the candles and the lantern. Numb, I cleaned the cups and dishes and got ready for bed. Part of me was very relieved. I lay in my hanging bed with my Lakra underneath and felt a certain lightness, a certain release. I was hurt but knew I was better off. Deep in my soul, I knew this would help me let go. But it would sting for a long while. If I had been close to an ice cream store I would have eaten a quart of Cherry Garcia. Instead, I fell sound asleep.

I woke the next morning with the sun, stretched and started to cry. All the sadness from inside me sort of exploded out. It was Sunday, my least favorite day. No one would visit and I always felt alone in the Mexican Sunday family culture. It was the day people got together and ate and drank and spent afternoons on the beach. I went to the beach with Lakra before anyone got there. The ocean was calm. The sun was hot. I did some drawing, some writing, hanging around, watering the plants. The day would not go fast enough. I called my mom and cried. I didn't dare to tell her why. I said it was all too much. She told me to come home, reminding me I needed to see my doctors. I decided to buy a ticket to do just that. Lakra and I went to town and I prayed I would not see Amador or Akim or Gisella or anyone else I knew or who knew me.

When I returned I chastised myself for being a wimp. Lakra and I shared quesadillas and I wondered who would take care of her for me. I wasn't running away, I reminded myself. I needed a break. Alot was waiting for me. It was early September and I had some doctor's appointments and fundraisers to prepare. I needed more contract work and without internet or any real way to contact the world outside, it was difficult. A short time in the US would be good. I could check on our condo in Miami and try to push that sale. I told myself again that it was just a break. And as I looked around, I told myself that actually things could not be better. I would find some workers. Other people would help me. I told myself that Amador was a liability and would only hold me back or mess something up. Better for me if he were with Akim. She could try to control him. I knew no one could. I gave my Lakra a big hug and got ready for the evening, lighting some candles, making tea.

I found my way for the next few days. It was solitary: no workers, no Amador, no outside influences, no pressure. It was heaven. My days kept the natural rhythm of the sun. I heard Amalio's cough in the night but even my neighbors were quiet. I had a hammock for the evening and the afternoons and I painted and wrote and practiced yoga as always. I had classes with Juan and Martha and we shared coffee afterwards. By Wednesday, I had healed from the melodrama. Thursday afternoon Amador came to the gate. He yelled my name at the door. I felt a pit in my stomach and stood still. He yelled again, forcefully as if demanding I answer the door. I knew I could wait it out. Lakra was howling to see him and when he called a third time I walked to the gate.

"You don' hear me?" he asked. I told him I was busy and asked him what he wanted.

"You not gonna let me in?" he said and I told him no.

And again I asked him what he wanted.

He said, "*Mami*, let me in. I just wanna talk with you."

I snapped. Anger overcame me and I told him, "I am not your *mami*, I am not your girlfriend, I am not even sure we are friends Amador, so really why would I let you in."

I took Lakra and walked back to the house leaving him there, like a person in a refugee camp, peeking behind the poles that made my gate. Lakra wanted to see him but I pulled her along with me and we went inside the house. I was shaking and was afraid to look to the gate. But I had done it. I had finally taken a stand. I smiled and sat down on the cooler, out of sight, almost hiding but almost not. It was an hour before I had the courage to look over to the gate to see if he was still there. He was not. I did not dare to open it in case he was waiting in the street. I wondered who was the prisoner as I walked to the back of my lot and climbed to the top of my shell of a penthouse and looked out over the magnificent swamp and thanked God for my health and my strength. I felt good even though I started to cry.

Chapter 12

I was finally able to focus and enjoy my projects for the army and my non-profit. I liked my work, all of it. I reminded myself how great that was. I went to town just about every day but made my visits short. I did not want to see Amador and knew that the longer I was in town the easier it was to bump into him. I walked with Lakra to Jade to teach yoga. We settled into a wonderfully solitary routine. I called my mom and my friend Sheba once or twice from town and made some plans to return to the US to work the foundation and get some more money to continue in Mexico.

One day leaving the supermarket San Francisco, my phone rang.

It was Akim. She wanted to have lunch. I told her I did not think it was a good idea but she persisted and said the magic word. So I agreed. I told her I was in town and we could meet at la Nave. I liked the place and was hungry so I agreed to meet there in half an hour. In the meantime I would take Lakra and walk the avenue.

I felt weird walking into la Nave. The Italian family that owned it was good friends with Akim. The Italians were a clique in Tulum. They took care of their own and helped each other. They had some of the nicest places on the beach so far and next to the Mexican *Don Cafetos'*, *la Nave* was the most popular restaurant on the *Avenida*. I sat down with Lakra under the table and waited for Akim. I left my back to the street unwisely and pretended not to wait. When the waiter came I ordered a glass of wine. Just as he delivered it, Akim touched me on the shoulder and sat down next to me. When she sat down several people who were already in the restaurant got up to say hello. I knew them all but she introduced me. They seemed not to remember me. I reminded myself that I was invisible, except for when the bill came. I asked her if she was hungry. She said no. I was starving but just as I was ready to order Amador came over. He was all smiles and kissed me on the cheek. I wanted to die. I got defensive and asked Akim if this was why she wanted to see me. She said no, apologizing for him. Amador asked what we were doing. I told him I was leaving and got up to pay for my wine. Akim asked me to please wait telling me we had things to discuss and that Amador would leave. But even the magic word had limits.

I paid the bill and told her, "perhaps another time or at least another place," as I left.

Lakra and I walked toward the car not caring if people were watching. Akim caught up with me and suggested we drive somewhere else. I stopped, looked at her and I am not sure if it was curiousity or sympathy but I agreed and mentioned the beach. As we got in the car, Amador came to my window and asked where we were going. Akim told him to give us some space, saying it was not fair. I started the car, put it in drive and left him. I lost my anxiety as soon as we were on the Avenue. I started to laugh, my nervous reaction to almost anything. Akim didn't know what to do but she smiled.

"This is ridiculous, you know that," I told her.

She asked me why. I told her we had nothing to discuss. I was happy. I didn't need Amador and she could have him. I laid it out for her. She looked straight ahead and was suddenly not the happy cute little girl anymore. I wasn't being nice like my reputation.

She told me, "We don't need to be enemies, Joanne."

I groaned and said, "We don't need to be friends either," without drama or anger.

I stated the fact. She told me I could use a few friends. I told her I had some and that I was fine.

We drove up the north beach road toward the Tulum Archaeological site and the *Playa Pescadores* and parked. Lakra ran out of the car towards the beach but I called her back. I really needed to eat something so if Akim and Lakra didn't mind we would go to the restaurant *Don Cafetos* on the beach. I took a table in the back. The place was empty and there was a gentle breeze coming off the ocean. A few tourists and campers wandered around the restaurant, looking for information or a bathroom or shower. The sun was setting and it cast long shadows along the sand from the palm trees.

I ordered quesadillas and another wine. She ordered a beer but no food saying they had eaten earlier. It stung a little that she said "we." I asked her what she wanted to talk about.

She stuttered before telling me, "Amador needs work," as if I should care.

I looked for the waiter to bring my wine and asked her what that was to me.

She looked down at the floor and said, "well, I thought you cared for him and you might need some help with your project."

I couldn't believe what I heard. I stared at her, speechless. The waiter brought the food and I ate in silence.

She continued to speak to me in broken English, telling me "We are good womens" and then she said how she and Amador liked me and could help me finish my project.

She finished saying, "when he is working, he is very good."

I gave my last quesadilla to Lakra and asked for the check. I looked at her, tried to be open-minded but couldn't imagine working with them. Honestly, I told her that I still had not recovered from the other night and that I was pretty sure I could manage my project with someone other than Amador. A part of me wanted to be big enough to work with them and pretend I never was Amador's lover. But I could not. I told her that he was not the only person who could manage a project and that he had very few credentials to do the work.

I surprised myself with my candor and my ability to lay it out for her. I wasn't sure I could do the same if Amador asked me for work but I would try.

I patted Lakra and watched Akim's face get red as I told her what I was pretty sure she already knew. It had an impact. She was not getting her way like she was used to. But I was pretty sure that mostly happened with men or perhaps with other Italian "womens." She told me that Amador could help me find workers or take care of things when I went to the states. She reminded me I would need someone. I still said nothing and she filled the silence saying that Amador needed a chance. I laughed when she said it. She looked shocked.

I laughed harder and said, "You would have me work with the guy who was two timing you and me for about 2 months and who chose you over me."

She told me there was no reason we could not be friends and work together to make my project a reality. Then she took my hand and told me she could only imagine how badly I felt but I should not let that stop me moving forward. I waited a moment, took my hand from her's and assured her I was not stopping work. I was only stopping work with Amador and that, in fact, my life was easier for it.

She repeated that I could use a friend and that I might not be so closed minded. I tried to soften my attitude and I explained to her that I was hurt and not ready to have their relationship thrown in my face.

The check came and she looked for money for her beer. I told her not to worry and paid the bill telling her I would take her back to town if she wanted. She told me no that she would stay there on the beach, said thanks for the beer and asked me to think about it. I told her not to expect anything. She went to talk to the guys at the cabanas and I took Lakra down to the water before we turned back to go home. I liked getting there before dark and we would make it if we left shortly.

We walked back up the sandy road toward the car and as we reached it, Akim came running up with a smile saying she had changed her mind. If I would take her back to town it would be great. I abandoned my idea of getting to the house before dark and opened a door for her. We didn't say much on the ride back but she asked me several questions about my life, about the project and when

I would go back to the states next. I answered her in one word answers where I could. Then it got so boring I started to talk with her like a friend. I told her a little about my life and my desire to bring survivors to Tulum. She was silent for a moment, and then, out of the blue, asked me why I didn't go out more. I told her I was happier at my house in the night.

She asked me, "But then how you gonna meet people to help you. How you gonna make friends?"

We were back in Tulum by this time so I asked her where she wanted to get out. I dropped her at a little bar on the avenue that sometimes had live music but always had the most colorful and interesting owner: *la Cubana*.

La Cubana would walk the Avenue in the middle of the day in leather shorty shorts with a tight vest holding the 2 biggest false breasts anyone in Tulum had ever seen. She was petite with false eyelashes and long brown hair almost to her knees. She generally wore thigh high boots with heels and the shorts combined with tops that looked like *bustierres*. She was the best show in town. At her bar, she was even more flamboyant, wearing negligees and very often dancing on the bar with her tits way ahead of her or pouring shots down the throats of male tourists and locals alike. She had a husband who was more like a bodyguard but who tolerated her behavior so long as it was paying. I guess he was more of a pimp.

I had only been to her bar a few times and it was always surreal. I could never take my eyes off her. Akim asked me if I wanted to come up and although tempted to witness the Feliniesque floor show that I knew would be happening in a few hours, I told her that I might go another time and said goodnight. She asked me to think about hiring Amador again and I shook my head. She left happily and kissed the cheeks of the bouncers as she headed up the stairs to the terrace bar. I drove back to the beach with Lakra, lit candles and star watched not missing la Cubana or any of the "friends" I could make in town. And when the mosquitoes got too bad, I went back to my screened in porch to sleep, Lakra by my side.

The next days I researched bringing Lakra to the states with me but since I really didn't have a place, I started looking for someone to take care of her in Tulum. I asked at Jade but they were not too enthusiastic and didn't think she would stick around. I didn't have too many other contacts, Akim's words "how you gonna meet people" echoed in my ears but still I did not go out. I knew I would find someone. I did not trust my neighbors but I had one friend at a coffee shop I could ask. I was running the options in my mind one afternoon when Amador came by again.

I was painting palm trees while sitting in the hammock and he shouted "hello" from the gate. I looked up and then exhaled heavily when I saw him. Lakra started to howl and ran to the gate. I got up feeling a heaviness overwhelm me and, not sure why, went to the gate. Maybe it was his little boy smile and his hair all tousled around his face, one curl coming down his forehead. He didn't say anything. Neither did I. We looked at each other like two people across a border who had so much history but had been separated by the world. I caught myself starting to cry and inhaled to stop.

He noticed and said, "Why you so sad *Mami*, you got everything goin' for you?"

Then I laughed. It was a big laugh and I smiled broadly and told him it showed how much he knew.

Then he said, "don' you wanna have a coffee with me?" and I admitted to myself that I did.

I wanted to sit with a man and talk and perhaps even hold his hand. Life had become so confusing, so in the moment, so fleeting. I wanted to forgive, forget and come back to that nice feeling of having a friend who was male. So I forgot for a moment that he was not a friend, that he was a predator, and I opened the door and let him in, again. We took our coffee out to the back structure and climbed to the top, Lakra waited below. And we sat there and had Mexican coffee from the Italian coffee maker poured into my Irish coffee cups served on the Elvis Presley tray with French cookies and looked out over the most magnificent space that I could remember seeing in my life.

Amador put his hand on top of mine and told me, "I just want to help you *Mami*." I didn't say anything for awhile.

I thought and finally told him, "Amador, I am not your *Mami*."

We both laughed.

Chapter 13

I walked Amador to the gate after our coffee and he asked if he could see me again. I told him anything was possible. He got angry.

Not a lot but enough to remind me who he was.

"C'mon Joanne, let me be your friend. You might need me," he told me.

I looked at this man who I believed had helped me change my life but who had hurt me so much. Surprising even myself, I told him OK, we could have a coffee again. He immediately asked about breakfast the next day and I told him that perhaps the day after since I had plans. He asked me what I could be doing in the morning, apparently jealous.

"I have a yoga class," I told him proudly. He smiled and asked if he could come. I told him of course, knowing he would never make it but not wanting to be rude. He asked about the following day. I opened the door and let him out. I did not commit to anything. I knew that to make a date with him meant waiting and near certain disappointment. I wanted neither. He gave me a hug. I hugged him back. And that was it. He crossed the street and started walking, looking for a ride, the happy man. I locked the gate behind him and wondered what had happened. But I could not deny that I felt good. It was nice to have a coffee and perhaps a friend. If I could only keep it that way, it might all work out.

He came two days later just as I was leaving for town. The man had timing. Lakra was in the car and I was closing the gate. He asked about breakfast. I told him it would be my second breakfast but why not, if he didn't mind going back to town. He never minded moving. He seemed to spend his days moving from one place to another looking for opportunities. If he wanted to stay somewhere, he did. If not, he moved on. We enjoyed breakfast at la Nave with Lakra under the table waiting for treats to fall from our breakfast. Before we finished a dog walked in front of us and Lakra ran out to assault her. I screamed, afraid she would be hit by a car. Amador laughed, amused at her ferocity not at all concerned with the implications.

As I pulled her back and put her leash on, Amador asked me what I was going to do now.

I began reciting my "to do" list when he interrupted me with, "No, I mean on the land. You gonna keep working?"

I paused, inhaled and said, honestly, that I didn't know. I was out of money and needed to go to the US and look for more work. I explained I needed to take care of my foundation and my books and the construction was taking too much of my time and money. He took my hand to get my attention, and asked if I would let him help me. Uncomfortable with the concept, I could not answer.

With great effort, I slowly told him, "that didn't work out too well before," and waited for his reaction.

He was silent and then said, "I know. But now it is different. I am different."

And I asked him bluntly, "Why? Because you are with Akim?"

And unbelieveably he had the balls to say yes.

I looked around for the check and told him that really, he had no experience and the times I had worked with him I always lost money and he always lost his mind. But he didn't give up.

As I stood up to go pay the bill, he asked me, "Don' you think people can change?"

He knew me so well. I sat back down and told him that I wanted to believe people could change. I mean, I listened to Garth Brooks over and over again while he sang, "some people change." I wished he could to my soul. He looked at me and asked me to give him a chance. He went to pat Lakra under the table.

I told him, "Listen, I don't want to construct now. I want to finish the house, put in windows, move the kitchen. Perhaps you can help me finish that. And I need someone to take care of Lakra. I will be away 3 weeks and I cannot leave her with anyone else. Can you do it?"

A huge smile crossed his face that was so contagious I couldn't help but smile and feel better.

He told me he could and then asked me what I would pay.

We settled on a price and then he asked me, "How am I gonna move?"

I didn't understand the question. He looked back at me and explained that he needed a car to get around. My joy at helping him faded fast. We had been through this many times before. I told him he would have to manage without a car. The work was simple enough, he had to organize it and get the people there to work and pay them. It didn't require a car and Felix had a car and could take care of most everything.

I believed he accepted it. I paid for breakfast and he asked to come along as I ran my errands. He said wanted to "hang" with me. It was a term Lynn and I had taught him and it was a good memory. We walked together to the internet. He waited outside and then he came with me to the bank and to the laundry and, finally, I told him I was going back to the beach. He asked for a ride to the supermarket and as we were waiting at the light, a black jeep pulled up next to us with a for sale sign on it.

"You could buy that one," he told me, "and think of all the money you could save from renting a car."

I looked at the car and then at Amador. In a perfect world it would make sense. But I knew it was not a perfect world. I smiled and looked at the car again. Amador told me he knew the owner and that we could go see him now if he wanted. Then he reached over and touched the horn to get the driver's attention.

He yelled over, "How much?" and the driver told him 20,000 pesos, less than $2,000 US. Amador talked with the driver until the light changed and I took the turn to San Francisco.

"It is a great deal," he told me and followed with, "think about it," as he got out of the car.

I looked back, patted Lakra and said "so long."

"See you," he said and he puckered his lips as if waiting for a kiss.

I laughed, put the car in reverse and backed out. He shrugged his shoulders and blew me a kiss. I blew one back and drove back to the beach with Lakra, not sure what I was doing but knowing that I had to trust someone to help me. I choose Amador once again.

I had about 5 days to prepare to go to the US. I always missed my people there but never wanted to leave when it came down to it. But it was more than time. The last nights Lakra and I sat under the stars and shared our quesadillas and chicken and I told her that I had to go and she needed to wait. I hoped she would. But I told myself that she was she at least healthy, if she decided to leave me. Too, I trusted Akim to take care of her more than Amador.

Two days before my flight, Amador came by with a carpenter to take measurements for the oversized windows in the house. They would give me an estimate the next day. Before they left, Amador asked if I had thought more about the jeep. I told him I had not, that I didn't have the money and that I didn't want one more thing to worry about. I had enough on my plate, I explained to him. He told me he would take care of it and that he had talked with the owner and that it was a great deal and in very good condition. He also said the owner would take payments. I thought about it, did the math and then told him no.

He said, "how about we go to town and talk to the guy."

I looked at him and asked, "what part of 'no' do you not understand."

He told me, "all of it," making a joke.

I shook my head in disbelief and went to the house for something. He sat in the hammock out front, hanging around. His ride, the carpenter, had left. I asked him if he had something to do but he didn't answer me.

I said to him, "well I do so if you want a ride back to town, I will give you one."

I wanted him out of my space and thought he might go to the beach or something but no, he just wanted to hang with me and push the idea of buying that car. We went to town, him talking about the car the entire way. I did the math in my head. I would pay a little more than 1000 US to have this rental car for so much time. I intended to come back for more time so it would be about the same all over again, if I rented a car. I really didn't want to have a car but I was finding it was a necessity. He gave me peace for awhile and I thought about it.

After a full 10 minutes, he asked me, "cmon Joanne, what you thinking?"

I told him that I was thinking that perhaps it was good idea and that perhaps he was right. He smiled and told me that of course he was right.

We went to talk to the owner who lived on the Avenue behind a building that sold car batteries and oil and whatever other thing you might need for a car. The day was hot and dry but on the street there was a breeze that sort of cooled the sweat off your body. Amador knocked several times on the big green colored gate. No one answered. A part of me was relieved. I would be spared. But as we turned to leave, the door opened and a fat balding guy poked his head out and said hello to Amador. Amador introduced me and we spoke about the car and how much. He lowered the price to 1800 and I thought it was a good deal but told him I didn't have the money with me and would have to pay him from the US or when I got back. He told me no problem and asked when I could give him a deposit. I asked to drive it first.

Amador, Lakra and I got into the car and took a drive. The

directionals didn't work, I noticed, nor the windshield wipers. But the motor sounded OK and it started several times in a row so I figured it was a good car. The breaks were squishy. When we went back I asked the guy to fix those things and told him we would come back tomorrow with a deposit. Amador wanted to do it all that day but I wanted at least directionals. The guy told me he would get it together and if I wanted to come by in the evening it would be ready. I told him tomorrow would be fine but Amador pushed me to come back at night.

"That way you have one day at the beach before you go back to US," he told me.

That sounded nice so I agreed and we settled on 7 p.m. to pick up the car.

When I came back in the evening Amador was waiting for me with the car owner. They had been talking. I said hello to both of them. The owner told me that he fixed the directional, and showed me how it was working but told me the wipers needed a motor and he was waiting on the part. He said he would fix it with Amador while I was away. I accepted that, we signed papers and he showed me the title. He told me that when I finished paying he would give it to me and he gave me his bank information. I gave him 5000 pesos and told him I would send the rest from the US.

The next day I knew I needed to give the carpenters a deposit and then I would go. I hoped I could get enough out of the bank to get home. There was a pit in my stomach as I left and Amador took the jeep, probably to go take Akim somewhere. In that moment I cared less.

I told him, "Listen Amador, I want that car to be here and in great condition when I come back. It is a work car and it is mine, understand?"

He cooed that it would be in great shape when I returned and then he got in and started it and took off. As I watched him drive away I remembered that he didn't even have a driver's license. I shook my head, feeling foolish and went home with my dog to enjoy the night. We stopped for a pizza on the way and as I ate it I congratulated myself: I now had a car in Mexico.

The next day Amador did not visit. The carpenter did. He had the estimate for the windows. I gave him a deposit, hoping they would be done when I got back. Lakra and I enjoyed our last night together and the next morning we walked on the beach before I packed up the car and drove her to where I knew Akim lived. I saw the black jeep in front of the house. I cannot say I liked it but I pushed the annoyance and jealousy from my mind. As I drove up the dirty, bumpy driveway towards the little concrete bunker that they called home, they came out to say hello. Akim was wrapped in a pareo, her long curly hair flowing behind her. Amador was in his surfer shorts with no shirt. The setting reminded me of one of those romantic Italian movies where the woman is waiting for sex in a dusty little beachside town.

I parked father away than necessary and brought Lakra to them. Akim promised to take care of her. Amador did too.

He walked me back to the car and asked for money saying, "How am I gonna work if I got nothing?"

I gave him 2000 pesos and told him that should be enough, that there wasn't much work to do and when he started something, I could send him more. He didn't look happy about it but he took it and told me he would be in touch. I took out a big bag of dog food for Lakra and gave it to them saying, "Just be good to the dog ok? And if you get something started with the kitchen, that would be great. Go by often to check the land too." I gave him the extra key to the gate and he gave me a hug. Akim knew better than to come over but she was patting Lakra and I waved goodbye to her and yelled, "take good care of her OK?" She shook her head yes and I got in the rental car to go to the airport. I cried for awhile and then took a deep breath and let it all go.

Chapter 14

I had booked my ticket through Pennsylvania to visit my partners Bathsheba and Paul. Sheba picked me up and we worked on That Barry Girl: leads on book sales and presenting a check for our first grant of $1000 dollars to a woman in treatment. We had made $2500 on book sales, but after the cost of books and the grant, we had only a little to pay for marketing. I had no fears of some accountant telling me I was out of line. I had not taken a cent, rather I had paid for t-shirts and pillow cases and some of the books that would not be reimbursed. But money had started to not mean much to me. I was spending so much that a part of me knew I could never stay on top of it. But another part told me I was OK. That part justified that I was not paying rent and I was investing in my future and a life I wanted. I was passionate about what I was doing and I knew I could figure it all out eventually.

We drove to Sheba's house in the suburbs and sat out back with a cup of tea. They had moved from Boston to buy a big old house on the outskirts of Philly that reminded me of the house I had grown up in. They had painted the house intensely beautiful colors with murals and accents that said artist in every square inch. Paul had put some of the best furniture designs from the 40's and 50's in the house. It was a pleasure to sit in the back yard under the pine trees and breathe. I wasn't sweating. The water was not salty and the bugs were not enormous. We talked about the foundation and ultimately Mexico. Paul asked me how it was going, reminding me that people were always fascinated by the idea. But he added that we could use a little more focus and that I had lots to do in the US. I told him that Mexico was going. I didn't tell him how really. I said it was slow. But I told them I was so happy there. They looked at each other and then at me and said we had lots to do if I were to go back so soon. I smiled knowing they would help me.

We made our grant with local press and interviews. Everyone congratulated me on my books, survivorship and then ultimately the questions went to Mexico. Nearly everyone told me it was a great idea. They wanted to know how we would select the people to go, where was Tulum, wasn't Mexico a little violent for recovering cancer patients. There were so many questions and I answered them all honestly.

In the back of my mind, my sister's voice echoed when she commented on my plan, "taking survivors to Mexico? What are you trying to do, kill them?"

I would smile politely and explain that this part of Mexico was different. It was more the Caribbean than Mexico. There were no drug cartels, I told the interviewer. I didn't think my little narco neighbors counted. After all, they seemed harmless enough to me.

We had planned a fundraiser on Nantucket where my sister lived. It would be fabulous. All my family was participating in what was called the Nantucket Ironman, a ridiculous race that included paddling a surf board and running in sand with a pack on your back. We had competed in it as a family for years and this year we had two teams and were raising money and awareness for my foundation. We had even made a banner that said, "That Barry Girl Foundation" with my bird logo on it. I hand painted our T-shirts and drew birds on them in bleach pens. We finished 5th and 8th of about 15 teams and had a lobster fest back at Calzi's house. The local paper came and interviewed us and took a picture of my clan in front of the banner that made it to the paper the next day. Things were moving ahead.

But Mexico haunted me through the entire trip. If I were not daydreaming of my house and dog there, I was looking for money to pay for the jeep or dealing with Amador's missed calls. I had a hard time finding the final payment for the car and so only sent $500. But I sent a note explaining that I would pay it all when I returned. It probably caused problems for Amador. But he was being such an ass that I really did not care. Away from his proximity, his mental and emotional grip over me lessened and I could think more clearly. Too, I had received an emotional slap in the face that day in the car on the outskirts of Pennslyvania with Sheba. She reminded me that I could be in an abusive relationship and needed to be careful. The thought had never occurred to me and I would not allow it to happen. That was not my life. Being among "my people" I thought more clearly and recognized the scams. After that call, I sent money directly to the people I had hoped Amador would pay, Felix, his wife and the jeep owner directly. I sent some money even to Akim but that was for Lakra. I needed to have her be taken care of and little by little, I realized that Amador would do anything to get what he wanted, even if it meant hurting her to hurt me.

But through it all, even with my family, the wonderful sense of security I had with them and the fabulous support they gave me for my foundation and my books, I felt lost back in the US. And I felt so found in Tulum even with all the drama and the craziness. There was something there that kept calling me. I got on the plane to return filled with a sort of eagerness and anticipation, not only for the beauty and energy of the place, but also to deal with Amador's drama and pull control from him.

I had hoped Amador would pick me up in my new jeep. But his last call was to ask for things for the jeep and to tell me that he doubted it would make the trip to Cancun. I was disappointed but a little happy to be independent. But I had this nagging fear that I had been scammed. Still, I had not paid the whole amount for the car. Amador had no papers and the only person who the owner would give them to was me, when I paid. I let that console me as I rented a car once again and said so long to the dream of saving money as I drove to Tulum. It was late October and still hot and I drove directly through town to where I know Akim lived. But there was no one there. As I drove back to town, I saw the jeep, parked in front of a pharmacy. I pulled over and as I did, Amador came out of the pharmacy with one of those drinks for babies, sort of like a gator aide but used to pump electrolytes, and sugar, I am sure, into dehydrated kids.

He smiled when he saw me.

I smiled back, saying, "Thanks for coming to get me," sarcastically.

He shrugged and told me that if I had sent him the money to fix the car, he could have gone. I sighed, tired of his attitude already and asked him for Lakra. As if it were nothing, he told me that she went to the beach one day and didn't come back. I couldn't believe it and when he saw how shocked and sad I was, he told me she left at least a week ago. I was crushed and started to get back into the car to look for her. Before I left, I asked him about the construction.

He told me the carpenter had not come back but that they were almost finished with the kitchen saying, "you cannot live there. There are no windows or screens and they took apart your little house to put in the real kitchen."

He said it with a certain happiness, as if he were gloating over the fact that I would need to look for a place. I told him I would find a place but first I wanted to find Lakra.

He said, "Lakra is OK. She probably find someone who not gonna leave her like you."

I wanted to throw up as he continued to tell me the jeep needed new tires and that we should go to Playa to buy them. I asked him if he meant at that moment, reminding him that I just got back. He reminded me we needed to get to work right away since once I fixed the jeep I could return the rental car. I wanted to look for Lakra at the beach. Amador told me she was fine and that the next day he would help me find her. He kept asking about the tires, pushing me like a little kid. There was a part of me that so wanted to do things with him. I believed that if I had some time with him, I could understand him better and have him understand me.

Too, without a house, without a dog, without Amador, I really didn't want to be in Tulum. I agreed to go to Playa to fix the car. I wondered where I would stay when I got back and how I could find my Lakra as I started to follow Amador driving north. Behind him I could see that one tire on the jeep was damaged. He could barely drive in a straight line. I flashed my lights and motioned for him to stop, pulled behind him and went to the driver side window and asked what had happened to the car. Defensively, he assured me he had taken good care of the car. I told him obviously not but wanted his help to fix it, get him out of it and get back to Tulum to find my dog and a place to stay.

He started driving again but we had barely gone 500 meters when he stopped and told me that the car couldn't make the trip. I told him to watch me, asked him to get out, got into the drivers seat and handed him the keys to the rental car and commanded him to follow me. I drove in the breakdown lane with the flashers on and the car wobbling ferociously all the way to Playa. Amador followed me in the breakdown lane with his flashers on. I kept telling myself that he was just another asshole man who would let me kill myself. And even though I told myself that more than a thousand times along the way to Playa from Tulum, somehow I still wanted a relationship with him. I still thought he could be a wonderful guy and I remembered the times he had been. That helped me believe I could fix him. For some reason, I would not let myself see that he was a selfish loser. Not yet anyway.

Sweating and dirty and tense, I drove into the tire place. I got out of the hot and sweaty car in my designer jeans and linen shirt and then Amador walked in behind me with his barefeet and surfer shorts, no shirt. He approached the manager of the shop with me behind him. They looked at us as if they knew the story. I was sure they did not but they told us the car would be ready tomorrow afternoon: 800 pesos for the work and 1700 for the two tires. I paid reluctantly and then decided to find a hotel. Amador said he would stay with me. I was actually happy about it. I hoped to talk about plans and enjoy our time together.

I asked Amador if he knew a good place but he shook his head no. I had seen a place on the 10th Avenue at the northern end where there were not too many tourists but some new hotels and restaurants. It had a pool and a restaurant. I drove us there and went in alone to ask for a room since all of a sudden, Amador could barely stay awake. A part of me wanted to leave him sleeping in the car. But a part of me was happy he was with me. For some reason I took great comfort in having him around. I got us a room using my limited Spanish and then went back to the car for my bag and for Amador. I am pretty certain that the owner regretted renting to me when he saw Amador come into the hotel lobby but I was oblivious to it. Amador hung on me like the old days when Fernando would tell me to "get a room." It was as if he had lost control of his muscles he was so wobbly and weak. The porter led us to the room and handed me the key.

I opened the door, threw my bag on the bed and ran into the bathroom to peel off my sweaty jeans and to pee. I was reaching for the toilet paper when Amador came in. I started to tell him to give me a minute but he and started kissing me as I was finishing on the toilet. I pushed him away, asking him what the hell he was doing but he laughed and called me "*mami*". I remembered how I used to love him calling me that. As I finished and tried to pull up my pants he grabbed me by the waist and pulled me into the shower. I told him to stop and started to fight him but he kissed me more and started speaking Spanish into my ear and pulling off my pants. He had turned the water on and it was soaking my clothes but it felt good and was cool. I partially fought him off but he was stronger.

I wanted a swim and tried to tell him that but he closed my mouth with one of his suction cup kisses and I stopped pushing him away for some ridiculous reason like I really wanted to have sex with him. I relaxed and decided to go for it. We had mad sex in the shower, more forceful and aggressive than ever. It was almost violent but I started to give it back to him, pushing into him and clawing at his back under the water. I actually could not get enough of him and I started to punch him and then to again push him away. But he held my hands back and pushed me against the wall, maintained contact and we came together.

He fell to the floor afterwards and I stood against the wall, gasping for air and letting the water fall against my face and body. Then I started to laugh. He looked up at me and smiled. I couldn't stop laughing for a little while but then I asked him to wash my back. He crawled to his feet and took the face towel from the sink and soap and made luscious soapy circles with it on my back. It felt like love and when he finished, I washed his back. Afterwards, we lay on the bed in clean white towels and slept.

I woke first but before I could ask myself what I had done, Amador woke and asked if I were hungry. I was and pulled myself off the bed to dress. In the next few moments, he changed. I could feel him getting angry and I wasn't sure at what or why, but I felt it. I didn't acknowledge it, denying that he would spoil such a great moment. I put on my favorite black flowing skirt and pink top. He made some comments on my outfit that made me feel less than beautiful. But I knew that my outfit was fabulous. Too, I had dissenting opinions on my style sense before.

I took his hand and he looked down at me and told me, "I gonna take you to a great place."

We walked like lovers on 10th Avenue and then walked a few blocks into the city to a steak house. When I asked for fish, he made a scene to the waiter telling me they didn't have fish, that they only have meat.

The waiter was embarrassed for him but told me, "We have fish and it is very good."

I felt vindicated and ordered some white wine. Amador ordered a cuba libre. I had seen him before when he was drinking rum and it was not pretty. Rum and coke was worse. But we had a delicious meal and I was happy to have something so wonderful.

During dinner, he got up to go talk to a friend in the kitchen. I waited for him alone. Amador knew I hated sitting alone in a restaurant. On more than one occasion I confided that to him and when he came back I was annoyed but noticed he looked somehow darker. He sat down and asked for a whisky, asking me if I didn't want one. I told him I would finish my wine and before the waiter could bring him something, he started to talk about socialism and communism in a way that was totally convoluted and anti-US. I couldn't follow it. I had never known him to be political or have communist views or hate America so much but it all came out in the next half hour.

I got tired of the insults and prepared to leave when he asked the waiter for desert. I told him no, I did not want any but I waited while he asked for something. Finally, when his dessert came, he told the waiter it was "shit." He sent it back with a hand motion and asked for the check like some aristocrat. I wanted to crawl into a crack in the floor but sat there, taking it all in. Finally, I mentioned that although he might not agree with capitalism, he certainly accepted the benefits of it through his "tours" and through me paying cash for a good meal. I thought he was open enough to grasp what I was talking about and I wanted to shut him up and put him down a little. As I said it, the check came.

I stared at him, challenging him to pay. I was tired of his bullshit and his ignorance. But he looked back at me with such hatred that I broke the stare, still happy I had made my point, and looked into my bag to pay. I knew he had no money. I put some bills on the table and looked up at him. He was still staring at me with a hatred that went right through me.

Then he said, "You think you better than me because you can pay?"

I told him not at all. He continued to stare at me. But I was not afraid. I was more disgusted and I told him he was a hypocrite for criticizing something while taking full advantage of it.

I stood up to go and put the money on the table and told him, "For example this dinner. For example, my jeep."

He put his hand on my arm to stop me. With the other hand, he took the money for the bill and told me he didn't care for money and threw it into the street as he let my arm go. I went to get it slowly, walking, thinking what to do. He laughed at me as I picked up the money from the street and again started talking political bullshit that I finally realized he got from his Italian socialist girlfriend. The realization pissed me off more. I took the money and the bill to the waiter, said *"gracias"* and walked out of the restaurant. Amador nearly fell out of his seat to follow me. I had no idea where I was but I started to walk toward the sea. I knew I could find my way back to the hotel from there counting the blocks back from 5th Avenue. He caught up to me quickly and started to talk about how he could have any woman he wanted.

"How about her," he said as he passed one woman with a friend.

I told him to go with whomever he wanted and tried to get away but he continued like that until he saw a Chinese place.

He said, "I want Chinese."

I kept walking and asked him how he would pay but he grabbed my arm and said meanly, "You gonna take me."

I pulled away from him but he pulled me to the restaurant and forced me to sit me down with him. He ordered something as I sat there, getting angrier by the second.

He asked me if I wasn't hungry and I told him, "For God's sake Mr. Comunist, you just ate a steak."

He was disgusting. I wondered if he were having a mental breakdown or something. I still wasn't afraid. I was annoyed, a little concerned but wondered how I would get rid of him. When he called me a "Capitalist whore," I pulled myself out of his grasp as he ate his chop suey and told him, "Fuck you," and walked away from him fast. I didn't care that people were staring. I nearly jogged away from him and felt good for a moment until I heard him coming behind me, his bare feet hitting the pavement hard. He grabbed me at the waist and pulled me into him in an almost embrace.

People may have confused us for lovers if they didn't look closely.

He was smiling a crazy smile and he said, "Oh no" and then loudly, *"Amor,"* so people could hear him.

And then he whispered that if I didn't go back to the restaurant the waiter would call the police and I would have trouble.

I spat back at him, "I didn't order anything, you did. You are the one who is gonna have trouble," I imitated him.

He pulled me close to him then. His face was in mine almost as if to kiss me but he was whispering in a threatening voice, "you gonna come back now or I gonna tell the police you have drugs. I left some in the room."

I actually smiled but I was shocked. I almost started laughing, I was so nervous when I realized he meant it. I pulled myself free of his grasp and told him he won but added, "this time." I walked freely back to the restaurant and paid the man saying, "*gracias.*"

Then I turned to walk back to the hotel. I didn't care that I didn't know where I was going. I wanted to get away from him. Amador followed and every so often he would grab my arm but I would pull it away. Then he started yelling. I cringed and shrank personally as he called my name and then said how he would fuck someone else, using that exact language in the street. Finally, I let him catch up to me.

"You wanna talk to me now?" he said. I looked at him and for some reason my anger subsided.

I inhaled and in a calm voice said, "Not really Amador." Then I asked him, "What is going on with you?"

I sincerely wanted to understand. And as I stood there waiting for an answer, he was taken aback.

He looked at his feet and said, "Nothing," like a child that had been caught playing a bad game.

Then he told me he didn't know what was going on but that I made him crazy.

I said to myself "always my fault" and asked if he meant the things he said.

"No baybe, no. But," he hesitated and then looked around him, suddenly paranoid.

Then he said he had to go. He was frightened. I asked him why, touching his arm and holding it for a second.

He told me, just like the time we had stayed in the Luxury Cabanas, "They gonna come and get me."

I pulled him toward me and told him that no one was going to hurt him. I told him I would take care of him, not understanding where that sympathy came from but knowing I wanted to help him feel better.

I pulled him toward me softly and said, "lets go back to the hotel."

He pushed me away, and screamed, "No! They will find me there," and ran away.

Sadly, I watched him run around a corner. I didn't feel anything. I was numb after the whole interchange but finally, I remembered the way to the hotel. Exhausted, I moved west two blocks and I recognized the hotel by the Laundromat next door. As I was turning the key in the door, I heard, "be careful," whispered into my ear. I jumped. It was Amador. I calmed down and asked him if he was OK but he looked around like a trapped animal. He didn't answer but I invited him in. He continued to look around but said he trusted me and would come inside. We walked past the scrutiny of the security guards and up the stairs to our room. Once inside, he fell onto the bed. I went into the bathroom to wash my face.

When I looked in the mirror I asked myself, "What the hell was that all about?"

But I had no answer. I went back into the room and looked at him laying on the bed like a baby. I wanted to lie down next to him and tell him it would all be OK. But I knew better. Instead, I put on my bathing suit and went to the pool downstairs and floated under the starry sky. I took my wallet and stuff with me. There was a part of me that wanted to help this person who was obviously messed up and then the other that wanted to protect myself. I looked up at the stars in the semi-urban sky and thanked God for getting me through the night. When I went back upstairs Amador was vomiting in the bathroom. I could hear it. I knocked on the door and went it. He was sitting on the toilet but he had shit and vomited all over the place. "What the hell is happening?" I asked.

He cried, "Help me baby, I don't know," as he projectile vomited and I stepped back to avoid a direct hit.

It was repulsive but I couldn't refuse helping him. I got the wastebasket and let him finish throwing up into it and, fighting the urge to do the same, grabbed some towels to clean up the floor and the wall. He slumped on the toilet seat, his head falling nearly between his legs.

"Wipe your butt and get into the shower," I commanded.

I turned on the water as he pulled himself toward the shower and I helped him get under the warm water. He stood against the wall, barely able to stand. I washed his body and then took one of the clean towels and wrapped him up in it after I shut the water off. Then I helped him to bed and asked him if he would be OK. He shook his head and hit the bed hard. I told him that if he needed to throw up he had to get out of the bed and into the bath. I put a wastebasket beside him just in case.

I started to go to my suitcase but he grabbed my arm and begged, "Don't leave me baybe. I sorry."

I looked at him and I saw a little boy, a small insecure messed up man boy. I wanted to heal him.

I pushed the wet hair from his face and kissed him on the forehead and assured him, "I won't leave you Amador," and told him to go to sleep.

I held his hand as I gently rested my head against a pillow beside him. I exhaled deeply and fell gently into a half sleep. I heard him start to snore and let myself sleep more soundly but before I finally fell to sleep, the voice in my head asked me "what the hell are you into now?"

Chapter 15

I woke early the next morning. Well, early enough. Amador had slept the night, no more projectile vomit or diarrhea. I had slept fitfully, dreaming of Chinese food and kidnapping by communists. I lay there for a moment, Amador's leg on top of my body. I used to love that but this morning it felt like a heavy weight on top of me, as if I were supporting his whole life. I pulled myself out from under him when I realized that was exactly what I was doing. I went into the bathroom. It was filthy and smelled badly. I washed my face and teeth and pulled on some clothes, opened the balcony doors to let air in and walked to the street to get a coffee. I wondered how this would play out. I wanted to return the rental car and get the jeep back. Amador was out of control, I finally realized. I wondered the role I had played in his current situation and wondered where was that happy beach bum I had met 3 years earlier.

But, I wanted my stuff back and to get away from him, disown the mess I hoped I had no part in creating. As I walked, I thought. It felt nice to be in a city where no one knew me. I went to a coffee shop and sat down for a relaxed breakfast alone. It felt good to be away from him. My shoulders relaxed and after the coffee, I walked out onto the street. It was after 9 but things were still just opening. I loved that, earlyish morning in the city: some people rushing to work, me strolling feeling wonderfully different. I window shopped for awhile and then got an anxious feeling and went back to the hotel. I felt something was up, or someone. I stopped for tea and water on my way, knowing Amador would want something, would need something.

When I got to the hotel room, he was in the bathroom, in the shower again. He had dropped the nearly clean towel on the floor in some remnant vomit and had used the last one to wrap around himself as he came out of the bathroom. He reached his hand out for me.

All I could say was, "I had saved that towel for me."

He didn't hear me and pulled me next to him on the bed telling me he felt badly. I lay there for a few moments, annoyed and uncomfortable and then got up and went out to write on the balcony. I didn't write much, my mind was racing and I couldn't think. I watched the hotel staff cleaning the pool and getting supplies for the rooms. I shuddered to think of the poor woman who would clean this one. I went back in and told Amador that it was nearly check out time. He ignored me. I told him I got him some water and an iced tea. He said thanks but rolled over and put his head into the pillow.

I was quiet for awhile and then there was a knock on the door, housekeeping. I opened the door a crack and asked her for more time. After about half an hour I was able to prop Amador up and get him dressed. I let him rest by the pool while I paid the bill and went for the car. He took full advantage of being an invalid but I knew he was getting better so I suggested getting the jeep. He agreed and I mentioned returning the rental car. He wanted to wait until Tulum. But I knew that if we got to Tulum with the two cars, I would never see the jeep again. I was tired of paying for things I didn't use. I reminded him that the point of fixing the jeep was to get rid of the rental car.

He said OK. He couldn't argue being so sick. I practically forced him to go for the jeep and then we went to return the rental car. They wanted an extra $100 US to return it in a different location but I didn't care. I would have my car in my hands and I knew that was the only way I would ever get to use it. Why I allowed this game of ownership to continue didn't enter my mind. I just knew I was in it. I signed the paperwork and my American express accepted the charges. I felt light as I walked back to the jeep and told him I would drive.

I got behind the wheel and he slumped down into the passenger seat. There was no rear view mirror and when I asked about it he grunted.

"I can't believe we bought this without a rearview mirror," I said as I started to drive to the highway.

Amador fell asleep. I was happy driving. It felt good, free. And I liked being in my own car. I told myself I had not made a big mistake buying it and that it was a good thing. I blocked visions of the night before and tried to stay present and enjoy the blue sky and the flowers on the road. Then, I noticed the gas gauge. Of course we needed gas. I got annoyed but then reminded myself that Amador was like a teenager. He never had any gas in his car. I sort of laughed at the thought and then looked at where we were to gauge the next gas station.

It reminded me of when we were driving back from Palenque and he had bought magic mushrooms to sell. Well, Amador bought them with my money. I had never even done mushrooms. Still haven't.

"It is a good opportunity," he told me and then continued, "You know what we could sell these for in Tulum?"

I didn't care. I didn't want to take them or sell them or anything but Amador wouldn't hear of it. When I said no he threw a fit and left me there in Palenque for the second time. But he always came back.

I remembered that promise from the first month I lived with him. "I always coming back to you, Joanne."

At the time it was comforting but more and more it seemed like a threat.

I had caved and bought the mushrooms for him. He always wore me down. But I remembered coasting on gas fumes for what seemed like miles on that road trip. Just like now, Amador had been sleeping next to me as I stressed about running out of gas in the middle of nowhere with a pile of mushrooms in the trunk. I could see the police who might have stopped to help us finding the mushrooms as they helped me with the spare. Amador would have run away and I would go to jail. What a guy, right? What the hell I was doing with him. Then I reminded myself that it didn't happen that way. We made it to a gas station in Palenque and there was one coming up soon here on this road. All my worrying was for nothing, as always. But sometimes it took me over.

I stopped at the gas station in Puerto Aventuras and turned the car off.

When I did so Amador woke up and asked frantically, "What you doing?"

I told him we needed gas. He told me that I should not turn the car off. I asked him why and he said it would not start again. I said "really" as I asked the attendant for gas and then told him it would not run without gas.

He mimicked me saying, "Really." and then followed with, "You are so stupid."

I was tired and had no patience to avoid the fight this time. I told him not to start and asked him how I could have known.

He said, meanly, "It is your car. You should know."

I ignored him, paid the attendant and then tried to start the car as he called me a "stupid bitch." I looked at him as if he had two heads and told him he could have told me before he passed out.

He pulled himself up from the seat as if to help me and said, "Fine. You fix it," as he opened the door, got out of the car and walked toward the highway.

I waited for him to come back. When he didn't, I sat for a moment more trying to get my bearings. I had been right. He would have left me on the highway back in Palenque and let me go to jail. "Asshole", I whispered as I tried the car again but no luck. The attendant came by and asked if I needed help. "*Si,*" I said earnestly. I needed a lot of help but he could help me start the car. He opened the engine, did some things and it started. He explained to me something about the radiator that I didn't understand but I was pretty sure he told me that when the car got too hot it wouldn't start. I said "*gracias*" and gave him 100 pesos and was on my way. Amador was long gone. I was flabbergasted and shocked but felt happy enough that I had gotten my car back, had gotten rid of Amador and could go look for Lakra without him.

I drove to Tulum feeling sure of myself and happy. As I turned to the beach road I knew a hotel where I would stay. I knew the owners. I hoped they would keep me away from Amador, somehow. I hoped they would want to help me. I wasn't sure how or why but maybe they thought I was a good person. Maybe. But I got a pit in my stomach as I entered town and realized that no one could keep me from him and that no one would want to help me.

I mean, why would they? I was just some tourist coming and going. Amador lived there. And then, there he was, waiting at the cross road when I pulled up to the light. He stared at me meanly and I smiled and took the left when the light changed. I would not talk to him. I would find my own place to stay where he didn't know and wouldn't find me. I would sleep well at least for that night, believing he would leave me alone.

I had a lot to figure out but I was exhausted and needed to find Lakra and a place to stay. Weary of the beach front hotels filled with lovers and honeymooners, I stayed at a little hotel on the jungle side in the settlement that many people called *"pueblo pequeno,"* little town. I talked to my friend Carlos at his restaurant. Of course he had rooms, he told me. Actually, he had no one in the hotel at all. He gave me a room for $40 US per night. I gladly took the room, back in the jungle and away from the road. It had only screen walls but I felt at home with that. The shower was good and the place was interesting at least. There was a little garden in front and it seemed safe enough. I asked him where I could park the car and if I could put it off the street. He found me a spot next to the hotel. But it was visible. I knew Amador would find it but for that night, I didn't care. I took my things and went up to the room, laid on the bed and fell asleep soundly, dreaming of cars and mushrooms and flying back home, wherever that was.

I was there at *Trece Luna* for three days before Amador found me. He probably knew where I was after the first night. I was so clueless about small towns that I thought I could really get away from him. He just wanted to do something else. He knew where I was and when he wanted or really needed something, he would come and bother me for it. But in those few days, the jeep started and stopped for me like a regular car. I liked driving around in it and getting construction stuff and seeing people. I was always looking out for Lakra, but I had not found her yet. I wasn't sure I had ever really been ready for a dog but I knew if I saw her, she would be mine. I decided she was happily with someone else and she would come when she needed me.

I liked living like this, making my way, doing my thing. I was lonely and hated eating alone and not having any real friends but I knew that would come in time. I visited my land every day to see what was or actually wasn't happening. I bumped into Felix the contractor on the road and he said he would find me and come out to take a look at what we needed to do. I still had no real windows. I needed a banister and doors. I needed to finish the floor and have some shelves and furniture. But, even so, I had a lot. I had big parts of the construction complete and even if I was alone, I knew some people and could muddle my way through.

One day, I was leaving my apartment and I saw Amador waiting for me. I surprised myself by being happy to see him. When I smiled, he smiled. I walked out and he gave me a big hug and a kiss. Once again, I kissed him back. I hugged him back. It felt good to have that physical contact and when he was good, he made me so happy. And I was so alone without him. As I left his embrace I thought I noticed people looking at us. Then I told myself it was my imagination but now I know it was real. All the people who I wanted to be my friends were watching. And the minute I took Amador's embrace, they took a step away from me once again. They knew better than to be around him and if I were going to allow him into my life, they would keep me at a distance. I didn't understand that then, but I do now.

He asked if we could talk. I was feeling open on that particular day and agreed. He wanted to go for a drink but I told him it was not a good idea. He complained, and said one beer wouldn't bother him as he took my hand and led me across the street to a bar called Zahra's. We sat outside and listened to the guy who played this instrument that looked like a zylaphone on legs. It was happy Mexican music and for once I was sitting with someone and not alone so I enjoyed it. I ordered food, taking advantage of having someone to eat with. I so hated eating alone.

Then I asked him, joking, "Did you invite me to this beer?"

Whoever invited paid. He told me he had invited me to the beer, but not to dinner. I laughed and ordered a glass of wine, happy to be out with a man, even if he was a madman. I thought I loved him and I somehow thought loving someone meant tolerating him. It was probably that 'better or worse' thing from Catholic marriages. I mean, what did that mean if not standing by your man? Weren't you supposed to tolerate their ups and downs as you worked together to have a better life? All these thoughts ran through my mind as I listened to Amador tell me he had a problem.

I told him I was sure of it and he looked at me meanly, and said,

"You gonna listen or I gonna go?"

I shook my head indicating that I would listen.

He told me he was not going to be with me. I wondered if he had hallucinated that he had been with me since I had not seen him for awhile.

He took my chin in his hand dramatically and forced me to look at him as he told me, "But I need a job."

I felt a deep hurt settle in as he stated that he knew I would help him. "Why?"

He took a deep breath then and told me he couldn't be with me since I made him crazy. I told him I understood that. I wanted to scream out why that meant I needed to employ him. The food came but I didn't want to eat anymore.

Then, as if nothing else mattered, he said, "So, let me work for you."

I laughed into what appeared like an earnest face and I told him, honestly and once again, that he had not done so well so far.

He got angry. His face changed. I hoped he would leave. Instead, he took a deep breath and continued to tell me I could hire him. I asked him what he would do and he told me he would get me workers and check on the project and manage things. I put my drink on the table and told him that was not what it was about, him being my worker. I reminded him that we were supposed to do this project together.

He said he understood, "But."

I told him, "But you don't love me is that it?"

I was angry and tired of the bullshit. I told him I was not enjoying this visit and got up to leave. He took my hand and told me he was not enjoying it either but that if I thought about it, we were no good for each other. I agreed and explained that I didn't want to be with him or to see him working for me every day while he went home to someone else. Then he reminded me I needed help.

Finally he told me, "Nobody else here gonna help you Joanne. Not the way I can."

I sat back down and looked at him. I took a bite of my now cold food and thought for a moment. He was right. A part of me knew he would make it that way, with threats and his reputation for being mad, and my reputation for always taking him back. We were like a local live soap opera in this small gossipy town. I knew it but couldn't stop it. I was quiet for awhile and ate my food. He said nothing. Finally, I wiped my mouth and asked him what he wanted. He smiled as if he had won the lottery. He told me a salary and the car.

I threw my napkin on the plate and stood up saying, "It is all about that fucking car and money, right?"

I finally realized he didn't give a shit about me and I started to understand that I really didn't give a shit about him. I didn't want him to suffer but I wanted him out of my life or in it on my terms.

As I stood to go he took my hand but gently this time and he said, "Sit Joanne. That is not the truth and you know it. But I need to live and if I am working for you all the time, what else I gonna do?"

I asked him what I would do without a car.

He told me we could share saying, "I help you and you help me."

I wanted to believe him so much. He continued to tell me that he had found a nice place on the beach that I could rent by the month. I could walk to the land from there to check on things. That way, he said, I wouldn't need the car that much. He told me we could go there now so that I could get out of the place I was staying. He looked over toward *Trece Lunas* where Carlos was pretending not to watch us.

"Why you go to rent with fucking Carlos anyway?" he asked.

I told him to stay to the point, surprising myself with my business like attitude and asked him how much it would cost me. He told me he could live on 500 a week. I asked him if that were dollars or pesos. He smiled and said dollars. I said impossible and got up to go.

"250" he said.

I told him $100 and that he could do other things. I reminded him that he didn't have to be there full time. He quickly agreed. I felt trapped and before I could back out, he asked me to come and see the place he knew on the beach. I agreed reluctantly as he asked for the check and I paid both the drinks and the food. We left in my jeep with Amador driving. I had lost it again, I knew.

We drove up the beach road and pulled into a barely discernable driveway before *La Nueva Vida*. We parked next to a white jeep and walked up a circular path lined with chit palms. In many places you had to duck to make it under them. Amador went ahead of me, walking faster and seeming to know the path. I reached the top of the small bluff to see a circular white house built up high on pilings. I did not see Amador. There was a little gate at the stairs that was half open but I didn't feel comfortable climbing into someone's house so I waited.

In a few moments, Amador came to the top of the stairs and motioned me to come up in that downward arm motion that I found so endearing. Something about it made me feel wanted and cared about, as if I would run to an embrace if I followed the direction. When he did this my heart caved with sadness, knowing I wouldn't have the embrace at the end. What I would have was the torture of seeing him each day and never being his. I started to imagine paying him each week so he could take someone else out.

I didn't think I could do it and told him so as I reached the top of the stairs. "Ay Joanne, give it a chance will you?" he said and then he followed with, "Please?"

The magic word. I said nothing but he assumed that meant yes.

He led me around a balcony to the front of the house where there were two women in hammocks looking out over the sea. The view was spectacular, directly in front of the white sandy beach and crystal blue Caribbean. The breeze cooled the sweat on my face and chest. I exhaled and felt my shoulders relax as Amador introduced me to Norby.

I extended my hand and she said, *"Mucho gusto, niña"* sincerely but talking as if I were actually a child.

It was funny, I felt like one around her. I smiled and then she started talking, loudly and pure Spanish. The blond hair blowing into her face every so often did not stop her or even slow her down. She kept pushing it out of her face and talking fast. She had a long, tanned face and was sitting in the hammock with her legs splayed out on both sides and a colorful pareo wrapped around her body. I had to focus intently on what she was saying to understand, especially since she was asking questions and Amador was answering for me. But I grasped most of what they were saying and every so often I tried to answer, mostly with '*sí*' or '*no*' to show I understood.

Little by little Norby started to talk to me directly. This made Amador mad I could tell but Norby handed him a joint to calm him down. She seemed to know him well and once he was smoking she asked me if I wanted 2 or 3 months. I hesitated looking for the words but she told me the most she could rent the house was 3 months and she offered to show it to me as she stood up from her hammock and climbed out of it. She went inside, grabbed a set of keys and we walked back down the stairs and to a house that was hidden among the palms. Amador followed. Norby opened one of the hurricane shutters that had been pulled closed along all sides of the house to show a double wood door that led to a beautifully tiled dining room, complete with sofa and two steps up to a full kitchen. We entered and she put on the lights, normal lights.

"We have solar," Norby explained to me, "So you need to conserve but we normally have lights 24 hours."

It was beyond anything I had seen in Tulum and, actually, seemed almost too nice. The bedroom had two double beds and a large closet and a balcony that accessed the wrap around porch and had a fabulous view to the sea.

The bath was tiled with colorful Mexican *talo vera*. The kitchen was lovely and had nearly everything I could need.

"I can rent it for $800 US per month," she said as we went back out onto the balcony.

It was getting dark but you could still see the white of the crashing waves and the pink hue on the clouds from the sunset on the opposite side of the peninsula. I asked if she could do better, knowing that with everything else I had going on, 800 would be tight. She agreed to 700 because I was, "Amador's friend." I smiled disengenously because I hated the words, "Amador's friend." I was his ex-lover or ex girlfriend or now boss or whatever but we were more than friends. I wanted the place certainly, but at that moment, I really wanted to leave the neighborhood and get out, abandon my project and go home.

Then that voice in my head reminded me, "You really don't have a home anymore."

I continued walking ahead of Norby until Amador grabbed my arm and said, "Well?" in a sort of irritated voice, as if I were being rude or something.

I told him I was thinking and pulled my arm from his.

"Womens," was all he said.

That made me laugh, the grammar was so wrong. But it pulled me from a dark place.

I stopped. "What do you think?"

He told me he thought it was a nice place for a good price.

Then he added, "You will be happy here and I gonna be around," which I wasn't sure was what I needed but I smiled and shook my head yes.

Norby was closing the front door and I told her the house was beautiful and I would take it. We settled on Friday as the day to move in. Two more nights with Carlos. Norby reminded me we needed to sign a contract and that I needed to leave a deposit. Then she told me she would see me Friday mentioning that she was not around all the time but when she was we shared the kitchen. She hoped that would be fine with me.

I was not sure how I felt about sharing but didn't see another option and suddenly, I wanted to live there. I nodded that it would be fine and we said goodbye. The jeep started right away and Amador drove me back to my hotel.

He kissed me on the lips to say goodbye and said, too happily, "see you tomorrow."

But before I left the vehicle I reminded him that we were sharing and that I would need the car by around 11 a.m. the next day.

"Of course," he cooed as I opened the door and got out.

Then I reminded him that I wanted to see Lakra and take her with me to Norby's. I told him he owed me that.

He agreed that we would go get her then next day saying, "Bob has her."

I knew he had left her with someone but all this time he had let me believe she was lost. I made a mental note of his cruelty as he blew me a kiss and I watched him drive down the road. Before I could cross the street to my apartment, I saw Carlos watching me from his restaurant. I waved hello and he waved back. Then I went up to my room deciding to wait until the next day to give him notice that I would be leaving.

Chapter 16

I moved into Norby's Friday afternoon. Amador came to help me but late, as usual. I was getting very good at waiting. I had breakfast and second breakfast while I wondered where he was and packed my bags. Carlos helped me bring them down to the street.

"Remember Joanne," he told me, "*cualquier cosa*. Whatever you need."

I thanked him. I appreciated it. But doubted I would take him up on it. I told him his place was wonderful and I hoped that he realized I couldn't live in a hotel forever. I was aching to have my own kitchen and to be closer to the beach. Carlos' place was across the street and had a beach access but the beach there was rocky, beautifully wild but not so good for walking and very far to walk to my land. I was excited to move into Norby's house where I was pretty much alone and the beach walk to my house was magnificently easy.

Carlos interrupted me before I finished explaining, and said, "I am not just talking about hotel living."

I knew he meant my relationship with Amador. I knew in my heart and even in my mind it was totally messed up. "Thanks," I said.

I went back into his garden reception and sat and wrote and waited until finally my black jeep came up the road. Amador got out, looking rough but he puffed out his chest in what seemed like an arrogant move but what I finally started to recognize as his attempt to gather courage to face the day. I watched as he inhaled deeply in this posture and walked over to me and gave me a kiss, asking if I wanted breakfast. Annoyed, I told him breakfast was two hours ago and I was ready to leave.

He didn't like my tone of voice and threw the car keys at me and said, "Then go," as if he didn't care. Bored with the drama, I took the opportunity to take my car back and told him, "Fine." Then I added, "I knew you couldn't handle honesty."

He called, "Bitch," to my back as I struggled to put my bag in the back seat while he watched.

I got in and started the car on the second try. He yelled to me with a smile on his face that I would need gas. I didn't even look at him. I was just happy the car started and I guessed I could make it to Norby's with what gas I had. I drove up the road angry at Amador but happy to have my car, even without gas. Sharing with him would have been a challenge so now I didn't have to. I could drop my things, go buy food and have my space. It would be better. I would change the locks on the gate to my land and find someone else to help me. It didn't matter that he had helped me find the place. I felt powerful and entitled to it after all his scams and disruptions as I pulled into the drive and parked next to Norby's car. I found her around front, sunning herself. I walked over to say hello but noticed I was shaking slightly, still unnerved by the exchange with Amador.

Norby smiled and said hello as she put on her top. She told me she had the contract and an inventory to sign and that she would be at the house over the weekend but then go to Cancun. I thought it would be perfect to have her there the first few nights and then nice to have her go. We walked to the house together. When she opened the doors, I noticed how the sun came into the living room. My shoulders softened as we walked into the bath and Norby's voice followed me advising that there was no hot water yet. She told me that it was so warm she didn't turn it on but that if I needed it, we could start the boiler. She reminded me that I would need to buy the gas. She showed me how to light the gas powered refridge in case it went out. We went through the house room by room so I would know everything I needed. She was thorough and happy, if a little talkative, but I liked her. She had positive energy and a big beautiful smile, even if her face was a little long. She was tanned and straightforward and reminded me that if I broke anything, I would have to pay as I signed an inventory of the things she had in her house.

I was disappointed when she told me that she would use the kitchen that night with her son but then she invited me to dinner. My mood changed and I accepted, happily. I had no plans, no illusions that Amador would come back and knew that if he did it would be to use the jeep again. She handed me the keys and then remembered the roof deck.

She showed me how to access it off the back door and cautioned me to be careful as we climbed up a rickety stairway. The view was amazing, crystal blue out to the reefs with the gentle white foam of breaking waves the only inturruption.

"I could practice yoga here in the morning," I said dreamily.

She asked me if I practiced yoga. I told her I taught. She asked for classes and we talked about it a little. For some reason I did not invite her to yoga at Jade. I was unsure she would fit in. But I told her she could join me when she wanted, unsure if I wanted company but then not sure she would ever take advantage of the invitation. Everyone "wanted" to start but very few people ever did. I looked out over the sea and imagined a sunrise practice and how good that could feel. It was bright and hot at the moment but I knew the morning would be cooler and more gentle.

Norby said she was gong town and asked me if I needed anything but I thanked her and told her I would go myself. I wanted to take my time shopping. She walked down the stairs to her house and I walked happily into mine. I went to get my things from the car and stopped abruptly when I saw Amador waiting there. He immediately apologized but I told him to save it. I knew he just wanted the car. He put his arms around my waist and kissed me on the neck. I wiggled free but really I liked the feel of it. I grabbed my bag from the back seat and he came to help me with it saying, "Let me help," in a way that I knew he wanted to do something for me. We walked to the house together, him following me saying, "Why you have to be like that?"

I turned to say to him, "Why you have to be like that?" As if we were little kids, play fighting.

Then I started to laugh, realizing it was ridiculous. I didn't think about all the hurt I had endured, all the sadness I had experienced with him, how much money he had taken from me. I didn't think about any of it. What I thought was how nice it was to have someone to laugh with. I didn't think about what a jerk he had been in the past or what anyone would think or even what would happen that evening, when I knew he would be with someone else. I let myself go and I laughed loudly. He helped me bring in my stuff up and as I was unpacking some things by the sink, he came behind me and held me from behind. I liked it and told him it was nice, meaning that the sentiment was nice. He thought I meant something else and he started to kiss the back of my neck. While it did feel nice, I didn't want that from him. I wanted to be free and after all, I was pretty much his boss at that point. He held me tightly but I managed to wiggle around to face him and he started to kiss me on the lips. I loved the attention but I knew this wasn't where we were in that moment and I tried to talk to him.

"*Amor*, how you gonna resist me?" he said to me.

I laughed out loud and told him he was not that irresistible.

I told him, "For one thing you smell badly."

He backed away. I was sorry if I had been rude but it was the truth.

When he saw me smiling he took me less seriously and came back at me saying, "Not so bad," and he kissed me again on the mouth.

I moved away saying "yes, that bad," but he kissed me on the neck and asked me,

"Why you got to be so hot?"

I laughed again, finding him ridiculous. For some reason I was undeniably happy. Suddenly, he picked me up, and carried me onto the unmade bed and literally pulled my clothes off. I admit, I wanted sex with him. I wanted love from him. I wanted to be someone's, for Gods sake. Here I was traveling the world alone again and I had tried so hard to be good and normal and get what other people had but I had failed again. I wanted a simple life with a man and to adopt that little black child. But it had gotten so complicated.

I stopped thinking and came back to happiness as he caressed my breasts and kissed my body and entered me with a force that gave me an orgasm quickly. We came together and then rested, as always his leg over mine, keeping me from escaping. But I didn't want to escape. I wanted that moment to last forever.

"Joanne?" he pulled me from my bliss saying he would need the jeep.

As happy as I had been, I got just that mad. I called him a motherfucker and told him to get out now.

He whined, "*Amor*".

I told him, "Don't *amor* me."

I lifted my body off the bed and put my feet to the floor but he pulled me back to him, spooning with me. It felt great but I f knew he would leave and even if he stayed, he would do something weird again, something crazy. I cursed myself then for sleeping with him because it affected me.

I moved around to face him and said, "What am I to you, anyway?"

"You are the best," he said and then continued, "But I got things to do and I need to use the car to do them. That is all. Don't take it personal."

I thought about it then. He was pretty much right. I mean, life here was a little difficult without a car. And what did I want, him just sitting there while I unpacked. I told him it was a little weird since he was living with another woman. He told me that he was but that he still loved me.

I asked him how that could be and he told me, "Well, you got to believe, you got to know," as he held me closely and told me he would always be there for me.

He had said it before. Other times it had brought me great comfort but now it made me sad and a little bit afraid. Before I could analyze my feelings he asked me if I wanted him to scrub my back and have a shower before he went. I smiled and told him that would be nice.

He smiled back and said, "I love you Joanne" and that was all I needed to hear.

I asked him if before he left we could go get Lakra and he agreed.

I was happy. At least I would get my dog.

We showered together and complained of the cold water. I dressed quickly and we went to town together. He talked about his friend Bob who was taking care of Lakra. I got nervous that he may not want to give her back but Amador told me not to worry. He told me that Bob loved Lakra but he would give her back. We drove to the back part of town where I had not been before. It was mostly forested, not too many houses, a few shacks with fires burning outside and chickens running in the street. A pig walked in front of us slowly and I laughed. Then we came to a house with a very high gate and Amador pulled over saying, "Wait me here." I didn't correct him. I smiled and waited.

After about 10 minutes he came out with Bob, a soft, thin man, taller than Amador, whiter skin and more European features but with very bad teeth that ruined his friendly smile. He had a funny posture as if his bones were brittle and he could break at any moment. His steps were light as if he were tiptoeing. He and Amador stopped in front of the car and I got out to meet them. But there was no Lakra. I introduced myself. Bob was polite but spoke only to Amador. I couldn't understand his Spanish, it was garbled as if he had marbles in his mouth and I suddenly remembered the time as a kid I put marbles in my mouth to make my voice lower and I had swallowed one. It took me two weeks of checking my poo to pass that marble. I wondered if Bob knew the danger of keeping marbles in his mouth when he looked at me again and said something like, "Are you really gonna take care of her? I got lots of dogs and she is no problem."

At least that was what I understood. I promised to take good care of her. Once I did so, he turned to the door and called her out. Lakra came out humbly as if she were mad at me. She slowly walked over to me. I started to cry. I had let her down. Bob thought I might abandon her again as well. After some coaxing, she wagged her tail and rubbed her head against me, giving me a dog hug that I took as a sign of forgiveness. I hugged her back and apologized for leaving her. Then I looked at Bob and thanked him. Amador said we needed to go so I took Lakra, helped her into the jeep, said goodbye to Bob and told Amador that we needed to stop for dog food as I patted her head and she sat happily next to me, her belly, now free of those pesky tumors, still hanging out between her legs.

I was happy. It was good to see her again and I would have company. She could come everywhere with me like before. It would be great. We got dog food, a few supplies and a thin red collar and leash just in case. When we got to the house, he took the car and I went inside and unpacked my things and then Norby came in with her son. She brought lasagna and heated it up in the oven for us. We had a nice meal with sporadic conversation half in English and half in Spanish. She told me Lakra was fine but could not get on the couch and that if she did any damage, it was my responsibility. I knew Lakra would not damage anything.

Later, Lakra and I sat under the stars on the balcony. She put her head on my thigh and I started to cry. I wasn't sure what I was doing but I knew I would be OK. I asked God for help and then went back to the other bed, not the one I had slept in with Amador, the one with my own clean sheets and a nice fresh blanket. I put a towel on top of my extra yoga mat for Lakra and she curled up. I slept like the dead until the sun wakened me through the window. It was a brand new day. I quoted Amador and said to Lakra, "Lets see what great things can happen" as I took my yoga mat to the roof and practiced there while I thanked God for being alive.

I had breakfast on the deck and enjoyed a slow morning. Then Lakra and I walked the beach to the land and I got my bicycle from the bodega. We walked the road back. Everyone who met her seemed to know her. We stopped at *El Viejo's* for a few things, but they didn't have much, some juice, dog food, in case I ever ran out, and Bimbo white bread. We walked past the *Casa Banana* restaurant of *Nueva Vida* and I told myself I could have a dinner there alone sometime or at least breakfast. It was not intimidating. When we got back, I locked my bike under the stairs and sat on the balcony with my dog once again: totally happy, even if the feeling only lasted that afternoon.

Chapter 17

I didn't see Amador until the following Sunday. I had been writing, attempting poetry in my solitude and drawing around my words on the front balcony when he came, kissed me on the lips and said, "Joanne, I need a favor."

I asked him if he had brought my car. I didn't say hello or ask how he was. I needed to do some things. He told me he would bring the jeep to me later but he needed 500 pesos in that moment. I told him angrily that it wasn't payday and walked into the kitchen.

He came after me like a lost child and said, "But baybe, Amalio is hurt and needs a doctor."

I asked him why that was my problem. Amador told me he knew I was not that way and pleaded for money. I told him he should go to a hospital. He asked me to come and see Amalio for myself.

I wondered if it was all a bluff and said, "OK, Lets go see him," as I put the coffee pot on the counter and we walked the path to the street together.

There was a white van in the drive and the door opened as we walked toward it. Amalio was there, inside, sitting in the back with his leg outstretched. It was bloody and bruised and looked bad but he looked worse. He was coughing and there was spittle on the sides of his mouth. He was obviously drunk and he smelled a combination of beer and I wasn't sure what else.

I poked my head inside and told him, "*Buenos dias*, Amalio."

He said, "Joanna, can you help me?" in Spanish as if he knew me.

We had never been formerly introduced but he knew my name and then told me he would pay me back. The guy in the driver's seat said hello in English and waved, then held out his hand and introduced himself as Chi Chi. His eyes were glassy and set into a round head that was too big for his body. He had a Cheshire cat smile on his face and a long, stringy black poney tail. But he was dirty and, although I didn't want to take his hand, I did, to be polite. There were two other people who I didn't recognize. I didn't want to recognize them again either so I did not introduce myself.

"I am not sure I can help you Amalio," I said honestly.

At that Amador grabbed my arm tightly and pulled me back telling the guys, "We be right back."

He pulled me close to him and told me, "Listen, these guys are dangerous."

I laughed and told him they were a bunch of drunks.

But Amador told me, "They bad."

I smiled at the line but he ignored me and told me I needed to help them so they would leave me alone.

I smiled and told him that I wasn't sure that giving them money would make them leave me alone saying, "it hasn't worked too well with you."

He got annoyed but puffed out his chest and told me not to worry that he would protect me. I smiled more and asked him if he would bring my car back. He told me that of course he would and he promised to take me shopping and then we could go for a meal.

I weighed my options and started walking to the house. I knew that he would not give up and I wondered if the rumors that Amalio was the "godfather" of Tulum were true. I figured for less than $50 US I might make a powerful friend and decided to risk it. If he never paid me back, I could use that the next time he asked for money. I had learned there would always be a next time. I gave Amador the money but told him to come back with my jeep.

As I handed him the 500 peso note he said, "you got 200 for me."

I told him to get out.

But he only became more determined it seemed and said, "please? I got nothing baybe."

I told him that neither did I but it didn't register.

He said, "*por favor.*"

I angrily told him I didn't have any more but he said, "Be that way," took the 500 and walked down the path to the car.

I heard the car screech away 2 minutes later. I walked out to the balcony and wondered what I should do.

He came back later with the jeep and told me Amalio was better. We went shopping together with Lakra. She loved a joy ride and I was happy going to town with my little family. But something was up, I could feel it. He watched me too closely at the ATM. He cooked me dinner and ate with me, although I could tell his mind was elsewhere.

After dinner he went to the beach, "I gotta see someone. I coming back," he told me.

I never knew if that meant 10 minutes or 10 hours but I knew he would eventually come back. I played music and started to paint and had almost forgotten him when he came behind me, kissed me on the neck and whispered, "bayby" in my ear. I jumped and turned around to see him. It was dark and he was with someone, but I couldn't see who.

He kissed me on the lips but I pulled myself away from him and said, "What's happening?"

He told me he just wanted to see me. Then he cocked his head toward the door and told me he was with his friend, Miguel and invited me to town with them. I was almost flattered. It had been a long time since anyone had asked me to go out and I did really want to go. But I could tell he was stoned or drunk or something and I knew if we went out with his friends I would end up paying, it always worked that way.

No thanks, I'm good here," I told him honestly.

I mentioned that I had started painting and although I knew my artwork wasn't great, I liked my "Outsider Art". Untrained artists did "Outsider Art". I felt the label bizarre somehow but it seemed to fit. I was never in with any group, an outsider in my engineering work with all my artistic tendencies and now an outsider in the art world with all my engineering training and ability to make money. I was not trained. I worked at a job I didn't like more than I painted and that made me feel inferior to most artists I knew who painted all day and worked their off hours.

Amador looked at my work and dismissed it, saying, "Isn't it better to paint in the daylight?"

He wrapped his arms around my waist and kissed me on the lips hard. I liked the attention and he had a point. I hadn't been out for awhile and who cared if I had to pay, I needed a break so I told him I would go and told him to give me a second to change.

"*No problemo*," was all he said.

I went into my room, put on a black dress and was ready in a second. It didn't take much in Tulum, a dress and flip-flops and I was ready to go. Amador told me that his friend Miguel would come with us. I said that was fine but asked him to introduce me first.

Amador told me it wasn't necessary saying, "He knows who you are and now you know him."

I told him that it was polite to introduce people who had not met each other.

He told me "You right baybe, you always right."

I answered honestly, "Well, I hate being right so why don't you be right for a change."

He took it as a joke. Apparently it was my job to be right.

When I came into the living room, Amador called Miguel in and introduced me. He was thin and tall with curly hair that fell below his ears. He had a pierced eyebrow and lip and his eyes were brown but I could hardly see them, he was that stoned. Like Amador, he had no shoes on and he was dressed in surfer shorts and a t-shirt. I wondered why I was dressed but then I reminded myself that I felt better that way. Too, I wasn't a Mexican beach bum. I just liked them.

"*Vamos?*" Amador said as I kissed Miguel on the cheek and said, "*Mucho Gusto,*" nice to meet you. I was excited. I felt like the kid who never gets asked out and finally I was popular. I cautioned Lakra to take care of the house and I locked the door. She hated that but I thought it was better for her to be inside. Amador drove and I sat in the middle. Miguel spoke some English and we chatted,. He was well mannered and Amador didn't want to talk so at least we weren't all quiet. When we arrived to town, Amador looked at Miguel and said, "*La Cubana?*" Miguel agreed and I confirmed that the bar's owner was the one with the big breasts. Amador and Miguel laughed like schoolboys and nodded their heads to confirm I was correct.

The bar was fairly empty. Amador told me Gisela would come soon as we sat down at a big table with a bench seat. The evening was cool and the moon was rising. I sat between the two Mexicans and Amador joked that they would protect me and not let me go anywhere. It was an obtuse reference to being kidnapped and I laughed, feeling slightly absurd. I ordered a margarita and Amador ordered a bucket of beers, a special *La Cubana* thing. When the beers arrived, Gisela and her boyfriend came with two other people. They sat with us and Amador ordered another bucket of beers. I knew I was paying. The dj played 80's music and we all started to dance. I had a great time as I looked up at the growing moon and thanked God to be alive.

I spoke Spanish with Gisela and we danced more, *La Cubana* was on the bar for a second or two, pouring a shot into some unexpecting tourists throat, her brown skin glistening with sweat and her oversized breasts nearly touching the man's forehead. Her husband stood glumly in the doorway, and watched. Finally, the music stopped and the check arrived, somehow in front of me. I was the kid that they invited to pay. The night's fun faded somehow and I felt more lonely than before. If I didn't pay there would be a scene. None of them had any cash. They all left, not even saying thanks. Not even acknowledging my contribution. Amador, Miguel and I went back to the beach. Miguel went to the camp-site Playa Selva next door and Amador walked me to my house.

"I gonna stay here with you tonight," Amador said as we came to the door.

I was surprised and not sure I wanted him in my house. I was pretty happy with not being around people and although the night had been sort of fun, the ending with me paying left me feeling sad and alone. I didn't need those emotions. And I was beginning to see that I didn't need Amador either.

I looked at him and said, "Are you asking if you can stay here with me?"

Incredulously, he said, "You don' want me?"

I looked at him and, admittedly I was a little drunk, but he looked good. He had a happy smile on his face and those curls around it made him adorable. And the fact that he could not believe someone wouldn't want him made me laugh. He reached out for me as if I could not resist him. I laughed and let him carry me to bed.

The sex that night was unremarkable. He was too drunk or too disinterested in my pleasure and only in his own. And for a guy who was only 36 years old, he had little stamina. At least that night. Other times I could remember he was incredibly persistent, exhausting me. Those nights made me feel beautiful, sexy, and alive. That was what I wanted in a man, sort of a savage dominance that so far no man could provide for me in other ways. I could do everything without them but that: enjoy and let go and be completely free. That was what sex with Amador had been at first. But I was getting bored with his drunken attempts at overwhelming me. I lay there on my back, enjoying the warm body next to me, loving the touch of a man, but totally confused and dissatisfied. I had made all these changes and worked so hard to get to this man and here I was, not really loving being around him. I pulled myself out from next to him and went to the balcony to look at the stars. It was chilly and the sky was clear and the stars incredible. I saw a shooting star make its arc slowly across the sky and I wished to be in love with that man again. Because if I didn't love him, what was all this about?

I didn't want to be wrong again, so I believed I could make it right. And if I couldn't change him, I believed I could change myself. I could be the woman he needed or mold him into the man I needed. I crawled back into bed and spooned with him.

He woke for a moment and asked, "Where you been baybe?"

I loved that he noticed my absence, if nothing else.

"Looking at the stars. Making a wish," I told him.

He told me not to let him wake up and not find me next to him, saying he hated it. I smiled, mistaking that possessiveness for love. The next morning was another story. He didn't waken with the sun like me. In fact, he wouldn't waken at all and although I wanted to be there with him, I couldn't stay in bed all day. I had things to do, perhaps not a lot of things but I wanted to get up and talk and have breakfast. I wiggled out of bed and went to make coffee. Then I did yoga and wrote and made some eggs and tried to waken him. He woke like a bear, slowly, but then moved into a space that was not happy. By the time I got him to get up I was exhausted from the effort.

We sat outside together.

He inhaled his food, said thank you and then, "I gotta go. You need anything from town?"

I reminded him about checking on the project but he said that we could go later finishing with his famous, "I coming back."

I told him it had better be soon because I needed to buy some things as well. He asked me what I needed, telling me he would shop for me. I told him I liked to shop for myself. He pushed the issue telling me I didn't need to leave the beach and he could get things for me, as if he didn't want me to be around other people, as if he didn't want me to meet anyone except his friends. I decided to let it go and see when he got back. If I needed something I would go to the little grocery store, *El Viejo*. They always had basics.

I walked him to the car and before he got in, stopped and asked, "So Amador, you think you are going to live here with me?"

He asked me what I would like. I hesitated for a moment and then I lied, trying to maintain what I had believed in the past, and told him I would love it.

He smiled, kissed me on the lips and said, "We'll see, ok? Step by step."

I hated him then. After I had put my heart on the line, he put me on hold.

I told him not to wait to long and explained that I need to figure things out. I told him that if he was with me, that was one thing and if not that was another.

I looked at him again and said, "I need to have my life."

I turned away from him and went into the bedroom, sulking, angry that I couldn't control things, especially him.

He came after me saying he was just being honest and please, "Don' be mad."

I wanted him to get away from me. I told him not to worry, that I was just being honest as well. He accepted that, said he had to go and then asked for 200 pesos.

I flipped.

All the resentment from the night before came at him as I spat out the words, "Amador, what do you think?"

I reminded him that I had paid for all their "fucking drinks" last night and that none of them had given me "a fucking peso."

I told him he had no concept of how I made my money or how hard it was for me to keep things together with him showing up and asking for cash as if I were some sort of ATM.

He stepped back from me and said, "Hey calm down. I just asked for 200 pesos."

I escaped from my body long enough to see myself: a raving lunatic who would deny her lover 20 dollars.

I inhaled, calmed down and went to my wallet saying, "Sorry. Sometimes I feel taken for granted."

I handed him 200 pesos.

As I did so, he looked into my wallet and said, "You got enough. What you gonna need here anyway. You got everything. Remember. You got me."

I smiled then and gave him a hug. He kissed me on the lips and said he had to go and reminded me to relax, as if I were the one with the problem. I nodded, wondered if I were while I played the good wife and let him leave. I turned to do the dishes and decided to go for a swim, walk to the land and check on the workers. Amador might be sure they were there but I was not.

I didn't see him again for 4 days. I was angry and hurt and didn't understand what had happened. I rode my bike to town for food and looked for him. As I exited the supermarket, Lakra was there, panting, looking for me and water. I poured some into my hand so she could slurp it up and then we practically had to walk back home. But we made it. I scolded her but actually, I was happy and a little proud that she would follow me. If I needed to save someone, better that it was her. But my mind always drifted back to Amador. I wasn't sure if he was OK or an asshole. I dreamt of him in jail or in the hospital. But each day I got a little better at accepting that there was nothing I could do. I counseled myself and told myself that if something had happened one of his "friends" would come to get me to pay or to help. So then, I was faced with the issue that he was probably with another woman, most likely the Italian. Fucking Akim. I preferred my illusion that he was in jail. But, after the 4th day I didn't care anymore. I found the papers for the jeep and was ready to go to the police to report it stolen. The night before I had steeled myself to that option, no matter how embarrassing it would be. For the first time in those 4 nights, I slept well.

I woke with the sun rising over the sea and Lakra on the dog bed I had made for her with a yoga mat and a blanket by the door. The sunrises never ceased to be anything but amazing. As I opened my eyes, the phone rang. No one called me, and never at that hour. I answered and a throaty voice called into the receiver, "*Amor*". I asked incredulously if it were Amador. He was almost crying as he said, "*Amor*," again. I asked him where he was and he told me he was in front of the house, on the beach.

I hung up the phone, stepped over Lakra and walked onto the balcony and down the stairs to the path between the palms that led to the beach as the sun rose. The white slip that I used for a nightgown softly brushed against my skin as the morning breeze cooled my body. The morning had the flavor of autumn. The sun was peaking over the horizon and the air somehow reminded me of waking on the boat at Semester at Sea. I could see foam on the shore and the water was greener than usual. The early light was soft and gave Amador an absurd halo as he waited by the gate. There was still sleep in his eyes like the first time I had met him, his hair tousled from God only knew what, little pieces of palm leaves sticking out of it. He was crying and told me he had been missing me. I laughed but wanted to believe it. I opened the gate, took him in my arms as if he were my son. He held me back and any loneliness disappeared. My heart felt whole again. It was as if the connection between my heart and my mind had been severed. I let myself go and embraced him, not realizing the pain I would need to embrace later.

He slept most of the day on Norby's sofa. I think she would have preferred Lakra sleeping there but the lease did not say, "no beach bums on my couch." He groaned from time to time. Lakra didn't want to be near him.

She escorted me around the house and out to the beach as if asking, "What are we doing bringing this guy here?"

I patted her and asked myself the same thing.

I didn't know where he had been but I knew it had been a binge, probably drugs, most likely cocaine. I let him sleep the entire day, realizing that the hangover from a 4 day drugfest would be fierce. He woke just before sunset. I had been writing and heard him in the fridge.

"How are you Amador?" I asked as I walked up behind him.

"Hungry," was all he said. And then he added, "And you got nothing in here."

I told him I was sorry that the hotel didn't live up to his expectations and then added, "Nice to see you too."

He grunted and said he would cook something. I told him that would be wonderful since I was hungry too. But I told him there was loads of food in the fridge and I opened the door and recited a list of eggs and bread and vegetables.

He grunted, pulled the eggs out of the fridge and broke one on the floor. I cursed and went to clean it, not able to resist the reflex. He let me and as I was on my hands and knees, trying to get egg white to resist its viscous force and move onto the paper towel, he pulled the milk from the fridge and started drinking from the container. I looked up at him and told him there were glasses. He shot me a mean look and continued drinking, letting milk slide down the sides of his face. I finished cleaning his dropped egg and then walked outside telling him to let me know if he needed help as I went back to writing. He grunted acknowledgement and I started thinking "how dare he!" and "what a jerk" and "ingrate" and "child" as I punched the keyboard on my computer. I heard a pot drop and him curse. I smiled.

In about 15 minutes he came out to the porch and said, "Ready" in an almost nice way.

At least he was smiling.

As I entered, he gave me a kiss and said, "Sorry. I not feeling too well."

I softened and said truthfully, "I can only imagine."

I could only imagine how badly he felt after probably not sleeping for three nights and pumping his body full of chemicals. I set the table and we sat down together to eat. He had created an egg mix of some sort with about everything that was in the fridge. There were tortillas and beans and when I looked over at the stove, a big mess.

He brought the pineapple juice to the table saying, "Why you drink this. It is totally sugar"

I laughed at the hipocracy of the statement and asked him how he could be concerned about sugar after what he had put in his body, finishing with, "Give me a break."

He looked angry and confused. Then he got the joke and laughed. I laughed as well and then asked him where he had been.

He told me it was "A party."

I asked if it were normal for him to have three-day parties.

"When I can," he said and smiled.

I remembered when we had first met and Lynn had asked him if he got stoned every day.

He replied with a smile, "I hope so."

We had all laughed. But this time I didn't laugh. I told him his body was a mess and he needed to think about how to salvage it. He stopped shoveling food into his mouth for a moment and looked at me.

I told him seriously, "Amador, you are polluted, it is obvious. Look at yourself."

"I don' look too good?" he asked me.

And I honestly told him he looked older than I did. Then I asked him how long he thought he could keep living that way. He shrugged, told me he was fine and that he didn't need a lecture. Finally, he asked me how the food was. I lied and told him delicious.

He said almost humbly that he only cooked the food. It was really mine. I watched a cloud pass over him and he repeated the phrase that everything was mine.

Then he got up from the table and almost ran out of the house. Confused, I called after him and ran out to the front porch. He was there on the beach. I walked up to him and asked if he were OK. He told me, with tears in his eyes that he was not OK and that he had to go. I put my arms around him and almost begged him not to go.

He gave me his famous, "I coming back."

I told him firmly "no" saying, "Not like yesterday Amador. Don't come back here like that again."

I had to put up some sort of boundary since I couldn't live with him coming home to sleep it off and then going out to start all over again. It was pathetic. He told me he needed to walk a little.

He kissed me then and said, "Go back inside," as if he were dismissing me.

I didn't fight over it. I turned and walked back to the dirty kitchen, threw my eggs in the garbage and started to clean up, happy he was gone. Suddenly, I didn't care if he ever came back. But I had forgotten to ask him about the car.

Later I walked over to Jade to see Juan and Martha. They were always cordial and since I generally brought a bottle of wine, I felt welcome. We talked a little and I practiced my Spanish. I appreciated the opportunity to see other people and to speak the language with people who were patient with me. They were marvelous. Plus they found my Spanish amusing. I made some pretty funny mistakes.

After awhile, Martha said to me, "Lets start our yoga classes again."

I told her that would be great and we set a schedule for 3 days a week at 730 a.m. We talked about inviting local people this time. I told Martha they would not pay 100 pesos and she said they could pay 50 reminding me that I could not give them something for nothing. "They will not appreciate it."

Life was teaching me that she was absolutely right. We finished the wine and I went back home excited to start teaching again. I sat down and sent some messages to invite people and that was it. I had a yoga class and a studio, of sorts. I hoped Amador would not come by so that I could be well rested and prepared. But later that night when he didn't, when he didn't even call or send me a text, I let myself be disappointed once again. I woke up in the middle of the night, went to the balcony to see the stars and talk to God and ask, "Why am I alone?" The stars twinkled back at me as if laughing.

Chapter 18

I didn't see Amador for a few days after that. Nor did I see my car. I decided to let him take it.

Jerry's words echoed in my head, "If you lie down like a carpet, people gonna walk on you."

I knew I wasn't standing up for myself but I didn't have the energy.

I smiled at myself in the mirror as I prepared to ride my bike to town and said, "At least you will never buy him a car again, right?"

I wouldn't let him bring me down. The first of my family were coming to visit me here in Mexico. My cousins from California would arrive that evening and I was excited but a little frightened. I wasn't sure what they expected and I wondered what we would do as I biked to town. I rented a car to meet them at the airport and as was heaving the bike into the trunk, I felt someone grab the back wheel to help me put it in. I turned to see Amador standing there with a smile. I pushed him out of the way and told him I could do it myself. He asked me why I had to be so mad.

I spat back at him, "Why do you have to be such an asshole?" and then asked him where the jeep was and why he wasn't working.

I finished, inhaled and waited for an answer.

Finally, he shrugged and admitted, "I am an asshole."

I pushed the bike a little deeper into the trunk and fixed a bungey cord around the closure to keep it from moving too much. Then I told him I didn't want to know an asshole so if he couldn't change he should stay away from me. I checked that the bike wouldn't fall out, got into the driver seat and closed the door. Then, as if I had told him he was the greatest thing on earth he ran up to the driver's window and asked if he could come with me. I told him I had family coming, that I was going to the airport and didn't need company.

He asked to come with me again. I wondered for a second if I had dreamed calling him an asshole. I thought I had remembered saying that I did not want to see him anymore. I was confused and started the car.

As I did he said to me, "Come on Joanne. You know it gonna be more fun with me around."

I wanted to be around him. I told him he could help me unload the bike first. My hip hurt from the ride to town and loading it in the car. I knew I needed some help getting it out. He jumped into the passenger side as I asked him about the jeep.

He said, "I gonna 'splain that later."

I laughed at his English and thought of the quote from "I Love Lucy;" "you got some 'splainin to do."

As we drove past Zama's I noticed a black and white dog that looked a lot like Lakra. As we got closer, I realized it was Lakra. She had followed my scent more than 2 km. to Zama's. I stopped the car and she jumped in, panting with thirst but wagging her tail with glee. She hated being left behind and had the habit of following me everywhere. While it was endearing, it frightened me. She had very bad street sense, always running in the middle of the road, looking over her shoulder for dogs that might attack her. And those times she made it all the way to San Francisco Supermarket and we had to come back the 6 km together, she would be exhausted for a day or two. I put her inside determined not to lose her again. But this afternoon, I took great pleasure that she was happier to see me than Amador. He noticed it too as we dropped the bike and the dog at the house. Inside, on the couch or off it, I knew that I wouldn't meet her on the highway as we came back from Cancun.

We drove out of the driveway and Amador asked me again if he could come to the airport and meet my family. I told him no, I would drop him at the traffic light. He pleaded with me and reminded me how much fun he was and told me he knew some great places to show my cousins. I thought about it. My cousins, twins from California, were very cool and open minded. I had no doubt they would accept Amador as my friend and perhaps even find him interesting in a beach bum sort of way. He knew I was considering it and he asked me again at the traffic light, just as I pulled over to let him out. I agreed only if he promised not to sleep the entire way. He smiled and took my hand and kissed it like some knight in shining armor would. I laughed.

As we passed the police checkpoint, I told him my yoga classes were filling. The comment didn't register. He told me he was hungry, wondering if I were hungry as well. My dream was coming true and all he could think about was food. I realized my dream was perhaps not so interesting for other people. But I didn't consider him, "other people," he was supposed to be my intimate soul-mate or something and he couldn't even be happy for my success. He mentioned there was a place close to the ruins where we could get slices of pizza. When I complained that we had no time, he told me it was close and directed me to turn right quickly. We drove into the parking lot where there was a new pizza place and indeed they sold slices. "I told you I show you some good places", Amador said as we ate the hot delicious pizza in the car.

I was pulling hot cheese into my mouth that had stretched off the slice on my last bite when Amador told me the jeep had been impounded, "in the *corralon*." I knew then that was why he came to find me. It had nothing to do with love or even like and everything to do with money. For some reason, I didn't call him on it. I was bored of the scams and decided to enjoy his company, pretend he was a nice fun guy and take advantage of his local knowledge, if he actually had any. I pulled a piece of tomato off my lap and he handed me a napkin. Then he lit a joint, took a few tokes and handed it to me. I took one toke. I handed it back but he said, "Take more," as if he knew what was good for me. I told him I was driving and reminded him that we needed to get to the airport. I asked him sarcastically if he had forgotten. He smiled, took the joint back and as he put it in the ashtray asked if I would help him get the jeep from the pound. I immediately answered, "No," and then, a little stoned, started to laugh.

He wasn't laughing. But I couldn't stop.

After a few minutes he said, "Ha Ha. Funny for you but you gonna lose your car."

That statement made me laugh even more. "My car?" I asked him. Still laughing, I told him it was hardly my car. I rarely got to drive it or see it and told him that it was a big waste of my money. But I couldn't stop laughing.

"We will see," was all he said.

I kept laughing and told him, "No you will see. I won't pay for that car anymore."

I was hysterically laughing and finally asked him what he had put in that pot. He smiled and repeated, "you will see."

Then he told me that "we" were not going to just leave the car with the police.

I giggled and told him to do whatever he wanted. I would not be held ransom to his poor behavior. I kept laughing. He eventually fell asleep.

We got to the airport just in time. I waited outside the customs line jumping up and down as my cousins were exiting. It felt good to have someone with me. And I was happy Amador was there too. We put their bags in the car and Amador suggested Puerto Morelos for lunch. He started playing tour guide and attentive boyfriend all of a sudden. But they didn't really care about him. We chatted about me and them and family. He was outside the conservation and as we walked the beach after lunch, he drifted off to talk to some fisherman and tour guides. My cousin Kari and I were in the car when Megan asked if he was coming back with us. I laughed again, this time from the margarita at lunch and looked around for him. He was jogging across the street to catch us, slightly annoyed that we had almost forgotten him.

I dropped Amador at the traffic light back in Tulum, feeling weird that he would go but also feeling happy that I would not have to share my cousins. We shopped for food, taking advantage of having a car and then drove out to the beach. They fell in love with the house and we had tea and cookies on the balcony with Lakra until we tired of talking and fell asleep.

But before we went to bed, Kari asked me, "So what is up with the guy, Amador, right?"

I didn't know what to say. Slightly embarrassed, slightly defensive I told her I really didn't know. Then I tried to explain how we had been together and how then we split up and how now he came to see me and that sometimes he helped me but I finished telling her, "it is pretty messed up."

She put her hand on my shoulder and asked me if I liked him. I wanted to give an honest direct answer but all I could come up with was, "Sometimes."

She waited for more. I tried to explain to her and to myself that he and I had history here and sometimes how I felt he was all I had. I confided in her that it was weird and then told her how he had been an asshole on more than one occasion.

"Well, honey, you don't need that," she said to me smiling. "You deserve a great guy and a great life. Look at me," she commanded.

Embarassed, I said, "we all do."

But she corrected me and said that was not actually true and that some people deserved to be, "kicked to the curb and put out of your life."

Then she took both her hands on my shoulders and told me directly, "You don't need his shit. I can see he sucks off of you."

I wanted to cry. Another bad choice for my family to witness. I wanted so badly to get it right. I did all the right things for all the right reasons but with all the wrong men. Megan came out from the bathroom, saw us both and asked what was going on. Kari said she would drop it and said she was really tired. And we all went to sleep.

After breakfast and a swim we walked the beach to my project. As we crested the dune and walked toward the street, I became nervous. The project reflected the crazy mess of people who had started and then given up or been fired. I was still not sure I could finish or sometimes, why I was even doing it. Under the scrutiny of my family, I was nervous and unsure. We walked onto the site and the dust from the dry soil kicked up around our feet even though it had rained in the night. It was a battleship grey colored, silty soil, not at all like the white and pinkish sand on the other side of the road. The scientist in me wondered how it had come here, by what hurricane or by what glacier.

There was construction debris everywhere. The concrete kitchen counter was not straight, the windows weren't square and I still had no front stairs. We wandered around and then climbed up the back to see the great swamp behind the house.

"Wow," Megan said as she reached the top floor and Kari whistled, "Impressive."

The vista made me happy and calm and somehow justified my commitment to being there. Coming down the ladder, I confided that I would have a hard time leaving the place.

But my cousin reminded me, "There are a million great places in the world."

I almost cried as I told them I had spent everything I had here.

Kari, clearly shocked, said, "You cannot just walk away."

She knew Amador would take it.

Lakra half jogged half floated up the stairs to join us in the puddle the rain had left on the second floor as she said, "You cannot let him take everything from you. You have to sell it."

I thought about what she said and, without realizing what it might take, I committed to not leaving until it was finished and I could sell. As we walked back between the palm trees on the dusty path in near silence, I decided that I would realize my dream of finishing the construction and bringing patients here and then perhaps sell. All it took was someone to believe in me.

We walked across the street, over the dune and strolled the beach back to the house. I left the girls at the beach with Lakra and went to town for groceries. As I drove along the road, I got this sick feeling, a nauseous from fear of seeing Amador. I knew I had to get him out of my life and start saying no but he seemed to always find me in my weakest moments. I needed a break to get my strength. Perhaps he knew that. It seemed each time I was almost ready, he showed up to break my will. Tonight, I shopped quickly, reading from the list that we had made. As I walked out to the car, I thought I saw him and a chill ran down my spine. But no, it was another beach bum, Angelo, who smiled and waved hello. Relieved, I waved back, loaded the groceries and drove back home where we cooked, ate and played poker like kids, using beans for money. It felt nice to not go out yet not be alone and to talk and laugh. Those two twins from my childhood fed my soul, loved where I was and, although they knew I was mixed up, believed I was OK and not totally crazy. I felt more whole than I had in a long time.

At about 3 in the morning I heard a knock on the door. Kari and I woke, looked at each other and I got up to see what it was. I turned on the light in the bathroom to guide me to the front door. Lakra stayed asleep in the bedroom with the girls. I looked through the glass on the door and saw Amador's halo. I opened it slowly and he said hello.

He was drunk and he had a little puppy in his arms which he pushed toward me saying, "Look *Amor*, I bring you a present."

Lakra finally came out from the bedroom, rubbed her head against my leg and then sniffed the puppy. I patted her and looked at this little yellow baby that was so cute but that I knew would be so much care. He had done this to me before when Helen and George were with me. He brought me that cute little puppy that I swore I saw Akim walking in town about a week ago. I started to get angry but then I looked at his face, his watery eyes that were the sign of someone drunk or stoned, and I looked at the curls of hair around

413

his face and the golden tipped dreadlocks and his little smile.

"What will I do with a puppy?" I asked, as he put it in my arms.

"It not gonna take much. You can love it," like a child who had no idea of what the world was about.

Then he kissed me and wrapped his arms around me and the puppy and I felt good. Lakra walked away and laid down in the kitchen, as if she couldn't believe what she was witnessing. Then suddenly he said he had to go. I told him it was 3 am and asked where he was going. He told me he needed to find some people and that a taxi was waiting for him.

Then, he said, "You got 200 pesos to pay him?"

It was like a slap in the face. I got furious and asked him how he could come here in the middle of the night with a dog for me to take care of and ask me to pay his taxi when he lived with another woman. I finished asking him if he were joking. He looked at me and smiled and said he knew I had it.

I imagined how my mom felt when my grandfather would show up drunk in a taxi and expect my mom to take care of him and the fare. At least she had my dad to sleep with. I would go back to bed alone, 200 pesos poorer. I vowed not to give him a cent and told him I would take the dog but not pay the taxi. He reached to grab the puppy from my arms and told me he would sell it to pay the fare. I instinctively pulled the puppy to my chest and asked him who would buy a dog at 3 in the morning. He reached for it, his face hard and angry and told me he would find someone.

We were wrestling with the dog when Kari came out of the bathroom and asked if everything was OK. I was embarrassed at having Amador there, at this little dog in my arms, at everything.

But she said, sleepily, "What you got there Jo Jo?" and came over to pat the dog as I explained that Amador had brought me a puppy.

With his words slurring, he denied it saying, "No. It is mines."
He reached for it but Kari took the animal out of my arms and cuddled it and said that it was a nice gift.

Amador looked at me and said, "You got the 200?"

Kari was staring at me. I didn't say a word but went to my bag and took out two 100 pesos bills and pushed them at and told him to never come back. He didn't care. He took the money and even said "Goodnight" to Kari. He tried to kiss me on the cheek, as if everything were fine, but I moved away and closed the door.

Kari smiled and said, "What are we gonna do with this little guy?" she held him up and we both started to laugh.

But I was weary. I had a cooler on the porch and we found some towels to put inside so that we could put him in it for the night. I told my cousin we would figure it out tomorrow.

She smiled at me and said, "giving him money is not the answer, sweetie."

I told her that sometimes it was easier and she gave me a hug before I could cry and told me, "But it is not gonna keep him away."

I took a deep breath, took the puppy from her and put him in the cooler and wearily said, "I know but I am not sure anything will. That is why I need to go."

And I wondered why I didn't just say no.

The next moring, like a little tribe, we all woke at sunrise and went to Jade to my yoga class. Lakra came with us. The puppy stayed in the cooler after a walk around the house. Lakra sat at the foot of my mat as we practiced: two tourists, Martha on a fur throw that she used for a mat, Kari and me. Megan took pictures and wandered around as we played. It was a great class and I made 200 pesos, less than 20 US but it was ok.

"You have to start somewhere," I told myself.

Kari left the next day. I told her it was too fast and she said it was better than nothing. I was grateful that Megan would stay a few more days. As we hugged at the airport, she told me to take care of myself and "keep that guy out of your life," before she reminded me I was, "way too good for him." I started to cry and she hugged me again. I explained that it was not so easy. She told me she understood but reminded me that I could sell and come to California and stay with her and her husband until I got set up.

Megan groaned, saying "Oh yeah, Dan will love that."

Kari reminded me that whatever I needed they would help me. Then she walked into the security line, her yellow pony tail bouncing from the back of her baseball cap with her bouncy step and thin cut jeans and waved to us before she disappeared into the airport. Megan and I waved back and then turned to go back to Tulum. We had a couple of dogs waiting for us.

On arrival, we stripped down and ran into the water with the two dogs running behind us. Then we sat on the porch, played with the puppy and talked about life, about Tulum and about how many other great places there were in the world. We discussed selling and although I knew it wouldn't be easy, there had to be a way. We thought it through over the next 5 days she was with me, between swims and lunches and long walks on the beach with the dogs. We discussed with Juan how I could do some advertising on Craig's list and perhaps with some local realtors. I still dreamt of finishing the houses and bringing cancer survivors to recuperate. I knew that if I could get away from Amador, I could make it happen. Megan reminded me, that if I got the opportunity, I should sell and do my project somewhere else.

She finished telling me, "He is a train wreck and I want you to get off board."

We had a wonderful 3 more days and evenings and Amador never showed again. We played with the dogs and even Lakra fell in love with the new little puppy.

"I think we will name him Diego," Megan told me one day.

I agreed. Diego was as good as any other name. But I worried what I would do with a little puppy and how the dog almost called Amador to come and harass me. I knew he would come back when I was alone, try to take the dog and ask me for more money. I confided in Megan and she decided to adopt him. We went to the vet's the next day. Megan was adamant and when the vet told us Diego would need shots and that there was no quarantine period between the US and Mexico, Megan was sold. We drove to Playa for a kennel for the plane. We decided that since she already had one dog at home, another would be no problem for my uncle. We got ready to take Diego to California.

But I was not ready to let them go. I knew that the minute I was alone again, Amador would come back. Another part of me was afraid that he wouldn't. I would just be alone. But one thing I knew as I walked to 7:30 yoga that morning with Lakra, I was loving my life and did not want to let it go for some crazy drug addict I had made the mistake of sleeping with and wanting to be a partner in my dream. I wasn't sure what his dream was, but I was going to make mine work, with him or without him. With Megan I was strong. I knew in my heart that alone I was could be just as strong.

Later that day, we waited in line at the airport check in. The attendant had a problem with the kennel fitting under the seat.

Megan assured her it would fit. We already had the dog, drugged and sleeping, in the kennel and Megan had already paid 100 US to have him ride with her. After about 5 minutes of conversation, the attendant told Megan she could try to fit the kennel onto the plane. But she told me to wait until the plane took off just in case. We hugged and she wandered off with her backpack on one arm and the little dog kennel on the other. She stopped only once to wave good-by. I watched the screen until the plane had taken off. They never came back and if not for Lakra waiting at home, I would have booked a flight home in that moment. But then again, I thought as I walked back to the rental car, where was that?

Chapter 19

I drove back to Tulum before dark and found my Lakra waiting. She seemed happy to be alone with me again without the puppy. I took a glass of wine and went with her to the beach. We watched the stars come out. Then I walked back to the house, fed the dog, opened a book and read until I fell asleep in the chair. When I woke with a snort later, I walked under the full night sky to lock the gate and returned to lock the house before I fell into bed exhausted. Lakra followed me everywhere s if she knew I were thinking of abandoning Tulum.

The next morning I walked the beach to my project after yoga class with Lakra walking close enough. She hated the water and hugged the shore while I waded in the clear shallows, enjoying the coolness of the clean Caribbean. We climbed the vegetated bluff, then ran down the other side between the chit palms and the sea grape trees and crossed the street to the property. No one was working but there really was not much left to do. I needed the windows and perhaps a little more work on the bar and counter but the house would be livable once I got the carpenter back. I looked for his number in my paperwork, climbed to the roof where I had cell phone coverage and called him. With my developing Spanish I got it across that I needed the doors and windows. I believed he said he could have them in 2 weeks but he needed money. Apparently the deposit I had paid had not been enough. I told him to come around and I would pay him directly. I was lost in thought walking back with Lakra. I thought Amador had paid more than enough for the deposit.

The next day the carpenter arrived at around 1 p.m. with my favorite of his workers. We discussed the windows again and I asked him about the deposit I had given him. He shook his head and said something about my "*esposo*" husband. I clarified, or at least I hoped I did, that Amador was never my "*esposo*". I wondered what the involvement was but told him I would pay more with the condition that he sign for the money and bring me the windows in 2 weeks. I tried to tell him that sooner would be better but in 2 weeks I had to leave. I hoped he understood. Regardless, I paid, he signed and we shook hands. I told him, "two weeks" putting up fingers for 2. He repeated the two weeks, held up 2 finders as well and the worker with him smiled. I was certain the translation was good.

They headed back to their town. I wondered what Amador had told him. Preoccupied, I took a walk around the property. Goliath, the dog from next door came by and we hung out for awhile. Lakra and I were happy to see him. I finished with my usual climb out back to look over what I now called 'my swamp' and then walked the beach home.

I began visiting the project each day to take a look, check things, see what I wanted to do, what I wanted to change. I would start the generator and check the water and the pipes. I continued to own the place, to make it mine. I watered the plants and checked their growth. Even though I wasn't living there, I would still be there. I was still a part of that place. Lakra and I accustomed ourselves to walking the beach to the project in the autumn sun. The water was generally calm and sparkeled differently from other months as the sun started its harvest profile. Normally the beach was ours, totally empty. I would splash through the water with Lakra walking along the perimeter.

One particular afternoon, I noticed something floating in the shallows and when I went to pick it up, found a $100 bill. I looked up and down the beach for the owner but no one was on the beach. I imagined that someone swimming had let it fall from a pocket. I laughed out loud and said to Lakra, "this is our lucky day." We skipped home and put the bill in my wallet to save it for a special day. I had not seen or even thought about the jeep. I was learning to let it all go. I was living my life in a cucoon in that little round house on the beach. Seeing my yoga friends in the morning, going to a project where nothing was really happening in the afternoon and then writing reports and journals or painting into the night. But it had to end. The lease terminated in November. Norby would rent to tourists and I would, once again, visit my doctors in the US. There, I had some foundation work and I had some deliverables on my engineering contract that really could not come from Mexico. I was still using the address of the condo in Miami for my work with them. I was afraid to tell them I lived in Mexico. But I still had nearly a month and I would make the most of it. I rode my bike to town almost every other day to get groceries and wine. I swam every day and practiced and taught yoga and poured my solitary self into the right now, into the moment and visited my nearly ready project.

One night, I was painting as the moon was rising. I was trying to capture the palm trees under the starry sky, trying to channel Van Gogh unsuccessfully but enjoying the effort. As I dotted yellow onto the midnight blue background, I heard footsteps on the front stairs: Amador. I had not seen him for a long time. Nor had I missed him. That was a giant step. I did not smile when I saw him either. Another leap. Something between us had died. That spark of a connection wasn't there.

He felt it and said, "What? Not happy to see me?"

I answered honestly, "no."

I was not happy to see him. I told him I didn't need the hassles he generally brought me. It didn't stop him. He smiled his little boy smile and walked up to me on the porch to see what I was doing. Shy, I covered the painting and told him it was dark and I was not finished.

He tugged the painting away from me and said, "it is not bad," as if he knew art.

I wanted to hit him. He asked me what I was doing, what had been going on. I told him not much and started to put my paints away, hoping he would leave. He asked if I had eaten yet and I told him no, that I was going to cook. I had been raised to be consummately polite and Amador always took advantage of it. I invited him to dinner because I didn't know what else to do. Too, I wanted to discuss the carpenter.

I had my back to him, cooking, and asked him, "you know, Amador. I go to the project every day. No workers come, no carpenters, none of the things you were supposed to take care of are getting done. So, why not you tell me what has been going on?"

He wasn't ready for that sort of directness. He told me he would leave if I wanted but I told him I would rather know what happened to the windows and doors and to the car as I put dinner on the table, patted Lakra and sat down. He stood there until I asked him to sit. We ate in relative silence.

At one point he put his fork down and told me, "You know. Things not so easy as you think."

I told him it was always the same story and to save it. He was surprised. We finished eating and I made tea and brought cookies for desert. He asked me if I wanted to play poker. I asked what we would play for. He had some coins and I went to get my wallet to see if I did as well. I brought the wallet to the table, turned it upside down to let any coins I had fall. About 35 pesos in coins gently dropped to the table and on top of them, my lucky 100 dollar bill, folded into a square so I would not spend it. His eyes lit up when he saw it. I knew I had made a mistake.

He said, "You doing OK with the yoga."

I laughed and told him it was not yoga money and put the bill quickly away and told him the story of how I found it and how it was my lucky bill.

I told him I was saving it and added, "a concept you wouldn't understand," as I shuffled the deck.

We played a few hands and I was enjoying myself when he said he had to go. I asked for one more hand and he said only if I played for my lucky bill. I looked at him and told him no and explained it would not be fair since he would not put up a $100. If I won, I just kept my money. I didn't win anything.

He looked confused and said, "So then why don' you just give it to me?"

I laughed and said "because it is mine."

He got up and walked around the room. I put the cards away, sorry we had ever started and said I knew he had to go. He looked at me then and asked for the 100 dollars. I told him no and he started whining about how he had people to pay and it was so hard to come see me and whatever stupid excuse he could think of that he thought he could justify taking the money from me.

Finally he told me "and it not yours anyway. You found it" as he grabbed my wallet from the table, opened it and took the money out.

I ran over, grabbed my wallet and went for the bill.

He held it up high so I could not get it and said, "Baybe you not need this but I really do," as he pushed me away so hard that I nearly fell.

Then he took off. I ran after him but he had disappeared into the night. I couldn't believe he had robbed me and nearly assaulted me. The idea of going to the police didn't occur to me. In the small town I was at a minimum his ex and probably he still told people we were married or at least working together. I started to cry and then stopped myself. I would never let him in my house again. I vowed to myself and swore to Lakra saying "never, never, never again." I locked the doors and put my bag under my pillow and went to sleep praying he would never come back.

And he didn't, at least not for the next two weeks. I made arrangements to go back to the US and Norby told me she would take care of Lakra. Juan and Martha told me they would look out for her too. I left her bed under Norby's house where she would have the shelter of the bodega. I left food with Norby and reminded them that she just needed a little love to stick around. I put what few things I had in the bodega at the house and kissed Lakra goodbye as I left with a taxi in the morning. Norby told me not to worry, that she loved animals. I wasn't sure they loved her back but it was the best I could do. I prayed Lakra would be OK as I headed onto the highway and back to the North East US.

Chapter 20

The November greyness was a stark contrast to the green of Tulum but I welcomed it. So much sun for a girl who grew up loving grey rainy days was exhausting. I had been missing my rainy days and my family. It was wonderful to see them both. We were a tribe and I was the only nomad so it was nice to hang at all of their houses. I shared myself with each of them, did some fundraising for That Barry Girl foundation and incorporated book sales meetings with visits to hospitals and doctors. I was opening doors for my projects and healing well.

But I was always preoccupied with Tulum. Thankfully, I heard nothing from Amador during that time. I was happy but concerned in the same moment. I had limited contact with Juan and Martha by email. They said things were good and wanted me back to teach yoga.

I had people asking for classes. They had seen Lakra a few times but I worried about her too. Norby told me she remembered the food and asked the workers to give her some when she was not there. But I knew the love was missing and that was what Lakra needed most. I finished my business in record time including a fabulous art show of my work at Lynn's shop and I headed back to Tulum. I was defining my success by Tulum. Regardless of how well things were going on my other endeavors, I would feel a failure until I succeeded there.

I headed back after Veteren's Day and rented a car at the airport. The sting of renting had faded although I knew the car I had bought was sitting in a lot waiting for redemption. I doubted Amador had it. The papers were still in my bodega and unless he totally forged things or bribed the officials, he would never get it. My only consolation was that he would have a hard time selling it if he had retrieved it. I drove to directly to the beach and started looking for a place to stay. I needed to cut back on my expenses and the high season was approaching. Zama's had one little bungalow across the street from the beach that was affordable. It was a private space with two beds and a desk with a shared bathroom outside the apartment. It had nice light in the afternoon and it would be wonderful to have coffee on that beach in the morning.

I took the room and then went directly to Norby's to look for Lakra. She was not there. I went to see Juan and Martha but they said they had not seen her for a few days. We scheduled a couple of yoga classes for that week. They were excited to start again. As the sun started to set, I drove to *Mar Caribe* to ask if they had seen her. Reyes was there with a bunch of his friends and I asked him about the dog. He said he had not seen her in an unkind way. He and his friends were not welcoming and I decided not to hang around. I went back to Zama's feeling a total shit and missing my dog. I vowed to look for her again the next day.

I drove to the *Mar Caribe* again in the morning to look for Lakra but again, no love from the gang and no Lakra. I went to town to work. My cousin Megan sent me an email saying she would come to visit again in 3 days. She said she found a fantastic fare and couldn't resist. I knew she thought I needed help and I knew I did. She called me on my shit with Amador, which was exactly what I needed. I prepared for her arrival and kept looking for Lakra wherever I went, ready to grab her. I was also looking out for Amador wherever I went, ready to hide.

I went to my property. No one had entered. The rain had helped the plants and they didn't seem to have missed me. I climbed to the top of the back structure to check the water levels and visit my favorite marsh in the world. It had not missed me either. I inhaled the tranquility of that huge body of green and, exhaling, said hello. I wasn't sure if I was happy or sad but took my time before going back downstairs. As I backed down the ladder, I noticed my neighbors had been building a little more but still no one was living there. I walked to the bodega, checked the generator and started it, afraid of an explosion but curious if it still ran. It started with a spark and pop but then ran smoothly. I smiled, feeling like a "greaser" as I checked the oil levels, sparkplugs and gas. Then I took a walk along the water pipes and noticed that they were growing some green slime. We had put in flexible, transparent piping. Moises had recommended it because it was easy to run and easy to maintain. But it looked like we needed to flush the tubes because the transparent nature of them allowed algae to grow with the sun. I made a mental note to look for the plumber.

Then Goliath came from behind in the *mangroves* and I started to cry, missing my Lakra. I sat with Goliath for a bit, listened to Amalio's cough and then decided to walk over to the beach. There was nothing I could do until I got my doors and windows. As I shut the door to the property, exhaustion overwhelmed me. I patted Goliath and told him, "let's go." We crossed the street, climbed the dune, inhaled the sea air and felt alive again. We walked a little, him running a lot, me following with my feet in the water and not a soul on the beach. I was not really happy, but not really sad. I felt at home however, free and energized. I knew I had a lot of work to do and I was really unsure where to begin but I felt a drive to do it and a confidence that I could. Goliath started to run for a tourist who was coming onto the beach. I called him back before he could attack and we went home. He crossed over to Amalio's. I got in my car to go back to Zama's or to town. I would decide which as I drove.

I reached the break by Zama's and decided to go to town and call the carpenter. I still had my phone with me but the reception was bad on the beach. Too, I wanted to get some food and check for work on-line. The Water Resource Institute had renewed my contract and I was hoping for more studies to review. The carpenter answered and even remembered me. In my remedial Spanish, I was pretty sure he told me he would have the windows and doors ready the following week. Excited, I told him the sooner the better. He told me he was waiting for a truck to bring them to Tulum and asked if I had one. I shook my head and said no, sadly. He told me not to worry, they would find a way, but that I might have to pay extra for the transport if he had to rent a truck. I was sure we could work it out. Although I had been studying Spanish, I hoped he was clear that I wanted the doors and windows and that I would pay extra to get them to the house. When we hung up I was dubious about everything.

I went to the San Francisco to buy a cooked chicken and some fruit and peanuts to eat so that I was not in the restaurant every moment. I got a bottle of bad red wine but figured that bad wine was better than no wine. I purposely did not go deeper into town and I checked my email at the internet café next to the supermarket. I did not want an "A" sighting and made my way back to the beach where I was just another blondish tourist in a rental car. In town I stood out and people recognized me. So I stayed away, believing I could stay anonymous at least until my cousin arrived. It was a small town, however, and with more than 1000 full time residents with very few of them living on the beach, two days without bumping into someone who knew Amador and recognized me was ambitious.

Regardless, I felt relatively comfortable in the bar at night ordering a pizza and glass of wine. It was still low season but I didn't want to hide. And I was not yet surrounded by lovers and vacationers which felt good. Afterwards, I marvelled at the stars as I walked back to my house. Lights went out with the electricity at 11 pm and in the darkness, I slept amazingly well. The second night, before sunrise there was a knock on my door. It entered my dreams and I ignored it until it became so loud that I realized it was in fact someone at my door. I was afraid for a moment and did not move until I heard the knock again and then "*amor.*" I knew it was Amador.

I debated getting up at all and rolled over to ignore it. He knocked harder and called again, "*amor.*" I realized he would not go away so I got up to tell him to leave. I opened the door to see him: barefoot, surfer shorts, hair touseled and eyes as bloodshot as the sunrise but with that little boy smile that made him less of a bum and more of the happy man.

He looked at me and said, "no, you not happy to see me."

I told him no, that it was 4 in the morning and I had been sleeping. I asked why he thought I should be happy to see him.

He said, "OK, then I go now."

And he turned and walked away. A part of me wanted to run behind him and catch him but another part of me held back and let him go. I watched him cross the street to the beach and disappear down the bluff. I sighed and then closed the door and went back to bed. But I could not sleep.

That voice inside my head told me, "Now he knows where you are. You will never have any peace."

I pushed the voice away and prayed that being in the hotel would protect me. Plus, I could always find another place. I stayed in bed until daylight and then dressed and went to the beach with my journal. I wrote until the restaurant opened and I could get a coffee.

I needed to make a plan now that I was not so anonymous. But a walk on the beach always helped. Zama's made great French toast and I ordered an extra large coffee to go with it. There was no one in the restaurant and I enjoyed the solitary morning. I spent the morning writing and organizing things on the computer and denying to myself that I was waiting for Amador or afraid to leave for fear of bumping into him.

However, the encounter that morning left me unnerved and I could not shake the feeling. True to form, as I opened the door to leave, Amador was on the other side, waiting. He smiled and asked why I was not so happy to see him that morning.

I inhaled, smiled back and told him "Some drunk waking me at 4 in the morning is supposed to make me happy?"

He laughed. So did I.

Then he put his arms around me and said, "but I your drunk."

I pushed him away and turned to lock the door and told him I knew better. I walked away and he called after me, asking me to have dinner with him that evening. I told him no. He asked why.

I said, "because" like a kid who had no reason to say no but did anyway.

He asked again and I asked him if he were buying. He said yes and then said, "please" and I agreed to meet him. He smiled and told me he would come for me at about 7 p.m. I was not sure what I was doing, but I at least had gotten rid of him for the moment.

Just before 7, he knocked at my door.

I answered it saying, "I am impressed."

He mentioned that the band at Zama's that night was good as he hugged me and handed me a small boquet of bugambilia he had picked from the road. I felt like a young woman on prom night, honestly happy to be out with a man and listening to live music. By myself I would not go, I would feel too weird, too alone, too whatever. I lacked the confidence to go out alone and, at this stage, I preferred feeling lonely in my house rather than looking and feeling alone in a restaurant or bar full of lovers. Even if I were out with a guy who had robbed me and abandoned me and cheated on me, I preferred to be with him than alone. That societal pressure to be with a man amazed me and I wondered where I got it as we crossed the street and took a table in the back. The restaurant already had only a few seats left. I ordered a margarita. Amador asked for a beer.

He looked nice, clean, and as put together as a guy who never wears shoes could be. I told him so as the waiter brought our drinks. He smiled and asked me, "think so?" We touched our glasses with, "cheers big ears" and the band started to warm up as the place filled. I sipped my margarita and wondered if we would dance as Amador's phone rang. He took the call as if he were some sort of businessman. I noticed that at least he had some money, clean clothes, and a cell phone. All the signs of what I thought I wanted were there. I blocked the thought that he had either sold a bunch of drugs or some more of my land to get it. I decided to enjoy the date and told that voice inside me to be quiet. Amador hung up the phone and, like an executive, said he needed to go see someone. He puckered his lips for a kiss and when I did not give it to him, he shrugged his shoulders and said, "I be back." He left his beer and I enjoyed the music knowing that at least I appeared to be with someone.

I asked the waiter to wait a moment for our order as people start to dance. Hungry, I looked for Amador several times, turning my head toward the road.

When the waiter came a second time and I told him I was waiting, he said, "I saw your friend get in a car just now. Are you sure you want to wait?"

The color left my face and my head started to hurt. I asked the waiter if he was sure. He shook his head yes. I inhaled and rather than cry, ordered pizza. Humiliated, I wondered why I allowed this man to manipulate me. I knew at this point it was my challenge but I was still unable to believe he was such a bastard. My pizza arrived and I ordered another margarita, "*en las rocas con sal.*" I almost cried with every bite. When the band took intermission, I asked for a check, self-consciously paid for my dinner and Amador's beer and left to go back to my cabana. My cousin would come the next day. I vowed to lose my susceptibility to Amador once and for all. I put on my p.j.s, journaled about what an asshole he was and then, happy about my resolve to abandon him for a change, drew some of the things in the room before I fell soundly asleep.

No one knocked on my door that night. I woke with the birds and practiced yoga between the bed and the desk before I crossed the street once again. The same waiter smiled as he served me coffee. Selfconscious, I enjoyed my coffee on the beach while I watched the waves crash on the rocky shore. I had time for a swim before I would drive to Cancun for my cousin. For most of the trip, the highway was 1 lane in each direction with a small breakdown lane. But often you needed to pass container trucks and slow vehicles, gauging the oncoming traffic as you did so. It generally gave me a heart attack so I would stay behind the trucks, afraid to pass. Therefor, I gave myself time, not wanting to be late or totally stressed when I arrived. I checked the locks on the doors and took my computer with me, just in case. I told myself I was not being paranoid. The voice on my shoulder congratulated me on being realistic.

Megan's flight arrived on time and I got there only a few minutes before she walked out the door from immigration looking lovely with her quick white smile, short dark brown hair and sweat pants. She always dressed in soccer clothes, forever the tomboy. At her sister's wedding I saw her for the first time in a dress and made up. She was absolutely gorgeous. When I told her, she told me not to get used to it, laughing.

We hugged fiercely even though I had seen her a month ago. I felt my backbone grow being near her. We started talking then and didn't stop. Megan told me how wonderful Diego was and how my uncle enjoyed him. I was relieved to know that my favorite uncle wasn't cursing me on a daily basis for some hyper-active puppy. Megan added that Diego was probably the only good thing Amador had ever done. The conversation shifted to Lakra and shameful, I told her she had run away from Norby's while I was away and I had not found her yet. Together we committed to finding her. So instead of going back to my cabana, we took the turn toward the ruins when we entered Tulum, "just in case" I had missed something. I was excited as we drove up the pothole filled road. It was a combination of desire to find Lakra but also fear to find Amador. He still colored my every move. Megan saw it and took my hand telling me I would be fine. I wondered that I was so transparent.

Once again, I parked the car by the *Don Cafeto's* where Lakra had originally jumped into it and walked casually down toward the beach. I asked the waiters if they had seen her. They shook their heads no. It was the same with the Mayan guy watching the cabanas. Megan commented that they probably wouldn't know one dog from another since they were so stoned and jaded to animals on the beach. I agreed and my positive attitude weakened. We walked to the beach and I yelled for Lakra, loudly, almost sadly. Nothing. A couple of hippies looked at me. I smiled, reminding myself that Lakra means horrible vagabond in Spanish. Regardless, I yelled again, this time almost depserately and I walked closer to the water, put my feet in and looked out to sea. I started to cry but then stopped myself, bored with that sad emotion. I turned back and yelled again as Megan walked toward me and then called "Look" and pointed to the dune where the tents and hippies were. Lakra was running down the dune towards me. I allowed myself to cry, this time with happiness.

She ran up to me howling like she used to and I got down on my knees to hug her. She started humping my arm. I laughed. Megan ran up to meet us. I stopped Lakra's show of affection and she rubbed her head against my thigh like old times. I had my dog back. We brought her to eat with us at *Don Cafeto's*. She sat under the table as I fed her bits of this and that. I couldn't remember being happier than there on the beach with my cousin and my dog, not eating alone. I reminded myself that life was beautiful.

Chapter 21

"So how long can you stay?" I asked Megan as we tucked ourselves into the two single beds in my cabana with Lakra on a yoga mat next to my bed.

The comfort and close quarters reminded me of being at my grandfather's summer house. She told me ten days and I started to plan where we would stay as I drifted off to sleep. I only had that cabana until the end of the week and my house might not be ready for another 2 weeks. I fell asleep committed to look for another place in the morning.

So after breakfast at Zama's, a long walk on the beach, yoga for me, some photographing for Megan, we explored our options. We took our time, had nowhere really to go. Lakra stayed with us, happy. We walked to a small hotel down the road and found a room at La Posada del Sol, more expensive but the room had 2 levels and a small balcony you could climb onto through a window. It was wonderful and artsy and was available for 3 nights. High season was beginning and I knew I needed to look for something more permanent. "A step at a time," my cousin said. I agreed but I was worried about spending the winter running from hotel to hotel, both financially and physically. The gypsy life was wearing me down. But for these 10 days I would enjoy my cousin and my life. We planned where to go for dinner, explored, talked and hung out. I kept the rental car and we snuck Lakra into the room after reception had closed in the evening. We visited my house more than a few times, just to see it. That part of the beach was so beautifully deserted. There we could take Lakra and Goliath walking as if we owned the beach. There was no one around for miles.

Our second day at La Posada del Sol, Amador found us. Not that we were hiding but neither one of us wanted to see him. Had we seen him first we would have walked in the other direction. I was on the balcony writing with Lakra. Megan was taking photos on the rocks in front of the hotel when he came into the room. The door was unlocked but closed. He didn't care. He had no limits, no boundaries. I made a mental note to always lock the door from then on. I didn't hear him walk up the stairs to my room, nor did Lakra, until he stuck his head through the window looking for me. I jumped back and he laughed loudly. Lakra howled hello and he went to pat her.

"Weird way to get out here," he said referring to the fact that you had to climb through a window.

I shrugged and I asked him what he was doing. He said he was looking for me.

I put down my book and told him, "Amador, after you left me the other night in Zama's I decided I never wanted to see you again." His smile faded. He patted Lakra's head as he accused me of focusing on "sad" things, "it is always sad things with you."

I asked him what else he gave me and he said, "You gonna see. You gonna need me soon. Real soon," his tone was threatening and he continued, "How you gonna find a place in the high season? You gonna live like me on the beach? I don' think so."

I told him I didn't need his shit and asked him to leave but I he had touched the frightened part of me. I got up and escorted him downstairs so he would go and to make sure he didn't take anything on the way out. Lakra stayed under the bed, she knew his moods better than I did.

He kept mumbling things the whole way down, "You gonna see. Only sad things, that why I can't be with you."

As I opened the door, Megan was coming in. She met us abruptly and although surprised, said hello to him politely. I walked him to the front of the hotel, passing the owners in their kitchen as we left. Amador said hello to the husband. They knew each other but I didn't care. We were leaving the next day.

I got to the street and looked around, "You got a car?" I asked him.

He immediately shifted his approach, telling me that was why he came. He said he met a guy who could help him get the jeep out of the pound if I gave him the papers and 3000 pesos. I laughed, not able to help myself. He was annoyed.

I didn't care and asked him, "what the fuck do you think I am? Stupid? Or a bank machine?"

He looked at me and told me to calm down.

I lowered my voice and told him "well, I am neither," and started to walk away.

From behind me he said, "You gonna give me those papers and I gonna get the jeep back," again, threatening me.

His tone made my skin crawl. I kept walking and did not look back.

Once I got inside, I reminded Megan that we needed to lock the doors. I told her how Amador walked in and came all the way upstairs. Lakra came down the stairs, her hind quarters nearly catching her front. When she heard me talking, she sensed it was safe.

I gave her a pat and continued to tell Megan that maybe we could take a drive and look for another place. She agreed so we put a leash on Lakra and took a drive down the road. I thought that perhaps at La Vita e Bella they might have something affordable. Too, I wanted Megan to experience where I had first come when I came to Tulum.

As we drove up the small hill heading back to town from La Posada del Sol, I noticed Amador hitching on the side of the road. As we passed he practically stood in front of us. I slowed and opened the window to see what he had to say. He got in the car opening the back door as if we had stopped to give him a ride.

I told him we were not going to town and he said, "I go with you wherever," and something about that made my heart melt.

I couldn't believe it. Megan smiled uncomfortably and we drove to *La Vita e Bella*. Amador asked what we were going to do here and I told him we were looking for a room. He told me he could help me and he jogged ahead to talk to the owner, whom he knew. He knew all the Italians. I told myself that if he could get me a good price, who cared, he needed to pay me back for so many things, not the least of them standing me up the other night.

He ran back to announce, "They gonna give you a great room for a great price."

I said "cool" and "thanks" and the owner, Sylvia, came out with keys to show me the room saying, "Ciao Bella," and giving me a kiss. I liked her. She had a mona lisa face, perfectly oval and for a woman who lived in the tropics, wonderfully white skin. She was loving and I never felt judged around her. She brought us to a small bungalow over the entrance where they had a shop. The stairway was in the back and the room had a nice view of the restaurant and then, over the *palapa*, the sea. There was a full bath and 2 beds: all we needed. Sylvia told us we could stay for 10 days at a price of $40 per night and the dog was no problem. I hugged her and even gave one to Amador. Megan loved the place and we left a deposit to come back the next day.

As we walked to the car, Amador asked for a ride to town. I thought it was the least we could do, so we gave him a lift.

When we got to the traffic light he touched me on the shoulder and said, "you can drop me here."

I pulled over and let him out.

He came over to my window and said, "Think about what I said.

I helped you. You could help me."

I didn't answer and before the light changed he kissed me on the lips and said, "*te quiero* Joanne."

The light changed and I drove away not knowing how to feel but wanting to forget all the "sad things" once again.

"What was that all about," my cousin asked, laughing.

I shook my head and we drove into town wondering about the interaction. We stopped at the Mar Caribe Supermarket and then took a walk around the town before we decided to have a margarita back on the beach to celebrate that we had a room. We drove back to spend our last night at la Posada del Sol. It was a moonlit night that cast a shadow on the floor as the light came through the little balcony window. Restless, I crawled out onto the balcony to see the moon and be outside. It was hard to see the stars for the brightness of it, but I knew they were there. I thought of the time Amador had come into the room at Amansala when I had first met him. Without making a noise, absolutely silent, all wet. I remembered how he told me he had walked and swum to see me. I had felt so loved then. Now, I felt confused. I couldn't wait to get away from him but was afraid that I needed him. I pushed the sad thoughts away, took another look up at the moon and then crawled back into my single bed and fell sound asleep.

The next morning we had another long walk on the beach, yoga on the balcony and a swim: my routine. Megan didn't want to be seen in a swimsuit. I couldn't believe it but that was the story. So her routine omitted the swim and focused on photography. Excited to check in at La Vita e Bella, we ate, filled the car and went to town for money. There were about 6 people in front of us at the ATM. We waited patiently in the sun and when I was next, Amador showed up. He was happy and smiled, kissing me on the cheek this time and Megan as well. Lakra howled to see him, but didn't hump his leg. I got nervous but tried to ignore it.

When it was my turn, I was somehow afraid and couldn't move. But Megan said, "Your turn," opened the door to help me in and then closed it behind me, staying outside with Lakra and Amador. I sighed and withdrew what I could to pay the hotel. The whole time, I tried to keep my back to the window so Amador couldn't see.

I told Amador we were going to check in and said *hasta luego* as Megan and I walked toward the car. But in the middle of the parking lot, he caught up with me and asked if I had thought much more about the Jeep. I told him I didn't need to. His mood changed and although I didn't see it, I could feel it. He took my arm and came very close to me as he took his sunglasses off so I could see his eyes. Megan waked ahead of me not realizing I had stopped.

Amador looked down at me and said, "You gonna help me get that Jeep," and he squeezed my arm.

I didn't say a word.

He raised his voice, swearing at me in Spanish, "*Puta*, you gonna do that for me *perra* because I do stuff for you."

People in the parking lot looked at us. I got embarrassed. Megan turned, noticed us and started to walk toward us with the dog. Amador kept squeezing my arm until it hurt. I tried to wiggle free and asked him to stop.

Loudly he told me, "*Puta*, I need the papers and if you don't give me them I gonna give you trouble."

Then he let me go.

My arm hurt but I was not taking his shit. I told him he would never see them and he got furious.

He threw the glasses onto the ground breaking them and yelled, "*Pinche puta perra*" but then softly, close to my face, looking me in the eyes with his eyes absolutely wild, "You no help me I gonna plant drugs in your room and tell the police. Then you have big problems and you really gonna need me."

I looked at him and felt my eyes narrowing.

Megan got to me and touched my shoulder saying, "hey, what is going on here?" more to Amador than to me.

She took my shoulders and led me away saying, lets get going, and she, Lakra and I walked to the car. Her intervention released Amador's grip on me emotionally.

But he kept staring and then when we got to the car he yelled to me, "*Puta*, remember what I said."

I felt the eyes of the entire parking lot on me: the *puta*, the whore. I shifted into reverse with the idea of hitting him but then changed my mind and pulled out into the traffic and drove home.

"Now that was something," my cousin said.

I started to laugh and then couldn't stop.

"Hold on tiger," Megan told me and I finally stopped laughing and started to talk, non-stop, about what he had said to me. When I finished, I patted the dog. We were both silent. Finally, Megan said he was all talk with very little follow through. But I knew how determined he was to get that car. And I knew that when he was determined, there was very little that could stop him. I didn't tell Megan but I was really afraid he would pull some stupid shit and at least get the police interested in me. And any more attention in Tulum was the last thing I wanted. We took the bags up to the room and dropped them there before going down again, locking the door and taking a walk on the beach as the sunset reflected in the clouds.

"So beautiful," I said to my cousin.

She said, "Yes it is. But there are a million gorgeous places in the world."

The night before she left, we started to make a plan to find them as Lakra ran ahead of us at the edge of the water.

That night, we discussed options. There was so much to do. I told Megan I had always wanted to drive across the county. We could bring Lakra and take photos the whole way back to the US. I had actually been thinking of that trip when I moved there. But between the bad press on Mexico and the fact that I would have to do the trip alone, I had put the idea on hold. But I still had that dream. We planned to leave when Megan had to go anyway. The time had gone so fast. We would go to the airport, see what the rental car would charge and if we could cross the border in it. If we could take the car, we would, and cancel Megan's flight and get started.

It was a great plan and would be a great adventure. Once we got the OK on the car, we would plan a beautiful route, take loads of photos and publish them in an oversized photo book called, "Escape from Paradise." I slept well that night knowing I had a way out.

We took Lakra to the Vet for her shots and papers so she could come. Juan remembered Megan. As we left she said to me, "Now he would be a great man for you".

I laughed and told her he was hardly interested.

"Plus he is too nice for me", I joked.

She shook her head as we wandered toward the main avenue to window shop and pass the time.

We ate in town that night, It felt risky but Megan laughed it off saying, "are you afraid of an A sighting?"

I laughed "no" but I was paranoid.

We went back to the hotel to pack our bags and get ready to go early in the morning. We didn't check out since I had paid another 5 days. But we were ready. First stop was the rental car agency. I asked him about taking the car to the US and he smiled nicely and said that it was not possible.

He told me, "You would need to leave the car at the border and walk across."

I laughed and asked him if he was serious. He assured me he was and told me there was another Hertz rental car agency on the other side where I could rent another to continue in the States.

I asked the magic question, "how much?"

He looked at some tables, checked his computer, pushed some buttons and came up with the number of $5285.50 US. I laughed nervously and asked him to repeat it. He did. I asked if that was only to the border or all the way. He smiled patiently and told me that was the cost to leave the car at the border. From there, I could rent another on the US side to drive in the US. I sighed, said thank you and went back to report to Megan who was waiting with Lakra in the car. I smiled and shook my head no. I told her the bad news and we both got very quiet.

"I guess we should go check in for your flight," I said sadly.

We took the car around to the terminal, checked in and then waited in the restaurant and shared a chicken club sandwich with fries, my comfort food. Something about French fries with catsup always made me feel better. I brought Megan to the security checkpoint and we hugged.

She told me, "It is still a great idea, the book, your stories, my photos. It would be really something."

I was starting to cry and she hugged me and said, "So lets do it another time soon," before she told me to be careful and to call if I needed anything.

She reminded me I could come to their house and bring Lakra. She assured me they would even send me a ticket.

Before she hugged me one more time, she repeated what she had told me so many times, "Stay away from that guy. He is a train wreck and I don't want you to be on board when he crashes."

I gave her a hug and then she walked to her gate. I watched the last of her disappear and then turned to go back to the car wondering how I could get off the train before it was a wreck.

Chapter 22

I cried most of the way from Cancun back to Tulum. When I wasn't crying I was talking to Lakra about the unfairness of it all. At least we still had a room at *La Vita e Bella*, I told her. When I got in, I brought my suitcase back upstairs, ordered a pizza and glass of red wine to go and went to the room with the dog. The night sky was full of fast moving clouds and the moon was about ¾ full. One of those stellar nights when the moonlight comes and goes as the clouds pass over it. I could hear the surf and when the waiter came with my pizza and wine, I gave Lakra her dinner and we ate together watching the moon glistening on the water until it would turn to black as the clouds passed. The pizza was good and the wine always took the edge off my sadness. I enjoyed the privilege of where I was and I thought, "why should I let this one guy drive me away?"

The thought made me feel stronger. I didn't feel so helpless. I remembered my dream of building and hosting survivors and I reminded myself why I came to Tulum in the first place: to heal. It was not to be with Amador, it was to take back my life. I acknowledged that he was part of it, certainly, but not the only part. I remembered the other reasons I loved it there; the fact that I knew I could die in Tulum; also the hope that I wouldn't. The place made me feel alive and energetic and good. Just as I committed to taking back my project and staying to finish it, Amador knocked on the door.

I didn't answer. He walked out onto the sandy patio below so he could see if I was home. He called my name. I still didn't answer. He called again and yelled up for me to talk to him.

Then he said, "please."

I sighed heavily and went down to open the door.

I looked out and said, "What?"

He was calm, a very different man than in the parking lot. But I knew he could switch at any moment and I reminded myself that too, now I was alone.

"Baby," he said and he started to apologize saying, "I don' know what happens back there but I so sorry."

He came toward me to give me a hug and then he started to cry on my shoulder. I hugged him back and told him it was OK, realizing that is who I am, not weak but terminally kind.

He moved back to look at my face and told me, "I come to apologize but you were gone. All the bags, everything. I thought I would never see you again."

A switch went off in my head. "You came upstairs?"

He told me that the guy at reception opened the door for him. He continued to explain that when he came upstairs there was nothing there. I made another mental note to move soon or at least to always carry my cards and money. I asked him what he needed now.

He said, "just you." He came closer. "Joanne, *te amo*."

I repeated that he had a funny way of showing it.

He smiled and apologized but put the blame on me again and said, "You make me so crazy." Then he asked to come upstairs.

I told him I wanted to be alone. He said just for a little while. He wanted to talk to me. I hoped we could discuss things and so conceded. We went up and sat on the bed and watched the moon on the water with Lakra. Absurdly, I felt better with him there. The voice in my head said, "this is fucked up" and, for once, I agreed.

After awhile of talking about nothing since he wouldn't discuss, "sad" things, he laid his head on my shoulder. Then he let himself fall onto his back with his head on my lap and fell sound asleep. I stroked his hair and wrapped the little blond tipped curl around my fingers, looking out at the moon and thinking. Lakra started to snore from under the bed. I smiled because in that moment, I somehow felt whole. And I smiled not only because it felt good but also because I knew it was something that I couldn't maintain.

Life was sometimes cruel. But I told myself it was also very beautiful. I reminded myself that it was my fault for not accepting people the way they were. Just then, Amador woke up and sat up quickly, putting his elbow into my thigh.

"Ouch!"

"Sorry, baybe, sorry I hurt you."

Then he started to look around, paranoid, and asked me if anyone had come for him. I told him no. He started again with that same paranoid line of, "they coming for me" and then, "they looking for me" and then he said he had to go. I figured it was the drugs.

"No, Amador, nothing will happen to you."

But he kept looking around like a trapped animal and finally said, "I gotta go."

I tried to calm him down to the point of holding his arms and telling him that no one was there and that he was fine. But then he got mean and told me I had no idea. And then I started to get paranoid and it became a circle of anxiety that fed on itself.

He was getting more agitated as he looked for the door and said, "I going. Don' worry. I be back. Can you give me 200?"

I wasn't even shocked by it anymore. I didn't get mad. "No Amador. I don't have 200."

He accepted it and nearly ran down the stairs. I watched him almost run across the sand patio in front. He reminded me of a werewolf from the movies, running away from the daylight in the shadow of the moon. I checked the door to make sure it locked when he left. Then I put a chair in front of it, patted Lakra and got ready for bed. I knew he would not be back. And then I prayed that I was right.

I didn't see Amador for the next 2 days. I was happy and I noticed it. I walked the beach in the morning with Lakra, me with my feet in the water and her hugging the edge of the sea but never letting even one paw enter. We had coffee together at Mar Caribe and sat by the tour boats and watched the waves. The weather was cool and clear. A north wind had blown in that calmed the sea and cooled the air so that you looked for the sun to get truly warm. The water was often warmer than the air. It was heaven. The nights were so cool that I took the blanket off Megan's bed to be warm. Lakra and I ate pizza most nights there in the room, back to my executive days of asking for room service in hotels rather than dining alone in a restaurant. I wanted to let as few people in this small town know I was there as possible. Lakra seemed to enjoy it and so did I.

One morning, feeling brave, Lakra and I took a drive to town for breakfast for a change. We sat on the avenue, Lakra under my table and me sipping a cappuccino. I thought it would be a great photo and wished that someone would take it for me. But then I remembered I had no camera. Amador had "lost" it long ago. Anyway, I told myself that some day I would paint the picture.

As I finished my coffee, Amador sat down in front of me. It was uncanny the way he could find me and the way he didn't care if I wanted to see him or not. I thought to myself, what a gift it must be to think that everyone wants to see you. I was so the opposite, always hoping I wasn't interrupting or bothering people. Amador assumed that everyone wanted to see him and that he could interrupt anyone's day or moment to have his needs met. He faced me with a big smile on his face. We exchanged greetings and then he asked me the usual, "What you doing now?" I told him I had a few errands to run. He asked me if I had a place to stay long term. I admitted that I had not found anything. I hadn't really been looking but I had asked around more than a few places. The ones I had found were horrible and the ones that were marginally acceptable were much more than I wanted to pay. He told me he knew of a place and that he could take me there now. The owner was working on it and he was there. He said, "It worth a look." I agreed.

I took Lakra's leash and we walked south on the avenue towards the end of town, past the police station, past several taco stands, past *La Cubana's* Bar and the little orange palapa called *Tacoqueto* where they made chicken stew and cheap Mexican breakfasts and lunches. We continued past a huge excavation site that was totally overgrown and looked like a sink hole from a decade ago. Finally, we took a left into the heart of the pueblo. There was a new hotel on the left called Luna that looked more like a boarding house than hotel. We walked past the hotel where on the other side of the road was a run down shack with a bunch of cars and chickens in the yard. Next to it was a 2 story *palapa* with a 2 meter high concrete orange wall around it and a small dark arched wooden entry. The house occupied the corner of the street. "This is it," Amador said. He knocked confidently on the door.

Lakra barked as we waited, pulled on her leash and escaped to chase the hens. I went after her as the owner came to the door. I caught her and came back but he and Amador had been talking. I hated that I wouldn't know what Amador had said about me. I introduced myself and Lakra. His name was Augustin. We shook hands, entered and took a look around. It was a cool house, not terribly efficient but interesting. There was a wraparound concrete couch in the living room as you entered and to the right.

A small galley kitchen was tucked in to the right and opposite was a small bath and shower. Behind the kitchen was the bedroom. It was dark but the owner assured me there was more light if you opened the windows, which had shutters on them. I could not imagine less. The bathroom was clean and outside it, there was a ladder to a balcony with a meter diameter circle cut into the extended outside wall as you went up. It looked out over nothing and everything. The entire dirty *pueblo* lay there for view. Across the street was a tarpaper shack where a woman was cooking over a fire, behind her was a flat screen television. There was a police kiosk one block over on the corner and the cemetery was behind the police station. A nice house sat directly in front with lots of kids playing outside it.

I went downstairs as Amador called me to the garden just off the living space. It was small with an empty fish pond. Augustin said he would fill it. There were loads of plants and then a spot to park a car with an automatic door that opened and closed like in the real world. I smiled and reminded myself that this was very real. The owner asked me when I wanted the place. I told him as soon as possible. He told me it could be ready December 1st and that he could rent it long term for 800 US. Then he reminded me that didn't include gas or electric and I told him I understood. But I told him I only wanted it for 3 months since I was building a place on the beach and hoped my place would be ready by February. He told me that was fine and to get him a deposit soon. We shook hands, exchanged contact information and I had a place. I thought that it could be a great temporary home and at least I could cook, and take out all my stuff. I gave Amador a hug and said thanks.

He said it was a pleasure, as he was accustomed to doing, rolling the "r" of pleasure. I said goodbye not really wanting to know where he was going and started walking with Lakra. This time I went slowly to get to know my neighborhood. It was funky, down to the Avenue and then some. Lakra barked at several dogs but she didn't try to get away. It was as if she were saying hello. We walked happily back to our car, girls on an adventure. I felt positive, good and happy. We asked to stay for awhile longer at *La Vita e Bella*. They said our cabana was booked in less than a week but that we could move to one closer to the water for the same rate. I was glad we wouldn't have to move far and happy I finally had a place to make a temporary home.

Chapter 23

Lakra and I spent four wonderful days in the little apartment above the "Confusion Shop" at *La Vita e Bella*. Amador didn't visit. I enjoyed my solitary existence surrounded by the sea and the sand and relatively kind people who had learned my name. We finally moved to a cabana on the north end of the property in the newer part of the hotel that lacked the charm of my attic place above the shop as well as the interaction with the staff. But it didn't lack for access to the Caribbean. I had a hammock in the palms and a direct ocean view. The bath was private and even though it was smaller, I told myself it was only for a week and I should enjoy it.

The week included Thanksgiving. I had never been a huge holiday person but if I had to pick a favorite holiday, Thanksgiving would be it. Filled with food, family, friends and fun with no excessive gift buying, it was my sort of holiday. I had no children and was not a huge shopper or baker so Christmas was always a bit of a challenge. Thanksgiving was generally a nice day for me. I could make a grand statement bringing wine and some specialty store dessert that you could only find in the city.

I had not been on my own for the holidays in about 20 years. That was in Germany where I had gone to visit Helen in Ireland. I had her big Irish family to celebrate with. This year would be different. I would be alone but for Lakra. But I vowed to be thankful for life first, then for the gift of Tulum and the possibility of life here. I told myself that soon everyone would be coming to my houses and they would all see how fabulous the place was. I reminded myself to enjoy the solitude and kept reading my daily affirmations for strength. The wind picked up from the north again right before Thanksgiving, bringing a cold front to Tulum. I laughed at people talking about it. I knew cold and 45F was not cold. What I forgot was that I was basically living outdoors. The thatched roof was hardly insulated and the glass doors and windows were not double paned. Even if they had been, the walls consisted of cement over poles with gaps at the top where the roof met the cement. The wind rode up the wall and into the cabana.

The first night I put on all my clothes and pulled Lakra into bed with me. All I had was a bedspread and thin polyester sheets. Once the sun came up the next morning, Lakra and I ran over the cold concrete floors to the beach to catch the sun and head north to Don Cafeto's for a hot extra large coffee. I managed to get a polyester filled comforter that served a little bit better against the cold the following night. But I was amazed that 45F could be so cold. I

wrapped Lakra in the towels and put her on a pillow on the floor.
Just as I fell to sleep, curled into a fetal ball and hugging my knees, I
heard a knock on the window. I ignored it not wanting to lose the
heat I had trapped into my center. Whoever it was knocked again and
then tried to open the door. Freaked out and afraid, I huddled deeper
into my fetal ball. Then I heard that scratchy voice call my name. It
was Amador. I sighed knowing he would not stop until I answered.
The voice on my shoulder advised, "Try it once. Don't answer."

I considered it, and relaxed back into my ball. Lakra didn't move
either and for a moment I thought he had gone away. But then
another knock and my name louder and all of a sudden, I knew, I
wanted to go. I wanted to see him.

I unraveled myself and wrapped the comforter around me and
went to the door. He was there with a woman. They both wore grey
hoody sweatshirts with grey sweatpants and for a moment I
wondered if I were dreaming and some elves had come to visit.
Amador smiled and pointed to the door to open it.

I opened it a crack and he pushed his way in saying "baybe it's
fucking freezing out there."

The girl came in after him. They were both stoned. Amador
looked at me and told me he brought this girl to give me a massage.
She was great, he told me and he said he wanted me to have that
experience. I told him thanks but it was too cold to be on a table
naked. He shook his head seeming to understand but said nothing. I
asked him if that was all. He said yes, that he had come to give me
that massage. His eyes were red and sort of rolling in his head, as if
he couldn't focus. The woman never introduced herself and with her
hood on I couldn't really see her face but she looked familiar. I was
pretty certain I had seen her in town with Amador and his buddies.
Regardless, I said thanks but perhaps another time.

Amador stood there. So did the woman. There was an awkward
moment of silence and I waited for someone to say something.
Finally Amador started to laugh and said that then they might be
going. He said she could come back tomorrow if I wanted. I told him
it was cold in the day too. He said that if there were sunshine she
could work in the sun. His words were weird somehow as if he had
no connection between his brain and his mouth, or at least the
connection was moving so slowly that it altered his speech. I told him
okay. As I suspected, he asked for money. I felt heartsick and almost

threw up on him but, instead, told him no. He said please and I told him again, "no".

Then he shrugged and said, "You no want to help me, ez okay."

His tone was not okay, however. It was that almost threatening tone I had begun to recognize and the girl started to giggle. They were giving me the creeps. He looked down at the floor and said, "Yeah. It okay."

He smiled and said, "We go now, okay? Maybe you get a massage tomorrow."

His words were still weird. Then he left. For a moment the girl stood there like she was going to be invited in, but when she noticed he was gone, she followed. They disappeared into the night. I went onto the deck and looked for them but there was no sign. I looked up at the stars and pinched myself to check to see if I was dreaming. I was not, it hurt and I didn't wake up. I went back inside and patted Lakra who had not moved. Her sense of who people were in the moment was uncanny. She was like one of those shamans who only saw energy, or who say they only see energy. Except, Lakra really did. She knew when not to make a move or recognize a person. I reminded myself to take my cues from her as I took my quilt and crawled back into my fetal position to fall soundly asleep.

The next day dawned magnificently: Thanksgiving. I stretched under my blankets and said thank you to God for the day. I rolled to one side and saw the water, it was even more blue than normal. Something about the cold and the north wind made it even more spectacular, deeper blue against the sand that seemed even whiter. I hurried out over the cold concrete floor to catch the sun in front of the cabana by sitting on the stoop. Lakra got up and did a down dog before coming to see me. She howled hello, as she always did and then went to pee in the sand, lifting her leg like a male. I watched her hustle away, rubbed my hands together and put my face to the sun to warm up. She came back and licked me on the face, asking for breakfast. I smiled, gave her a hug and got up to get her food. She howled until I put it down for her. I smiled until and after I did and said thank you for Lakra as well.

I found a warm sunny corner of the balcony to practice yoga and Lakra licked my face to pull me from savasana. I went with her to the waters edge. We turned left to Don Cafeto's for a coffee and what they called a croissant: heavy dough in the shape of a horn. I sat by the tour boats that had been pulled up onto the sand while Lakra looked for her dog pals. I enjoyed the croissant with strawberry jam and said thank you for every bite. The beach was wide and open with its hard packed pinky white sand so it was easy to walk. There were a few palms to offer shade but no one was looking for it in that moment. Everyone wanted the warmth of the sun.

Hippies crawled out of their tents to find it in their Guatamalan jackets and Indian Shirpa hats. The workers raking seaweed were wearing ski parkas and would stop every so many meters to move their face toward the sun and warm up a little more. The tourists in their bikinis and beach dresses were running to get as much of it as possible. Even Reyes the hammock man came down toward the water to be in the sun. Then he saw me and walked back toward reception with his head down. I felt a sad about that but it was his fault that he had jumped my fence. I had been more than kind to him and he knew it. I wondered about kindness and how my brother T-Bird had told me on more than one occasion, normally playfully but sometimes seriously, "Don't mistake kindness for weakness. Many people do."

A slow ache grew in my heart for my bro who normally would be running with me before a huge Thanksgiving dinner. Then I told myself to put it away and to remember that he would come see me and even maybe work with me here one day. I finished my coffee, called Lakra and walked back to the cabana with a plan to go to town for a roast chicken. After all, it was Thanksgiving.

As I was about to leave, Amador and that girl came up the path, still in their hoodies, talking to each other, not even noticing that I was in the door until they got to it. I waited. When they saw me they stopped and started to laugh.

I smiled and Amador said, "Hey baybe, she come back for your massage."

They were still stoned and I told them I was about to leave. Amador asked if I couldn't go later and didn't I want a massage. I thought about it and decided, yes, I could go later and I would love a massage. I asked where her table was. They looked at each other with shock on their faces. I laughed since it was something out of a Cheech and Chong movie, each one sort of asking the other, "you got the table?" and the other answering, "no, you got the table."

Until finally Amador told me that she could use the bed for a table. I told him no thank-you. I liked a massage on a table. They stood there stupidly and couldn't think of anything more to say. Sometimes stoners were so boring. I called Lakra and went to lock the door but she didn't want to come. Then I noticed Amador looked angry.

Lakra must have known something was up before he started but suddenly he was mumbling, "nothing good enough for you."

Then, the mumbling got a little louder. I called Lakra again but she wouldn't come out.

And Amador came closer to me and said loudly and to my face, "You think you so much better than everyone."

A statement but also a sort of challenge and I told him that I didn't. He wanted to argue and said "Oh yes. You do."

I told him, "Okay, whatever you say," and went in to get Lakra with the leash.

He followed me inside the cabana. I knew I had made a mistake. Lakra went under the bed. His friend stayed outside playing with her hair while looking at the ground.

Amador said, "Why you be like that?" repeating it over and over until I told him I was being honest.

I interrupted him and said loudly, "I do not want a massage on my bed from that woman."

He became quiet. Then he started to back out of the cabana saying, "If that how you feel. She a great masseuse but you can do what you want."

I was shaking but happy he was moving in the right direction. It was as if the storm inside him had passed.

He backed out, suddenly calm, saying, "I just trying to be nice like I hope you be with me but it okay. I think of another thing to be good to you. So you can help me one day, okay?"

I had the idea he was trying to leverage something and in that moment I knew. He was back onto getting the jeep out from the pound. I sighed and asked myself when it would end. But he left for that day.

He went to the balcony and touched the woman on the arm and said, "She no want a massage from you" and they left.

The woman didn't take it as an insult and told me, "another time sister, another time."

I felt like I had been transported to New Orleans with the

"sister" stuff. I watched them walk down the path until they were out of sight. I exhaled and turned to see Lakra coming out from under the bed to come with me. She walked up to me and touched my thigh with her head to give me a dog hug. I patted her and noticed that my hands were still shaking.

"Too much coffee" I told myself but knew that was not it. I locked the door and we walked the sandy path to the rental car to go to town.

We drove the *Avenida Tulum* looking for a lot of nothing. People were in sweaters and huddling over coffee in sunny spots. I stopped for a bottle of mediocre wine in the Mar Caribe Supermarket. No one had good wine in Tulum. Then I walked to *Pollo Bronco,* Fernando's favorite place.

I got a roast chicken to go. I asked for a roasted onion too, my favorite. I waited distractedly, hoping that Amador wouldn't find me. I loaded the car and stopped at Stop and Go for dessert: Teddy Grahams. Even if he charged almost $5 for a box that in the US cost about $2, I decided I was worth it. I had my Thanksgiving feast. I headed back to the beach. No "A" sightings. No issues. I would have a relaxing, if cold and solitary, Thanksgiving.

Lakra and I took a long walk on the beach before I took my Thanksgiving swim. The water was calm and warmer than the air. The sky was blue with puffy clouds floating by. When they passed over you could feel the temperature drop but then when the sun came back, you could bask in it. It was heaven until I got out. The chilly air enveloped me and gave me goose bumps so I ran for the shower and turned the hot water on full. It dripped out but at least it was hot and I squeezed my entire body under that one dripping column, nearly scalding the part of my body that caught the water directly but warming the rest of me. The steamy heat in the bathroom faded quickly as I dried myself, dressed in as many clothes as felt comfortable and took my feast to the deck and the hammock. Lakra laid under the hammock and I shared the roast chicken with her, drank the mediocre wine out of a regular glass and enjoyed the starry night.

I decided to call my sister since, after all, it was Thanksgiving. I needed to talk to a family member. They were having their dinner as well. I could hear the chatter and the laughter behind her voice on the phone. I became so homesick I started to cry.

"What am I doing here?" I asked my little sister.

She listened as I told her how messed up it was with Amador and what a hard time I was having. But I told her that I had found a place and would move in a week so at least I would have a home and my things. I rambled on and she listened. It came to a point where we both were laughing at how absurd it all was.

Then she said, "Fanny? You know you can come home whenever you want to. No one is judging you here, ok? We love you."

I started to cry again and she told me our favorite good bye line, "now go on, get out of here. I love you."

It was a sort of cult thing from the Saturday Night Live of our 20's and I repeated it back to her. We hung up. I cried envisioning my whole family at the table and my place empty. Lakra looked at me for more chicken. I fed the rest to her, poured some more wine and ate my Teddie Grahams under the stars that twinkled in the cobalt blue sky.

Chapter 24

I opened the gate and inhaled the peacefulness of my property. I had checked out of *La Vita e Bella* that morning and took a drive to my unfinished house. I noticed that the tranquility of the jungle side was different from the peace on the beach. Everything was a bit softer. I wanted to feel that soft "home" before I went to live in town. I had stopped making the daily trips to my house since they made me sad, so much left to do and so little progress. But I needed to touch it that morning. I walked around, wandered down the 50 meters to the back and climbed up to the top of that incomplete structure. There I talked to my dad and to God and cried a little. I finally pulled myself together, said thank you to the area and went to the bodega for the Elvis tray, my Spanish wine glasses and the Italian coffee maker. I started the generator to make sure it still worked and let it run while I loaded the car.

I finished, heard Amalio's cough and decided it was time to go to my house in town. The concept startled me a little. I could not believe I was moving to town but knew it was only temporary. I turned the generator off and went to lock the gate. As I fumbled with the chain, my neighbor, Irij, called hello to me. She was coming from the beach and waved. I waved back and she came over to speak with me. We saw each other from time to time but that was the extent of our relationship. She and her husband had crammed a small house into a third of the lot next to me. I couldn't help but disrespect them for it. It was built exactly on my property line and had pipes and cables running along the wall on my side creating the ugly vista I had tried to hide with a garden. Too, she had that New York thing going where they are so hip and so efficient that they always have somewhere to be and rarely time to say hello. Today was different, apparently.

"Hey," she said as she came up to me, "I wanted to invite you to meet some people tonight. We are making dinner in town."

I asked Irij what I could bring and she told me how to get there. It sounded like the place I had seen Moises and Amador ages ago in what they called the "scarey house." I didn't say anything since people had started to fix everything in Tulum. I decided to keep my story to myself. Irij told me she had to go, just like a New Yorker, but that she would see me around 8 p.m. I called Lakra who had wandered off toward the beach, finished locking the door and we headed home: to town.

We stopped at San Francisco for groceries: a little wine, beer in case I had company, coffee and some other basics before heading to my new house. I had picked the keys up when I had paid the rent and deposit two days earlier. Augustine didn't want to come to Tulum on Sunday. I pulled up to the garage doors and tried the clicker. It worked. Amazed, I pulled in and it closed behind me. Impressed, I got out of the car. Lakra jumped out after me. Together, we looked around the garden. There was a table for coffee in the morning with the wooden chairs I had seen carpenters selling in the street. They would put a bed on top of a bike or a wheelbarrow and then stack chairs and tables on top of it. It was an amazing balancing act and I wondered if some of them were drop outs from the circus that came to Tulum every year.

I was surrounded by some excellent tropical plants but the goldfish pond was still empty. It looked sad so I decided to ignore it. We unpacked our things, opened all the windows to let in light, put my favorite sheets on the bed and hung a few pictures to make the place mine. I decided to make a cup of tea and sit outside with Lakra.

We looked around and both thought, "now what." It was a weird feeling being off the beach. Instead of the sound of waves and Malio's cough, we had kids laughing and Mexican folk music coming from the neighbors. Often there was the sound of a car braking before the speed bump, or tope, just before the house. I sipped my tea and closed my eyes to bring back the sea. It was there in my mind and I meditated that way for a few moments, hearing the waves, feeling the breeze. I remembered that tomorrow I had to return the rental car. I knew that would leave us slightly stranded. I bent down and patted Lakra on the head and told her, "don't worry baby, we will work it out," before I went in to unpack.

About 7:30 p.m. I locked Lakra in and walked to have dinner with my neighbor's friends, exploring my neighborhood. It was funky. Leaving toward the left, you passed a couple of nice-ish houses and then came into a big square with an open area for sports and a huge palapa that I would later learn was the Mayan Church. They had a corral in front but no animals in it. There was an enormous tree on the right called a Ceiba that reminded me of a hobbit house. But the empty place in the trunk where a hobbit could enter was at that moment blocked by a drunk sleeping in that cozy crevice of this ancient, sacred tree.

On the far left were some apartments that looked like the getto: tar paper roofs, one place exactly next to the other, dirt floors and then a few shops in the front that reminded me of Chinatown in Boston with animals, mostly chickens, hanging from the ceilings. There was a bike maintenance shop and a place that repaired watches and a place that took passport photos. I passed a few taco places and a point in the road where a tree grew in the middle. The cars moved to either side to pass. I loved that they had let the tree grow in the middle of the road and smiled as I looked for a drunk at its base. Thankfully, there was no one and I continued past more small shops selling everything from sewing needles to holy candles embossed with the Virgin or Sacred Heart.

On the next corner, I found the place where Amador took me to get a fruit water in a bag. The same store, *La Michuacana*, also sold ice cream popsicles or "*paletas*." The area opened up across the street to a slightly unkempt park with soccer fields to the left and a Catholic Church on the right. I looked into the Catholic Church, almost wanting to enter. Thousands of flickering candles called me but people were going in for mass. I became nervous and felt decidedly foreign. I decided to go another time and continued to the next block, crossing an intersection to the main avenue. I passed a fruit stand on the corner and then a town office called *"ministerio publico."* That was my landmark. The house was one more block. I passed the Hotel Latino where I had stayed ages ago before Amador and I had bought the land. Just after the hotel, I saw the house and Irij's car. I went to the door and knocked. Before anyone answered I took a good look and realized that yes, it had been the "scarey" house. I hoped it was not so "scarey" anymore.

An attractive woman answered the door, saying "You must be Joanne. Welcome." She opened the gate and introduced herself as Kim and her husband, Felix. They were from Texas. She was perfectly made up and dressed up and appeared a little older than I was. But I couldn't tell how much. Her husband had grey hair, a charming smile and a welcoming way about him. It was the Texas thing. He told me "Y'all make yourself at home." I smiled, handed him the wine I had brought and he offered me a special cocktail as he led me through the house to their outdoor kitchen and bar. Irij and Filip were already there. Starved, I attacked the cocktail nuts and listened to their stories about driving from NY to Tulum in a van.

Just as they were telling me about crossing the border, a group of cool people came in. I felt totally out hipped by these *Chilango's* from Mexico City. Irij introduced me to Lina, her brother Roberto, their friend from Italy, Christian, Lina's sister Laura and another friend Angie. They were beautiful people and easy to talk to. Their English was slow and well accented. I felt I belonged. I could let my guard down. They weren't asking me for anything more than to interact and enjoy. We all had a few drinks before the food came out. We laughed and then ate like kings. Kim and Felix loved to cook and Lina was a chef in town. She brought some amazing *chile relleno* and chicken with a *mole* sauce. The flavors mixed perfectly with the good company. I had not had such a wonderful meal with such interesting people since I left the states. At about midnight, Irij and Filip gave me a ride home and waited until I got inside my house before driving away in their big cross country van. I felt cared for and gave Lakra a hug before I went to bed telling her, "not so bad for our first night in town."

I slept soundly until about 3 a.m. when I heard shouting from my neighbor's house. The noise had a drugged and drunk energy that was frightening. There were several voices yelling and then laughing. House music started. I put the pillow over my ears and tried to go back to sleep but it was impossible. Between the noise and my fear, I just laid there, pretending to sleep. But my mind played all the possible absurd scenarios over and over in my head. Frustrated, at 5:30, I got up and made coffee. The music stopped at 6 a.m. I started yoga at 7 in down dog with a slight hangover and began my life in the little pueblo of Tulum.

I began a pattern of writing, working at the internet café down the street and making a few friends with whom I was comfortable. But I had this subtle discomfort as if I could feel Amador around. I watched out for him, for his friends, for people who wanted to scam me or borrow money, or just know too much about me as if I sensed him taking account of what I was doing. There was a part of me that wanted to see him. I still wanted to see if he was OK, if he was alive or dead or in jail and too if he still even cared about me. I somehow felt I owed him that. I believed I should at least be his witness of sorts, in case he had any trouble. But there was a bigger part of me that didn't. And I would remind myself to listen to that part, to remember he was dangerous and that I didn't owe him anything or need him. However, those two voices were in constant conversation.

And in this small town where no one was anonymous, I generally felt that if Amador were not watching me, someone else was doing it for him. Sometimes, I told myself I was being paranoid but the sensation was still there. However, most days, coming back from shopping with Lakra close behind, I would arrive at the street where I lived without incident, no "A-sighting." I said hello to the kids playing in front of the house on the street. They looked at me as if I were an alien. I felt their parents watching from the doorway to make sure I didn't bother them. But once inside, I would open all the windows and relax. The house was dark and even with the windows open it felt slightly like a cave. But the garden received nice light and was warm. From the roof I could see the sunset and watch the stars come out and dream about finishing my project on the beach.

More than a week passed that way: totally uneventful, *"tranquilo."* I went to my house on the beach a few times by taxi. It felt strange to walk the beach without Lakra. Very few taxis would take her. Fewer wanted to drive the dirt road to my house. So I didn't go often. Lakra and I walked in town and explored around our neighborhood. She would follow me a little behind, like she used to on the beach. When dogs would run to attack her I would jump in and yell at them to get away. People looked at me as if I were crazy. Maybe they thought I was over reacting or doing the dog's work but I didn't let it stop me. Those townie dogs would not get my girl.

People still recognized Lakra on the street. I met some very interesting people that way. They would stare at her as she sat at my feet and then, after awhile, come over and call her. She would look up when they called her name and when I smiled, they would ask if it were Lakra. When I confirmed, they patted her and told me how they knew her: camping, a 3 day party on the beach where she slept with them, a month at "Santa Fe" beach where she shared their cabana. I loved the stories but more, I loved telling them she was mine now. And generally, they were all happy she had a home.

We settled into a fairly happy existence. I called the carpenter every day until he finally answered. He told me his car was still broken but that as soon as he had a truck he would bring my windows and doors. I asked him when that might be. He told me after Christmas since the mechanic had already gone back to Tabasco for the holidays. There were still 2 weeks before Christmas but he explained that the festival of the Virgin was December 12th. That was why I was seeing so many people on bicycles and running with T-shirts of the Virgin Mary. I pictured the mechanic in his car with a big statue of the Virgin on top and a torch out the window while he followed some poor bastard running all the way to Tabasco. He would not be back until around the 6th of January, the day of the 3 Kings. I hung up the phone and shook my head, almost amused. Lakra stretched and came to give me a hug, rubbing her head against my thigh. She understood that it was not easy. Then someone lit off a firecracker and she ran under the bed, trembling and afraid. It would be a long holiday season for both of us.

On one of my daily work trips to the internet, I had a message from my sister, Susan. I loved getting family mail and opened it before anything else. She told me she was coming to see me in January. I squealed and clapped my hands together. Half the place looked at me. The other half was wearing headphones and didn't notice. I apologized meekly, finished my work, paid the bill and headed home, floating with happiness. Lakra sensed my happiness and kept up, almost running along with me. As we crossed the street and took the left to my house, I noticed someone leaning on my front door. I slowed my pace and called to Lakra so that we could see who it was. I took a deep breath when I recognized Amador's silouette. I stopped, thought about changing direction but then decided to confront him. After all, it was my house.

He smiled and something about him brought back all the great memories and allowed me to temporarily forgot all the bad ones. When I got closer he said, "I been waiting on you for awhile."

He tried to kiss me but I turned my cheek. I said nothing and waited for him to speak.

His smile faded and he asked me, "You gonna invite me in?"

I hesitated for a second and he said, "Come on Joanne."

I stopped thinking and moved from my instinct. Company would be nice so I told him, "sure," and opened the door.

I asked him if he wanted a coffee while I put down my things. He opened the refrigerator and said he would rather have a beer. It was rude but rather than be impolite myself, I told him of course. I made coffee and sat on the couch while he walked around, looking at things as if he were casing the place or waiting for a moment to tell me something. Then he sat next to me like a child would and told me the place looked good as he took another swallow of beer. He was waiting for the right moment for something. But then, as if he couldn't wait any longer, he asked me if I was missing a car. I told him yes and no. I missed being mobile but I did not miss all the problems I had with the jeep. He reminded me that "we" had a car that was sitting in the pound. I shook my head and reminded him in detail about my experiences and expenses with it and told him "we" didn't have anything. I had a big loss. I watched him get angry then and wished I had never let him into my house. But there he was.

He finished his beer then and went to the fridge for another. I told him I had not offered him the second but he didn't care. He was walking around the place like a caged animal all of a sudden and lectured me on why I should help him get the car out of the pound. First he told me he had helped me get the house, as if I owed him. Then, he told me he needed to move and we could share the car. I asked him why would we share it if it were my car. He got angrier and told me that was the deal. I reminded him that he was not working with me any more. I stayed calm and tried to be clear. He stopped talking but his face stayed ugly.

He sat down next to me and said, "Listen. You know I got to move and you know you bought that car for me. I wanna get it and you can let me use it sometimes. I gonna help you more than you know, I promise. All you need to do is give me the papers and a little cash."

I hesitated, weary of the whole issue, wishing I had never bought the foolish car. I told him I would give him the papers but he stopped listening when I said I had no money. I felt it even though he was looking at me. I reminded him that it was still my car and I would need to use it at least 3 days a week. He told me that was OK. I went to get the papers from the closet and when I came close enough, he pulled them from my hands. Then, he walked out the door without saying goodbye. I closed the door behind him and leaned against it for a moment. I knew I had just lost the car. But then I told myself to get real, I never had it. At least for now, I had some peace.

Wednesday, I met Irij and Kim for cocktails at *la Cubana*. We sat downstairs on the sidewalk where you could sit until they were open upstairs. Irij asked me about Amador and I told her I still saw him as a friend. She looked down at her drink when I said it as if she believed otherwise. Kim asked if he was that guy who was always hanging around the crack house in her neighborhood. I cringed. Irij smiled. I said "perhaps." I still wasn't sure he was smoking crack. I mean, who did that?

I said as much to Kim. She asked how I knew him and I told her we were lovers for almost a year, more if you count distance relationships. She raised an eyebrow and told me she was surprised that a person like me was with him. I hated the classist tone and told her so. I told her he wasn't always so abusive with drugs and that he had helped me a lot when I was first starting here. Then I changed the subject to my project on the beach. We talked a little about what had brought us all Tulum. The common thread was freedom, although the concept was different for each of us.

I got bored after awhile and told them I needed to leave. I didn't want any more questions about my life.

As we stood to go, Kim apologized for sounding class conscious but told me, "You seem so together and strong. You don't need an addict pulling you down, take it from me."

I wondered how she knew but decided to forgive her. I liked her. For one thing she was right on, telling me how she felt without working around things. And she was more sensitive than she appeared. She was like a big sister that I certainly could use in this small town. We left committing to see each other again soon.

The next day I was walking along the *Avenida* with Lakra when a car pulled up behind us and beeped. I grabbed Lakra, attached her leash and got onto the sidewalk to let it pass, cursing at how rude some drivers were. Then I looked at the car. It was Amador in the jeep, smiling that little boy, happy man smile that I loved. I grinned and he pulled over and asked me if I wanted a ride. I told him I really was not going far. He said to please get in. I hesitated but then decided to take the ride and let Lakra in the back. I sat up front with him and congratulated him on getting the car back. Then, I asked if I could take it to the beach. He told me he was busy, but tomorrow I could take it. I did not believe him but congratulated myself for asking. We talked and laughed. When he was in a good mood, he was still wonderful. But the voice in my head told me, "And when not, absolutely not." But in this moment he was happy so life was beautiful.

He asked me if I wanted an ice cream and he parked. I had almost forgotten how good it felt to do things with someone. It was wonderful to have an ice cream with him on the avenue with Lakra sitting under our feet. Then he asked me if I wanted to watch a movie. I finished my ice cream and thought it would be nice. Believing his good mood would last, I agreed. We got back into the car to go to the video store but when he turned the key in the ignition, nothing happened. He tried again. And again. Still nothing. I got uncomfortable as he started to swear and sweat. I got out of the car and took the dog. His attitude frightened me. Finally he stopped trying and looked at me, standing outside with the dog. I apologized for no reason but the fact was that I was sorry it was happening. He told me, "not your fault" and then smiled and said, "but at least it is out of the *coralon*." I agreed and started to walk away with Lakra but he called to me to wait. He suggested we walk to get a movie and later he could have a mechanic come for it. I hesitated but he said, "please." I said OK and we walked down the *Avenida* to a video store by the bus station.

I waited on a bench out front with Lakra while he chose a film.

Lakra lay under the bench next to my brown suede backpack. The pack closed loosely on the top with a tie and I took out my journal, placed my wallet inside and rested my feet on top of the pack. I wrote and watched the people coming and going to the bus station in the heat under the blue sky. I was imagining their destinations when Amador called me in to see his selections. I tied Lakra up, grabbed the pack and went in.

We decided on two videos and he asked me to pay. I reluctantly took money from my bag, he looked inside and asked me for another 20 for popcorn. I handed him the money and went back outside trying to let go of feeling used. I rested my backpack on the tree that was behind the bench and leaned on it, resting my head. When Amador finally came out, I got up, stretched, put it on my back and we started to walk, Lakra behind me with Amador. After a little while, he told me he wanted to take a taxi. His feet hurt. I laughed at him, started to argue but then gave up. Unlike with me, for Amador, the taxi driver allowed Lakra on the floor and we started the 4 block drive to the house.

I had place my backpack on my lap in front of me and let Lakra sit on my feet. Amador put his arm around me and I leaned into him, feeling a little weird but a little good. Then the weird part took over so I leaned forward and looked into my pack for my wallet to make sure I had enough to pay the cab. It wasn't there. I dug deeper since there was a bunch of stuff in there but still, no wallet. I got nauseous and checked again. It was the wallet I had chosen with Sheba and Paul to carry all my money to Mexico. I had everything in there. The Iranian salesman's voice echoed in my head telling me about the security of the clip. Normally I wore it around my neck butI had been careless and had thrown it into my backpack to walk home.

I told Amador, "I've lost my wallet."

His smile faded and he said, "What?"

I told him that I couldn't find my wallet as I looked behind me on the seat, under Lakra, everywhere in that little space.

He asked the driver to take us back to the video store. I ran in to ask but they didn't have it. I was out of my mind. All my credit cards, my passport and driver's license were there. I had no idea how I had lost it. I wanted to cry but didn't dare. Amador had enough money to pay the taxi and when we got out at the house he started to yell at me telling me how could I be so careless with all my things. I told him I didn't need a lecture. He threw the videos onto the bed and called me a stupid bitch. I asked him to leave. He did, happily and fast and I locked the door behind him.

Then I sat down to cry, wondering what I would do. I ignored the knock on the door as Amador called my name and apologized for being an ass. He went to the garage door by the garden and called there and then went back to the front door and knocked again, called again and apologized again. Finally, I opened the door and looked at him as if to say "what." After the few moments of awkward silence, he told me that he was sorry but he got crazy and annoyed. I told him it was a hell of a time to leave me. He apologized, reminding me that he was an asshole. I told him I knew. Then I waited in silence to see what he wanted. Finally, he offered to go to the police station and file a report. Perhaps I would get my bag or my passport back. Too, I knew I needed a police report for filing my lost credit cards. I started to cry. Amador came over, held me and said not to worry, that it would all be OK. I started to sob because I was not sure it would be. I had nothing. I couldn't even pay for a phone call and I told him so. He said he would help me and not to worry. But I wondered how this beach bum who never had anything other than a nice smile and sometimes a great attitude could help me.

Chapter 25

I stood in front of the desk where the police officer was filling out paperwork by hand and filing it in a cardboard box below his desk. When he looked up, I explained that my wallet had been stolen. He looked at me suspiciously and then looked at Amador and asked my relationship to him. "*Amigo*," I replied, for once happy to say the word. Amador wanted to correct me but didn't dare. After all, I made him crazy and we could not be together. He had told me so on more than one occasion. If I was learning to accept the "*amiga*" status, he could too.

The officer gave me some forms and Amador helped me fill them out. I brought them back to the officer who stamped them, put one in the box under his desk, one in the basket on his desk and gave one to me. I waited for him to say something but he didn't. Finally he told me I could go saying they would call if they found anything. I said "*gracias*" and left the building tying to figure out my next steps: cancelling the credit cards was first, calling home was the second, asking for help would be the third. But then I realized asking for help would be first. I asked Amador if he had money for the internet. He emptied his pockets to find 30 pesos, about $3 US and gave me 20, telling me he needed something. I wanted to cry. That voice on my shoulder started talking, "You wanted a beach bum, right?" I told it to shut up and tried to stay focused.

I thanked him for the help and told him I would see him later. I needed to start fixing the mess I was in. He asked me if I wanted company, but I told him no. I had a strong intuition that told me not to let him watch me filing the reports on the cards. I found it weird but I followed it. Lakra came with me instead. I managed to complete things in 5 pesos worth of internet time. We walked home together with 15 pesos in our pockets. I doubted Amador would come back and was unsure if I really wanted him to. I had this unnerving feeling that he was somehow responsible. I made dinner with whatever we had in the fridge and obsessed over what to do next.

I needed to go to the US Consul in Cancun, but without my cards and my license it would be difficult to rent a car. Without money, it would be impossible to hire a driver. I had a map and I had found a booklet of checks from my US bank. I was hoping that the consul would cash one so that I could have money and replace my passport. I hoped they would accept the copy of my passport as identification. I had a copy of the police report so they would know I was legitimate. Too, I believed they would allow me to call my mom and let her know what had happened. She could forward the replacement cards when they came. That was what consulates were for right? Helping the citizens of their country.

As I sifted through my folders I found a credit card for That Barry Girl foundation and a second license. I had lost one before and then, as is the way, once I received the new license found the old one again. I squealed with joy realizing I could rent a car. I walked to the Hertz Rental Car agency where I had rented cars so many times before and asked for a deal. Rodrigo, who was nearly a friend by now, gave me a red Atos. It was a rollerskate of a car and as I was leaving, car keys in hand, he called after me to stop putting the dog in my cars. They were full of dog hairs when I returned them. I smiled, said nothing and went to take Lakra from the bike rack where she had been tied and slipped her into the back seat.

Early that next morning, I left for Cancun. About 2 and a half hours later, I found the consul within a maze of shopping malls and office buildings on the outskirts of the hotel zone. Driving in Cancun was a nightmare. I was exhausted by the time I arrived. All I wanted was to stop at the Starbucks I had passed and get a latte. But I had no money. I hated that sensation. The voice on my shoulder told me, "Get used to it" as I entered the US Consul in Cancun sure they would help me. With optimism, I took a number and a seat. I waited a short time before a youngish Mexican man called me.

I spoke with him about my situation but he looked at me without emotion and said nothing. I took out my checks, prepared to write one but he cut me off saying, "We don't do that sort of thing, madam." It was as if someone had let the air out of my balloon. I stuttered and then asked him how he could help me. He told me I should call my family. I asked him if he could help me make a call. He said flatly, "no." My eyes narrowed and I went from nervous tourist to US Citizen bitch and I asked him what he could do for me. He told me that basically he couldn't do much. He didn't apologize. He only explained that the Cancun office was not a full service consulate. I interjected, "obviously."

He ignored my remark and told me their role was to answer questions and direct tourists to the police. He continued to say that with the copy of my passport, I had the right to enter the US as a citizen. He suggested that I buy a ticket within Mexico using cash, where I would not need identification, and get to the border. There, I could walk across into my country and get my family to help me. I was stunned. I couldn't even answer him bitchily. I asked him genuinely if he knew geography. He shook his head yes and then looked at some papers on his desk to ignore me. I told him that my family was from the north-eastern US and it was a very long walk from the border to Boston, Massachusetts. I stood there and waited for him to suggest something. He didn't.

He looked back at me and said "You might have better luck if you go to the consulate in Merida. They have a full office and can at a minimum process your request for a replacement passport."

I put my checks back into my bag, said thank you and walked away, absolutely devastated.

I cried most of the way back to Tulum. I still had 15 pesos so I went to the house, had a peanut butter sandwich and then took Lakra to the internet. I logged on, got into my Skype account and called my mother. When she answered I started to cry. I told her what had happened and where I was and blurted out everything to her. The woman in the internet was listening but I didn't care. My mom, of course, was sympathetic. She was my angel and asked how she could help. I inhaled deeply, told her I needed some money to get everything sorted and that I could pay her back as soon as I got my next paycheck. I hated to but I asked my mother to send me money from Western Union. I knew the place she would have to go since I had been there to send money to Amador.

It was about half an hour from her house and while not at all the getto, the people who waited for Western Union were not the people my mom was used to being around. I pictured her with her blue wool suit, Perry shoes, and blond hair in a ponytail waiting in the line with foreigners sending money home, welfare recipients and the unemployed to send me 600 US. I hated myself for putting here there. But I did it. She promised she would go the next day. I said thank-you more than a few times and then we had our historic long good-byes filled with "love you, love you, love you" until we had to count to hang up the phone simultaneously. I felt blessed to have her on my side and wondered why I had put myself so far away.

The next few days were full of organizing and travel. Irij helped me pick up the money after I remembered that I could not receive it without a passport. Fortunately, I caught my mom before she had waited in line with the welfare people and the immigrants. After several iterations of the spelling, she put the money in Irij's name and I reminded her she had to carry cash.

"Oh my," she said in her little correct voice, "That is a lot to carry around."

I heard the nervousness in her tone and wanted to crawl under a rock but convinced myself it would be a big adventure for her.

Irij was kind enough to wait the 30 minutes in line to pick up the money and come to Merida with me. It was a forced trip to a beautiful Spanish Colonial city, full of culture and art. But I knew the consul there would not cash a check either. At least I had That Barry Girl Foundation card to pay the passport fees, food, gas and hotel. We would miss any shopping in the *mercados* of Merida, but managed to buy some great veggies that were unavailable in Tulum. In 6 weeks

I would have my new passport. I counted the months and held back tears as visions of an unhappy Christmas alone in a rental house, poor in a poor pueblo ran through my mind. But Irij told me it would be OK and we talked the entire way back to Tulum and became friends on that trip.

I dropped her at her house and dashed home to mine to find Lakra waiting. She ran outside to pee before inhaling her food. At least she had water. I consoled myself that I was not such a bad owner. It felt somehow strange to be penniless but I decided I would be OK. I made a tea, wrote in my journal, and then started to cry. Life seemed to be crashing down on me and I couldn't see what I was doing wrong. Then that voice on my shoulder spoke up and told me to relax, reminding me that at least I had shelter, food and clothing, quoting Mazlov's hierarchy of needs from Grad school. I smiled. Laughing always helped. I went to the roof to see the stars and thank God for being alive.

The next few days were uneventful. No A sightings. I had a drink with Kim and Irij again. They bought. Kim invited me to Christmas at her house. They were cooking an entire pig and, although I found it disgusting, I wanted to be with people I liked. I accepted. We would celebrate on the 24th, in Mexican fashion. I reluctantly returned the rental car, afraid that I would never be able to pay my credit cards but knowing I would miss it. Walking home from the Hertz agency, I felt broke and sensitive to the holiday consumer spirit in which I could not participate. As I passed one of the bars on the avenue that had karaoke 24 hours a day, I heard my name. I stopped and turned to see Amador come running out to say hello. I was happy to see someone, even if I was dubious about him. He invited me in for a beer but I told him I had no money and, in case he didn't remember, I didn't drink beer. He looked at me as if he cared and told me he would like to buy me a margarita.

In that moment, I realized why I hadn't seen him in awhile. He had money. I wondered how. But I didn't go to the place that suspected him of robbing me. I couldn't. I exhaled and looked into his glassy brown eyes, let my eyes drift to the blond tips on his hair and then to his white smile. I accepted because I really wanted to have a drink at a bar with a man. And I liked being in this dive bar called Don Karonte's that was weird and different and interesting. And I liked being with Amador because he was pretty weird, definitely different and, sometimes very interesting. The bar was just a roof and a wall in the back and the air cleansed it of cigarette smoke and probably the smell of urine. There were a few sleezey people and a big screen that displayed bubbles passing by until someone decided to sing.

The drinks came. I relaxed and allowed myself to enjoy a moment or two of voyeurism as two drunks came to the microphone and started to sing Sonny and Cher, "I Got You Babe." We laughed. I actually started to sing along. It felt good and fun and easy until Amador asked if he could come home with me. I stopped singing, trying to understand what he meant. He had a half smile on his face. I decided not to understand. It was too much to take in right then. I was having fun, tequila was running through my veins and I was finally comfortable with our *"amigo"* relationship. I dodged the question saying I didn't have much for dinner but he was welcome to visit.

He smiled and said, "No, baybe. I want to come home like living there wit' you."

I shook my head, not believing what I heard and told him slowly it was not a good idea. He took my hand and asked me why not. I looked at him and let silence speak for me. I thought, took a sip of my margarita, licked the salt on the rim and asked slowly if his girlfriend had kicked him out. He told me no: he missed me and that he was always better with me and went on about how much he really loved me and kept going on about "us" in one big run on sentence. He said all the things I wanted to hear and wanted to believe but in my more rational moments knew were impossible and untrue.

When he finished I told him again that I didn't think it was a very good idea and he said, "Please. Just give it a try."

I was so lonely and it felt good to think someone missed me and that I might not wake up and go to sleep every night alone. And it helped me believe I would not die alone. I inhaled, smiled and said OK.

But followed with, "just to see how it goes."

When I said it, that sense of life crashing down on me suddenly lifted. He kissed me, paid the bill and we walked home together, him holding my hand, me feeling as if I belonged. To what, I was still unsure. But it felt good. In that dusty borderline 3rd world village, I would at least have my 3rd world lover.

Lakra was happy to see him. She loved this guy when he was good, sort of like me. I made dinner and we planned to watch a movie but he fell asleep before we could even turn on the computer. I actually had visions of his face falling into the plate over dinner he seemed so exhausted. I tucked him in like a baby, worked and then crawled into bed with him. The second he felt me in the bed he rolled over, put his leg over me and pinned me to the bed. I felt safe and loved. Hours later when the party bus passed my house repeatedly, I didn't feel so annoyed. And when my crazy neighbors started screaming and partying around 4:30 a.m. I was not so afraid.

The next couple of days he went out to either work, which he never told me what that meant and I did not want to know, or he had to "do things." But we had coffee in the sunny spot outside in the morning and pretended to be a couple for those first few hours of those first few days. For two nights he came back, I made food and we slept. I noticed how much he was sleeping, as if he was catching up on something. We didn't have sex. We slept. The third day he didn't go out but I had to. I left him in the house sleeping and went to the internet café down the street, where the nice fat girl worked who was becoming my sort of friend. At least she would say hello when I came in and goodbye when I left. I didn't need much. The entire time leaving him in the house, I was nervous but couldn't figure out why. I hurried home rather than taking my time and stopping for the usual second coffee at *La Nave*.

When I got to the house, the door was open. I swore under my breath and went in calling Amador's name. Lakra met me but Amador didn't answer. There was a strange smell in the house, not dope, definitely not cigarettes. It was smokey and plastic-like but I didn't recognize it. I went sniffing around the house, calling Amador's name but still no answer. Then I heard a knock on the door. It was Amador. He asked why I had locked him out. I told him I didn't lock him out. I had locked the door behind me. Amador shrugged my response off and sat down on the couch and opened a magazine.

I went into the bathroom and when I put my paper in the trash-can, I noticed a can of coke in there. I pulled it out since we could sell aluminum and I love recycling and doing business with trash. As I did so, I noticed the can was bent to open the middle and there was a little screen in a hole that someone had made there. It was a pipe. I bent it once or twice, sniffed it and then it dawned on me that it was a crack pipe even though I had never seen one. In a flash, I knew what the smell was. The realization took my breath away.

Then I wanted to vomit and said out loud, "He has been smoking crack in my house."

I ran out of the bathroom with the coke can in my hand to confront him but Amador wasn't there any more. The door was open and I saw him about running toward the avenue, as if he were escaping. I felt a combination of disgust, fear and self-loathing. I wanted to scream and wondered how I could be so stupid. Then I wondered how he could be so stupid. But then I realized that he wanted me to know. Or he wanted to throw it in my face, that he was smoking *"piedra,"* as they called it in Tulum, in my home. He was telling me he could do whatever he wanted. I sat down to cry but then had a sick paranoid feeling.

I checked my closet to see if I still had the little money I had hidden there. I rustled through the clothes folded on top of the small bag and found it. Then I checked my computer, hidden poorly under a pile of books and magazines. But everything was there. I went to the fridge and noticed he had either taken or drunk the beer. But that was his style. The sign of an alcoholic: you can never keep liquor in the house. I sat on the couch and put my head in my hands. Lakra came over to give me a hug, rubbing her head against my leg. I patted her, let go of my sadness and told myself, "well girlfriend, now we know for sure, right? No more with this guy. He really is a crack head."

It was a week before Christmas. The party bus came by every night now, not just the weekends. My neighbor came home at dawn to party 5 nights out of 7, similarly not just on the weekends. I could not wait to move. But I was not more afraid because Amador wasn't there. I was happy to be alone and unafraid until one night at 5 a.m. when I heard a loud knock on my door. Then, I heard that familiar scratchy voice call my name.

I rolled over but he knocked again. I struggled to consciousness and shuffled in a sleepy fog to answer. I didn't think about not opening the door. When I did, I gasped. He was covered in blood. He had sunglasses on but there was blood dripping down his cheeks. It was obvious that someone had punched him more than once in the face. I lifted the glasses off his face to see two black eyes. I wanted to cry and hold him and bring him inside and save him from all the badness that had taken over my happy man.

When I asked him what had happened, he asked me to please help him. How could I say no? I brought him in, helped him take a shower, looked for any old clothes he had left in my place and put him in my clean bed while I tried to get blood out of his shirt. As I was scrubbing his shirt in the bathroom sink, he came behind me and kissed me on the neck. I got nervous and I told him to go back to bed but he said he didn't want to sleep so I made coffee and eggs. I wrapped my hands around the coffee cup and sat down at the little kitchen bar while he told me how some guys had beaten him up outside *la Cubana*. I didn't ask why. I was sure he was a lot to blame.

But I wanted to hold onto him in that moment and keep him there with me. Protect him. He didn't eat and barely drank the coffee and just as I thought I was reaching him on an emotional level, he got paranoid and said, "I got to go." I recognized the paranoia from other times, in the Luxury Cabanas and in La Vita e Bella, and when he ran from the house the other day. There was a palpable energy to it. I realized then, he had been smoking crack all those times. It made me so sad.

Then he said it again, "I got to go."

His eyes looked around like a trapped animal and he got up to leave. I didn't argue with him. I let him go, opening the door for him. He kissed me like an outlaw, a dramatic kiss on the lips and then he said, "ouch," smiling but looking over his shoulder as he put his sunglasses back on. I watched him walk away, his chest puffed out to play the macho man but always looking over his shoulder for who was there. I watched until he turned the corner to the avenue. When he did, I prayed he would never come back.

He didn't for awhile, at least not before Christmas. Part of me missed him. It was like someone had died. I had presents for him. I thought it would have been nice if he could come to Christmas with me at Kim and Feelix's house. I would have loved to have a walk on the beach with him or have someone to shop with. But I chastised myself each time I started down that delusionary path. I told myself to step out of fantasy land and remember that all the things I wanted to do with him were impossible. He was a crackhead and no matter how much I wanted that not to be true, I had to face it.

So, I was happy that I never saw him: no A-sightings or drive by's with the jeep. His friend Sylvia visited me one night. I was happy to see her wonderful smile and hear her accented English that showed her German heritage. Her hair was a touseled blond mass of curls that fell over her shoulders. On this night she wore it down and looked elegant. But there were dark circles under her eyes and her skin was grey rather than the glowing peach complexion she normally had. I offered her some wine and she accepted a tea, saying she was a little "off" alcohol. We both laughed at the descriptive phrase, "a little." We talked about Tulum, about Mexican men and then she asked about Amador. I told her we were done. She raised her eyebrow and told me it wasn't always so easy to be "done" with a Mexican. I laughed, not understanding but assured her that I was. She didn't say anything more.

We drank our tea gossiping about more than half the people in Tulum. It made me feel part of something, even if it was a messed up Mexican pueblo. Then she said she had to go but as she was leaving she stopped and asked if I could do her a favor. I said sure and she asked me to borrow 200 pesos. I was a shocked and saddened at the same time. I knew she had money and I hated that people thought I did. Now apparently, even the wealthy people in Tulum wanted to borrow from me. She noticed and told me that she would pay me back but that at the moment she was short on cash. That was all. I went to see if I had 200 pesos.

I did and I loaned it to her saying, "It is not like I really have this to give away or I would. So please pay me back when you get some money, OK?"

She nodded, kissed me on the cheek and I watched her walk away while that voice in my head told me, "kiss that 200 goodbye." I didn't tell it to be quiet. I asked that smart ass voice where it was when I needed the balls to say no.

Chapter 26

The week between Christmas and New Year was uneventful. No one worked again until the 6th so it was as if it were a long school vacation for everyone. I did lots of writing, met Kim and Iraj a few times, visited my house on the beach and developed a holiday rhythm to my life. New Year's Eve, I rode the bike in my party dress to Kim and Feelix's house, happy to be on my girls' bike in a dress and smallish heels that had a pink leapord skin pattern. I was who I wanted to be in that moment on my bike.

When I pulled up to the door, Felix smiled and said, "Well lookie here," in a Texas accent and started to laugh saying, "You really don't give a shit."

I lied and told him no, I really did not. The party for New Year was subdued but we had a fantastic meal, lots to drink once again, champagne at midnight and a very good time. I left at 2 a.m. on my chariot of a bike and drove home between those firecrackers and fires in the streets that must have been leftover from Christmas. There were drunks and crazy people all around. I had never seen anything like it. It reminded me of a Mad Max movie with drunks staggering into my pathway, people throwing firecrackers in front of me and general mayhem.

I got home to find Lakra once again under the bed shaking from the noise. I locked the door and prayed that it was not a riot or some revolution that I was in the middle of but by 4 a.m. things settled down. The firecrackers got less frequent and Lakra and I could sleep. I realized that it was the way these people party: ferociously. When I finally drifted off to sleep, I vowed to get back to the beach as soon as possible where the lights went out at 10 and no one threw firecrackers into the road.

New Year's morning was a quiet, cool and clear day. Everyone was resting. Lakra and I had breakfast in the sun together sitting in the garden. I pulled some weeds and wrote and enjoyed the stillness of everything. Just before noon, I heard a knock on the door. I went to open it with out thinking and found Amador standing there. I didn't know how to behave. I reminded myself that he was a crack head. I couldn't even believe I had to say it to myself but then I started reciting all the cautions in my brain: he will rob you, scam you, hit you and so on until I told myself to stop. He didn't seem happy to see me, he seemed ugly somehow and I wondered why he had come. His eye had healed and I told him Happy New Year but I didn't invite him in. He said it back but reservedly, almost as if he had rehearsed what he was about to say.

Then he asked if I spent it with my "friends" putting a nasty accent to the word. I was surprised he knew but told myself to get used to life in a small town. I didn't answer but invited him in for a coffee. For once, he had things to do.

Then he said to me, "Listen Joanne, listen good, OK? I need money and I got some things I gonna do that you not gonna like."

I stood there quietly as he told me he had rights to the land on the beach and he wanted me to pay for those rights.

I said, "Really?" and reminded him he had been paid for his "rights" when he sold my land.

He got angry, raised his voice and told me I needed to pay him $10,000 US or he would take my land away. I looked at him and a nervous pit started to grow in my stomach. I told him I didn't have that kind of money and reminded him that he had taken just about everything I had. He told me meanly that I had better find it. He said he could give me 2 weeks but that if I didn't pay he would come with some other men and "take you out." I wondered what he meant by that since I was barely in, but decided not to ask. He finished his sentence putting his forefinger on my chest like he was making a point and then he said "get it?" and walked away.

I wondered if I were dreaming but then I panicked, closed the door and ran after him. I caught up with him on the Avenue and called to him to wait. In that short time he was already with some woman. She was dirty and her eyes were red. Her shirt had stains on it and she had her dirty hair wrapped in some sort of scarf. She smiled when she saw me.

I nodded hello to her and grabbed Amador's arm saying, "You cannot do this."

He told me he could and he was. I told him he had no right, that I couldn't pay and asked him "how could he?" I went on like a mad woman. He enjoyed it, I could tell. He shook free of me and told me that was the way it was. If I didn't pay, he was going to make trouble. Then a black car with dark windows pulled up beside us. He got in and left me there, shaking with anger and fear. Not knowing what else to do, I walked home to feel at least safe.

I waited 3 days before I did anything. I didn't tell anyone. I was ashamed and afraid and I did not know what to do. I had rented a house for my sister who would come in another week and a half. I went to see the real estate guy to check on it. I had given a deposit and wanted to confirm that the house would be ready. I knew my sister would not want to be in town and my house on the beach was not ready. I still had a few days to wait for the carpenter to fix his truck. The 6th was almost upon us but even if I had windows and doors, I didn't have beds or furniture. I was happy I had rented something decent for us.

Marco, the real estate guy told me the house was ready and I could pay the day Sue arrived. We chatted for awhile about life and Mexico. He was from Canada and was in Tulum with his girlfriend. I told him about my project and my books and then got ready to leave. I told him thanks and then, without having planned it, I asked him if he knew a good real estate lawyer in Tulum. He gave me the card of the lawyer they worked with and said he was pretty good, at least he had a good reputation. I looked at the card as Marco told me he had opened an office in Tulum at the end of town by *Tia Maria*.

I walked the avenue toward the attorney named Octavio's office. I enjoyed the walk and took it slow. No A sightings or drive-bys, my metric for a good day. I had decided I would not pay Amador. It was an easy decision since I didn't have the money. But I decided to stand up to him, finally. I would not be intimidated or abused any longer. I got to the small office in a white building and pushed open the glass door. The secretary was there and introduced herself as Flor. We shook hands and in my limited Spanish I asked for Octavio. She said he would be back in the afternoon around 4 pm. I told her I would be back then.

Later, I walked with Lakra to the office and waited. He came in at about 4:15 apologizing for being late. We shook hands and he brought me to his office in the back room. He was pudgy and soft, bald and very white for a Mexican. His English was good and I explained what was going on with Amador. When he said he knew him, I felt self conscious as I told the story of our "involvement." Then he asked me if I had my "constancia de possession" and under whose name it was if I had it. I didn't have it yet but it was in process and Amador had signed things over to another person awhile ago. He shook his head as if he understood. He told me, "Listen. Legally he cannot do anything." I felt better. He told me that my *constancia de possession* under someone else's name would take Amador's presence off of the property. Octavio told me that without the *constancia* in another person's name, Amador could cause problems. He reminded me to get a contract with the new person like I already had with my new *preste nombre* so that she gave me the rights that the *ejido* would give to her. I nodded that I understood and he wrote some names and numbers on a paper and handed them to me explaining they were the *ejiditarios* who I should call to start the process. They would charge 10,000 pesos, about $1000 US.

Then Octavio told me that perhaps I wanted to consider a private contract with Amador that said he would leave me alone. He was sure I would need to pay but he could help me to negotiate the amount.

Then he added, "Although, ten thousand to secure your property and have him leave you alone doesn't seem too bad."

I told him I didn't have that kind of money to give to a petty criminal. He shrugged and told me it was my decision.

But he finished saying, "Those sort of people can make your life difficult here. Sometimes it is better to give a little than to lose a lot."

I held back tears and thanked him for his advice. As I got up to leave, I asked him what I owed him. He said nothing. If I wanted the contract with Amador he would do it for 2500 pesos, about 250 US. I said thanks and meant it. It was one of the few times anyone had done anything for me without charge. But if I took his advice I would pay heavily. Lakra and I took the long way home as the sun started to go down and the lights came on in the little pueblo of Tulum.

Chapter 27

My sister arrived a week and a half later. The carpenter had come, finally, with the doors and windows and the house was enclosed anyway. It was not the job I had asked for and there were gaping holes between the wood of the windows and the concrete of the walls but I settled for it. After having waited nearly two months, I did not dare to send them back. I was starting to see a pattern with these carpenters and masons and the workers in general. They would make you wait so long that you were happy with whatever you got, so long as it was something fairly similar to what you wanted. Regardless, I was ready to move in. I needed to hang the bed, redo the kitchen and get some furniture and a million other things. But those were things I could do alone. First, Susie, Tom and I would have a week at the beach house down the road. After all, it was their vacation. I took the bus to meet them and they rented a car so we could drive back together. I waited in the area where people come out from customs ready to burst with excitement. I jumped for joy when I saw them and made one of those scandals that I love seeing at airports: the pure joy and love of people re-united. Finally, I had family in Tulum.

Amador called a few times in the weeks before, pressuring me to pay. I saw the attorney and he reminded me that Amador could make real trouble for me. He was more certain that I should do the contract and I wondered about his advice. Too, I didn't want to focus on that with my sister visiting. So I stalled and denied that anything could happen. Deep down, I didn't want to believe that Amador would do this. I still believed he was not so bad a person and blamed it on the crack. Once, with that monkey mind analyzing and going over every possible outcome, I said to myself in the mirror, "it is just the crack." I caught myself and had to shake my head and put the thought away not believing I was even thinking it. Crack cocaine was out of my league.

Driving back from the airport with Sue and Tom, I answered my phone to hear Amador's scratchy voice at the other end. A pit grew in my stomache.

"I hear you got visitors," he said to me.

I had no idea how he knew.

I had barely told anyone about my sister coming. Kim and Feelix and Irij knew and perhaps I had mentioned something to the lawyer. But I didn't think so. I didn't say anything but he continued to tell me he was in Playa del Carmen and if I didn't stop and give him some money he would find us and put drugs in our car and report it to the police. My heart stopped.

"What?" I said.

He told me, "You heard me right, *puta*. You gonna start to pay or I gonna give you problems."

He told me to stop in Playa del Carmen at the *Plaza de los Pelicanos* and he would find me there. Then he hung up the phone. I felt like I was dealing with a wild animal in some strange tele-novella. Susie looked in the rearview mirror and asked me if I was OK.

"You look a little pale there, Fans," she told me.

I smiled and said I needed to stop to meet someone in Playa and asked if that would be alright. Tom said "sure" and Susie said, "whatever." I told them that it would not take too much time. Susie had given me all my cards when we arrived telling me she was sure I would need them. She had carried the ATM with the pin number and I could use it right away. She gave it to me smiling and said, "I know you are not supposed to carry these two together but I figured I would live dangerously." I smiled remembering her words. She had no idea.

I wanted to die and crawl into a crack in the pavement as we pulled off the main highway and made our way down *Constituyentes* to 10th Avenue and double parked in front of *Plaza de los Pelicano's*. I told them I would be a minute as I got out and looked around. I felt like I was in a bad B rated spy film as I walked into the plaza and Amador came up behind me and touched me on the shoulder saying, "*Amor.*"

I was startled and turned to look at him and said, "Don't you dare call me that."

I explained to him that I could only give him a portion of the money. He told me that was no good. I told him that was too bad then and I started to walk away but he grabbed my arm hard. It hurt and I told him to let me go.

Susie got out of the car and called to me, "You okay, Fans?" Amador let me go.

I looked back and told her yes. He told me to introduce him. Susie was walking over to us anyway, so I did. He shook her hand and made small talk, asking if it were her first time to Mexico and some other questions that I didn't want her to answer, like where we were staying and for how long. I interrupted her and told her I owed Amador some money and was going to pay him and then we could go. Before I could tell him to come with me, he walked over to the car and introduced himself to my brother in law as well. He was absolutely charming and now he knew who they were and where we were staying. I felt totally screwed.

We went to the ATM and I took out 5000 pesos.

He looked at it and said, "Not enough."

I told him "too bad."

"I coming for more," he threatened.

I told him to give me a break and he said he had been talking with the *ejiditarios*, those tribal pirates from whom I had bought, that owned most of the land on the beach and were selling it in narrow lots like mine. They were famous for fishing, drug dealing and selling the same land over and over to unaware foreigners and sometimes cutting the problematic ones up with machetes. The Mexican government had given them the land on the Tulum beach back in the late 70's in efforts to populate the peninsula. Instead, they sold the land and used the money to buy big trucks, alcohol, drugs and the odd wide screen TV. He told me that they were "gonna give him the *constancia*" and then I would get nothing. He said it as if he enjoyed seeing me in pain, seeing me suffer. I told him I doubted it and turned to leave. He caught me again, this time standing in front of me to block my way and spoke to me in a tone reserved for a bad dog. Finally, he barked, "*Perra*, you gonna pay me or you gonna be sorry." I stepped back from the spit of his words and walked around him to the car.

I must have been paler than white when I reached the car. My sister looked back and asked me what that was all about. I told her, "lets get out of here and get to the beach." I directed them back to the highway and Susie reached back to hold my hand. I took it, put my head back and closed my eyes, exhausted by the episode. We made it to Tulum, stopped for groceries, picked up Lakra from my house in town with a crate I had bought for her since Susie was allergic, and went right to the house called, Los Arcos.

It was a funny little house on the water with a weird design, almost as if it had been built for a reception area but later turned into a house. You entered from the driveway into a dining area and kitchen on the right and a bathroom on the left. The floor was covered in the big tiles that were common in Tulum. I saw them everywhere and imagined that one day about 10 years earlier more than a few truck loads of the 9x9 tiles had come through town when the drivers crashed and sold all the merchandise cheaply. They were the shiney kind that looked slippery even when not wet. These were an orangey color and seemed cleaner than the cement floors anyway. At the dining table were three or four stairs down to two side-by-side platforms with a bed on either side, separated by a curtain. Then you stepped three or four more stairs down and there was a sort of wrap around couch, big glass windows and a door out to the beach.

But right in front of us the waves were crashing and the sun was setting and that made the design superfluous. At the beach, there was a plastic picnic table and chairs and a barbeque in an area nestled into a few sea grape trees that hugged the house. Off to the side was a clothes line and a hose. We had arrived.

"Don't need much more than this," Tom said happily.

None of us wanted to cook so we walked the beach to *Dos Ceibas*, where I had spent the month of July the year before. There we had 2 for 1 margaritas and dinner. I relaxed. Susie and Tom were happy, I could tell. We didn't talk about Amador. No one wanted to bring it up. So we made plans for the week ahead, focusing on good things. Playa del Carmen and he seemed far away. We walked back under the stars with a warm breeze on our face and our feet in the water making circles with the phosphorous while Lakra chased translucent crabs that came out at night.

We laughed at her until we got to the house and I put her into the crate for the night. Before we went to bed, Susie asked if I were OK. I shook my head yes and she handed me a present. I started to cry but she gave me a hug and told me it was for Christmas and she knew I would love it: Origins Skin Cream.

"It is my favorite," I told her. We hugged and I apologized for not having anything for her.

She opened her arms wide, taking in the house. "Look what you have given us."

I smiled, told her it was a pretty weird house but it would be adequate and she agreed. I washed up, used my new cream and we found our way into those two funny beds next to each other. We mimicked the Walton Family like we used to on our ski vacations, saying, "goodnight John-boy" and "goodnight Susie Q." Tom wouldn't play, he chuckled at our childishness. But we were happy to rest and forget about Amador.

The next two days we hung out at the beach. Tom loved sitting under the palm tree and looking out at the sea. It was rough and you could see the waves of the gulf stream on the horizon. He was dreaming of sailing there, I could tell. They were planning to move onto their sailboat and he was focused on that. But for now, he would enjoy the warmth of this part of the Caribbean and dream of Key West and the Bahamas. Kim and Feelix invited us for dinner. Sue and Tom enjoyed their company. They were people I could be proud to know and Susan was happy I had some friends who were not trying to steal money from me. I wasn't sure how much she understood about Amador, but she knew something was going on.

Another night Kim and Feelix came over and we barbequed at the house with them. The next day they came back with a cooler to cure our hangovers, "hair of the dog", and we took Sue and Tom to the biosphere. Feelix had fishing rods and we sat on the dock and pretended to fish while we drank and relaxed. We came back to

Tulum after dark and Tom reminded us we needed beer. But Sunday in Tulum on the beach you could not buy beers after 2 pm.

Felix told me, "Let me show you something."

We passed the house and drove over to the little grocery store called "*El Viejo del Mar,*" or "*El Viejo*" for short. The doors were open and there were candles lit inside.

Felix called "*hola*" and went in.

Tom followed. I had to go in too and then Susie followed me. El Viejo was behind the register. He was a sun bronzed brown color and had wrinkles on top of his wrinkles. His white hair was more bleached than grey but it was a full head of hair. He was missing all his upper teeth but he had a friendly sort of smile. When we asked for beers, he motioned to follow him. His son, Miguel, who I knew, walked out front I assumed to check for police. He charged double for the beers bought on Sunday but no one was bothered. We made our way out back and we counted our change to buy two six packs.

He whispered the price and we passed him the money. He didn't look at us, put it into a tin and said, "*mota?*" Tom looked at me for translation, but I said no. Susie and Tom loved it. We took the beers and walked out past the candles and into the waiting Land Rover as if we were smuggling cocaine across the US border. In the car, Susie said she felt like an outlaw. I smiled and for the first time in my life I felt the more experienced sister.

The next morning, she and I walked to my house to practice yoga. Tom came along since I wanted to show them what I had done so far, something I was proud of. Too, I needed ideas. We practiced in the second floor area out back where I wanted to eventually live. We brought incense and thought we could put some "positive energy" into the place. While we practiced Tom looked around the house and then told me how I could fix what the carpenter had gotten wrong. We talked and laughed and enjoyed looking at the construction and discussing how different it was from back up north. Tom was skeptical that I could pull anything off, I could tell. Susie wanted to take me home and put me safely back into an office. But she held back on saying it. I believed in my idea and they knew that to argue with me was pointless. And I think they thought that bringing survivors there was a good idea too. It was all the logistics and hurdles I had to jump. And then there was this extortion issue.

After awhile and more than a few mosquito bites, we closed the gate, crossed the dirt road and climbed the dune to get back to the beach and back to our little house up the road. The wind was raging and the waves were huge but Susie and I swam before having sandwiches and margaritas at the plastic picnic table on the beach. Tom was happiest looking at the waves and reminding us once again that the Gulf Stream was on the other side of the reef. After the first margarita, he shared some sailing stories until we all slept in the sun. The lazy afternoon melted into evening as the sun started to set and we got cold. Lakra had climbed into her crate hours earlier to stay warm on her blanket inside. As the moon rose, we ate leftovers and played cards into the night, finishing the tequila before we climbed into bed. It had been the perfect day.

The next day Tom and I went to town for supplies. I also wanted to pass by the attorney's office. Susie told Tom not to let me go alone. After we loaded the car with groceries, we drove the avenue to the attorney's office. I ran in and talked to him a little about my doubts and about Amador harassing me.

He was not surprised and told me, "Take a look at this and get back to me after your sister leaves."

I told him I would and ran back to the car noticing that he knew she was here. I wondered if he had spoken with Amador but pushed the thought from my mind. We headed back up the avenue toward the beach. Tom stopped to let someone pass at the rotary, or *glorieta* as they called them.

In that moment, Amador came to my window from nowhere and said, "*hola.*"

I jumped. Tom did too. Amador smiled.

I said "*hola*" back.

Tom waited for the person to pass and Amador asked me, "You got something for me?"

I shook my head no.

His eyes narrowed and he said to me, "you gonna pay."

At that moment, the person passed from in front of the car and Tom moved forward leaving Amador at the side of the road. I watched him in the rearview mirror and he watched back. I wished so much that he was not such an asshole.

Tom looked at me and said, "That guy is a creep."

"He is now," I told Tom remembering how nice it used to be with him, and then I mumbled, "It's just the crack."

476

Tom asked, "What?"

I told him it was an old memory and that Amador had been a very different person when I first met him.

"Not such a criminal, right?" he commented with a smile.

Somehow he was absolutely correct.

I replied, "Yeah, something like that."

We drove back in relative silence with me thinking Amador would put drugs in the car if he hadn't already. When we passed the police checkpoint I got ready for an inspection but nothing happened. I was learning that Amador was not so connected as he thought.

Sue and Tom left the day after. The last day they helped me move some things to the beach house. As we were packing the car in town, I was nervous that Amador would come by. We pretty much raced to get the stuff out of the house and over to the beach. Tom helped me get the mattress set up and one of the workers came to help hang the bed upstairs. Susie and I put the mosquito net up and my special sheets on the bed. I was ready. I would bring them to the airport and then come back to live in my own little house.

"You sure you will be OK here Fans?" Susie asked as we finished moving stuff.

There was really nothing. But I had two big wooden double doors upstairs and downstairs that would at least keep animals out. I had the same cloth clothes closet that had been working for me all along. We moved it upstairs. I had the small stove and little gas tank from when Moises was working with me. And I had hot water and a toilet. The windows were big and had screens and locks on them. Compared to what I had before, I was secure. And I had Lakra. We could walk the beach every day.

"I will have a beautiful life here," I told Susie.

She gave me a hug and told me she hoped so.

We ate our dinner that last night once again at *Dos Ceibas*. It had become Tom's favorite place. And the next day we all drove to the airport. I would take the bus back but we had breakfast there and hung around until the very last minute. Susie and I cried and Tom said, "Come on. You will see her soon." Then they left. I felt deflated, as if someone had taken everything I had. Emotionally it was true. But I inhaled deeply, and got a taxi to the *ejido* office. My plan was to meet the "*comisario*" and ask about what I needed to do to get my "*constancia de posesion*" and to see if Amador really had any right to it.

The taxi found the place easily next to the Toyota dealership in downtown Cancun. It was a 2 story plain white concrete office building and seemed almost vacant. I entered and looked on the directory for the *ejido* offices. They were listed on the second floor. I walked the two flights of stairs and down a narrow corridor to find the office. I pushed the glass door open and entered an airy office space with big windows, nice art and a couple of very comfortable seats. The secretary was pleasant and when I asked for the *comisario* she asked me to wait. The exchange was all in Spanish and we understood each other. As I waited I looked at the walls. They were filled with maps of the Caribbean and the properties on either side. There were some obviously surveyed maps and then some great aerial photography. It was not at all what I had expected or what people had led me to believe about the *ejido*. They were professional and knew every centimeter of their property, at least at the level of *comisario*.

After about 10 minutes, a tall, handsome man with brown hair and brown eyes but lighter skin than most Mayans came out and shook my hand. He introduced himself as Augustine, *comisario* for the *Ejido*. I started to speak to him in Spanish and he invited me into his office. Then he told me he spoke English and asked me what he could do for me. I had a copy of the map of my property and all my contracts and I started to explain the situation. I did not mention Amador's name. Halfway through my explanation he told me he was familiar with the lot and the story. I told him I wanted to get my *constancia de possession* and asked if Amador had contacted them.

He asked me to wait for a moment and left the room. When he returned he told me there was no register for a *constancia* for this lot but if I wanted to do it, it would be in the person's name on the contract and cost me 10,000 pesos. He said we could start the process that afternoon and they would finalize it in about 2 months. I would need to leave a deposit of 2,500 pesos.

I wanted to jump for joy. Finally I had found my way to people who understood me. Even better, I understood them. I had barely enough money to pay the deposit and get the bus back to Tulum. We completed all the paperwork, I took my receipt, shook hands and Augustine told me, "*estamos en contacto.*" I was in process and left the office optimistic. I got back to Tulum before dark, bought groceries and ice at the San Francisco supermarket and went to my beach house to cook something with Lakra.

Just before the sun went down, we walked the beach and I swam. We ran back to the house to light candles and make something for dinner before I watched the stars, this time from the lawn in front of the house. I climbed upstairs to crawl under the mosquito netting on my hanging bed and fell asleep solidly moving gently side to side. Lakra slept underneath me. The front gate was locked. I had both doors to the house locked and a machete at the foot of my bed. I had my cell phone under the pillow with the police number already selected, just in case. Before I went to sleep I visualized the entire property surrounded by light. I moved over every square meter and put light into it until I got to myself and Lakra and I put light around us. I was totally secure.

Chapter 28

The night passed uneventfully. At about 4 a.m. I heard car doors close and a few men's muffled voices next door but nothing to keep me awake, except the odd coughing from Amalio. Lakra barked softly from under my bed but almost as if she were dreaming. We were both accustomed to their rhythm and noise and after so much time in town, the disruption to the quiet was almost comforting. The sun woke me the next morning. I took a coffee and Lakra across the street and over the dune to the beach. Lakra ran and barked and I inhaled and smiled. We walked. I swam. I picked some blue wild flowers from the dune walking back. I had returned home.

After breakfast, I organized things, wrote and got to know my improved house a little better. On a spur of the moment decision, I had the carpenter put a deck onto the front porch when he did the windows. We had discussed it on the phone before he came and we gave it a curve to match the windows. The wood was the same beautiful dark tropical hardwood called *zapote* that he used to make the doors and windows. It was high and without stairs but it gave an elegance to the house that before looked unfinished and common. They had completed the work in one day, cutting and carving the long planks with a chainsaw or a machete. It was incredible. I was surprised when they had a drill to install the big doors and heavy windows. Now, when I walked onto the property from the beach, I saw that the house had closure. I loved the big windows that let enough light in but still protected me. I loved the doors that made me feel secure. I loved my life and I had managed to finish my house.

The next few days were gloriously quiet. My neighbors to the north did not visit their houses. Amalio and his band of lost boys had gone fishing, in a manner of speaking, and Amador perhaps could not make it to the beach. I had my bike and rode to the El Viejo store for juice and eggs and the odd avocado or tomato if they had one. I spent the days happily until the ice and food ran out and then I took a taxi to town to buy groceries. Since I was going, I visited Kim and Felix and we planned a cookout for the next day.

They arrived at about 1 p.m. I was far from ready but Kim and Feelix had brought everything, even a portable grill. I felt so loved when they showed up. We went to the beach and at about 3:30 started the grill. It would be dark by 6 and they knew I had no lights so Feelix wanted to cook in the daylight.

"Want to see what it is I am eating, if you don't mind," he told me in his Texas accent laughing and opening a beer as he nurtured the coals to life.

Kim and I sipped tequila and as he was about to put the burgers on, we heard a loud car pull into the driveway: Amador. My heart stopped and I paled.

Kim asked me, "you OK?"

I told her "Not really" and waited for the knock.

"You want me to get that?" Felix asked me.

I told him no and walked to the gate to see what Amador wanted, even though I already knew. Kim told Feelix to mind the fire.

I walked to the gate and saw a black chevy two-door with lots of dents parked in front of the house. Amador was leaning on one side of it with 2 small Mayan men talking to him.

When I said hello, he puffed his chest out and came closer and said, "*Hola*, Joanne."

I thought to myself that at least he didn't say *amor*. He immediately asked if I had anything for him. I told him no. After going to the *ejido* and realizing I would get my *constancia* and that Amador was talking trash, I had no intention of paying him. Regardless, I didn't have it. I watched him get angry like a storm coming in over the sea. He actually thought I would hand him over money through the gate, just like that. He called to his friends who came to the gate on either side of him. Both had a machete in their hands. He looked at me with narrow eyes and said in English, these guys gonna chop you into pieces if you don't give me that money or get off this land.

I inhaled sharply, shocked. Adrenalin started to flow but I started to laugh, my stress reaction and once again, not the best. Amador got angrier as I laughed and told him I didn't have the money. I couldn't control the laughter. I knew it was pissing him off but couldn't do anything about it. He told me to leave. I got more nervous and started to laugh harder. He got furious and told the guys to start chopping at my fence. They did. They actually started to hit the little posts with their machetes with the goal of cutting them down.

I said, "Really, Amador?"

Then, one of the poles fell over and I screamed. Feelix came running to the door and Amador got angrier. They started yelling at each other in Spanish. I couldn't understand what they were saying but I recognized the swears.

Then Amalio appeared in the street. I saw him stride up, shirtless, his bowed legs jutting out from under too big surfer shorts as he coughed his way almost over to my gate and yelled to Amador, "*Oye Cabron*," and then a litany of Spanish as Amadors' buddies put down their machetes and Amador went to talk to Amalio. They talked angrily for about 3 minutes, their faces so close I was sure that the next day Amador would be coughing like Amalio, having caught whatever it was Amalio had. Felix stayed with me on the other side of the fence and held me on the shoulder saying not to worry.

I was shaking nervously as I watched Amador and Amalio shout at each other. Finally Amador yelled something, spat on the ground and walked back to the car looking angrily at me. He started the loud engine, told his guys to get in and skidded into the potholes to back out yelling "You gonna see me soon. This not over." He put the car in drive and passed close to Amalio who made a hand gesture as Amador drove toward the biosphere. In about 2 minutes, Amador passed again in the opposite direction, too fast for the potholed road, putting dust up as he skidding in front of the house and then he was gone.

I went to talk to Amalio, Kim was calling Felix and he went to see what she needed. I told Amalio thanks and in my limited Spanish asked his opinion about the whole thing. I understood him to say that Amador was a "*mamon*", mommies boy, and that I didn't need to worry. He finished by touching my shoulder with his dark hand and long fingernails and told me not to worry, he wouldn't let anything happen to me. I exhaled when he said it, "*no pasa nada, no te preocupes. Yo te cuido.*" Perhaps paying that doctor bill a long time ago was a good ide.

"What the hell was that all about?" Kim asked me as I came back to the house.

Then I started to cry. Felix was minding the fire, about to start cooking and he said, "Oh boy," with a chuckle as if he knew tears were coming.

I couldn't help it. I started to sob and told them the whole story up until I went to the *Ejido* in Cancun and what they had told me.

"Jeez girl," Felix said, "you got some balls."

I really didn't see what he was talking about since I felt like a coward, crying like a baby in front of them.

Kim gave me a hug and told me, "That asshole couldn't get his shit together enough to plant drugs on you or your car. You have to remember that."

I was not so sure. Regardless, we had burgers, more than enough tequila and they stayed with me until the moon came up and the stars came out. Felix had brought a little radio and we sang some songs with the candlelight until they remembered that they had their dogs at home. We gave Lakra the last of the hamburger and they left, asking me if I would be OK. I told them, "I am home, remember?"

They smiled, hugged me and took off. I got ready for bed. Checked the gate and the doors to make sure they were locked and listened for Amalio's cough. Once I heard it, I could fall asleep.

For the next month, I walked the beach every day and locked the gate every night. Amador stayed away, although some nights I thought I heard his voice at the camp for lost boys next door with Amalio. When I did, a pit formed in my stomach and I couldn't move until I didn't hear it anymore and heard Amalio's cough. I kept visualizing surrounding my little property with light, making the shape in light in my head and including me and Lakra in it to keep that darkness away.

Little by little, I found furniture and I brought home driftwood to serve as tables and stepping stones. Some of the stuff I brought home I painted, some I left as it was. Lakra and I walked the beach pretty much alone and I was free to be as weird as I wanted. No one was judging me except perhaps the guys cleaning the beach in front of the few hotels that were there at the time: *Las Ranitas, Dos Ceibas, Hamaca Loca, Tierra del Sol* and of course, *Luxury Cabanas*. I imagined they found me amusing if they noticed me at all. I used some concrete blocks to support some of the planks and made myself a little table on the deck. Kim and Felix passed by one day with two bar stools they had bought for me in Cancun. "Girl, we need something to sit on when we visit," Felix said with a smile. My home was becoming a home.

One afternoon I came back from my swim at the beach and noticed the moon nearly full. I had left Lakra in the house since she had the habit of not wanting to come back and it had been a quick swim. I needed a dip to feel the salt and rinse the sweat from my body. The moon was rising in the east in a still soft blue sky with a hint of pink from the sunset to the west. I could see the red-orange through the palm trees as I walked into my property. When I stepped on one of my driftwood stepping stones I heard a rustle and stopped. The noise stopped too but it sounded like about a thousand little legs walking on the earth softly. I took another step and it started again. When I stopped it stopped. In the dusk I couldn't distinguish but it seemed that the earth itself was moving with me. I got to the house in that rhythm of stopping and looking and starting, opened the door and got the flashlight.

Lakra barked hello and rubbed her head against my leg as I shined the flashlight into the property towards the gate and we saw them: blue crabs, hundreds of them. They froze when I shone the light. Lakra barked at them and I pulled her back into the house as they ran to the edges of the property, passing under the house that was raised about 2 feet above the earth. It was freaky. I closed Lakra in again and went to the edge of the deck and shone the light on them again, disturbing their retreat.

They were amazing: a deep blue color with their black eyes protruding from that blue shell. They had big claws, one bigger than the other and they scurried fast once they got used to the light. They went under the rocks and the house and along the fence to escape me. "Don't worry little guys," I told them, "I won't bother you." And I went back into the house and closed the door. I lit the candles for the evening and gave Lakra her dinner. I had quesadillas and red wine sitting on my new bar stools and decided I loved living in the jungle.

When I woke the next day there was very little sign of all my blue friends. I was in the habit of saving the dishwater for the plants since I hated starting the generator to pump water. I conserved as much as I could and wanted a garden that would tolerate the dry season. When I threw the water on one little tree that I had planted, I noticed the shell of a crab upside down. I walked over to it and saw that something had eaten it. When I walked out to the back of the property I notice holes in the ground and saw the crabs ducking into them when they felt the vibration of my footsteps. There had to be at least 200 holes and if I stopped and was still, the blue crabs would poke their eyes out to see me.

I told them again that they didn't need to worry and went back to my house for some compost, noticing a few more dead ones along the way. Some animal had crab for dinner under the full moon last night. "Life in the jungle," I told myself. I grabbed the compost of a few tomato ends, apple peels and some scraps of tortillas and I tossed it out towards the crab holes. When it hit the earth, they all ducked in but then I waited. They came out, slowly but surely, and hustled along the earth, grabbed the compost and brought it back to their holes. I was fascinated and excited to have my very own garbage disposal: the blue crabs.

Chapter 29

I locked Lakra in the house after our morning walk and took the bus to meet my mom. She was escaping the February cold in New England. I was excited but at the same time nervous. I wasn't sure the house was good enough. Before she came I bought a bed for her in Sam's, a place I hate to admit I started shopping. They have stuff. No one in Tulum had much of anything. Kim and Feelix helped me bring the bed home and we set the room up so my mom had a small table even if it was recycled wood on concrete blocks. I bought a lounge chair for a sort of belated birthday gift so she could put her feet up while sitting on the front porch. It was a mix of rustic Caribbean meets college dorm meets recycled kitch.

Tears filled my eyes when I saw her coming out of immigration in her blue wool pants and white shirt, soft pony tail and gentle smile looking for me through the gauntlet of tour salesmen and taxi drivers. I ran to meet her, hugged and once again, displayed a reunion full of love. We rented a car and drove directly to Tulum. She gasped at the beach, just as I had when I first saw it. It was nearly dark when we got to the house, freed the howling Lakra and unloaded the luggage and groceries we had bought. I put water on for tea and started to light the candles. My mom wandered around kind of tiptoeing and looking at the things I had. I finished lighting the candles, made tea, and asked if she remembered my tea cups. She remembered them well and after tea we decided to go out for dinner at *las Ranitas*. Lakra came with us because in those days she could.

We crossed the dirt road to the beach and walked about 800 meters under the stars to the hotel that was one of the original hotels on the beach. My mom sang as we walked, me with my feet in the water, she and Lakra trying to avoid getting their feet wet. They walked in little arcs as the waves came in and sent them further up the beach and then receded and lured them closer to the water. I laughed at the two of them. We held hands for half the dinner, Lakra sitting under the table and a gentle breeze coming off the water. At every pause in the conversation, my mom would look at the stars and tell me how beautiful it was.

My mom was never direct unless it was absolutely necessary. So she never mentioned to me that Susan had reported my problems with Amador to the family. She didn't comment how Susie had described the town as a dirty place full of drug addicts. She never told me that Susan had also mentioned with glee to the entire family how I knew where to get beer on Sunday afternoon on the beach and how, generally, she and Tom had decided I was becoming a degenerate who dealt with narco's and addicts. I would later learn that they believed I really didn't work much and that I should come home to New England. My mom would never tell me that. It was too unhappy a topic to discuss, especially on our first night together in so long. Instead, she listened to my plans, nodding and talking when I asked her opinion. But she never told me I should get out. We walked back the beach and crossed the raod to my house with ease. The gate that marked the entrance to my access was half off its hinges and always open. The sign, "*dona monica*" was tacked on with one rusty nail. No one knew the *dona* but we all appreciated her allowing us access to the beach. We saw a shooting star before we reached the house and we both made our private wishes. With a few candles still lit, we got ready for bed.

I brought a candle to the bathroom and was showing my mom where to put her things by the sink when I noticed a black scorpion about 1.5 inches long on the wall next to her shoulder. I told her to hold still and gently moved her back holding both shoulders. When she was a few feet away, I showed her the insect. She gasped, "oh dear," and I laughed like a seasoned veteran of all things tropical insect related.

I got a yogurt container and put it over the scorpion and then slowly put a piece of cardboard under the container to move him onto the porch for the night telling my mom, "We can figure out what to do with that guy later." My mother smiled and let me lead her up the stairs to the bed. It was not like me to be so cool with a big biting insect. The last time she had seen me with a bug that size was in Miami when a "palmetto bug," or flying cockroach as I like to call them, came into the apartment. I spent hours trying to find him before I could sleep. And before I could, I took all the sheets off the bed to make sure he was not inside. She laughed at me the entire time. Now, we both went directly to bed with that animal waiting there.

The next morning we had coffee on the porch and continued our conversation as if it had never stopped from the night before. Later, we went to the beach and swam and walked and kept on talking. It was heaven. We stopped at *Las Ranitas* for a drink and then searched for shade. I wrote while she napped and we got ready for dinner. Juan and Martha at Jade had invited us and I was looking forward to having my mom meet them. They were respectable, good people even if they were different. But before we went, we climbed to the top of my structure out back and took a look out over the swamp. I told her I spoke with my father there.

She told me wistfully, "I speak to him everywhere."

We sat for a nostaligic while longer before we climbed down. I showed her the crab holes and told her how they ate everything. We laughed like kids and then had a wonderful seafood soup with salad of local chaya and tomatoes with Juan and Martha. We brought wine and Fabio ate with us. It felt like old times with Juan playing guitar, shots of tequila, us all singing along and Lakra howling to the music. When we finally left, Martha reminded me we had yoga the next day and we made a plan to have class later than usual. I was sure I would be hung-over.

As predicted, I was foggy the next morning. We drove to yoga and I put my mom in a lounge chair on the beach. Juan and Martha and 2 guests were waiting for me and we started the practice standing, proceeded through several sun salutations, twists, balances and warriors before we were on our backs in savasana, everyone sweating, cleansed and relaxed. Lakra had stayed with my mom and the three of us walked for breakfast to Tita Tulum. Tita barely tolerated dogs but made an exception for us probably because my mom was there. Had it only been me, she would have sent Lakra and me both away. She had seen me with Amador on more than one occasion and there were many people on the beach like her who didn't want anything to do with him. Since he was known as my stalker, it meant they didn't want anything to do with me. We hung out at Jade afterwards and then went swimming before we went back home. We planned on going to Zama's for dinner. Javier, who I had met at *Saphiro*, and his band would play and I thought it would be fun to see them.

We arrived at Zama's shortly before the band started and grabbed a seat close to the stage. I wondered if Javier would remember me. And then realized probably not as we ordered and he came onto the stage to check the microphones. As I waved to him, I felt a hand on my shoulder and turned to see Amador. "You know him?" he asked me and then gave me a kiss on the cheek. I was surprised and the look on my face told my mom that it was not a pleasant surprise. But Amador went over to her and took her hand as he introduced himself saying that she must be my mom. He used that word, saying "Hi, Mom," as if he could adopt her or something. A chill went up my spine as he took the seat between us and settled in for what seemed like the show. We were both too polite to say anything. My mom didn't even raise an eyebrow and when the waiter came with our drinks, Amador asked for a beer and he repeated the original question, did I know Javier. I told him yes and reminded him of the time I stayed in *Saphiro* and Javier was there. "The time we stayed," he told me and smiled at my mother.

It was uncomfortable to say the least but the band started to play and we listened to the first set over our pizzas. We had another round of drinks with the food. Amador didn't eat but kept ordering drinks. I wished he would leave. At the end of the first set he said he would be right back and I told my mom, "lets go," telling Amador we were leaving anyway. We asked for the check and he said good night to my mother saying, "goodnight mom." I paid for everything. I was humiliated but we left happily enough. Javier finally recognized me and came over to say "thanks for coming" but nothing more. As we got to the car, Amador came up behind me again and whispered, "You sure you only know him from *Saphiro*?" I jumped and when I saw him, breathed a sigh of relief and asked him whom he was talking about. Then I realized he was talking about Javier and assured him that I only knew Javier from the one night we had all spent together.

I opened the door and as I rolled down the window Amador stuck his head inside and suggested we should do something together. I told him maybe but he pushed the issue asking my mom if she didn't want to see Valladoloid. She told him that might be nice but she prefered to stay at the beach, her very kind and obtuse way of saying "no thank-you". But he didn't get that approach and told her that it was supposed to rain the next day so we should see some sights around Tulum and Valladoloid was a nice colonial city.

I told him we would think about it but he wanted to close the sale and said, "I be by for you in the morning." I blurted "no" a little too fast and too loud and I noticed he started to get angry.

I did not want my sweet mother to witness an outburst so I followed with, "We can meet you in town. There is no need for you to come all the way to the beach. But only if it is raining."

And so it seemed we made a rainy day plan. As we drove home under the starry sky, I prayed for sun.

We woke to the normally wonderful sound of rain on the roof. But on this morning, the sound made me want to hide. We took a long walk on the beach when the rain subsided and then went to town for lunch. I was hoping that Amador would forget us and we sat down at a new café on the *Avenida*. I thought we had escaped. But just as we were served, he found us and once again sat down to join our meal.

"You certainly have a good sense of timing," my mother said.

Her sarcasm was lost on him. He agreed with her, asked for a lime soup and then asked about Valladoloid. For some reason I was afraid to tell him we didn't want to go. Well, I know the reason. I was afraid of one of his scenes and too, I really didn't know what to do with my mom, although she would be happy doing anything or nothing. I wanted her to see some things and I liked the drive to Valladoloid and actually liked having Amador on board to help me navigate, if he was good. But lately he never was. I took a chance that he could be and we decided to go. My mom and I sat in front and he sat in the back. After about 10 minutes, he lay down and fell solidly asleep.

"So much for my navigator," I thought.

We made it to Valladoloid but the rain got harder.

As we waited at the first traffic light, Amador woke and poked his head between the seats saying, "We could go see the hammocks at the prison."

I wanted a new hammock and did not want to walk around the town square in the rain so we drove around the square to see the colonial architecture and the cathedral. We drove slowly, like the tourists we were, and then took the road out of town that wound up a slight hill and then curved down between rows of poor housing to find the prison. There were rows and rows of colorful hammocks lined up, some hanging vertically and some open as if you could rent one for a nap. They were under tarps to keep them dry and there was one person selling.

Amador went to talk to him as my mom and I started looking at the colors. The patterns were amazing. I asked my mom if she wanted one and she reminded me of the day I found the hammock I had given her from my first visit to Tulum still in the bag at the bottom of her closet totally eaten by moths.

"Right" I said as Amador returned with prices and one that he wanted.

He said to my mother, "buy this one for me will you mom?"

I nearly died.

My mother, said to him, "You can buy that yourself young man."

I wanted to explode laughing but was afraid to.

Unphased, he said to me, "but you gonna buy it for me right *mamasita?*"

I told him to back off but he persisted and showed it to me and told me how he needed a hammock and then he whispered in my ear as my mom walked back to the car disgusted, "you gonna buy this one so you not gonna have trouble."

I wanted to stab him in the eye but instead, as my mom got in the car, I paid for his hammock. Before I could he took a blue one from the rack next to me and told the salesman he wanted that one too.

He looked at me meanly and said, "one for you too."

I inhaled, paid the man and walked back to the car. I wanted to drive away leaving Amador there.

But he ran up behind me and said, "let's go home."

I ignored him and got in the car, my mom next to me and with him in the back. I was preoccupied the entire drive home, chastising myself and feeling stupid in front of my mother. Amador fell asleep. You could hear him snoring. My mom and I talked. I could tell she was angry and concerned and I hated it. We dropped Amador at the Hotelito on the avenue.

As he got out of the car my mother said her famous, "good riddance."

I finished with "to bad rubbish" and we both laughed.

When we got to the house we hugged Lakra and then went to dinner at *las Ranitas* again. I vowed not to go back to town until my mother left. I would get groceries and we would cook at home or eat on the beach. That was enough.

The next morning we were lazy. The sun was out and it felt good to sit on the porch in the shade. As we sat there with Lakra under my Mom's chair we heard a scratching and crying at the door. I went to see who it was, nervous that it might be something to do with Amador. I opened the door and there was my pal Goliath, the first dog I really knew in Tulum, emaciated and dragging one leg that was sort of dangling there.

"Goli," I cried and he hobbled into the land and then up to the house and lay down on the porch, "what happened?"

I explained to my mom how Goliath was the dog who made me commit to coming here, how he had been in the photos that Moises had sent to me when he first asked to work with me and design the house. He was a love but at that moment he was a mess of bruises and cuts and his hind leg on the left side looked as if it were dislocated or something. I put his head on my lap.

As I stroked him, my mom said to me, "what are you going to do with him?"

I said, "What else can I do? I will keep him."

She shook her head as I told her I loved him anyway and Lakra needed some company.

We took him to the vet in town that afternoon. He told me that Goliath had suffered multiple contusions on his body and that his hind leg had been dislocated. He explained to me that it would go back into place on its own if he had rest and moderate exercise. We had him vaccinated and Juan the vet told me he needed to gain some weight and to take it easy for a while and he could be fine.

Then he asked me, "Isn't this Amalio's dog?"

I told him not any more. He smiled and told me that I should check that out with Amalio if I wanted to stay on good terms. I paid him, thanked him for the advice and took Goli limping back to the car.

We got home and I brought Goliath slowly into the house, made him a nice comfy bed, fed both dogs and watched them.

"The vet told me I should ask Amalio about taking Goliath," I told my mom.

"He's probably right."

I started to argue about how they mistreated the dog and how I fed him more than anyone and how he would be better off with me and a few other reasons I had for keeping him.

"Just go ask," my mom said.

The entire walk over I planned what to say. It would have been hard enough in English but I had to figure out the Spanish. Before I entered their community, I listened for Amador's voice. I heard only Amalio's coughing so I continued. His property had a 2 meter high concrete wall in front with an arched entryway. There was no door. It was open to enter. The sides and the back had chain link fencing.

I went under the arch calling, "*Buenas tardes*" and saw Amalio lying on the front porch of his small *palapa* in a hammock.

As I got closer I noticed he was naked.

He invited me to enter saying, "*pasale* Joanna" and he sort of wrapped the hammock around his private parts and leaned up to talk to me.

They had an open-air kitchen and his friend and I think drug runner Chi Chi was making something over a fire. Chi Chi saluted me as well and spoke to me in English asking how I was. I told them both fine in my best Spanish and then tried to tell them about Goliath.

The minute they heard the name, Amalio started yelling, "*pinche perro*" and "*no vale Madre*" and some other words I knew were not terms of endearment.

When he finished, I asked if I could have the dog, at least that is what I was trying to say. Chi Chi translated for me and Amalio told me in a funny English annunciating with lips and tongue reminiscent of Mick Jagger and gesturing dramatically with his hands whose fingernails were about half an inch long and a dirty yellow, "Be my guest."

Then he showed me a bite mark on his calf that he claimed was from Goliath and told me "*cuidado con esta perro*," "be careful with that dog."

I said thank you and good-bye. Chi Chi told me to say hi to my "*mami*" as I left.

I told I him would, realizing that the entire village knew my mom was visiting. There were no secrets in Tulum.

I went back to my house happily and as I entered the gate, saw my mom patting the two black and white dogs and enjoying their company.

I strolled joyfully onto the property and announced, "He's

mine!"

My mother said that at least he was a nice dog.

Chapter 30

The remaining days of my mom's visit went by without an A-sighting. And I ended each such day with a grateful prayer to God and the universe. I wanted no more drama, no more internal conflict. It was easier if I just didn't see him. My mom and I walked the beach with the dogs, cooked in and hung out. Goli's leg started to heal as my nervousness about Amador's behavior disappeared. Slowly, the dog could walk better and even run. I was able to relax. He was a funny guy, black and white like Lakra but his head was more square and he was lean where Lakra was chubby. Most of the dogs I had met in Mexico, like Lakra, were aggressive toward locals, Mayans especially, and not so much so toward tourists. But I soon learned that Goliath took attitude with tourists and not so much with locals, probably from his days with Amalio.

One day on our walk, a model type walked toward us in a bright red pareo and black bikini. She was a postcard walking along the shore, her feet splashing in the water. Even my mom commented on the contrast with the blue of the sea, the red in her pareo and the black of her bikini, the pinky white sand and the blue sky. She walked past us. We all said hello. I kept Goli on the leash until she was well ahead of us. Then, since there was no one else around, I let him loose. In a second he was running funnily with his limpy leg toward that woman. I didn't believe he was going for her so I didn't call him until it was too late. He reached her, grabbed her red *pareo* in his mouth and ripped it off her body. Apparently he noticed the contrast as well. By the time I reached them, she was in a tug of war with Goliath for the *pareo*. I calmed him down, took the material from his mouth and handed it to her apologizing. My mother jogged up to meet me as the women angrily told me to keep my dog on a leash. We laughed about it as the model huffed away. But I put Goliath back on his leash and did so every time we passed a tourist for a long time.

Before my mom left, I took her to the land I had bought with Fernando and Lynn in the town called Francisco Hu Mai. It was on the highway to the archaeological site in Coba, pretty much in the middle of nowhere. We thought it was cool at the time and the owners of the land had built a couple of modest homes close by. There was one carpenter's shop and a few small grocery stores but nothing much really other than a place to get fresh coconuts and juices on the corner.

The land was new growth, forested jungle and there was a dirt access road we had paid to put in. We bumped along to what I believed was my land and stopped, listened and looked at the trees. It was peaceful and calm, yet neither of us could imagine me living there: the only white woman for miles among the coffee colored Mayans, so much more of a freak than where I lived on the beach. And my project with cancer survivors? It would be peaceful, certainly, and there was an energy there that could be healing. But I knew people would rather come to the jungle side of the beach than the jungle side of the jungle.

Serge, who I had met at Jade and had demonstrated remarkable skills on the spoons when full of tequila, had built a beautiful postmodern house with a fabulous pool and garden at the end of the road. We went to visit him and he showed us the potential of the area. For now, I decided, I had my hands full on the beach. I was not ready for even a part time life in the jungle: nowhere to walk, no one to really meet and nowhere to shop unless you got in the car to go. None of those were reasons I had come to Mexico. But we enjoyed my neighbor's hospitality, his pool and the idea that I could have a getaway house. But building one house had been enough of a challenge and I kept bringing myself back to the purpose: hosting women with breast cancer.

When I took my mom back to the airport we stopped in Playa del Carmen, that hot, dirty, boomtown that had grown without a plan and where I knew only two streets: 10th Avenue for my attorney's office and 35th Avenue where Amador had been in the hospital in what seemed like another time. We left a copy of the paperwork for my *constancia de possession* with Mario Vela, my attorney. It was in his paralegal's name so I wanted her to have a copy. I already had a contract with her that gave me all the rights and responsibilities to the land. I was not bothered by the fact that it was in someone else's name. Many people used *"preste nombres"* as I did. Not many had ever used Amador and I now knew why.

Mario told me I could relax since that was all the paperwork I could get to secure the land.

Nothing more existed so, "be there and if you have any trouble, call me," he told me.

I wondered why I had ever asked Octavio for help but told myself it was always good to get a second opinion. My mom seemed satisfied that I had some help.

Before she got into the line at security, she told me, "You know Joanne, I was so worried about you here by yourself. But now I see why you are here. It really is paradise and you can have a good life here. You just need to be more careful."

I gave her a hug and started to cry and told her I would try to be better. She reminded me that it was not about being better, just being careful. When she handed the security guard her passport and walked into the line to pass security, I resolved once again to avoid Amador. I knew I could make a good life in Tulum, but I had to keep away from him and cultivate friends who could help me. If it seemed to be social climbing, that was too bad, I told myself, as I watched my mom slip through the security screen and wave to me from the other side. She was my angel, the only one I knew who had a tailored blue suit and ponytail and I wanted her to come back and stay with me. She never would if Amador was around.

On the bus ride home from the airport, I started to make plans. Confident I could succeed, I focused on a strategy to stay away from Amador. I realized that every time I saw him, I gave him my power. He knew it too. We both could feel it. I realized I had to look for ways to break that hold. Thinking how, I fell asleep until the bus got to Playa. Then I took the *colectivo* to Tulum and pensively enjoyed the sun setting in the fields to the right on the highway.

The taxi from the bus station dropped me at home and as I opened the door, I notice the two dogs had been digging under the gate to get out. I scolded them both, went inside and relaxed in the hammock, feeling my house. It was wonderful to be there. And now, it had my mom's energy. I missed her but the dogs gave it life as well. I lit candles before I showered and then watched the stars come out as the dogs ate. Amalio's cough reminded me it was real, not a dream. I smiled when I heard that labored cough because strangely, that cough from cigarettes, crack cocaine and who knows what else, made me feel safe.

For nearly a week I lived quietly in a certain sort of solitary bliss practicing and teaching yoga, writing and walking the beach with my dogs until one night I heard a knock on the door and my name called loudly. It was a woman's voice and I went to the gate. My friend Millie was peaking her head through the poles of wood that made the gate. I was happy to see her but surprised. I had no idea she was house sitting across the street for my neighbors at *Casa LaHa*. I was a little embarrassed about my empty house and the lack of furniture, but I invited her in. I could at least serve her a tequila in the candlelight. Millie had the restaurant in town called *Azafran* in front of Kim and Felix's house and one of the few places you could get a decent cup of coffee and great bread. Of German descent, she somehow found the right yeast, flour and butter to make solid German black bread that she served with about three different kinds of breakfast eggs. When I could, I had breakfast there. And even if I went alone, half the town was there having breakfast so you could spend an hour or two with people you knew.

We sat on the floor and talked about nothing in particular until she told me she had clients who wanted yoga classes. They were living up the road, she told me, and they were very nice. I thanked her more than once, took their number and told her that I would talk to them. I mentioned my class at Jade in the morning but she told me they wanted something in the evening. But she told me to work directly with them. We had another shot of Tequila before I walked her back to her house under the stars.

The next day, I called the number Millie had given me and talked to Mary at a project in the biosphere called *Palencar*. She told me there were about 8 to 10 workers on the construction job who would like classes in the evening at about 7 pm. She wanted to know if I could get a studio. We talked price and I told her I would get back to her about the place. She said the sooner the better and we settled on Friday for a class. I had 3 days to work something out with Juan and Martha. When we spoke, I knew they were not exactly thrilled with the idea but they agreed. I would pay them a commission of 50 pesos per person and I would allow their guests to attend as well. It seemed fair and we settled on 3 nights a week starting that Friday, like Mary wanted.

The old campsite down the road called *la Zebra* was being turned into a petite hotel with a bar and restaurant. I often stopped for lunch there since they also had Internet and electricity. I could sit at the large wooden bar and work while charging my computer and cell phone. It was expensive Internet but the view was fabulous: direct ocean view of the Mexican Caribbean. The people were lovely and they liked me. As I looked out toward the sea, I remembered camping there and shivered at the memory of the horrible place, the abuse from Amador, and the memory of those used condoms outside the tent. I waited for a juice and *huevos energeticos*. The manager Lina and I talked about my new class. She knew Mary and told me they came there often for champagne dinners. I realized that I was charging too little but resigned to do at least the first few classes. Eventually, I would make more or at least be invited to their champagne dinners.

Friday night I arrived to Jade early to sweep sawdust and a few cockroaches from the floor of my fabulous "studio". Juan had built the huge *palapa* 2.5 meters above the ground, like his rooms. It was surrounded by sea grape trees that entered the space over the railings and hugged the sides. It was built with trunks of trees about half a meter thick and some of them 6 meters tall. It floated over the sandy dune, touching it only with the support beams which were about 14 meters long. The solar lights were low and I lit candles and placed some mats on the floor to show how I wanted to orient the practice: facing the sea, east, new beginnings, new energy.

The shadows from the trees played in the candlelight and the dark wood turned a pearlescent shade of coffee with the yellow of the candles. I lit some copal incense and people started to arrive. About 12 people came, most of them super fit yet inflexible males who worked construction. Many were climbers or surfers and they all wanted to move. The 3 women had been dancers at some point in their lives and were flexible in contrast to the men who were super muscular but very tight. We had a fabulous class and almost all of them were all excited for Monday. They paid me and I paid Martha and we all were pretty happy. I rode home on my bike under the stars about as content as anyone could be.

The following Monday, 12 people came again. Juan and Martha were happy when I paid but seemed to not like having outsiders come to their hotel. My intuition told me they would prefer I find something else. I ignored it because I didn't know where else we could go. Wednesday and Friday passed and the class numbers did not dwindle. Nor did my feeling that we were not all that welcome. On Friday night, Juan and Martha watched a movie with the volume full force while we were upstairs practicing. No one in the class complained but the situation was less than ideal. I did not dare to complain but felt a certain passive aggressiveness from Juan and Martha.

We were into week 2 before Amador found me. We were about to finish practice and in the final twist when I saw him come up the stairs to the studio. He looked stoned but almost exactly as I remembered from when I stayed there about a year before. His hair was a mess but the candlelight highlighted the blond tips and gave him almost a halo. The pearl of his teeth caught the candlelight as well when he smiled. It was as if there were a ghost of him there. I ignored him and finished the class. I was not sure if anyone in the class was bothered but I didn't like it. My stomach was in knots and I thanked God we were almost finished. When I chanted "*Om*" and said "*Namaste*" to the group, I looked over and he was gone. I wondered if I had imagined him there.

I got on my bike after saying goodnight to Juan and Martha and paying them. At the end of the long narrow driveway that marked the entrance to Jade, I heard my name called in a whisper from behind their sign. It was that gravelly velvet voice that pulled at me from a place deep inside. Amador was waiting there. I put my feet to the floor to stop the bike and said hello. He walked out from behind the palms and when I asked him what he was doing there, he said he was waiting for me. I didn't know how to feel. A part of me wanted to hug him and then another part of me wanted to slap him.

Then he told me, "You are so beautiful when you teach. It is amazing."

I laughed and asked him if I was not beautiful when I was not teaching.

He told me, "it is as if the yoga flows through you. You become like the light."

I told him thank you and before I got more confused, told him I had to leave. He asked me if he could come home with me and I got angry. A ball of fire formed in my gut and I wanted to hit him and pound him into the earth for messing up all my plans and our lives. I fought not to act on it but told him no, that it was not a good idea. And then my feelings shifted and I wanted to take care of him again, give him a home, make him well. I was a mess of emotions as he asked to see me sometime. I told him OK but to please not come to my classes. I told him it was upsetting for me and for my students.

He looked me in the eye and said straight to my face, "you no love me anymore."

I said, "You are too hard to love, Amador."

I pushed my foot into the pedal on the bike and rode away before I could feel or say another thing.

Chapter 31

We had 3 more classes at Jade. It was something that no one ever mentioned but when my clients would come, Martha and Juan would get tense. I felt it. The loud movies and one time live music interfered with the classes as well. The group had dwindled to about 8 carpenters imported from the US working on the project in the Biosphere for an ex-movie star. Juan and Martha hated the concept and transferred it to the imported laborers in my class.

The guys all lived together in a place called *Villas Sian Kaan*or as they called it, VSK. It was a lovely house on the water with 5 suites, 3 decks, full kitchen and patio. The final night, after we overheard a B-Movie gun-fight during *savasana*, John, one of the guys in the class, asked me if I would bring the yoga to them. It was no further away from my house, they had enough space in front of the house on a level patio and it would be easier and definitely more conducive to relaxing.

"More money for you as well," he told me, since I would not have to pay Juan and Martha. I agreed and started to teach yoga there instead.

Juan and Martha were not sad to see us go. Fabio perhaps was but I didn't get the chance to see him after our last class. He and Juan were distant and I wondered what had happened. But, it was not my place to ask. Juan and Martha wanted to continue with the morning classes but were thrilled that we would not be there at night. It worked for every one and Amador would not have access to me at VSK. Only invited people were allowed in. I settled into a wonderful routine of writing, working, yoga and life on Tulum Beach.

The next Wednesday morning, as I was leaving for Jade on my bike, there was a small, chubby yellow lab hanging out in front of the house. She was sweet and friendly but my dogs wanted to kill her. I told her she was lovely but needed to go and then pedaled away on my bike. When I came back she was still there. I told her she could not stay and went in without letting the dogs know she was still out front. We would walk later. I couldn't get my mind off her during the day and wondered about the parallel between my love for stray animals and the men I chose in my life. I pushed those thoughts away when, around noon, I put some water by the road for her when I checked to see if she was still there. She devoured the water. I told her I was sorry but she could not stay. I patted her on the head and went back to the house to work and organize some things for the evening's class.

I spent the day working at home until 7 when I left to teach at VSK, as the guys called it. The dog was still there. She was curled up under a car that had parked in the drive. She came out to see me, with her pleading brown eyes and wagging tail. I patted her and explained that I already had 2 dogs. She followed me on the bike to VSK and I again tried, unsuccessfully, to get one of the guys to adopt her. She followed me.

Before I went into the house, I patted her and told her, "You must be somebody's you are so nice."

I figured someone would come for her or she would go find them in the night.

The next morning we went to walk the beach and that little yellow lab was still there. Goli attacked her. Lakra wanted to but I held her back and yelled for Goli. The lab ran up the road but not too far. When we came back she was waiting again. I gave her water but did not let her in. As I fed my dogs I kept thinking of her and then I put some food out for her. She inhaled it.

"Poor thing", I thought but I could not see having three dogs and my dogs were so aggressive toward her.

That voice on my shoulder told me, "Lakra was that way with Goliath too."

Three was too much. I thought of my sister's comment about the "crazy cat lady" when I brought her that stray cat more than year ago and "crazy dog lady" echoed in my head. But that yellow dog was persistent. She followed me to yoga at Jade. Their dog chased her away. I thought she might be gone for good but when I came home, she was there waiting. In the evening she came to VSK and waited for me at the door. The guys loved her but no one wanted the responsibility of another dog. As I rode home from class with her trotting behind me I thought to myself, "I have to do something." The next morning she followed us to the beach and every time my dogs saw her, they chased her away. But still, she tried.

Working that afternoon, I heard Amalio yell and I heard something like stones dropping on the ground. Then I heard a dog yelp. I ran to the door and saw that it was that yellow lab. I knew Amalio had a sling shot. They were shooting at her. I got so angry that I went to the door and walked over to Amalio's house. The dog was on the other side of the road with her tail between her legs and a paper bag full of tortillas in her mouth. When she saw me she dropped the bag and came over to greet me.

Her pretty yellow face had a slight white half moon on her forehead and a white spot on her butt. "Okay," I said, "You win. If you want to give it a try, you can come stay with us."

I would not have Amalio abuse another dog.

I opened the gate and she came shyly in. Lakra and Goli ran to attack her but I stood between them, explaining that we were going to let her in, as if they could understand. She sat inside but in front of the gate and each time she moved they would run to send her back. She stayed there that whole first day. At night I wanted to bring her in but each time I brought her close I had to referee the dogs so they didn't attack her. I put a blanket and water by the gate and left here there. She didn't make a sound all night and when I woke the next day, she was curled up in her bed and happy to see me. The 4 of us took a walk.

She followed me pretty closely although I really didn't mind if she took off. I thought perhaps she would find her old owners. But no, when we turned to climb the dune to the house, she was right behind me. We entered and I anticipated a fight but the dogs let her to the deck on the second day. I told myself they were becoming friends. That was, until evening when I tried to bring her up to sleep under the bed. Lakra would not have it and I was too tired to referee all night.

For 3 nights she slept at the foot of the outdoor staircase on a little bed I made for her. Finally, on the 4th night, she climbed to the top of the stairs and waited at the door off the balcony. Lakra growled but I slapped her on the butt and told her to share. And she did. She stopped growling and when I opened the door, Ama walked slowly in. It was wonderful. I put her bed next to the door and we all had a quiet night, that tribe of 3 stray dogs and one crazy lady, sleeping in the tropical Mexican jungle.

We became a family, me and my dogs. They each had their personalities and we got to know each other. Lakra was the more mature who, although she would greet me at the door when I came home, was more laid back. She slept under the bed. Goliath slept by the door and he would run to see me when I came home but then would try to escape into the road. When I left them alone at the house, Goli would try to tunnel, several times successfully, under the gate. Ama, as I finally named the yellow dog, was a love. She always wanted to lick people. It was funny and endearing but sometimes embarassing. When I would come out of the shower, she would chase me around and try to lick the cream off my legs. When people would visit, she would lick their feet as they sat at the bar. One friend told me it was a sign that she was mentally retarded. I did not love her less for it. When I came home, she ran to the door and stayed with me, licking whatever part of me was not covered by clothing.

Ama and Goliath would chase runners on the beach. Lakra would bark behind them or alert them to someone coming but rarely join the chase. I was generally prepared but on the occasions when I was relaxed or watching the sun sparkling on the water they would attack some person running. After the apologies and running to put them on leashes, I would smile, because I always thanked Tulum for stopping me from running. It never felt right here and my body thanked me for walking and practicing yoga. I told the dogs they were helping those crazy people.

We enjoyed our morning walks on the beach together and the days passed with us all working on the houses, writing, painting and planning. They surrounded me in my yoga practices in the morning. The evenings and nights passed quietly as we watched the sunsets together from the back structure and lit candles before the darkness enveloped us. I woke with the sun most mornings and had coffee before we started the routine over, bothering the odd tourist that dared to venture onto the beach when we were there. It was the most beautiful life I could imagine.

Chapter 32

I opened my eyes and looked at the sun peaking through the awning of the *palapa* roof and stretched, enjoying the peace. I listened to the birds chirp and my dogs snore. Then, I heard a car pull into my driveway, the door open and close and my name called in that throaty voice I knew so well: Amador. My heart stopped and a pit grew in my stomach: fear. It was familiar but not at all nice. I was paralyzed.

The voice called again, this time louder, and then followed with, "*Mami*, answer me."

I told myself to not be so dramatic. After all, it was just my ex. But the voice on my shoulder reminded me that it was my ex who had robbed me, abandoned me, tried to extort money from me and most recently, threatened to "chop me up". I needed to be careful.

I pushed my feet from under the mosquito net and onto the floor and patted Lakra who was sleeping there next to me. I stretched and the voice called again. A big part of me hoped he would get back in his car and go. But when he wanted something he would be patient. A part of me wanted to see him. It had been a while. I walked to the door, saluting Ama and Goli on the way, each on a dog bed made of rags, went downstairs in my pajamas, and walked slowly to the gate. I saw his hair, the gold tips shining in the sun, his face pushing against the gate, his smile exactly fitting between the thin poles. I smiled back, unable to help myself. He said good morning as if it were the best day in the world and as if nothing he had done before mattered. It was as if he felt the newness of each moment and we should all forget how it had been. I loved that attitude and tried to use the tone to reply to him but I could not forget how it all had been. I kept the door closed.

"Can we talk?" he asked me.

I asked him what more we had to talk about.

"Come on, Joanne. I need a friend."

When he said it like that I could not refuse him. I opened the gate, gave him a hug hello and we walked back to the house. Lakra howled and then humped his leg with glee. But Goliath and Ama both barked. He yelled at them. That made them bark more until I told them to stop. I patted the dogs and they quieted down but did not come close to him. I was glad. I needed someone fully on my side, especially since I was so nebulous about how I felt about him.

It was the first time he had visited since I had moved upstairs and changed the kitchen. The last time he had come into the house was the time he left with Akim. He left me alone and heartbroken with a house to finish and a dream that seemed bigger than me alone. Compared to then, the house was a mansion. I offered him a coffee as he looked around exclaiming over the changes. I felt the envy in his exclamations but tried not to let it bother me. I had some cookies and served us both coffee from the Italian coffee maker in my favorite mugs with sheep on them from Ireland.

"You like that coffee maker now, *verdad?*" he said referring to how he had shown me how to use it back when I lived in Cesiak.

It was a nice memory. I smiled and told him, yes, it was my favorite. He took a sip of his coffee and looked around and told me my house was nice. I had nothing to say.

Then he looked at me and said, "My moms died yesterday."

I inhaled deeply and said I was so sorry. She was only about 10 years older than I was. I asked him how it had happened. He started to sob into his coffee and said he really didn't know but his sister had called him and told him yesterday. He told me he needed to talk to someone. I gave him a hug and let him cry on my shoulder. When he stopped crying, he released me from the embrace and I handed him the box of Kleenex. He blew his nose forcefully and told me that the worst thing was that they did not have the money to bury her. I prepared myself for the next question.

He told me that if they didn't pay, the government would put her into a mass grave. I was shocked and told him I didn't believe it. He shook his head and said he didn't want to believe it either but that was how they took care of dead people with no money. I flashed back to the time he was in the accident and I found him handcuffed to the bed until I could pay for him to be released. I knew the Mexican government was brutal.

Then I asked the million dollar question: how much. He told me that his sister Hayyde had told him 5000 pesos; the exact amount I could take from the bank in one day. I told him that he needed to put her in a proper place or at least cremate her. He told me that his family could not pay and that Hayyde was going to see if the authorities would wait but they wanted to send the body to the mass grave tomorrow unless they received the money. I asked how he could even get it there before tomorrow. But he said, from all his experience, that he could do it with Western Union. He shook his head and told me he could not believe that his mother was dead and he started to sob.

I held him and thought about it. It disgusted me. I asked him if he were sure this was happening, not believing we were still in an age when it could. He got angry and asked if I doubted him. When I said I couldn't believe it he flipped and asked me if I thought he was lying. Exasperated, I told him it was an expression in English and one he should learn. I noticed how nothing he did un-nerved me anymore. Here I was talking with this guy who had caused me so much pain and appeared to be ready to lose it once again. I was calm and I forced myself to remember the times he had helped me as well. I smiled. He calmed down and smiled back. The smile broadened when I asked him how I could help. He paused to think about it.

But it was very clear how I could help: pay 5000 pesos. Then, as if he read my mind, he told me that he didn't expect me to pay. He wanted to talk with someone, he told me as he came over and gave me a hug. I hugged him back and he kissed my neck. I did not feel that electric reaction from before. It felt nice, to be sure, but I did not have that need to let him drag me up the stairs to bed. I congratulated myself and moved away from him. He noticed that I did not want more and for once he accepted it. I couldn't imagine making love with the image of his mother in a mass grave floating in my mind and I was happy that I had not lost all semblance of civility.

He sat back down. I walked to the door and looked out over the rough garden I had managed to carve into a little less than raw jungle, the palm trees, the lilies that I had planted after one hurricane had left them on the beach like little pebbles. I had carried about 100 of them back in small bags that cloudy day with Lakra.

For a moment, I was unaware that he was even there as I let my mind escape the horror he was talking about until he said, "I got to go Joanne." He stood up to go and said thanks for the coffee.

On total impulse, I told him, "I will help you with the money Amador. Your mom deserves more than that."

He looked at me and said, "You don' got to do that."

I smiled at his bad English. I told him that I wanted to. I wanted to help him. And even if I didn't want to sleep with him right then, I still wanted to save him. I still wanted to make him better, "more appropriate". And I believed that making him better would make me better too. Although why I needed to be better I still do not understand.

We went first to the ATM and then to Western Union. I gave him the money and as I waited in the car noticed it was Akim's. There was a little dream catcher on the dash that wouldn't be Amador's, a comb that would never get through his hair, a lipstick that looked like the shade I remembered her using.

That voice on my shoulder told me, "What did you expect."

I tried to answer but couldn't and put my head back on the headrest and waited, exhausted all of a sudden. Before long he came back in and leaned over and kissed me on the lips.

I was surprised and even more so when he pulled away and said, "Thanks baby. That gonna help a lot."

I felt good. I had saved the day.

He drove me back to the beach and left me at the house saying he had things to do. Before he shifted into drive to go, he asked me if we could have dinner that night. Not thinking clearly, I told him it would be nice. Then, I told him frankly, I would prefer that he not come if he could not commit to it. I had spent too many nights waiting for him to want that. He smiled and told me he would be there at 8.

I remembered that first night when he came back to meet Lynn and I at *La Vita e Bella*. I remembered the nervousness before he came and then the relief when he showed up.

I gave him a hug in the car and told him "*hasta luego*, then."
As he drove away, I told myself not to wait for him to come back. I made a pact with myself that after 8:05, I would not answer the door.

Chapter 33

At 7:45, I heard a car pull into the drive and figured it was someone turning around. Practically no one came down the road at night. It was unpaved still and full of potholes big enough to eat cars. Plus there was nothing around and no reason really to go there other than to get drugs from Amalio or to visit the few hotels up the road. I heard the car door close and wondered if Amador had actually come back on time. Lakra was resting quietly under the hammock where I was relaxing in the candlelight. But Goli and Ama barked and ran to the door. My heart beat faster. I reminded it to slow down, sat up in the hammock and put my feet on the ground. Slowly Lakra and I walked out to the gate with the dogs barking. Lakra started to howl. I got to the gate and smiled.

"I am not late, am I?" he asked as I opened the gate to let him in.

"I don't have much to eat but we can make something," I told him, "I really didn't expect you to come."

He took my hand and told me he had brought chicken and potatoes. We walked together to the house. I was happy to have him there, happy for the company and happy that he had brought food. And I allowed myself to be happy that he did not stand me up.

We shared a simple dinner on the porch with candle light and a slight breeze coming over the dune and through the palm trees.

"You done a good job here," he told me as he finished his potato and waited for me to fill his wine glass.

Then he started, just like a guy would, to tell me how to make the place better. He told me I should turn the bathrooms Gerry had built into a house pointing out that if "we" built on top of the concrete box "we" could put a *palapa* and make it into a nice apartment. I was not sure about the "we" word. Part of me liked it and the other more sensible part feared it. I told him it might be good but that "we" had no money to do it. He smiled when I said it and stopped talking about it.

After a moment of silence, I looked at him and asked, "Why did you leave me, Amador?"

He was surprised but regained his balance quickly and told me, "You always leaving me, Joanne. You go here and there and I always the one here. It not so easy."

I understood. It was not me, it was my lifestyle and that made me feel better, less undesirable.

Yet, I could not see changing that part of me. It was a lot of what I liked about myself. Then he continued to tell me how Akim liked to go out more and was more social. I defended myself saying I liked to go out.

Then he hit me with, "and she like to fuck a lot."

I wished I had never asked the question as he continued, "she fuck me when I am sleeping," as if I were some guy friend in whom he could confide.

I suddenly hated him and told him to stop, please. Shocked and interested at the same time, I felt square and old-fashioned and conservative.

But at the same time asked myself, "what is the point?"

I still had that romantic notion that sex, or fucking as Amador liked to say, was supposed to be something two people shared. It was supposed to be something special and with love behind it, not sitting on some erect pole while the man slept so that you could get off. And I wondered if it could really happen that way. My mind started to analyze the whole act and I had this almost comic vision of Akim jumping up and down on top of Amador snoring. Almost comic because he had left me for her I got up to clear the table.

I am not sure Amador even understood that I had been hurt. His culture, and part of what I liked about Tulum, was this hedonistic acceptance that if you liked something you continued to do it. It was a lot of why I was there. I had abandoned my work, any sense of stability that I had in the Western world, my friends and family to pursue this feeling I liked: sun on my face, warm days and starry nights, and at the beginning, Amador. For me it may have been love but I was beginning to understand it may have been just another obsession. And I started to realize that for him too I was just another thing that made him feel good, like a joint or cracking open a beer or a swim first thing in the morning. I started to wash the dishes, not wanting to hear any more. But I also wanted details. I wanted to understand this culture and believed I wanted to join it.

Amador came up behind me and put his arms around my waist. I wiggled free, confused and not up to the challenge of "fucking him while sleeping." It intimidated me, intrigued me and repulsed me all at once. I walked back to the porch and sat down. He told me he was tired and asked if he could sleep with me. He saw the hesitation in my face and quickly said he would sleep in the other bed if I wanted. I was not sure what I wanted. It was all too confusing. He told me he was too tired to drive back to town. I asked him if that was the only reason he wanted to stay.

He looked at me and said, "No, Joanne, I would like to stay with you. You got to know that."

It was what I wanted to hear. I looked at Lakra at his feet and thought about how good it would feel not to be alone, to hear someone else snoring besides the dogs, and to make coffee for a man in the morning. I said OK but I asked him to sleep in the other bed since he was actually with another woman.

Then, I told him frankly, "I won't fuck you in your sleep," still fascinated with the concept.

He didn't deny that he was still with her, so I knew it was true but I decided I would at least have the company. He could share the house with me for the night. When I agreed, he went directly upstairs as I washed up and hustled the dogs up the stairs so they would not bark through night. As I looked up from the little balcony toward the stars, I thought how my life had changed. I felt the warm air on my skin and looked for a shooting star as a sign that this was OK. That it was OK to be friends with someone who had hurt me so badly and was so erratic and volatile.

That voice on my shoulder told me it was OK so long as I didn't let him hurt me and, "so long as you don't fuck him in his sleep."

I smiled and went into my bed with the three dogs close by and Amador in the next room.

The thing about *palapa* roofs is that you hear pretty much everything. And in my little house the walls didn't go all the way to the ceiling. I had never put doors on the rooms, so it was even more open. When you walked into the upstairs there was a space that I used for a sort of dressing, sitting area. Then there were two bedrooms that came off that area that shared a common wall about 5 feet high. It had a wave design on the top and the air moved freely through the oversized windows to both spaces. But so did the noise. And as I listened to Amador snoring in the room next door I remembered that the next day Isaac and Sylvia from Jade were coming to help me clean the land. Too, he was sleeping in my mom's bed and somehow I felt I had betrayed her letting him in.

"You don't always have to be so nice," I heard my friend Susanna's voice say to me.

She was commenting one day on how I could be polite and almost friendly to my neighbors who had robbed me of the frontage of my house.

"They don't deserve your courtesy," she said.

I thought about it as I felt for my wallet under the pillow and reminded myself that I left the upstairs door unlocked just in case I had to leave. I barely slept. Annoyed at myself for letting him in, I told myself to accept it and go to sleep. Finally I fell into a fitful sleep. I woke with the sun and his snores determined to tell Amador that this was a one time courtesy. I made coffee for 2 and waited for him to waken while I obsessed about what Sylvia and Isaac would think when they saw him. Once again, I quoted the self-help books that said that what other people think of you is not important. But had learned that in a small town, what other people thought of me was important.

Chapter 34

I drank both cups of coffee and made some toast while listening for motion from upstairs to signal that Amador was awake. But all I heard was snoring, loud and congested. Finally, I packed my wallet into a bag and took the dogs to the beach while he continued to sleep. Even carrying my wallet, I worried that he would take something or mess something up or leave without saying goodbye. And even though as I put my feet into the sand, I nearly forgot everything else but that beautiful morning, we had a shorter than usual walk on the nearly empty beach as the sun moved higher into a blue sky. I noticed some wispy clouds on the horizon and the waves that were forming well past the reef, about a kilometer off the shore: Sue and Tom's gulfstream. Somehow those waves that looked like the backs of elephants joined together and moving north connected me to all the people and places I loved. Their presence on the horizon gave me a peaceful feeling. It made me feel insignificant enough to know that everything would be OK.

I rounded up the dogs and when I got back to the house Amador was still sleeping. I checked on him, sat next to him on the bed and whispered his name but nothing. I went back downstairs and customarily threw the old coffee grinds into the garden to help the soil. I started another pot of coffee but then abandoned the idea realizing I had already had enough for 2 people and my hands were shaking. I wrote in my journal while he snored upstairs.

I was exploring the concept of being too kind, as I wrote and then stopped to draw the dogs or a gecko or a plant before writing again when I heard my name at the door. It was almost noon and I peered toward the front of the house to see Sylvia from Jade coming to help me clean. She brought her son, Isaac, with her. Sylvia and I often talked after my yoga sessions when Juan and Martha were absorbed in their computers with their coffee. We had funny discussions since she barely spoke English and my Spanish was bad. But Fabio would translate when we got stuck and we laughed a lot.

She had a pretty face, was chubby bordering on fat and, like most of the Latin overweight women I had encountered, she wore clothes that hugged her body and showed every curve. She had ten children from I don't know how many fathers but she had one man that she called her *"esposo"* or husband who was living in the US and sending them money. She also had loads of taxi driver "friends" but her last 3 kids at least were from the husband in the US.

The situation blew my mind but I enjoyed her company. She had come to my house after class once. We had lunch together and as she smoked a cigarette on the porch, she offered her son to work for me. She told me I needed help maintaining the land. I had to agree. Raking was my nemesis. It made my back ache and gave me blisters. Sweeping was almost as bad and I had never been good at cleaning house. She told me Isaac could come once or twice a week to clean and I could pay him what I wanted. Then she looked into the house and said she would come by as well to help me. I smiled, not at all embarrassed, and explained that cleaning was not my thing. It was one thing I knew about myself and I liked the fact that I did not conform to the "woman" role. When I finished telling her, she said my name and laughed, as if I were an anomaly.

They had come as promised and I went to the door to let them in. I told myself she had no room to throw stones over Amador after the 10 kids thing. And actually, I knew they only worried about my safety. At that point I could not even figure why I had let him back in.

I smiled hello and opened the gate as the voice on my shoulder answered, "you were just lonely."

I gave Sylvia a customary kiss on the cheek and then she introduced me to her son. He was beautiful. Tall, dark, thin and with a smile that would melt any girl's heart, Isaac said hello and shook my hand. He was dressed in a white shirt, black jeans and nice shoes as if he were going to an office. I wondered how he would work in the yard dressed like that but he did not hesitate to take up a rake and start to move the leaves into an organized pile. He added any fallen palm fronds and then started burning it all. I was nervous but Sylvia told me to relax and went into the house to do the dishes.

I had nothing but Ajax for the toilet, dishwashing soap and a broom and mop. Sylvia laughed and asked if I had a "*jallador*" or sort of squeegee that we used to clean windows only longer and with a broom handle. We figured it out with hand signals and pen and paper. Here, they used it for cleaning the floors. When I finally understood, I laughed and vowed to get one the next time we went to town. She started to clean and I walked out onto the porch to look at the fire Isaac had started. I had one fire extinguisher that Amador had recommended I buy when we started building but I had no idea if it was functional or not. Actually, I had no idea if I could use one or not. But I figured that if the roof caught fire I would figure it out.

The smoke was rising and the orange flames were shooting from the burning leaves and I listened to nothing much except the waves on the beach over the crackling of the fire. The bell from the ice cream man interrupted that rhythmic crashing as he came down the road.

I had almost forgotten Amador was upstairs when he came down and said, "*Buenos Dias*," and then kissed me on the lips in front of Sylvia.

He greeted her without the kiss and asked in English if I had coffee. I was annoyed with him sleeping so late while we were all working and functioning and he was expecting coffee like some sort of king. I told him I had made him coffee at about 9 but he could make one if he wanted.

"It is all right there," I told him and went back to getting Sylvia organized.

When I finished, Amador was in the hammock relaxing. I sensed he was waiting for me to make him a coffee. I could not be rude, so I asked him if he wanted me to make coffee for him.

He said "*Si, porfavor.*"

As I prepared it, I was slightly nostalgic for those days at Cesiak when we would have coffee each morning by the sea. I lit the stove under the coffee maker and went to talk to Isaac about some more things I needed help with. Amador didn't move to help me. The ice cream man was coming back after making his route to the entry of the biosphere and you could hear the bell as he returned, bumping down the road. Amador stood up, burped loudly and asked me for 20 pesos for an ice cream. At first I ignored him. He asked again and I told him no.

He said, "come on *mami*".

I told him to check on the coffee.

He walked over to me and Isaak and with a mean look on his face said to me, "You not gonna buy me an ice cream?"

Isaak walked away.

I looked at him and said, "No, I am not," and he slapped me in the face, hard.

I had never been hit before. I was stunned, hurt and when I touched where he hit me it was hot. I felt as if I were in a dream. Amador called me a "fucking bitch" and turned and walked to the front door. Sylvia and Isaac looked at the ground, embarrassed for me. I couldn't believe what had just happened was real. But then something inside me clicked and I ran to the door with the dogs chasing after me as he was leaving. As he pulled away, I ran to the middle of the road and yelled after him to never come back.

I walked back ashamed for myself. My hands were shaking and I had started to sob. Sylvia came over, hugged me and told me it would be OK. I knew she wondered why I had let him into my house. I wondered the same thing. She offered me a cigarette to calm me down. I was so upset it sounded good and I accepted. The only time I had been hit was in a fight in high school but that was with a woman and I am pretty sure I hit her first. My parents had never hit any of us. She handed me a Benson and Hedges. Isaac lit it for me and we watched the leaves burn as tears rolled down my face.

I felt a sting in my throat, coughed and told myself, "This sort of thing doesn't happen to my people."

I rubbed my cheek where he had slapped me until I remembered the coffee on the stove, dropped the cigarette and went in to turn it off.

We finished cleaning, had a coffee and Sylvia left me another cigarette. The land looked so much better after the raking. Before we finished, Sylvia asked me what I was going to do with the little concrete structure that was my bodega. I didn't have an idea and explained how it was supposed to be bathrooms when I was contemplating a bigger project. She suggested I make it into a little house.

I told her that was funny, Amador had said the same thing. She said that it was still a good idea as she stood up to leave. We walked to the door together and I asked them what they charged. They told me it was whatever I wanted to pay. I had no idea what to pay so I saw what I had in my bag and gave them most of it. I am pretty sure that was their strategy: to have me give more than the going rate which I knew was embarrassingly low. Too, I was happy they had been there. Although witnesses were not what I had been hoping for, I didn't want to think what might have happened had I been alone. I closed and locked the gate behind them and walked back to the porch and sat with the dogs. I tried to not think of what had happened. But I knew I had crossed a line.

Chapter 35

I crested the bluff on the beach access with the dogs running ahead of me and let my gaze move from the horizon down the crystal blue Caribbean across the interminable pinkish white sand to the foot of the dune and noticed a body wrapped in a blanket. Bare feet stuck out from under it. Goli and Ama passed but Lakra ran towards him. I caught her before she could waken the person who I hoped was only sleeping. As I grabbed her collar, I noticed the matty brown dreadlockish hair with the golden tips sticking out the end of the blanket. That was Amador.

I inhaled sharply, pulled Lakra away and then started to run. Lakra stood still, confused. I kept running. I didn't call her for fear of waking him up, but I made that wonderful underhand movement with my arm that Amador had taught me and started skipping backwards with the other two dogs a little in front of me. Lakra stayed behind, still hesitating to come. It made me angry she wanted to see him but I couldn't blame her. I actually wanted to see him too. But I had made a pact with myself to stop. She looked at me with her head cocked to one side and then sort of jumped in place and put all her paws a little wider on the ground to come into an almost squat when she landed. Then she took off after us. It was fabulous, as if she were bracing herself to get more momentum before taking off. Before too long she was leading the pack and we walked along the shore, enjoying the sea and the sand. I tried to forget that Amador was there, sleeping in front of my place but I made a mental note to get her on the leash on the way back.

I retuned to the spot with all the dogs on leashes but Amador had left. I imagined him waking, looking at the sea and then having a swim, impulsive, irresponsible. With envy, I looked out to the ocean to see if he was there. He was. I saw him doing this breathing exercise we loved doing together. You bobbed up and down in the water inhaling as you came up of course and then exhaling slowly as you went under. It was almost a pranayama practice and if you used your arms you could go down deep. We would do about 30 of them and come up a little lightheaded but totally invigorated.

I felt a nostalgic desire to jump into the sea with him and play, but instead pulled the dogs along the path to escape before he would finish. I don't know if he saw us but I did not look back as we crested the dune and crossed the road. I closed the gate behind us, shaking. I shook my head in disbelief that he affected me so much and went to feed the dogs and have a coffee. I was almost waiting for him to knock on the door the entire day and I was almost always preparing in my mind what I would say when he did. And I was almost always chastising myself for giving him so much of my mind.

I quickly became accustomed to checking both ways as I left the house to see if he was around. Where before I let the dogs charge down the dune, now I kept the dogs on the leash until we were well onto the beach. I didn't want them waking him if he were sleeping there. Some days he was curled up under the palm tree that grew close to the fence I crossed to get to the beach. Other days he was inside the dune, as we would enter and I would tip toe past him, pulling the dogs with me.

I imagined letting Goliath, the only male in the group, pee on him but then thought better of it. Other mornings I would see him walking up the beach and go in the other direction, almost running with the dogs to get away, then stopping, telling myself not to over react or be so dramatic. Sometimes he was nowhere and I was never sure that was better since I wondered where he was and carried this slight fear of a confrontation into all the things that gave me so much pleasure. But even though I was always looking over my shoulder, it could never take away the beauty of those morning walks. I would risk more than an "A sighting" and even an "A confrontation" to put my feet into the sea and let the dogs run in front of me while we felt the sun and the warm air on our faces and bodies. I was in heaven on that beach and would not let him take that from me.

We moved around like that for more than a month before he came to the door one day. I was painting on the deck, sitting in the hammock to paint the palm trees in the yard on an old canvas I had. When I heard the knock and then the throaty voice call my name, I froze, afraid of him. But I felt something more and realized I was afraid of myself. I was afraid of my tendency to let him in, my desire to forget all the shit he had done, afraid of my tendency to pretend it was not real or important. I couldn't move for a moment. He called again. I knew he wouldn't leave. He would wait outside for me to leave or for another opportunity to talk to me about whatever it was he wanted.

Resigned, I put down my artwork and paints, climbed out of the hammock and walked slowly to the door. He could see me coming through the poles that made the fence. I could see his hair, his smile but I didn't smile back. I was annoyed and a little afraid.

"Hola *Mami*," he said to me happily.

I sighed and told him I was not his "*mami*."

And then he went away, and I wondered what he had wanted.

"He is a master at this," I told myself as I walked back to the house.

I couldn't help but wait to see if he would come back. He was on my mind for the rest of the day and into the night. Not in a good way, but definitely on my mind.

When I scooted the dogs up the stairs for bed, I took my cell phone and checked that I had the number of the police on it, ready to dial at any moment. I had stopped at the tourist police one day and asked them for a number to call if I had problems. The entire time I was looking behind me to see if Amador was around. Thankfully, he was not and they gave me a number I saved on my phone. I locked downstairs, which was always a bummer when I had to get up to pee in the middle of the night, but decided to do it anyway. I locked upstairs behind me as I crawled under the mosquito netting, put the phone under the pillow and drifted into a shallow sleep with every noise waking me. Before I knew it, the birds were calling to announce the day. I congratulated myself on making it through the night.

When I pulled the phone out from under the pillow, I felt silly but told myself, "whatever it takes."

The three dogs and I trotted down the stairs, into the house and then out to the beach.

He was nowhere that morning or for several days after. It felt like the calm before the storm but I relished it, sometimes even singing Neil Young's, *Hurricane*, as I walked the beach. It's beauty made everything pale: Amador, all the cons, cancer, loss, everything. It was that lover that you have to have and will do anything to keep. I was an addict to the free feeling it gave me each morning, shuffling in the water along the shore, my dogs in front of me, the sun on my back and my hair getting lighter with every step.

Some mornings when we had walked far enough, I would strip naked and walk into the water, feeling the sand under my toes and the coolness as the sea enveloped me. I imagined becoming one with it, water entering my pores and accepting me and supporting me as part of it for a moment. I would lie there looking at the sky and the frigate birds floating higher than I ever thought possible. The dogs would search around and then finally sit and wait for me. Ama would come into the sea after me but only until her feet would not touch the ground. Then she would turn and go back, roll around in the sand and finally, sit with Lakra and Goli.

Leaving, I would look up and down the beach for people before I would walk naked from the sea and stand in *tadasana* on the shore and let the sun dry me, whitish body glistening, eyes closed, hands open to the sun. In those moments, I was never afraid. I was bliss. There was nothing like it and I would risk everything to keep it, no matter how short lived it was. A bark from one of the dogs would pull me from my meditation as a tourist or fisherman came up the beach. I would inhale out of the pose and get dressed.

After about a month, as I was coming home over the dune confident that he had left us alone, he was waiting at the door. I inhaled deeply, took the leashes in my hand and started playing with the keys as I continued walking towards the door.

He stood in my path and said, "Joanne. Talk to me a minute, will you?"

I melted. Perhaps it was his direct tone, or the fact that I had just had my fix of peace and light and love from this magnificent beach and I said OK. He asked me if I could make him a coffee. I said sure.

We sat on the porch. I did not let him into the house.

I didn't say anything but he told me, "I could help you build a house over those *banos* if you wanted. I got someone who needs work. He make a real nice *palapa*."

I listened to him and then looked at the little concrete block that was supposed to be communal toilets for my spa, another lost dream.

I had to do something with it. Amador continued talking about how it would be good to have another rental. I started thinking it could be the place for my cancer survivors. I envisioned an outdoor kitchen and bath downstairs and a nice loft bedroom upstairs, just enough, not too much, a nice little bungalow house.

He was still talking when I came back from my vision and I told him, "Go talk to your *palapero* and come back with an estimate."

He smiled and told me I would not be sorry. He kissed me on the lips, said thanks for the coffee, and nearly ran for the gate saying he would be back in an hour or two. I looked at the palm trees in the garden and wondered if I had made a mistake or not.

"Time will tell," the voice on my shoulder told me.

I finished the coffee, sighed and started to write in my journal. It was the only way to get the insecurity out off my mind.

Chapter 36

About noon, Amador yelled at the front gate and interrupted my work.

"Here we go," I said to myself and went to open the gate.

"This gate needs some work too," he told me as he entered the property with a short fat Mayan guy whom he introduced as Efrain.

His skin was a dark cherry color and his face was wide and chubby. His eyes were nearly Asian and when he smiled they narrowed to slits as he took my hand and greeted me with "*mucho gusto*."

The three of us walked over to where the concrete box of a building was and we started to plan. We talked about putting in a floor in front where the property was pretty open anyway except for one small chit palm that we would work around. I would not cut the palm trees on principle and because it was illegal. I felt enough of a renegade doing everything without permits, finally understanding all the people I thought were "oh-so-bad" back when I worked in wetland permitting.

I planned a circular stairway to access a loft space upstairs with a *palapa* roof of *guano*, the palm fronds I had used on the house. I liked it better than the cheaper *zacate* that many people on the beach were using. *Guano* was more expensive, and nearly endangered I would later find out, but cleaner and easier to work with. We would change the door on one of the bathroom areas and leave the other one like a bodega for storage, the way I had it now. After we finished talking, Efrain sat on the palm trees that created a nice bench as they grew along the jungle floor before climbing up to the sunlight to do his estimate.

During the 20 minutes that Amador was talking to me about the gate, Efrain finished his estimate. I gladly finished the conversation with Amador and looked at the estimate, asked a few questions, took out a few things and then told him to let me think about it. Amador was disappointed that I would not jump into the project immediately. I told him that I needed to see where I would get the money and that I did not have the deposit but I could talk to Efrain tomorrow.

He got angry and told me that if I didn't want to do the project I should not have made them come to the house. He even kicked the dirt dramatically before he walked out the gate to wait in the street. I spoke to Efrain in my poor Spanish.

I knew he understood and told him we would talk the next day, "*Hablamos manana*, OK?"

His eyes went to slits as he nodded his head and shook my hand saying *gracias* several times. Then he went to his car, a beaten up little black Chevrolet something, against which Amador was leaning, still angry that I would not give him a deposit. The only thing that would make him happy was to give him money. I decided not to do that.

As I started to shut the gate, Amador came over to me and asked me what I was going to do.

I looked at him with a question on my face and he finished the sentence saying, "about the building."

I told him I was going to review the proposal, see if I liked it and if I could afford it. It seemed logical but he got angry, telling me I moved too slowly and embarrassed him in front of people. I told him that he should not bring me people if they were not ready to let me feel comfortable starting a job. I was calm about it but he continued to almost yell at me.

"You think these guys come here to wait? They ready to work," he told me starting to get hysterical.

I looked at him annoyed and told him that they could start the next day. He started yelling and I forced the door shut, pushing him out.

I locked it and told him, honestly, "I do not care."

He exploded then and started to yell that he didn't care either and that he would not help me anymore. I walked away and left him there with the Mayan guys witnessing his meltdown. I heard their car drive away and I assumed he left.

I put my head in my hands and sat at the table wondering if I could manage this. I told myself yes, but did I want to, as I looked at the estimate, written on a piece of crumpled notepaper in a nearly illegible hand. I checked the numbers against what I was pretty sure I had in the bank and what I would earn that month. The two figures almost came together, almost. I told myself I could live off the yoga classes and would start work whenever Efrain told me he could. I lifted my head toward the front door to see Amador there. His hands on the poles as if he were in a prison cell or something, looking into my property. Perhaps it was his perseverance, perhaps it was my *naivete* that thought he was waiting for me and not the deposit. I am still not sure why, but my first glimpse of him made me smile. What happened after could be any number of emotions but to see him at first made me happy.

I asked him what he was doing.

He said, "You *cabrona, mami.*"

I said, "There is nothing *cabrona* in doing things well."

He wanted to talk to me and I said only if he would be polite and kind. As usual he promised something he could not guarantee delivering. For my part, I let him inside knowing full well that he could not keep that promise.

We walked to the deck and he sat in the hammock. I sat in a chair at the table until he opened the hammock and asked me to sit with him. I told him I was fine but he persisted and so I lay in the hammock next to him; big mistake. We were like that for a little while as he told me a million things about how good the guys were and how they would do a good job and how I needed to think bigger and take care of myself and how my survivors could stay there. It was a seemingly endless verbal barrage. I kept listening and relaxing into his body. I was so comfortable with him it amazed me. Finally, after his monologue, I said OK. I couldn't see his face but I felt his body smile. He was happy and it made me happy as well. I cannot even explain why I cared that this man was happy. But I did. And for the next 3 minutes we laid happily together until he said he wanted to go for the deposit now. I had other ideas for our afternoon but hoisted myself out of the hammock. He jumped out and we prepared to leave. We would hitch to town since he had let the guys and the car go before.

We waited by the side of the road with shade and he took my hand. I leaned closer to him when he did it and we both looked for oncoming cars. When no one appeared immediately we began to walk. We strolled leisurely, both sure a ride would come soon, but nothing appeared. There was no one on the road. Instead we saw things: Caribbean blue jays, butterflies, people Amador knew, my neighbor's walking back with big jugs of water on their bikes or their shoulders. It added a dimension to the trip that allowed you to surrender to circumstance. There was no way to rush, no way to say when or how you would get there. It was a totally zen way of travel. Finally, a pickup truck came around the bend, slowed and motioned for us to get in the back. Amador helped me get into the truck and get comfortable sitting against the cab, then tapped the back window as a signal we were ready to move. We bumped gratefully along the road. As we neared the traffic light at town, Amador hit the window again lightly, gave the guy a thumbs up to say thanks and helped me get out of the truck. I felt the adventurer, the wanderer, the traveller, you name it but I felt good hitching. It was something that had been forbidden my entire life, but here it seemed such a great idea. Another great thing Amador had shown me. Before I became confused, I resolved to try it on my own the next time I was stuck for a ride.

The truck turned right and we headed left to town and the bank. The only bank in town was at the other end. We strolled until the sun became too much. Then we jumped into a taxi. I went into the bank while Amador called Efrain. Then I ran across to a *papeleria* for paper and a pen to write a description of the work and the amounts and for Efrain's signature. In about 10 minutes, Efrain arrived in his black sedan with the guys still in the back seat looking hot and bored. We signed, I counted out the money, he double checked it and then he left saying he would start in 2 days. He explained how he had to cut the wood and prepare workers etc. I did not mind, actually. I hated workers on my land so I was happy for a day or two to prepare. We shook hands and they left, presumably to go cut some wood.

Amador said, "great" and got ready to leave.

"You are going?" I asked him, hurt but I reminded myself he

was only around me for the money.

I had to accept that and work with that concept in the front of my mind or I would be miserable. But it was not easy. I wanted some company, someone to hang out with.

He took my hand and said, "Baybe, I got things to do. I see you tomorrow."

I pulled my hand away and told him okay. By the time I looked back, he had disappeared. He was amazingly fast when he wanted to be.

I walked to Mar Caribe Supermarket to buy some things for the house and then took a taxi home, leaving my solo hitching commitment for another day. I was suddenly exhausted.

Amador didn't show for a few days. But Efrain did. He was fairly punctual and after two peaceful mornings, I once again had workers on my land. They arrived at about 8 am. I was ready and had a place for them to put the supplies and a big trash barrel for their empty coke bottles. I still could not get used to how much the workers drank Coca-Cola. The country of Mexico had a love affair with it. Some workers even put it in as a requirement for working with you. I noticed that whenever I brought it, productivity went up. It was horrible but I figured that whatever they wanted to do with their bodies was their business. But I would not have their plastic trash on my property.

Once they settled in, Efrain wanted to talk about more money. I was prepared for that too, having learned more than I wanted to admit. I was patient with him and let him tell me what he wanted. I knew that no one liked a know-it-all, particularly a woman, particularly in Mexico. Too, I had learned that people, men in particular, liked to have their say. And I needed to take some time to focus on his Spanish to really understand it. When he finished, I told him I would pay for the materials and then pay the balance of his labor at the end, like it said in his proposal. I had known he would try to change once we got started because it had happened to me before. And what I also knew from experience, was that once I paid I would never see him again, at least not until he needed more money for another job. He looked at his feet when I told him exactly what he had initially agreed to and then he agreed, giving me a smile but not one big enough to make his eyes disappear. He was obviously not that happy.

By day 3, the roof was framed and they started to build the stairway. It would be a circular stairway or "*caracol*" as they called it in Spanish. They brought a magnificent trunk that would be in the center. "*Puro curazon*," Efrain told me as they dragged the 15-inch diameter pole over and began to put it into a hole filled with rocks and then poured concrete into it. I understood that meant it was strong and figured it was what we called "heart wood" back north. Regardless, I had respect for the wood and for the guys carrying it and placing it into the foundation. They were not big men but they were strong. They had those fire hydrant bodies that could be mistaken as fat but were solid muscle. By noon they had their shirts hiked up over their bellies to cool themselves and had placed the trunk into a meter deep hole filled with cement and stones and began carving the stairs with a chainsaw. I was astonished at the artistic carving but could not take the noise and took the dogs to the beach to relax. I locked the house and took my journal so that I could spend some time.

Coming over the bluff, I took my customary inhale as I viewed the nearly empty beach and the magnificent Caribbean Sea. We walked before I sat on the sand, looking out at the water. Once again, I felt so blessed.

"Even with all the shit, my life here is still so damned good," I said to myself.

Then I stripped down to my underwear, self consciously looking over my shoulder, and ran into the waves. It was heaven. I swam and floated and then came back and let the sun dry me before writing and then laying back and enjoying the sun. But in not too long a time, I got anxious about leaving the guys. Something bothered me and I felt the need to go back.

The dogs came with me easily once I dragged Lakra from her shady spot. She never liked the sun on her body. She must have understood she had skin cancer since whenever we went to the beach outside of early morning or late afternoon, she would find shade to walk or relax in. She naturally knew to take care of herself. Ama was always right with me and Goli would stay close, at least until a tourist came by.

But they all were happy to go back to the shade of the jungle and they followed me back over the dune and along the winding path through the flowery weeds and chit palms stunted by the constant wind and salt. I checked for traffic before we crossed. When I entered, I saw Amador talking animatedly with Efrain. It did not feel right. But when I came closer, they both appeared fine. Perhaps I had mistaken their body language but then I knew I had not when I moved closer and felt the thickness of the air around them. They had been arguing.

I told Amador hello, kissed him on the cheek and then asked Efrain if everything were OK saying, *"todo bien?"* He smiled big enough to make his eyes slits, said yes and went back to work. Amador asked me how it was going. I told him well and asked where he had been.

He answered me a little too defensively that he had "things to do." I could only imagine but didn't want to so I walked over to the deck.

He followed me closely asking, "They working well, no?" I went to get a treat for the dogs.

I finished making the dogs sit and told him that it seemed so. He seemed ill at ease for a man who was so relaxed nearly everywhere, and I asked him about it. He said he had lots to do and decided to leave. He kissed me on the lips and said goodbye. I wasn't sure how to feel. Everything about our relationship was confusing. I asked him if he didn't want to stay for dinner and regretted it the minute the words left my mouth. I was acting as if nothing he had done meant anything to me. He said he couldn't stay so I was relieved but felt rejected still. I torn by my feelings and felt all over the place with them.

I walked him to the gate and closed the door behind him as he said, "I coming back."

I had heard that too many times. I knew he always would but I couldn't help wonder when. And that voice on my shoulder told me that it would be at the worst time possible.

The next week they progressed slowly, very slowly. I wasn't sure what had happened but for 2 days they didn't even come to work. I couldn't get cell phone signal so I waited until 10 am and then let it go, enjoyed the silence and being on my own. When the workers finally returned, Efrain told me he would start the concrete walls soon and we would need cement.

He wanted me to leave my credit card at Cocopesa, the construction store, so he could get supplies whenever he needed them. I had been down that road with Bali and he had used my money to buy all the supplies to build his own house, not mine. I was not going to let that happen again. I told Efrain truthfully that I didn't mind coming with him to buy supplies. I liked the construction store with all the guys buying stuff and I liked to see people working and actually, to have a trip to town. Efrain was not as excited, but we went in his little dumpy black car, bought more cement than I thought we would need, ordered the "*polvo*" to mix with it and a little gravel as well.

Before we left town he asked me for more money explaining that his expenses were high and he needed to pay the workers. I explained to him that when he finished I would pay him. I stayed firm. It was one of the most difficult things for me about these construction projects. My tendency was to trust that the guys would do the work even if I had already paid most of their wages. But experience had taught me that it never worked that way: not in Mexico, not in the US. This time I was going to get it right and wait. I settled into the seat and we drove to the beach. The guys unloaded the cement, put it in a dry place and then left. I waited for the truck to come later with the *polvo* and the gravel. Efrain promised me he would be back the next day.

During this time I had been preparing to go to the states for a fundraiser for breast cancer called "Wine Women and Shoes". My friend Meg was on the organizing committee for the event. She had nominated me to participate in a fashion show where you got to wear Jimmy Choo shoes and designer dresses, based on the "look good / feel good" concept in which I believed. There would be a wine tasting and lecture and there would be some wealthy philanthropists there. I was excited, sure it would be a breakthrough for my foundation and my books. I had been sending letters and email inquiries daily and my mom was sending books to lists of influential people who had breast cancer or who were involved somehow with the disease. Still no one had jumped on buying a million of them. I was sure it could happen at this event. If it didn't, I would have a night out, re-connect with my childhood friend and meet some cool people.

I had instantly committed when Meg called the year before. But I had not realized I would have so many lose ends in Tulum. Kim and Felix said they would take care of the dogs but I had not yet approached them about taking care of the construction. I had not told them that Amador had found Efrain for me. Nor had I mentioned that he hit me that day. Saying it to someone made it more real than I could handle. I was still trying to put it into that "never happened" folder that I had in the back of my brain. So I asked them if they could help me deal with Efrain. I had not seen Amador for nearly a week and I had a feeling he would not come back until I paid. Felix was actually excited about managing the project and being at the beach. They would stay at the house and I knew I could count on them to take care of my dogs.

We went over things to do one afternoon when Feelix and Kim came by to have a swim and a few beers on the beach. I had a flight for the next week and told him that perhaps the construction would be finished. Somehow when I said it I knew it was an unrealizable dream. But as we spoke the truck from Cocopesa came and dumped a few more meters of gravel and *polvo* into the entryway. At least if Efrain showed, he would have materials. The dogs loved the light reddish brown *polvo* and all peed into it and then dug holes and sat on top as if on lookout. I scolded them, imagining the cement might smell of pee if they continued and we all went for a walk on the beach.

Felix took the cooler and his chairs. I grabbed towels and some bags for poop and we crossed the street noticing the pink hues to the clouds as they reflected the setting sun. I had a swim and then we sat and talked about life. Feelix had perspective on many things. He had been in Viet Nam and had nearly died there. He knew what made a difference and shared that with me as he opened a bottle of wine for me and a beer for himself. We watched the moon rise under the pink clouds with the dogs sitting around us and touched our beverages in a toast: "It doesn't get much better than this," he said, quoting my father.

Chapter 37

I abandoned ideas of finishing the construction work before I left when Efrain showed up three days later with 2 workers instead of the 4 he had before. They put stucko, or *masia*, onto the walls to cover the concrete blocks that formed the structure. But they were moving incredibly slowly, so much so that I couldn't even watch. I left for the beach after checking where they would put windows and the door. We discussed the floor for the downstairs area and I asked him if he knew how to make a floor with stones. I had seen these fabulous floors and walls made of a flat, chiseled stone called *"vista maya."* I thought it would be nice for the floor in the outdoor kitchen space, working the motif of the stones I had used in the garden into the kitchen.

Efrain jumped on the idea, telling me he could get the stones and he would bring me samples that afternoon. He left the 2 guys working and took off with an enthusiasm I had not expected. When I came back from the beach, he had returned with about 4 or 5 stones to show me. He told me that he could get more and they cost 10 pesos each, about one dollar. I would need 300. I told him I would think about it in my characteristic need to think about things before I spent. He got anxious and told me it was a good price and how they were good stones and they were not so easy to find. He followed me to my house talking, trying to get me to commit immediately until I stopped moving, looked at him and repeated that I would think about it and tell him the next day. I asked him if he planned on working.

He told me *"claro que sí"*, of course.

I said, *"bueno"* and then commented on how slow the guys were. He kicked the dirt and told me told me good work took time. I nodded agreement but I liked him less every day.

The following morning he arrived at about 9 with the same 2 guys. I had gone over my numbers and was comfortable buying the stones. I told him so. He happily ran off to get them once I gave him a deposit. When he came back, I introduced him to Felix and Kim who had come to visit and go over things with the house and the dogs. After he met them he asked me about Amador. I told him he was not there. My language skills did not permit me to elaborate so I said, *"no esta,"* he is not here. My reply seemed to make him happy and I wondered why he had asked.

But I had no time to wonder more about Efrain's relation to Amador since I would be leaving in 2 days. There was a lot to manage before hand. I knew Kim and Felix could handle things so long as Amador stayed away. I prayed that he would. They were happy to be in my beach house and the dogs loved them. They stayed with me the night before I left. Early that Wednesday morning I took the dogs to the beach, had a swim and waited for taxi number 517 to take me to the airport. Manuel was Sylvia's friend and a great contact for a relatively cheap fare. He was chubby, his shirt barely met his pants when he opened the door for me and his smile was missing 2 front teeth. But it was a real smile and he was a happy person. Sylvia had mentioned that he could help me with just about anything. He had contacts. I would not need his help more than to get me to the airport. But I reminded myself to perhaps call him before I called the police.

I was sad to leave my house and my dogs but I was excited about the event and my role in it. I would meet new people, people who were influential in the medical and non-profit world. I hoped to meet collaborators. We would save the world together. I still had that vision: selling a million books, no matter how many people told me to lower my expectations.

One friend told me, "isn't one million a lot?"

I answered, "yes, but so was 100,000 and at the end of the day, 1,000,000 was just a number".

The goal was to help a lot of people and share what I had learned. I knew my experience was not universal, some women had totally different needs. But the feelings were universal. And my booklets were the best thing I had ever done. I was sure the world needed them and I needed some money to do something even better. I was certain it would all work out.

In the states, I stayed with my younger brother in his new house on a beautiful salt marsh on the south shore of Massachusetts. He loaned me his car to go to meetings and lunches and rehearsals where I would put on thousand dollar dresses and shoes and feel amazingly beautiful. I was having a ball. In the mornings I did yoga against the backdrop of his lawn that extended to the salt marsh and then the Jones River that meandered out to the Plymouth Bay. I would sit in their oversized windows with a coffee working until I had a meeting or luncheon. When I could, I saw family in the evening or worked more. I was passionate about the entire project.

About 2 weeks into my stay, a few days before the event, I got an email from Kim that said Amador had been by and was looking for me. She said that fortunately, Felix had not been there. Amador was polite with Kim but he was looking for Efrain. Kim told me that

Efrain had come back for several days after I left but then asked Felix for money. When Felix said no, he never returned. My shoulders fell and I slouched in my chair as I read the message. All my enthusiasm shifted into a ball of anxiety and disappointment.

She mentioned that Efrain told Felix he had been paying a commission to Amador for getting him the work. Efrain said that Amador wanted to be paid every week and it was cutting into the quality of the job. I couldn't believe it. I couldn't understand why he wouldn't get out of my life and go.

"Because you pay him in so many different ways," the voice on my shoulder told me.

But I didn't understand how not to pay him. He was a leech that was sucking me dry emotionally and financially and I couldn't get him off my back.

Kim finished the email telling me not to worry but that if things got crazy for them at the house with Amador, they would take the dogs to town and lock up. She was afraid for Felix's temper and didn't want to deal with "Amador's bullshit". I started to cry. They would leave my property and I would have to figure it out. I had a little less than 2 weeks still in the states and I was not going to let Amador mess this up for me. I committed to finishing what I was doing, thanked Kim for telling me, apologized for Amador's presence and told her I understood whatever she needed to do.

I asked if she could check on the place every so often if they were not there then told her I appreciated it and to please stay in touch. And then I closed the computer, cried a little and let it go. I reminded myself that there was nothing I could do from my brother's and unless I wanted to let all this work go out the window and my foundation fall on itself, I needed to "let go and let God" as my daily affirmation book told me. My new mantra became, "if it is meant to be, it will be." And I practiced it daily, hourly, sometimes non-stop. But sometimes I did not need to.

For example, the day I went to try on dresses for the show. I put on an emerald green silk dress with heels from Jimmy Choo and felt so fabulous that nothing could burst the bubble. The dress was about $3,000 and there were people in the audience who would spend that easily. The shoes were $900 and there was a silent auction for them. They would probably go for more. In my life, I had never valued spending that much on clothes. It seemed exaggerated and not wise.

But when I put that dress on, the way I felt was indescribable and, had I the money, I would have bought it. Even if I just put it on in the evening after a long day at work to feel beautiful.

My friend Meg took me to lunch and introduced me to the board of directors. My foundation and my bio would go into the program. Every item on the list of "to-do's" for successful PR and non-profits was there. I could feel myself and my goals growing and becoming healthier with every step. The day of the show, I climbed into my sister-in-law's Toyota and drove myself into the Hynes Auditorium. As I pulled around the corner of their house where you could glimpse the Jones River and New England houses meeting corn-fields, the phone rang. I answered happily and then inhaled, it was Amador.

I pulled the car over so I could concentrate and tried to explain where I was and how important this was to me. He wanted to discuss the construction and why I was not there. I told him I did not need to discuss it with him. He got angry, I could hear it in his voice. I told him I would take care of things when I got back. He told me I needed to do it now, that things were not moving forward.

When I asked him why he cared, he went ballistic and said, "You got to send me money to make this work and keep Efrain."

I smiled, even though I wanted to cry, and I was shaking as I said it but I said, "No. I do not need to send anything."

There was silence on the line for a second or two and then he said, "No? You don' think so? I show you then."

And he hung up. I couldn't believe it and I repeated his name several times until I heard the ring tone. I started to panic and cry but then pulled myself together, repeated the "let go and let God" mantra and shifted back into drive so that I could get on the highway and make the event on time.

The entire drive, I worried about what he would do, if he would hurt Kim and Feelix or the dogs or perhaps go in and take over my land. Finally, after 45 minutes, I walked into the hall with all the beautiful people and their beautiful husbands and wives and let myself forget it. I stood tall and looked for my friend Meg behind stage and pretended nothing was wrong so that I could enjoy the night. But at the final part of the show, as I looked out on the audience full of husbands and families with flowers for their survivors and saw no one of mine, I knew I was "paying the price for my own voluntary decisions," as my dad used to say. I was responsible for where I was: alone. Even if I was working toward a dream, I was alone because of choices I had made. In that moment, I was hardly sure they were the right ones.

After the party and silent auction and all the families and couples and me alone, I drove home and made a cup of tea in my brother's kitchen. He came out from his bedroom and asked me how things went. We sat together on his couch and looked out over the field and the river. It was spectacular.

I finished my tea with his dogs and congratulated myself on at least doing things my way. Whether or not I had done things right, and even though I was paying the price for my own voluntary decisions, that voice on my shoulder told me I would be okay.

The next week was full of last minute errands and obligations. I followed up with everyone I had met at the event and received several copies of the programs with publicity for my non-profit. I was in touch with other non-profits and some philanthropists and business people. But I was not any closer to selling a million books to hospitals or cancer patients. On the contrary, I was receiving requests for money from many of the same non-profits I was hoping to approach to help me. It was depressing and nearly time to head back to Mexico. My doctors said I was well, superb even. But I was dragging emotionally. They loved my idea about bringing patients to Mexico and the counseling group told me they would publicize the program and help me find people who could benefit from my offer of a week or two on the Caribbean. But they had no money for books. I had to figure out another way to sell one million and keep my dream alive financially.

In that time, I had pushed some doors open and some had closed in my face. I was tired and I missed my dogs, my house, the beach and my dream. I needed to touch it again and I decided to stay with my mom for a night or two before heading back to Mexico. I packed the car and waited for my brother to come back from work to say goodbye and thank him. He was surprised to see me there, car full, waiting with his dogs.

"Fanny," he said.

We hugged and I told him I was leaving and that I so appreciated everything he had done for me. I invited him to come see me in Mexico.

He looked at me and said, "I thought you would stay longer, you know, to get your shit together."

I smiled. I told him I thought I pretty much had it together and this was what I wanted to do. He understood his *faux pas*.

We had a deal. He would let me make my own mistakes. I gave him a hug, told him I loved him and that my mom would return the car the day I left so he should be ready with dinner. We laughed and I left feeling powerful and for a moment, so very sure of myself. I had my shit together. I just needed a little more time to demonstrate it.

Chapter 38

There was a fabulously distressed 1998 VW bug that my friend offered to sell me. The "*vocho,*" as they called them in Mexico, was spray painted grey and yellow on top of it's original forest green. Elise had used the rest of the yellow spray paint to transform the formerly green and black interior into a spotted green leapord pattern. I loved it on many different levels. It ran and was affordable, $1,000 US, as well as so distinctive that no one would steal it. It was so loud that I often joked with her that I could hear her coming to class 20 minutes before she got there. But it was the type of car that belied class. It was not for rich girls and I did not want to be seen as one, although my reputation so far in Tulum was some one who did not take care of her money. I sent her a deposit from the states and organized to pick it up when I returned from my brother's.

On the way to the airport, I told my mom I would have a car. She raised an eyebrow and asked if I had not already bought one or two. I exhaled and told her it was only one car that Amador had stolen from me.

My mother, concerned, said, "Darling" without adding anything.

I had not pressed charges because I did not want to hurt him. Too, I never had the paperwork correct or the desire to put him in jail. Crazy, right? He had lost it finally to the police in an act of pure idiocy. I told my mom this time would be different. I was done with Amador and he would not want this car, I knew it. She told me she hoped so. I smiled and told her not to worry.

I was excited to leave the northeast. I had planted seeds for That Barry Girl Foundation and knew I could maintain my contacts from Mexico. Sheba and Paul seemed happy with the work I was doing, although not happy with sales or with the money coming in. Neither was I. But I knew that with time something would happen financially. I asked them to be patient. But I wondered if we could be. Regardless, I needed to get back to see what shape my house was in. I had contacted Beth Israel's oncology social work center and I would get some candidates to come to Mexico soon. Things were happening. They just were not happening fast enough and we were all running out of money.

As I changed planes in Miami, in line at a Starbucks, my phone rang. It was Kim asking when I would come back. When I told her I was on my way, she sounded relieved. I planned on taking the bus and picking up my new car in town to get home. She laughed when I told her the car I had bought. Everyone knew that car. She told me she would wait for me at the house and mentioned there had been some problems but said we should talk about it when I arrived. I knew from Amador's calls that he had acted out, for lack of a better term, but I hoped it was not so bad. When I hung up the phone and got back in line, I had a sick feeling that things were not going to be so easy back in Tulum. To help me cope, I bought 2 bags of Organic Mexican coffee with my latté, paid with a credit card that I hoped would work and stuffed them into my carry on, intent to succeed.

The crossing from Florida to Mexico was relatively short and incredibly beautiful. Each time I made that trip, I had something on my mind that the view allowed me to clear. The sea was generally so transparent as you came close to Cancun that in places you could see the bottom, notice the gradual and not so gradual changes in depth and imagine, if not see, all the marine life there. This day there were gentle white caps on the waves but you could easily see the sandy bottom migrating with the currents. It was mesmerizing right into the moment of the landing. The plane was relatively empty and the lines at customs were short. I rapidly passed for my baggage and leaving, pushed the traffic light button that allowed you to either pass without inspection or pass with inspection. I got the green light but nonetheless had missed the bus and would have to wait another hour for the next one. Lazy and a little anxious, I hired a driver to take me back justifying that my time and my back were valuable too. The change in Playa alone with my over sized, over stuffed bag would challenge my back and my energy.

The taxi driver dropped me in front of the bus station where I saw my grey, green and yellow VW bug and my friend's marvelously big brown hair. We hugged, exchanged papers and she showed me a few of the nuances of the car, like the passenger side door not really closing and the trick to getting it to stay shut and then to opening it again. I would eventually put a bungee cord on to hold it shut but for now she showed me how to lift the latch and get it to work well. Then she told me that if the engine got wet, it would not start so that I needed to keep a plastic bag handy and cover it every night in case of rain. I asked her if there was anything else.

She shrugged and said to me, "Over time everything here wears out."

Tired of Tulum, she was heading back to DC to try something new. I believed she would be back.

I started the engine feeling slightly embarrassed of the noise but very happy to be mobile. Elise waved and walked away as I shifted into reverse and then jumped into first gear and drove down the interior part of the *Avenida Tulum* heading south. The car jumped slightly when I shifted into second. I was not used to a clutch, or this go cart of a car but I was smiling. Something about the car made me happy. People noticed me; for the noise and the car. It was really a work of art: distressed art but art none the less.

I jumped through a U-turn to head back to the beach and plodded along the beach road with cars passing me. I nearly stalled at every speed bump. They had paved the road in my absence and, although I was not sure I agreed, it made it easier for me to drive and I was grateful. Finally, I made it to my door. I wanted to hug that big wooden gate and just as I arrived, Kim opened it and started to laugh. "Look at you" she said to me.

I smiled and ran out of the car to give her a hug. We both laughed. She suggested I put the car inside. I realized something was up but we decided it was a good idea. It fit perfectly. The dogs were howling with glee and Ama was literally jumping up and down. I was home.

I gave the dogs their share of love, gave Kim one of the organic coffees and we sat down at the dining table.

"How'd it go?" I asked.

She said there were some issues but that first she wanted to hear from me. I told her about the event, all the people I had met and how amazing it was to put on a $3,000 dress. She shook her head agreeing. Kim had been an attorney in Texas. She had owned a radio station and race horses and she knew the value of expensive clothes. But she also knew how to drive a bargain. We both knew that it didn't really matter in the end and that was what made us good friends.

I finished telling her that I thought it had been a good investment of time for the foundation and great to see my family. Then I let her speak. She told me that Amador had come back. He and Felix did not fight but Amador was surprised to see them. He mostly wanted to talk with Efrain and when they did, they had an animated discussion. She assured me she had not left the house when Amador was there and I thanked her. Apologizing, I told her Amador had called me for money and that I told him no. I assumed it was after the call that he came by. She told me that later Felix had spoken with Efrain and it seemed, at least according to Efrain, that Amador was asking Efrain to pay him a portion of their earnings, like a commission for getting them the job. I felt my energy slip through my chest and out into the garden. How could I have been so stupid, I asked myself. Kim put her hand on my shoulder. I inhaled and then understood why Efrain could not keep guys working and why he was constantly asking for money. It was Amador sucking him dry.

Kim went on to tell me that Amador had come by another afternoon when Efrain was not there and asked to talk to Felix. He was not aggressive and just had some questions about me. Felix did not answer and when Amador asked how the job was going and about life on the beach, Felix said good and ended the conversation. Kim told me that Felix came back shaking his head wondering what it had all been about. Otherwise, she told me, it was pretty quiet and lovely at my house. I did not mention how Amador had threatened me over the phone or how he had ruined my night.

We walked over to see the construction and Kim took a bottle of tequila from her bag. I ran back to grab two shot glasses saying I did not want to drink from the bottle. The circular stairway was finished and they had completed a beautiful sink formed of concrete in the kitchen. The floor was not well done. I didn't want to count the stones but I was sure he had short changed me on that.

"You could just pour concrete over it," Kim said to me and continued, "Felix tried to make them work well but that Efrain is something else."

Upstairs, the loft space was perfect. We had put in long, thinish rectangular windows on the side facing my neighbors and one horizontal one on the side facing the street. One day they might build on that space they had stolen from me. The other two sides were open. The side facing the garden had a big deck and a beautiful window. The palm leaves nearly entered. And the side facing the house was one big open window. It was fabulously just what I wanted. I didn't care that the kitchen floor was a bit uneven and more concrete than "*vista maya*" or that the bathroom was directly off the kitchen and downstairs. The upstairs space was fabulous. People could heal here and I was happy that I had built it. The *palapa* was high enough to give the illusion of much more space and the *guano* they had used to build it was fresh and somehow exotic. I gave Kim a hug before she poured us two shots of tequila. We toasted to good friends and big adventures and to surviving. I knew she had survived more than she had ever let me know and I admired her for it. Then she put her tequila in her bag and told me she had to go home. Felix was waiting.

When I closed the gate behind her after waving her away down the road, I walked back to the house content and ready to move forward. I was nearly ready to host my first survivor. It was exciting and energizing. The three dogs were on the porch wagging their tails. I asked them if they wanted to go to the beach and Ama jumped up and down, Lakra howled and Goli ran to the gate. I kicked off my shoes and we crossed to the beach. It was nearly dark and the last bits of sunset were reflecting in the clouds.

I had forgotten that Amador might be anywhere around and I let the dogs off their leashes as soon as we crossed the street. They ran up the dune fast and then I heard Lakra barking on the other side. I hurried to reach the top of the bluff to see what was happening and it was Lakra and Goli running after Pelicans. They were chasing them back and forth, Ama watching, knowing better than to think she could catch one. Goli was in the water but Lakra kept running up and down the shore where there were about 4 Pelicans fishing. I laughed and looked out past them to the horizon to see the Gulf Stream. I said thanks to God and Jesus and then added Buddha and Mohammed. The tequila had made me magnanimous. Then I ran down the bluff and called the dogs to join me. I was happy to be home, no matter what shit might be waiting for me the next day.

Chapter 39

Over the next month, I found a carpenter to install windows and I tiled the bar myself since I didn't have the money or patience to pay anyone. Travel, credit card bills, health insurance and Amador had sucked me dry. Too, Kim said she and I could do it. She had all the tools and had done some tiling in the past. There was no end to what this woman could do and how generous she was with her time. I wanted a mosaic on the kitchen bar and white tiles around the kitchen sink in the house; simple and clean. Kim told me the mosaic was not hard but that I needed to break more than a few tiles to make it happen. I had not really thought about it but knew I could at least break tiles.

We bought the tiles in Playa, using her red Land Rover since the *vocho* would never make the drive. When we walked into the display shop, I immediately felt underdressed, understyled or under-something. I noticed my dirty nails as I touched oversized marble tiles. I could never keep them clean in the jungle. I felt this yearning in the center of my chest for times gone by as I saw the green soap stone I put in my bathroom in Boston. When I brought my hand to feel the coolness of the stone and touch the gentle discolorations that made it so exotic, the shop person asked if she could help me. I inhaled and looking down at my dirty feet in flip flops brought myself back to my current reality. I wanted basic. The sales person brought me to the back of the store. I found exactly the tile I wanted and bought 3 boxes each of blue and of white. I was happy with the colors and that the charge went through on my credit card. I told myself work would come this week and to make the time to do it.

When we got home, Kim showed me how to break the tiles. She wrapped 4 or 5 in a thick towel, took a hammer and started to whack them with it. It was noisy but very liberating. I practiced.

Kim approved and told me, "when you have 2 cases done, give me a shout and we'll start. For now, lets do the whole tiles."

We started the next morning after coffee. Kim showed me how to put down the adhesive and then, with her tile cutter, how to cut the tiles and place them, using the same trick my dad had shown me in what seemed another lifetime: coins for spacers. My dad used nickels but Kim used 5 peso coins. The result was the same: a perfectly aligned line of tiles that moved your eye into a clean white space. Then we went to the beach to let it dry.

When we came back, the tiles were set. We made the grout and put it between them. It was a blue grey color that matched the concrete in the bathroom and you had to push it into the space between the tiles. It was hard work. As the sun set, we were tired and sweaty and both ready to quit. But we were done with that portion and we stood back and admired our work.

"Like I said, it isn't difficult but it is work" she told me in her Texas accent with her hands on her hips.

Then she reminded me that when I finished breaking all those other tiles, I could call her to do the mosaic. She was a gift from God.

The carpenter was actually Kim's find. Jose Louis had built cabinets and doors and even put a little dog door in for Kim. I was sure he could frame a few windows and a door for me. His estimate was not too high and I knew I would have a deposit from work at the end of the month. It seemed I was going through money quickly again and with 2 days work per week, I was barely keeping up with my expenses. But I had faith it would all work out. I had my yoga classes for food and then my engineering work was paying everything else. We had managed enough with fundraisers to donate some books and make our first cash grant to a woman in treatment but I was the one responsible for Mexico. Nothing from my non-profit could be used to build here. I had this annoying fear that people and the IRS, would think I was building a house for myself with the money from my foundation. I could not let that happen. Too, the more my partners knew about the project in Mexico and my involvement with Amador, the less they wanted to do with it. I kept the costs separate but it was straining me.

I managed to give Jose Louis a deposit in the next week and he told me that in one week he would install the windows. We discussed some shelving and a piece of furniture for the upstairs. But I only had enough for the windows and door. Too, I reminded myself I had to get a bed, stock the kitchen and get a table and chairs. Fortunately, no one was coming yet. I had a little time. So I poured all those frustrating moments worrying about money and remembering how much Amador had stolen from me into breaking tiles for my mosaic. I would envision his face in the towel full of tiles as I hit it hard and broke everything inside. Some nights my arm was sore from my remedial but functional therapy.

I had been back nearly a month and I had not seen Amador. After the way he treated me when I was in the states I was happier not to have him around. I noticed that the longer he stayed away, the happier I was. The more tiles I broke, the less I needed to break them. Little by little, I worked out other issues with the tiles and let Amador slip from my consciousness. I was soon able to tell Kim I had enough tiles for the mosaic and we were ready to begin.

Mosaic tiling is not just throwing the tiles down into cement like I thought. Each piece has to be selected to fit into the larger piece. It is sort of a puzzle that has about a million pieces. I had never really had the patience for puzzles and thought that 45 was late to start. But Kim guided me through the first round. The thing with the mosaic is that you still need to move quickly so that the cement doesn't dry. So you only put a small amount of cement down as you fill in the pieces. Then you need to keep the cement wet to put it down little by little. Kim and I started and then she left me on my own telling me she would come back when I was ready to grout.

"And don't forget: the spacing between each piece needs to be the same. Use your pesos," she called to me as she got into her car.

I settled into the work and hours passed before I got much done. My shoulders and neck ached and my fingers were bleeding by the end of the first day and I had only covered half the bar. It had not helped that I started at noon and was ready for a swim by 4. I packed things up and covered the cement with cellophane so that I could take the dogs to the beach and wash my sweaty body in the ocean before bed. I vowed to start earlier the next day.

It took me two more days to finish the bar. Kim came over and we grouted together and then she reminded me about the front and the sides.

"Don't you want them done as well? It looks a little bit lonely with out that part finished," she told me as she cleaned her hands from the grout we had just placed.

I was tired of the whole thing. She could tell. Too, I needed to break more tiles before we could start again. The work was good but it was hot and the *tabanos*, those biting red flies, were in season. It was impossible to whack them with the cement and tiles in your hand so you had to let them bite. Kim's bites turned into grapefruit sized mounds on her legs as we worked. I had lemon size mounds that itched for about an hour and then went away. How she wanted to continue was beyond me. I told her we should go to the beach and think about it. The sun would be down soon and I could break tiles in the cool of the night and start again tomorrow.

We took the dogs to the beach and then relaxed with a tequila as we looked at our work. It was lovely and it changed the kitchen immensely. Where it was super rustic before, now it was rustic but artsy. We decided to do the front and sides. Maybe it was the tequila or perhaps it was just me but I told her I would like to put a peace sign on the front. When you entered the kitchen it would be the first thing you saw. She laughed but said it was a good idea. To start the next day, I needed to start breaking tiles.

I was ready for her the next day but the *tabanos* were crippling Kim. Between the heat and the bugs, she was miserable. I asked her to let me do the rest on my own and when I finished I would call her to critique. After all, how long could it take? She limped home after finishing the sides with me and left me to do the peace sign in front. I was happy with that. I could take my time and do things the way I wanted. I sat on the floor with my coffee the next morning and began placing the tiles in cement. I used white for the background and did the peace sign in blue. The work went slowly but well.

Nearly two hours into the work, I stood up to stretch and take a look. I smiled to see it. But then I heard my name yelled at the front gate: Amador. He was there with Chito, a mutual friend. I liked Chito but when he was drinking or on drugs he was frightening, like most of the guys around me. There was a small Mayan man behind him with a package.

"I bring you a present," Amador told me and then told the guy to come in with the package.

Amador was stoned and dirty. His shirt looked as if it had not seen a washer in weeks and his face was smudged with dust or something. But his smile was infectious, probably like his clothing but I tried not to think about it. I turned my cheek as he gave me a kiss. The small Mayan man brought the package to the deck and Amador had me open it. It was a cage of some sorts and inside was a baby toucan. I wasn't happy and I told Amador that it was illegal to take these birds.

He said, "But look, baybe, look. He no have a mom or anything.

We saved him."

I wondered. Regardless, the bird was adorable and nearly tame. I took it in my hands and stroked his black feathers as he made a clucking sound. His feet were wonderfully blue and he rubbed his long beak onto my breast.

"But where will I put him?" I asked.

Chito, always resourceful, noticed the dog crate and said that he could stay there until we built a bigger space. We took a tree branch and put it inside so that the bird could have a perch while he was safe from the dogs and other animals. He jumped up onto it immediately and started to hop around inside. It was fabulous to see him and I was smiling from ear to ear. I put the crate on the table and asked the Mayan man what I fed him. He told me fruit and *masa*. I had no idea what *masa* was, but we cut up some papaya and put it into a little bowl inside. The poor toucan was starving and he pecked at the food until he had eaten it all.

When we had finished watching him, I put some water in and he gently dipped his beak in and then tipped it back to let the water run down his throat. I told Amador thank you and walked them to the door.

Chito said goodbye but before Amador left he said, "Baybe, there is just one thing with this bird. You got to pay for it."

I lost my mind in that moment and asked him, "What?" as if I didn't understand. "Did you say you brought me a present and I have to pay for it?"

He smiled and told me he was sorry but he didn't have the money but wanted to bring me something. He continued to tell me that if I didn't want the bird the guy would take him back and sell him somewhere else. I couldn't believe what he was saying or doing. I looked at him with scorn and anger and whatever else I could muster and asked him how much.

He told me it was just "2500 pesos," almost 250 dollars.

I sank emotionally and physically and sat on the ground by the door. I barely had that much in the bank and he would take it from me.

I looked at the bird but could not imagine putting it back into that undersized cage. I told Amador I needed to go to the bank to get the money. We went in the white van he was driving. When I asked him who's car it was, he told me "mines," in his not so adorable anymore bad English. I corrected him but he was too stoned to understand. I didn't talk to any of them on the way to the bank. When I paid Amador, he told me the bird was worth twice the amount. I told him I didn't care and to leave me alone. When he offered me a ride back to the beach, I told him I would find a cab. I was sick of him. I took a walk in town looking for *masa* before I went back to the beach, my dogs, my mosaic and my new toucan.

Lakra, Ama and Goliath were waiting for me when I came home. I sat down with Lakra, looked at the Toucan in his crate and started to cry. I sobbed and asked myself how I could be so stupid and gullible and then asked myself how Amador could be such a jerk. Lakra didn't say a word. She looked at me with sympathetic eyes that didn't judge. That was why I loved her so much. But I felt so very beaten. I had a cup of tea and started to make the *masa* into little balls that the toucan could eat. I had found the *masa* on the street behind the fruit store Pool, pronounced 'pole' in Tulum. The woman sold it from her house and had a little handwritten sign above the door saying '*masa*', nothing more. I asked her if she knew that toucan's liked it. She told me yes and then she showed me how to make the little balls for them. The interaction lifted my spirits and reminded me that kind people still existed. It was just a shame I happened to have slept with the biggest asshole in town.

When I finished about a dozen little *masa* balls, I went to the cage and put some inside, next to the remains of the papaya. The baby toucan hopped over to it on his blue legs, took a piece in his long beak, ate some and made a mess with the rest. I put another one in to watch him do the same. We went through 6 of the 12 before he and I both tired of the game and I put the others in the cooler for the morning. I was suddenly exhausted, hungry and in need of a swim. I grabbed a banana, put on my suit and took the dogs to the beach. We came home and I made quesadillas, drank a half bottle of wine and went to bed with the three dogs around or under me and the toucan gently perched on the crooked little stick in his crate. I was not quite sure what I would do with the baby but I knew God would help me. I was sure of it.

I developed a gentle rhythm with the toucan, feeding him after the dogs, buying more fruit than usual and becoming very good friends with the woman who sold *masa*. My mosaic was going slowly but it was progressing and I loved it and worked on it for about 2 hours each day after the "feedings." I had half the peace sign finished when Chito came by to see how the toucan was. I didn't want to let him in and I had not told many people I had the bird. The story was embarrassing: my ex conned me into buying a toucan from a poacher. But I could not deny to Chito that it was true and he had brought materials to help me build a cage. He suggested we use the posts under the deck of the new house with the floor of the deck being the roof. We enclosed the space with chicken wire and found some poles and sticks to build perches. Amador came by once to see what Chito was doing but I didn't speak to him. He pretended to help for about half an hour and then left. But at the end of the afternoon, the toucan had a nice space to live in. It was raised off the ground and Chito even made a little gate to open and close to feed him.

By the time he had finished, I had forgiven him and gave him a hug. Before leaving, Chito asked me his name, I told him I called him Toucan after a track friend I used to have in college. He laughed and we put him in his new space. He clucked almost like a chicken but deeper and hopped on his 2 wonderful blue feet along the perches. He was adorable hopping from side to side, up and down along the poles.

I put my finger into the cage to say hello and he came up to me and touched me with his beak. He probably thought my finger was *masa* but I imagined he knew I was his friend and it was our greeting. Chito told me to be careful since the toucan's beak was so strong he could break my finger. I kept my hands inside more after that but kept calling him Toucan.

About 3 days later, I was still at the mural, nearly finished and getting ready to push grout into the peace sign when Amador yelled my name at the gate. I didn't move. He yelled again and this time said "please" so I went to answer, always a sucker for politeness. I opened the gate and he pushed himself inside rather than waiting for me to invite him. I didn't like it and told him so. He said sorry but he asked me if he could please use my bathroom, confiding that he was sick and needed to use it. I told him to get sick in his own bathroom but he was running for mine before I could finish the sentence.

"Here we go," I said to myself and slowly followed him into the house.

"You have no right to just come in here Amador and use my

toilet. It isn't yours and I am not here for you to do whatever you need to in my house," I told him.

He stayed in the bathroom and told me he knew saying, "Sorry baybe, sorry."

I went out to the deck since I still only had a curtain for the bathroom door and didn't want to be a witness to his health issues. I remembered him calling me in DC from the toilet in San Francisco Supermarket and telling me how he was so happy to take a shit. He was a piece of work. My smile faded as I heard a police siren. It was strange. You barely heard police sirens in the town, let alone here on the beach. Even stranger was that it seemed to stop in front of my house.

I figured my neighbors had done something when I heard Amador call me and say, "Baybe, if they looking for me. Tell them I not here."

I inhaled before I poked my head into the bathroom and, trying not to exhale, asked him what he meant. He said to please not tell the police he was here. I couldn't believe it. After he had conned me and now was clogging my septic tank he wanted me to hide him from the police. Internally, I refused. But so far they had not knocked on my door. Amador grunted. I waited on the porch for him to come out before I asked him to leave. But still no knock on the door. I believed he was just messing with me, making things more dramatic than they were. It was so Mexican.

Then I heard it: a loud knock on the front gate and a call, "Policia."

I told myself to let them in and see what they would find. Then I remembered I had no building permits and the toucan. I heard my father say to me "guilt by association" and I got more uncomfortable with each step closer to the gate. There were two police officers at the door and I greeted them as I opened the door. They asked me if a man named Amador was inside.

"No."

I couldn't believe I was saying it and as the lie came out of my mouth, I felt dirty but also a little dangerous and more interesting. Then they showed me a very bad picture of him and I shook my head. I was in the movies. One of the two poked his head into the gate and I invited him inside. The other officer told me that it was not necessary and then thanked me for my time. I closed the gate both loving and hating myself and it would have appeared Amador as well.

When I got to the house, I heard the toilet flush and Amador came out saying, "thanks baybe, I know you not turn me in," and then he puckered his lips for a kiss.

It was comical, a bad B movie. He came at me for his kiss with his arms open. I pushed him away and told him to get out. He took the push as a sort of detour and walked a little more slowly saying he knew I loved him. I sat down at the table, put my head in my hands and asked myself how much weirder things could get.

Chapter 40

I may have still loved him, but it was nice not to see him for a while. Nearly a month passed with no A sighting or A visit. I had my toucan and the dogs and my few friends. I had my *vocho* so that even when they would close the entrance to the beach, as the new owners had started to do, I could take the dogs up to the biosphere and we could run. I actually liked it better. The beach there was rugged and we rarely saw anyone while more and more tourists were coming to the beach by my house. It was an outing. The dogs loved getting into that car and I loved driving it. There was something adventurous and romantic about it. You had to drive slowly, it didn't go that fast. The car had a great turning radius so you could get around potholes easily. It was small enough to park anywhere and it was actually quite rugged in the sand. I never got stuck. And everyone smiled to see it. Whether they were laughing at me or smiling with me, it made me happy to add smiles to the world and to be mobile in doing so.

Kim and Felix came to visit and often invited me for dinner. We laughed a lot with each other. We drank a lot too and some nights I had to say no. I suffered after many of those nights, each morning swearing off drink until someone invited me for one. And I had my yoga daily with or without a hangover. I had my classes at VSK and started classes in the structure behind the house on the mornings I would not go to Jade. At 7:30 a few friends came over and we practiced together. It became a my routine, my comfort and a great way to do something besides drinking with people I liked. My yogi carpenters would be here for another few months and they were

545

advancing in their practice, although one or two had already gone back to the US. Their project was finishing. Soon a new chapter would start for each of them. I would miss them and our times together. But I was learning to trust the flow of things. I appreciated each day, each new person in my life, each time I placed my foot into the sand and the ocean and I reminded myself that it would not last forever.

I finally finished the new house, my casita. It was a sweet place. Somedays, if it were rainy or too buggy, we would do the morning yoga class there behind the screened walls. I had no furniture yet and about 6 people could fit. I believed I was adding good energy to the place. Although Bali had knocked on the gate and called my name one afternoon. I barely wanted to talk to him ever again. He had robbed me of so much and justified it by saying it was my fault for being with Amador. I took that responsibility although he used it to his advantage. That day, I slowly walked to the gate and without opening it, asked him what he wanted. He said they would start to build shortly and I would need to move my fence. I told him I didn't have money to move it and he said his workers could do it. I asked him to make sure I was here when they did. We left it at that.

They came later that week and I showed them where to put the posts and watched them take over the piece they had stolen in front of my property. I cried until they finished. Then I blew my nose and went to the beach and screamed into the sea. The dogs waited for me on the beach as I bobbed up and down and with each descent screamed loose some anger from my body. I did not want it to stay inside and knew the sea could neutralize it. I had so much hatred for them I wanted to get it out of me. In doing so, I remembered that I was not a victim. I was responsible. But that voice on my shoulder reminded me, "so was Amador."

He came to see me again after they moved the fence. The wound over him selling my land was raw and recently opened with the fence issue. He had brought a friend with him and when he introduced him, I said hello and shook his hand firmly. I made a point to make eye contact and used body language to tell him, "don't mess with me." Amador felt my vibe and sort of puffed out his chest as he told me that his friend might want to buy my land. I got angry thinking about Amador selling the land. I realized how hard it would be to get any money out of the deal if it were his buyer. I only had to hear it to get furious.

I told Amador loudly, in front of his "buyer," that he was not selling my land. I used a condescending tone that put him down. Then I told him he had no right to even be on the property. His "buyer" stopped moving and looked at him with a face that I am not sure was anger or disbelief or annoyance at having come to the property for nothing. Amador's face I knew: anger.

He moved closer to me in a threatening way, and I told him again "I think you should leave."

His face contorted into something monstrous in contrast to the backdrop of the detailed beauty on the leaf of the coco palm that framed him. Things moved in slow motion as he looked at me and asked me to repeat myself.

I did it easily and told him, "For the last time, Amador, you cannot sell my land and you should go."

His lip curled then and he hit me hard enough to knock me down. I was in front of Bali's workers and I got up as quickly as I could but held my hand to my face and yelled at him to get out before I called the police. His client had already walked away.

Amador said, "bitch," and followed him.

The workers looked away, not knowing what to do but not wanting to get involved. I couldn't believe it had happened, again. This was the second time he had hit me. I was shaking and wanted to cry but wouldn't let myself. I looked over to them but they did not make any eye contact and seemed to be working harder, probably so that I wouldn't talk to them. I felt my face where he had hit me. It was hot and I imagined red. My butt was sore from where I had fallen and my whole being felt assaulted. I focused on an ant walking over to the palm tree. It helped my mind relax. I inhaled and then took my focus off the ant, looked around nervously and asked the workers to leave. The head guy told me they were finishing. I asked him to hurry up and went to lock the gate.

I looked for Amador and his client on the road but they had gone. I imagined them laughing and having a beer over the issue. I slowly walked out back to the top of the three story shell of a structure so I could talk to God. I stopped for the cigarette I had hidden that Sylvia had given me the last time he hit me. I had saved it. As I climbed the hand made ladder to the roof, I started to cry. I clutched the cigarette and matches in one hand and took a deep breath as I reached the top. I looked out over the jungle that had lured me there, the jungle that had enticed me to come to Mexico and it seemed, had finally trapped me here. The soft shades of green from the palms and the *manglers* were sparkling, their salty leaves in the sun blurred as the tears flowed freely down my face. Several white birds flew past.

I lit the cigarette and inhaled, loving it and but hating myself for it.

"Its only one" I said to myself but then countered, "One a day is 365 a year."

I stopped crying and said out loud, "Shut up, please. Just shut up."

I smashed the cigarette into the concrete and threw it into the dirt below as I looked out over the jungle and wondered what I would do now. I had been hit. I had a stalker. I had been robbed and conned and I was on my own in this crazy wonderful but dangerous place. My mind went back to my dad in bed a day or two before he died.

"Is it ok if Harry helps me spread that mulch we have down there?" I asked him.

He looked at me and smiled some knowing sort of smile as he played with my thumbnail pushing his thumbnail underneath mine. I hated the feeling but I loved the intimacy and would never pull my hand away.

"Joanneo?" I stared into his steel blue eyes as he continued, "Joanneo, you can do whatever you want."

He held my gaze for a few moments to communicate silently that it was about more than the mulch.

I reminded myself of that then; "You can do whatever you want."

I cried harder the more I thought about it. I could have done whatever I wanted and look, here I was. I took my cell phone from my pocket and checked to see if I had reception. Up so high it was pretty good. I called Kim and told her what had happened. She seemed to know it would happen eventually and told me to come to her house so we could all go to file a *demanda* against Amador. This was the beginning.

I told her I would come as soon as the workers left. I heard Feelix in the background saying he would come get me and then Kim confirmed for him. I still had friends and I hung up the phone feeling better but wondering if I could handle it all. Filing charges here would be interesting if I could stay detached. But it was about me, so it would most likely be humiliating. However, it was something I needed to do.

I worried about Amador's reaction. I knew that Kim and Felix loved me but the reality of the situation was that I was alone most of the time. Amador knew it and he knew how to get to me. He was a mad man in his own town and I was a nearly rational woman in a foreign country. As I thought about it, I heard Amalio cough and decided to talk to him before Felix came by. I climbed down the ladder, walked past the workers nearly ready to leave and went over to Amalio's place.

He was sitting there in his hammock reading the paper. I asked for permission to enter his place.

"Joanna" he said to me, *"Que paso?"*

I tried to explain about Amador hitting me and how I would go to the police. Then I asked if he thought it was a good idea. He told me to go see the police and that it was important that Amador know I would do something. Then he told me not to worry.

He said, *"Yo te cuido,* Joanna," "I will take care of you."

I wanted to cry but didn't. Instead, I took his hand and we shook. Then I gave him the customary kiss on the cheek but held my breath so as not to catch whatever lung disease he had and said, *"gracias."*

I was not sure if it was a good thing or not but at least I had somewhere to run if Amador came back. For some reason, Amalio liked me. I decided it was a good thing and went back to let the workers out and check the relocated fence.

Felix came by in about an hour and said, "little sis, we gotta put this thing to rest," as he gave me a hug.

I knew he was right and got ready to leave. I put the dogs in the house and gave them each a bone telling them I would be back soon. They seemed to understand, in fact, Lakra gave me a look that said, "get your shit together" and my brother's words echoed in my head. I told her I would take care of things as I tucked her into her bed on the floor: a yoga mat and 2 towels that had seen better days. I told myself this was my chance as I put the *vocho* inside the gate, locked the door and Feelix and I got into his red Land Rover and headed for town.

We went first to the police station on the first floor of a 2 story white concrete municipal building on the *Avenida* Tulum. The jail was behind it then. They looked at me when I entered and then went back to whatever paperwork they were reviewing. Feelix and I waited in front of the desk for acknowledgement that we could talk.

The policeman didn't look up even when Felix said, "*Buenas tardes.*"

He sort of nodded and kept working for a few uncomfortable minutes. Felix was getting angry, I was still nervous and a little embarrassed but did not want more of a scene.

I said "*Buenas tardes?*" again.

Finally the man in the blue uniform looked at us. Felix explained for me since he spoke better Spanish. It was not a long explanation but it was correct. At the end the policeman asked me to see the mark where Amador had hit me. I looked at him, hurt and embarrassed to be questioned that way, and told him it was my face but that it had been hours ago so it was not still red. He told me it didn't look like much and went back to his paperwork. Felix inhaled to stay patient and explained that we wanted to get a restraining order against the man who had hit me. The office looked up, not seeming interested or concerned, and told us to go to the *Ministerio Publico* across the road. They handled that sort of thing, he explained.

Felix put his arm around me as we left the police station and we walked across the municipal park to the *Ministerio Publico*. I felt horrible and numb at the same time. It was as if I were walking through jello. Every step took effort and had a sort of squishiness about it. He assured me that this was something we had to do. I was becoming unsure. Regardless, we arrived and took a seat as the secretary was with someone else. Felix called Kim from outside as I waited my turn. When the couple in front of the secretary left, she motioned to me to wait, stood up and went to what looked like an office behind her desk. Felix came back and sat next to me asking where she had gone. Before I could tell him, she came back and called us to the desk and asked how she could help.

I started to cry so Felix explained how my ex boyfriend had hit me and we wanted to put a restraining order against him. Felix explained how Amador had come to the house, entered without permission and when I asked him to leave had hit me in the face and knocked me down. I sniffed myself back to some semblance of a conscious human being as Kim walked in and the secretary asked us to wait. Kim hugged me, asked how I was and told me this was all a good thing really. I was unsure. I sat next to her with my head on her shoulder, quiet for awhile. Then she told me how she had seen a couch I wanted on sale at Walmart and we could go later if I wanted. She was trying to change the subject but I started to cry again, not because of the issue with Amador but because I had been reduced to shopping at Walmart and even having to save money and wait for things to go on sale to do so. I felt such a failure but told her that yes, perhaps we could go after all this shit. I used the word because I felt that was what it was: shit. And I felt stuck in it. The voice on my shoulder told me I could be at the beach if I had not let Amador back into my life and I just told it to "fuck off." I was in no mood for a helpful second opinion.

Finally, a fat Mayan man who introduced himself as the *Ministerio Publico* came into the room and called my name, pronouncing it so badly I was not sure it was me. But there was no one else there so the three of us stood to answer him. He asked which one of us was "Joeahnney". I raised my hand and he told me he would take my statement. He went over the process for a restraining order: he would write everything and then they would arrest Amador if we wanted to press charges. I inhaled. Feelix answered for me that yes, we wanted to press charges. Then he explained how they could not keep him long for this sort of behavior but they could keep him 48 hours. At the end of this meeting he would give me a restraining order and Amador would not be able to come within 50 meters of me. He explained that I needed to post the paper on my door at the beach and if Amador came into a public space where I was, I had to show him the paper and ask him to leave. I asked him to repeat that statement, thinking I heard incorrectly. He repeated it and Felix, reading my mind, said, "Yeah. He said you need to put it on the door and carry a copy with you."

I shook my head started to sob again when the *Ministerio Publico* said it would be 356 pesos. I nearly fainted. I had to pay to get it going. Stunned, I took out the money. He gave me a receipt and my change and began to enter my information into his computer, typing slowly, with one index finger. I fought the urge to do it for him, since I knew this would take the time I had to get my couch. But I sat on my hands and answered his questions, one by one.

He finally finished and asked me to read it before he printed it, explaining he and I would both sign it. I looked at the statement, all the dates and names started to blur together but I told him it was fine. He shook his head and said something that I figured was "OK, then" and he hit the print button. He went to the back room to retrieve the document. The three of us waited until he came back with 3 copies, one, he said was for me, the other for him and one for the file.

"Triplicate," I said to myself and smiled at the beauocratic nature of things, familiar with that culture.

The *Ministerio* said that once they picked up Amador they would call me and I could come back to press charges. When I realized they would arrest Amador and I would have to confront him, I became very much afraid and totally abandoned the couch idea.

One of my biggest fears was confrontation, including confronting a lunatic ex-lover who had already hit me twice. I regretted ever coming and I moved closer to the door to escape. Kim knew exactly what I was thinking and in a low voice assured me that I had to do this to show some backbone and protect myself. I knew she was right but I was not sure I could do it. As we started to walk out the door, the phone on the table rang and the *Ministerio* picked it up, said "*sí*" several times and then, "*bueno*" and then as he hung up, called to us.

He told Felix that the police had picked Amador up and would be here shortly. He told us to wait. I started to tremble and my stomach started to ache. I could not believe they would bring him here and that I had to see him. We waited in the street since there was no waiting room and the *Ministerio* was taking the statement from some other people. I wanted to give them some privacy and I wanted to talk to Kim and Felix, so we stepped outside.

Police cars came and went, each one enveloping us in a cloud of dust as they pulled behind the building with their cargo: mostly dark skinned men. I had to leave the scene mentally so I thought about the dust clogging my pores and used that excuse to distance myself from the scene physically. I walked farther away from the building. Again, Kim read my mind and stayed with me as I drifted along the side of the road. After about 10 minutes, I saw Amador sitting in the back of a police truck as it pulled behind the building. His head was down and his hands were behind his back, probably handcuffed, and it was my fault. I could not believe it had come to this.

Gratefully, I became numb. I would not let it touch me and sort of stepped outside myself. When the police officer called us to come back in, I walked confidently into the room. They said my name and I nodded and then they brought Amador out.

He looked at me without anger and said in English, "Baybe, why you do this? I no hurt you."

The police officer told him to be quiet and the *Ministerio Publico* started to read the charges against him, basically assault. I felt uncomfortable and started to think about what I considered assault. He had slapped me and knocked me down but it wasn't really assault. And I just wanted him to stay away from me, not go to jail. I wanted to save him, I reminded myself, not put him further into a hole. When the *Ministerio Publico* finished he asked me to affirm that those were the charges.

Before I could say anything, Amador started, this time in Spanish, "*porfavor, no haces eso, porfavor.*"

I started to cry. He apologized and told me he wasn't sure what had happened but that he was sorry. The *Ministerio Publico* asked me again to confirm the charges.

I sniffed, said "*sí*" and then started to cry harder, my shoulders hiccupping as I tried to control myself without success.

Kim put her arm around me and Amador continued to say "Baybe, *perdoname. No fue intencional.*"

But in a moment of clarity, I saw through his acting. The *Ministerio Publico* asked if I wanted to bring any witnesses. I told him no. I knew that the workers would not testify against Amador, if that was even what they had to do. When I told him no, he told me, against the back drop of Amador crying and pleading with me, that they would hold him for 48 hours and after he could not come within 500 meters of my house. He explained that in public, there was not much that they could control. But that I should carry the restraining order with me and if Amador should approach me, after I asked him not to, they could put him in jail again. But, he mentioned to me, that I should try to get witnesses to help them protect me if that happened. I felt as if I were the prisoner now.

As we finished, Amador said he loved me and asked forgiveness. Finally, the police officer told him to be quiet. They led him out of the room as the *Ministerio Publico* handed me the restraining order and told me to make copies and reminded me to put one on the front door to my house. He told me if I liked, I could give one to places I went often and they could keep him away from me. I couldn't imagine giving one to the people at *la Nave* or *Cocodrillos* or any of those places and decided to stay in for the next few weeks until the whole issue blew over. I took a final look at my Amador, handcuffed, hair wild, eyes pleading with me, tears running down his face.

He called loudly, *"te quiero mucho, amor,"* and I nearly melted.

I could not believe it but every muscle in my body wanted to embrace him, rip the handcuffs off and run away with him.

Kim sensed something because she put her arm around me and whispered, "Lets go."

I followed her remembering the stories my dad had told me about how he would go to scenes of domestic abuse and try to arrest the woman beater only to have the girlfriend or wife attack him as he did so. I never understood it then and I still did not understand, but I knew what it felt like and I sympathized with my Dad. It was a totally illogical and irrational impulse and he had spent years of his life fighting with people who could not be rational. I heard the door close behind me. Felix was behind me with the paperwork. The dusty street seemed surreal and Kim asked me if I wanted her to come home with me.

I looked at her and surprised myself by saying, "do we still have time to go to Walmart for that couch?"

Chapter 41

Over the next weeks, I became somewhat reclusive. My neighbors built a concrete wall where they had stolen my land. Where before I had coco and chit palms and the breeze and the birds could pass to visit me, now each day I had less. They were filling in my open space and it broke my heart. I was sad and furious and shamed all at once every morning. I spent more time in the back house, looking over the marsh and talking with my dad, wondering how I could have been so stupid and wanting to run away. But how, I kept asking myself. The answer didn't come.

Too, I started to avoid people to avoid Amador. It seemed that he found me everywhere. He was always "around" somehow. He would never do much, but that wasn't the point. I changed when I saw him. Sometimes at a bar with friends, he asked me to dance or sent me a drink, although I knew it would be on my bill if I accepted. So I would not. But I felt a mix of emotions when I saw him, mostly shame and fear but there was always that desire for reconciliation and for things to be the way I wanted them, not the way they were. It was confusing and I dealt with it by hiding from nearly everyone. At times, I even hid from Kim and Felix. I didn't want to know what I had to do and they generally had advice. I wanted Amador to leave me alone or I wanted him to come back and have things be the way I had planned. I wanted to escape all the bad and, now with the construction, I couldn't. It stared me in the face 24 hours a day.

There were still many times, with my dogs on the beach or teaching yoga on the balcony at VSK or walking home on the beach under a full moon, witnessing a turtle coming up to lay her eggs or a great blue heron standing in front of me, letting me pass, that I knew I was in the right place. I found a peace that I knew was worth whatever sacrifice I had to make to keep it. And for the other times filled with construction and inconsideration and cons and bad memories, I told myself I had to figure it out, be patient, breathe into it and go with the flow.

Walking along the shoreline one morning, Goli started to run but then stopped, burped loudly, gagged and sat down. I sat with him for awhile, his brown eyes a little sad. Then he seemed better. He jogged off behind the girls and even chased a tourist. I figured it was something he had eaten and smiled as the tourist ran into the water. When I called he came happily back to me and the tourist ran away. But that night he had another attack and again recovered fairly fast. I made sure he was comfy next to my bed and he slept the night without an incident. The next day nothing happened until evening but the burps seemed more painful and sort of gagging. Afterwards he seemed more tired and sad.

The next morning, he didn't eat and he had another round of what seemed like some gastro-intestinal reflux or something, so I hustled the dogs into the *vochho* and we headed into town to see Juan the vet. As we passed the *El Viejo* store, Amador was there, standing in the road, doing nothing. But it killed me to pass him. I was afraid of another of his outbursts and then ashamed that he wouldn't even look at me. I used all my energy to keep my foot on the gas pedal and not turn back. Then, as I got to where he was standing, I bent over to check Goliath so I would not have to see him or acknowledge him. I didn't know what else to do so I pretended he wasn't there. It was uncanny. I was shaking after I drove past and had to tell myself 'fake it til you make it' about a hundred times until I calmed down. I congratulated myself, realizing it would get easier with time. That realization allowed me to enjoy the drive with my dogs. In that car, it was an outing.

We got to the *Casa Azul*, where Juan's veterinary office was located, and I pulled Ama and Goli into the property. Lakra walked in on her own. She loved going to the vet. After all her adventures and operations I would have thought the vet would frighten her. But she and Juan were good friends. She howled to see him and humped his leg like she would with Amador.

Juan told me it seemed Goli had indigestion but that he needed an X-ray. The only X-ray machine was in Playa del Carmen and my car wouldn't make it. My shoulders dropped and I fought feelings of inadequacy as I called Kim to ask for help, again. She could take me the next day. The X-ray would be 600 pesos that I didn't have. I couldn't believe I had dropped so low but I needed to save my little guy. I dipped into my overdraft. I could figure it out later.

We put Goliath in the back of Kim's car early the next morning. She seemed tired, perhaps tired of me. But I let that feeling go. I needed the help. When she asked me how Goli was I told her he had been worse the last two days. Then she asked about me, how I was. I couldn't lie to her and told her how hard it was to have Amador always lurking around. She agreed but also told me that I gave him way too much credit and power over me. I knew she was right but didn't know how to stop feeling so afraid when he came around. She told me I would find a way.

"Own your power," she told me.

I agreed and patted Goliath in the seat behind.

We arrived in Playa del Carmen and searched *Avenida* 30 for the Vet's office. It was a part of town I did not know, past the Walmart I hated and the veggie store, Dac, that I loved. We drove through the bicycle district and into a neighborhood with fewer shops. The houses started to look sadder until we found the vet in a three-story row house. The buildings reminded me of lower Mass Avenue in the

90's when I swam at City Hospital: cool and almost comfortable, but not quite. There was a definite edge to the neighborhood. We parked the car and brought Goli inside to find the young doctor who was very polite but spoke very little English. I did my best to translate "burp" and "gag' but mostly pantomimed how Goli acted to the delight of Kim and the doctor. I found myself pretty amusing as well.

We took Goliath upstairs for the X-ray and the doctor asked me to help. I had no idea what I was getting into. It made a mammogram look comfortable in comparison. We stretched Goli on a table in a way that hurt his body. The doctor strapped him down and he was crying and howling. I had to hold his legs so that the doctor could get a good picture. I was crying and sweating and telling the doctor to hurry or stop. I couldn't wait to get out of there.

Kim stayed downstairs but when we finally got the pictures and went back she looked at me nervously and said, "Everyone okay?"

I wasn't sure who was worse, Goli or me, but I shook my head yes. The doctor said we could have the X-rays in an hour, so Kim and I took Goliath and went for a lemonade on the street. I confided in her that it was brutal and described how we had manipulated poor Goliath. He sat next to me on the street and I put my arm around him as he rested his head on my thigh.

When we got back to Tulum, Juan read the X-rays for me: Goli had a hernia between his stomach and his lungs. It was probably from the trauma he suffered with Amalio nearly two years before. I wanted to know how to fix it. It was a big operation and Juan said he could do it but it cost 1200 pesos. I asked him to give me time. I had no money but I could not let my dog die. I thought of people here with kids who had absolutely no money and imagined how hard that would be. Before I got too depressed, I took Goliath back to the beach. I hustled to get into my suit and get the girls ready for a walk before dark. We crested the beach with Ama and Lakra running but Goliath walked sadly next to me and then stopped. The girls ran along the shore and I sat down with him. I put my arm over his shoulders and we watched the waves coming in and the white caps farther out.

I told him, "Okay Goli. This is no fun so let's try to make you better."

I called the dogs and we went back to the house to call Juan. He told me to bring him the next morning before breakfast.

I hung up, frightened, not knowing what to do. I was afraid for Goli, for me, for money, for everything. My heart had butterflies. Then the phone rang. It was my friend Erika, Chito's girlfriend who was back in the states. She loved Goliath and one time wanted to take him back to New York but then we decided he was better with me. I told her about his operation and she told me she could send me some money to help pay. I had to accept and it killed me. But it made things possible. Too, she said she would post something on Craig's list so that we could get more prayers for him. I smiled about it but liked the idea. She was such a positive person. I knew it would all work out.

We got to Juan's office early and waited in the car, Goli and me sitting in that funny car.

I talked to him about nothing and then said to him, "you know Goli, I would never be here but for you."

He rested his head on my shoulder as if to say he knew. And I reminded us both of how Moises sent me his photo entitled, "funny pet," back when Moises wanted to work with me. The opportunity to have that "funny pet" helped me make the decision to come and live in Tulum. It may have seemed frivolous to some people, but for me, it meant the world to have my own dog in my own house close to the beach. I hugged Goli and we got out of the car as the Vet's assistant came around the corner on her bike. I left him there at about 9:30 in his crate with a big towel from me to make him comfortable. I left praying that everything would go well.

I was home and upstairs after 2 pm when the phone rang: Juan. I asked if I should come for Goli and Juan told me he had "*mal noticia,*" bad news. He explained some things that I didn't understand and then said he was sorry. I asked him what exactly was he saying before I understood that Goli had died. When I did, I started to sob and couldn't stop. I told Juan I would call him back. I finally got my grip and called back. He told me Goli had died on the operating table. It was too much for him. There was silence on the line for a moment before he told me they could bury him or I could come for him. I couldn't imagine leaving him there and I told him I would come for him before I started to cry again. I cried the whole way to the vet's office in my distressed *vocho*.

When I arrived, Dr. Juan led me around to the operating room to a garbage bag on the table.

"Is that him?" I asked incredulously, "In that garbage bag?"

Juan explained that they didn't have anything else, as if I should be more practical. He hoisted Goliath into his arms and walked with me to the car.

"We will give you a refund," he puffed matter of factly as he pushed Goliath in. "We couldn't operate, he died before the anesthesia."

I started to cry again, feeling as if I had let everyone down and thinking if only I could have gotten the X-ray sooner, Goli would still be alive. I wanted to hit myself for not having my life more together.

"It is okay," Juan said and gave me a hug.

I took the refund and cried my way home with my little man dead in the seat next to me in a garbage bag. I reached over and touched his fur as we passed Zama's. Then I pulled over to see the ocean with him one more time, tears running down my face.

Sylvia was leaving work at Jade just as I was passing. When she saw my state, she came to help me and together, we put Goliath on the new dining table in the new house. I brought out tequila and we sat watch for my Goli as we waited for Silvia's friend Hilario to come help us dig a grave. After awhile and 2 shots in relative silence, Sylvia lit a cigarette, got up, walked over to the spot we had selected. She took the pick ax over her head to start slashing into the dirt. The glow of the cigarette in her mouth reflected in the sequins on her always too tight shirt. I couldn't take my eyes off her. But my hand was on my dog in the bag.

After 4 or 5 swings Hilario arrived with 2 oversized beers and took the tool away from her. I stood by Sylvia watching him dig and then reached into the bag to touch Goli again. I withdrew my hand. His body was stiff. It was time to say goodbye. We took Goliath out of the bag wrapped in the towel I had put in his crate to keep him cozy while he waited for surgery. I started to cry again and Sylvia put her hand on my shoulder as Hilario lowered him into the hole. I dropped some *bugambilia* flowers I had cut into the grave on top of Goli and lit a candle. Hilario covered the body as I thanked God for my friends.

We had another shot of tequila, they finished the beers and left.

That was it. The finality of things always escaped me as I looked for redemption or some miracle that would undo those endings that were permanent. I got into the hammock with my two dogs on either side of me and hoped for Goli to return, for my neighbors to give me back my land or for Amador to be the man I wanted. It was impossible and though I knew it, I never quite accepted it. Some days it seemed I was waiting for miracles, knowing they were all around me, yet wanting just one more.

Chapter 42

I didn't call Kim about Goli until the next day. I was tired and felt that she was tired of me. I had to call Erica. She had people praying for Goli from across the globe. But it seemed their prayers didn't work. Too, she had sent me money and now I had to send it back. A part of me wanted to not tell her about the refund. I scolded myself to not sink to Amador's level. But the voice on my shoulder told me I could use the money. I ignored the idea. When I called Kim, she offered to take me for a beer but I wanted to be alone. She told me to call if I changed my mind.

Erica cried with me, told me to keep the money saying, "It would be too much trouble to send it back," and said she would post something on Craig's list later.

We were done.

I wandered around, made a sculpture of drift wood and conch shells on Goli's grave and then took the dogs to the beach, worked a little, cleaned a little, went through the motions of my day. I decided to go to town for some food and went out to the *vocho* to have a drive, to take my mind of things. I opened the door and sat in the drivers seat without "*animo*" as they say in Mexico, without energy. I turned the key and nothing happened. I sat there, not believing that the car wouldn't start. So I turned the key again and got a weak noise, sort of a grind.

"Battery," I said to myself and checked to see if I had lights but no.

Puzzled, I took the key out of the ignition and opened the door. I wanted to move and thought about how. I needed more than I could fit on my bike. I stood next to the car and thought how I had hitched many times with Amador. I decided it was time to try on my own. I closed the car door, locked it and walked across the street to wait.

I remembered the last time Amador and I had hitched and I

tried to channel the enjoyment of that. Instead I got afraid. One car with a couple of tourists passed my extended thumb. I pushed the feelings of rejection away and wondered if I were doing it right as I waited for another car. In about 5 minutes, just before quitting, a silver grey pickup came around the corner. I stuck my hand out again and tried to look confident but not too eager. The truck slowed. I was elated. I thought I would jump in the back like I had done with Amador.

But the driver opened the front door saying, "Hey, get in front. With that dress on you will get all dirty in the back."

It was a tall blonde with big breasts and a low cut shirt. She had a huge and contagious Cheshire cat smile and blue eyes that were captivating. She was tanned and her hair was nearly white from the sun. I introduced myself and she said she had heard of me. Then she extended her hand and said, "Gina." She told me she had a house up the road as she hit the accelerator and we bumped and squeaked down the road.

She asked if I were going to town. I told her yes and then she told me again she knew me. I smiled and said I didn't think we had met.

She agreed but said, "No. I know you from around, *chisme*, you know, gossip. Weren't you with Amador?"

I wanted to jump out the car door regardless of how fast she was going. Before I could answer she hit the break to talk to a friend whose hotel and shop was on the road. She introduced me to Christina who had dark hair, dark eyes, a thin face and a nice smile. I knew her from *la Posdad del Sol* where Megan and I had stayed. Luckily, she didn't remember me. They chatted awhile before we moved on.

As we were cresting the last tope before the gentle hill that led to the road to town, she looked over at me and said, "yeah, you used to be with Amador, right? Strange guy."

I could not escape. I told her yes I was but not for a long while now. I wanted to cry and couldn't believe it. But I swallowed my tears and sat there.

"You ok?" she asked me and I shook my head yes.

Then she said, "Honey, do not worry about that man. I saw him the other day and he looks like shit," she laughed, "He used to be pretty cute, but now? I don't think so."

She finished somewhat nostalgically and then went on to tell me how she knew the entire group: Amalio, Chito, Chi Chi and Amador. She had some fun facts about each one telling me Amalio couldn't get an erection any longer since he had done so many drugs. She said that Chi Chi was from a nearly extinct tribe in the northern mountains of Mexico and that she had dated Chito for awhile but his drug use got to be too much for her. She told me Amador was a *mammon* who couldn't even fight.

I forgot about crying and we laughed together. By the time we got to the traffic light, we were friends. She asked me what I was doing in town. I told her about my car not working and said I was only getting groceries so she could drop me there at the light. She was going for a movie and then heading back and asked me if I needed a ride home. She also mentioned that her friend was a mechanic and could help with the car. She gave me his number and said that I could call and tell him she sent me. I thanked her, told her a ride back would be great and that I would wait in front of San Francisco.

She came back with a popped bag of microwave popcorn and we drove back to the beach like old friends, gossiping and eating popcorn. She made me laugh and feel comfortable. We talked about what I did here and how construction was going.

She mentioned she was still finishing her house up the road, saying, "things take forever here."

When I told her I taught yoga, she asked if we could practice. She promised to come the next day to my 7:30 practice. I was excited about having a new person in the class and excited about having a new friend. When she dropped me off, I was no longer sad. I felt as if I belonged somewhere and that good things could still happen. I went inside to feed the dogs and myself and then rest up.

Gina arrived at the door early for the 7:30 class. It made me grouchy since I liked to prepare for class alone. But we shared a coffee and when we finished, people were arriving for the class. We went out back to my studio, that open space on the second floor. We lit incense, placed the mats on the concrete floor and began. The filtered early morning sunlight shone into the space through the chit palms. Lakra and Ama sat in the corners in their own space and we moved through a blissful practice. When we finished in *savasana*, Ama licked Gina on the face and brought her back with a laugh. Our little group was used to the dogs and it was as if Gina had received an initiation. We finished, shared breakfast and she offered to drive me in to see her mechanic friend, Gabrielle about my car.

Gabrielle lived on one of the back streets behind the *Avenida* Tulum. He was a quiet man, with long hair. He made jewelry and repaired VW's. He was not so much a mechanic as he was an *affectionado* of VW Bugs, *vochos*. He followed us to the house and he told us it was the battery. He had brought one with him since the cars had a tendency to go through batteries rapidly. Eight hundred pesos later, I was mobile again.

We had a coffee and Gina asked about yoga. I had started teaching at Maya Tulum and she decided she would come to that class too. She arrived early again the next day and we biked to class. For about the next 3 months we rode our bikes to the classes I taught or we practiced in my yoga space. Gina invited me for dinners and movies and even tried to fix me up with a man. She was fabulous about household things and her boyfriend could wield a chain saw unbelievably well to cut whatever it was I might need into form. Too, she had some great workers and introduced me to many of them before she loaned me one or two to help with projects around the house: repairing the deck, repairing screens, cleaning the yard.

One day she honked at the gate and when I opened it carried in about 15 sapling trees called "*despinatas.*" They were a type of palm that had curly leaves and looked like something out of a Dr. Suess book. She and I planted them along the path between the lilies. Then she took out a few orchids and told me, "Happy Birthday." I couldn't believe she remembered or even knew. I took a piece of driftwood I had salvaged from the beach and put one of the orchids into a small bend in the piece and then balanced it on Goli's grave. The house looked cared for and welcoming. Finally, I was ready to host my first survivor.

My contact at Beth Israel hospital had sent me the name of a woman who wanted to visit. Joan was coming in about a week. Gina sold me a small inverter with a used battery so Joan could have light in the evening. I charged the battery in the day so she could have one light at night. For me, candlelight was enough, actually better. But Gina reminded me that Joan was accustomed to the city and might need some light. We hooked it up and, *voila*, Joan would have all the comforts of home. Well, perhaps not all, but that wasn't the point. I wanted her to feel the energy of Tulum, to feel the sun on her face and the breeze and jump into the Caribbean, to touch the earth and remember that life was good. I wanted to share all the good things with her; the beach, the dogs, the sun, the freedom. She would be with me for Thanksgiving and we both had so much to be thankful for.

The next Thursday, I took the bus to the airport to meet her. I was late, as usual. Well, the bus was late but I was on it. I was worried since coming into Cancun could be a challenge. Exiting immigration could be intimidating with the gauntlet of salespeople nearly assaulting you from outside the fence, taxi drivers shouting to you for a ride, hotels calling to offer you a room, vans yelling to say they could take you where you wanted to go. Then there was the myriad of regularish people looking for their friends or family. I say regularish since after a few years on the beach, whether Cancun, Playa del Carmen or Tulum, people started to look different. Some had bare feet even at the airport. Often, their hair was burnt nearly white or a shade of orange or even almost pink from the sun depending on whether they used chemicals or not. People had sunburnt skin and often lots of silver and big jewelry that went with the total tan. They blended minimally with the dark skinned locals who wore long pants and button down T shirts that said the hotel or time share or resort name in the breast pocket.

It was a movie scene and when you walked off the plane after hours of travel and alone, it could be unnerving. I hoped Joan would not be too shell shocked to come back with me. I got a message on my cell as I was arriving and running to the meeting point. She was there and was looking for me. I texted her back just as my phone battery died. I sighed and thought what next. But then I saw her, waiting on the corner, suitcase by her side, looking a little lost but still confident. I called her name and she smiled, a big white South Boston smile. She had that Irish American look: blond hair, freckles, nearly translucent white skin. I reminded myself to bathe her in sunscreen every day as I hurried to meet her.

I hugged her immediately. I was that happy to see her. She might have been surprised but she hugged me back.

I apologized for not being there on time but said, "Welcome to Mexico," and let that explain everything.

She had rented a car and we went to pick it up. I was sorry my car was not good enough to pick her up but she told me, "Friends of mine are renting this for me. People have been so kind and really wanted me to come."

I prayed things would be okay. We got back to Tulum before the sun went down and she put her things in the little house, which now had a nice bed with a place to hang your clothes, one light and a hammock. The kitchen had a table, two chairs, a coffee maker, pans and plates but I told Joan that we could eat together. We talked. She smoked. I wanted to.

Then we crossed the street to take the dogs to the beach, ate something and both went to sleep in our respective houses. She asked to have Ama sleep with her. I told her if Ama would go, that was fine. Ama, the love, went happily until about 2 am when she cryed to come back and sleep with Lakra and me. I left a candle lit by Goli's grave. Before I fell asleep, I prayed that we would have a quiet night and thanked God for letting Joan come. My dream was coming true. I had done something right.

Joan was in the middle of reconstructive surgery for her removed breast and was in some discomfort from it. Every month she had to see the doctor to check how things were going and they did some "expanding' of the prosthesis. I had remembered my sister Carolyn telling me that if I had to have a mastectomy we would have reconstruction afterwards, as if it were simple. I naively pictured doctors sort of sticking a fake breast onto the scar where they might cut my cancerous breast away. Nothing could be further from the truth.

Joan explained how they tried to put the new breast in under the skin using a sort of balloon that they put in flat and then gradually filled to expand the muscle and the skin. At that point in the process, Joan's reconstructed breast was uneven and weird looking. She had been waiting months to start and it would take months to get it right. But she was wonderfully confident and happy to be alive. She had a bikini for the beach and if people noticed that one breast was higher and smaller than the other, they didn't show it. We went out at night or stayed in, walked the beach, relaxed in the hammock and laughed.

She shared her past, her difficult times with addictions and men and her much more difficult time with breast cancer. I confided in her about Amador. The day after I told her about him, as was my fear when I would even say his name, he came to the door. We had enjoyed 3 wonderfully peaceful days together before he called my name at the gate. My hands started to shake with fear when I heard him. Joan and I had been sitting at the kitchen table when he knocked. I knew my expression changed. I tried to ignore him but then he called again.

Joan said, "I think there is someone at the door."

The day was cloudy and we had massages from my friend Suzanna. I had been relaxed and didn't need or want an interaction with him. But I didn't know what else to do.

I walked to the door as he called my name again and I saw his face through the fence. His smile still melted my heart. I fought the urge to smile back and give him a hug even though he was not allowed within 500 meters of my house. I asked him what he wanted. He became almost angry. I could see it. He told me he had some plants for me and reminded me that I needed them in my garden. Regardless, I opened the door to take a look. There were loads of lily bulbs, the same ones I had picked up off the beach once after a hurricane. He also had some *bugambilias* which I desperately wanted and a hibiscus bush.

"They cheap," he told me.

I should have known that it was about money again.

"I don't have any money, Amador," I told him truthfully and went to close the door.

But he stuck his foot into it and told me in a threatening voice that I hardly recognized, "Then you better find some."

I asked if he were threatening me. He told me no, he was telling me the truth. He told me he needed 500 pesos and that I could take the plants or not but he wanted the money or he would make trouble for me. He knew I had a guest. I wanted to spit at him.

My eyes narrowed and I stood my ground, for a moment anyway, as I thought things through. I didn't want trouble for Joan or for me. I knew I could call the police, but I decided it would be easier to buy the plants and get rid of him. I told him to wait as I jogged to the house. He didn't. He followed me inside and I looked back at him as he got to where Joan's house was and I called to him to wait. I did not want him in my house. Ama barked and Lakra howled. I left him there to deal with the dogs as I went upstairs to where I kept some money hidden. It was in the stuffed animal pig that my nieces had given me ages ago. It had a pouch in its stomach where the maker had put baby pigs. Now she had piglets and all my cash in her belly.

I took out a 500 peso note, went back down and handed it to him, telling him he could leave the plants and go. He took the money, but didn't go. I knew Joan was watching. She was sitting a few meters away, having moved from the house to her balcony. I did not want a scene and told Amador to please help me put the plants inside. But I was afraid to tell him I could have him put in jail.

He turned slowly and told me, "I can do whatever I want here. This my country, not yours."

I prayed that he would go. And he did. He looked up to where Joan was on the balcony before he walked to the door and walked out. I took the plants and pulled them inside the door, shaking, and then locked it and went back to my house, calling the dogs after me. I sat on the porch and put my head in my hands. Joan came over and asked if things were alright. I told her yes but asked her for a cigarette. She told me she felt as if she were corrupting me and I told her no, that had been done long ago.

Chapter 43

I decided that hitching was like being at a dance without a boyfriend: you open yourself to rejection with every passerby. I had never liked going to dances and so I liked it less when my *vocho* wouldn't work again and I reverted to hitching. I was out of money and could have called Gina but sometimes, I liked doing things on my own. Joan had left the week before after a wonderful week. I needed to resume the legal search for some sort of security about my land ownership. I had an appointment at 9:30 and something was up with the car, again. It didn't like the rain and sometimes the engine needed to dry out but if I didn't get going, I would be later than the allowed 15 minutes. This was Mexico. Not much happened in a day. Less happened on time. But people wouldn't wait forever.

I started to walk, looking back every 5 minutes to look for an oncoming car. Finally, a silver SUV passed, slowed and stopped ahead of me. I jogged to catch it.

As I reached the window the driver said, "*Wie Gehts.*"

I responded, "*Gut,*" thinking he was German and waited for him to invite me in.

Instead, he smiled at me. I waited and noticed the car was packed full of stuff: what looked like a tent, two guitar cases, bags of food and a cooler crammed the way back. A dog, a child and sundry clothing filled the back seat and the balding driver and a blond male sat in front.

Finally, I asked, "*Vas al pueblo?* in Spanish not remembering how to say it in German, "Are you going to town?"

He replied "yes" and then asked where I was from telling his friend, "Oh I love Americans," when I told him I was from the US.

He still had not invited me in. Finally, I asked him if he had stopped to give me a ride as I saw another car approaching.

"Well, it depends on her," he answered motioning to the dog in back and reaching from the drivers side to open the door.

When he did a few blankets and tee shirts fell to the ground. The dog jumped out. I picked up his things and put them back into the car as he called the dog and told me that if she liked me, I could have a ride. If not, he was sorry, but he would not give me one. I told him that dogs generally liked me as she jumped back in. I went to sit next to her. She gave me barely enough space but allowed me to sit. The driver told me I had a ride to town. I smiled, closed the door and he started to drive. There was a mound of clothing that separated me from the child sitting in the back. I waved at him from over the top of it. He stared at me. Uncomfortable, I looked away and patted the dog as the driver asked my name.

Nonchalantly he told me, "I am Sam and this is Gabriel and his son Lucas. My dog's name is Mero."

Then he asked me where I was from and when I told him I lived in Tulum asked me where exactly. I gave him a general description of where, not wanting to be too specific. Then he asked if I owned the property.

I told him, "as much as a foreigner can own anything here, yes, I own it," referring to the *ejido* issue.

He smiled and went back to driving very slowly. He seemed stoned. His friend didn't say anything. The child started to cry. Gabriel turned to see what was wrong, gave me a half smile and then undid the straps for the seat belt and brought the child to the front to sit on his lap. I looked over at the dog, who was sitting looking straight ahead. I patted her and looked back out my window as Sam continued his inquisition asking me if I built my house. I told him I was still in process and mentioned that it wasn't so easy to do things here. He asked me what I meant by that and I told him that I had been ripped off several times and the legal issues were formidable. I mentioned that I was on my way to my laywer's.

He agreed saing, "Yeah, Mexico is different."

He told me he had been in Mexico for awhile but was from Chicago originally. He told me he had lived in Mahahual, a beach community close to Belize, before Hurricane Dean made landfall there. Now he was traveling. They had been camping in the biosphere. I told him how I loved the biosphere and he agreed that there was something magical about it. We talked about Mahahual a bit. I had driven through it after the hurricane and knew it had been devastated. He shook his head in agreement and told me he had a great house on the water but it had disappeared. The hurricane was how he had found the dog.

He explained, "She found me actually. We are both displaced hurricane victims," as he took the left turn off the beach road towards town.

We started to move a little faster. He said a few words to his friend and then asked me where I was going.

"The end, towards Carillo," I said mentioning the name of the next town down the road, Carillo Puerto.

He told me that he would take me there if I didn't mind bringing Gabriel home first. Since I was only almost on time, I decided to take the ride. I liked talking to him. I was alone most of the time and it was nice to be around someone who was more or less normal. Too, I found him mildly attractive. He had small round eyeglasses, the kind John Lennon wore and his hair was wispy and soft around his face but receding at the hairline. He was cuter than John Lennon but not stunning at all. He was slight, you could tell that by his shoulders, or lack there-of, and he had a small, impish nose and unspectacular lips. But he had a nice smile and was amusing. So I stayed in the car as we dropped his friend off and then he took me back to town.

As we waited at the traffic light he asked me about my business with the attorney. I told him I was still waiting for my *constancia*, or permission from the *ejido*.

When I said the word he said, "Shit. You bought *ejido* land."

I was somehow embarrassed but nodded my head yes.

"Well you are braver than most," he said. I felt more stupid and I defended myself saying I had no idea what I had gotten into when I bought it. He told me not to beat myself up over it and that Mexico had a way of educating people.

He finished saying, "I bet you are not so naïve anymore."

I smiled, liking him more for defending me. Then I told him I constantly amazed myself at my ability to forget some of life's lessons and admitted to myself as much as to him that I had made some huge mistakes.

He looked over at me with a smile and said, "Get on board."

I liked him and it was empowering to like another man. But at the same time, I felt a little nervous about it. It was strange because I hadn't slept with Amador for a over year. But he was always around, looking for something. And he considered me his. He threatened men who talked with me. One man friend told me so. And although people told me Amador was a poor fighter, he seemed crazy and people were afraid of him. It still was never for some reason. Regardless, I noticed that I was looking over my shoulder as I gave Sam my number and got out of his car at the attorney's office only to find that, after all that work to get there, he had cancelled. I walked slowly to breakfast at *Don Cafeto's*.

Sam sent me a text the following night. "The moon is beautiful tonight, no?"

I looked up at the sky, smiled and texted him back that it was magnificent. Then he told me to have a good night. I told him the same and felt that warm glow inside when you feel you have met a new friend. The next day Sam texted me again to invite me to the beach in the biosphere. I was working on a new tiling project and thought about Coco beach, as I called it. I put down my tools and decided to go on my bike. When I arrived, I saw his silver SUV parked in the most remote corner of the parking area by a bluff that offered protection from the sea. It was where I would have put my tent if I were to camp there. I called to him as I pushed my bike through the sand. I noticed he was stoned but didn't seem too spacey.

"Hey. I didn't think you would come. Cool that you did."

The dog, Mero, ran up to me to say hello and he commented that she liked me.

"Dogs generally do. I told you that," I said as I bent down to pat her.

He offered me an iced tea and I sat down on a log by his tent telling him how much I loved that beach. I cracked open the tea and then asked him how he had come to Mexico.

He smiled and said, "I blame it on a waiter."

I asked him to explain, thinking for a moment he was gay and he fell in love. He continued to tell me how he came to Cozumel for a weekend before he was to be married. He was looking at the sky, reminiscing almost as if he had forgotten I was there. He told me that the day his flight was scheduled to go back, he was at the beach having his last margarita. He still had enough time to catch the flight when the waiter asked him if he wanted another.

He told me, "I thought about it and answered honestly, 'Yes'."

Then he told me that as he had sipped that second margarita, he saw the plane fly overhead and knew that he would stay in Mexico for awhile. I didn't quite believe him and asked him if he seriously didn't go to his wedding.

He said it had been a "bit of a mess" with a mischievous smile on his face.

I told him it was a "bit of an asshole move".

He agreed, "Yeah. But I did it."

There was a short silence before he asked me how I came to Mexico.

I told him it was a long story. Then confided that I was going to be married here. I thought of Amador asking me to marry him on several different occasions, telling Sam, "thank God, that didn't happen," before I explained that I had come to Tulum sort of for a man but more for myself.

I felt comfortable with him and told him how I had been sick with cancer and found that I felt good here so kept coming back. I told him how I bought that land with my ex who turned out to be a con artist and a drug addict and that was the end of the story.

Then I said with a laugh, "Or rather not end of story. He hassles me all the time and I am trying to sell my place and get away but so far no luck."

He looked over at me with his stoned eyes looking through those little John Lennon glasses and said, "Interesting."

But then he wanted to know what I meant by "hassling." I got suddenly sad and told him what had happened to me at the internet the other day, mentioning that Amador had come in while I was there. I explained to Sam and a little to myself that I tried to be friends with my ex since we live in the same small town. Sam nodded as if that were logical. I felt better about it and continued to tell him that also there is a part of me that wanted Amador to be okay. I never mentioned Amador's name and didn't want to. I told him that Amador made a phone call. I knew he did it only because he was so loud about it. I explained to Sam that I tried not to pay attention since I had a restraining order and wanted to get away. But I could hear him talking. When I went to pay my bill, it was about 200 pesos.. Amador was waiting outside the store. I mentioned his name.

Sam interrupted me, "Amador is his name?"

I asked if Sam knew him. He asked if he hung out with Chi Chi and Malio and those guys and I nodded yes.

He shook his head. "Wow. You sure know how to pick em."

"He picked me,"I said defensively. I told him that Amador had told the internet guy to put his call to Italy, where his girlfriend lives, on my bill.

Sam laughed. I didn't appreciate the humor and explained that it was not so funny since when I confronted Amador with the issue in front of the store, he went ballistic. I told Sam how Amador started screaming in the street and calling me a whore. I decided to walk away. But he wouldn't let me go. I looked down at the dog and patted her and told Sam how Amador followed me yelling, "*Pinche puta perra*" and all these other horrible curses until I ran away from him. But he ran after me.

Sam chuckled and shook his head. But I told him how Amador would not stop and how he chased me for almost 3 blocks yelling swears at me and telling me how he would put drugs in my friend's car and send them to jail and do the same to me and take my dog. Then, finally, I touched Sam on the knee and told him that Amador sat on the curb in front of me, blocking my way and started hitting himself. Punching himself in the face and he saying he would tell the police I did it.

Sam was not chuckling any more. And he probably was no longer interested in me. But I told myself he was probably an asshole after what he did to his bride to be. I continued with the story explaining that Amador finally stopped, talked to me and asked me for money so he could get the car he had stolen from me out of the *corralon.*

I finished asking him, "Can you believe it?"

Sam shook his head and cursed. I told him I had given him some money and then ran home. I played in the sand with my feet and told him that the bummer really was that Amador got what he wanted and that I still didn't know how to handle the situation.

He patted his dog and took a long drink of his beer before looking back at me and saying, "You need someone to kick his ass."

It was one thing to think that to myself, it was another thing altogether to have someone else say it aloud. I told him if it were just Amador it might be easier but that he was hanging around with Amalio these days and people really didn't mess with those guys. "And,"I said, " I am nobody here."

He touched me on the shoulder and told me there were things that I could do. I agreed with him and said the thing to do for me was to sell my house and get out. I changed the topic and confided that I loved Tulum most of the time. I explained to Sam how I taught yoga, which was my dream, and how I built my houses and I brought a cancer survivor there to recuperate which was my dream too.

Then we were silent for awhile, each of us thinking until Sam said, "Sometimes dreams turn into nightmares."

I told him I wanted to travel and write a book mentioning that I was a writer. I was about to leave when he told me he could help me sell my house. I was not convinced but he told me I would have to pay him. Then I believed him more. I made a mental note of that psychological reality: people do not value when they do not pay. I told him of course I would pay him a commission and he asked to come by and see the house. I agreed and stood up, feeling I had said too much and it was time for me to go.

"What about tomorrow?"

I would make lunch if he sent me a text before he came. He stood do give me a hug before I pushed my bike through the sand to the dirt road and rode back to the house. As I passed my neighbor Amalio's little camp of lost boys, I heard Amador laughing.

I told myself it was bad coincidence that he chose to live next door. Well, he really didn't live there and I knew there were no coincidences. And I knew I could call the police, but I also knew it was futile. He was right: it was his country. He would come to Amalio's to hang out for a few days of partying and then leave. But he always made himself apparent, letting me know he was there by driving by when I was leaving. Or he would be walking past as I was coming in or opening the door to put out the trash. It was weird. He seemed to know every move I made. It wasn't difficult, I told myself. Amalio's camp was only 10 meters away and I could see them in the outdoor shower they made by their well: a bucket they could drop into the well and pull back up to dump over themselves. I heard them squeal when the cold water poured over them. At night, I heard the car doors slam and the women's laughter and the bottles dropping to the floor. And of course I heard Amalio's incessant coughing.

That afternoon, when I closed the gate behind me, I prayed, "please make him stay away".

I knew if he came over I would want to fix him or fix me so that I still wanted him to be the man I needed instead of who he was and asked God to give me a break. I prayed for Amador to go away and to sell my houses and start a different adventure. I knew Sam was coming tomorrow to help me do it. I was sure he was a messenger from God: a short skinny Jew from Chicago. I laughed at the thought of it and prepared for my yoga class.

The next afternoon Sam showed up on time but with a friend he introduced as his ex-girlfriend Heather. He explained that they were both refugees from Mahahual. Under her feet was a little puppy, all legs with paws bigger than each leg it seemed. I said hello and bent down to pat her adorable dog and invited them in but asked her to hold the puppy in case my dogs got territorial.

We walked the property while Sam took visual notes. My dogs nipped at Heather's heels trying to get the puppy from her so I put them in the house. We climbed to the top of what would have been my penthouse suite with Amador. I laughed to think of it but it pained me that his scams were the reason I hadn't finished it. We got to the top, the puppy waiting at the foot of the ladder and me helping Heather to finish the climb.

"Spectacular," said Sam and when Heather got to the top, she said, "Wow."

Somehow I was immensely proud of the great swamp behind my house, as if I had discovered it. I loved it back there. Sam told me there was definitely a market for the place even with the *ejido* thing. I was heartened until he asked about the shape of the lot and why it seemed as if a piece had been taken out of the front. I had naively hoped he wouldn't notice. I was tired of explaining but began to tell him how Amador had been my *preste nombre* and that to get out of jail, he sold the front piece to my neighbors. Sam's eyes widened more when I told him that he had sold it for $1000 and a car.

He shook his head and I said, "Can you believe it?" and then explained to him how I had offered them $10,000 to get it back but they wouldn't take it.

I finished saying, "So I am still not sure which is more the asshole. My neighbors or Amador."

"Wow" was all he could say until he asked me if Amador was still my "*preste nombre.*"

Thankfully I could say no, that he had signed everything over to me. I told him that when he wasn't on drugs he was a pretty good guy, trying to rationalize how he could have done that.

Sam chuckled and said, "Yeah, but when is he not on drugs?"

We heard a loud laugh from next door and then Amalio's cough. The laugh was Amador's. I got nervous and asked them if they wanted lunch explaining how I had made some pasta with black olives, tomatoes and chicken.

Sam said we could talk more while we ate. As he said it, we heard a thump and a cry. Heather looked down and saw her puppy on the ground three levels down and she screamed that he had fallen. I cursed and we rushed down the ladder and the stairs to find the little dog getting up, wimpering. Heather picked her up and checked to see if she was OK and touched her legs and belly to make sure nothing was broken. I suggested we bring her to the house and let her rest on the couch.

We had lunch and laughed and talked about life in Mexico. I didn't want them to leave. The puppy was sleeping and my dogs, Lakra and Goliath, had accepted her as a visitor. It was a nice home for the moment. Sam told me his ideas on how to torment my neighbors and get them back for all they had done to me, like buying the biggest speakers I could and playing music at about 7 am.

"Blast the shit out of them." he said.

I questioned my attraction to him. And his "ex" didn't seem to be too "exy." I laughed at his ideas and walked them to the gate. When I opened the door I saw Amador's white van blocking them in. I swore to myself. Worse, he was in the car, sitting behind the wheel, looking straight ahead. I felt sick and shakey and asked them to wait while I asked Amador to move.

"Is that him?" Sam asked. I shook my head yes and walked toward the car.

Before I could, Amador's friend Chi Chi came out from Malio's place yelling Amador's name. He was drunk and he angrily sort of half walked half ran to the van. I stopped. He opened the driver's side door and pulled Amador into the street. They started to fight in front of us. Amador took Chi Chi's head and pushed it into the pavement. Then Chi Chi pulled him down on the road. They were punching each other and scrambling along as a taxi drove past, beeping and driving around them, as if it were a normal occurrence. I screamed to stop but they didn't listen. Finally, Amador stood up and kicked Chi Chi in the stomach, got back into the van and drove away. It was surreal.

Sam and Heather got into their car quickly then and said, "See you."

I filled in the "Wouldn't want to be you."

Sam backed out and told me to be careful. I nodded and watched them drive off.

The little voice on my shoulder said, "So much for your messenger from God."

I should have known God wouldn't send anyone from Chicago.

Chapter 44

I heard nothing from Sam for the next three weeks. My tourist friends from Oregon came to rent the new house. I felt better having someone there. Marcia and Pat were organic people, and I knew that in a pinch they would help me. They were kind and over Christmas we took a drive to the biosphere together with the dogs. They invited me for drinks on more than one occasion and they made my solitary Christmas less lonesome. In those days, the beach became tense with rumors of invasions and take-overs on properties. The neighbors closed the access to the beach in front. Pat and Marcia were not bothered since they had other people staying up the beach and they were so cool that not much got on their nerves. Not even the odd visits from Amador. He started to wait in a white van in front of the house. I am pretty sure he was living in it but sometimes he would park either across the street or in front of my car, blocking my exit.

I tried not to let it bother me. But of course it did. A lot. One morning Pat and I took the dogs to the biosphere to walk and the van was blocking my car. Pat showed me how to drive my car around the van and get it out. When we came back, Amador was no longer there. I would have liked to see his face figuring out how we got the car around him.

"That guy is a real pain in the ass," Pat told me in an accent that made the statement seem way too nice.

When they left after the New Year, I missed them incredibly but I decided to try to support my project for breast cancer survivors with rentals. I still had my contract with the Corps of Engineers and I had my yoga classes so I figured that with the rentals, I could save for solar panels and keep the place looking good while buying furniture for the houses, even if it came from Walmart.

I had nearly forgotten Sam and figured he had forgotten me, when on a Saturday afternoon, I got a message from him asking me to meet him at Zama's, the restaurant by the ocean as you entered the southern beach. I had been tiling again and was ready for a break. I happily jumped on my bike and met him and the dog. We sat in the back at the tables that overlooked the rocks to one side and the bumper pool table on the other.

"How've you been?" Sam asked me as we sat down.

I told him that things had been pretty quiet and I was managing. He told me he wished he could say the same and then told me he had been arrested in Playa for drugs. I was surprised.

He acknowledged he had a joint in his wallet but told me they took the car, "with the dog inside" and put them both in the *corralon*, the famous Mexican holding area for cars.

He was agitated and told me, "They didn't give a shit that the dog would die in there."

Then he told me he contacted a friend who had keys and they let him in to get Mero, he said as he patted her head. He had spent three days in jail and then another three running around "getting papers and attorneys and paying 3000 pesos in fines and now my stomach is a mess," he said sadly.

I wanted to give him a hug and tell him everything would be OK but I saw no evidence of that.

He and said flatly, "I am getting the fuck out of this country," and then, "You want to come?"

I was shocked and flattered and frightened all together. I started to mumble that I had all this stuff here and asked him if we could bring two more dogs. I was beginning to toy with the idea when reality intruded. "I can't leave until I sell this place. Remember? You were supposed to help me."

I took a sip of my wine and let the view ease my disappointment.

He said he could help me from wherever he went telling me it was just marketing and stuff he could do on the internet. But he had lost his appeal. I asked him if he really believed he had to leave. He said he would go to Guatamala where he had lived before.

"The cops there are normal, or as normal as can be," he said.

"Be careful," I told him, "My father was a cop."

"A real Boston cop?" he asked, surprised and the police conversation died before it started.

He likened his ordeal to a kidnapping and reminded me that the dog could have died.

I finished my wine and asked him when he would leave. He told me he would go as soon as possible. And just like that, the guy who I thought might save me and who I thought could be my adventure boyfriend was leaving my life. All of a sudden, I didn't respect him anymore. He told me to think about coming with him. I couldn't imagine it now.

He tried to convince me saying, "I mean, it is crazy for you here. The police will do nothing for you if that asshole comes back into your life."

I told him I did not think that anything would happen and I believed it. I caught the waiter's attention and motioned for a check. When he put it on the table, I waited for Sam to take it. He didn't move.

I wearily told him, "It's okay, I will buy. Save your money for Guatamala," as I couldn't help but think he was more guy who would suck me dry.

The concept exhausted me and I reprimanded myself for being sad he was leaving. I walked to the car with him and his dog, gave him a hug and rode my bike back home.

The next week, I heard from him again. I was finishing the bathroom floor tiles when I got a text, "Can you meet me at San

Francisco in 15 minutes?"

I read the text not quite understanding and called him back. He said he was leaving today and wanted to talk to me and say goodbye. I asked him if he couldn't come to my house. I was tired and wanted to finish my project. He always interrupted me. He pleaded into the phone for me to come so I agreed to meet him in 30 minutes. I got ready to go, happy to be at least remembered if nothing else.

When I pulled the *vocho* noisily into San Francisco Supermarket parking, he was leaning on his car smoking. He wore jeans, a white tee shirt and his John Lennon glasses. He looked pretty sexy, actually, and I was almost attracted to him again. Except for the fact that he didn't want to buy me that drink. I was so tired of mooches. I walked up to him and kissed him on the cheek saying that it was nice to see him.

"Great," he said distractedly, "Let's walk inside."

I asked him if he needed me to help him buy something. I thought it was strange that he would invite me to come into town to grocery shop but I was happy to have a guy to talk with at the least.

We walked into the supermarket and he said to me, "Pretend you are looking for something."

I told him that if he told me what he needed, I could find it for him. He told me he wanted people to think we were shopping.

"But we are," I said.

He told me that was right, pretend to shop. I was confused as he paused, looked over his shoulder and continued to talk as I examined the sugar as if I were searching for a particular brand.. Then he told me he had a friend in Guatamala.

"Remember?" he asked. "I told you about him."

"Might have," I responded and then smiled, "Is this what you were looking for?" as I handed him a bag.

"Nice touch," he said to me.

Then told he me that his Guatamalan friend could help me take care of my problem. I inhaled, immediately understanding. He was talking about his friend who killed people. I nearly fainted as he told me the guy was a professional and reached down for sweet and low. He shook the package and told me the person was ex-military and he would come here and take care of things. I felt dizzy and took down a box of sugar cubes to have something to focus on.

I told him honestly, "I don't know Sam. I never signed up for this."

He got excited then and started to almost yell, "You didn't sign up for that asshole either. Listen, you would be doing this town a great favor and no one would miss him."

I told Sam that Amador had a family at least. He countered that he was probably a burden for them as well.

He justified, "you don't deserve to live with him tormenting you. There is no reason to not take care of it. It's not like he is helping anyone and there will be no trace with this guy."

I reminded him he was talking about killing someone and then said, "That is not the sort of thing I do."

He took my shoulders to make me look at him, "Better you get him before he gets you."

I was quiet as the enormity and the hopelessness of things sank in. I asked him how much. He said $10,000 U.S.

I said, "I don't have that kind of money," starting to get angry.

He continued trying to sell me on the idea and told me, "Well, you might think about trying to get it."

He wanted me to think he was helping me. Then, all of a sudden, he was in a rush and told me to email him in a day or two since we still had time. He reminded me that the guy was a pro.

And then said, "Think about it: no more stalker, no more pressure, no more any one trying to kill you or threaten you again."

I wanted to cry as he continued.

"And don't kid yourself, this guy is using you and will continue to torment you until you go away or he kills you. It is that simple and I have seen it before."

I started to be afraid and stared at the sugar as he said all FBI like, "I am going to leave now. Stay here for another few moments before going. Think about it. I want to help you."

He bent down and gave me a kiss on the lips, and told me I could still come to Guatamala with him. But, he warned me, I needed to do something. I watched him leave and took the box of sugar cubes to the check out. I liked sugar cubes. As I paid, I asked for a pack of Camel cigarettes. I moved in slow motion as I walked to the car.

Part of me so wanted to have Amador, "taken care of."

I drove to the beach, sat there and smoked one and then two cigarettes in a row, thinking how I could get $10,000. I still had credit. I could do it. But something wasn't right.

As I finished my second cig, feeling nauseous and lightheaded, I told myself, "What are you thinking? It is murder. Stop."

I walked to the car, throwing the cigarettes in a trash barrel as I did and drove to the internet. I sent Sam a message: "'Judgement is mine, sayeth the Lord.' I cannot do it." I read it five times before I hit send, got into my *vocho* and went home to take the dogs to the beach.

Chapter 45

I was nearly asleep when the phone rang the following night, number unknown. I pulled it from under my pillow and answered it.

"Your car is ugly."

I responded, "I know, Amador. That way maybe you won't steal it from me."

He laughed loudly and told me he knew it and then, happily as if we were good old friends, he asked to see me, in a dreamy voice calling me baybe the way he used to. I sighed and told him no, it was not a good idea and then hung up the phone. I didn't get mad, I actually wanted to see him, but I knew it was not good for me. I congratulated myself on saying no and fell soundly asleep.

I spent the next month working and laying low. I had little money but when I did I went to la Zebra to use their internet and have a glass of wine with my friend, the manager, Lina. She would often share a cigarette with me and always gave me more wine than I paid for. La Zebra at that time was the pulse of the beach, at least on the southern end. Their Sunday dance parties were legendary for tourists and locals alike and if there was something going on, Lina would know and she would almost always invite me. Too, she would not speak English with me and always corrected my improving but still imperfect Spanish. Many afternoons turned into evenings we would laugh together and she would tell me things about Mexico. She had long dark hair and light skin. Lina hardly ever went to the beach and loved to cook. She managed the kitchen and would let me taste whatever new dish she was contemplating for the menu. We were becoming good friends.

One Sunday afternoon, I was at the bar before the salsa dance party. It had been a cloudy day and Lina and I had been looking at something on line. I had been working and she had distracted me with a question about food when Amador walked in. I got obviously nervous and afraid. It was as if he stole my spirit somehow, or I gave it to him. Whichever, I lost it. Lina looked at me and asked me if everything were okay. She probably knew about my relationship with Amador but we had never discussed it.

As I answered her with a nod, she looked over at Amador and said, "*Chango-leon,*" with a smile.

I wondered what the word meant before she told me, "He looks like a *chango* or monkey, and smells like a lion, *leon.*"

I smiled and lost my self-consciousness as we both broke into laughter. Amador noticed and walked through the restaurant with his chest puffed out, looking around, pretending to ignore us. He did not say hello but walked out to the beach and left. As he walked down the stairs and onto the nearly empty beach, seemingly looking for someone, Lina told me not to be afraid of him.

"That is what they want. You cannot be afraid or they win," she said, lighting a cigarette.

She was my Mexican angel in her embroidered Mexican shirt, a flower in her long dark hair, dark eyes scanning the horizon and cigarette always in her hand.

She was right and I knew it. I resolved to be more like her; wise, beautiful and tough. She motioned to the barman to fill my glass as she went to check on some guests and to make sure that Amador had passed through the property and moved on. I went back to work until she invited me to eat with her.

She had made fabulous *chile relleno* once again, like she had whenI met her at Kim's. Then, as if we were celebrating something, she brought out my favorite coconut flan and I realized we were celebrating something: the ability to recognize and avoid *chango-leones.*

I was preparing to leave when Lina took my computer and put it in her back office saying, "The dance lesson is beginning."

Manuel had arrived and the tourists were lining up on the deck out front for salsa lessons.

"You need to go," she told me and I easily obeyed.

I loved dancing there and was learning more every Sunday that I practiced. Manuel was funny, a little lewd but kind and a superb dancer. He was a master at working the crowd and he got the group going on their 123 4567 quickly, placing his portable stereo on the deck next to one of the two palm trees that came through the wooden floor. People laughed, danced and Lina put a full glass of wine on the corner of the dance floor for me. Leo the bar man got my attention as he left it. I smiled and felt very much at home.

Two hours later the bar was packed, the beach nearly so and an 8 piece salsa band was playing under the stars. The dance floor was full and other *change-leones* were dancing with tourist girls. Several asked to dance with me and we laughed and danced until I got tired and went in to see my friends. Lina's family was there. She had 3 gorgeous sisters who were at the bar. All with dark hair, same light complexion and strong but kind eyes. But Lina was the matriarch. We were talking and drinking when I felt a touch on my shoulder. I turned to find Amador behind me. I inhaled and he asked me to dance.

I hesitated and said "No thank-you." I had been talking with Laura, Lina's little sister. She was watching him as I turned back to continue and moved closer to the bar.

Amador hung around for a little while and the sisters moved around me to push him away. It was as if I had entered a protective circle and he could not cross the line. I reached for a water from the bar and when I looked back he was gone. Laura smiled at me, then the other sister, Mirriam did. They knew. I was embarrassed but thanked them. They acted as if they had no idea what I was talking about and we went back to discussing where to buy the best bikinis.

Before I knew it, the bar was clearing out and the band packing up. Lina had set up some shots of tequila at a table. When she motioned to me to sit, I shook my head and told her thanks but I had to go. I got my computer from behind the office and jumped on my pink bike to go home. The road was dark but the stars were brilliant. I felt warm from the dancing and the alcohol and I resolved not to be afraid anymore. There was a gentle moon setting on my side of the road and into the *manglers* and I knew I had a wonderful life if I could move past my fear of the *chango-leon*.

The next day I was slightly hung over. I fed the animals and had a swim in the ocean: instant cure. I came back to the house clear, a little tired but no traces of the headache and general malaise from before. I loved my life. I had just started to work when my friend Erica called to tell me she was in Tulum. I had not seen her since Goliath died. Happy to have a friend, I invited her to stay with me.

She brought Chito, her boyfriend now. I liked him but only when he was not drinking or taking drugs. Like most addicts, he had two sides. One was genuinely endearing. He was generous, smart and helpful, like when he built the house for Toucan. When he was on something he was mean, unpredictable and crazy. No other words for it. They were wonderful together, but had their moments. Like the time Chito left Erica in the house and took her wallet and car so that he could go score more of whatever. Or the time Chito had decided to kill her for something she said and she had to literally escape from her cabana and come to my door for sanctuary.

But I was happy to touch my culture, if only remotely. Erica was from Eastern Europe but lived in Jersey City, close enough to Manhattan to be nearly a New Yorker. She was an artist and sold real estate and had been coming to Tulum for long enough to know nearly everyone. It was still a time when there were re-curring tourists who were nearly locals. They came often and always brought something that you couldn't get in Tulum. That was who I was supposed to have been: jet setting, back and forth, famous in New York, semi-anonymous in Tulum. That had been the plan but I couldn't seem to fulfill it. I was becoming nearly famous in Tulum and totally anonymous everywhere else.

They arrived in a rental car with loads of groceries even though I didn't have a fridge. We found space for everything and allowed ourselves to eat most of what wouldn't fit in the cooler. We had wine and talked and enjoyed the evening. Later we went to the beach to look for turtles. Chito put a hammock in the 2 palms trees that grew just as you entered the beach and after about half an hour, I left Erica and him there. They were laying in the hammock, nearly entertwined and I felt as if I were intruding into their space. I walked home feeling a little lonely but not for Amador, just wondering what I had done wrong in regards to men. Then the voice on my shoulder chimed in and told me not to be fooled by one nice session in the hammock: Erika suffered for Chito. It was clear and simple. I came home and before I went to bed lit a candle in front of Goliath's grave. I missed that dog. My girls and I went up to bed together.

They stayed another 3 nights. Erica and I cooked and painted. It was nice having them there. Chito left for town around noon one day and came back around 4 pm. When he walked in the gate I smiled but then saw Amador behind him and my smile faded quickly to anger. Lakra howled and Ama started to bark.

"How could he do this?" I asked Erica.

She said to calm down and she would talk to him. But before she could Amador was at the porch with the two dogs still going wild. He asked to talk to me, nicely. I told him we didn't have much to talk about.

He disagreed and said he wanted to apologize for how he had behaved on so many occasions, "I just crazy but I still love you."

I looked at him more closely: that same matted hair but this time with less gold on the tips. He had not been to the beach much lately. His skin was paler, his feet cleaner and he was wearing sandals. Part of me softened but part of me knew that it could never work. I didn't want to lose all my new friends and the life I was building. And deep down, I didn't want to take care of this addict any more: cleaning up after him, tolerating him, supporting him. But, I still wanted him to be well. Before I could say anything, he asked me to let him help at the house. He said he wanted to do something to make up for all the shit. I told him that was impossible.

He said, "Let me try."

Chito and Erica came up behind him then and Erica commented that I needed a privacy screen and that perhaps Amador could build one with me. I said I would think about it. They wanted to cook and invited us to eat with them. Us. I reluctantly said okay and Amador sat down to pat Lakra and then he asked me to show him what I wanted. We went inside so that I could explain it to him. He seemed calm as I told him what I wanted and then food was ready. Erica had set up the table out front and put a huge pan of pasta with shrimp and white wine onto the table for us. She poured white wine for me and for her and in her Eastern European accent told the guys they couldn't have any, laughing. We touched glasses, Chito opened a couple of beers saying something about us and the wine that I didn't hear but I decided I didn't need to. It was a wonderful lunch and we ate every last bit.

After the meal, we talked. Erica smoked. I wanted to but was giving up on cigarettes. They bothered my throat and my conscience and made me sick. After about 30 minutes, Amador stood to leave. Chito asked if he could give him a ride to town in Erica's car and they left.

Erica lit another cigarette, filled my glass with wine and said,

"What do you think?"

I was confused, I confided, but really wasn't sure that he could repair all the damage he had done.

I told her how he had hit me on 2 occasions and then I used Fernando's line from so long ago, "He really doesn't bring much to the table."

I hated that sort of weighing people's worth in what they could do for you but I was at a place where I needed help. I needed to be with people who were going to do something for me in whatever form.

Then I told her, "He brings me down."

She agreed but told me he really loved me and that people change. I took a deep breath and told her people do and I had. She asked me to give him a chance. I wasn't sure why but it was almost as if she thought that if I could work it out with Amador, perhaps her love affair with Chito could work as well. I knew I always thought the same when I saw them together. I always asked myself why it couldn't work for me. I imagined she did the same. We cleared the table, did the dishes together and took the dogs to the beach.

The next day Amador came by in the morning. I was surprised to see him and went to open the gate. He tried to kiss me but I offered him my cheek. It was easy to do all of a sudden and I waited for his reaction. He accepted it. He told me he wanted to take some measurements so we could start to make the screen. I had other plans but when he asked me to take him to town to buy the wood I said OK. He explained that had no money or he would have gotten it while he was there. I detected a hint of an accusation in his voice, as if he were saying I should have given him the money the night before, but I ignored it. I could not afford to throw any more money down the toilet.

When we came back, I went upstairs to work and he worked on the project downstairs. Erica and Chito had gone into the biosphere. It was their last day. I would miss them. I worked quietly upstairs listening to the sound of Amador's saw and hammer. It felt OK but something was not right. He called to me for help and I held some wood while he hammered. We worked together, had a few laughs and I knew he was waiting for the chemistry to kick in because I was too. But I felt nothing and I didn't want him to try anything. I mostly wanted him to leave. But it was only almost.

He almost finished when Erica and Chito came back with fish to grill. We abandoned the project and started the charcoal. He left after dinner saying he would see me the next day. I hoped so since the project was half finished. Erica and Chito went to their house and I went to the beach. It was a beautiful night. I left the dogs in case there were turtles. I didn't want the dogs chasing them or disturbing them. I felt the darkness and the stars. And when I saw a shooting star, I wished for strength, not for Amador or any man, just for the strength and courage to follow my best self. I laughed when I said it, told myself I had come a long way from wishing for men on stars and decided to go to bed. Walking back into the property I notice the silhouette of Erica and Chito having sex on the balcony of their house. They must have thought I would be longer. I smiled, was jealous for a bit but then decided no and took the dogs quietly upstairs to sleep.

Amador came later the next morning. Erica and Chito had left early for the airport. He started work with only a coffee and toast. Erica was not there to cook and that was breakfast for me. Later I heard a curse and some tools fall. He had hit his thumb with the hammer. I smiled and went down to help him. Over the course of a day and several interruptions, we finished a room divider between my living room and bathroom. I helped him stretch fabric behind it and it was almost the one I had seen in Crate and Barrel. He asked if we could have dinner together that night. I told him yes. I planned to see what exactly he thought were his next steps. Fortunately he didn't ask for money to go back to town. He said he had to do some things. I always wondered what "things" he could be doing but let it go and told him I would be here later. I had some food in the fridge cooler and it would be nice to eat together.

He came back as the sun was going down and we went out back to watch the sunset, that painting in the sky of rose, orange, red and yellow with the hint of blue above. I loved watching it but it made us both think, perhaps too much. We walked back to the house in silence and I started to cook. He asked about my yoga guys jealously and asked if he could practice with me. I told him yes and joked that I wouldn't even charge him. He didn't like that, I could tell. I poured us some wine and he helped me serve the pasta. He started to talk about some land deals he was working on. I didn't let the idea that I would help him enter my mind but I knew he wanted me to say something about it. I had always been fascinated by real estate but now I knew I could not do anything with him. It made me happy that I had learned, finally.

As we finished dinner he started to get strange, perhaps it was the wine. I couldn't tell. He told me how people would kill for a piece of land like mine. Then he described how they would skin you alive. At first I laughed asking him what movie he got that from but he looked at me seriously and said, "I no joking."

I was quiet and after a few moments he said, "They coming for me, you know."

He had said that before at Las Ranitas and Luxury cabanas and at Zamas when he was waiting for more drugs, I remembered. But this time it frightened me more.

"They maybe come for you too," he told me.

I asked him to stop and told him it was time for him to go.

"They do anything for a piece of land here," he said, not moving and I told him he was frightening me and asked him to stop.

He said, "I go now" and got off the chair and started to walk to the gate.

I went with him nervously. He had changed from one moment to the next and I did not like it. He kissed me on the cheek as he left without even trying to kiss me on the lips. He seemed as if he were in a trance. I asked him if he were OK and he said he was fine and puffed out his chest.

"I don' need a woman," he told me as he turned his back to me and walked away.

I let him go. He had no car and I watched him walk across the street to the beach.

I closed the gate behind him, locked it securely and then walked back to my dogs. I cleaned up the kitchen, admired the new room divider and brushed my teeth while checking it out. It was not that sturdy but it didn't matter. It was functional and clean. I liked it for now and that was all that counted. And finally, Amador had done something good in my house. It was a sort of victory. But then I thought of how he had left and knew it was not. I hustled the dogs up the stairs and locked both doors. As I was ready to blow out a candle, I heard a piercing scream on the beach. I knew it was him. It was very like a scream I heard my brother make when he was first experiencing the traumas of schizophrenia. My brother had run from his bedroom, rushed into the street and screamed for what seemed like 10 minutes. KB was exhausted and distressed from the voices inside his head and the mental illness. This time, I heard the same agony and pain in Amador's scream. It was his addiction torturing him. I felt only sadness and sat by the candle with the dogs thinking, not ready to go to bed yet.

Chapter 46

I was reading under the mosquito netting when I heard footsteps and turned to grab the flashlight I kept by my bed. The candle was still burning on the nightstand but I needed more light so I crawled from under the netting and stood in the oversized window. I filled the yard with light and saw the moving shadow of a man. I felt a sudden chill despite the hot jungle night air. My dogs, sensed my fear and came to the window next to me and panted at my feet. Ama let out a nervous bark as the shadow, not caring he had been discovered, continued moving toward us. It was Amador. I froze. The dogs didn't move. Even the geckos stopped chirping as he moved closer.

I finally yelled, "Amador, go away," through what felt like a desert in my mouth.

"No. I no go. I want to talk to you," he responded, continuing to progress toward me.

I prayed he would leave. But a part of me loved that he wanted me, loved that he yearned to possess me. It was a sickness born of some sort of insecurity and low self-esteem, I knew. I had read the books, been to therapy, talked to myself in the mirror. I knew I was better than this. I was successful, I was together, I had hired and fired men with real credentials, real values. Amador didn't even wear shoes. God knew the last time he had brushed his teeth. I had more to offer than he would ever be able to handle or would ever care about knowing. Yet, even now, I loved him from somewhere deep in my soul.

His throaty, sweet, heavily accented English terrified me now and I finally understood everything. Where before, his voice had called to my heart and had seduced me into thinking he was the man I wanted, now I knew he was a selfish predator. The man I had believed in was my own creation and Amador had become that man on occasion, long enough to get what he wanted from me, anyway. I finally understood how I had given him status, access, money to feed his addiction, comfort to quiet his pain.

I had been his *mujer*, his rich *gringa*—smart, beautiful, capable of taking care of herself, a writer and an artist, an engineer who was an expert in her field. I scolded myself and reminded myself that I had testified before Congress on environmental issues. The voice on my shoulder told me that it didn't matter. It cautioned me that I was dealing with the drama of a drug addict who had taken all my money and most of my love. And for so long, I had been clinging to the notion that he could love me, that he did love me, that I was capable of getting and keeping real love, that love could work. But now, we had crossed the line from love to hate. I was no longer rich and he was no longer loveable. I held Ama's mouth to keep her quiet. Her barking would only make it worse.

I told him, "I don't want to talk to you, Amador. Go away."

He advanced onto the porch and I strained to listen as he came up the wooden stairs. I jumped at the sound of breaking glass as he kicked a votive candle on the way. He was on the balcony outside the upstairs bedroom. I silently cursed myself. I had repeatedly vowed never again to live in these dramatic episodes, the victim of his tirades, an addict to the drama. Yet, here I was, like another fallen junkie. I had let him back into my life and now my hands were trembling in anticipation. I went to the double door and could see the outline of his body through the cracks in the oversized planks of dark tropical wood. I could hear his breath as I tried to control my own. I put my back against the door, more to support myself than to keep him out and then, I exhaled heavily and leaned my head against the door, closed my eyes, and tried to gain the strength to refuse to engage him.

His voice suddenly snapped, "Open the door."

I stood motionless. He commanded in a tone I barely recognized, "*Oye, puta, abrir la puerta,*" "Listen, cunt, open the door."

I put my back closer to it and tried to close my ears to his insults and told him no.

I said firmly, "I don't want to talk to you." and then in a whisper, as if praying, "Please, just go away."

"I not going anywhere *puta*. Open the door." he said forcefully but then, as if he really didn't mean the insult, he added in a voice filled with fatigue, "I just want my dry clothes."

The tone was filled with pleading and reason as if I were over reacting. I hesitated, weighing my options and stayed silent, knowing it could not be so simple. Still, every nerve of my being was on fire with fear and anticipation of what could happen next. I unglued my body from the door and went to the bed, reached under the mosquito netting, and lifted my cell phone from the covers. I thought about calling the police but knew that he would hear me dial and it would infuriate him. I reminded myself that they were 30 to 45 minutes away and that their concept of emergency did not include domestic disputes. I remembered how they had left me feeling victimized and wasted by the people I hoped would protect me. Additionally, those encounters had cost me cash that I no longer had.

I kept the phone in my hand and walked to the open closet to pull Amador's clean, dry clothes from the shelf where I had put them that morning with love. Since he had been working downstairs I had washed his clothes still thinking that we could be friends. I carried the clothes toward the bolted double door but I was afraid to open it. Instead, I looked to the oversized screen window, opened that and handed the orange shorts and white shirt to him around the wooden support column. My hands were shaking as he took his things from me gently, touching my hands as if to hold them. He didn't grab me. He touched me, in an almost loving way. I was confused and thought that perhaps I was over reacting. There was quiet for a moment. I exhaled and imagined that was really all he wanted and he would quietly leave the way he had come.

But suddenly, he pounded his fist on the door. I screamed, a high-pitched, girlish sound and then inhaled and chastised myself for the cry's weakness, as if it really mattered. No one was listening.

I pressed my body back into the door and he commanded, "Don't scream *puta*."

As I listened from he the crack between the double doors, I could hear the spittle on the sides of his mouth and realized he was a rabid animal, more *leon* than *chango*. I screamed again, fear overtaking my reflexes, and prayed for help. But only the jungle heard me. My neighbors were close on either side but one set would ignore me, believing I deserved what I got from my ex for repeatedly letting him back into my life. On the other side were Amador's buddies and they generally returned well after 3 am. Regardless, I knew their routine and abuse was part of it. It would take a lot for them to do anything to help me.

I jumped and screamed again when he yelled, "Don't scream or I gonna knock the door and kill you."

This time my instinctive scream was loud and forceful. I searched for the correct buttons on the phone to dial the police. Even in Mexico, they don't condone killing their women. I hit the send key as the door slammed against my back from outside and I fell to the floor, clutching the phone. The splintered deadbolt hit the floor next to me. Amador followed, an animal looking for its prey. When he saw me in the corner, he slowed and smiled cruelly as I pressed the phone to my ear. He reached me in the exact moment that the call was connecting and, with the same twisted smile, ripped the phone from my hand and threw it against the far wall. I screamed loudly in a rage of frustration but he grabbed my throat, forcing me to stop. I started to choke under his grip. His face turned to an old photo negative and then disappeared as I lost consciousness.

Chapter 47

I opened my eyes to see Amador sitting in my oversized bamboo chair patting my Lakra. He looked weary, exhausted. I felt trapped, afraid to move but needing to. I helped myself sit up.

He looked over at me and said, "I got to go," as if he had been waiting to tell me before he left.

Warily, I told him that was okay. He could go. My throat hurt and my whole body was heavy but I was aware of every second. I watched him stand and Lakra came over and put her head against my chest. I wondered what to do as I patted her, trying to appear calm as my mind raced frantically to figure out how to save us.

"Yeah, I got to go," he repeated and went toward the door.

I helped myself to stand unsteadily and followed, staying well behind him. Lakra didn't move. I silently counted each step he took to get down the stairs. He stepped off the porch, my heart started to lighten and I almost felt victorious. He was out of the house.

But just as quickly as I began to almost celebrate, he stopped and said, "No. No. I not going. You," he turned to me and repeated, "You. You going."

I inhaled and then caught his gaze again, afraid to lose sight of him. I told him okay. I was shaking, weary and in my nightgown but told him I would go and get the dogs. I called to Lakra and Ama but he said no again. He said the word forcefully and with meanness in his tone.

"Lakra, she mines," he told me.

I felt a courage or an idiocy overtake me and told him, "No. Lakra is mine. If I leave she comes with me."

I did not care anymore.

He took two steps towards me but I did not back down. He and I realized something then. I could see it in his eyes and I felt it. He was not so powerful and I was. I planted my feet and stood there.

He took a step back and said, "No" and then paused and looked around before he continued saying, "I hate your house and I hate you."

I winced at the word, hate, but didn't move or say anything.

He continued, "I sleep there in the house I helped build," referring to the cottage I had built for cancer survivors.

I couldn't believe that I thought about it but I knew there were no sheets on the bed. Unbelievably I commanded him to wait so I could get him sheets. I felt ridiculous but almost robotic as I climbed back up the stairs to get them scolding myself the entire time. But still, I opened the black chest for clean sheets and told myself it was good, I would not have his dirty feet on my clean mattress. Something about working so hard to have each item in my place made me need to take care of it. The voice on my shoulder asked me what the hell I was doing and I grabbed my yellow Calvin Klein sheet that I used for the dogs. It had been damaged by bleach and we used it at the beach. I took two clean pillow cases as well and caught him before he got in the bed. He grabbed the pillows from me and just as I put the sheet over the mattress, fell into the mosquito netting with his dirty feet hanging outside. I hoped the mosquitoes would be eat him alive as I walked down the stairs and left him there.

Part of me wanted to run and leave him but the other part of me would not abandon my place to him. Plus, where would we go? The sky was still dark and there were stars shining in the middle of the yard that made me feel taken care of. I crossed the yard in my favorite black nightgown, now soiled with one strap torn and I walked up the stairs, looked at the broken door and went inside where the dogs were waiting for me. I heard the tails happily tapping the floor. They were afraid to come out. I closed the door as best I could, patted them and went to bed. I fell asleep soundly and didn't wake until well after 9 am wondering if it had all been a dream.

From my shelter under the mosquito netting, everything appeared perfect. Nothing was amiss. I stretched and swallowed and knew I had not been dreaming. My throat was swollen and sore. I climbed out from under the mosquito netting, put my feet on the cool floor as the dogs came up to say hello. I hugged them both and whispered that we would go get some breakfast. My voice was scratchy and it hurt to talk. I looked over at the broken door.

I started to cry and mumbled, "what the fuck," as I picked up the broken deadbolt still attached to a piece of the wooden door. Then I inhaled sharply remembering that he was still here, still in my space. Without thinking too much about it, I went downstairs, had a drink of water, made coffee and fed the dogs. I sat on the porch, drank my coffee and tried to figure out where to go from here. He was still sleeping. I could not stand having him there. I finished the coffee, stood and walked over to where he was sleeping, moving quietly up the circular stairway. His feet were still sticking out from under the mosquito netting and he was curled up in the yellow sheet and white blanket I had given him what seemed like ages ago. I wanted to cry but was too afraid. I was not only afraid of Amador but of my reaction to him: I wanted to forget the whole thing and climb in next to him and hold him, like lovers do. The realization repulsed me. I scolded myself and then called his name loudly to waken him. He didn't stir so I called his name again. He started to stretch and so I walked a little closer and grabbed his foot, pulling on it. He moved and tried to kick me before he wined, "what," like an adolescent child whose mother wanted him to get out of bed. I straightened my spine and prepared myself for the verbal abuse I knew would follow.

I told him "I want you out of my house."

He rolled over and looked around, he looked at the yellow sheet and the blanket and then through the mosquito netting at me. I thought I saw sadness in his eyes but reminded myself he was hung over from whatever he had the night before.

Then his eyes changed to meanness and he said to me, "This place sucks. I go now."

I didn't say a word. I walked back down the circular stairs before he could bother me more. I sat on the palm trees that were joined together in the front yard and waited. Lakra and Ama came to me. I patted them and waited. Before too long I heard a big fart and then feet on the floor. The door slammed against the wall and I heard the slow, unsteady footsteps coming down the stairs. I heard a loud burp with the last step and then waited. I heard pee in the toilet and then another fart and the seat went down before I heard the echo of him taking a dump in my bathroom. I heard the toilet flush and him sniffing as if to spit, but he did not. I thanked God since that would have put me over the edge. I waited. He walked behind me and over to the door and didn't look at me.

From his back he called, "This place is shit," as he went up the path and stood at the door, waiting for me to unlock it.

I had the keys and I walked up, nearly afraid of him but not. Again, more afraid of myself but this time not to hug him, to beat him until his face was a mess of blood and bruises. My reaction frightened me more than he ever could.

Neither of us said a thing. He walked out and I closed and locked the door behind him. Then I started to cry. I leaned my back against the gate and slid down it to sit on the ground and sobbed. I looked up and asked God to please help me. I waited for an answer but neither felt nor heard anything. It seemed even my dad wasn't talking to me any more. Then I knew, it was up to me. I stood up and took the dogs to the beach. I desperately needed a swim.

I walked with them along the shore and found Hilario, Sylvia's boyfriend who had buried Goliath with us. I told him what had happened and asked if he could come and help me. I was having trouble keeping it all together but he said he would come by in about an hour. I told him thanks and continued to walk the beach until the spot past VSK where there was no one: no hotel, no house, just pure dune. I stripped and walked slowly into the water and swam. The dogs waited. I floated, feeling the sun and water on my skin, moving gently up and down, my naked body enveloped by the sea, my eyes closed against the brightness of the sun. I felt as if I had been resurrected. This time God talked to me. Or my dad. Or myself. Whoever it was told me I would be okay, that I had the power, that I always had the power. I just had to use it.

Chapter 48

I closed the gate behind the dogs and crossed the street. As we entered the path to the beach, I noticed the small blue flowers growing in between the sea grapes and chit palms and I smiled. I followed a gecko's path as he ran in front of me along the sand and then inhaled sharply as my eyes latched onto the feet of a man: Amador. I would know those feet anywhere. My eyes ran up his legs, past his shorts to his bare chest and then to his dirty face. He had awakened and was walking to the road with his blanket and his scruffy hair and that ugly face that I loved. I didn't want to look at him but I couldn't help myself.

"Joanne," throaty, sweet, broad 'a' and accent on the 'anne', he called to me.

I stopped, and surprised myself by smiling when I realized he would never change. Then I looked away, knowing that I would not either. I walked past him, pulling the dogs with me.

"Wait me, Joanne," he called to me.

I stopped. I had not seen him since he had tried to choke me about a month before.

"Can I have a hold?" he asked like a child. I smiled again, this time at his accent and incorrect English. Why did I love that he sounded so foreign, perhaps so ignorant? I continued to walk away from him.

"*Porfavor?*" he called.

I asked him why.

He answered me, "Because, I really need it."

I stopped. He reached for me and I reached out and hugged him back. It felt more than good, it was warm and comforting and familiar like I hadn't felt in a while.

"Can we walk a little? On the beach?" he asked while still holding onto me strongly.

I pulled away from him and said yes. I wanted to hear what he had to say even though I knew it could never be enough. The voice on my shoulder told me that people would see, that people would know. In the time that I had not been with him, my life went well. I had friends, a social life, a manageable work life. I was content. The dogs were happy. I knew everyone on the beach as we walked towards the biosphere in the morning. Things seemed to have settled for me. I had few interactions with my neighbors, their ugly construction was nearly done. My peace sign mosaic as you entered the house glowed with the energy that it was in fact a house of peace. As I walked with him, I wondered if the people who had stood by me might not again. But I still wanted to be next to him, to be close to him, to hear what he had to say.

"Wait me," he said, "I put this away" he motioned to the blanket.

It was the same white one I had given him. I remembered how it felt to buy things for him and told him I would wait on the beach. I walked over the bluff with a confused heart and mind and sat with the dogs. The Caribbean welcomed me and lightened my heart and attitude, telling me anything was possible. He came over the dune. I didn't move. He held his hand to help me up and asked me to walk with him.

I told him I would, "for a little bit. I am walking anyway with the dogs."

I did not take his hand and helped myself up. We walked slowly. It felt good to be beside him. He reached for my hand but I pulled away. I was still afraid of him and so very confused.

"Okay," he said, "I understand."

I walked with him and felt the power of silence. But I felt his energy too. Once again, I felt possessed and I liked it.

"Swimming?" he asked. "Want to swimming?"

I smiled again, at the idea and at his English and told him I would love it. We stopped. The dogs stopped with us and they sat on the sand as we entered the crystal blue waters of the Caribbean, my home. It was calm, marvelously warm yet cooling at the same time. He swam out toward the reef. I swam along the shore.

Suddenly, I wanted to be away from him. It had been a mistake to engage him. It was more than I could handle. He started to swim toward me and I turned to go in. He caught up to me and reached to touch me. I wanted to have him hold me so badly, to have him love me, to love him back, to be in that place where I felt good with him, to be touched by someone I loved and could trust. I ached for that feeling so much that I could taste it. But it had all been replaced with treachery and mistrust and dirt and darkness and everything bad from so much beauty. That was the tragedy. I felt the electric tingle of his touch and then swam away. He felt it too, all of it. The chemistry and the spoiled softness of a good thing gone very bad. He treaded water and looked down into it as I swam for the shore where I sat in the sand, letting the waves gently wash over my legs and onto my belly. I had nowhere to go. I was confused and felt empty. The sun and the water were healing but they could only do so much. I had to move on alone and I was weary of it, weary of the effort, weary of not getting my way. He swam up and sat beside me.

"Amador?"

"*Si mami*," he crooned back.

I told him not to call me that.

"*Si*, Joanne," he mocked me like an obedient schoolboy.

"Amador, remember when I told you I wanted to die here with you?" referring to the first time he took me past the arch to Sian Kann and to a deserted beach where we swam and slept. The minute I had put my feet into the sand, I told him I could die there and I meant it. At the time death felt very close, a comforting promise, the one thing I could count on. Now it was a memory, still something to count on but hopefully far away.

He nodded yes.

"I didn't mean I wanted you to kill me."

We both laughed and then we stopped. I didn't want the moment to end. It was heaven being next to him on this beach. I could forget everything, forgive everything, if I only thought it could work, if I only thought it had a chance. But I knew better.

"Amador?" I asked him again.

"*Si, mami.*"

And then I asked him what I could have done differently? I asked him what I could have done to make it work.

"*Oye*, Joanne, *mami*," he said with sympathy as if I were a child, "Nothing, *mamasita*. It was all me, all my fault."

I knew he was wrong. It was our fault and I hated that I had enabled our pain. I shook my head and looked down at my belly and then toward my feet. The water washed over them. The sand stuck to them, small grains of granite and coral shimmering in the sun. I looked back up at him and into his eyes. I felt nothing. The longing was gone.

He had to look away.

I stood up, said goodbye, called the dogs and walked myself home.

ABOUT THE AUTHOR

Fanny Barry is a native of Boston Massachusetts who first discovered Tulum Mexico in 2003 after surviving breast cancer. She is a writer, artist, engineer and yoga teacher who re-built her life from the ground up in Tulum, Mexico against some fairly steep odds. She recently built a yoga studio in Tulum called Tribal (www.tribaltulum.com) and she blogs at her web site www.thatbarrygirl.com . She wrote 3 emotional support booklets for breast cancer patients called, *I Wish I Knew,* and has contributed articles to several yoga magazines.

95009384R00361

Made in the USA
Lexington, KY
04 August 2018